THE DEVELOPMENT AGENDA

THE DEVELOPMENT AGENDA

GLOBAL INTELLECTUAL PROPERTY AND DEVELOPING COUNTRIES

EDITED BY NEIL WEINSTOCK NETANEL

OXFORD UNIVERSITY PRESS

OXFORD
UNIVERSITY PRESS

Oxford University Press, Inc., publishes works that further Oxford University's objective of excellence in research, scholarship, and education.

Oxford New York
Auckland Cape Town Dar es Salaam Hong Kong Karachi Kuala Lumpur Madrid Melbourne Mexico City Nairobi New Delhi Shanghai Taipei Toronto

With offices in
Argentina Austria Brazil Chile Czech Republic France Greece Guatemala Hungary Italy Japan Poland Portugal Singapore South Korea Switzerland Thailand Turkey Ukraine Vietnam

Published by Oxford University Press, Inc.
198 Madison Avenue, New York, New York 10016

Library of Congress Cataloging-in-Publication Data
The development agenda: global intellectual property and developing countries / editor, Neil Weinstock Netanel.
p. cm.
Includes bibliographical references and index.
ISBN 978-0-19-534210-9 ((hardback) : alk. paper)
1. Intellectual property (International law) 2. World Intellectual Property Organization.
3. Intellectual property—Developing countries. 4. Law and economic development. I. Netanel, Neil.
K1401.D478 2009
346. 04'8—dc22
2008030811

---

1 2 3 4 5 6 7 8 9

Printed in the United States of America on acid-free paper

Note to Readers

This publication is designed to provide accurate and authoritative information in regard to the subject matter covered. It is based upon sources believed to be accurate and reliable and is intended to be current as of the time it was written. It is sold with the understanding that the publisher is not engaged in rendering legal, accounting, or other professional services. If legal advice or other expert assistance is required, the services of a competent professional person should be sought. Also, to confirm that the information has not been affected or changed by recent developments, traditional legal research techniques should be used, including checking primary sources where appropriate.

(Based on the Declaration of Principles jointly adopted by a Committee of the American Bar Association and a Committee of Publishers and Associations.)

CONTENTS

PREFACE AND ACKNOWLEDGMENTS

NEIL WEINSTOCK NETANEL

Do broad, universal intellectual property rights bring the benefits of innovation, creativity, technical know-how, and foreign investment to developing countries? Or do treaties that require developing countries to accord greater intellectual property (IP) protection actually stifle development and impede access to the knowledge and essential medicines that the world's poor so desperately need? The debate over such questions has raged for decades among scholars and diplomats, lawmakers and policymakers, nongovernmental organizations and international agencies, IP industries and development policy analysts. In parallel, countries have tussled repeatedly over IP and development issues within the international treaty arena. They have argued before the World Intellectual Property Organization (WIPO), a special agency of the United Nations charged with "promoting creative intellectual activity and facilitating the transfer of technology related to industrial property to developing countries"; before the World Trade Organization, overseer of "TRIPS," the Agreement on Trade-Related Aspects of Intellectual Property, which requires countries to provide specified minimum intellectual property protections or face trade sanctions; and before the United Nations Commission on Human Rights, which has cautioned that TRIPS might run counter to countries' obligations under the International Covenant on Social, Economic, and Cultural Rights, including countries' obligation to ensure access to essential medicines so as to provide their citizens with the "highest attainable standard of physical and mental health."

The WIPO Development Agenda is the fruition of developing countries' most recent campaign to ensure that the intellectual property treaty regime permits—and, indeed, empowers—developing countries to tailor their intellectual property laws as they deem necessary to promote development and serve the welfare of their citizens. The Agenda's adoption by the WIPO General Assembly in September 2007 may well constitute an historic watershed for that organization, which has long viewed its mandate as the unequivocal promotion of greater intellectual property rights throughout the world. If so, this book, a collection of essays about the complex issues that underlie the Development Agenda and what the Agenda might portend, has been a part of that history in the making. It began in March 2007 with a conference, "Intellectual Property and Developing Countries: The WIPO Development Agenda," at the University of California at Los Angeles. Representatives of WIPO and the governments of Brazil, Nigeria, and the United States began the conference by reporting on recent progress made toward agreement on a Development Agenda for WIPO but cautioned that many obstacles remained. The first drafts of many of this book's chapters were prepared without knowing in what form, or even whether, the Agenda would be adopted. Yet as published, this book both looks back upon WIPO's adoption of the Agenda in its final form and assesses some of the initial currents that the Agenda has unleashed within WIPO and elsewhere.

The debate over IP and development has often been infused with ideological fervor. It has pitted a faith in the efficacy of markets against a belief in government as guarantor of social welfare. It has juxtaposed a belief in the rights of authors and inventors to the fruits of their intellectual creations against the view that access to knowledge and invention is a fundamental human right.

In that vein, for better or for worse, WIPO itself has been animated by a fervent belief in intellectual property rights. The cupola of WIPO's headquarters in Geneva bears a Latin inscription penned by the organization's renowned director general, Arpad Bogsch. In English translation, it reads:

> HUMAN GENIUS IS THE SOURCE OF ALL WORKS OF ART AND INVENTION * THESE WORKS ARE THE GUARANTEE OF A LIFE WORTHY OF MEN * IT IS THE DUTY OF THE STATE TO ENSURE WITH DILIGENCE THE PROTECTION OF THE ARTS AND INVENTIONS.[1]

The Development Agenda does not erase that marble inscription. Nor does it deny the value of creative arts and invention. But it does insist that intellectual property law be placed in the service of development. And, as such, it calls for a nuanced account of how intellectual property law actually operates in developing countries. It recognizes, and demands that WIPO recognize, that creativity and innovation require access to existing knowledge and that a robust public domain can be no less crucial to development than are intellectual property rights. It thus insists that countries have the flexibility to fashion intellectual property law in line with their level of development and the shape of their indigenous industries. It is in that spirit that this book presents a granular, multidisciplinary study of how and when intellectual property rights promote—or impede—development.

This book would not have been possible without the generous support of the Ann C. Rosenfield Symposium Fund of the UCLA School of Law and the UCLA Anderson CIBER Center for International Business Education and Research, which co-sponsored the conference from which this book arose, and of the UCLA Dean's Fund for its funding of this book's initial copyediting. I am very grateful for their support. In particular, I want to thank Robert Spich, Faculty Program Director of the Center for International Business Education and Research at the UCLA Anderson School of Management, for his personal assistance in bringing together scholars, policy analysts, and diplomats from various disciplines and countries for our conference, and Michael Schill, Dean of the UCLA School of

1. See Gerald J. Mossinghoff and Ralph Oman, The World Intellectual Property Organization: A United Nations Success Story, 160 World Affairs 104 (1997).

Law, for his enthusiastic support of scholarship at UCLA, including my own, and for making the School of Law funding available for this project. I also thank Wyatt Sloan-Tribe and Elke Kolodinski for their fine work in copyediting this book's chapters and, of course, my wonderful Oxford University Press editors, Sarah Bloxham and Chris Collins.

CONTRIBUTORS

DIANA V. BARROWCLOUGH

United Nations Conference on Trade and Development

Diana V. Barrowclough is an economist at the United Nations Conference on Trade and Development, Geneva. She has been responsible for research and policy analysis on topics relating to trade, finance, investment and development; including advising on national and multilateral policy and writing for numerous UNCTAD publications. Before joining UNCTAD in 2001, she lectured economics at the Faculty of Economics and Politics at the University of Cambridge, where she was appointed a Fellow of St John's College. Prior to moving to Cambridge, Dr Barrowclough worked in London for the international consultancy National Economic Research Associates, focusing on issues relating to liberalization and privatization. She has been a consultant to a wide range of enterprises, governments, and supra-national organizations and institutions. Her recent textbook (authored with Michelle Baddeley) *'Running regressions: A practical guide to quantitative research in Economics, Finance and Development Studies'*, (Cambridge University Press, 2008) reflects her interest in combining theory and practical economics. She is also co-author and co-editor (with Zeljka Kozul-Wright) of *'Creative Industries and Developing Countries: Voice, Choice and Economic Growth'* (Routledge Studies in Contemporary Political Economy, 2007), and co-author (with Anne Miroux and Hafiz Mirza) of *'FDI in tourism: the development dimension' (United Nations, 2007)*. Dr Barrowclough holds a PhD in Economics (University of Cambridge), an M-Phil in economics (University of Cambridge), and a BA in economics and political science (University of Auckland). This paper represents her personal, and not UNCTAD official, views.

JOHN H. BARTON

Stanford University

John H. Barton is the George E. Osborne Professor of Law, Emeritus, at Stanford Law School. Professor Barton has devoted his academic career to the examination of questions at the intersection of science and the law. A fellow of the American Association for the Advancement of Science, Professor Barton has focused his scholarship on international law concerns ranging from national defense to issues surrounding the distribution of intellectual property across the developed and undeveloped world. His current work involves the study of the transfer of technologies, including vaccines, steel, and climate change technologies, between scientifically sophisticated and developing nations, and the development of a political theory of international organization and globalization. Professor Barton has chaired or been a member of more than a dozen academic and international advisory commissions, most recently heading up the International Commission on Intellectual Property Rights. Before joining the Stanford Law School faculty in 1969, Professor Barton was an engineer with Sylvania Electronic Defense Laboratories.

MICHAEL D. BIRNHACK

Tel-Aviv University

Michael D. Birnhack is a senior lecturer at the Faculty of Law, Tel-Aviv University. Prior to joining Tel Aviv University, he was a senior lecturer at the University of Haifa, where he served as co-director of the Haifa Center of Law & Technology. His research interests are intellectual property, law and technology, and privacy law. He writes, teaches, and lectures about these topics. He edited a book on freedom of speech in Israel (Hebrew), and is currently engaged in editing books on the new Israeli Copyright Act and Law and Technology. Dr. Birnhack is a member of the Israeli Public Council for the Protection of Privacy, served in a Ministry of Justice committee on data protection, served as a sub-contractor to the EU Commission on the matter of adequacy of the Israeli data protection regime, and advised several public agencies on matters of online journalistic ethics, web-access in public libraries, and patent law.

OTÁVIO BRANDELLI

Brazilian Ministry of External Relations

Otávio Brandelli is a Brazilian career diplomat who headed the Intellectual Property Division of the Brazilian Ministry of External Relations from 2004 to January of 2008. During that time, he was responsible for the coordination of Brazilian positions on IPR in international fora and he represented the said Ministry in the Brazilian Interministerial Group on Intellectual Property and the National Council on Combating Piracy and Other Offences to IPR. From 1992 to 1996 he was a member of the different interministerial committees which developed the Brazilian bill of laws proposed by the executive branch to the Congress, concerning the TRIPS Agreement implementation. He also worked at Brazil's Permanent Mission to the European Communities (Brussels) from 1996 to 2000, and at the Permanent Delegation of Brazil to the Latin American Integration Association and to the Common Market of the South–MERCOSUL (Montevideo) from 2000 to 2004. He is currently posted for a second term at the Permanent Delegation of Brazil in Montevideo, Uruguay.

LEONARDO BURLAMAQUI

State University of Rio de Janeiro and Ford Foundation

Leonardo Burlamaqui is a Program Officer at The Ford Foundation in New York and is responsible for the *Global Economic Governance* portfolio.

Previous to this appointment, Leonardo held academic appointments as a professor and research director of the law and economics program at the Candido Mendes

University and associate professor of economics at the State University of Rio de Janeiro (on leave) and spells at WIPO (the World Intellectual Property Organization), WIDER (the World Institute for Development Economics Research) in Helsinki, IDE (the Institute for Developing Economies in Tokyo), and SUM (the Centre for Development and the Environment at the University of Oslo).

His books include *Organized Capitalism in Japan* (IPEA/CEPAL, coauthored with Maria da Conceição Tavares and Ernani Torres) and *Institutions and the Role of State* (E. Elgar, coedited with Ana Célia Castro and Ha-Joon Chang). His latest publications include the chapter "Banking and the Financing of Development: A Schumpeterian and Minskyian perspective," coauthored with Jan Kregel, in *Re-imagining Growth: Toward a Renewal of the Idea of Development*, edited by Gary Dymski and Silvana de Paula (Zed Books, 2005); the essay "Innovation, Competition and Financial Vulnerability," also coauthored with Jan Kregel, published in the *Brazilian Journal of Political Economy* (autumn 2005); and the chapter "The Rise And Halt of Economic Development In Brazil, 1945–2004 Industrial Catching–up, Institutional Innovation and Financial Fragility" in the book *Institutional Change and Economic Development*, edited by H.J. Chang (United Nations University Press, 2007). His forthcoming publications include the book *Schumpeter's Capitalism—Evolutionary Economics, Economic Sociology and Competition in Politics* (Edward Elgar, 2009).

SUDIP CHAUDHURI

Indian Institute of Management

Sudip Chaudhuri is professor of economics at the Indian Institute of Management Calcutta. He has conducted research in industrial policy, globalization and liberalization, reforms of insolvency procedures, WTO, TRIPS, and the patent regime. His latest book is *The WTO and India's Pharmaceuticals Industry: Patent Protection, TRIPS and Developing Countries* (Oxford University Press, 2005). He has done studies for different organizations including the World Health Organization, the Reserve Bank of India, UNICEF, and the Government of India.

CARLOS M. CORREA

University of Buenos Aires

Carlos M. Correa is professor and the director of the Centre for Interdisciplinary Studies on Industrial Property and Economics Law at the University of Buenos Aires. Professor Correa is the author of several books and numerous articles on law and economics, particularly on investment, technology, and intellectual property. Professor Correa served as Under-Secretary of State for Informatics and Development in the Argentine national government from 1984 to 1989. During that period he was coordinator of the Inter-ministerial Group on Intellectual Property. He was also, from 1988 to 1991, an Argentinian government delegate in international negotiations on intellectual property (including the Washington Treaty on integrated circuits and the TRIPS Agreement).

Professor Correa has been a consultant to several regional and international organizations in different areas of law and economics. At different times he has advised governments on these matters. He was a member of the UK International Commission on Intellectual Property, established in 2001 and of the Commission on Intellectual Property, Innovation and Public Health established by the World Health Assembly in 2003.

CAROLYN DEERE

Oxford University

Carolyn Deere is a senior researcher at the Global Economic Governance Programme at the University of Oxford, where she is the director of the global trade governance project. She is also a resident scholar at the International Centre for Trade and Sustainable Development (ICTSD) in Geneva, Switzerland, and the founder and chair of the board of Intellectual Property Watch. Dr. Deere previously served as the assistant director of the Global Inclusion Programme at the Rockefeller Foundation in New York. In partnership with colleagues across the Foundation, she designed and coordinated the Foundation's initiative to Promote a Fairer Course for Intellectual Property Policy and launched the Bellagio Series on Intellectual Property Policy and Sustainable Development. During this time, Dr. Deere also co-founded the Funders Network on Trade and Globalization (FNTG). Prior to joining the Rockefeller Foundation, she was the manager of the Congressional Staff Forum on International Development at the Overseas Development Council (ODC) in Washington, D.C. Dr. Deere is author of *The Implementation Game: The TRIPS Agreement and the Global Politics of IP Reform in Developing Countries* (OUP, 2008), the coeditor (with Dan Esty) of *Greening the Americas: NAFTA's Lessons for Hemispheric Trade* (MIT Press, 2001), and coauthor (with Elizabeth Havice) of *Fisheries, International Trade and Sustainable Development* (ICTSD, 2006). She has been a consultant to UNDP's Office of the Human Development Report, the National Wildlife Federation, the Yale Center for Environmental Law and Policy, the Open Society Institute, and the South Centre. Dr. Deere holds a DPhil in international relations (University College, Oxford) and an MA in international relations (Johns Hopkins School of Advanced International Studies).

DANIEL J. GERVAIS

University of Ottawa

Daniel J. Gervais is professor of law and director of the Technology and Entertainment Law program at Vanderbilt University. Until June 2008 he was acting dean and Osler Professor of Intellectual Property and Technology Law at the University of Ottawa Faculty of Law, Common Law Section. In 1990, he became Consultant-Legal Officer at the World Trade Organization (GATT) and was actively involved in the TRIPS Agreement negotiations. In 1992, in joined the World Intellectual Property Organization and was promoted the following year to head of the Copyright Projects Section, where he prepared WIPO studies and international meetings on the impact of digital technology on copyright and neighboring rights. In 1995, Dr. Gervais joined the International Confederation of Societies of Authors and Composers as assistant secretary general and in 1997 moved to the United States to become director of international relations at the Copyright Clearance Center. Professor Gervais joined the Faculty of Law of the University of Ottawa in 2001. He has published several peer-reviewed articles, in six languages, on various intellectual property topics. He is the Editor-in-Chief of the *Journal of World Intellectual Property* and the author of a reference book on the TRIPS Agreement published by Sweet & Maxwell in London.

P. BERNT HUGENHOLTZ

University of Amsterdam

P. Bernt Hugenholtz is professor of law and director of the Institute for Information Law (IViR) at the University of Amsterdam, where he teaches courses in copyright law, industrial property law, and international copyright law. He also occasionally teaches at the Munich Intellectual Property Law Center (Munich), Fordham Law School (New York), Monash University (Melbourne), and the University of Bergen (Norway). Dr. Hugenholtz is the general editor of the Information Law Series, published by Kluwer Law International. He was a member of the Amsterdam Bar from 1990 to 1998 and has been an advisor to WIPO, the European Commission, the European Parliament, the Ministry of Justice of the Netherlands, and various private firms. He is also an adjunct judge at the Court of Appeals in Arnhem (Netherlands). Professor Hugenholtz has written numerous books, studies, and articles focusing on topics involving copyright and information technology, notably on the protection of databases, on copyright problems relating to the digital networked environment, and on copyright contract law. Professor Hugenholtz received his doctorate cum laude from the University of Amsterdam.

B. ZORINA KHAN

Bowdoin College

B. Zorina Khan is associate professor of economics at Bowdoin College and research associate at the National Bureau of Economic Research. Professor Khan has been a Fulbright Scholar, Griliches Fellow, and visiting scholar at Harvard University and the UC Berkeley and UCLA Schools of Law. She has served as a consultant to the World Bank, the British Commission on Intellectual Property Rights, and the Commonwealth Secretariat. Her publications include journal articles on the economics of law and legal systems, intellectual property rights, antitrust, and technology. Her recent book, *The Democratization of Invention: Patents and Copyrights in American Economic Development, 1790–1920* (Cambridge University Press and NBER, 2005), was awarded the 2006 Alice Hanson Jones Prize for the best book in American economic history over the past two years.

FRANCESCO LAFORGIA

Brescia University

Centre for Research on Innovation & Internationalisation, Bocconi University

Francesco Laforgia recently earned his PhD in economics for production development from Insubria University, Italy. He currently serves as a junior researcher on Innovation in Pharmaceutical, Biotech and ICT Industries at Brescia University and at the Centre of Research on Innovation and Internationalization at Bocconi University. His writing focuses on innovation in high-tech sectors, intellectual property rights systems, mobility of knowledge workers, and patterns of knowledge diffusion.

KEITH E. MASKUS

University of Colorado

Keith E. Maskus is professor of economics and associate dean of social sciences at the University of Colorado, Boulder. He has been a lead economist in the Development Research Group at the World Bank. He is also a research fellow at the Peterson Institute for International Economics. He has been a visiting senior economist at the U.S. Department of State and a visiting professor at the University of Adelaide, and he serves as a consultant for the World Bank, the United Nations Conference on Trade and Development, and the World Health Organization. He was the editor of *The World Economy: The Americas.* Maskus received his PhD in economics from the University of Michigan in 1981. He has written extensively about various aspects of international trade, including empirical testing of trade models and determinants of foreign direct investment. His current research focuses on the international economic aspects of protecting intellectual property rights. He is the author of *Intellectual Property Rights in the Global Economy*, published by the Institute for International Economics, and coeditor of *International Public Goods and the Transfer of Technology under a Globalized Intellectual Property Regime*, published by Cambridge University Press.

FABIO MONTOBBIO

University of Insubria

Centre for Research on Innovation & Internationalisation, Bocconi University

Fabio Montobbio is associate professor of economics at Insubria University, Varese, Italy; contract professor at Bocconi University, Milan; and researcher at the Centre for Research on Innovation & Internationalisation at Bocconi University. Professor Montobbio earned his PhD in economics in 2001 at the University of Manchester, where he wrote his dissertation on technological spillovers and structural change. Since then, his research interests have extended to the economics of patents, university technology transfer, the new economics of science, and finally, technology and development. His teaching centers upon two main disciplinary areas: industrial economics and innovation and intellectual property rights. Professor Montobbio has published in *World Development,*

Economics of Innovation and New Technology, Cambridge Journal of Economics, Journal of Evolutionary Economics, and *Structural Change and Economic Dynamics.*

HENRIQUE CHOER MORAES

Brazil Ministry of External Relations

Henrique Choer Moraes is a career diplomat currently working at the Permanent Mission of Brazil to the European Communities (Brussels). Prior to that, he worked at the Intellectual Property Division of Brazil's Ministry of External Relations, where he served from 2004 to 2007. In that capacity, Mr. Moraes has served as Brazilian delegate to the XXXII, XXXIII, and XXXIV General Assemblies of the World Organization on Intellectual Property, held during 2005, 2006, and 2007 in Geneva, Switzerland, and to the meetings, assemblies, provisional committees, and other events on the Agenda for Development held during 2005, 2006, and 2007 in Geneva, Switzerland. He also took part in the negotiations on patents, copyrights, and biodiversity at the World Intellectual Property Organization, biodiversity and intellectual property at the World Trade Organization, and intellectual property, access, and benefits sharing at the Convention on Biological Diversity. Mr. Moraes was professor of international public law at the University Ritter dos Reis, Porto Alegre, RS, from 2000 to 2004. He holds a master's degree in integration and business international law from Universidade Federal do Rio Grande do Sul (Porto Alegre).

NEIL WEINSTOCK NETANEL

University of California at Los Angeles

Neil Weinstock Netanel joined the UCLA School of Law faculty in fall 2004. He teaches copyright, international intellectual property, and intellectual property scholarship. Prior to joining UCLA Law, Professor Netanel served for a decade on the faculty of the University of Texas at Austin School of Law, where he was the Arnold, White & Durkee Centennial Professor of Law. He has also taught at the law schools of Haifa University, the Hebrew University of Jerusalem, Tel-Aviv University, Harvard University, the University of Toronto, and New York University. Professor Netanel's most recent scholarship includes *Copyright's Paradox* (Oxford University Press, 2008); "Why Has Copyright Expanded? Analysis and Critique," in 6 *New Directions in Copyright Law* (Fiona Macmillan, ed., Edward Elgar, 2007); and "Copyright and the First Amendment; What Eldred Misses—and Portends," in *Copyright and Free Speech: Comparative and International Analyses* (J. Griffiths & U. Suthersanen, eds., Oxford University Press, 2005). His primary work-in-progress is *From Maimonides to Microsoft; The Jewish Law of Copyright Since the Birth of Print* (Oxford University Press, forthcoming 2010) (with David Nimmer). Professor Netanel received his undergraduate degree from Yale University and his graduate degrees (JD and JSD) from UC Berkeley and Stanford University.

RUTH L. OKEDIJI

University of Minnesota

Ruth L. Okediji is the William L. Prosser Professor of Law and Solly Robins Distinguished Research Fellow at the University of Minnesota Law School where she teaches copyright, trademarks, contracts, and international intellectual property law. Prior to joining the University of Minnesota in 2003, Professor Okediji held the Edith Gaylord Harper Presidential Professorship at the University of Oklahoma College of Law. She has also been a visiting professor at the Duke University School of Law. Professor Okediji's research and scholarship focus particularly on development issues in the global economic regulatory framework, including the impact of the international intellectual property system on innovation prospects of developing and least-developed countries. She has written and lectured extensively on various aspects of international copyright law, the TRIPS Agreement, and the relationship between international trade and intellectual property regulation.

Professor Okediji is past-chair of the Intellectual Property Section and the Section on Law and Computers of the Association of American Law Schools. In addition to numerous articles, book chapters, and monographs, Professor Okediji is the author of *Copyright in a Global Information Economy* (with J. Cohen, L. Loren, and M. O'Rourke, Aspen Publishers, 2002) and two forthcoming books, *Global Perspectives on Patent Law* (with M. Bagley and J. Erstling, Oxford University Press, 2009) and *Global Perspectives on Intellectual Property* (Oxford University Press, 2009). Her most recent article, *WIPO-WTO Relations and the Future of Global Intellectual Property Norms* is forthcoming in the 2008 Netherlands Yearbook of International Law. Professor Okediji has served as a consultant to various UN agencies, and other international organizations, on projects addressing the interests of developing countries in the international intellectual property system. She has also served as Advisor on Trade-Related Aspects of Intellectual Property Rights to member countries of the South African Development Cooperation, and other countries, under the auspices of the Commercial Law Development Program, U.S. Department of Commerce. Professor Okediji holds an LL.B. degree from the University of Jos, and LL.M and S.J.D degrees from Harvard Law School.

LUIGI ORSENIGO

University of Brescia

Centre for Research on Innovation & Internationalisation, Bocconi University

Luigi Orsenigo is a full professor of applied economics at the University of Brescia and member of the board of directors of the Centre for Research on Innovation & Internationalisation at the University of Bocconi. Professor Orsenigo has been involved in advisory activities on issues related to industrial policies, science and technology policies, and regional planning for various national and international institutions. His main research fields are in the areas of the economics of innovation, industrial dynamics, and evolutionary theory, both theoretically and empirically. Professor Orsenigo is the author of *The Emergence of Biotechnology: Institutions and Markets in Industrial Innovation* (Pinter Publishers, 1989). He obtained his PhD at the Science Policy Research Unit, University of Sussex, Brighton, United Kingdom, in 1989.

YI QIAN

Northwestern University

Yi Qian is Kraft Research Professor and assistant professor of marketing at the Kellogg School of Management, Northwestern University. She received her undergraduate degree in economics, master's degree in statistics, and doctorate in economics from Harvard University. Professor Qian is the author of "Do National Patent Laws Stimulate Domestic Innovation in a Global Patenting Environment?—A Cross-Country Analysis of Pharmaceutical Patent Protection, 1978–2002," *Review of Economics and Statistics (RESTAT)*, MIT (August 2007), and "Impacts of Entry by Counterfeiters," Quarterly Journal of Economics (QJE), MIT (November 2008). Her research interests include intellectual property rights, innovation and international trade, and foreign direct investment.

NAGLA RIZK

American University in Cairo

Nagla Rizk is associate professor of economics at the American University in Cairo. Her area of research is the economics of knowledge, technological change, and development with emphasis on the economics of intellectual property, access to knowledge, and human development in Egypt and the Arab world. Of particular interest is the potential role of information and communication technology (ICT) as a source of empowerment and a driver for development. She has done extensive work on the assessment of e-readiness of small and medium enterprises in the Egyptian industry and is presently working on a macroeconomic study on information technology, productivity, and economic growth in Egypt. Her current research includes work on Egypt's open source software and copyright in the Arab music industry and is done in partnership with the Information Society Project of Yale Law School where she is the team leader, contributor, and coeditor for Egypt's A2K country study. She is a core author for the Arab Knowledge Report (2008). She has served as chair of the economics department of the American University in Cairo, research advisor on Egypt's e-readiness at the Ministry of Communication and Information Technology, and is currently the leader of Egypt's research team within the Research ICT Africa Network and a member of the Research and Strategy Advisory Group of Iqsensato research and policy think tank. She received her PhD from McMaster University in Canada and has also taught at the University of Toronto.

PEDRO ROFFE

International Centre for Trade and Sustainable Development

Pedro Roffe is Senior Fellow on Intellectual Property and Development at the International Centre for Trade and Sustainable Development (ICTSD) and a former staff member of the United Nations Conference on Trade and Development (UNCTAD). He graduated from the Faculty of Law of the Universidad de Chile and pursued postgraduate studies at New York University, Europa Institute (University of Amsterdam), and the Graduate Institute of International Studies (Geneva). His work has focused on international aspects of transfer of technology, intellectual property, and foreign direct investment. He is the author of articles and books and is responsible for a number of United Nations–related publications. Published contributions in which he has recently been involved include *International Technology Transfer: The Origins and Aftermath of the United Nations Negotiations on a Draft Code of Conduct*; *Bilateral Agreements and a TRIPS-Plus World: The Chile-USA Free Trade Agreement*; *Resource Book on TRIPS and Development*; and *Negotiating Health: Intellectual Property and Access to Medicines*.

KENNETH L. SOKOLOFF

University of California at Los Angeles

The late Kenneth L. Sokoloff was professor of economics at the University of California, Los Angeles; director of the UCLA Center for the Study of Entrepreneurial Activity in Economic History and Development; and research associate at the National Bureau of Economic Research. He was a fellow of the American Academy of Arts and Sciences, and published many articles and books on the processes of early industrialization in the United States; the development of a market for new technological knowledge and its impact on the organization and rate of inventive activity in the United States; the evolution of intellectual property institutions over the nineteenth century; the record and sources of productivity growth in newly industrializing East Asian economies; and the effects of the extent of inequality in the Americas on the paths of long-run institutional and economic development. He received his PhD from Harvard University in 1982, and was a visiting professor at the California Institute of Technology, the Ecole des Hautes Etudes en Sciences Sociales, Tel Aviv University, and Harvard University.

MADHAVI SUNDER

University of California at Davis

Madhavi Sunder is professor of law at the University of California, Davis, School of Law. Professor Sunder teaches intellectual property, international intellectual property, and women's human rights. She is a leading scholar in the legal regulation of culture. Her work traverses numerous legal fields, from intellectual property and cultural property to human rights law and the First Amendment. Her recent publications include "IP^3," *Stanford Law Review* (2006); "The Invention of Traditional Knowledge," *Duke Journal of Law & Contemporary Problems* (2007); "The Romance of the Public Domain," *California Law Review* (2004); "Piercing the Veil," *Yale Law Journal* (2003); and "Cultural Dissent," *Stanford Law Review* (2001). She has authored numerous comments and chapters in books and is the editor of *Gender and Feminist Theory in Law and Society* (2006). In 2006 Professor Sunder was awarded a prestigious Carnegie Corporation Scholarship. Professor Sunder has been a visiting professor of law at Yale, the University of Chicago, and Cornell. Professor Sunder received her bachelor's degree in social studies, magna cum laude, from Harvard in 1992 and her JD from Stanford Law School in 1997. While at Stanford, she was an articles editor for the *Stanford Law Review*. Sunder clerked for Judge Harry Pregerson of the Ninth Circuit Court of Appeals and practiced law in New York City with the firm of Cleary, Gottlieb, Steen & Hamilton.

GINA VEA

International Centre for Trade and Sustainable Development

Gina Vea joined ICTSD in Geneva in 2006, where she assumed the position of Programme Officer, Intellectual Property & Technology. Her work has focused on the nexus between intellectual property and public health, particularly in relation to the development of new medical technologies and access to essential health products. This has involved managing projects aimed at increasing understanding of the relationship between patents and the price of medicines, monitoring and analyzing negotiations at WHO, WIPO, and WTO, and facilitating meetings between policy makers, academics, industry representatives and other stakeholders.

Ms. Vea's experience also includes providing outreach and communications planning for international organizations and coordinating academic programs on global governance and health. At the domestic policy level, she has served as an analyst, consultant, and legislative director. Ms. Vea received a BA in history from University of California and a master's in public policy from Duke University.

HONG XUE

University of Hong Kong

Hong Xue is associate professor at the University of Hong Kong and Fellow of Yale Information Society Project. Dr. Xue was elected as one of the Ten Nationally Distinguished Young Jurists by the China Law Society and granted the Special Governmental Allowance for prominent contribution to social science by the State Council. She also received the Outstanding Young Researcher Award from the University of Hong Kong. Internationally, she works in many governmental and nongovernmental organizations. She is one of the three Asia-Pacific Representatives in the At-large Advisory Committee of the Internet Corporation for Assigned Names and Numbers (ICANN) and the Member of the Executive Committee of the International Association for Promotion of the Advanced Teaching and Research of Intellectual Property (ATRIP).

1. INTRODUCTION
The WIPO Development Agenda and Its Development Policy Context

NEIL WEINSTOCK NETANEL*

The World Intellectual Property Organization General Assembly adopted the Development Agenda in September 2007, after three years of often acrimonious debate.[1] The Agenda radically transforms WIPO's mandate and reverberates throughout the international intellectual property regime, including in ongoing battles within the World Trade Organization over the future direction of "TRIPS," the Agreement on Trade-Related Aspects of Intellectual Property. Yet despite its powerful symbolic message, the full extent of the Development Agenda's actual impact on the ground, both within WIPO and without, remains to be seen.

In 1967, the Convention Establishing the World Intellectual Property Organization provided unequivocally that WIPO's central mission would be "to promote the protection of intellectual property throughout the world."[2] In that vein, WIPO has long favored the "upward harmonization of intellectual property laws"—ever greater intellectual property protection and enforcement in developing and developed countries alike. WIPO's IP maximalist approach remained constant even after 1974 when WIPO became a specialized agency of the United Nations. In 1974, the United Nations stood at the center of the New International Economic Order (NIEO), a far reaching program for revamping the global economic system to jumpstart third world development, which included calls for

* Professor, UCLA School of Law.

1. WIPO Doc. A/43/16 Annex A. The 45 proposals adopted as the Development Agenda are reproduced as Appendix A to this Introduction.

2. Convention Establishing the World Intellectual Property Organization, July 14, 1967, 21 U.S.T. 1749, 828 U.N.T.S. 3.

compulsory transfers of technology.[3] In language responding to those calls, the UN-WIPO agreement gave WIPO responsibility for "promoting creative intellectual activity and facilitating the transfer of technology related to industrial property to developing countries in order to accelerate economic, social and cultural development."[4] Yet WIPO's leadership refused to recognize any contradiction between the organization's assigned task as UN agency of spurring development versus its traditional core objective of extending greater copyright and patent protection "over the world."[5] Rather WIPO has insisted that promoting greater, universal IP rights *is* the means by which the organization facilitates technology transfer and promotes development. As a 2003 WIPO publication, authored by then Director General Kamal Idris, proclaimed, "intellectual property is a 'power tool' for economic development and wealth creation," one "that is not yet being used to optimal effect in all countries, particularly in the developing world."[6]

The Development Agenda decisively rejects that IP-centric view. It posits that strong intellectual property protection does not consistently promote creative activity, facilitate technology transfer, or accelerate development. The Development Agenda accordingly places the benefits of a rich and accessible public domain, national flexibilities in implementing IP treaty norms, access to knowledge, UN development goals, curbing of IP-related anti-competitive practices, and the need to balance the costs and benefits of intellectual property protection firmly within WIPO's central mission. The Development Agenda by no means abandons the idea that intellectual property rights can fuel creativity, innovation, and development under some local conditions. But for the first time in WIPO's history, it places the need for balance, flexibility, and a robust public domain on par with promoting IP protection in all WIPO matters affecting developing countries.

The Development Agenda is not only a rebuke of WIPO's uncritical promotion of intellectual property rights. It reflects developing countries' growing

---

3. *See*, generally, THE NEW INTERNATIONAL ECONOMIC ORDER: THE NORTH-SOUTH DEBATE (Jagdish N. Bhagwati ed., MIT Press 1977).

4. Agreement between the UNITED NATIONS and the World Intellectual Property Organization, Art. 1, entered into effect, Dec. 17, 1974 [hereinafter UN-WIPO Agreement].

5. WIPO officials viewed WIPO's UN agency status as a means to further the organization's mission of having copyright and patent protection "extended over the world, or at least to the great majority of countries." Arpad Bogsch, The First Twenty-Five Years of the World Intellectual Property Organization from 1967 to 1992, at 28 (WIPO Publication No. 881 (E), 1992), quoted in Debora J. Halbert, *The World Intellectual Property Organization: Past, Present, and Future*, 54 J. Copyright Soc'y U.S.A. 253, 261 (2007). Bogsch was WIPO's Director General when the UN-WIPO agreement took effect.

6. KAMIL IDRIS, INTELLECTUAL PROPERTY: A POWER TOOL FOR ECONOMIC GROWTH 1 (World Intellectual Property Organization 2002). Kamil Idris is the outgoing Director General of WIPO.

resistance to the upward harmonization of IP protection required by the TRIPS and subsequent "TRIPS-plus" bilateral free trade agreements as well. Indeed, the WIPO Development Agenda should be understood as part of a broad, multipronged rejection of the "Washington Consensus" that shunted aside the NIEO and came to dominate development policy in the 1980s and early 1990s. That neoliberal approach advanced an ironclad belief that unregulated markets, unhindered cross-border trade, and the spread of formal property rights are the best tool to promote economic growth and development.[7] But in the last decade, in the wake of the spectacular failure of that approach in a number of areas, the World Bank and other international economic institutions have moved away from the Consensus's sweeping free market prescriptions. They have embraced instead a new development framework that eschews across-the-board solutions in favor of nuanced consideration of local conditions, recognizes the need for governments actively to assist developing countries to reap the benefits of liberalized trade, and, in line with Amartya Sen's seminal argument for "development as freedom,"[8] intertwines issues of social justice and human rights with the goal of generating economic growth.[9] This development-as-freedom lodestar also infuses the United Nations Development Programme, which assesses development in terms of life expectancy, education, literacy, gender equality, and political participation, in addition to gross national product.[10]

In line with this new development framework, the WIPO Development Agenda similarly rejects the notion that unregulated markets in the products of creative expression and innovation, secured by countries' uniform enforcement of broad, proprietary rights in those products, will promote development. It posits, rather, that a robust public domain and national government flexibility in defining and delimiting IP rights will best serve developing countries' needs.

In its embrace of UN development goals, indeed, the WIPO Development Agenda jettisons the unregulated market approach to intellectual property along the same two fronts as development agencies have distanced themselves from the Washington Consensus in the arena of development policy generally. First, the Development Agenda rebuffs the neoliberal belief, which has been a driving force behind TRIPS as well WIPO treaty initiatives, that broad IP rights will

---

7. *See* David Kennedy, *The "Rule of Law," Political Choices, and Development Common Sense, in* The New Law and Economic Development; A Critical Appraisal 95, 128–150 (David M. Trubek and Alvaro Santos eds., Cambridge Univ. Press 2006).

8. Amartya Sen, Development as Freedom (Alfred A. Knopf 1999).

9. *See* Kennedy, *supra* note 7, at 151–58. *See also* Joseph E. Stiglitz & Andrew Charlton, Fair Trade For All; How Trade Can Promote Development (Oxford Univ. Press 2005) (presenting a mainstream criticism of the Washington Consensus and presenting a detailed proposal for a liberalized trade regime that is geared toward the special interests of developing countries).

10. *See* United Nations Development Programme, Human Development Indices, http://hdr.undp.org/en/humandev/hdi.

bring affordable technology, innovation, and foreign direct investment to developing countries. Although not eschewing IP's potential for promoting innovation and economic growth in certain local circumstances, the Agenda views technology transfer through ready access to knowledge, unimpeded by exclusive IP rights, as no less a cornerstone of economic development.

Second, the Agenda calls into question whether economic development and wealth creation are the sole metrics for measuring development. The Agenda itself and the developing country campaign to bring the Agenda before WIPO have been informed by a new development framework that seeks to attain social, material, and political conditions conducive to human freedom, of which economic growth is an important contributing factor, but not an end in and of itself.[11] The initial "Friends of Development" proposal for a WIPO Development Agenda explicitly underscores that view: "As a United Nations specialized agency, WIPO has an obligation to ensure that its technical cooperation activities are geared towards implementing all relevant UN development objectives, which are not limited to economic development alone."[12]

As the new development framework posits, there is no single path to development. A configuration of government regulation, market, and intellectual property rights that spurs development in one country might be ill suited to economic conditions, market and governmental institutions, and cultural traditions in another. So, too, does the WIPO Development Agenda require WIPO to work toward intellectual property norms that "take into account different levels of development" and to assist Member States in tailoring intellectual property laws to their "country specific" conditions, reflecting "the priorities and special needs of developing countries." It is no longer WIPO's mission to serve intellectual property producers' interest in obtaining uniformly high levels of protection throughout the world. WIPO, rather, must henceforth be guided by distinct, country-specific understandings—for example, that patent law norms that well serve pharmaceutical industries and innovation in the United States and Europe might be less than optimal in China, wholly ill suited to India, and inimical to Senegal.

Academic studies support the Development Agenda's rejection of the neoliberal belief that developing countries' across-the-board adoption of robust IP protection will bring economic growth, foreign direct investment, and technology transfer. Even those who contend that IP rights can enhance technology transfer under certain conditions concede that empirical evidence for that proposition is mixed and that strong IP rights can merely impose costs without bringing technology

11. For illuminating discussion of the Development Agenda's rejection of WIPO's "unreflective alignment with a model of development as growth," see Denis Borges Barbosa et al., *Slouching Towards Development in International Intellectual Property*, 2007 Mich. St. L. Rev. 71, 120–23.

12. WIPO, Proposal by Argentina and Brazil for the Establishment of a Development Agenda for WIPO, WO/GA/31/11 (Aug. 27, 2004), Annex, ¶ VII, at 4.

transfer or other efficiency benefits when, as is typically the case with pharmaceuticals, related know-how is not needed for the diffusion of the technology product.[13] Indeed, some studies show that a developing country's expansion of IP rights and enforcement can even lead foreign firms to close manufacturing facilities in those countries because increased protection makes it more feasible to import IP-rich products produced elsewhere, thus blunting technology transfer and foreign direct investment.[14] For these reasons, there appears to be consensus among leading, mainstream development economists that uniformly strong levels of IP protection are highly detrimental to developing countries. As Joseph Stiglitz and Andrew Charlton state,

> The TRIPS Agreement has considerable implications for technological and industrial policy. By strengthening intellectual property rights in developing countries, it is likely to increase the royalty payments demanded by technology holders there, and also to create or reinforce monopolistic positions in small markets. It also restricts reverse engineering and other important methods of imitating innovation, thereby limiting the ability of firms in developing countries to reduce their technological disadvantage.[15]

Similarly, Jagdish Bhagwati, a prominent proponent of liberalized global trade, summarizes,

> As regards intellectual property protection (IPP), demanded insistently by the United States and then by other rich countries, most economists believe that having patents at twenty-year length (as put into the WTO) is, from the viewpoint of worldwide efficiency, suboptimal, just as having no patents almost certainly is. Many also consider it to be a transfer from most of the poor countries to the rich ones and hence as an item that does not belong to the WTO, whose organizing principles should be the inclusion of mutually gainful transactions, as indeed noncoercive trade is.[16]

To emphasize: that is *not* to say the IP protection is inimical to development as applied to every developing country and industry. Indeed, as several contributors to this volume point out, robust IP protection may well spur economic growth in

---

13. *See* Ashish Arora et al., *Markets for Technology, Intellectual Property Rights, and Development, in* International Public Goods and Transfer of Technology in a Globalized Intellectual Property Regime 321 (Keith E. Maskus & Jerome E. Reichman eds., Cambridge Univ. Press 2005) [hereafter International Public Goods]. See also Lee G. Branstetter, *Do Stronger Patents Induce More Local Innovation? in* International Public Goods at 309 (finding that economic studies fail to find evidence that stronger patents spur domestic innovation).

14. Carlos M. Correa, *Can TRIPS Foster Technology Transfer?* in International Public Goods, *supra* note 13, at 227, 231.

15. Stiglitz & Charlton, *supra* note 9, at 103.

16. Jagdish Bhagwati, Free Trade Today 75–76 (Princeton Univ. Press 2002).

developing countries with large domestic markets and emerging economies and may nourish cultural industries even in least developed countries. Nonetheless, it is apparent that the neoliberal one-size-fits-all approach to property and markets has no more purchase as it pertains to intellectual property than it does with respect to development generally. Thus, to determine how the Development Agenda should be implemented, WIPO officials, national governments, nongovernmental organizations, and scholars need to focus on granular, empirical study. They must understand how intellectual property law might differentially impact particular countries, institutions, markets, cultural traditions, and creative sectors. General economic theories of how intellectual property law can be expected to promote innovation and development continue to provide a helpful analytic perspective. But such theories, current thinking on development tells us, only go so far.

This book aims to further that granular study. Its contributions address issues of intellectual property and development from a variety of disciplinary and national perspectives. The contributors use case study, empirical research, and sector- and country-specific analysis to shed light on how intellectual property can impact development.

My introduction to this anthology of illuminating, varied contributions unfolds in two sections. I first present and explicate the principal features of the WIPO Development Agenda. I then present an outline of the chapters to come.

I. THE WIPO DEVELOPMENT AGENDA

The Development Agenda adopted by the WIPO General Assembly in September 2007 contains 45 items divided into 6 "clusters." Of these, the Assembly identified 19 items for immediate implementation, but without implying that the remaining 26 are of lesser priority.[17] I have reproduced the Agenda in full in the appendix to this introduction and noted in bold the items that are set for immediate implementation. I focus here on the Agenda's overall themes and most important provisions.

A. "Technical Assistance and Capacity Building"

The Development Agenda provides that "WIPO technical assistance shall be, inter alia, development-oriented, demand-driven, and transparent, taking into account the priorities and the special needs of developing countries, especially LDCs,

17. The 19 items were chosen primarily because their immediate implementation does not require the engagement of additional staff or financial resources. *See* Provisional Committee on Proposals Related to a WIPO Development Agenda (PCDA), WIPO Development Agenda; Preliminary Implementation Report in Respect of 19 Proposals, Feb. 28, 2008, at 1, available at http://ip-watch.org/files/WIPO%20comments%20 on %20DA%20recs%20-%20part%201.pdf [hereafter "Preliminary Implementation Report"].

as well as the different levels of development of Member States." In particular, WIPO must assist Member States in "making national IP institutions more efficient" and in promoting "fair balance between IP protection and the public interest."

To the uninitiated, "WIPO technical assistance" might sound like mundane bureaucratic activity. In fact, its importance can hardly be overestimated. Developing countries often lack the resources and expertise required independently to evaluate and implement intellectual property treaty obligations in a manner that best serves their national interests. As a result, they rely heavily on WIPO for guidance. Over the years, WIPO has accordingly advised developing countries on how WIPO-administered treaties are to be implemented, assisted in drafting national legislation, generated model intellectual property laws, trained officials and lawyers, and sought to bolster the competency and efficiency of national intellectual property offices.[18] Of particular importance, pursuant to its cooperation agreement and joint initiative with the World Trade Organization, WIPO provides developing countries legal-technical assistance regarding their obligations under TRIPS.[19]

In line with its mission of promoting "the protection of intellectual property throughout the world," WIPO has historically provided that technical assistance with single-minded devotion to teaching developing country officials and citizens why intellectual property protection is in their best interests. In that regard, WIPO has viewed strong intellectual property rights as unequivocally conducive to economic growth and development. As WIPO's Intellectual Property Handbook states, "The protection afforded by intellectual property laws results in more creations, innovations and inventions, more investment and effort in research and development (R&D) in technical fields, leading to technological improvements, and thereby to improvement in the quality of industrial output, and by greater access to creations of foreign origin, in an educational and cultural climate that promotes development in general."[20] Among the many examples of how this view has impacted WIPO's advice to developing countries, the Handbook's chapter on intellectual property and development contains a lengthy section on licensing and technology transfer that focuses entirely on voluntary commercial licensing. It makes no mention of the compulsory licenses that are permitted under TRIPS and other intellectual property treaties and that developing countries view as crucial means for gaining access to knowledge, medicines, and technology.

---

18. *See* World Intellectual Property Organization, WIPO Intellectual Property Handbook: Policy, Law and Use 196–203 (WIPO Publication No. 489, 2d ed., 2004), available at http://www.wipo.int/about-ip/en/iprm [hereinafter WIPO Handbook].

19. *See* WTO-WIPO Cooperation Agreement, Art. 4 (Legal-Technical Assistance and Technical Cooperation), entered into force Jan. 1, 1996. Pursuant to their Cooperation Agreement, WIPO and the WTO launched a joint initiative in July 1998 to assist developing countries in complying with TRIPS. *See* Handbook, *supra* note 18, at 359–60.

20. *See* Handbook, *supra* note 18, at 200.

The Development Agenda mandates a wholesale revision of that approach. It requires WIPO to provide assistance in line with what developing countries identify as their specific needs rather than aiming to promote a one-size-fits-all model of intellectual property. It also calls upon WIPO to assist developing countries in taking advantage of the leeway given to them under IP treaties to tailor their intellectual property laws to best promote development, including through the use of competition law to define and combat anti-competitive IP licensing and through maintaining a balance of IP protection and a robust public domain. In particular, the Agenda provides that "[w]ithin the framework of the agreement between WIPO and the WTO, WIPO shall make available advice to developing countries and LDCs, on . . . the understanding and use of flexibilities contained in the TRIPS Agreement." Such flexibilities are found in TRIPS provisions permitting various exceptions and limitations to intellectual property rights, requiring that intellectual property laws serve broader societal interests, and providing least developed countries a moratorium on TRIPS compliance until the date determined by the TRIPS Council, currently January 1, 2013, for copyright, trademark, and patent generally, and 2016 for pharmaceutical patents.

The WIPO General Assembly designated the fundamental change in WIPO's approach to technical assistance as one of the items requiring immediate implementation. In response, WIPO's Preliminary Implementation Report states that the organization has already "been reorienting its programs and activities by consistently and comprehensively taking into account country specific needs, priorities and the level of development, particular the special needs of Least Developed Countries."[21] With respect to TRIPS, the Report notes that WIPO "will organize meetings to deal specifically with flexible implementation of TRIPS obligations" and that it already provides advice to specific developing countries and LDCs on "the legal options provided under the TRIPS Agreement," including those regarding the provisions for compulsory licensing of pharmaceutical patents pursuant to "the TRIPS Doha Declaration on Public Health."[22] Moreover, although WIPO views its primarily role under the WIPO/WTO Agreement as furthering countries' "understanding and informed implementation" of TRIPS, the development-oriented technical assistance mandated by the Development Agenda suggests that WIPO should assist developing countries in gaining the expertise needed to further a development agenda within the WTO as well. On that score, the Preliminary Implementation Report states that WIPO will also advise developing countries "in relation to ongoing discussion on various TRIPS related matters in WTO."[23] At the same time, of course, like in other areas, it remains to be seen whether the Agenda's broad revision of WIPO's mandate

21. Preliminary Implementation Report, *supra* note 17, at Annex, p. 1.

22. Id., Annex, p. 22.

23. Id.

regarding technical assistance will truly work a fundamental reorientation of the way WIPO provides technical assistance on the ground.

B. Norm-Setting

Cluster B of the Development Agenda governs WIPO norm-setting. WIPO is actively involved in organizing negotiations and preparing drafts and working papers for new intellectual property treaties. The Development Agenda requires WIPO norm-setting to "take into account different levels of development," "take into consideration a balance between costs and benefits," "support a robust public domain," "take into account flexibilities in international IP agreements," and "initiate discussions on how, within WIPO's mandate, to further facilitate access to knowledge and technology for developing countries and LDCs." In addition to those substantive requirements, the Agenda also requires that WIPO norm-setting be more transparent and inclusive. It requires that WIPO's work in preparing and setting agendas for new treaties and protocols must "be a participatory process, which takes into consideration the interests and priorities of all WIPO Member States and the viewpoints of other stakeholders, including accredited inter-governmental organizations and non-governmental organizations." The Agenda further provides that "WIPO shall conduct informal, open and balanced consultations, as appropriate, prior to any new norm-setting activities, through a member-driven process, promoting the participation of experts from Member States, particularly developing countries and LDCs."

In principle WIPO norm-setting has always been, in WIPO parlance, "member driven." WIPO acts as a neutral facilitator and expert to assist its members in coming to agreement on treaty norms. But in practice, WIPO has sponsored treaty initiatives, produced treaty drafts and working papers, and drafted model laws either at the behest or closely aligned with the positions of the United States and Europe. For example, in preparation for the December 1996 diplomatic conference aimed at updating WIPO treaties to the digital age, WIPO produced draft treaties and working papers that would have substantially implemented the United States' IP maximalist digital agenda, together with some European gloss.[24] Pointing to the IP protectionism that has been endemic to WIPO norm setting, commentators have also expressed concern that WIPO's ongoing efforts to promote patent law harmonization through agreement on a Substantive Patent Law Treaty would, if successful, sharply constrain developing countries' leeway to craft their domestic patent laws to narrow patentable subject matter, set a high bar to inventiveness for patentability, limit patent holders' exclusive rights, and impose compulsory licenses.[25]

---

24. Pamela Samuelson, *The U.S. Digital Agenda at WIPO*, 37 Va. J. Int'l L. 369, 374 (1977).

25. Jerome H. Reichman & Rochelle Cooper Dreyfuss, *Harmonization without Consensus: Critical Reflections on Drafting a Substantive Patent Law Treaty*, 57 Duke L. J. 85, 93–102 (2007).

This IP maximalist bias partly reflects WIPO's traditional institutional mission to "promote the protection of intellectual property throughout the world" and WIPO officials' personal commitment to that mission. Yet it has also arisen from WIPO's norm-setting procedures, which, like those of the WTO, have been widely perceived to favor developed countries.[26] The preparatory groundwork for new WIPO treaties is carried out by one of the organization's standing committees, such as the Standing Committee on the Law of Patents or the Standing Committee on Copyright and Related Rights. The WIPO General Assembly does not decide to convene a diplomatic conference to consider a new international instrument unless and until the appropriate standing committee determines that sufficient progress has been made toward treaty adoption.[27] Although developing countries are formally represented on the standing committees, their impact on treaty preparation is severely hampered by their lack of resources and expertise. For developing countries, it is often prohibitively costly to send an expert to Geneva to attend committee meetings. As a result, the developing country representative is often a lowly official from the country's diplomatic mission in Geneva. WIPO does sponsor a number of delegates from developing countries to attend norm-setting meetings. But, as a seasoned observer notes, "the truth remains that most of the delegates from developing countries attending Standing Committee meetings are members of the diplomatic corps and are not versed in intellectual property."[28] The "well-resourced and technically proficient delegations of developed countries, such as the United States," stand in sharp contrast.[29] The Development Agenda seeks to remedy this disparity by requiring WIPO both to promote participation of developing country experts and to consider the viewpoints of inter-governmental organizations and NGOs that give voice to the interests of IP users and developing countries.

C. WIPO's Governance and Relation to Other Organizations

The Development Agenda firmly places WIPO's mission of promoting intellectual property protection in the service of—and subject to—an overriding mandate of fostering development. To that end, the Agenda also aims to further integrate WIPO within an overarching framework of agencies devoted to development.

WIPO was established as a successor to the United International Bureaus for the Protection of Intellectual Property, an independent international agency,

---

26. *See* Stiglitz & Charlton, *supra* note 9, at 82 (discussing the infamous "green room" methods of the Uruguay Round of WTO negotiations and continuing disabilities faced by developing countries within the WTO).

27. *See* Geoffrey Yu, *The Structure and Process of Negotiations at the World Intellectual Property Organization*, 82 Chi.-Kent L. Rev. 1445 (2007).

28. Coenraad Visser, *The Policy-Making Dynamics in Intergovernmental Organizations*, 82 Chi-Kent L. Rev. 1457, 1459 (2007).

29. Id.

known by its French acronym, BIRPI, formed in 1893 to administer the Berne and Paris Conventions. BIRPI was founded as an organization serving intellectual property owners under the supervision of the Swiss Federal Government.[30] WIPO effectively reconstituted the organization as an association of sovereign states. Importantly in that regard, WIPO succeeded BIRPI in 1967 as a free-standing, autonomous international agency. Nor did WIPO's designation as a specialized agency of the United Nations in 1974 fundamentally detract from WIPO's independence. As WIPO's Handbook emphasizes, "Each specialized agency has its own constitution, its own governing bodies, its own elected executive head, its own income, its own budget, its own staff, its own programs and activities. Machinery exists for coordinating the activities of all the specialized agencies, among themselves and with the United Nations, but basically each agency remains responsible, under its own constitution, to its own governing bodies, which are the States members of the organization." Nonetheless, WIPO's agreement with the UN does commit WIPO to cooperating and consulting with the UN and its various organs. In particular, the agreement provides that WIPO shall "co-operate within the field of its competence with the United Nations and its organs, particularly the United Nations Conference on Trade and Development, the United Nations Development Programme and the United Nations Industrial Development Organization . . . in promoting and facilitating the transfer of technology to developing countries in such a manner as to assist these countries in attaining their objectives in the fields of science and technology and trade and development."[31]

The Development Agenda does not diminish WIPO's formal institutional autonomy as a specialized agency of the United Nations. But it does bring the development policies of other agencies and regimes to bear more forcefully on WIPO norm-setting and procedure. In particular, the Agenda provides that "WIPO's norm-setting activities should be supportive of the development goals agreed within the UN system, including those contained in the Millennium Declaration."[32] It also calls upon WIPO "to intensify its cooperation on IP related issues with UN agencies, according to Member States' orientation, in particular UNCTAD, UNEP, WHO, UNIDO, UNESCO, and other relevant international organizations,

---

30. *See* WIPO Handbook, *supra* note 18, at 4; Paul Joan George Kapteyn, International Organization and Integration: Annotated Basic Documents I (Brill 1984).

31. UN-WIPO Agreement, *supra* note 4, Art. 10.

32. Proposed language that would have required WIPO to ensure that its norm-setting activities are "fully compatible" with other international instruments that advance development objectives, including international human rights instruments, was not adopted as part of the Development Agenda. See WIPO, Working Document for the Provisional Committee on Proposals Related to a WIPO Development Agenda (PCDA), WIPO Doc. PCDA/3/2, Annex B, ¶ 28, pp. 14–15, Feb. 20, 2007 [hereinafter "Provisional Committee Working Document"].

especially WTO in order to strengthen the coordination for maximum efficiency in undertaking development programs."

Significantly, although the UN's development goals do not refer to intellectual property per se, they embrace an understanding of development as freedom that stands at odds with one-dimensional support for broad intellectual property rights.[33] On that score, a UN-commissioned independent report on achieving the Millennium Development Goals expressly criticizes TRIPS for taking "too little account of levels of development and varying interests and priorities" and for providing for insufficient flexibility in implementing the Agreement's requirements.[34] Furthermore, almost all the UN agencies identified in the Development Agenda's call for intensified cooperation have taken positions at odds with IP maximalism. Both WHO and UNESCO have expressed concern that uniformly strong IP rights run counter to human rights, particularly with regard to access to essential medicines; UNCTAD has sharply criticized the erosion of least developed countries' flexibilities in setting IP policies, particularly under TRIPS-plus agreements, as erecting barriers to development; and UNIDO has placed a premium on promoting technology transfer to least developed countries.[35]

One would thus expect that WIPO's close cooperation with other UN agencies would reinforce the Development Agenda's fundamental reorientation of

33. UN General Assembly Resolution 55/2—The United Nations Millennium Declaration, Sept. 18, 2000. The UN has since expressed concern that the benefits of economic growth in emerging developing countries have been unequally shared in those countries as well as in the world at large. United Nations, The Millennium Development Goals Report 2007 4–5 (2007).

34. Millennium Project, Investing in Development: A Practical Plan to Achieve the Millennium Development Goals 219 (2005). Of import for WIPO's role in advising developing countries regarding TRIPS, the report refers to the recent need to renegotiate TRIPS rules on access to essential medicines and strongly suggests that TRIPS remains ill suited to developing-country needs: "There is a clear case for revisiting more of the rules to examine their impact on developing countries and any additional flexibility required. This remains relevant for access to essential medicines." Id.

35. *See* World Health Organization, Globalization, TRIPs and Access to Pharmaceuticals, WHO Policy Perspectives on Medicines, No. 3, WHO/EDM/2001.2 at 5 (Mar. 2001) (asserting that "[a]ccess to essential drugs is a human right" and encouraging countries to take advantage of existing TRIPS "safeguards" to "enhance the affordability and availability" of patented pharmaceuticals); UNESCO, Report on the Experts' Meeting on the Right to Enjoy the Benefits of Scientific Progress and its Applications 3–4 (UNESCO Pub. SHS-2007/WS/13, June 7–8, 2007) (reporting UNESCO's support for a right to enjoy the benefits of scientific progress and concern over the tension between that right and intellectual property); United Nations Conference on Trade and Development, Least Developed Countries Report 2007 128–29 (UNCTAD/LDC/2007 2007); United Nations Industrial Development Organization, Strategic Long-Term Vision Statement, GC11/8/Add.1, Oct. 14, 2005, ¶ 5(A)(h) (noting focus on "assistance in diffusion and transfer of modern and relevant technologies").

WIPO's goals and priorities. But the Agenda's general call for greater cooperation leaves considerable room for variable interpretation and implementation. WIPO's report on Development Agenda items not listed for immediate implementation states that the organization is "already engaged in enhanced cooperation with UN agencies and other international organizations."[36] Yet it is too soon to gauge the extent of that cooperation or its potential impact on WIPO's work and objectives.

In addition to pressing WIPO to intensify its cooperation with UN agencies, the Development Agenda requires that the organization "ensure wide participation of civil society at large in WIPO activities in accordance with its criteria regarding NGO acceptance and accreditation."[37] Similarly, as noted above, the Agenda requires that WIPO norm-setting "be a participatory process," which takes into account the viewpoints of non-state "stakeholders, including accredited inter-governmental and non-governmental organizations."[38]

WIPO has long worked closely with NGOs. Indeed, some two dozen NGOs were observers at the meetings at which WIPO was established. But following on its BIRPI heritage, WIPO has traditionally consulted only organizations representing intellectual property producers, as evidenced by the fact that the NGOs present at WIPO's formation were all unions and associations devoted to lobbying for greater intellectual property rights.[39] In 2005, WIPO caused an uproar when it announced that it would bar numerous public interest organizations from discussions on the Development Agenda because those organizations were not accredited as permanent WIPO observers.[40] Since then, however, WIPO has considerably broadened civil society participation. It has now accredited some 250 NGOs as permanent observers, and these include groups, such as the Electronic Frontier Foundation, that typically oppose broad IP rights as well as those favoring such rights.[41] The Development Agenda seeks to deepen and solidify this participatory trend in WIPO norm-setting procedures.

D. Technology Transfer

The Development Agenda contains a number of action items related to technology transfer. A seasoned observer comments that technology transfer is

---

36. *See* Provisional Committee on Proposals Related to a WIPO Development Agenda (PCDA), WIPO Development Agenda; Initial Working Document for Implementation of Agreed Proposals, Feb. 29, 2008, at 29, available at http://ip-watch.org/files/WIPO%20comments%20on%20DA%20recs%20-%20part%201.pdf [hereinafter "Initial Working Document for Implementation"].

37. Development Agenda, ¶ 42.

38. Development Agenda, ¶ 15.

39. *See* Bogsch, *supra* note 5, at 125 (listing observers).

40. Electronic Frontier Foundation, *WIPO Shutting Out Public Interest Organizations*, Mar. 5, 2005, http://www.eff.org/press/archives/2005/03/07.

41. WIPO, Observers, NGOs, IGOs, http://www.wipo.int/members/en/admission/observers.html.

"an issue hitherto viewed with disdain in WIPO."[42] Yet WIPO's leadership seems not to have misprized technology transfer per se, but simply to have adhered unquestioningly to the neoliberal notion that developing countries can better acquire technological know-how and direct investment in local technology production by legislating strong IP rights than by implementing compulsory licensing.

Although the Development Agenda certainly does not forswear further promotion of intellectual property rights as a possible tool for technology transfer, it does put an end to WIPO's monolithic "IP as power tool of development" approach. In particular, the Agenda ties "IP-related policies and initiatives necessary to promote the transfer and dissemination of technology" with taking "appropriate measures to enable developing countries to fully understand and benefit from . . . flexibilities provided for in international agreements," including, no doubt, compulsory licensing.[43] In response to that action item, WIPO proposes both to "undertake empirical economic studies that seek to understand the role of IP rights in international technology transfer in different contexts," including "country-specific and industry-specific studies," and to "provide assistance and advice by exploring and explaining all legal and policy options available to each country under relevant international treaties, while keeping in view the country's international obligations and its national priorities."[44] More specifically, the Development Agenda instructs WIPO to advise LDCs on how to gain access to and make use of IP-related technology and to "undertake initiatives agreed by Member States, which contribute to transfer of technology to developing countries, such as requesting WIPO to facilitate better access to publicly available patent information."[45]

Although the Development Agenda creates openings for WIPO to promote technology transfer through cracks in and limitations on IP rights, it stops far short of supporting wholesale compulsory licensing to bring technology and know-how to developing countries. As I will shortly discuss, indeed, a number of more far-reaching proposals, including one calling for a Treaty on Access to Knowledge and Technology, were not incorporated into the Agenda. Critics have long bemoaned what they view as the lip service paid to technology transfer, followed by inaction on every front except that asserting that greater IP rights provide incentives for IP holding firms to disseminate know-how and technology. As in other areas, the jury is still out on whether the Development Agenda will lead to concrete steps to enhance developing countries' access to knowledge and technology in a more direct and proactive manner.

42. Sisule F. Musungu, *WIPO Development Agenda—As the Dust Settles*, Thoughts in Colours Blog, July 9, 2007, http://thoughtsincolours.blogspot.com/2007/07/wipo-development-agenda-as-dust.html.

43. Development Agenda, ¶ 25.

44. Initial Working Document for Implementation, *supra* note 36, at 17–18.

45. Development Agenda, ¶¶ 30 and 31.

E. Competition Policy

The Development Agenda contains a number of items regarding the potential conflicts between intellectual property and competition policy. With regard to technical assistance, for example, the Agenda provides that WIPO must "promote measures that will help countries deal with IP related anti-competitive practices" by assisting developing countries "to better understand the interface between intellectual property rights and competition policies."[46]

Competition law and policy represent a largely untapped area that developing countries might deploy to limit what they regard as overreaching and overly constraining intellectual property rights. Intellectual property rights have long been seen to pose possible conflicts with competition policies. As William Landes and Richard Posner describe it, indeed, the traditional view in the United States is that "intellectual property law and antitrust law are enemies—that intellectual property authorizes patent and copyright (and perhaps also trademark and trade secret) monopolies that offend antitrust principles."[47] That antagonism has significantly subsided in developed countries. Much current thinking is that antitrust and intellectual property law fall within a common rubric of innovation policy and that, in the new information economy, each focuses on dynamic efficiency.[48] Certainly in the United States, moreover, in contrast to antitrust's traditional antipathy toward the limited monopolies that intellectual property law makes possible, contemporary antitrust jurisprudence recognizes that innovation may often be fueled by the prospect and proper exercise of market power.[49]

Yet even developed countries take different approaches to competition issues. For example, European competition law is typically more protective of competitors and views vertical restraints considerably more harshly than does U.S. antitrust law.[50] Accordingly, there would appear to be ample room for developing

---

46. Development Agenda, ¶ 7.

47. William M. Landes & Richard A. Posner, The Economic Structure of Intellectual Property Law 372 (Harvard Univ. Press 2003).

48. The current, express position of the U.S. federal antitrust enforcement agencies is that "[t]he intellectual property laws and the antitrust laws share the common purpose of promoting innovation and enhancing consumer welfare." United States Dept. of Justice and Fed. Trade Commission (1995), *Antitrust Guidelines for the Licensing of Intellectual Property*, §1.0, available at www.usdoj.gov/atr/public/guidelines/ipguide.htm.

49. *See*, generally, Robert Pitofsky, *Antitrust and Intellectual Property: Unresolved Issues at the Heart of the New Economy*, 16 Berkeley Tech. L. J. 535 (2001); Richard A. Posner, *Antitrust in the New Economy*, 58 Antitrust J. 925 (2001). *See also* Massimo Motta, Competition Policy; Theory and Practice 55–66 (Cambridge Univ. Press 2004) (demonstrating that although established monopolists might have a lesser incentive to innovate, the expectation of market power to appropriate investments in R&D, such as can be gained through intellectual property rights, may be a critical incentive to make those investments).

50. *See* Eleanor Fox, *Antitrust and Regulatory Federalism: Races Up, Down, and Sideways*, 75 N.Y.U. L. Rev. 1781, 1791–92 (2000); James C. Cooper et al., *A Comparative Study of*

countries to tailor their competition laws in line with their national priorities and to use competition law far more aggressively than do either the United States or the European Union in defining as anti-competitive various uses of broad intellectual property rights, including IP holder refusals to license others to use IP on commercially reasonable terms.

TRIPS recognizes but does not define the scope of such leeway. Article 8 of TRIPS provides, "Appropriate measures, provided that they are consistent with the provisions of this Agreement, may be needed to prevent the abuse of intellectual property rights by right holders or the resort to practices which unreasonably restrain trade or adversely affect the international transfer of technology."[51] The Development Agenda does not further specify what might qualify as an abuse of IP rights or which types of licensing practices constitute unreasonable restraints of trade—and a proposal that would have required WIPO to "promote model approaches on how to implement the relevant provisions on anti-competitive practices of the TRIPS Agreement" was deleted prior to the September 2008 meeting of the General Assembly.[52] But the Development Agenda, as adopted, does commit WIPO to raising awareness of possibilities for crafting competition law and policy to better serve developing country interests in delimiting exclusive IP rights.

F. Genetic Resources and Traditional Knowledge

The protection of genetic resources, traditional knowledge, and folklore has been a high priority for developing countries for a number of years. Although developing countries generally oppose the upward harmonization of patent, copyright, and trademark, they regard international treaty recognition of proprietary rights in genetic resources, traditional knowledge, and folklore as an opportunity for requiring protection of resources that they have in relative abundance. However, the United States and other industrialized countries have thus far blocked any commitment to adopt a treaty recognizing such rights.[53]

Discussions on a possible treaty have continued apace. In 2000, the WIPO General Assembly established the Intergovernmental Committee on Intellectual Property and Genetic Resources, Traditional Knowledge and Folklore (IGC) to progress toward a "shared international understanding" of how best to protect

---

United States and European Union Approaches to Vertical Policy, 13 GEO. MASON L. REV. 289 (2005).

51. Agreement on Trade-Related Aspects of Intellectual Property Rights, Art. 8.2, Apr. 15, 1994, Marrakesh Agreement Establishing the World Trade Organization, Annex 1C, Legal Instruments, Results of the Uruguay Round vol. 31, 33 I.L.M. 81 (1994).

52. Provisional Committee Working Document, *supra* note 32, Annex B ¶ 16, p. 7.

53. *Assembly Approves Work on Development Agenda, Broadcast Treaty, Traditional Knowledge*, BNA International World Intellectual Property Report, Nov. 2007, http://www.hostref4.com/nxt/gateway.dll?f=templates&fn=default.htm&vid=BNAI:10.1048/Enu.

traditional knowledge and genetic resources "against misappropriation and misuse."[54] The World Trade Organization has also waded into this area, directing the TRIPS Council "to examine . . . the protection of traditional knowledge and folklore."[55] Meanwhile, a number of developing countries have enacted domestic legislation protecting traditional cultural expression and knowledge, but advocates for protection have been frustrated by the lack of progress on an international treaty.

The proposed Development Agenda action item in this area would have requested WIPO to adopt a treaty for the protection of genetic resources, traditional knowledge, and folklore "in the nearest future."[56] That language was diluted in the negotiations leading to adoption of the Development Agenda. As adopted, the Development Agenda provides that WIPO must "urge the IGC to accelerate the process on the protection of genetic resources, traditional knowledge, and folklore, without prejudice to any outcome, including the possible development of an international instrument or instruments."

The IGC met for its 12th session in February 2008, following adoption of the Development Agenda. It is apparent that there remains considerable disagreement over how, if at all, genetic resources, traditional knowledge, and folklore should receive international recognition and protection in areas within WIPO's purview. Options on the table, assuming consensus can be reached on substance, include model laws, a nonbinding "soft law" instrument, and a political declaration of principles, as possible alternatives to a binding international treaty.[57]

G. Bolstering Exceptions to IP Rights: Rejected but Still Under Consideration

A number of proposed action items that would have significantly bolstered exceptions and limitations to IP rights were not included in the Development Agenda as presented to the General Assembly. These included, most prominently, requirements that WIPO (1) provide technical assistance to "ensure . . . that flexibilities existing in international treaties are taken full advantage of,"[58] (2) maintain "a list of essential technologies, know-how, processes, and methods

---

54. WIPO Member States Extend International Work on Protection of Traditional Knowledge, Genetic Resources, and Folklore, World Intellectual Property Organization; available at www.wipo.int/pressroom/en/articles/2007/article_0072.html (last visited Nov. 25, 2007).

55. World Trade Organization, Ministerial Declaration of 14 November 2001, WT/MIN(01)/DEC/1, 41 I.L.M. 746 (2002), available at http://www.wto.org/english/thewto_e/minist_e/min01_e/mindecl_e.htm.

56. Provisional Committee Working Document, *supra* note 32, Annex B ¶ 18, p. 9.

57. WIPO Intergovernmental Committee on Intellectual Property and Genetic Resources, Traditional Knowledge, and Folklore, Summary of Options for the International Dimension of the Committee's Work, Dec. 6, 2007, WIPO/GRTKF/IC/12/6.

58. Provisional Committee Working Document, *supra* note 32, Annex B ¶ 3, p. 3.

that are necessary to meet the basic development needs of African countries,"[59] and (3) "establish a Treaty on Access to Knowledge and Technology."[60] By assisting developing countries actually to take full advantage of treaty flexibilities, WIPO would need both to define the full scope of those flexibilities and to advise developing countries to refrain from entering into bilateral TRIPS-plus agreements that trump the flexibilities found in TRIPS and other international instruments. By maintaining a list of essential technologies, WIPO would provide African countries a solid basis for imposing compulsory licenses to obtain such technologies under TRIPS. By moving to establishing a treaty on access to knowledge, WIPO would likely fuel calls to embed minimum, mandatory requirements for proscribed exceptions and limitations to copyright.[61]

Although these proposals were not incorporated into the Agenda, somewhat diluted versions were. For example, an item for immediate action under norm-setting requires WIPO "to initiate discussions on how, within WIPO's mandate, to further facilitate access to knowledge and technology for developing countries and LDCs."[62] Further, as noted in WIPO's implementation report, the issue of mandatory limitations and exceptions to copyright is under consideration in the Standing Committee on Copyright and Related Rights. Indeed, the SCCRR has given priority to considering a proposal by Brazil, Chile, Nicaragua, and Uruguay to evaluate the possible need for mandatory exceptions and limitations.[63]

II. CONTRIBUTIONS TO THIS VOLUME

Our study of the issues surrounding the Development Agenda encompasses a rich variety of insights and perspectives. Our contributors hale from 14 countries, some developed, some developing, some emerging. They include political scientists, economists, lawyers, historians, policy analysts, and diplomats. Their chapters explore the Development Agenda's background, content, and ramifications, guiding us to understand the Agenda in its historical, geopolitical, and development policy context. Their studies span a broad range—from the Agenda itself, to WIPO's interaction with developing countries, to TRIPS, to how particular

59. Provisional Committee Working Document, *supra* note 32, Annex B ¶ 43, p. 18.

60. Provisional Committee Working Document, *supra* note 32, Annex B ¶ 35, p. 16.

61. The draft Treaty on Access to Knowledge, May 9, 2005, which was prepared by civil society groups and presented to WIPO, contains various such provisions. The draft is available at http://www.cptech.org/a2k/a2k_treaty_may9.pdf. For discussion, see Laurence A. Helfer, *Towards a Human Rights Framework for Intellectual Property*, 40 U.C. Davis L. Rev. 971, 1012–14 (2007).

62. Development Agenda, ¶ 19.

63. WIPO Press Release PR/2008/541, Member States Consider Future Work of Copyright Committee, Mar. 13, 2008, http://www.wipo.int/pressroom/en/articles/2008/article_0013.html.

countries and industries grapple with issues of development and intellectual property, to the interplay between IP and competition law in the development arena.

We begin by examining the Development Agenda in the context of the international IP treaty regime. We are especially fortunate to have Henrique Choer Moraes and Otávio Brandelli, two Brazilian diplomats with extensive firsthand knowledge of their country's efforts to promote the Development Agenda, present their personal assessment of the IP treaty regime issues that fueled the Agenda proposal and analysis of the Agenda's potential impost. Daniel J. Gervais, who recently moved to Vanderbilt University from the University of Ottawa, then places the Development Agenda within the ongoing debate about whether TRIPS and robust IP protection benefit developing countries. The answer, he underscores, is that there is no across-the-board answer. We have moved beyond both the "addition narratives" of early TRIPS proponents, according to which universally high levels of IP protection would jumpstart economic growth in developing countries, and the "subtraction narratives" of TRIPS critics, in whose opinion the lesser the impact of TRIPS, the better developing countries would be. We are now in a third phase, one informed by "calibration narratives," which recognize that IP protection may benefit certain developing countries but not others, and thus that we need different implementations of TRIPS, tailored to level and nature of development, instead of "cookie cutter" norm implants.

Part II examines the Development Agenda in historical and institutional context. Pedro Roffe and Gina Vea, of the International Centre for Trade and Sustainable Development, find parallels in the late nineteenth and mid-twentieth-century negotiations over the Paris Convention to current debates over how to strike a balance between public and private interests in a way that promotes development. Their focus is the Paris Convention's evolving treatment of "working requirements," countries' requirements that patent holders actually use patents in local production or face patent forfeiture or compulsory license. Roffe and Vea note the connection between such working requirements and the emphasis on local production found in the import substitution industrialization policies that Latin American countries favored as a means of development through the 1970s. As the authors highlight, many of the arguments that developing countries have traditionally advanced for imposing such working requirements find echoes in the Development Agenda today.

Carolyn Deere, of Oxford University and Intellectual Property Watch, situates the Development Agenda firmly within the political realities on the ground in developing countries. As Deere insightfully reminds us, the Development Agenda's implementation will rely heavily on the political process and organization of IP decision-making at the national and regional levels in developing countries, including the specific ways in which WIPO's activities influence the IP reform process. Developing country governments vary considerably in the degree of national debate regarding IP norms, the internal organization and capacity of government agencies to weigh the benefits and costs of IP protection, and the degree of coordination with other governments and international fora. As Deere details, far beyond whatever the Development Agenda might provide, these country-specific factors heavily impact developing countries' abilities to carve out IP policies that suit their national interests rather than caving in to the considerable pressure to rubber stamp universally high levels of IP protection.

Part III then presents two cautionary notes regarding the Development Agenda, each coming from a different direction. Ruth L. Okediji, of the University of Minnesota, hails the Agenda as a potentially important milestone within WIPO but expresses some skepticism that the values, coalitions, and priorities that ensured the Agenda's adoption will resonate deeply within WIPO's infrastructure. Okediji then places the Agenda within the framework of development policy generally. She considers lessons learned from the failure of the New International Economic Order—what she characterizes as the transnational development "experiment" of the 1970s—and proposes some ways in which IP might be re-envisioned to promote human welfare in the digital age.

Keith E. Maskus, of the University of Colorado, similarly believes that the Development Agenda may herald some desirable reforms in WIPO, an agency he describes as "excessively hidebound and insular," and may enable governments to recognize officially that IP policies impact development and need to be varied across national levels of per-capita income and technological attainment. Maskus warns, however, that developing country governments should not view IP flexibilities as a substitute for sound development policy. Middle-income and larger developing countries, he argues, do appear to be generally well served by high levels of IP protection and the voluntary technology transfer that such protection engenders. And although lesser protection is an appropriate policy for poorer developing countries, such countries must couple that policy with transparent enforcement and judicial procedures to ensure that what IP rights are on offer are actually protected because transparency and certainty are significant factors in attracting foreign direct investment and other forms of technology transfer.

Part IV examines IP and development from the perspective of various countries. Hong Xue, of the University of Hong Kong, presents a case study of how developing countries acquiesce in demands for greater IP protection. She examines China and its Internet Copyright Regulations, which were enacted to implement the WIPO Copyright Treaty. Xue concludes that China has incorporated wholesale many features of the U.S. Digital Millennium Copyright Act even though it was not required to so by the Treaty. She argues, on the basis of this example, that developing countries too readily view the way of developed countries as the prescribed path, failing in the process to develop their own internal capacity for normative innovation.

Yi Qian, of Northwestern University, evaluates the effects of patent protection and technology transfers on pharmaceutical innovations for 26 countries that established pharmaceutical patent laws during the period from 1978 to 2002. She concludes, based on her regression analysis, that national patent protection alone does not stimulate domestic innovation or the establishment of new multinational subsidiaries. However, domestic innovation accelerates in countries with higher levels of economic development, educational attainment, and economic freedom. Additionally, Qian finds, there appears to be an optimal level of intellectual property rights regulation above which further enhancement actually reduces innovative activities.

B. Zorina Khan, of Bowdoin College, and the late Kenneth L. Sokoloff, of UCLA, also present a sweeping comparative analysis of patent law, but, as befitting of economic historians, theirs assesses the evolution of institutions designed to stimulate innovation across countries over the past two centuries. Their study highlights the extent to which countries have tailored such institutions to suit their particular social and economic circumstances. They note, for example, that the United States took a more democratic approach to patent law than did its European industrialized country counterparts, charging relatively low fees to apply for and maintain patents and eschewing working requirements, thus making it easier for individual inventors to obtain patents and share a stake in the patent system. They suggest, in conclusion, that developed countries' current efforts to achieve upward harmonization of patent law stands in contrast to the leeway those countries have historically enjoyed to tailor patent law to their own needs and ideologies and that restricting the menu of choices available to developing countries is likely to constrain development.

Part V addresses an issue that, arguably, has been the primary driving force behind developing countries' growing resistance to upward harmonization: access to medicine. Carlos Correa, of the University of Buenos Aires, provides a granular account of the linkage between pharmaceutical patents and drug registration, particularly how that linkage can effectively broaden the scope and lengthen the period of market exclusivity for a patented pharmaceutical. Like all drugs, generic pharmaceuticals must typically receive regulatory drug safety and efficacy approval before being put on the market to compete with the pharmaceutical for which the patent has expired. Because such approval can take a couple years, the generic producers' ability to work the patent in order to obtain regulatory approval upon or prior to expiration of the patent term is critical to reducing drug prices through competition at the earliest possible date. In addition, questions may arise regarding whether a new drug infringes on the patented pharmaceutical at all and thus whether the new drug may be put on the market during the patent term. Drug regulatory agencies are ill suited to consider patent disputes. As Professor Correa points out, however, the United States Trade Representative has consistently acted, through bilateral free trade agreements and the threat of unilateral trade sanctions, to require developing countries to accord pharmaceutical patent holders with far-reaching rights, extending even beyond those that patent holders enjoy in the United States itself.

Sudip Chaudhuri, of the Indian Institute of Management in Calcutta, studies the impact of TRIPS on India's pharmaceutical industry. Until India revised its patent law in 2005—the deadline for developing countries (but not least developed countries) to comply with TRIPS—India was a leading producer of generic drugs. Professor Chaudhuri finds that research and development expenditures have increased dramatically for a segment of India's pharmaceutical industry since TRIPS took effect in the mid-1990s. He finds, moreover, that whereas Indian firms' R&D efforts were previously engaged primarily in developing new processes for drug manufacture, they are increasingly involved in developing new, sometimes patentable chemical entities. Professor Chaudhuri attributes this increase and change in R&D to pharmaceutical patent protection in developed countries, where the primary markets for pharmaceuticals lay, not to TRIPS compliant patent regimes in developing countries. While Indian pharmaceutical companies have demonstrated their ability to produce generics, they have yet to prove their competence in innovating new products. He concludes, accordingly, that India's experience does not justify stronger patent protection for R&D and innovation.

Francesco Laforgia, Fabio Montobbio, and Luigi Orsenigo, all of the Centre of Research on Innovation and Internationalization and Bocconi University, examine pharmaceutical patenting in Brazil after TRIPS. Based on their case study, they conclude that there are, indeed, profound trade-offs between providing incentives to innovate and ensuring public access to medicines, trade-offs for which no obvious and simple solutions exist. In line with that recognition of complexity, they argue that the effects of strengthening patent protection depend on a wide variety of conditions in any given country and that, with pharmaceutical patents in particular, the existence of price controls, the nature of health-care delivery systems, the state of basic research, and other country-specific factors play key roles in determining whether increased protection will yield net benefits.

Part VI moves from medicines to culture. Diana V. Barrowclough, of the United Nations Conference on Trade and Development, presents evidence that some developing countries, far from being only consumers of intellectual property, have the potential to be extremely dynamic players in the new markets for creative industries. They are already producing and exporting at an extremely rapid rate of growth, much greater than in older, more conventional goods and services. Creative industries offers new opportunities for employment growth, both direct and indirect, and can be an important postal into the global knowledge economy—with the appropriate industrial policies in place. Hence, she argues, the WIPO Development Agenda debate is subtly different in the creative-industries context, given the nature of its products and the fact that developing countries can be producers as well as consumers. In the cultural industries–copyright context, therefore, policies geared toward boosting creativity and getting creative ideas into marketable form are as important as policies geared toward capturing or liberating IP—indeed, maybe more so. At the same time, she maintains, there is a need to seek more equitable and fair methods of rewarding creators than those existing under current regimes.

Nagla Rizk, of the American University in Cairo, takes a close look at the Arab music industry in light of the region's sociocultural, economic, political, and legal realities. In so doing, she compares and contrasts popular stars with underground musicians. Given the lack of published data on the Arab music industry, her research is based primarily on extensive interviews with music industry players and government officials in Egypt. Along the way, she describes models for disseminating Arab music that emanate from the actual practices on the ground rather than being imposed from the top. Given the ethic of sharing that permeates the culture of much Arab music, she characterizes these models as a "de facto commons." Professor Rizk concludes that such models for Arab music should be acknowledged and accommodated through flexible IP systems that maximize access to users and reward the music creator rather than record labels.

Michael D. Birnhack, of Tel-Aviv University, explores the clash between a global copyright regime that views copyright law as an instrument of trade and the complex set of local factors that form each country's culture. Using Israel as a case study, he focuses on what he calls "foreign leverage," the process by which local interest groups turn to global players, including both lobbying associations and foreign governments, to pressure local government to grant high levels of copyright protection sought by those particular interest groups. Professor Birnhack's conclusion, as he describes it, is "rather dim." Copyright used to be about culture, education, and human flourishing, but it has become a matter of trade, promoting the material flourishing of certain industries over the interests of the public at large.

Part VII looks at issues of industry structure, innovation, and access. John H. Barton, of Stanford University, assesses whether it would serve developing countries' economic interests to counter the upward harmonization of IP protection that TRIPS and other treaties demand with a strong antitrust law (or what is called in Europe and elsewhere "competition law"). In examining the actions that developing countries might take in the antitrust area, he looks both at national legislation and international arrangement and presents approaches that reflect sound economic analysis while still comporting with current law. Professor Barton considers three important contexts where antitrust might be employed to blunt abusive uses of IP rights: the response to a (generally foreign) monopolist, the response to a (generally primarily foreign) global oligopoly or cartel, and the management of relations between a major (generally foreign) firm and a local licensee. His analysis is specific to each scenario, but he concludes generally that the current process of national enforcement of antitrust law is suboptimal from a traditional competition-law perspective and thus that developing nations should explore possibilities for an international agreement, either in the form of a WTO antitrust agreement or of a WIPO intellectual property/antitrust agreement.

Leonardo Burlamaqui, of the Ford Foundation and the State University of Rio de Janeiro, analyses the interactions among IP issues, innovation, and development from a Schumpeterian perspective. In so doing, he aims to build a more coherent framework within which the discussions of both institutional building and policy design toward development can proceed. In particular, Professor Burlamaqui introduces the concept of a "market features approach" for structuring competition policies that support both innovation *and* a less restrictive IP regime. He devotes special attention to how competition policies should address intellectual property issues under a market feature's approach and to the institutional design of public agencies dealing with intellectual property issues.

Part VIII presents two perspectives on intellectual property and developing-country citizens' freedom. Madhavi Sunder, of the University of California at Davis, builds upon Amartya Sen's influential vision of "development as freedom." She argues, accordingly, that the "development agenda" for intellectual property must focus as much on freedom, equality, health, and participation as on economic prosperity. At the same time, Professor Sunder cautions, the development agenda should not focus solely on limited IP rights. Rather, Sen's vision highlights the importance of recognizing and rewarding the cultural creations of the poor as we think about development in a Knowledge Age. A broader understanding of intellectual property and development as freedom would recognize the importance of not just producing more knowledge goods, but also of participating in the process of knowledge creation.

P. Bernt Hugenholtz, of the University of Amsterdam, and Ruth L. Okediji, of the University of Minnesota, take up the proposal, which following the Development Agenda is now before the WIPO Standing Committee on Copyright and Related Rights, for an international instrument that would require minimum limitations and exceptions to copyrights. They sketch the rationales for such a multilateral approach to the question of exceptions and limitations and explore the flexibilities within the current international copyright treaty regime, particularly the three-step test that has become the standard for demarcating the permissible scope of countries' exceptions and limitations to copyrights. In so doing, they assess the three-step test's import for the validity of a proposed international instrument that would not only allow, but would actually require, certain minimum limitations and exceptions to copyright. They then provide a preliminary proposal setting out the basic contours of such an instrument, taking into account feasibility, political sustainability, and normative priorities.

As should be apparent from my summary descriptions, our contributors do not present a common perspective regarding how the Development Agenda should be implemented or how intellectual property rights should be tailored to promote development. Rather, as befitting their diverse disciplines, professions, and nationalities, they tackle multiple facets of the Development Agenda and the issues it raises, and do so from a variety of approaches and viewpoints. If there is anything held in common in their perspective, it is that intellectual property and development must be understood from the bottom up. Experience since TRIPS teaches us—and the Development Agenda recognizes—that the optimal scope and nature of intellectual property protection varies from one industry, country, and level of development to another.

APPENDIX

The WIPO Development Agenda
Items for Immediate Implementation are in bold

CLUSTER A: TECHNICAL ASSISTANCE AND CAPACITY BUILDING

1. **WIPO technical assistance shall be, *inter alia*, development-oriented, demand-driven and transparent, taking into account the priorities and the special needs of developing countries, especially LDCs, as well as the different levels of development of Member States and activities should include time frames for completion. In this regard, design, delivery mechanisms and evaluation processes of technical assistance programs should be country specific.**
2. Provide additional assistance to WIPO through donor funding, and establish Trust-Funds or other voluntary funds within WIPO specifically for LDCs, while continuing to accord high priority to finance activities in Africa through budgetary and extra-budgetary resources, to promote, *inter alia*, the legal, commercial, cultural, and economic exploitation of intellectual property in these countries.
3. **Increase human and financial allocation for technical assistance programs in WIPO for promoting a, *inter alia*, development-oriented IP culture, with an emphasis on introducing intellectual property at different academic levels and on generating greater public awareness on IP.**
4. **Place particular emphasis on the needs of SMEs and institutions dealing with scientific research and cultural industries and assist Member States, at their request, in setting-up appropriate national strategies in the field of IP.**
5. WIPO shall display general information on all technical assistance activities on its website, and shall provide, on request from Member States, details of specific activities, with the consent of the Member State(s) and other recipients concerned, for which the activity was implemented.
6. **WIPO's technical assistance staff and consultants shall continue to be neutral and accountable, by paying particular attention to the existing Code of Ethics, and by avoiding potential conflicts of interest. WIPO shall draw up and make widely known to the Member States a roster of consultants for technical assistance available with WIPO.**
7. **Promote measures that will help countries deal with IP related anti-competitive practices, by providing technical cooperation to developing countries, especially LDCs, at their request, in order to better understand the interface between intellectual property rights and competition policies.**
8. Request WIPO to develop agreements with research institutions and with private enterprises with a view to facilitating the national offices of developing countries, especially LDCs, as well as their regional and sub-regional IP organizations to access specialized databases for the purposes of patent searches.
9. Request WIPO to create, in coordination with Member States, a database to match specific IP-related development needs with available resources, thereby

expanding the scope of its technical assistance programs, aimed at bridging the digital divide.

10. To assist Member States to develop and improve national IP institutional capacity through further development of infrastructure and other facilities with a view to making national IP institutions more efficient and promote fair balance between IP protection and the public interest. This technical assistance should also be extended to sub-regional and regional organizations dealing with IP.

11. To assist Member States to strengthen national capacity for protection of domestic creations, innovations and inventions and to support development of national scientific and technological infrastructure, where appropriate, in accordance with WIPO's mandate.

12. To further mainstream development considerations into WIPO's substantive and technical assistance activities and debates, in accordance with its mandate.

13. WIPO's legislative assistance shall be, *inter alia*, development-oriented and demand-driven, taking into account the priorities and the special needs of developing countries, especially LDCs, as well as the different levels of development of Member States and activities should include time frames for completion.

14. Within the framework of the agreement between WIPO and the WTO, WIPO shall make available advice to developing countries and LDCs, on the implementation and operation of the rights and obligations and the understanding and use of flexibilities contained in the TRIPS Agreement.

CLUSTER B: NORM-SETTING, FLEXIBILITIES, PUBLIC POLICY AND PUBLIC DOMAIN

15. Norm-setting activities shall:

- **be inclusive and member driven;**
- **take into account different levels of development;**
- **take into consideration a balance between costs and benefits;**
- **be a participatory process, which takes into consideration the interests and priorities of all WIPO Member States and the viewpoints of other stakeholders, including accredited inter-governmental organizations and non-governmental organizations; and**
- **be in line with the principle of neutrality of the WIPO Secretariat.**

16. Consider the preservation of the public domain within WIPO's normative processes and deepen the analysis of the implications and benefits of a rich and accessible public domain.

17. In its activities, including norm-setting, WIPO should take into account the flexibilities in international IP agreements, especially those which are of interest to developing countries and LDCs.

18. To urge the IGC to accelerate the process on the protection of genetic resources, traditional knowledge and folklore, without prejudice to any outcome, including the possible development of an international instrument or instruments.

19. To initiate discussions on how, within WIPO's mandate, to further facilitate access to knowledge and technology for developing countries and LDCs to foster creativity and innovation and to strengthen such existing activities within WIPO.
20. To promote norm-setting activities related to IP that support a robust public domain in WIPO's Member States, including the possibility of preparing guidelines which could assist interested Member States in identifying subject matters that have fallen into the public domain within their respective jurisdictions.
21. WIPO shall conduct informal, open and balanced consultations, as appropriate, prior to any new norm-setting activities, through a member-driven process, promoting the participation of experts from Member States, particularly developing countries and LDCs.
22. WIPO's norm-setting activities should be supportive of the development goals agreed within the UN system, including those contained in the Millennium Declaration.

The WIPO Secretariat, without prejudice to the outcome of Member States considerations, should address in its working documents for norm-setting activities, as appropriate and as directed by Member States, issues such as: (a) safeguarding national implementation of intellectual property rules (b) links between IP and competition (c) IP-related transfer of technology (d) potential flexibilities, exceptions and limitations for Member States and (e) the possibility of additional special provisions for developing countries and LDCs.
23. To consider how to better promote pro-competitive IP licensing practices, particularly with a view to fostering creativity, innovation and the transfer and dissemination of technology to interested countries, in particular developing countries and LDCs.

CLUSTER C: TECHNOLOGY TRANSFER, INFORMATION AND COMMUNICATION TECHNOLOGIES (ICT) AND ACCESS TO KNOWLEDGE

24. To request WIPO, within its mandate, to expand the scope of its activities aimed at bridging the digital divide, in accordance with the outcomes of the World Summit on the Information Society (WSIS) also taking into account the significance of the Digital Solidarity Fund (DSF).
25. To explore IP-related policies and initiatives necessary to promote the transfer and dissemination of technology, to the benefit of developing countries and to take appropriate measures to enable developing countries to fully understand and benefit from different provisions, pertaining to flexibilities provided for in international agreements, as appropriate.
26. To encourage Member States, especially developed countries, to urge their research and scientific institutions to enhance cooperation and exchange with research and development institutions in developing countries, especially LDCs.
27. Facilitating IP-related aspects of ICT for growth and development: Provide for, in an appropriate WIPO body, discussions focused on the importance of IP-related

aspects of ICT, and its role in economic and cultural development, with specific attention focused on assisting Member States to identify practical IP-related strategies to use ICT for economic, social and cultural development.
28. To explore supportive IP-related policies and measures Member States, especially developed countries, could adopt for promoting transfer and dissemination of technology to developing countries.
29. To include discussions on IP-related technology transfer issues within the mandate of an appropriate WIPO body.
30. WIPO should cooperate with other intergovernmental organizations to provide to developing countries, including LDCs, upon request, advice on how to gain access to and make use of IP-related information on technology, particularly in areas of special interest to the requesting parties.
31. To undertake initiatives agreed by Member States, which contribute to transfer of technology to developing countries, such as requesting WIPO to facilitate better access to publicly available patent information.
32. To have within WIPO opportunity for exchange of national and regional experiences and information on the links between IP rights and competition policies.

CLUSTER D: ASSESSMENT, EVALUATION AND IMPACT STUDIES

33. To request WIPO to develop an effective yearly review and evaluation mechanism for the assessment of all its development-oriented activities, including those related to technical assistance, establishing for that purpose specific indicators and benchmarks, where appropriate.
34. With a view to assisting Member States in creating substantial national programs, to request WIPO to conduct a study on constraints to intellectual property protection in the informal economy, including the tangible costs and benefits of IP protection in particular in relation to generation of employment.
35. To request WIPO to undertake, upon request of Member States, new studies to assess the economic, social and cultural impact of the use of intellectual property systems in these States.
36. To exchange experiences on open collaborative projects such as the Human Genome Project as well as on IP models.
37. Upon request and as directed by Member States, WIPO may conduct studies on the protection of intellectual property, to identify the possible links and impacts between IP and development.
38. To strengthen WIPO's capacity to perform objective assessments of the impact of the organization's activities on development.

CLUSTER E: INSTITUTIONAL MATTERS INCLUDING MANDATE AND GOVERNANCE

39. To request WIPO, within its core competence and mission, to assist developing countries, especially African countries, in cooperation with relevant international organizations, by conducting studies on brain drain and make recommendations accordingly.

40. To request WIPO to intensify its cooperation on IP related issues with UN agencies, according to Member States' orientation, in particular UNCTAD, UNEP, WHO, UNIDO, UNESCO and other relevant international organizations, especially WTO in order to strengthen the coordination for maximum efficiency in undertaking development programs.
41. To conduct a review of current WIPO technical assistance activities in the area of cooperation and development.
42. To enhance measures that ensure wide participation of civil society at large in WIPO activities in accordance with its criteria regarding NGO acceptance and accreditation, keeping the issue under review.
43. To consider how to improve WIPO's role in finding partners to fund and execute projects for IP-related assistance in a transparent and member-driven process and without prejudice to ongoing WIPO activities.
44. In accordance with WIPO's member-driven nature as a United Nations Specialized Agency, formal and informal meetings or consultations relating to norm-setting activities in WIPO, organized by the International Bureau, upon request of the Member States, should be held primarily in Geneva, in a manner open and transparent to all Members. Where such meetings are to take place outside of Geneva, Member States shall be informed through official channels, well in advance, and consulted on the draft agenda and program.

CLUSTER F: OTHER ISSUES

45. To approach intellectual property enforcement in the context of broader societal interests and especially development-oriented concerns, with a view that "the protection and enforcement of intellectual property rights should contribute to the promotion of technological innovation and to the transfer and dissemination of technology, to the mutual advantage of producers and users of technological knowledge and in a manner conducive to social and economic welfare, and to a balance of rights and obligations," in accordance with Article 7 of the TRIPS Agreement.

PART ONE

THE DEVELOPMENT AGENDA AND THE INTERNATIONAL IP TREATY REGIME

2. THE DEVELOPMENT AGENDA AT WIPO
Context and Origins

HENRIQUE CHOER MORAES AND OTÁVIO BRANDELLI*

I. INTRODUCTION

Since the inception of the regime established by the TRIPS Agreement in 1994,[1] international intellectual property (IP) discussions have pointed in basically two directions. Discussions in one direction favor the strengthening and international harmonization of intellectual property rights (IPRs) beyond the standards set out in the TRIPS Agreement, the proponents of which assume strong IPRs to be automatically conducive to the technological, economic, and social development of those countries that adhere to stricter rules regarding IP. In this view, IP is perceived as a purely technical matter, one that should not be tainted by "alien" concerns emerging in other issue areas that are nonetheless affected by IPRs, such as public health, environment, culture, and access to knowledge and education. From this perspective, IP discussions should be confined to IP-specialized fora (which would currently mean the World Trade Organization [WTO] and the World Intellectual Property Organization [WIPO]).

* Henrique Choer Moraes and Otávio Brandelli are diplomats with the Brazilian Ministry of External Relations. All opinions expressed in this paper are the authors' exclusively and do not necessarily reflect those of the Brazilian Government.

1. "Agreement on Trade-Related Aspects of Intellectual Property Rights," Agreement Establishing the World Trade Organization, Annex 1C, Legal Instruments. *Results of the Uruguay Round*, vol. 31, 33 I.L.M. 81 (Marrakesh: April 15, 1994).

Although not seeking to detract from the need for compliance with international agreements, discussions pointing in a different direction highlight the difficulties inherent in putting TRIPS commitments into practice. They also attest to the shortcomings of the current IP system in living up to the alleged promise of inducing technological, economic, and social development. A pervasive element in these discussions is the perception that attempts to strengthen IPR protection should be preceded by cautious and rigorous assessment, lest the delicate balance between rights, obligations, and public interest become undone. From this perspective, IP is not an insulated subject area, and it therefore deserves to be scrutinized with an open mind in all fora that might be affected by the policies created to address it—fora such as the World Health Organization (WHO); the Convention on Biological Diversity (CBD); and the United Nations Educational, Scientific, and Cultural Organization (UNESCO). Actors supporting discussions in this direction have sometimes been mistakenly dubbed "IP-skeptics." As we shall see below, the group of actors that takes a critical approach to the pressure to strengthen IPR protections, an approach which is disseminated across developed and developing countries, would be better described as skeptics of the reflexive "the more IP, the better" approach: it should be noted that this way of seeing the strengthening of IPR protection is entirely legitimate in a transparent, democratic debate and by no means represents an attack against the IP system itself.

The proposal to establish a "development agenda" in WIPO, initially tabled by Brazil and Argentina, is largely a product of this debate.[2] The initiative introducing the development dimension into IP discussions is not an isolated fact. On the contrary, it follows a trend we can identify in other fora, both domestic and international, in developed and developing countries alike.

A panoramic view of the discussions representing both directions mentioned should give us a clear picture of where the current WIPO "development agenda" stands and provide some hints of what could be achieved from this process.

We begin by quickly analyzing the moves toward strengthening and harmonizing IPR protection. We then present views from international organizations, experts, and scholars demonstrating that the IP system, as it is, needs to go through some adjustments if it is meant to work as a tool to foster socioeconomic and technological development. This is followed by facts and figures that question the case for the strengthening of IPR protection—a case that, so far, has not been made convincingly. These chapters provide the background that explains the timeliness of the Development Agenda as an initiative that reflects the trend toward incorporating development issues into the agenda of international organizations. We conclude by highlighting the results achieved,

2. "Proposal by Argentina and Brazil for the Establishment of a Development Agenda for WIPO," WIPO Doc. No. WO/GA/31/11 (Geneva: August 27, 2004); http://www.wipo.int/documents/en/document/govbody/wo_gb_ga/pdf/wo_ga_31_11.pdf.

in particular the adoption of the "Development Agenda" by the 2007 General Assembly, as incorporated in the set of 45 recommendations for concrete action.

II. RECENT INITIATIVES TO STRENGTHEN AND HARMONIZE IPRs

The TRIPS Agreement has significantly strengthened IPR protection by, for example, requiring the patentability of products and processes "in all fields of technology." Despite provisions such as this (from Article 27.1), the TRIPS Agreement contains flexibilities that ensure a certain balance of rights and obligations while affording developing countries some leeway in implementing the Agreement's commitments in line with their national circumstances. These include, for example, Article 1.1, on the freedom countries enjoy regarding form of implementation of the obligations stemming from the Agreement; Article 6, on the exhaustion of IPRs; Articles 7 and 8, on objectives and principles, which accommodate the concern that IP should be used as an incentive for technological, economic, and social development; and Article 31, on the possibility of resorting to compulsory licensing of patents.

Nonetheless, the TRIPS Agreement's taking effect has not meant the end of international IP negotiations. The current international agenda shows a host of negotiations under way in which some countries seek the elevation of IPR-standard protection to a degree superior to that set out by the TRIPS Agreement—a "TRIPS-plus" agenda, the effect of which might be the erosion of many of the flexibilities enshrined in TRIPS. Such negotiations are pursued especially in WIPO and in free trade agreements.

Negotiations in WIPO have until recently followed two sets of "agendas": the Patent Agenda and the Digital Agenda. Each is ultimately aimed at filling the spaces that the TRIPS Agreement deliberately left to each state's discretion in order to better accommodate the international commitments to states' national specificities. The Patent Agenda and Digital Agenda assume that harmonization of IP rules, on an international scale, is beneficial to all countries.

In the context of WIPO's Digital Agenda, the WIPO Copyright Treaty (WCT), and the WIPO Performances and Phonograms Treaty (WPPT) were adopted in 1996.[3] Yet since then, the Digital Agenda has largely stalled. In 2000 the diplomatic conference convened to adopt a treaty on the protection of audiovisual performances reached a stalemate and ultimately failed because an agreed result on the subject could not be brokered.[4] As of June 2007, after about 10 years of negotiations, WIPO members have not been able to agree on essential elements

3. WIPO Copyright Treaty, 36 I.L.M. 65 (Geneva: December 20, 1996); WIPO Performances and Phonograms Treaty, 36 I.L.M. 76 (Geneva: December 20, 1996).

4. "A Diplomatic Conference on the Protection of Audiovisual Performances held in December 2000 was unable to reach agreement on all articles of a proposed treaty aimed at strengthening the rights of performers in their audiovisual performances,"

of a proposed broadcasters' treaty; they voted to send the proposal back to the committee drawing board.

In the field of patents, the Patent Law Treaty was adopted in 2000, and the draft Substantive Patent Law Treaty (SPLT) is foreshadowed in WIPO's negotiating agenda. The SPLT aims, inter alia, to harmonize important concepts of patent law, such as "novelty," "state of art," and "inventiveness," whose implications would extend far beyond the purely technical level of the patent examinations.

Aside from the multilateral negotiations, it is important to note that a host of bilateral trade agreements containing a diverse range of "TRIPS-plus" provisions have been signed since the 1990s. These agreements reflect the strategy of leading IP proponents to raise the bar on IP protection in settings other than the multilateral organizations. The TRIPS-plus provisions significantly limit the flexibilities provided for in the TRIPS Agreement; for example, pharmaceuticals companies may seek to extend de facto the patent term of protection on particular drugs, consequently impeding the entry of cheap generic medicines into the market. On their face, these provisions aim to grant exclusive protection to such things as clinical test data, or to require the establishment of a "linkage" provision, whereby generic producers must wait for the expiration of a patent term before applying for marketing approval for similar products. (This rule and the lengthy regulatory examination that follows also impede the entry of generic medicines into the market.)

These prescriptions are not only "TRIPS-plus": they might threaten the very balance underlying the patent system. This poses some important risks, as discussed below.

III. THE CURRENT GLOBAL IP SYSTEM: ITS EFFECTIVENESS AND STRENGTHENING

The move toward strengthening IPRs collides with concerns raised in recent years by international organizations, public agencies, and expert and academic groups, all of which express caution regarding the shortcomings of the current IP system, as well as concern over the possible negative effects that its strengthening could have on public policies in countries seeking to foster development. Such perceptions are shared both in developed and developing countries.

A. The Current IP System and Innovation: Criticism

Critical views that point to the subversion of the IP system as an incentive for creative activity are disseminated worldwide. We begin with a brief overview of the patent field.

The rationale that is normally evoked to justify the granting of patents (i.e., affording temporary exclusivity against the disclosure of the invention) appears

---

WIPO Doc. No. WO/GA/32/4 (Geneva: September 27 to October 5, 2004); http://www.wipo.int/documents/en/document/govbody/wo_gb_ga/doc/wo_ga_31_4.doc.

to have been inadequately transformed over the years, in the sense that it is growingly far from clear whether the benefits touted by "strong IP" harbingers do actually materialize as promised when countries adopt the muscled intellectual property protection proposed by the latter. As stated in the 2002 Report of the U.K. IPR Commission, IP anticompetitive practices

> may lead to behaviour by companies or public institutions that appears perverse from a social point of view. Organisations may patent in order to prevent others gaining access to areas of research or to ensure that other organisations cannot block their research.[5]

In a number of developed countries, the low quality of patents, the novelty or inventiveness of which are disputable, has aroused much criticism. As can be easily imagined, the increase in the number of low-quality patents negatively affects the public domain, and this, of course, runs contrary to the rationale that has made scientific and technological development possible over time.

The adverse effects on innovation provoked by low-quality patents have been addressed by a report released in 2003 by the U.S. Federal Trade Commission, which provides insightful analysis on the interplay of patents, anticompetitive practices, and consumers' rights. According to the report:

> Firms in the biotech industry reported that they avoid infringing questionable patents and therefore will refrain from entering or continuing with a particular field of research that such patents appear to cover.[6]

The Report concludes that:

> More patents in more industries and with greater breadth are not always the best ways to maximize consumer welfare.[7]

The normal practice of companies, nevertheless, is driven toward increasing the number of applications for low-quality patents, as revealed by a study conducted by the OECD, according to which:

> More than three-quarters of ICT firms in the survey reported that they now patent technologies they would not have patented a decade ago—even if the technology had been patentable then.[8]

---

5. "Integrating intellectual property rights and development policy" (London: Commission on Intellectual Property Rights, 2002): 138; http://www.iprcommission.org/graphic/documents/final_report.htm.

6. "To promote innovation: the proper balance of competition and patent law and policy" (Federal Trade Commission, 2003): 5; http://www.ftc.gov/os/2003/10/innovationrptsummary.pdf.

7. Ibid., p. 18.

8. "Patents and innovation: trends and policy challenges" (Paris: Organisation for Economic Co-operation and Development, 2004): 25; http://www.oecd.org/dataoecd/48/12/24508541.pdf.

The OECD report maintains that:

> An initial economic investigation of the working of the patent system reveals limitations in the adequacy of this system for enhancing innovation and diffusion of technology.[9]

The U.S. Supreme Court has also recently expressed concern for preserving patent quality. In *KSR Int'l Co. v. Teleflex*, decided in 2007, the Court reversed application of the "obviousness" test (the so-called Teaching, Suggesting, and Motivating test, or "TSM") by the Federal Circuit Court of Appeals on the grounds that it allowed for the granting of substandard patents. According to the Supreme Court:

> Granting patent protection to advances that would occur in the ordinary course without real innovation retards progress and may, in the case of patents combining previously known elements, deprive prior inventions of their value or utility. . . .
>
> The flaws in the analysis of the Court of Appeals relate for the most part to the court's narrow conception of the obviousness inquiry reflected in its application of the TSM test.[10]

One field in which abundant concerns with the adequacy of the patent system have been addressed, vis-à-vis its purported ends, is the public health sector: The capability of patents to provide increased access to medicines to those in need in the developing world is the subject of much debate. In this context, the Doha Declaration on TRIPS and Public Health (2001) features as a prominent example of the need to limit the encroachment of the patent system over society's ability to manage public health issues.[11] This, in turn, translates into the importance of preserving the flexibilities foreseen in the TRIPS Agreement to ensure countries the leeway necessary to put in place public health policies commensurate with the challenges they face.

In 2005, in response to the debate over the current IP system's impact on development, a group of scholars and civil-society institutions issued the "Adelphi Charter" under the auspices of the Royal Society for the Encouragement of Arts, Manufactures, and Commerce (RSA). The Charter calls upon countries to take into consideration certain principles in the IP discussions, among which it is worth mentioning the following:[12]

> Laws regulating intellectual property must serve as means of achieving creative, social and economic ends and not as ends in themselves. . . .

---

9. Ibid., p. 28.

10. KSR Int'l Co. v. Teleflex Inc., 127 S. Ct. 1727, 1741 (2007).

11. "Declaration on the TRIPS Agreement and Public Health" (World Trade Organization, November 14, 2001); http://www.wto.org/English/thewto_e/minist_e/min01_e/mindecl_trips_e.htm.

12. "Adelphi Charter on creativity, innovation and intellectual property" (Royal Society for the encouragement of Arts, Manufactures & Commerce, October 13, 2005); http://www.rsa.org.uk/acrobat/adelphi_charter.pdf.

8. Intellectual property laws must take account of developing countries' social and economic circumstances.

9. In making decisions about intellectual property law, governments should adhere to these rules:

* There must be an automatic presumption against creating new areas of intellectual property protection, extending existing privileges or extending the duration of rights.

* Change must be allowed only if a rigorous analysis clearly demonstrates that it will promote people's basic rights and economic well-being.

When the Charter was released, the British weekly journal *The Economist* highlighted the fact that the document aimed at the right target by promoting the idea that good policy is not only about creating more rights: rather, it is about keeping the balance between IP and the public domain.[13]

The current functioning of the IP system raises enough concerns to spur a considerable deal of criticism. As the next section reveals, the logic of the demand for strengthened IP protection faces even more difficulties, in view of the many questions left unanswered.

B. Strengthening of IPRs: Criticism

The case for the strengthening of IPR protection is commonly based on an alleged causal link between strong IPR protection and the attraction of foreign direct investment (FDI). Yet this assertion is backed by scant evidence. For example, the World Bank's 2005 Global Economic Prospects report[14] states:

> Evidence is inconclusive about the responsiveness of FDI to intellectual property regimes.

In fact, studies express widespread *concerns* regarding the strengthening of IPR protection, especially because concrete evidence showing the need to strengthen IPRs is lacking. Let us refer back to the OECD study. Regarding patent law, it says:

> Most of the changes to patent regimes implemented over the past two decades were not based on hard evidence or economic analysis.[15]

A similar position can be found in the previously mentioned FTC report:

> Decisionmakers should ask whether granting patents on certain subject matter in fact will promote such progress or instead will hinder competition that can effectively spur innovation.[16]

---

13. "Free ideas," *The Economist* (October 13, 2005); http://www.economist.com/business/displayStory.cfm?story_id=5032375.

14. Op. cit., p. 110; http://siteresources.worldbank.org/INTGEP2005/Resources/GEP107053_Ch05.pdf.

15. Op. cit., p. 26.

16. Op. cit., p. 15.

The 2001 Nobel Prize winner for economics, Joseph Stiglitz, questions whether a strengthening of patent protection would, in fact, induce the claimed positive effects on innovation:

> As difficult as it may be to assess the costs of the inefficiencies arising from patent protection, it is perhaps even more difficult to assess the extent to which [strengthened] intellectual property rights might lead to higher innovation.[17]

Stiglitz's fellow Nobel Prize winner Sir John Sulston, the eminent physician who played a leading role in the Human Genome Project, draws attention to the disputable nature of the relationship between patents and development. According to Sulston:

> Many statements affirm the value of patents by showing parallelism between the growth of patenting and increasing prosperity. But proof of causality is usually missing.[18]

In the copyright area, the World Bank's 2005 Global Economic Prospects argues that:

> The welfare effects of stronger and new copyright protection standards are ambiguous.[19]

The IP negotiations pursued in the framework of FTAs are also a cause of concern because they, more often than not, lead to the adoption of TRIPS-plus obligations and are not always accompanied by an assessment of their effects on development. In this context, it is useful to recall that one of the recommendations of the WHO's Intellectual Property Commission is:

> 4.26 Bilateral trade agreements should not seek to incorporate TRIPS-plus protection in ways that may reduce access to medicines in developing countries.[20]

---

17. Joseph E. Stiglitz, "Towards a pro-development and balanced intellectual property regime," (Seoul: WIPO Ministerial Conference on Intellectual Property for Least Developed Countries, October 25, 2004); http://www2.gsb.columbia.edu/faculty/jstiglitz/download/2004_TOWARDS_A_PRO_DEVELOPMENT.htm.

18. John E. Sulston, "International Patent Law Harmonisation, Development and Policy Space for Flexibility," presentation delivered at the Open Forum on the Draft Substantive Patent Law Treaty (Geneva: March 1–3, 2006); http://www.wipo.int/export/sites/www/meetings/en/2006/scp_of_ge_06/presentations/scp_of_ge_06_sulston1.pdf.

19. Op. cit., p. 110.

20. "Public health, innovation and intellectual property rights," World Health Organization, Report of the Commission on Intellectual Property Rights, Innovation and Public Health (Geneva: 2006); http://www.who.int/intellectualproperty/documents/thereport/ENPublicHealthReport.pdf.

A Resolution adopted in July 2006 by the European Parliament follows the same line, stating:

> 19. [The European Parliament] criticises bilateral and regional trade agreements which restrict, if not eliminate, the safeguards established by the Doha Declaration; stresses the need to ensure the primacy of health over commercial interests; points out the responsibility of those countries, in particular the United States, that put pressure on developing countries to sign such free-trade agreements. . . .[21]

In sum, if we are to engage in an informed debate, the case for strengthened IP protection should be backed by concrete data pointing to its timeliness and to the positive effects that could ensue. Yet the feedback we obtain from the experience of developing countries with the strengthening of IP protection engendered by TRIPS does not endorse so unequivocally the case for ratcheting up IP rules.

After more than a decade following the approval of the TRIPS Agreement, developing countries have become more aware of the consequences engendered by increased IPR protection. The criticisms we have just mentioned reflect the situation on the ground in both developed and developing countries, as demonstrated below.

Increased IPR protection in developing countries, as required by the TRIPS Agreement, has apparently led to the concentration of innovative activities in a handful of developed countries and has consequently diminished innovative production in developing countries.

According to the World Bank's 2005 Global Economic Prospects report:

> Although surveys of foreign investors typically indicate concerns for IPRs, this is often of secondary priority. . . . Finger and Nogues (2002), in fact, argue that the introduction of patent protection for drugs in Chile made several multinational pharmaceutical companies stop production and investment and source this market from other locations.[22]

Data collected by the United Nations Industrial Development Organization (UNIDO) reveal that investment flows in the biotechnology sector in Brazil have decreased from US$28 million in 1994 to US$15 million in 2003, whereas investments in the pharmaceutical sector have plummeted from US$91 million in 1994 to US$37 million in 2003.[23]

---

21. "AIDS—Time to deliver," Resolution of the European Parliament (Strasbourg: July 6, 2006); http://www.europarl.europa.eu/sides/getDoc.do?objRefId=124436&language=EN.

22. Op. cit., p. 110.

23. Benjamin Zycher and Timothy Wolfe, "Biotechnological and pharmaceutical research and development investment under a patent-based access and benefit-sharing regime" (Pacific Research Institute, May 2005): p. D7; http://www.wipo.int/export/sites/www/meetings/en/2006/scp_of_ge_06/presentations/scp_of_ge_06_zycher.pdf.

It is quite telling to recall that between 1996 and 1998 Brazil updated many aspects of its IP legislation: in 1997 a new industrial-property act and a plant-variety protection act took effect; in 1998 new copyright and software laws were enacted. Despite these significant improvements in Brazilian legislation, according to a North American researcher and former advisor to President Bill Clinton, Brazil's position in the ranking of countries' ability to attract FDI fell from 2nd in 1998 to 17th in 2004. This expert argues that the downgrading Brazil experienced was mostly the result of allegedly feeble IP protection. As this alleged downgrading took place soon after the enactment of updated legislation in Brazil, we can easily see that the claimed link between strong IP protection and FDIs is debatable.[24]

The adoption of the TRIPS Agreement also suggests an increase in rent-seeking behavior by companies headquartered in developed countries.

The World Bank's 2002 Global Economic Prospects report presents an estimate of the net transfer of capital effected by the TRIPS Agreement and its IPR regulations. According to the report, the United States figured as the major winner, having received US$19 billion in transferred capital, followed by Germany's US$6.7 billion, Japan's US$5.6 billion, France's US$3.3 billion, and the United Kingdom's US$2.9 billion. Conversely, other countries would become net exporters of capital: South Korea would lead the group with remittances reaching US$15 billion, Greece with US$7.7 billion, and China with US$5.1 billion.[25]

In Brazil, royalties' remittances related to IPR have surged in the years since 1993: they have increased from US$146 million in 1993 to US$1.6 billion in 2004, according to data collected by the Brazilian Central Bank.[26]

This framework shows the importance of ensuring a balance of interests in IP discussions, in particular to safeguard the existing flexibilities that, despite all the constraints contained in the TRIPS Agreement, by and large afford countries the necessary margin to implement development policies adapted to their needs. This line of reasoning is echoed by the following excerpt from the World Bank's 2005 Global Economic Prospects report:

> All in all, the general conclusion is that countries have to develop an IPR strategy appropriate to their level of development. . . . [27]

In sum, numerous studies and leading development experts concur that countries must have flexibility to tailor IPR to their development needs. Given this broad consensus, it is not surprising that the development dimension has stood

---

24. A. T. Kearney and Robert Shapiro, *"Ataque aos Piratas,"* Interview with Cátia Luz. *Época* (São Paulo: September 12, 2005): p. 56.

25. "Global Economic Prospects 2002," World Bank, p. 133; http://siteresources.worldbank.org/INTGEP2002/Resources/gep2002complete.pdf.

26. Figures provided by the Brazilian Central Bank, available at http://www.mj.gov.br/data/Pages/MJ7DB451B5ITEMID911BEE061103415AB6EE6CF153D50A0EPTBRIE.htm.

27. Op. cit., p. 111.

at the center of the IP discussions taking place in many international fora. A quick glance at the agendas of some relevant international organizations will suffice to demonstrate a trend to this effect and provide the elements to support our claim that WIPO should follow the same path.

IV. INTERNATIONAL DEVELOPMENT AND THE WIPO DEVELOPMENT AGENDA

In the year 2000, the UN adopted a set of eight goals, the Millennium Development Goals (MDGs), which should be met by 2015. These goals were set to attain minimum objectives worldwide in areas that range from hunger elimination to poverty eradication, from environment protection to the fight against AIDS, in order to reach a partnership for social and economic development. Some UN goals encompass issues affected by IP rules (such as Goal 8: "combat HIV/AIDS"), giving IP protection influence over their achievement.[28]

Additionally, the UN General Assembly adopted a Political Declaration at the Follow-up Meeting on the Declaration of Commitment on HIV/AIDS in 2006. The Declaration reaffirms that the TRIPS Agreement "does not and should not prevent members from taking measures now and in the future to protect public health," and, in this regard, "reaffirms the right to use, to the full, the provisions in the TRIPS Agreement, the Doha Declaration on TRIPS Agreement and Public Health and the World Trade Organization's General Council Decision of 2003 and the amendments to Article 31, which provide flexibilities for this purpose."

Furthermore, it is important to recall that the concern with reaching development-oriented outcomes pervades the WTO negotiation agenda. The need to render international trade beneficial to all countries led to the launching of the Doha Development Round in 2001, which has introduced into the work of the WTO the need to ensure development for all. Also in the WTO, an amendment to the TRIPS Agreement was approved in December 2005 as a result of discussions mandated by the Doha Declaration on TRIPS and Public Health, in what could be regarded as an acknowledgement of the need to render fully effective the flexibilities in the IP system. The amendment incorporates provisions to the TRIPS Agreement to facilitate the export of pharmaceutical products to countries with insufficient, or no, manufacturing capacities in the pharmaceutical sector.

---

28. One of the recommendations for action agreed upon at the IV session of the Provisional Committee on Proposals Related to a WIPO Development Agenda (June 11–15, 2007) prescribes WIPO's norm-setting activities to be "supportive of the development goals agreed within the UN system, including those contained in the Millennium Declaration." (Consolidated list of PCDA recommendations, document A/43/13, recommendation number 22.) See http://www.wipo.int/ip-development/en/agenda/pcda07_session4.html.

The World Health Organization has likewise addressed the development dimension. The 2006 World Health Assembly adopted a recommendation, pursuant to which member states were urged:

> (4) to encourage trade agreements to take into account the flexibilities contained in the Agreement on Trade-Related Aspects of Intellectual Property Rights and recognized by the Doha Ministerial Declaration on the TRIPS Agreement and Public Health. . . .[29]

The Final Report of the Expert Commission convened by the WHO to discuss IP, innovation, and public health adopts a similar position.[30] It highlights the need to ensure a balance between patents and public health concerns, as well as the importance of safeguarding the policy space necessary for countries to pursue their national development policies.

A. The WIPO Development Agenda

As the previous panorama makes clear, the proposal to establish a Development Agenda in WIPO, submitted at the 2004 General Assembly, did not represent an isolated incident. Rather, it followed a trend identified in many international and national fora, both in developed and developing countries, in the direction of discussing IP as a means to development and not as an end in itself. In this connection, the adoption of the "Agenda" by the 2007 General Assembly could represent one step to steer the work of WIPO in the direction followed by other international organizations.

Until recently, the international IP agenda did not reflect the development concerns highlighted above. The Doha Declaration on TRIPS and Public Health could be seen, in this respect, as a landmark that raised awareness of the possible deleterious effect that IP might have if the flexibilities and balance in the system are not preserved.

The WIPO Development Agenda is co-sponsored by Brazil, Argentina, Bolivia, Cuba, Dominican Republic, Ecuador, Egypt, Iran, Kenya, Peru, Sierra Leone, South Africa, Tanzania, Venezuela, and Uruguay—a group called the "Friends of Development." Other countries that do not officially sponsor the initiative, such as India, have nonetheless expressed support for it. The declaration issued at the Third Trilateral Commission of the India-Brazil-South Africa (IBSA) Dialogue Forum, a concertation group of the three countries, which took place on March 30, 2006, states that:

> 32. They recognized the importance of incorporating the development dimension in international discussions concerning intellectual property, as a means to

29. "Resolution WHA 59.24," World Health Organization; http://www.who.int/gb/ebwha/pdf_files/WHA59/A59_R24-en.pdf.

30. "Public Health, Innovation and Intellectual Property Rights," World Health Organization, Report of the Commission on Intellectual Property Rights, Innovation, and Public Health (April 2006); http://www.who.int/intellectualproperty/documents/thereport/ENPublicHealthReport.pdf.

> preserve the policy space that countries enjoy in ensuring access to knowledge, health, culture and a sustainable environment. In this context, they welcomed the launching of a "Development Agenda in the World Intellectual Property Organization" and reaffirmed their hope that the aforementioned Organization incorporates effectively the development dimension in all its bodies.[31]

The Development Agenda is aimed at incorporating into WIPO the concerns previously mentioned with regard to the effects of IP on development. It also seeks to restore the balance in the activities being conducted at WIPO, considering that, after the entry into force of the TRIPS Agreement, the Organization dedicated its work mainly to the proposals directed toward increasing IPR protection, as is the case with the Digital and Patent Agendas. Because there is no evidence to show that increased IPR protection plays a compelling role in engendering technological, economic, and social development, it seems legitimate and logical to turn WIPO's attention to IP issues in a development-oriented manner. The Development Agenda seeks, therefore, to preserve public-interest flexibilities, which, despite being crucial tools for the pursuit of public policies, are threatened by increased IPR protection.

The Agenda is meant to have a cross-cutting nature (i.e., it should be taken into account in all WIPO's activities) and should be considered as an ongoing process, because development concerns are supposed to be inscribed permanently into the work of WIPO. True incorporation of the development dimension means putting in place measures that not only enable countries to make full use of the inherent flexibilities but also that preserve these flexibilities. This means discussing measures on norm-setting activities, technical assistance, impact assessment, and institutional features of WIPO.

The proposal initially put forward by the "Friends of Development" which was largely adopted by the General Assembly in September 2007, envisages concrete steps to incorporate the Development Agenda under four issue areas. Briefly, these include:

1. Mandate and Governance in WIPO According to the Agreement by which the UN acknowledged WIPO as one of its specialized agencies, the mandate entrusted to WIPO includes, inter alia:

> promoting creative intellectual activity and . . . facilitating the transfer of technology related to industrial property to the developing countries in order to accelerate economic, social and cultural development, subject to the competence and responsibilities of the United Nations and its organs. . . .

Considering that WIPO is part of the UN system, its activities should be driven toward implementing the UN Millennium Development Goals as far as IP is concerned—something that has apparently been overlooked, as evidenced by the direction taken by the SPLT negotiations and other WIPO initiatives.

31. Available at http://www.mre.gov.br/portugues/imprensa/nota_detalhe3.asp?ID_RELEASE=3657.

Another set of proposals regarding governance in WIPO seeks to widen and enhance participation of civil society in WIPO discussions. Traditionally, civil society representatives in WIPO have predominantly represented rights-holders' associations. Only recently have organizations defending public interest grown aware of what is at stake in IP negotiations. As IP expands its scope to encroach upon other issue areas (such as health, environment, access to culture, and so on), it is important that stakeholders defending the public interest be afforded the opportunity to contribute. Allowing the participation of organizations defending the public interest also increases the accountability of the IP system.

2. Norm-Setting Activities As we have outlined earlier, there is widespread concern with the appropriateness of the current IP regime as a means of inducing development in all countries. There is also concern regarding the effects of increased IP protection on development-oriented national policies. Therefore, the demand for increased harmonization of IP international norms should be scrutinized in view of the effects such actions might impose on development in individual nations. In this context, the Development Agenda proposes to recognize certain negotiating principles in order to maintain the balance of rights and obligations already enshrined in the TRIPS Agreement and supported by other international agencies. Also, we propose that, in view of the dispute surrounding the need for increased IP norms, norm-setting activities be preceded by impact assessments that better inform countries about the risks involved.

3. Technical Assistance WIPO plays an important role in delivering technical assistance to countries in complying with their international IP obligations. International IP norms also foresee flexibilities that countries need to be empowered to exercise. These include compulsory licenses, anticompetitive rules to curb abuse of IPRs, exceptions to patent rights, and others. WIPO's top-quality technical staff should be given clear instructions by the organization's membership in the direction of encouraging and enabling the full use of these flexibilities. Otherwise, the balance reached at the negotiating table risks being lost as a result of developing countries' inability to effectively implement the safeguard clauses they are entitled to use.

4. Transfer of Technology and Anticompetitive Practices We can no more overlook the interface between IP and competition rules than we can disregard the inextricable relationship between IP and the transfer of technology. It is, thus, somewhat surprising that we see very few activities in WIPO that are dedicated to these issues. In that vein, the Development Agenda proposes that in the framework of WIPO, we (a) pursue IP-related measures to enable developing countries to absorb technology, such as, for example, building capacity to effectively use information disclosed in patents; (b) examine possible measures to facilitate access to knowledge generated by public funding; and (c) address anticompetitive practices that hinder the transfer of technology, and propose ways to overcome these practices.

B. The Development Agenda and WIPO: Discussions and Recommendations

The presentation of the Development Agenda was followed by a rich debate involving the entire WIPO membership, evincing the need to incorporate the development dimension into the activities of the organization.

The inter-sessional intergovernmental meetings, which took place in 2005, followed by the meetings of the Provisional Committee on the Development Agenda (PCDA) in 2006 and 2007, have shown that there is a great deal of work to do if we are to streamline WIPO's work regarding development. Some proposals have translated into concrete action during the process of the discussions and are worth noting, such as the convening of an open forum to discuss issues related to the negotiation of the SPLT, reflecting the concern to submit norm-setting activities to open-ended debate on issues under negotiation.

In September 2007, the General Assembly adopted a set of 45 recommendations that distill the three years of debate on the "Development Agenda."[32] These action-oriented recommendations cover all the issue areas mentioned above (technical assistance, norm-setting, mandate, transfer of technology, and impact studies) and incorporate most of the concerns enumerated by the "Friends of Development." The General Assembly's adoption of these proposals could be considered as the first stage of the Development Agenda process, setting the stage for WIPO´s implementation of the "Agenda" and the reorientation towards the needs of developing countries.

First, it should be noted that many of the 45 recommendations are designed to *level the playing field* in IP discussions: despite all the technicalities that surround the debates on IP, this is not an arcane issue anymore, and all countries should be equipped to actively participate in IP discussions—in particular to approach IP from a development-oriented perspective. In this regard, a good number of recommendations address the need to make all countries cognizant of the flexibilities they are entitled to use and to actually empower them to take advantage of these flexibilities. In fact, the recommendations incorporate the concern of preserving flexibilities at both the *negotiation* and the *implementation* levels, both preventing norm-setting activities from eroding the safeguards and allowing technical assistance to be harnessed as a tool to effectively put into practice the flexibilities existing in the IP regime.

Recommendations along these lines include the following: "In its activities, including norm-setting, WIPO should take into account the flexibilities in international IP agreements." Also, "WIPO shall make available advice on the implementation and operation of the rights and obligations and the understanding and use of flexibilities contained in the TRIPS Agreement." According to the recommendations, developing countries could also be provided with the

32. The 45 recommendations are reproduced in full in the Appendix to the Introduction.

necessary technical expertise to curb anticompetitive practices ("Promote measures that will help countries deal with IP related anti-competitive practices, by providing technical cooperation to developing countries"), an area where IP could certainly be approached from a development-oriented perspective.

Furthermore, a number of recommendations have been designed to better inform the discussions taking place at WIPO, with a view toward improving transparency during norm-setting activities and in the provision of technical assistance. In addition, measures were recommended to require the gathering of concrete data relating to WIPO's activities so as to facilitate, inter alia, assessment of their impacts on development. These recommendations include statements that "WIPO shall conduct informal, open and balanced consultations, as appropriate, prior to any new norm-setting activities" and "strengthen WIPO's capacity to perform objective assessments of the impact of the organization's activities on development."

As a response to concerns about the enclosure of the public domain, some recommendations have sought to touch upon the importance of avoiding its depletion. One of them requires WIPO "[t]o promote norm-setting activities related to IP that support a robust public domain in WIPO's Member States."

Although the complete implementation of the recommendations identified lies ahead, the outcome achieved thus far is very positive, especially because it has resulted from a consensus-based process with the participation of all WIPO members.

We conclude that the Development Agenda contributes to a better understanding of the complexities and nuances of IP, an issue area that affects countries differently and that has achieved a considerably expanded reach in the past decade.

V. CONCLUSION

First, we would like to underscore that the Development Agenda is not moved by any desire for confrontation. We believe this has become clear over recent years, when discussions on the proposals submitted by a number of members have shown a true interest in improving the way WIPO tackles development issues.

The Development Agenda is premised on the concerns disseminated worldwide about the adverse effects that might stem from upwardly harmonized, "one size fits all" IP rules. The Agenda is a serious attempt to bring this debate into the purview of WIPO in a cross-cutting and permanent manner. As such, it seeks to render the IP system beneficial to all countries. A precondition to this end is that countries must continue to enjoy the margins of action necessary to accommodate their public policies. This freedom of action is currently provided by flexibilities built into the IP system but is threatened by recent TRIPS-plus initiatives.

IP rules have become too pervasive in everyone's lives to continue to be crafted by a small group of experts. The reach of IP has widened to affect many domains—from health to culture to the environment—and, because of that, discussions pertaining to IP cannot continue to be based on the same dogmas that have prevailed in the past and which have proven to be disputable. One of these perverse dogmas is the assumption that any criticism directed toward IP is a sort of heresy, aimed at undermining the IP system altogether. This approach rules out any possibility of establishing an honest, evidence-based debate.

Of course, differences in perception on the issues at hand are legitimate, especially in an international organization comprising countries with enormous diversity in terms of levels of development.

Considering that a number of international organizations have already incorporated the goal of development into their activities, perhaps the proposal for a Development Agenda in WIPO might have taken too long to see the light of day. In any event, the U.K. Intellectual Property Commission concludes:

> We believe that the system will only improve from a development perspective if we can develop a deeper understanding of the relationships between IP and development. It is important, therefore, for the community of research sponsors and practitioners around the world to meet this challenge.[33]

We think that the Development Agenda is one firm step in this direction. Hopefully, its adoption in 2007 will usher in a new era in WIPO.

---

33. Op. cit., p. 179.

3. TRIPS 3.0
Policy Calibration and Innovation Displacement

DANIEL J. GERVAIS*

I. INTRODUCTION

The Agreement on Trade-Related Intellectual Property Rights (TRIPS)[1] is now entering its third phase. The first phase began with a well-documented push by the U.S. government,[2] supported by the European Commission and the Japanese government, to link intellectual property and trade rules in the World Trade Organization (WTO) as part of the Uruguay Round of Multilateral Trade Negotiations, which ended in Marrakesh in April 1994 with the signing of the Agreement Establishing the WTO, Annex 1C of which is the TRIPS Agreement. Phase I did not end with the Round, however. It continued for a few years after the establishment of the WTO, as a number of developing countries (very few of

* Professor of Law and Director of the Technology and Entertainment Law Program, Vanderbilt University.

1. "Agreement on Trade-Related Aspects of Intellectual Property Rights," 1869 UNTS 299, 33 ILM 1197 (1994) (hereinafter referred to as "TRIPS Agreement" or "TRIPS").

2. See Gervais, *The TRIPS Agreement: Drafting History and Interpretation*, 2d. ed. (Andover, UK: Sweet & Maxwell, 2003); Susan K. Sell, *Private Power, Public Law* 96–120 (Cambridge: Cambridge University Press, 2003); Christopher May, *A Global Political Economy of Intellectual Property Rights: The New Enclosures?* (New York: Routledge, 2000); Peter Drahos and John Braithwaite, *Information Feudalism: Who Owns the Knowledge Economy?* (New York: New Press, 2003); and A. Koury Menescal, *Those Behind the TRIPS Agreement: The Influence of the ICC and the AIPPI on International Property Decisions*, 2 Intellectual Property Quarterly 155 (Andover, UK: Sweet & Maxwell, 2005).

whom had been active participants in the negotiations)[3] began to grasp the detailed scope of their TRIPS commitments. From the perspective of TRIPS proponents, Phase I was informed by *addition narratives*, according to which adding high levels of intellectual property to the laws of developing and least-developed nations (a) would protect the property of intellectual property holders in both richer and poorer countries (and, by generating additional profits, would in turn lead to more research and development), and (b) was necessary to jumpstart economic growth in those countries (intellectual property being seen as a necessary ingredient of development).

Phase II began just before the new millennium. It was characterized initially by highly critical analyses of the TRIPS negotiation process. For many developing nations this was their first complete multilateral trade negotiation, a difficulty compounded by their lack of intellectual property expertise.[4] Not surprisingly, the negotiations were said to have been heavily influenced by coercion of developing nations and their ignorance of the matters at hand—thus producing a very bad "bargain" for the developing world.

The Uruguay Round was the first example—on such a scale, at least—of sectoral reciprocity: TRIPS (and the General Agreement on Trade in Services [GATS]) in exchange for agriculture and textiles. Critics who emphasize the coercive character of the bargaining process point to various threats posed during the Round to isolate developing countries from the global trading system or to impose punitive unilateral sanctions if they did not accede to the demands of the West.[5]

Some critics opined that intellectual property was not proper subject matter for the WTO.[6] An extension of this critique sees the Uruguay Round as the last major multilateral trade negotiations round, or at least the last in which the West was able to obtain more than it conceded to the developing world, specifically because of the WTO's foray into the atypical area of intellectual property and the developing world's reaction to it. Others argued that, given its impact on the global economy, the WTO needed a "stronger transnational and supranational mandate for governance."[7]

However, the majority of critics underscored the absence of empirical data to justify the addition narratives; they rejected the transfer of (partly) empirically based justificatory theories from industrialized to developing nations. Many of them also tried to demonstrate the inadequacy of Western intellectual property

---

3. Gervais, pp. 12–26 (cited in note 3).

4. Gervais, p. 375.

5. Put differently, TRIPS was perceived by a number of developing nations as a lesser evil than isolation and loss of MFN status. See Bernard Hoekman, *Services and intellectual property rights* in Susan M. Collins and Barry Busworth, eds., *The New GATT: Implications for the United States* 113 (Washington, DC: Brookings Institution, 1994).

6. Jagdish Bhagwati, *In Defense of Globalization* 182–85 (Oxford University Press, 2004).

7. Jürgen Habermas, *The Divided West* 134 (Cambridge: Polity Press, 2006).

norms to protect certain forms of traditional medicinal knowledge or traditional cultural expression (sometimes referred to jointly as "traditional knowledge").[8] This discourse went much further than the casuistry and polite obfuscation so prevalent in international diplomacy. A sense of outrage pervaded many of the discussions. Not surprisingly, it led to a recommendation that TRIPS should be resisted and new norms developed. Phase II was informed by *subtraction narratives*: in short, the lesser the impact of TRIPS, the better the situation of developing countries would be.[9] Several books, articles, and reports were published[10] to explain how TRIPS could be "fought" both within the WTO (for example, by coalescing or insisting on technology transfers) and without (for example, by fostering the emergence of alternative instruments in other forums, such as the Convention on Biological Diversity [CBD]),[11] either as countervailing international law norms or as hermeneutic tools for TRIPS exegetes. Phase II confronted head-on a fundamental two-pronged query, namely (a) what is the causal relationship between intellectual property protection and foreign direct investment (FDI), and (b) does increased FDI necessarily spur innovation in the recipient country? The query is important because it targets an assumption that underpins much of the pro–intellectual property discourse.

In parallel, multilateral norm-making designed to increase protection levels (and reduce some of the flexibilities that remain in the TRIPS Agreement), a process known as "TRIPS-plus," became increasingly difficult. Given the widespread outrage over pharmaceutical companies' ill-advised attempt to enforce patent rights in the face of thousands of developing-country patients being unable to afford antiretroviral or antimalarial therapies, increasing multilateral levels of patent protection has become exceedingly difficult, at least for the predictable future.[12] Initial suggestions in the Doha Round to strengthen the enforcement section of TRIPS and incorporate two treaties negotiated in 1996 under the auspices of the World Intellectual Property Organization (WIPO)[13]

---

8. J. Michael Finger and Philip Schuler, *Poor People's Knowledge: Promoting Intellectual Property in Developing Countries* (Washington, DC: The World Bank and Oxford, 2004). On possible solutions within the TRIPS framework, see Daniel J. Gervais, "Traditional Knowledge & Intellectual Property: A TRIPS-Compatible Approach," *Michigan State Law Review* 137 (Spring 2005).

9. For a detailed discussion of how Egypt's pharmaceutical industry and access to medicines was done more harm than good by TRIPS, see Basma I. Abdelgafar, *The Illusive Trade-Off: Intellectual Property Rights, Innovations Systems and Egypt's Pharmaceutical Industry* (Toronto: University of Toronto Press, 2006). At pp. 15–23, she discusses the emergence of TRIPS.

10. See the list of TRIPS-related books and articles on www.tripsagreement.net.

11. Convention on Biological Diversity, 1760 UNTS 143, 31 ILM 818 (1992).

12. Measures announced in 2006 and 2007 by the governments of Thailand and Brazil demonstrate that the issue is far from resolved.

13. WIPO Copyright Treaty, 122 Stat 2860, 35 ILM 65 (1996); WIPO Performances and Phonograms Treaty, 36 ILM 65 (1996).

dealing with copyright on the Internet were all but abandoned. Efforts in WIPO to negotiate new treaties (for example, on database protection, harmonization of substantive patent law, and the rights of broadcasters and webcasters) have met with strong opposition, in particular from developing countries. As an additional sign of the shift brought about by Phase II, while the WTO attempted to address some of the concerns raised by the developing world (for example, by adopting Article 31*bis*, which, in the wake of the Doha Declaration, limits the scope of the prohibition to issue compulsory licenses on certain pharmaceuticals for export purposes,[14] or allowing the TRIPS Council to work on the relationship between TRIPS and the CBD and insisting on documenting compliance with the industrialized countries' technology-transfer obligations), WIPO started work on a "Development Agenda" designed to align the Organization's work with the interests of the developing world.[15] As of this writing, work on the Agenda was accelerating, but its fate remained uncertain.

Yet during the second phase, the TRIPS proponents did not abandon their efforts to continue to increase the international intellectual property baseline. They began using their political ammunition in *bilateral* negotiations to negotiate trade and investment treaties. Recent bilateral agreements signed by the European Union and the United States almost always contain TRIPS-plus norms, including undertakings by developing countries not to use specific TRIPS flexibilities.

TRIPS has now entered a third phase, one that is informed by *calibration narratives*, against a backdrop of shifting geocommercial realities, including exponential outsourcing by Western enterprises and the growing clout, and tactical capabilities, of developing countries in trade and other multilateral discussions.

The building blocks of the calibration process that is under way are many: (a) the recognition that developing countries are very different—from Chile to China, from Bolivia to Burkina Faso, or from Egypt to India—and, consequently, may need different implementations of TRIPS, instead of "cookie cutter" norm implants; (b) the recognition that, below certain developmental thresholds, the introduction of high levels of intellectual property protection will not generate

---

14. World Trade Organization, "Decision of the General Council of 30 August 2003," WT/L/540 (2003), online at http://www.wto.org/english/tratop_ e/trips_e/implem_para6_e.htm. The Decision was incorporated into TRIPS as Article 31*bis*, together with an Annex and an Appendix.

15. WIPO, *Proposal by Argentina and Brazil for the Establishment of a Development Agenda for WIPO* (Aug. 27, 2004; WO/GA/31/11) (hereafter *AB Proposal*); see also WIPO, *Report on the Thirty-First (15th Extraordinary) Session* (Oct. 5, 2004; WO/GA/31/15) 33–37. This proposal was joined by 12 other member states (Bolivia, Cuba, Dominican Republic, Ecuador, Egypt, Iran, Kenya, Peru, Sierra Leone, South Africa, Tanzania, and Venezuela). See WIPO, *Report of the First Session of the Provisional Committee on Proposals Related to a WIPO Development Agenda* (February 20–24, 2006; PCDA/1/6 Prov 2, including an Annex containing all the proposals).

positive impacts (as was evidenced by the extension of transitional periods available for least-developed WTO members); (c) the growing belief that intellectual property protection is necessary to develop innovation and draw foreign direct investment (including technology transfers) but in itself is insufficient to achieve developmental objectives; (d) consequently, the recognition that any complete TRIPS implementation must form part of a broader strategic initiative; and, finally, (e) the recognition that the sudden introduction of high levels of protection and enforcement may induce significant negative welfare impacts, which must also be managed.

The thesis explored in this chapter builds on these foundations. It argues that we are on the cusp of a significant displacement of research and innovation to certain developing countries. Initially, this will constitute research by or for multinational companies currently dominant in Western research and development efforts, but it seems likely that research intensity in developing-country firms will increase in parallel, though perhaps with a time lag. The first part of the chapter discusses the impact of TRIPS on investment and innovation enhancement in developing countries. We then turn to our attention to the geographical displacement of innovation, which is the result, at least in part, of the implementation of TRIPS-compliant norms and standards. The last part of the chapter suggests a classification to determine which countries are likely to benefit from the displacement.

II. MEASURING THE IMPACTS OF TRIPS ON DEVELOPMENT

The introduction, or updating, of intellectual property norms in all member countries and territories of the World Trade Organization (WTO), as a result of the adoption of the TRIPS Agreement, sparked a relatively new field of study, namely the impact of the introduction of intellectual property norms on the social, cultural, and economic development of developing and least-developed countries. TRIPS is used here as the flag bearer because, backed by the WTO dispute-settlement system,[16] it has forced several dozen nations to adopt higher intellectual property protection measures in a relatively short timeframe.

Two notable institutional contributions to the analysis include a World Bank report on the impact of intellectual property on economic development[17] and a report published by the U.K. Commission on Intellectual Property Rights.[18]

16. Although the first case filed under TRIPS was against India, there have been relatively few TRIPS disputes involving developing countries.

17. Carsten Fink and Keith E. Maskus, eds., *Intellectual Property and Development: Lessons from Recent Economic Research* (Washington, DC: The World Bank, 2004).

18. Commission on Intellectual Property Rights, *Integrating Intellectual Property Rights and Development Policy* (2002). Available online at http://www.iprcommission.org/papers/pdfs/final_report/CIPRfullfinal.pdf (hereafter UK IPR Commission Report).

There have also been scholarly initiatives to explain the origins of the push to have intellectual property included as part of the Uruguay Round package[19] and to provide a deeper understanding of the impact of intellectual property on developing and emerging economies.[20]

A. Overview of Recent Analyses

Recent studies, including those just mentioned, offer a blurred and complex picture of the advantages of (high) intellectual property protection in developing economies.[21] It now seems clear that TRIPS put the policy cart before the empirical horse, as it were, [22] because the Agreement was informed more by the *belief* that introducing Western IP norms would induce development than by actual supporting analyses and data. We now know that a simple equation cannot be drawn between an increase in trade following the introduction of TRIPS-compatible IP protection, on one hand, and economic development on the other, especially when measured in terms of social welfare gains.[23] We also know that innovation (the generation and application of new ideas) is but one of the five main drivers of economic development, although in the longer term it is probably the strongest one.[24]

---

19. See note 2.

20. Many of the contributors to this book have published extensively on this topic. One could also mention Suzanne Scotchmer, "The Political Economy of Intellectual Property Treaties," 20 *Journal of Law, Economics and Organization* 415, 435–36 (2004).

21. *The Impact of Trade-Related Intellectual Property Rights on Trade and Foreign Direct Investment in Developing Countries,* OECD Working Party of the Trade Committee, Document TD/TC/WP(2002)42/FINAL (May 28, 2003), online at http://www.oecd.org/dataoecd/59/46/2960051.pdf; Walter G. Park and Douglas Lippoldt, *International Licensing and the Strengthening of Intellectual Property Rights in Developing Countries* (OECD document TD/TC/WP(2004)31/FINAL, Dec. 21, 2004); UK IPR Commission Report (cited in note 18); World Bank study (cited in note 17); Will Martin and L. Alan Winters, eds., *The Uruguay Round and the Developing Economies* (Washington, DC: The World Bank, 1995), available online at http://econ.worldbank.org; Scotchmer, 20 J L Econ & Org 415, 435–36 (cited in note 21); OECD Science, Technology and Industry Outlook 2004 (2004); Organization for Economic Co-operation and Development, Patents, Innovation and Economic Performance: OECD Conference Proceedings (2004); Carliene Brenner, *Intellectual Property Rights and Technology Transfer in Developing Country Agriculture: Rhetoric and Reality* (OECD Development Centre Working Paper 133, CD/DOC(98)3 March 1998).

22. See Park and Lippoldt (note 21, page 1).

23. See Carsten Fink and Carlos A. Primo Braga, "How Stronger Protection of Intellectual Property Rights Affects International Trade Flows," in Fink and Maskus, *Intellectual Property and Development* (cited in note 17), p. 21.

24. The other drivers are trade, finance, migration and aid. See Ian Goldin and Kenneth Reinert. *Globalization for Development, Revised Edition: Trade, Finance, Aid, Migration, and Policy* (World Bank/Palgrave Macmillan, 2007).

B. The Link between IP and FDI

The traditional view on the effect of intellectual property, which is supported by case studies in countries such as postwar Japan, is that higher IP protection, especially of patent rights, will lead to higher inward FDI, which often has a significant technology-transfer/intellectual property component.[25] Essentially, the conventional wisdom is that foreign firms invest internationally if there are location advantages and if it is more profitable for them to produce in another country rather than licensing their IP. Firms are more apt to invest in countries that implement strong IP protections (and to bring their IP or allow for licenses in such countries). Transnational firms may also choose to invest in vertical FDI (where some plants produce products that can be used by the plants "above" them as inputs to their products).[26] Yet this traditional IP/FDI correlation is not universally supported (and it is harder still to establish causation) by available data because there are several other key factors in play. Economic analysis demonstrates that, in most cases, sufficient IP protection is an essential component of increased inward FDI and trade flows in IP-sensitive goods for countries above a certain economic development threshold.[27] However, those studies also show that (a) the trade regime (especially tariffs and non-tariff barriers), tax, and competition laws are also potent, and often dominant, influences, and (b) in certain cases, such as China, geopolitical and commercial forces may trump weaknesses in TRIPS-compliant intellectual property protection. Indeed, in a recent analysis of the FDI component and its relation to IP, Professor Maskus concluded that other factors influencing FDI and technology-transfer decisions include market liberalization and deregulation, technology development policies, competition regimes, and a low level of corruption.[28] Other studies indicate that, in China's case, the growth of FDI does not seem to be correlated with increases in the level of intellectual property protection or with political reforms.[29]

---

25. See Park and Lippoldt (cited to in note 21), p. 2, and Keith E. Maskus, "Intellectual Property Rights and Economic Development," 32 *Case Western Reserve Journal of International Law* 471, 481–85 (2000); Keith E. Maskus and Christine McDaniel, "Impacts of the Japanese Patent System on Productivity Growth," 11 *Japan & World Economy* 557 (1999).

26. See Carlos A. Primo Braga and Carsten Fink, "The Relationship between Intellectual Property Rights and Foreign Direct Investment," 9 *Duke J Comp & Int'l L* 163, 172–73 (1998).

27. See Thomas Cottier, "From Progressive Liberalization to Progressive Regulation in WTO Law," 9 *J Int'l Econ L* 779, 802 (2006).

28. Keith E. Maskus, "Intellectual Property Rights in Encouraging FDI and Technology Transfer," in *Intellectual Property and Development* (cited in note 17), 70–71; see also Carsten Fink, *Patent Protection, Transnational Corporations, and Market Structure: A Simulation Study of the Indian Pharmaceutical Industry*, *id.*, pp. 250–51.

29. See Yahong Li, Comment, "Pushing For Greater Protection: The Trend Toward Greater Protection of Intellectual Property in the Chinese Software Industry and the Implications for Rule of Law in China," 23 *University of Pennsylvania Journal of International*

Correlatively, the U.K. IPR Commission Report[30] stresses that it is important not to consider developing countries as a homogeneous group.[31] It suggests that a sequencing phenomenon can be observed. In an impoverished country, there is little rent that foreign firms can extract and limited innovation potential—with the possible exception of the exploitation of genetic resources or traditional knowledge. Furthermore, technology to copy or improve on high-technology goods is often scarce, and it is thus unlikely that such a country can benefit (as an innovator) from technology transfer. Technology-intensive FDI is unlikely because of factors unrelated to IP, such as poor infrastructure or absence of a viable domestic market. International firms take notice when a country becomes both a piracy threat *and* a potential market, even if the threat is limited to a fairly small percentage of the population.[32] Although countries that implement IP norms may benefit from increased local development and inward FDI, they may also incur job losses in established copycat industries and welfare costs associated with higher local prices. However, consumers benefit from knowing they are purchasing the genuine product, especially in areas where the quality of the goods is essential.

C. Policy Lessons of Recent Analyses

At this juncture, we must differentiate two phenomena that are linked by a causal relationship but are markedly different, if only because one is measured at the macro level and the other visible at the micro level. The first is the increase of FDI after the introduction of TRIPS-compliant protection; the second is the decision by a particular transnational corporation (TNC) of whether or not to invest in a country because of its perceived need for protection, or lack thereof (an example is Novartis's decision to announce a move of research expenditures from India to China after the refusal of a patent on Gleevec®).[33] The difficulties

---

Economic Law 637, 638–41 (2002); Keith E. Maskus, "The Role of Intellectual Property Rights in Encouraging Foreign Direct Investment and Technology Transfer," 9 *Duke Journal of Comparative and International Law* 109, 115–19 (1998) (noting that FDI increased tenfold in China prior to the introduction of TRIPS-compatible norms); Mikhaelle Schiappacasse, "Intellectual Property Rights in China: Technology Transfers and Economic Development," 2 *Buffalo Intellectual Property Law Journal* 164 (2004); Peter K. Yu et al., "China and the WTO: Progress, Perils, and Prospects," 17 *Columbia Journal of Asian Law* 1 (2003).

30. Cited in note 18.

31. Id., pp. 2–3.

32. For a discussion on the situation in Kenya, see J. M. Migai Akech, "The African Growth Opportunity Act: Implications for Kenya's Trade and Development," 33 *NYU J Int'l L & Pol* 651 (2001).

33. Gleevec (or Glivec) is the beta-crystal form of cancer drug imatinib, a known substance. The patent application described the enhanced efficacy of the crystal form, which was found not novel enough by the Indian Patent Office. The company's CEO Daniel

posed by each analysis are different: In the former instance, one must try to isolate the role of the IP factor. In the latter instance, the data is almost necessarily anecdotal in nature (i.e., one generally gathers a set of discrete decisions, which may perhaps be aggregated but with required caution because each decision is also multifactorial). Both phenomena may make it impossible to determine precisely the impact of the introduction of TRIPS-compliant norms (isolated from other factors). One can nevertheless acknowledge TRIPS as a causal element, whether as a normative matter or as part of a broader, heuristic effect of encouraging developing countries to emulate and adapt innovation policies that are successful in the West. Those policies are linked, if only rhetorically, to a high level of intellectual property protection.

Turning to policy outcomes, it seems fair to conclude that when stronger IP rules allow foreign firms to begin exporting IP-sensitive goods and services to a country, local consumers and industries gain lawful access to those products and services. This may result in welfare gains, although it also leads to price increases when goods whose status changes to "pirate" or "counterfeit" after the introduction of IPR protection are displaced by genuine goods. Increased trade flows may lead to new jobs in distributorships and the retail sector, but these are likely to be low-skilled, low-paying positions that displace jobs in imitation-based (and possibly also piracy-based) industries. However, there may be significant gains in terms of product quality and reliability.

It also seems fair to draw the conclusion that FDI is a more powerful development lever than trade because it directly transfers technology and usually creates jobs requiring a higher skill level. This may be the case for the manufacturing of technology-intensive goods, which requires engineering and quality-control positions, as well as management and other softer skill sets. In the best-case scenario, some research and development jobs are created, which may have spillover effects in areas such as higher education or local laboratories.

At the sectoral level, one may reasonably conclude that, in the absence of sufficient copyright protection and enforcement, music, films, and books are unlikely to be distributed, and national cultural industries are unlikely to develop. In these areas, the gains generated by establishing sufficient protection are "unambiguous."[34] However, the introduction or beginning of enforcement of

---

Vasella said, "This [ruling] is not an invitation to invest in Indian research and development, which we would have done. We will invest more in countries where we have protection. It's not a punishment. It's just a question of the culture for investment." However, Professor Brook Baker commented that it was "virtually impossible to imagine this decision [to shift investment to China] given the other business conditions taken into consideration, such as the low cost of clinical trials and researchers." *BRIDGES Trade Weekly Digest*, vol. 11, no. 29, Sept. 5, 2007.

34. Keith E. Maskus, "Strengthening Intellectual Property Rights in Lebanon," in *Intellectual Property and Development* (cited in note 17), pp. 286–89.

copyrights may also lead to the closure of businesses that rely on copying, thus displacing (mostly unskilled) workers. Ideally, some of those workers will be able to find work in the new, creative industry jobs made possible by the adequate protection of copyrights. Although there is often little economic benefit derived from selling counterfeit DVDs or luxury goods (whether in terms of jobs or income or sales taxes, which may not always be paid), there are clear risks in selling counterfeit spare parts for automobiles or pharmaceuticals. In addition, new jobs created by new IP-based industries are likely to pay higher wages and stimulate creativity, as well as reduce the expatriation of local creators to countries with IPR protection.[35]

Introducing trademark protection as part of TRIPS implementation may, as in the case of copyright, lead to the closure of businesses producing counterfeit goods. Some of the higher-end former counterfeiters may be able to produce legitimate goods (either legal goods of the same class, or licensed goods legally bearing the trademark). Counterfeit economic activity may be partly replaced by jobs in distribution, retail, and franchises. These are, however, often low-level, low-skilled jobs. Trademark protection should benefit consumers who will have access to "genuine" goods, that is, goods that come with the perceived assurance of quality associated with the mark via domestic or international advertising and reputation, but this access will generally come at a higher price. Over time, the experience in product assembly, delivery, servicing, and management acquired through franchise and distributorship arrangements may be transferred to new, local businesses.

Patents do not ensure that new products will be supplied in the short term to a country introducing TRIPS-compliant protection. In fact, when patent protection is unavailable, products that would otherwise infringe can be made available legally for the domestic market without the patent rent. In terms of FDI, however, the impact is exactly the opposite because global firms relying on patent protection traditionally need assurances about the level of protection and enforcement before considering any significant technology transfer. Patent protection and enforcement often will be seen, therefore, as a prerequisite (though in itself is insufficient) to generate technology-intensive FDI increases.

The impact of patents on innovation is not straightforward.[36] Fully exploiting a patent often requires expertise that is not fully disclosed in the published patent or patent application. Ongoing research and variants of the patented inventions

35. If not physically, at least industrially. For example, a book published by an author who is not a national of a Berne- (or WTO-) member country may still be protected if the book is first published in a member country, thus benefiting the industry of the country of publication.

36. See Adam B. Jaffe, *Innovation and Its Discontents: How Our Broken Patent System is Endangering Innovation and Progress, and What to Do About It* (Princeton, NJ: Princeton University Press, 2004).

may also exist. For this reason, firms also consider the level of protection of trade secrets for information that, for strategic or other reasons, is not disclosed in a patent. In fact, for certain process patents, even in the presence of a presumption that a product not previously available results from a new patented process, many companies prefer not to disclose new processes in patent applications.[37] That said, direct patent-related FDI is often the best way to create high-paying, highly skilled jobs, and it is therefore highly sought after by many governments, which are willing to go to great lengths to attract foreign firms.[38]

Introducing patent protection may produce a shock on the economy. Like trademark protection, it will lead to closures of businesses that were copying/adapting (legally, before patents were issued) products or using processes developed by foreign inventors. In certain cases, they may, like in the area of trademarks, become legal manufacturers. In other cases, the process may lead economic players to move from imitation-based models to innovation-based models, thus contributing to the displacement effect discussed in the next section.

It is also worth noting that introducing patents may not help R&D efforts based on imitation, because commercial exploitation of the results of imitation (at least beyond experimental use) would require a license. Moving from a lax, indigenous, imitative base to a "foreign seed" base model thus arguably favors countries (mostly in the West) that currently own the bulk of global patented knowledge. But shifts remain possible as innovation capacity builds up faster in some parts of the developing world, where research costs are lower. This is the topic of the next section.

III. THE DISPLACEMENT EFFECTS OF TRIPS

A. The Role of the Demanders

The multinational companies that successfully lobbied to establish a linkage between IP and trade, first in the domestic U.S. context and then in the WTO,[39]

---

37. Article 34(1) of the TRIPS Agreement reads in relevant part: "[I]f the subject matter of a patent is a process for obtaining a product, the judicial authorities shall have the authority to order the defendant to prove that the process to obtain an identical product is different from the patented process." See Stephen A. Merrill et al., eds., *A Patent System for the 21st Century* 20, 23 (The National Academies Press, 2004), available online at http://www.nap.edu/html/patentsystem/0309089107.pdf.

38. Beata K. Smarzynska Javorcik, "The Composition of Foreign Direct Investment and Protection of Intellectual Property Rights: Evidence from Transition Economies," 48 *European Economic Revue* 39, 60 (2004).

39. Their decision to use the multilateral forum may be explained by the lack of alternatives: They could not easily lobby developing countries individually (having, in most cases, little to offer in exchange for higher intellectual property protection).

did so because of their desire to increase profit and markets—or, to put it differently, to maximize rent extraction and increase the number of foreign territories into which they could consider expanding their commercial or industrial activities. They argued that the failure to protect foreign intellectual property rights (IPRs) acts as an implicit subsidy to domestic production. However, imposing this harsh medicine on developing countries created difficult situations, especially in less industrialized nations.[40]

I suggest that, as more developing nations on the receiving end of technology transfers and inward FDI develop the ability to innovate and compete, new competitors for the same companies that lobbied for TRIPS consequently emerge. Combined with a healthy dose of economic nationalism,[41] the medium-term impacts of TRIPS and related measures (e.g., free-trade agreements and bilateral investment treaties, the purpose of which is to induce developing countries to adopt Western-style IP systems) are certainly worth pondering. Consider Japan after World War II and now, or China in 2000 and China circa 2025.[42]

There is a consensus assumption that the West will continue to dominate, and that the clout that follows from such dominance will allow the West to impose its will on the developing world—or, at least, allow it to resist norm-making attempts not supported by Western stakeholders. As examples of the latter, one might consider WIPO's work on Traditional Knowledge or a Development Agenda (to the extent that it tries to influence future norm-making and interpretation beyond capacity building and technology-transfer commitments), where work is slow as a result of lukewarm support from several Western countries. Bilateral-trade and investment treaties would be an example of the former.

If the current rates of economic growth are maintained, this assumption will hold, at least in part. As Table 3.1 shows, according to the World Bank and OECD predictions, by 2030 the United States, with a GDP of $25 trillion, will still largely dominate the world economy. China, however, will have moved from fourth to second place, ahead of all European countries and Japan, and India will be seventh, ahead of Canada. As was pointed out recently by the *New York Times*:

> China surpassed Canada in the first two months of this year as the largest exporter to the United States. According to statistics released by the World

40. Now subject, however, to the postponement of the deadline to implement TRIPS accorded least-developed nations until July 2013 (TRIPS Council Decision of November 29, 2005, Extension of the Transition Period Under Article 66.1 For Least-Developed Country Members, document IP/C/40).

41. Kenneth J. Vandevelde, "The Political Economy of a Bilateral Investment Treaty," 92 *Am J Int'l L* 621, 621–23 (1998).

42. Joseph Straus, "The Impact of the New World Order on Economic Development: The Role of Intellectual Property Rights System," 6 *John Marshall Rev of Intellectual Property Law* 1, 5–9 (2006), where Prof. Straus describes "China's commanding, complex, and almost scary development."

TABLE 3.1 PROJECTED GDP GROWTH RATES

RANK	8	7	6	5	4	3	2	1
	India	Canada	France	UK	China	Germany	Japan	US
pop 2006 (in millions)	1,094.60	32.6	60.7	60	1,304.50	82.5	128	300
GDP 2006 (in $US billions)	$785.00	$1,115.20	$2,110.20	$2,192.60	$2,228.90	$2,781.90	$4,505.90	$12,455.10
GNI (atlas) (in $US)	$720.00	$32,600.00	$34,810.00	$37,600.00	$1,740.00	$34,580.00	$38,980.00	$43,740.00
GDP per capita (in $US)	$717.16	$34,208.59	$34,764.42	$36,543.33	$1,708.62	$33,720.00	$35,202.34	$41,517.00
	Canada	India	France	UK	Germany	Japan	China	US
pop 2030 (in millions)	38	1,400	68	67.5	85	130	1,350	360
GDP growth/yr (% assumed annual growth)	3.00%	5.50%	2.50%	2.50%	2.50%	2.00%	6.00%	3.00%
GDP 2030 (in $US billions)	$2,266.00	$2,837.00	$3,816.00	$3,964.00	$5,030.00	$7,246.00	$9,021.00	$25,318.00
GDP per capita (in $US)	$59,631.58	$2,026.43	$56,117.65	$58,725.93	$59,176.47	$55,738.46	$6,682.22	$70,327.78

Source: World Bank Statistics/OECD.

> Trade Organization last Thursday, China also overtook the United States in the second half of 2006 to become the world's second-largest exporter of goods over all, after Germany. China is still nearly 25 times as dependent on exports to the United States as a percentage of its total economic output as the United States is on exports to China. Given that the Chinese economy is less than a quarter the size of the American economy, it is all the more striking that Chinese exports to the United States are worth more than six times American exports to China.[43]

Although one may naturally question such growth assumptions, the thesis explored in this paper is that we are on the cusp of a significant displacement of research and innovation to certain developing countries. This should cause a regional spillover effect, which, in turn will increase the gravitational pull of such regions for global business and generate new competitors based in such regions. In other words, the rather short-term determinants that drove multinational corporations in the pharmaceuticals, software, and entertainment sectors to "multilateralize" Western intellectual property norms has created a playing field that allows them to gradually move higher-knowledge functions to developing countries with an abundance of brainpower, a large supply of Western-educated (and, increasingly, locally trained in excellent institutions) workers, and much lower labor and regulatory compliance costs.

There is at least anecdotal support for this thesis. For example, *Business Week* reported in May 2007 that:

> more than three-quarters of new research and development sites to be set up over the next three years will be in China and India, according to a new study by Booz Allen Hamilton and business school INSEAD . . . A survey of 186 companies worldwide found a general trend of innovation moving east and predicts that China and India are on the verge of overtaking Western Europe as the most important locations for foreign R&D for U.S. businesses. . . .[44]

By the end of 2007, China and India combined will account for almost a third (31 percent) of global R&D staff, up from 19 percent in 2004.[45] Another sign is the constant string of strategic, governmental investment in R&D in developing countries. For example, in June 2007, a number of European governments announced a significant investment in research and development in Egypt, ostensibly as a contribution to development, but also, perhaps, to "stake a claim." Interestingly, when the investment was announced, officials refused to speak of

---

43. Keith Bradsher, "China Leans Less on US Trade," *New York Times* (Apr. 18, 2007).

44. "Europe Losing to China and India in R&D," *BusinessWeek* (May 26, 2007), available online at http://www.businessweek.com/globalbiz/content/may2006/gb20060526_804863.htm.

45. Id.

a "brain drain," insisting instead on "brain circulation" (i.e., recognizing the mobility in both directions of scientists).[46]

Then again, under pressure to increase quarterly profits and shareholder value, the multinational companies that sowed the TRIPS seed probably have no choice but to pursue massive outsourcing to developing countries.[47] With a higher level of intellectual property protection in place, those companies consider these countries first and foremost as new export markets, and possibly also as lower-cost production centers, while they seek to maintain the technological superiority of the West (where R&D is based), and hence, continue Western economic dominance through the control of outsourced industries. According to this view, as Professor Scotchmer noted:

> intellectual property rights are no longer a way to encourage domestic innovation. They also become a strategic instrument to affect profit flows among nations. To affect profit flows favourably, each country wants the strongest possible protections in foreign countries, and the weakest possible protections for foreigners in its own domestic market.[48]

Yet one may also question the ability of Western companies to prevent technology from being appropriated, transformed, and exploited in the recipient countries—or indeed their willingness to do so if those countries prove to be innovative, lower-cost environments.

B. The Transfer of R&D to Developing Countries

The TRIPS proponents' plan to harmonize the intellectual property playing field in order to create new markets where commercial (mis-)appropriation of their intellectual property would become increasingly difficult, coupled with opportunities to outsource technological development and manufacturing, is totally understandable from a business standpoint.[49] Yet it may very well be that the

---

46. Deena Douara, "EU Backs Egypt's Science, Technology with LE 135 mln," *The Daily Star* (Egypt, June 19, 2007).

47. Multinational (or, perhaps more accurately, *trans*national) corporations "account for a major share of global R&D. Indeed, with $310 billion spent in 2002 (United Kingdom, DTI 2004), the 700 largest R&D spending firms of the world—of which at least 98% are TNCs—accounted for close to half (46%) of the world's total R&D expenditure and more than two-thirds (69%) of the world's business R&D." *World Investment Report 2005: Transnational Corporations and the Internationalization of R&D* 119 (UNCTAD 2005), available online at http://www.unctad.org/Templates/webflyer.asp?docid=6087&intItemID=3489&lang=1&mode=toc.

48. Suzanne Scotchmer, *Innovation and Incentives* 329 (Cambridge, MA: The MIT Press, 2004).

49. See Robert M. Sherwood, "Some Things Cannot Be Legislated," 10 *Cardozo Journal of International and Comparative Law* 37, 39–40 (2002), and, by the same author, "Global Prospects for the Role of Intellectual Property in Technology Transfer," 42 IDEA 27, 34 (2002).

powers of innovation, once unleashed and properly supported, will cut Western dominance short. From this perspective, the end result of TRIPS for many developing countries, and for global welfare, would be very positive overall, especially compared with otherwise bleak economic outlooks. As Michael Ryan noted:

> In the foreword to the 1998/99 World Development Report: Knowledge for Development, [then] World Bank president James Wolfensohn states that "economies are built not merely through the accumulation of physical capital and human skill, but on a foundation of information, learning, and adaptation" and declares that in this new world economy that the "globalization of trade, finance, and information flows is intensifying competition, raising the danger that the poorest countries and communities will fall behind more rapidly than ever before." . . . The WDR recommends that closing knowledge gaps depends upon (1) the acquisition of knowledge through trade, foreign direct investment, and licensing, (2) the absorption of knowledge through education, and (3) the communication of knowledge through advanced information technologies. Developing countries intent upon closing knowledge gaps and reducing information problems will do so with the help [of] intellectual property institutions—trademark to facilitate consumer knowledge, patent to facilitate technology transfer, copyright to facilitate literary, artistic, and informational expression.[50]

In other words, and as India's "Silicon Valley" centered around Bangalore and Beijing's "Z-Park"[51] have begun to demonstrate, the appropriation process that began by the limited outsourcing of low-innovation coding[52] or other functions (for example, "customer care" call centers) tends to evolve to progressively more complex coding tasks and higher innovation activities, leading to significant innovations in the recipient (outsourced-to) country. The outsourced low innovation becomes a form of technology transfer and serves as a stepping stone to

50. Michael P. Ryan, "Knowledge-Economy Elites, the International Law of Intellectual Property and Trade, and Economic Development," *10 Cardozo J Int'l & Comp L* 271, 303 (2002).

51. Claire Juliette-Beale, "Z-Park: China's Silicon Valley," *BusinessWeek* (June 5, 2007), available online at http://www.businessweek.com/innovate/content/jun2007/id20070605_039465.htm. This section focuses on China and India, but similar observations could be made with respect to several other countries—though each one has a different industrial infrastructure—including Brazil, Egypt, South Africa, South Korea, Thailand, and many others.

52. One well-known commentator attributes the acceleration of outsourcing to India to the need of Western companies to deal with the Y2K "bug," which required extensive but fairly straightforward coding. In that case, the deadline was self-evidently unmovable. See Thomas Friedman, *The World Is Flat: The Globalized World in the Twenty-First Century* 131–37 (New York: Penguin Books, 2005).

higher-innovation functions, and eventually to world-class competitiveness.[53] Whereas the transfer of low-innovation functions may not require high levels of intellectual property protection, the (perceived) need for protection becomes greater as the level of technology becomes more complex.

Although a majority of the initial client base of India's programming powerhouse may have been foreign, mostly U.S. and European entities, the potential for homegrown innovation-based industries has now increased very significantly. The same could be said of China's manufacturing industries, and more recently of the exponential growth of its information technology and telecommunications sectors.[54]

China's R&D efforts are increasing rapidly: it plans to match U.S. R&D spending levels (relative to GDP) by 2020[55] and should have the largest number of researchers of any country by that date.[56] Its information technology industry "has been an engine of economic growth—growing two to three times faster than GDP over the past 10 years."[57] Multinationals are adapting.[58]

---

53. As UNCTAD's *World Investment Report 2005* noted: "Research and development (R&D) is one source of innovation (box III.1). In the early stages of technological activity, enterprises need not set up formal R&D departments. As they mature, however, it becomes increasingly desirable to monitor, import and implement technologies. R&D as a distinct activity may appear as early as the second level of complexity, where multifaceted technologies are involved or if local conditions demand significant adaptation. In a developing country, such R&D is feasible once the operation is fairly large scale and the necessary technical skills are available. The role of formal R&D then grows as the firm attempts significant technological improvements to introduce new products or processes," at 102 (cited in note 48).

54. Christine Zhen-Wei Qiang, China's *Information Revolution: Managing the Economic and Social Transformation* (Washington, DC: World Bank, 2007).

55. According to the China Blawg, "The OECD (see http://www.oecd.org/document/26/0,2340,en_2649_201185_37770522_1_1_1_1,00.html) recently announced that, this year, China's R&D spending will surpass that of Japan. Estimates have China's 2006 spending of U.S. $136 billion edging out Japan's U.S. $130 billion investment. . . . The rapid increase in R&D spending in China is one aspect of its current economic-development policy that is designed to make China a major innovative force in the near future. The government announced a 15-year plan last February that has R&D spending rising to 2% of GDP by 2010 and 2.5% of GDP by 2020. This would put China's R&D spending as a percentage of GDP at U.S. levels by 2020." Available online at http://blawg.lehmanlaw.com/english/archives/2006/12/05/199.html.

56. According to the same OECD report, "China, the number of researchers increased by 77% between 1995 and 2004. China now ranks second worldwide with 926,000 researchers, just behind the United States (more than 1.3 million)." The Gartner Group recently ranked India's Infosys as the most innovative software company worldwide.

57. Christine Zhen-Wei Qiang, *China's Information Revolution: Managing the Economic and Social Transformation* (Washington, DC: World Bank, 2007).

58. See Victor Mallet, "Watch for the New Timelords of Global Business," *Financial Times* (Apr. 19, 2007).

Another, related question worth asking is whether Western economic and political institutions and capitalism are coterminous, or whether they are just an instantiation of a (somewhat "free") market economy. Perhaps technological innovation can be woven into different social and economic fabrics, thus creating what Charles Taylor refers to as "multifaceted" capitalism—the South may be redefining capitalism, and the broadly held assumption that a free market can not exist without certain rights and freedoms (for example, the freedom of expression) may very well be proven wrong. Arguably, China, which is much less free than India, for instance, has been doing better over the past 10 years.

What seems inescapable, however, is the move toward modernity, which I would define for the purposes of this article, and using Taylorian terminology again, as moving to a rational moral order in which, following neo-Stoic teachings (Grotius) and Locke, "economic (i.e., ordered, peaceful, productive) activity has become the model for human behaviour and the key to harmonious existence."[59] Ideology or religion-based social orders, including those interpreted as excluding women, or social classes, or fearing innovation and change, cannot hope to succeed in this scenario.[60] This child of the Enlightenment we call *modernity* is not something that innovative societies can easily avoid inviting to their economic dinner table. "The Eighteenth-century transition is in a sense a crucial one in the development of Western modernity . . . [it] generated new, stadial theories of history, which saw human societies developing through a series of stages, defined by the form of their economy (e.g., hunter-gatherer, agricultural), culminating in the contemporary commercial society."[61]

Globalization also has an impact on governance. The globalization of media, in particular the Internet, feeds the various social imaginaries. For one thing, it provides new images of what is, and of what is possible. This is crucial because, as Taylor's insightful analyses have shown, a perception of what is possible widens the array of norms that are realizable. In other words, people don't fight for utopia but can move into action for something they know they can achieve.

The passage of time likely will show that some of the (Western) institutions we associate with an innovation-based capitalist economy are not, in fact, a necessary ingredient of a society that is able to compete (using the same science, of course) with the West. It will be interesting to see whether Western-style democracy is but an idiosyncratic variant of modernity. Put differently, although stadial analysis is indeed inexorable, there may not be a single path forward and the very direction of technological progress may be altered as a result.

---

59. Charles Taylor, *Modern Social Imaginaries* 15 (Durham, NC: Duke University Press, 2005).

60. To quote Taylor again: "Individualism and mutual benefit are the evident residual ideas that remain after you have sloughed off the older religions and metaphysics." Id., p. 18.

61. Id., p. 48.

C. Developing Countries as Global Competitors

It is not unrealistic to see a future where Indian, Chinese, and other companies compete head-to-head with innovation-based Western enterprises (in fact, in certain industries, this process has already begun). The innovation-displacement effect of TRIPS and TRIPS-plus agreements may be accelerated when considering that a very significant proportion of researchers in Western laboratories are nationals of developing countries (such as India).[62] Because the West cannot compete in terms of manufacturing costs if (when) it loses its competitive-innovation advantage, the picture of the global economy may be profoundly altered, with a shift in the center of gravity. To a certain extent, such a process would prove that those who pushed for the application of TRIPS-compliant norms to the developing world were right (at least for countries counted as success stories). As we have seen, TRIPS proponents were largely U.S.- and European-based multinationals. It would amount to historical irony if they should end up losing their economic dominance as a result.[63]

Perhaps the plan is that, through investment and acquisition, the same capital, though geographically reconfigured (an issue for Western tax authorities—which may have to move massively to sales-based taxes to replace income-based revenues—but not for the companies involved) will remain dominant in most industries.[64] That would explain why both in bilateral discussions and multilaterally (to the extent that the WTO remains a viable negotiation forum for new areas), where MNCs seem to be able to steer the U.S. agenda, there is such an emphasis on investment liberalization.[65] However, it may call into question the assumption that governs U.S. bilateral and multinational intellectual property

62. The *Financial Times* reports that in order to compensate for the shortage of first-rate talent, the "clamour for brains is driving elite employers in the UK to behave like football talent scouts in India and elsewhere." Alicia Clegg, "In Hot Pursuit of the Best Brains," *Financial Times* (Mar. 14, 2007).

63. Joseph Stiglitz reports that both the Council of Economic Advisers and the Office of Science and Technology Policy in the White House had deep reservations about TRIPS, and that he believes "the way the intellectual property regime has evolved is not good for the United States and the EU; but even more, I believe it is not in the interests of the developing countries," in Joseph E. Stiglitz, *Making Globalization Work* (New York: W. W. Norton & Co., 2006), 116–17.

64. One author argues that, once the proper legal system and protection is in place—and especially what he refers to as the invisible infrastructure of "asset management"—the conditions required for a Western, capitalist model to be moveable and for innovation fully to emerge will be present. See Hernando de Soto, *The Mystery of Capital: Why Capitalism Triumphs in the West and Fails Everywhere Else* (New York: Basic Books, 2003).

65. UNCTAD maintains a database of bilateral investment treaties. The list is impressive. As of June 1, 2006, it listed 48 bilateral treaties involving the United States alone. Available online at http://www.unctadxi.org/templates/DocSearch____779.aspx.

negotiations that U.S. domestic interests are coextensive with those of multinational corporations.[66] Multinational corporations that label themselves as American companies, rightly or not, still need the U.S. government (and, occasionally, its military arm) to spur growth of new markets and to level their outsourcing playing field.

In light of the high mobility of capital and innovation, the relative lack of scientists (especially compared to very high enrollment in science and engineering programs in a number of developing countries, including China),[67] and the higher level of business regulation and the associated compliance costs in the United States,[68] is it fair to ask whether U.S. prominence in innovation (and its insistence that other countries continually increase their levels of IP protection) will endure.[69] Is it clear that the pharmaceutical companies that drive U.S.

---

66. Christopher J. Forster, *China's Secret Weapon: Science Policy and Global Power* 29–30 (London: The Foreign Policy Center, 2006): "While policymakers regard S&T [science and technology] as a race between nations in a zero-sum game, businesses see themselves as part of a global information network. . . . Government officials are more concerned about stemming the flow of technologies to competitors and possible rivals who might use it for military objectives. . . . However, firms and businesses prefer a system that leads to the dissemination of knowledge, including to political rivals."

67. *World Investment Report 2005* (note 48 above) 159 and following. One should also consider the number of students from developing countries enrolled in programs in industrialized countries. The *World Investment Report* notes a growth of employment in R&D in developing countries (by local and foreign entities) of 20% per year compared to approximately 2% in the West. The cumulative effect of this growth over 20 years seems to support the displacement effect theory.

68. One well-known example would the Sarbanes-Oxley Act of 2002 (*Public Company Accounting Reform and Investor Protection Act of 2002*, Pub L No 107-204, 116 Stat 745 (codified in 15 USC 7243 [Supp III 2003]). See Gideon Rachman, "How to help the huddled masses through immigration," *Financial Times* blog entry (Mar. 13, 2007). Available online at http://blogs.ft.com/rachmanblog/2007/03/how_to_help_the.html.

69. As of 2003, the United States was (still) home to 42.3% of the top 700 R&D firms worldwide (*World Investment Report 2005*, note 48 above, 121). But the figure is on dollars spent, which obscures two key factors—how efficiently the research dollars are spent, and how far a research dollar can be stretched in one country compared to another—per employee expenditures of U.S. firms are significantly lower in their overseas laboratories (id. at 122), and recent surveys show that cost and lack of humanpower in industrialized nations (which slows time to market) have become major drivers of decisions about the location of R&D (id. 159). The recent announcement by Intel that it was moving design and manufacturing operations to Dalian (China) (though at this stage at least not for the most advanced chips) at a cost of $2.5 billion is yet another example of a trend that is likely to accelerate. See "Intel given green light for 2.5-billion-U.S.-dollar wafer facility in NE China," *People's Daily* (Mar. 15, 2007), available online at http://english.people.com.cn/200703/15/eng20070315_358013.html. Intel set up Intel China Labs in 2000 and also formed an alliance with Baidu.com, a major Chinese search engine, in April 2006, to develop search applications for laptops, mobile phones, and home PCs. See "Intel,

foreign intellectual property policy will forever remain U.S. or, more broadly, Western companies? As Chris Patten, former Governor of Hong Kong and European Commissioner for External Relations, noted recently, "If the Western front has fundamentally changed, or been broken by events and cultural disjuncture, what international configuration will emerge during the short interval of years before the rise of China and India reshapes the world's power politics?"[70]

D. Was It TRIPS?

Naturally, one may question whether a causal link between increased FDI, outsourcing of increasingly high-knowledge functions (and resulting technology transfers), and the development of local innovation that ensues exists. India's pharmaceuticals industry started well before 2005, when it introduced pharmaceuticals patent protection, and it is built on the foundations of a generics industry.[71] The United States and Europe, among others, began outsourcing to China before that country had achieved a level of intellectual property protection and enforcement that these countries considered sufficient. Indeed, a recent complaint shows that that level has not yet been reached.[72] Clearly, there are geopolitical (or "geocommercial") factors at play. Government-subsidized research laboratories were also created prior to TRIPS in those countries. Yet I suggest that TRIPS (a) led to the emergence of what is a relatively new field of study, namely the impact of introducing Western intellectual property protection into the normative, judicial, and administrative fabric of developing countries (at various stages of economic development), and (b) by forcing developing countries to adopt intellectual property protection at that level, is prompting them—though in almost all cases after, and not as part of, TRIPS implementation—to develop or revise their national innovation policies,[73] which is evidenced, inter alia,

---

Baidu to jointly develop search apps," *InfoWorld* (Apr. 13, 2006), available online at http://www.infoworld.com/article/06/04/13/77407_HNintelbaidusearch_1.html.

70. Christopher Patten. *Not Quite the Diplomat: Home Truths about World Affairs* 2 (New York: Penguin Books, 2006).

71. Jagdish N. Bhagwati and Sukhamoy Chakravarty, *Contributions to Indian Economic Analysis: A Survey* (New Delhi: Lalvani Publishing, 1972).

72. *China—Measures Affecting the Protection and Enforcement of Intellectual Property Rights: Request for Consultations by the United States.* WTO Document WT/DS362/1, Apr. 16, 2007.

73. Stan Metcalfe provides a more complete definition: a "set of distinct institutions which jointly and individually contribute to the development and diffusion of new technologies and which provides the framework within which governments form and implement policies to influence the innovation process. As such it is a system of interconnected institutions to create, store and transfer the knowledge, skills and artefacts which define new technologies." J. Stan Metcalfe, "The Economic Foundations of Technology Policy: Equilibrium and Evolutionary Perspectives," in Paul Stoneman, ed., *Handbook of the Economics of Innovation and Technological Change* (Oxford: Blackwell Publishing, 1995).

by the recent efforts on WIPO's Development Agenda and global development. In addition, the increase in FDI and outsourcing of intellectual property–sensitive issues is partly dependent on TRIPS compliance. It thus seems fair to link TRIPS to the increased innovation-based activity in several developing nations. Yet the point of this chapter is not to prove this causal link, nor *a fortiori* to quantify it. As mentioned above, TRIPS is used here as a credible flag bearer in the march toward increased intellectual property protection and awareness among policy makers since its adoption. TRIPS had a normative effect, as well as a heuristic one. In developing a calibrated, rather than a mechanical, implementation of TRIPS, developing countries have sought to emulate policies beyond protection and geared toward innovation of technologies, including through imitation and customization made possible, in many cases, by the outsourcing of Western research, development, and manufacturing that prompted, from the demanders' perspective, the negotiation and adoption of TRIPS.

E. Distribution of Innovation Development

The net effect of TRIPS implementation in several developing nations had been a new outflow of royalty (rent) payments by developing countries to Western interests, whether because of the patent and trademark rights of the pharmaceuticals industry or the copyright rights of the software, entertainment, and publishing industries. This was documented in numerous Phase II efforts, and the lessons learned are increasingly being applied to calibration efforts undertaken in Phase III. That said, calibration means more than limiting welfare and transition costs. It includes developing a national innovation policy to maximize the benefits, in addition to minimizing the drawbacks. This is, in fact, the very definition of full calibration. The equation is hard to solve because, for countries with finite resources, the immediate impact of additional rent payments reduces resources available to develop domestic innovation. However, the emergence of a number of successful examples tends to show that the circle can be squared.

Against that backdrop, for the purposes of this chapter, I would group WTO Members into four categories:

1. Industrialized nations, beneficiaries of additional rent made possible by TRIPS-compliant protection;
2. Developing countries where innovation benefits outweigh additional rent extraction (by Group 1) made possible by TRIPS;

See also Organisation for Economic Co-operation and Development (OECD), *National Innovations Systems* (OECD. *National Innovation Systems*) (OECD, 1997), available online at http://www.oecd.org/dataoecd/35/56/2101733.pdf); Daniele Archibugi and Simona Iammarino, "The Globalization of Technology and National Policies," in Daniele Archibugi and Bengt-Ake Lundvall, eds., *The Globalizing Learning Economy* (Oxford: Oxford University Press, 2002).

3. Developing countries where additional rent extraction (mostly by Group 1) made possible by TRIPS outweighs innovation benefits;
4. Least-developed countries below the threshold at which substantial industrial innovation benefits are likely to develop and which are now also exempt from most TRIPS obligations (and consequently from additional rent extraction).[74]

This grouping takes account of the fact that "development policies must be directed to ensure the sequencing of global market integration, particularly of capital markets long-term investment in health care, human capital and physical infrastructure and the development of transparent, accountable, political institutions."[75] This sequencing is precisely what TRIPS reflected very imperfectly (as a normative matter, relying essentially on broad "bands" of transitional periods), and which the calibration process emerging in Phase III of TRIPS is attempting to correct.

I leave out from my analysis Group 1 (because most, if not all, members were essentially TRIPS compliant before TRIPS and gradually increased their level of protection over several decades) and Group 4, which is no longer directly concerned with TRIPS, although it must be borne in mind for the future.

I suggest that the aim of a global development agenda should be to move as many countries as possible from Group 3 to Group 2. This can be achieved in part by measures to limit welfare impacts of TRIPS. However, in the longer term, it can be sustained only by developing domestic industrial-innovation potential.

It is also essential to note that displacement is not a zero-sum game. In other words, not every additional R&D dollar invested in country B means an equal loss in country A. Research can be amplified by the new inputs, vision, and human abilities of researchers in country B. Second, globalization is leading to the emergence of mobile researchers, often having the nationality of country B, and working in country A for most of their time, but traveling often to their home country and to third countries. In a best-case scenario, this should create numerous cross-fertilization opportunities.

IV. CONCLUSION

The latest developments in China, India, and others—such as Brazil and, perhaps, Russia[76]—beg the question whether imitation is a necessary phase of

---

74. See note 40 above.

75. David Held, *Global Covenant: The Social Democratic Alternative to the Washington Consensus* (Cambridge: Polity Press, 2004), p. 58.

76. The four so-called BRIC countries. It seems the term was first prominently used by Goldman Sachs investment bank in 2001 in Global Economics Paper No 99: *Dreaming*

industrial development (defined here as a movement toward Western-style capitalism with a strong emphasis on innovation). Imitation is still widely practiced in the West, most notably in the form of reverse engineering. Indeed, especially in smaller or less advanced markets, innovation often proceeds along the following sequence: first, a country imitates foreign technology (the *imitation* phase), which itself requires some technical skills; then, it modifies the foreign technology to suit domestic needs and markets (the *local innovation* phase); and then it produces innovations (whether new products or processes or improvements of existing ones) which are globally competitive (the *global innovation* phase). A strong intellectual property system is usually required to support the third phase, unless other considerations become dominant, as may have been the case in China. It could be particularly helpful in the second phase. Conflicts that may arise as a result of the need to license the foreign technology to which an improvement is made or applied often can be solved through licensing (market forces) or, if that fails, by the issuance of a dependent patent compulsory license (as allowed under TRIPS Article 31(l)).

The imitation phase is essential to internalize the "global" state of the art in any given field. In other words, before one can begin to innovate, one must ascertain the level of innovation in the field concerned worldwide to determine what can be used without a license and what could be improved upon, either by localizing a product or by making it better for the global market.[77] Then, perhaps, one can obtain intellectual property protection on such improvements. Naturally, one must have the intellectual, technical, and material tools to access and process this global state of the art before improvements or adaptations can be envisaged. This explains the heavy emphasis put on education, training, and technical assistance in recent analyses.

To take an example, the notion of novelty in patent law is generally defined as worldwide novelty, meaning that any element of prior art anticipating the invention claimed anywhere in the world will be sufficient to refuse the application. As a result, and also owing to the global nature of trade flows (especially in ideational goods and services), innovation is necessarily a global business. Possible exceptions are products and services, including variants of

---

with BRICs: The Path to 2050, available online at http://www2.goldmansachs.com/ideas/brics/book/99-dreaming.pdf. See also *The BRICs Dream: Web Tour*, (July 2006), available online at http://www2.goldmansachs.com/ideas/global-growth/brics/tour.html. See also Robert C. Bird, "Defending Intellectual Property Rights in the BRIC Economies," 43 *Am Bus L J* 317, 347 (2006).

77. To benefit from the patent system, innovators must be aware of the global state of the art. To do so, they should familiarize themselves with published patents and applications (most of which are published 18 months after filing). See Adam B. Jaffe and Manuel Trajtenberg, *Patents, Citations and Innovations: A Window on the Knowledge Economy* 337–76 (Cambridge, MA: The MIT Press, 2002), 2.

existing ones, developed to cater to the needs of consumers in a specific developing country or region. If that is correct, then those countries that had begun their growth and the imitation phase prior to TRIPS implementation may have benefited from a head start. For now, however, large exporting firms are the clearest winners.[78]

78. Evelyn Su, "The Winners and the Losers: The Agreement on the Trade-Related Aspects of Intellectual Property Rights and Its Effects on Developing Countries," 23 *Houston Journal of International Law* 169, 214 (2000).

PART TWO

THE DEVELOPMENT AGENDA IN HISTORICAL AND INSTITUTIONAL CONTEXT

4. THE WIPO DEVELOPMENT AGENDA IN AN HISTORICAL AND POLITICAL CONTEXT

PEDRO ROFFE AND GINA VEA

I. INTRODUCTION

International rules on intellectual property (IP) affect the flow of knowledge between countries. They influence trade, licensing agreements, and information shared about products and new technologies. They award exclusive rights to produce and sell products for a minimum period of time. In an international context, IP obligations impose a set of rules on countries that they may or may not have the capacity to implement, much less enforce.

The challenge of designing balanced international IP standards, suitable for all countries, remains an unfinished task. It involves an array of interested parties, including businesses for which IP is fundamental to profitability and groups striving to promote development by addressing problems such as food security, the Digital Divide, and the lack of affordable essential medicines and education materials.

In response to this challenge, in 2004, Brazil and Argentina introduced a proposal calling for "immediate action in providing for the incorporation of a Development Agenda" into the work program of the World Intellectual Property Organization (WIPO).[1] They were joined by 13 other countries, together comprising

1. WIPO General Assembly, Proposal by Argentina and Brazil for the Establishment of a Development Agenda for WIPO, (WO/GA/31/11) Geneva: September 27–October 5, 2004.

a group known as the "Friends of Development." Three years later, the members of the WIPO General Assembly adopted a package of concrete recommendations and the establishment of a permanent committee on Development and IP. The recommendations relate to a range of subjects including technology transfer, technical assistance, institutional governance, and issues such as competition, public domain, and access to knowledge.

Although the initiative for a WIPO Development Agenda is relatively new, the objective of striking a balance between public and private interests in a way that promotes development is not. At the birth of the modern IP system in the late 19th century, both "developed" and "developing" countries (using today's parlance) were involved in a similar conversation. Beginning with the establishment of the Paris Convention for the Protection of Industrial Property in 1883, industrialization was central to the debate on IP and development, and, ultimately, to the evolution of the international IP system. Furthermore, in the middle of the 20th century, developing countries were engaged in a similar debate in the context of reforms of their own patent systems, as well as in negotiations on the reform of the Paris Convention. These historical parallels shed light on how countries have grappled with IP and development, and particularly with the challenge of balancing public interests and private rights in the international IP system, beginning with the Paris Convention and continuing through today with the WIPO "Development Agenda."

This chapter attempts to show that the WIPO Development Agenda is part of a long chain of events and a broad political discussion that has been at the center of the ongoing evolution of international IP architecture. It illustrates the tensions that prevailed around striking an appropriate balance between the legitimate interests of rights holders and those of national economies, particularly in the context of the emerging international system in the last quarter of the 19th century. Furthermore, it shows that the establishment of the Paris Convention was the result of a compromise between those who wanted to promote the recognition of patents beyond national boundaries and those who feared that outright protection of foreign inventions might hamper local industrialization. This compromise was reflected in what is today Article 5A of the Paris Convention, dealing with measures that countries might take to correct possible abuses resulting from the exclusive rights attributed by law to rights holders.

Intellectual property laws established primarily in Europe spread to almost all countries, particularly former colonies and new, independent countries. Once these countries became more assertive of their rights and aware of their international obligations, they began to question the prevailing international rules and demanded changes to the system. In this respect, efforts in the 1970s focused on national reforms in some countries and on attempts to revise the classical conventions governing copyright and patents. These efforts did not succeed, and, contrary to the original intentions of the developing countries, international rules on IP were strengthened, namely as a result of the WTO Agreement on Trade-Related Aspects of Intellectual Property Rights (TRIPS) Agreement.

The Development Agenda constitutes a new chapter in this chain of events. It is an effort by developing countries to restore balance to the system and enhance its evolution by allowing full integration of countries at different levels of development. This paper essays to provide, from this historical and political perspective, an interpretation of the events that have culminated in the initiative for a Development Agenda.

We begin with the establishment of the Paris Convention in 1883 and its rationale, and then explain the so-called "strategic compromise" reached at that time. We examine how the notion of "local working" has evolved and how the concept of "compulsory licensing" was later incorporated in the Convention by examining the different revision conferences of the Paris Convention and corresponding changes to the local-working principle in Article 5A. The chapter then centers on what we characterize as the reformist movement of developing countries that led to the unsuccessful attempt to reform the Paris Convention, particularly the revamping of Article 5A and the restoration of the principle of local working as a fundamental aspect of the patent system. This attempt was superseded by the advent of TRIPS. We also review events subsequent to the implementation of TRIPS and discuss how these events in our view explain the emergence of the Development Agenda.

II. THE EVOLUTION OF THE INTERNATIONAL IP SYSTEM

The international IP system has been controversial since its inception, particularly with respect to industrial property and the patent system. The controversy finds its roots in the impact that such a system would have on industrial development.

In the 19th century, the Industrial Revolution in Europe and North America, and the growth of international trade, marked a pivotal moment in the history of intellectual property. In 1873, at the world exhibition in Vienna, countries were invited to showcase their technological and scientific achievements. Governments and potential exhibitors raised concerns over the possibility that visitors might copy some of the inventions. In response, the United States proposed an international convention on industrial property, stating that:

> We live no longer in the day of Industrial action, which is strictly confined and is removed from foreign competition, and where slow communication prevents or delays the utilization of inventions. We live at a time of liberal Customs policy; Steam and Electricity have newly united once isolated seats of industry in a way undreamt of; and the mutual exchange of goods shows today a magnitude which a generation ago one could not have imagined. Under such altered relations the Patent granted for an invention in one country becomes in fact a restriction, unprofitable and obstructive, if that invention without limitation or increase in price, becomes in an adjoining country

> common property. The artisan, who in one country must work with the auxiliary material there patented and dearer in price, will suffer an essential injury as soon as the same material is produced in the other country, not only without restriction, but also with a damaging competition. Moreover, a continuance of the hitherto antagonist views and measures would scarcely conduce to the preservation of general harmony; and if, for example, Patent protection were maintained in one country, so as to attract thereby skilled operatives from another, then the danger of disturbance of the International industrial balance might readily be apprehended. Such and similar inconveniences can only be met by the common action of all civilized States, disposed to the maintenance of Patent protection.[2]

Yet whereas the United States viewed international patent protection as fundamental to international trade, others across the Atlantic considered patents a hindrance to free trade. The anti-patent critics in Europe considered the patent mechanism to be one that restricts, rather than promotes, trade. They argued that it distorts the market by protecting certain economic interests over others. Some critics asserted that national patent laws, by granting temporary monopolies, acted in the same way as "prohibitive tariffs."[3] For example, French economist Michael Chevalier said that both tariffs and patents "stem from the same doctrine and result in the same abuses."[4] The majority of members of Parliament in the Netherlands concluded that a "good law of patents is an impossibility," leading to the abolishment of the existing law in 1869. (The patent law was not reintroduced until 1912.) The controversy raged vehemently in Switzerland where, under its constitution, the federal government could not establish a general patent law without a referendum. Calls for such referendums were rejected in 1849, 1851, 1854, and twice in 1863. In referendums called in 1866 and 1882, the proposals to give the federal legislature the authority to pass laws on patents were defeated. It was not until 1887 that a national law on the protection of patents was passed by Switzerland's congress.[5]

Patent opponents also questioned how property rights could be assigned to ideas in the same way that they are assigned to material things. In 1851 *The London Economist* argued that "the public will learn that patents are artificial stimuli to improvident exertions; that they cheat people by promising what they

---

2. Heinrich Kronstein and Irene Till, "Reevaluation of the International Patent Convention," 12(4) *Law and Contemporary Problems*, 768 (Autumn 1947).

3. See Surendra J. Patel, "The Patent System and the Third World," 2(9) *World Development* (Special Issue on Patents), 4 (September 1974).

4. Fritz Machlup and Edith Penrose, "The Patent Controversy in the Nineteenth Century," 10(1) *The Journal of Economic History*, 9 (May 1950).

5. See United Nations, "The role of the patent system in the transfer of technology to developing countries," UN Publications: E.75.II.D.6, 1975, at 32–33 (citing different sources).

cannot perform; that they rarely give security to really good inventions, and elevate into importance a number of trifles. . . . [N]o possible good can ever come of a Patent Law, however admirably it may be framed."[6] Others suggested that incentives were not needed to encourage inventions, but that "the seeds of invention exist, as it were, in the air, ready to germinate whenever suitable conditions arise, and no legislative interference is needed to ensure their growth in proper season."[7] Another argument suggested that inventors should be rewarded, but that perhaps a more appropriate system might involve bonuses issued by governments or professional associations.[8] The benefit of being the first to bring a product to market or having a "head-start" was considered a sufficient reward by other patent critics.

In brief, patent advocates were interested in a geographic extension of the exclusive rights granted by patents, and thus in a system that would make it easier to secure patent protection in foreign markets. Advocates for industrialization were interested in domestic production and were therefore opposed to a system that would protect the importer from the domestic producer, instead of the producer from the importer.[9]

As a result of the U.S. initiative for the Vienna exhibition, the preparatory work toward a multilateral arrangement for patent protection began precisely with the International Conference held at Vienna in 1873. Subsequent to the Vienna meeting, further conferences were held in Paris. Finally, the International Convention for the Protection of Industrial Property (the "Paris Convention") was adopted in 1883. Among the original signatories to the Convention were Belgium, France, Great Britain, Italy, the Netherlands, Portugal, Serbia, Spain, and Switzerland (from Europe); Brazil, Ecuador, Guatemala, and El Salvador (from Latin America); and Tunisia (from North Africa). The United States acceded four years later. As a French protectorate, Tunisia became a member through adherence. Of the four Latin American signatories to the Convention, Ecuador, El Salvador, and Guatemala withdrew from the Convention in 1886, 1887, and 1895, respectively.[10] These three countries returned to the Paris Convention more than 100 years later, after the adoption of the TRIPS Agreement.

It is striking that a number of original signatories to the Convention did not have a national patent system at that time. These included three European countries: the Netherlands, Switzerland, and Serbia.[11] They also included the

---

6. "Imitation v inspiration," *The Economist* (September 12, 2002).

7. Machlup and Penrose, 10(1) *J Econ Hist* at 22 (supra note 4).

8. Id. at 19.

9. See Fritz Machlup, *An Economic Review of the Patent System* 17 (United States Government Printing Office, 1958).

10. See Patel, 2(9) *World Development* (Special Issue on Patents) (supra note 3).

11. See E. Schiff, *Industrialization without National Patents: The Netherlands, 1869–1912; Switzerland, 1850–1907* (Princeton University Press, 1971).

three Latin American countries that withdrew their adherence to the Convention shortly after signing. In short, almost half of the original members did not have national regimes for the protection of patents.

The number of contracting parties to the Paris Convention increased to 47 by 1958 and to 80 in 1973. Today's membership is more than 170. By 1900, using today's definitions, three developing countries were members. The number had risen to nine by 1934 and to 15 by 1958. It had increased to 44 by 1973.[12]

Many African countries adhered to the Paris Convention after independence. More than half of the current African membership joined the Paris Convention during the 1960s and 1970s.[13] Some of the largest developing countries, including Bangladesh, China, India, Malaysia, Pakistan, the Republic of Korea, Sudan, and Thailand, are relative newcomers. Their adherence to the Convention began in the 1980s. India, for example, became a member in December 1998 and Pakistan as recently as 2004.

The Latin American and Caribbean countries (LAC) constitute an interesting case for analysis. The adoption of national laws dealing with the protection of IPRs began as early as 1820 (in the case of Mexico), and then spread throughout the region in the late 19th and early 20th centuries. The spread of national laws was unrelated to adherence to international conventions. Membership to international instruments was not widespread in the region. In the mid-1960s, only five LAC countries were members of the Paris Convention: Brazil (one of the founding members), Cuba, Mexico, the Dominican Republic, and Trinidad and Tobago. In 1967 Argentina and Uruguay became members. Venezuela joined only in 1995. Similarly, LAC countries were reticent to join the other major, classical IP treaty, the Berne Convention for the Protection of Literary and Artistic Works of 1886. In the mid-1960s, Brazil was the only LAC member of the Berne Convention, having joined in 1922. The majority of LAC countries joined in the 1990s. In short, beginning in the late 1960s, LAC countries became part of the international IP architecture slowly and cautiously, for the most part; just after the adoption of the TRIPS Agreement in 1994, however, they joined to a greater extent by adhering to the two major conventions (Paris and Berne).[14]

It should be noted, however, that in the case of copyright, an important number of countries in the region were members of the Universal Copyright Convention (UNESCO) of 1952 together with the United States, which only joined the Berne Convention in the late 1980s. With respect to the Paris Convention, the general view was that there would be no benefit to joining a convention that was not flexible enough to accommodate the needs of the local economy, such as the need to locally exploit foreign inventions. It was also felt

---

12. See "Role of the Patent System in Technology Transfer" (supra note 5).

13. Egypt, Morocco, and Tunisia became members before 1960.

14. See Pedro Roffe, "America Latina y la Nueva Arquitectura Internacional de la Propiedad Intelectual," *La Ley* (Buenos Aires: 2007).

that the national-treatment principle of the Paris Convention constituted a barrier to the design of national regimes dealing with industrial property. Furthermore, the prevailing economic thinking in those days in Latin America favored import substitution industrialization policies. Under these premises, local production was a key ingredient to this approach. As discussed later, in the case of the Andean Group, countries were only allowed to join international conventions on patents through a joint decision of all countries.

III. THE PARIS CONVENTION: THE WORKING REQUIREMENT AND THE COMPULSORY LICENSING SYSTEM

According to economist Fritz Machlup, the European anti-patent movement collapsed after an impressive propaganda campaign by the groups interested in patent protection.[15] It ended during the negotiations on the Paris Convention in 1883, during which countries reached a strategic compromise around the working of a patented invention in the country of importation. This concept of "local working" evolved during the various revision conferences of the Paris Convention. In the same context, the instrument of "compulsory licensing" was later formally introduced in the text of the Convention as one of the measures that countries could adopt to remedy possible abuses resulting from the exclusive rights conferred by patents, including, for example, failure to work. This strategic compromise was constructed in what is today Article 5A of the Convention. In its present version, Article 5A views compulsory licenses as a possible remedy to prevent abuses of the patent monopoly. As we examine below, Article 5A has been the most debated provision in the history of the Paris Convention.[16] Some observers have suggested that the Convention's entire history is represented by the evolution of and debate over, this provision.[17] As British economist Edith Penrose observed in 1951:

> These provisions have had a turbulent history because they touch directly on the conflict between the interest of the national economy as a whole and the interest of the individual patentee in obtaining the maximum return from his patent.[18]

This conflict is apparent in how Article 5A has been addressed and amended at each of the Paris Convention's revisions. The Convention, as adopted in 1883,

---

15. See Machlup, *An Economic Review* at 5 (supra note 9).

16. See Pedro Roffe, "Abuses of Patent Monopoly: A Legal Appraisal," 2(9) *World Development* (Special Issue on Patents) 15 (September 1974).

17. See Casimir Akerman, "L'obligation d'exploiter et la licence obligatoire en matière de brevets d'invention," Librairie du Recueil Sirey (Paris, 1936).

18. Edith Penrose, *The Economics of the International Patent System* (Johns Hopkins, 1951; reprinted by Greenwood, 1973).

was revised in 1900 (Brussels), 1911 (Washington), 1925 (The Hague), 1934 (London), and 1958 (Lisbon). At present, the Paris Convention as a whole has been incorporated into the WTO TRIPS Agreement of 1994, which has introduced new modalities for compulsory licensing.[19] The different texts of Article 5A of the Paris Convention, as revised by the relevant conferences, are reviewed here. The Stockholm Conference of 1967 introduced some formal corrections to the text. The latest unsuccessful attempt to revise Article 5A was made—as discussed in detail in a subsequent section—before the adoption of the TRIPS Agreement by an initiative of developing countries in the late 1970s. The latter initiative is part of the chain of events that culminates in the present discussion over a Development Agenda.

A. The Original Compromise

The "strategic compromise" referred to by Machlup was reflected in the original version of the Convention, as adopted in 1883.

1. *The introduction by the patentee into the country where the patent has been granted of objects manufactured in any of the States of the Union shall not entail forfeiture.*
2. *Nevertheless, the patentee shall remain bound to work his patent in conformity with the laws of the country into which he introduces the patented objects.*

The Convention in its original version provided that the patentee was obligated to exploit his or her patent in accordance with the laws of the country of importation of the patented article. The Convention did not refer specifically to compulsory licenses but recognized the working requirement, subject to the laws of the importing country. The broad limitation established by the Convention, as stated in Paragraph 1, is the only provision that has remained practically unchanged during its entire history. It affirms that importation could not be sanctioned by the forfeiture or revocation of the patent. The Convention, within these broad parameters, recognized that States had the ability to shape their patent laws according to their national conditions by introducing, for example, a compulsory-licensing system or directly deciding on the forfeiture or revocation of the patent in case working did not take place.

Furthermore, the Convention did not define what the term "work" meant, leaving each member to articulate its meaning in national law. According to law professor Jerome Reichman, the policies behind the working requirement have

19. See UNCTAD-ICTSD, *Resource Book on TRIPS and Development*, Chapter 25 (Cambridge, 2005).

been controversial, especially with regard to foreigners. They could be required not only to work the patent, as such, within a specified period of time, but "to work the patent locally" as well, entailing manufacturing or organizing the industrial use of the patented invention in the country that issued the patent.[20]

B. The 1911 Revision Conference

Over time, the flexibility of national governments to design their own patent laws was attenuated. In 1911, at the Washington Conference, paragraph 2 of the relevant provision of the Convention was amended.

> 2. Nevertheless, the patentee shall remain bound to work his patent in conformity with the laws of the country into which he introduces the patented objects, *but with the restriction that the patent may not be forfeited for non-working in one of the countries of the Union until after a period of three years from the date of filing the application in that country, and only in case the patentee cannot justify his inaction.*

The new text retained the obligation to work the patented invention in accordance with the laws of the country into which the patentee had introduced the patented objects. However, a major limitation was introduced to the forfeiture or revocation procedures. The revocation procedures based on the failure to work the patent could only take place after a period of three years from the date of filing the application and, in those cases, when the patentee could not justify inaction.

The weakening of the obligation-to-work principle, as embodied in the original Convention, began at this Revision Conference. However, the provision allowing local working was retained at the insistence of the French delegation, which pointed out

> that the obligation to work corresponds to an economic necessity, that of feeding the national industry of each country with the discoveries and inventions which have been made the object of patents in that country: that France is not in principle hostile to the idea of tempering the regulation of compulsory working but that far-reaching studies had not yet unearthed any means of reaching this end.[21]

20. Jerome H. Reichman and C. Hasenzahl, *Non-Voluntary Licensing of Patented Inventions: Historical Perspective, Legal Framework under TRIPS, and an Overview of the Practice in Canada and the United States of America*, Issue Paper No. 5, ICTSD-UNCTAD.

21. Roffe, 2(9) *World Development* at 23 (supra note 16).

C. The Hague Revision of 1925

> 2. Nevertheless, each contracting country shall have *the right to take the necessary legislative measures to prevent the abuses, which might result from the exclusive rights conferred by the patent, for example, failure to work.*
> 3. *These measures shall not provide for forfeiture of the patent unless the grant of compulsory licenses is insufficient to prevent such abuses.*
> 4. In any case, the patent may not be subjected to such measures before the expiration of at least three years from the date of *grant* or if the patentee proves the existence of *legitimate excuses.*

The Hague Revision of 1925 incorporated substantive changes to Article 5. Specifically, it (a) maintained, unchanged, the first clause of the original text of 1883 (importation of patented objects should not entail forfeiture); (b) recognized the right of each country to adopt necessary measures to prevent the abuses that might result from the exclusive rights of the patentee, as, for example, failure to work; (c) formally introduced the concept of compulsory licensing by providing that patents should not be revoked unless the grant of a compulsory license is insufficient to prevent the abuse; (d) retained the period of three years for the revocation procedures, but counted from the date of granting, and not from the date of filing, of the application, as in the 1911 text; and (e) permitted the patentee to prove the existence of legitimate excuses in the case of inaction.

The reference to "failure to work" in the text is cited as an example of possible abuses resulting from the exclusive rights conferred by the patent. According to Professor Bodenhausen, a former director general of WIPO, the official proceedings of The Hague Conference reveal that other examples of abuses participants had in mind included refusal to grant licenses on reasonable terms, thereby hampering industrial development; failure of patentees to supply national market with sufficient quantities of the patented product; and demanding of excessive prices by patentees for such products.[22]

According to Reichman, the crux of the Hague reform was that forfeiture or revocation as remedies for abuse were not allowed unless the grant of a compulsory license had failed to prevent abuse. In any case, neither sanction could apply for a period of at least three years from the date of filing the respective patent application. In brief, this resulted in discrediting the use of revocation as a remedy for abuse.[23] Another commentator stresses that, by diluting further the

22. See G. H. C. Bodenhausen, *Guide to the Application of the Paris Convention for the Protection of Industrial Property*, at 71 (BIRPI, 1968).

23. Reichmann, "Non-Voluntary Licensing," at 11 (supra note 21).

local working requirement, the final outcome of the Hague revision was to advance the interests of patentees, as opposed to those of society.[24]

D. The London Conference of 1934

> 4. In any case, the patent may not be subjected to such measures before the expiration of at least three years from the date of grant or if the patentee proves the existence of legitimate excuses. *No proceedings for the forfeiture or revocation of a patent may be instituted before the expiration of two years from the grant of the first compulsory license.*

The London Conference further limited countries' ability to revoke patents for lack of local working, while strengthening the compulsory-licensing remedy. The revised text provided that a patent may not be revoked before the expiration of two years from the granting of the first compulsory license. The net result was to ensure that any demonstrable claim of abuse had first to be addressed by issuing a compulsory license, building further upon the 1925 Hague Revision provision that forfeiture or revocation may not be imposed to prevent patent abuse "except in cases where the grant of compulsory licenses would not have been sufficient to prevent such abuses."[25]

The London Conference has been praised for making substantive steps toward the total abolition of revocation and for the universal recognition of compulsory licenses.[26]

E. The Lisbon and Stockholm Conferences

> #### The Lisbon Amendments
>
> 1. The *importation* by the patentee into the country where the patent has been granted of articles manufactured in any of the countries of the Union shall not entail forfeiture of the patent.
> 2. Each country of the Union shall have the right to take legislative measures *providing for the grant of compulsory licenses* to prevent the abuses, which might

24. See Ulf Anderfelt, *International Patent Legislation and Developing Countries,* 83–84 (The Hague: Martinus Nijhoff, 1971).

25. Reichmann, "Non-Voluntary Licensing," at 11 (supra note 21).

26. See Akerman, "L'obligation d'exploiter," at 151 (supra note 17).

result from the exclusive rights conferred by the patent, for example, failure to work.

3. Forfeiture of the patent shall not be prescribed except in cases where the grant of compulsory licenses would not have been sufficient to prevent such abuses. No proceeding for the forfeiture or revocation of a patent may be instituted before the expiration of two years from the grant of the first compulsory license.
4. An application for a *compulsory license* may not be made on the ground of failure to work or insufficient working before the expiration of a period of *four years from the date of filing* of the patent application or three years from the date of the grant of the patent, whichever period last expires; it shall be refused if the patentee justifies his inaction by legitimate reasons. *Such a compulsory license shall be non-exclusive and shall not be transferable, even in the form of the grant of a sub-license, except with that part of the enterprise or goodwill using such license.*
5. *The foregoing provisions shall be applicable, mutatis mutandis, to utility models.*

Except for the initiative of the 1970s, discussed later, the Lisbon Conference of 1958 was the last major event marking the evolution of the Convention with respect to the original "strategic compromise" made in 1883. The word "introduction" was swapped for "importation" in the first paragraph signaling the sole change to that paragraph in the more than 120 years of the Convention. Paragraph 2 restricted the scope of legislative measures a country might take to prevent abuses to the remedy of compulsory licensing. Paragraph 3 specified that no proceedings for the revocation of a patent could be instituted before the expiration of two years from the grant of the compulsory license. This formal change meant a rearrangement of the paragraphs as agreed in the London Conference. This rearrangement meant that the new paragraph 4 dealt exclusively with the application of compulsory licenses on grounds of failure to work or insufficient working that could not be made before the expiration of a period of four years from the date of filing of the patent application or three years from the date of the grant of the patent. These periods, as clarified in the deliberations at Lisbon, did not apply on grounds of public interest (health, military security, or affecting national or international planning).[27] The new text added also that licenses should be of a non-exclusive nature.

The clarifications made at the Lisbon Conference—that countries had the freedom to grant compulsory licenses in the public interest without the observation

27. See Bureau de l'Union Internationale pour la Protection de la Propriete Industrielle, *Actes de la Conference de Lisbonne* 393 (October 6–31, 1958). See Bodenhausen, *Guide to the Application of the Paris Convention*, at 70 (supra note 23).

of any date—have been commended as reaffirming the "flexibility" of the Convention and weakening the arguments advanced by some representatives of developing countries that the Convention needed to be revised on account of its not providing governments with sufficient freedom to resort to compulsory licenses in cases of public interest.[28] A relevant U.K. judicial decision of those days permeated the discussions at the Lisbon Conference. [29] In *Parke, Davis and Co v Comptroller of Patents,*[30] it was held that, in spite of the Paris Convention and the relevant English law, an application for licenses of a patented medicine can be made at any time, whereas the application for a license on grounds of an "abuse of monopoly" can be made only after the expiration of three years from the date of the grant of the patent.

At the Lisbon Conference, the International Bureau of the Paris Union made a proposal to insert into Article 5A a clause abolishing forfeiture as a sanction for failure to work. This initiative, as in previous conferences, was opposed by several delegations.[31]

Finally, the Stockholm Act of 1967 consolidated the changes made through the various revision conferences into the new Article 5A. As such, it was incorporated by reference into the WTO Agreement on Trade Related Aspects of Intellectual Property Rights (TRIPS), together with all other substantive provisions of the Paris Convention. The 1967 version made no substantial modifications to the text that emerged from the Lisbon Conference, except for minor changes in the use of some terms, as reflected in the following box and marked in italics.

The Current Article 5A of the Paris Convention, as Amended in Stockholm

1. Importation by the patentee into the country where the patent has been granted of articles manufactured in any of the countries of the Union shall not entail forfeiture of the patent.
2. Each country of the Union shall have the right to take legislative measures providing for the grant of compulsory licenses to prevent the abuses, which

28. See Frederick-Karl Beier, "La importancia del derecho de patentes en la transferencia de tecnología a los paises en desarrollo," 22–23 *Revista Mexicana de la Propiedad Industrial y Artística,* Numero Especial 55, 60 (Enero-Diciembre, 1973).

29. See *Actes de la Conference de Lisbonne,* at 394 (supra note 28).

30. *Parke Davis & Co v Controller-General of Patents, Designs and Trademarks,* 2 WLR 531 (1954).

31. Roffe, 2(9) *World Development,* at 23 (supra note 17).

might result from the *exercise of* the exclusive rights conferred by the patent, for example, failure to work.

3. Forfeiture of the patent shall not be *provided for* except in cases where the grant of compulsory licenses would not have been sufficient to prevent the said abuses. No proceedings for the forfeiture or revocation of a patent may be instituted before the expiration of two years from the grant of the first compulsory license.
4. A *compulsory license* may not be applied for on the ground of failure to work or insufficient working before the expiration of a period of four years from the date of filing of the patent application or three years from the date of the grant of the patent, whichever period expires last; it shall be refused if the patentee justifies his inaction by legitimate reasons. Such a compulsory license shall be non-exclusive and shall not be transferable, even in the form of the grant of a sub-license, except with that part of the enterprise or goodwill which exploits such license.
5. The foregoing provisions shall be applicable, mutatis mutandis, to utility models.

In brief, taking into account the said flexibilities, the five revision conferences watered-down the essence of what constituted the historical "strategic compromise" of 1883. The final text is considerably more rigid than the original one, which left countries free to determine the rules under which local exploitation could take place.

IV. THE REFORMIST MOVEMENT IN DEVELOPING COUNTRIES

The 1970s witnessed a wave of legal reforms in developing countries that translated into important changes in IP-related legislation in a number of countries. These include, for example, the strengthening of the working requirement and the expansion of measures to prevent so-called patent abuses and promote the transfer of technology. This was the case in Latin American countries, particularly Argentina, Brazil, Mexico, and the countries of the Andean Group. India, immediately after independence, commissioned a number of inquiries on how to make the patent system more suitable for the specific needs of the country.[32] The 1970 Indian Patent Law was an icon of the thinking that prevailed in terms of patent reform. For example, the law differentiated areas of social concern,

32. See N. Rajagopala Ayyangar, *Report on the Revision of the Patent Law* (Government of India, 1959).

such as health and food, where patents would be granted for only 7 years, as opposed to 14 years in other areas.[33]

The case of the Andean Group of countries provides an interesting illustration of how some developing countries dealt with patent reform. The Andean Group was established in 1969 between Bolivia, Chile, Colombia, Ecuador, and Peru. Venezuela joined years later. As one of its foundations, the Group adopted common rules for the treatment of foreign capital, trademarks, patents, licenses, and royalties. These rules were embodied in the well-publicized Decision 24 and in subsequent regulations and decisions on the treatment of IP and the transfer of technology.[34] The framers conceived the Decision as an important step in contributing to the integration of the Andean community by regulating international capital in a way that influenced the distribution of benefits of the integration process. By dealing with various aspects of economic foreign collaboration, including foreign direct investment, licensing agreements, and the treatment of intellectual property rights, the Andean Group sought mainly to extract benefits from the technological skills of transnational corporations as a springboard to the upgrading of local firms. It was perceived that this could be achieved with a more selective screening of foreign direct investment (FDI) and technologies that could contribute to the national development of the five countries. In order to fully understand the rationale behind these reforms, one needs to consider the political and economic context. Those years where characterized by a resentment toward foreign capital in Latin America, with respect to unfair conditions prevailing in the exploitation of natural resources. The Andean Group's regulations sought to remedy such conditions by establishing, among others things, performance requirements for foreign capital, such as to facilitate access to foreign technology and train local firms, as a condition of its establishment in the region. Law professor Frederick Abbott has characterized these legal instruments as:

> an attempt by the member countries to make modern technology more freely accessible to commercial enterprises in the region. The regulations . . . represent a radical departure from the traditional concept that patent ownership rights should be afforded the highest degree of protection. In effect, the patent licensing rules . . . mean that [member] country governments are free to give away a registered patent to any enterprise which desires so, so long as this procedure is considered in the interest of the member countries' development plans, and so long as some specified form of compensation is provided to the patent owner. The rules do not specify that "compulsory licenses" may be issued solely to [Andean] national investors, and it appears that a foreign

33. See Pedro Roffe, "The Political Economy of Intellectual Property Rights—An Historical Perspective," in J. Faundez, M. E. Footer, and Joseph J. Norton, eds., *Governance, Development and Globalization* (Blackstone, 2000).

34. See Bernard Remiche, *Le Rôle du Système des Brevets dans le Développement: Le cas des pays andins*, 13 (Libraires Techniques, 1982).

investor's registered patents may even be licensed to other foreign enterprises in [the Andean Community].[35]

The Andean regulations dealt with technology issues in three main respects: institutional structure, the management and commercialization of technology, and the role of the IP system. The institutional structure was related mainly to situations involving the importation of technology in which national agencies were established to execute common policies in coordination with those on FDI. One principal function was to evaluate and approve transfer-of-technology contracts against a number of criteria that included their contribution to regional development and the ability of the recipient firm to use the technology without conditions attached. On the management and commercialization of technology, the common policies addressed issues such as those of imperfect information regarding prices of goods (spare parts, accessories, components) and services provided by foreign firms that should be in line with international pricing. Restricted guidelines were provided with respect to the capitalization of technology that was not permitted, and royalties between related firms were not allowed. Equally, a closer scrutiny of restrictive practices in technology-transfer contracts was established.

With respect to industrial property, the common regulations for the Andean countries delineated the legal rights that ownership of patents could confer. For example, patents could not be granted for certain types of products, such as pharmaceuticals and, in general, inventions affecting the development of the country. Patent applications needed to include "a clear and complete description of the invention enabling a person skilled in the art to carry it out." Patents could be granted for a maximum period of 10 years with renewal and proof of exploitation required after the first 5 years from the grant. The patent conferred on the owner the exclusive right to work the invention in the recipient country, to grant licenses for its exploitation, and to receive royalties or compensation for its exploitation. At the same time, the regulations explicitly stated that patents did not confer to the rights holder the exclusive right to import a patented product or a product manufactured under a patented process. By excluding the right of importation—today recognized in TRIPS as an inherent right of patent holders—the Andean regulations recognized the obligation of the local working of a patent.

At the same time, the patentee assumed obligations, such as to work the patent and to register contracts according to their use. With respect to the obligation to work, the patentee, within three years from the date of the grant, was to notify the national authorities of the commencement of working. Lacking such notification, the working was presumed not to have begun for the purpose of the grant of compulsory licenses. Working was understood to mean "the permanent and regular use of the patented processes or the manufacture of the product

35. Frederick M. Abbott, "Bargaining Power and Strategy in the Foreign Investment Process: A Current Andean Code Analysis," 3(2) *Syracuse Journal of International Law and Commerce*, 349 (Fall 1975).

covered by the patent in order to put the end result on the market under reasonable marketing conditions, provided that such acts have occurred on the territory of the Member Country which granted the patent" (Articles 30 and 31, Decision 85, May 1974, of the Commission of the Cartagena Agreement).

With respect to compulsory licenses, they were available in the following cases: (a) the patented invention was not worked in the country; (b) the working of the invention was suspended for more than one year; (c) the working of the invention did not meet the demand of the national market on reasonable terms as to quantity, quality, or price; and (d) the patentee did not grant contractual licenses on reasonable terms to meet the demand of the national market on similar reasonable terms (Article 34, Decision 85).

Finally, reflecting uneasiness with membership in international conventions and organizations, the countries of the Andean Community were not entitled to unilaterally conclude agreements on IP with third-party countries or with international organizations, considered contrary to the common policies. This meant, in practical terms, that no individual country could become a member of the Paris Convention. None of the Andean Group countries were members at the time of the Convention.

V. ATTEMPTS TO REFORM THE INTERNATIONAL SYSTEM

Whereas national laws on IP were adopted at an early stage, developing countries' adherence to international IP conventions was slower. A majority of them, and even some members of the main conventions, remained skeptical of the multilateral IP architecture, particularly of the patent system and the merits of the Paris Convention in advancing industrialization.

The wave of national reforms of IP regimes, described earlier, had an impact on the international front. An important event took place in 1961. Brazil, the only Latin American country that had belonged to the Paris Convention since its establishment, launched a debate at the United Nations General Assembly on the relationship between the patent system and the economic development of developing countries. By raising the issue in this political forum, Brazil expected that further action could be undertaken at the technical level with the view of reforming the IP international conventions. As a result of this initiative, the General Assembly passed a resolution requesting that the Secretary General prepare a report on the effects of patents on the economies of underdeveloped countries. According to the resolution of the General Assembly,[36] the report was to include:

a) A survey of patent legislation in selected developed and underdeveloped countries, with primary emphasis on the treatment given to foreign patents;

36. UNGA resolution 1713 (XVI), "The Role of Patents in the Transfer of Technology to Underdeveloped Countries" (December 19, 1961).

b) An analysis of the characteristics of patent legislation of underdeveloped countries in light of economic-development objectives, taking into account the need for the rapid absorption of new products and technology, and the rise in the productivity level of their economies;
c) A recommendation on the advisability of holding an international conference in order to examine the problems of granting, protection, and use of patents, taking into consideration the provisions of existing international conventions and the special needs of developing countries, and utilizing the existing machinery of the International Union for the Protection of Industrial Property.

The UN Department of Economic and Social Affairs (DESA) published the requested report in 1964 under the title "The Role of Patents and the Transfer of Technology to Developing Countries." The report did not make concrete recommendations on holding an international conference to consider the revision of international conventions, as was the original intention of Brazil in raising this matter before the General Assembly. In one of its conclusions, the report stated that the problems connected with the transfer of technology went beyond the operation of patent systems and that more could be achieved through action at the national level than by convening an international conference, which could only deal with the limited aspects of granting, protecting, and using patents.[37] In other words, the 1964 report was of the view that international conventions, namely the Paris Convention, were not in need of reform for purposes of addressing the special problems of developing countries. Capacity-building effort at the domestic level was the major issue, not the reform of the international system. It should be noted, as discussed earlier, that by this time the Paris Convention had already experienced an important revision at the Lisbon conference of 1958.

Not satisfied with the outcome of the earlier deliberations or with the conclusions of the UN report of 1964, developing countries again took up the question of revising multilateral IP instruments in the context of deliberations on an international development strategy for the Second UN Development Decade. Paragraph 64 of the Strategy reemphasized the issue raised by Brazil in 1961 and called for a "review of international conventions on patents."[38] The International Development Strategy was not binding on governments and could not have an effect on the reform of the Paris Convention, as such. It was of a hortatory nature and became part of the chain of events ultimately leading up to the WIPO Development Agenda.

In the Latin American context, an important event took place in 1972 at a conference on science and technology organized by the Organization of American

37. See Patel, 2(9) *World Development* (Special Issue on Patents), at 10 (supra note 3).
38. Id.

States in Brazil. The Consensus of Brasilia was adopted, reaching the conclusion, among others, that IP regimes "have become inadequate and have been exploited by technology exporters to impose consumption patterns and obtain production, distribution and trade privileges." It proposed the revision of national regimes and inter-American treaties on patents and trademarks to assist in promoting social and economic development objectives.[39]

During the same year, at the third meeting of the UN Conference on Trade and Development (UNCTAD), the Conference recommended an update of the 1964 study prepared by UN DESA, with a view toward providing a better understanding of the role of the international patent system in technology transfer and in order to inform a future revision of the system. When the study was released in 1975, it contained more categorical conclusions on the revision of international conventions than did the study of 1964.

As a result of national IP reforms, the UN debates, and the 1975 UNCTAD report, developing countries took firmer steps to reevaluate the multilateral IP framework and to look for opportunities to reclaim some of the flexibilities lost in the numerous and substantial revisions to Article 5A of the Paris Convention.

At the same time, the debates on reform in WIPO gained momentum, as membership in international conventions increased. Many of the new members were former colonies, which expressed concern about the lack of sufficient access to information and knowledge. Led by India, these countries demanded "that unless some major copyright concessions were made for developing countries, they would have to make drastic changes in their international copyright arrangements."[40] The 1967 WIPO Stockholm conference became the venue for these countries "to adjust the system of protection under the Berne Convention to [their] economic, social and cultural needs."[41]

Under the 1967 Stockholm Act, the Berne Convention established a Protocol Regarding Developing Countries, which sought to enable those countries to broadly limit rights of translation and reproduction. The Protocol was not supported by developed-country members and was never ratified. A less ambitious Appendix adopted in Paris that constitutes an integral part of the Berne Convention superseded this attempt four years later.

---

39. See Eduardo White, *La Cuestión de la Propiedad Industrial en América Latina y su Papel en el Proceso de Desarrollo e Integración Económica: Un examen de las actuales tendencias legislativas, con especial referencia al tratamiento de las patentes*, trabajo preparado por el Instituto para la Integración de América Latina, Banco Interamericano de Desarrollo, como una contribución a las reunión de expertos sobre El Papel del Sistema de patentes, convocada por la UNCTAD (August 20, 1975).

40. Peter K. Yu, "Currents and Crosscurrents in the International Intellectual Property Regime," 38 *Loyola of Los Angeles Law Review*, 323 (2004).

41. Id.

With respect to possible reform of the Paris Convention, the WIPO secretariat adopted a rather cautious position, advocating instead for new international instruments. In a 1973 Report, the Director General of WIPO stated:

> In view of the requirements of unanimity of most existing conventions, it would probably be more practical to concentrate on new international instruments which could be better geared to the solution of some problems of transfer of technology, restrictive business practices, etc. However, if a revision of existing conventions would appear more desirable, and feasible, such revision, even if substantial, would be possible. . . . The recent revision at Paris in 1971 of the Berne Convention for the Protection of Literary and Artistic Works offers an example: the Berne Convention was then revised by adding to it, as an integral part and not as an option, preferential provisions, on a non-reciprocal basis, in favour of developing countries for the purpose of translation and reproduction of works protected by copyrights.[42]

VI. THE LAST ATTEMPT TO REVISE THE PARIS CONVENTION

The reform movement advanced further in WIPO when governments agreed finally to launch a new revision process of the Paris Convention to respond to the development needs of developing countries. A major impetus to this process was provided by the 1975 UNCTAD report on *The Role of the Patent System in the Transfer of Technology to Developing Countries*. The report concluded:

> The set of practices of the international system and its specific impact on the developing countries . . . require a revision of the current patent laws and administrative practices of the developing countries. The purpose of any such revision will have to be that of making patent laws and practices capable of effectively complementing other instruments of policy for national development. Of particular relevance in this connexion are, among others, the following aspects: treatment of nationals and foreigners; independence of patents; rights conferred by a patent; policies concerning the subject of patentability; duration of patent grants; adequate and effective provisions to prevent and correct the abuses resulting from the exercise of the rights conferred by the patent; using patent fees as a flexible instrument of patent policy; introduction of inventors' certificate, utility models, and other relevant means for promoting national scientific and technological capabilities. . . . Further significance attaches in this connexion to the position now being clarified at the international level concerning the promotion of new international and

42. Report of 1973 by Director General of WIPO to ECOSOC, Relations between the UN and WIPO.

> national systems of intellectual property, specially oriented toward the interest of developing countries; such systems could involve new international arrangements [reference to the Appendix to the Berne Convention] or substantial changes in the existing conventions.[43]

The idea of a possible revision of the Paris Convention was first advanced in June 1974 when the Director General of WIPO was instructed to create and convene an Ad Hoc Group of Governmental Experts. It met for the first time in 1975. At a meeting in December 1977, the Group adopted a Declaration, which served as the guiding instrument for the Diplomatic Conference on the revision of the Paris Convention. The 1977 Declaration of Objectives is reproduced below and provides insight into the development needs of countries at that time. The Declaration, an important episode in the chain of events leading up the WIPO Development Agenda, took into consideration a number of the recommendations made in the UNCTAD 1975 report and provided significant guidance with respect to a "new orientation in the industrial property field," in particular with respect to any review of the Paris Convention.

The Declaration also implied that there was a need to consider cases in which exceptions and corrections to the principle of national treatment and preferential treatment toward developing countries should be allowed. Access to technology, transfer of technology, and dissemination of knowledge were at the heart of the Declaration. A conspicuous element of the "1970s developing countries' agenda" was the establishment of an international code of conduct on the transfer of technology that would establish a framework for cooperation and would lay out general principles on commercial technology transactions, including the use of fair terms and conditions in contractual relationships.[44] Finally, the Declaration constitutes an interesting document that acknowledged the past debate in the UN and the need to address important relevant issues raised by developing countries in their national-reform processes. A remarkable parallel can be drawn between that consensual, international declaration and the developing-country claims made almost 30 years later in the context of the WIPO Development Agenda.

The Ad Hoc Group of Experts fundamentally sought to bring a convention that was established during the Industrial Revolution in line with the current economic realities of the 1970s and the development needs of a great majority of its membership.

On the basis of a recommendation made by the Group of Experts, WIPO established in 1976 the Preparatory Intergovernmental Committee on the Revision of the

43. United Nations, "The Role of the Patent System," at 64 (supra note 5).

44. See Surendra Patel, Pedro Roffe, and Abulqawi Yusuf, eds., *International Technology Transfer: The Origins and Aftermath of the United Nations Negotiations on a Draft Code of Conduct* (Kluwer: The Hague, 2000).

Objectives of the Revision of the Paris Convention

1. The revision of the Paris Convention should aim to contribute to the establishment of a new economic order in the world in which social justice prevails and economic inequalities between nations are reduced.
2. Industrial property, in particular as it relates to inventions, should constitute an element in the process of the transfer of technology and should contribute to the achievement of new technological advances. It should serve the goals of a new economic order, in particular through the industrialization of developing countries.
3. Thus, any new orientation in the industrial property field, in particular any revision of the Paris Convention and the model laws for developing countries, should be undertaken taking into account inter alia the following objectives:

   (i) to give full recognition to the needs for economic and social development of countries and to ensure a proper balance between these needs and the rights granted by patents;
   (ii) to promote the actual working of inventions in each country itself;
   (iii) to establish the principal obligations and rights of the owners of intellectual property rights;
   (iv) to facilitate the development of technology by developing countries and to improve the conditions for the transfer of technology from industrialized to developing countries under fair and reasonable terms;
   (v) to encourage inventive activity in the developing countries;
   (vi) to increase the potential of developing countries: in judging the real value of inventions for which protection is requested; in screening and controlling licensing agreements; in improving information for local industry;
   (vii) to contribute to the building of institutional infrastructure in developing countries designed to serve the above purposes, particularly the modernization or creation of industrial property offices, technical documentation centers and information services at the disposal of national industry and national inventors;
   (viii) to enable member countries to take all appropriate measures in order to prevent abusive practices in the field of industrial property;
   (ix) in general to ensure that all forms of industrial property, including trademarks, be designed to facilitate economic development and to ensure cooperation between countries having different systems of industrial property protection.

4. As far as the revision of the Paris Convention is concerned, consideration is to be given to certain defined cases in which exceptions and/or correctives to the principles of national treatment and independence of patents, and preferential treatment for developing countries should be allowed.

5. One of the principal immediate and continuing tasks with regard to industrial property should be, by establishing within the Paris Convention and by strengthening within WIPO special services for developing countries, to provide in the shortest possible time the necessary technical assistance to help developing countries strengthen their scientific and technological infrastructure, and to train their specialists.
6. Consideration should be given to the question of equality of treatment for all existing forms of protection of industrial property.
7. The international treaties within the competence of WIPO, in particular the Paris Convention, should be framed in the light of the above objectives, leaving maximum degree of liberty to each country to adopt appropriate measures on the legislative and administrative levels consistent with its needs and social, economic and development policy.
8. The principal lines of this declaration should be considered for incorporation as part of any Preamble to the Paris Convention in order to redefine industrial property concepts in an effort to better meet the needs and aspirations of developing countries.

Source: WIPO, Document PR/DC/3, 25 June 1979, Diplomatic Conference for the Revision of the Paris Convention: Basic Proposals.

Paris Convention. The preparatory work was entrusted to different working groups resulting in the preparation of the basic proposals finally submitted to the revision conference that met for the first time in 1981. As noted, Article 5A of the Convention was again a central issue of the revision process. The Basic Proposals dealing with Article 5A were an attempt to fundamentally reshape the Convention by revisiting the notions of local working, remedies to abuses, and the relationship between compulsory licenses and forfeiture or revocation of patents. It was the most radical attempt to revise the Convention in its entire history. Some issues raised at that time resurfaced during the negotiations of the TRIPS Agreement and subsequent discussions on the relationship between IP protection and access to medicines. For developing countries, the proposal to revise Article 5A constituted one expression of the claims made as early as in 1961 in the UN General Assembly.

The proposed new text included provisions authorizing national laws to take corrective measures in three cases, namely, those in which patent rights are abused; the patented invention was not, or was not sufficiently, worked in the country where the patent was granted; and the public interest was involved. In each case, the laws and competent authorities would have been able to apply several measures within the limitations established in the proposal. For cases of failure to work or insufficient working, it would have been possible for any country to provide for the grant of "non-voluntary licenses"—as compulsory licenses were renamed—to work the patented invention. Other measures included forfeiture and revocation of the patent in cases of abuse of patent rights, and—as a subsidiary measure—forfeiture and revocation for cases of non-working of the patented invention, as well. Moreover, in cases in which the public interest required exploitation of the invention—as was already clarified at Lisbon but not explicitly incorporated into the text of Article 5A—the proposal allowed national laws to provide for the grant of authorization to exploit, or work, the invention by the state or by any person designated by the competent authorities. Finally, Paragraph 8 of the Basic Proposals recognized special treatment for developing countries in dealing with issues such as local working and issuance of "non-voluntary" licenses. A full understanding of the implications of the proposal would require a full grasp of the various reservations and understandings made during the Preparatory Committee.[45]

Notably, at the time of the Preparatory Committee, Canada and Spain, among others, expressed the view that the special provisions in favor of developing countries, such as Paragraph 8 of the new Article 5A, should not simply apply to developing countries but should be of general application.

The proposed revisions to Article 5A of the late 1970s constitute yet another important historical incident in the chain of events that, in our view, are relevant antecedents to the WIPO Development Agenda. The text of the proposed revision follows.

The last meeting of the Diplomatic Conference for the Sixth Revision of the Paris Convention was held in 1983. Notwithstanding the important work achieved by the Preparatory Committee, no genuine progress was ultimately made on the issues dear to developing countries, such as preferential and differential treatment, particularly with respect to the reform of Article 5A.

Article 5A: Text Adopted or Forwarded by the Preparatory Committee to the Diplomatic Conference

(1) (a) Any country of the Union has the right to require by its national law that the inventions for which that country has granted a patent, or in the case of countries providing for a deferred examination when a provisional protection has been granted, be worked in the territory by the owner of the patent or under his authorization.

45. For a comprehensive review of the Basic Proposals, see WIPO, Document PR/DC/3, Diplomatic Conference on the Revision of the Paris Convention, Geneva, February 4–March 4, 1980 (June 25, 1979).

(b) Importation of articles incorporating the patented invention or made by the patented process does not constitute working of the patented invention. However, any country of the Union has the right to regard the importation of articles incorporating the patented invention or made by the patented process as fulfilling the requirements of working the patented invention.

(2) (a) For purposes of this Article, "non-voluntary license" means a license to work a patented invention without the authorization of the owner of the patent; it also means a license to work a patented invention given by the owner of the patent where the national law obliges him to give such a license.

(b) Any country oh the Union has the right to adopt legislative measures to prevent abuses resulting from the exercising of the right granted by the patent. However, importation into the country where the patent has been granted of articles manufactured in any of the countries of the Union shall not, in the absence of circumstances constituting abuse of the patent rights, entail forfeiture of the patent.

(3) Forfeiture of the patent shall not be provided for except in cases where the grant of non-voluntary licenses would not have been sufficient to prevent the said abuses. No proceedings for the forfeiture or revocation of the patent may be instituted before the expiration of two years from the grant of the first non-voluntary license.

(4) A non-voluntary license may not be applied for on the ground of failure to work or insufficient working before the expiration of a period of four years from the date of filing the patent application or three years from the date of the grant of the patent, whichever period expires last; it shall be refused if the patentee justifies his inaction by legitimate reasons.

(5) Any country of the Union has the right to provide in its national law, where the exploitation of the patented invention is required by reason of public interest, in particular national security, nutrition, health or the development of other vital sectors of the national economy, for the possibility of exploitation, at any time, of the patented invention by the government of that country or by the person authorized by it.

(6) An non-voluntary license shall generally be non-exclusive and shall not be transferable, even in the form of a grant of a sub-license, except with that part of the enterprise or goodwill which exploits such license. However, in special cases where exclusive licenses are necessary to ensure local working, such exclusive licenses may be granted for a period of up to [six] [three] years subject to the condition that the patent may not be forfeited or revoked for insufficient working for a period of [one] [two] years after the expiration of the exclusive license.

(7) Any decision relating to the grant of a non-voluntary license or to exploitation in the public interest, including the amount of the just payment to which the patentee is entitled or any decision relating to the revocation or forfeiture of a patent shall be subject to review at a distinct higher level in accordance with the applicable national law.

(8) Notwithstanding anything contained in paragraphs (3) and (4), developing countries have the right to apply the following provisions:

(a) Any developing country has the right to grant non-voluntary licenses where the patented invention is not worked, or is not sufficiently worked, by the owner of the patent or by another person acting under his authorization in the territory of the country within [two] [three] years from the grant of the patent in that country, unless the patentee can satisfy the national authorities competent to grant non-voluntary licenses that there are circumstances which justify the non-working of the patent. Where the national law provides for deferred examination of patentability and the procedure for such examination has not been initiated within three years from the filing of the patent application, the time limit referred to in the preceding sentence shall be [four] [five] years from the filing of the said application.

(b) Any developing country has the right to provide in its national law that the patent may be forfeited or revoked where the patented invention is not worked, or is not sufficiently worked, in the country before the expiration of [three] [five] years from the grant of the patent in that country, provided that the national law of the country provides for a system of non-voluntary licenses applicable to that patent, unless the patentee has been able to convince the national authorities competent for the forfeiture or revocation that circumstances exist which justify the non-working of the patent.

Source: WIPO, Document PR/DC/3, 25 June 1979, Diplomatic Conference for the Revision of the Paris Convention: Basic Proposals.

In evaluating the tensions of the time, Reichman provides the following interpretation:

> [I]n this period, the developing countries were as intent on lowering the international minimum standards of patent protection as the developed countries were resolved to elevate the same standards. Especially controversial were proposals to strengthen the capacity of member countries to impose non-voluntary licenses generally, and to restrict the ability of affected patentees to remain in the market with the designated licensees. In the end, such proposals led to the collapse of the Paris Revision Conference, and they were instrumental in the decision to remove efforts to reform international industrial property law from the exclusive

jurisdiction of WIPO and to bring them within the legislative and judicial jurisdiction of the GATT and its successor institution, the WTO.[46]

To the frustration of developing countries, in the middle of the Paris Convention revision process, there emerged an event that sidetracked the general revision. In June 1983, the Director General proposed a new complementary treaty to the Paris Convention that would consider the legal effects of public disclosure of an invention prior to the date of application. The Expert Group appointed to look at this matter seized the opportunity to widen the scope of issues that would be subject to the new treaty and included issues such as the unity of invention, the first-to-file versus the first-to-invent criteria, the minimum duration of rights, enforcement issues, exclusion of certain fields of technology from patentability, and the rights and obligations of patentees.

A diplomatic conference for such a complementary treaty was convened in The Hague in June 1991 to consider the work of the Expert Group. This effort ran counter to the initiative of developing countries to reform the main convention. Ultimately, efforts to revise the main convention and the initiative for a complementary treaty were both superseded by the move by developed countries to incorporate intellectual property rights (IPRs) as an integral part of the world trade regime in the new Round of Multilateral Trade Negotiations launched in Punta del Este in 1986.[47] Some of the issues raised in the complementary treaty surfaced and were incorporated in the TRIPS Agreement negotiations. Others not covered by TRIPS have been resurrected in discussions on the WIPO Substantive Patent Law Treaty. The issues raised by developing countries in the reform process, and well encapsulated in the 1977 Declaration of Objectives of the Revision of the Paris Convention, did not find answers in the TRIPS negotiations.

VII. THE ADVENT OF THE TRIPS AGREEMENT AND ITS IMPLICATIONS

The TRIPS Agreement marked a major event in the evolution of the international IP system. It represented a shift in international policymaking from the bottom-up approach of the Paris Convention toward the creation of a new set of minimum international standards and toward protection and enforcement of intellectual property rights. Also, it meant the full incorporation of IP into the international trading system, authorizing trade sanctions in cases of noncompliance.

In contrast to developing countries' activism in the period of reform that preceded the negotiations of the TRIPS Agreement, the role of these countries in the drafting and negotiation of TRIPS was extremely limited—and almost

46. Reichmann, "Non-Voluntary Licensing," at 13 (supra note 21).

47. See Susan K. Sell, *Private Power, Public Law: The Globalization of Intellectual Property Rights* (Cambridge, 2003).

entirely defensive. For a long period, the developing countries took the position that, except for counterfeiting and issues related to anticompetitive behavior, the subject of IPRs was simply not appropriate for discussion within the General Agreement on Tariffs and Trade system. To this end, they defended the appropriateness of WIPO to serve as the international specialized body to deal with IP issues. Developing countries finally accepted the TRIPS deal as part of the single-undertaking principle that prevailed in the Uruguay Round negotiations (a deal involving a single package of issues on improved access to markets—in general, markets for agriculture and textile goods, services, and investment); in exchange they received marginal concessions in terms of flexibilities in the implementation of its provisions, including transitional periods for the full implementation of the Agreement.

More recently, developing countries have sought to integrate a development perspective in the WTO and specifically within the TRIPS Agreement. At the Fourth WTO Ministerial Conference in Doha, Qatar, in November 2001, members adopted a Declaration recognizing the need of all people "to benefit from the increased opportunities and welfare gains that the multilateral trading system generates." The Declaration sets out a work program aimed at ensuring that "developing countries, and especially the least-developed among them, secure a share in the growth of world trade commensurate with the needs of their economic development."[48] Furthermore, members adopted a Declaration on the TRIPS Agreement and public health, which recognizes the "gravity of public health problems afflicting many developing and least-developed countries" and agrees that "the TRIPS Agreement does not and should not prevent members from taking measures to protect public health." It affirms the right of members to use flexibilities in the TRIPS Agreement to protect public health, including power to "grant compulsory licenses and the freedom to determine the grounds upon which such licenses are granted."[49] Most recently, in December 2005, governments agreed on the first amendment to TRIPS by incorporating Article 31*bis*, which deals with the situation of countries that lack (or have insufficient) manufacturing capacity to resort locally to a system of non-voluntary licenses, thus necessitating the importation of medicines from abroad.

Nevertheless, the challenges of implementation posed by TRIPS have been exacerbated by the new generation of free trade agreements (FTAs) that include IP obligations exceeding the minimum standards set out in TRIPS.[50] For example, such bilateral agreements extend the duration of patents beyond 20 years, restrict the use of compulsory licensing, and prohibit the use of test data on the

48. Doha WTO Ministerial Declaration, 14 November 2001: WT/MIN(01)/DEC/1.

49. Doha WTO Ministerial, 14 November 2001: WT/MIN(01)/DEC/2.

50. See Pedro Roffe, David Vivas, and Gina Vea, "Maintaining Policy Space for Development: A Case Study on IP Technical Assistance in FTAs," ICTSD Programme on IPRs and Sustainable Development Series, Issue Paper No. 19 (2007).

safety and efficacy of products by companies seeking marketing approval for generic products. These provisions have been a major source of concern for countries attempting to tailor policies according to their development needs, particularly those aimed at improving public health.[51] Yet developing countries are often willing to commit to stronger intellectual property rules as a quid pro quo for concessions in other areas—most notably, preferential access to developed countries' markets for agricultural and manufactured products. In addition to TRIPS and FTAs, new international agreements, such as the WIPO Internet treaties of 1996, and initiatives, such as the Substantive Patent Law Treaty (SPLT), have contributed to the controversial evolution of the international IP system, the anxieties of developing countries with respect to IP rules, and, perhaps ultimately, to the initiative for a WIPO Development Agenda.

Issues that developing countries raised decades ago have reemerged in the WIPO Development agenda. Parallels with the 1977 Declaration of Objectives of the Revision of the Paris Convention, if not obvious, are at least remarkable. References to issues such as technology transfer, capacity building, flexibilities based on countries' levels of development, access to knowledge, the preservation of the public domain, and access to new technologies (such as information and communication technology) are reminders of past events. However, one should not easily fall into the trap of simplifying scenarios. Today, there is a new context: Technology is faster and easier to copy; the supply chain is dispersed across the globe; people are better educated; and more actors are playing more prominent roles in the economy and in IP policy-making, including developing countries, civil society, and academia. The scenarios are different, but some of the central issues remain unchanged.

VIII. CONCLUSIONS

This chapter has attempted to draw some parallels between the evolution of the international IP system, particularly the Paris Convention, the trend to reform initiated by developing countries in the 1970s, and the initiative undertaken recently in WIPO on a Development Agenda. The establishment of the Paris Convention more than 120 years ago was the result of an initiative by a number

---

51. This is not the place to deal with the broad issue of why countries enter into and accept TRIPS-plus obligations, such as those incorporated in FTAs. FTAs between developed and developing countries are an important recent phenomenon in which countries, for a number of reasons (including the slow progress of multilateral trade negotiations) and with the purpose of gaining market access with major trading partners, conclude agreements that incorporate provisions that, in the case of IP, go beyond the minimum standards provided for in the TRIPS Agreement. In the case of the United States, chapters dealing with IP in FTAs are essential components of the FTAs.

of more advanced countries seeking protection for inventions beyond national boundaries. At that time, however, because national conditions differed and local industrialization was an important goal, a strategic compromise was reached on the need to balance the international recognition of foreign inventions with the need for local working. Each member country was left to decide how this working requirement would operate, including the possibility of resorting to compulsory licenses for failure to work. The subsequent revision conferences weakened the original compromise.

Political independence and collective action in the United Nations made developing countries more assertive in international fora. At the same time, they became more aware of their rights, and attempts were made to influence policy-making. This took the form of national-reform processes and later initiatives to revise international conventions to take into account their economic conditions. The climax for reform was reached in the late 1970s with the Declaration of Objectives of the Revision of the Paris Convention, among others, and the elaboration by its Preparatory Committee of the Basic Proposals, among others, on the revision of Article 5A dealing with the issue of working and the consequences of failure to work the patent. Contrary to developing countries' hopes and expectations, that initiative not only failed, but also spurred a campaign for upward harmonization of minimum standards of protection and enforcement of IPR, culminating with the successful conclusion of the TRIPS negotiations in 1994. Developing countries' original demands have not garnered the same level of attention as their more recent efforts to ensure that the international IP regime contains sufficient flexibilities to meet the needs of development. Endeavors such as the WTO Doha Declaration, the Declaration on TRIPS and Public Health, and the WIPO Development Agenda are reminders of the unfinished agenda of the 1970s.

When compared with current international IP standards, the Paris Convention might be perceived as a pro-development instrument. As noted by Bodenhausen:

> In the field of patents, for example, the Convention leaves the Member States entirely free to establish the criteria of patentability, to decide whether patent applications should or should not be examined in order to determine, before the patent is granted, whether these criteria have been met, whether the patent should be granted to the first inventor or to the first applicant for a patent, or whether patents should be granted for products only, for processes only, or for both, and in which fields of industry and for what term.[52]

Some aspects of the flexibility referred to by Bodenhausen in 1968 are no longer available today. In the 1970s scenario, developing countries felt that the Paris Convention did not fully take into account their respective levels of development.

52. Bodenhausen, *Guide to the Application of the Paris Convention* (supra note 23).

Moreover, Article 5A was perceived as extremely cumbersome for dealing with questions of abuses, including, for example, for the non-working of a patent.

At the time of writing, the prospects for implementing the WIPO Development Agenda appear promising. Let us hope that this latest occurrence in the chain of events meets the expectations of originators in contributing to a more inclusive IP system that takes into account, in a balanced manner, the interests of society, producers, consumers, and users.

5. THE POLITICS OF INTELLECTUAL PROPERTY REFORM IN DEVELOPING COUNTRIES
The Relevance of the World Intellectual Property Organization

CAROLYN DEERE*

I. INTRODUCTION

The September 2007 decision by WIPO member states to adopt 45 recommendations on the WIPO Development Agenda bodes well for the improved responsiveness of the global IP system to the varying circumstances and needs of developing countries.[1]

Many of the Development Agenda recommendations have implications for IP decision-making at the national level. Indeed, a number of recommendations specifically call for national improvements, including enhanced institutional capacity and efficiency on IP matters; a fair balance between IP protection and the public interest in national laws; coherence between IP laws and public policy goals in areas of innovation, science and technology, health, education, cultural industries, food security, and rural development; development-oriented and demand-driven capacity building; and development impact assessments of proposed IP rules. Progress on the implementation of the WIPO Development Agenda will therefore rely heavily on the political *process* and *organization* of IP decision-making at the national and regional levels in developing countries.

---

* Dr. Carolyn Deere is the Director of the Global Trade Governance Project at the Global Economic Governance Programme, University College, Oxford. The author would like to thank Ahmed Abdel Latif, Neil Netanel, Pedro Roffe and Caitlin Zaino for substantive and editorial suggestions. The author can be contacted at carolyn.deere@politics.ox.ac.uk.

1. See New 2007.

Despite the emphasis of international IP treaties, such as the TRIPS Agreement, on common minimum IP standards,[2] considerable diversity exists among developing countries regarding the nature and scope of IP standards, approaches to administration and enforcement,[3] and the responsiveness of national IP laws to development needs.[4] Although scholars have shown considerable interest in the politics of international IP agreements,[5] to date, there has been surprisingly little attention to the politics of their implementation and, more generally, to the political aspects of IP reform in developing countries. Where scholarly efforts to address these *politics* have emerged, they have mostly focussed on the implementation of one area of IP protection or on one particular country. Examples include discussions of the political history of the adoption of plant-variety protection legislation in the Philippines, the politics of TRIPS implementation in India, and IP enforcement in China.[6] Most other studies of IP politics focus on the coercive dynamics of the international negotiations and detail mechanisms through which external pressures impact treaty implementation, including bilateral trade pressures, corporate lobbying, and technical assistance.[7] Only more recently have political scientists taken up the task of systematically explaining variance in IP reforms in developing countries.[8]

For the WIPO Development Agenda to translate into meaningful development-oriented reforms at WIPO and also on the ground in developing countries, deeper analysis is needed of the political dynamics that impact IP decision-making at the national level, including the specific ways WIPO's activities influence the reform process. To aid in this task, section II of this chapter reviews how the process and organization of decision-making varies among developing countries, noting the ways this affects IP policy and reforms. It also outlines how national politics intersect with a range of international pressures on countries. Section III explores how WIPO's activities influence the politics of IP reforms in developing countries, highlighting the distinctive relationship between national IP offices and the WIPO Secretariat. The chapter concludes with a set of policy-oriented

2. For a comprehensive analysis of specific TRIPS provisions and their negotiating history, see Pengelly 2005 and Correa 2007.

3. See Deere 2008.

4. For debates on IP policies and development objectives, see CIPR 2002, Correa 2000, UNDP 2003: 203–34, UNCTAD 1996, and Watal 2001.

5. The origins and process of the TRIPS negotiations have attracted significant scholarly attention. See, for example, Beier and Schicker 1996; Drahos 1995; Gervais 1998; Matthews 2002; Ryan 1998; Sell 1995, 1998, and 2003b; Stewart 1993; and Wolfhard 1991.

6. Andersen 2006a and 2006b, Das 2003, Ramanna 2005, Mertha 2005, and Mertha and Pahre 2005.

7. See Drahos 1995, 1997, and 2003; Matthews 2005; May 2004 and 2006a; and Sell 2003b.

8. See Deere 2008, Shadlen et al. 2005 and Shadlen 2006.

recommendations for those working to advance a Development Agenda at WIPO and, ultimately, development-oriented IP policies at the national level.

II. THE POLITICS OF IP REFORMS IN DEVELOPING COUNTRIES

At the national level, three core factors make a difference to the kinds of IP reforms governments pursue: (i) the degree of public engagement; (ii) the internal capacity of governments on IP matters; and (iii) the degree of government coordination. These variables also influence the susceptibility of national governments to international pressures, as well as their capacity to filter and manage them. This section begins with a review of the national political dimensions and then introduces some of the key international pressures.

A. National Politics

1. Public Engagement The degree of public engagement on IP decision-making affects the pace and nature of national IP reforms. Across the developing world, the degree of debate in national legislatures in IP decision-making processes varies significantly, as does the responsiveness of both the executive and legislative branches of government to interest groups and parliament.

The speed of the IP reform process depends on the technical capacity of the government department charged with drafting and preparing legislation, and its relative influence within national governments. The strength and nature of relationships between the legislative and executive branches also influences the pace of IP reforms. Where executive branches exercise strong control over the legislature, reforms are swifter. The pace of reform may also depend heavily on the legislative calendar of the country in question and the range of other items for parliamentary attention. In many developing countries, the parliamentary process for review of national legislation is very weak. In addition, in some cases, international agreements have "direct effect" in national laws. In the agreements such as TRIPS, this means that beyond ratification of the international treaty in question, parliaments are not involved in the process of IP reform. Although a growing number of countries have parliamentary committees to address matters related to trade and IP, most countries do not. Even where such processes exist, few members of parliament have detailed knowledge of the IP issues under debate. Several governments have delayed bringing legislation forward where they fear that there will be staunch parliamentary resistance.

In some developing countries, proposed IP bills move through legislative processes more or less concurrently, but often different aspects of IP reforms are handled through independent pieces of legislation. In the case of TRIPS, most developing country governments amended or adopted several discrete pieces of legislation to address different aspects of implementation (e.g., copyright, plant-variety protection, industrial property, or trade secrets). In India, for example, some 10 different national laws have a bearing on the country's approach to TRIPS implementation, including the Biological Diversity Act (2002), the Copyright Act (1957), the Design Act (2000), the Geographical Indications of Goods (Registration and Protection) Act (1999), the Patents Act (1970), the Protection of Plant Varieties and Farmers' Rights Act (2001), the Semiconductor Integrated Circuit Layout Design Act (2000), and the Trade Marks Act (1999). IP is also dealt with under trade-secrets laws and the Indian Contract Act. In some cases, developing countries advance a suite of IP reforms in full knowledge that outstanding issues remain for later amendments.

Interest group politics can also generate variation in IP decision-making, most notably in those countries with civil society campaigns on aspects of IP policy and/or industry lobbies in favor of either higher or lower IP protection. Depending on the country, civil society actors may include associations of academics, consumer organizations, scientists, inventors, creators, musicians, authors, and IP attorneys. Such groups exert influence in several ways, including lobbying parliamentarians and government officials, and public education campaigns.

Although the level of activity and priorities of civil society groups vary by country, there are common themes across the developing world. In the Americas, Asia, and Africa, interest groups have emerged in response to specific challenges, such as improved access to essential medicines and the misappropriation of indigenous knowledge. In India, Brazil, and the Philippines, civil society engagement on IP issues began with apprehensions about biopiracy and opposition to patents on life forms. In South Africa, the push for affordable access to HIV/AIDS medicines galvanized civil society interest in IP issues. As the focus of global debates on IP policy has broadened from concerns about biodiversity and agriculture to public health, education, and access to knowledge, the diversity of civil society organizations involved and the intensity of national debates have increased.[9]

Evolving business opportunities have expanded the range of industry perspectives on IP reform in some developing countries. In Argentina, Brazil, and India, domestic generic-drug industries have long lobbied their governments to oppose stronger IP protection for pharmaceuticals. Yet, with new prospects for research contracts outsourced by multinational R&D companies, views on IP protection have diversified. Further, the emergence of lucrative new domestic and export opportunities—such as in the Brazilian, Indian, and Nigerian movie industries, and the Indian software industry—has galvanized a new set of stakeholders advocating stronger IP protection.

Interest group politics also sway the level of effort that governments devote to the enforcement of IP laws. In some countries, the subsidiaries of powerful multinational companies use their economic weight to lobby government agencies

9. See Sell 2002, 2003a, and 2006; Sell and Prakash 2004.

and parliaments to step-up enforcement efforts.[10] On the other hand, where moves to tackle piracy and counterfeiting threaten the livelihoods and employment of those involved in copying and imitation, some governments face public outcry. In certain instances, clamping down on piracy and counterfeit activities carries the risk of losing the support of important domestic voting constituencies. In Venezuela, for example, a pro-piracy NGO challenges the government's attempts to clamp down on piracy, arguing that the primary beneficiaries of boosted enforcement are foreign companies.[11]

Importantly, national interest groups often have strong links with international lobbies keen to advance their agendas within developing countries. Apparently 'local' interest groups sometimes serve as a conduit for the interests of international NGOs and industry coalitions that either favor or oppose stronger IP reforms.[12] Such groups forge alliances with local affiliates, research centers, NGOs, and scholars. In some cases, national actors are in fact subsidiaries of international organizations or members of international networks (i.e., Oxfam or the Business Software Alliance). Further, national governments often engage local scholars to provide advice regarding TRIPS implementation, who are simultaneously employed by foreign companies, NGOs, law firms, or international organizations.

2. Government Capacity A second aspect of national politics that contributes to variation in the nature of IP reforms in developing countries is the capacity of national governments. The key variables here are the level of technical IP capacity in governments, the strength and efficiency of government institutions, and the relative autonomy of IP offices responsible for TRIPS implementation.

Most developing countries suffer from weak institutional, technical, and financial capacity on IP issues. In many countries, the challenges associated with weak IP capacity are further compounded by problems of corruption, civil unrest, and political elites preoccupied with economic and political survival.

At the national level, governments usually delegate responsibility for IP issues to national IP offices, which are typically divided between an industrial property office located within the ministry of trade/industry and a copyright office located within the ministry of culture. With few exceptions, technical IP expertise in developing countries is concentrated in these IP offices and resides in individuals trained in IP law and practice but not in broader public policy goals. Most governments defer to these technocrats for advice on technical and legal IP matters, bolstering their dominance in national IP decision-making. This practice

---

10. For recent discussions of enforcement efforts in developing countries, see Drahos 2005, Endeshaw 2005, Knapp 2000, Li 2006, and Mertha 2005.

11. See http://eriubrighid.blogspot.com/2007/10/legalizar-la-piratera.html.

12. Conversely, in some cases *national* NGOs also have interests that extend beyond their national borders and are part of transnational campaigns to influence not just national IP reforms but also international IP regulation.

also serves to reinforce the notion that IP is a technical issue rather than one that warrants broader public policy discussion. A further consequence of this delegation to IP offices is that IP decision-making is often driven more by concerns for compliance with international law rather than the challenge of tailoring implementation to national development needs.

The concentration of a suite of functions in IP offices strengthens their relative power and authority on IP matters. In many cases, national industrial property or copyright offices have responsibility for drafting national laws, administering laws, adjudicating disputes, coordinating public outreach regarding the international IP system, and participating in international norm-setting negotiations, as well as securing technical assistance and capacity building from international donors.

The public accountability of IP offices is constrained by the low incidence of consultation with the full range of relevant stakeholders, experts, and interest groups. In most countries, local innovators and consumers have little involvement in discussions on the IP system. Indeed, the *insider governance*[13] of IP offices makes them prime candidates for regulatory capture. The vulnerability stems firstly from the fact that key IP decisions are made by a narrow group of technical experts, examiners, and patent attorneys, all of whom rely on actors outside government for their financing. Second, most IP offices generate the majority of their income from fees collected from private IP rights holders (i.e., for industrial property applications and maintenance), financial support from donors, or from in-kind support for training from private industry and/or foreign donors.

Across developing countries, an IP-centric perspective pervades not only the community of staff in national copyright and industrial property offices, but also the IP attorneys with whom they interact. Although IP attorneys do not have the economic weight of their industry clients, they are powerful by virtue of the *expertise* they lend to industry lobbyists, which few public interest actors on the domestic political stage can equal.[14] The command that such experts exert over IP decision-making in most countries generates a discourse on IP issues framed primarily in technical and legal terms. This further reinforces the notion that IP decision-making is a subject best left to experts rather than one of general public policy importance with a range of social and economic implications. Finally, although IP lawyers in developing countries generally have fewer resources than

---

13. See Drahos 2007.

14. Graham Dutfield similarly observes that "Members of the patent community speak the same language and share basic assumptions about patent law. . . . With the enormous economic power of some members arrayed alongside the 'objective' expertise of others, it would hardly be surprising if one particular perspective on patent law became the conventional wisdom within regulatory agencies and processes, government trade and industry departments, and throughout society." See Dutfield 2000.

their counterparts in developed countries to devote to influencing IP decision-making, they frequently serve as the local partners and allies for the broader international pro-IP community. There is only ocassionally a voice for IP consumers among the community of IP experts in developing countries.

3. **Government Coordination** The third element of national politics that affects variation in the approaches developing countries take to IP decision-making is coordination within government. This includes coordination between the internal and external faces of governments in respect of relationships with foreign donors and international organizations at the regional and multilateral level.

In general, internal coordination within developing countries on IP matters is weak, both with respect to internal IP issues and to positions taken in international fora. In some developing countries, there are sporadic debates that engage ministries of health, culture, agriculture, and industry on IP matters, but most developing nations lack a broader policy framework through which compliance with international norms is considered. The absence of such a framework and of internal coordination heightens the potential influence of external donors on national reforms, particularly because it serves to consolidate the relative influence of IP offices.[15] In some countries, Geneva-based diplomats charged with monitoring WTO discussions on TRIPS and WIPO have taken proactive steps to collaborate with national IP officials and to share technical and political expertise gathered in Geneva. The ministries responsible for foreign affairs and international trade, which are responsible for government relations with the WTO and WIPO, also sometimes play a central role. In most instances, however, the challenges of long-distance coordination frustrate the prospect of collaboration between diplomats and capital-based officials. Internal coordination at the national level is further complicated by resource constraints, turf battles, and lack of awareness of relevant issues. Among developing countries, Brazil stands out for having a deliberate and strategic approach to IP decision-making based on a broad policy framework for development and industrial policies, and a long history of informed discussion about appropriate IP policies.

A second aspect of government coordination concerns the character of the relationship between officials charged with IP reforms in national capitals and those responsible for interacting with foreign donors and international organizations. The degree to which governments coordinate their internal and external faces is particularly important in cases where countries delegate significant responsibility for IP matters to the regional level. Most member states of the two regional IP organizations in Africa, for instance, have limited capacity to monitor and guide the work of their agency. In both Francophone Africa and Anglophone Africa, the delegation of technical matters relating to the granting of IP rights

15. See Abdel Latif 2005.

has consolidated the accumulation of expertise at the regional level relative to the national level. In the case of the African Regional Intellectual Property Organization (ARIPO), this gap in technical expertise makes it difficult for national governments to ensure that their regional Secretariat's activities and recommendations are consistent with their respective national laws. In Francophone Africa, the weak national capacity of most governments on IP issues means that the regional Secretariat of the African Intellectual Property Organization (OAPI) operates without the oversight necessary to ensure accountability to member states or the public.[16] Furthermore, the OAPI secretariat has developed close ties with international providers of technical assistance and capacity building. In the case of TRIPS implementation, for instance, weak capacity left national governments susceptible to the preferences of the OAPI secretariat and external providers of capacity building (namely, WIPO, and the French National Industrial Property Institute, among others), which were in favor of stronger IP protection and successfully pushed through a TRIPS-plus approach to IP reforms.

B. International Pressures on Developing Countries

The international pressures on IP decision-making in developing countries come in two forms: economic and ideational. Economic pressures include those in which actors—states and industry—use their economic resources and associated political power to push countries to make decisions they would not have otherwise pursued. Such pressures include TRIPS-plus trade, investment and IP agreements, the use of the dispute settlement proceedings at the WTO, unilateral trade sanctions and threats (such as through the US-Special 301 process), industry threats regarding the withdrawal or withholding of investment, and diplomatic pressures.

Trade and investment deals and trade threats are extensively used by developed countries to push developing countries to go beyond minimum TRIPS implementation, to sacrifice the use of TRIPS flexibilities, and to add new, stronger IP standards to their domestic laws.[17] Most often this occurs when the United States and Europe link progress on IP reforms to concessions or assistance on

16. For a comprehensive analysis of the politics of TRIPS implementation in francophone Africa, see Deere 2008.

17. Several leading IP scholars discuss the use of coercion to influence international IP negotiations and IP standards in developing countries. See, for example, the work of Drahos 2001, 2002, and 2003; Abbott 2003; and Correa 2004a and 2004b. For similar analyses of *bullying* by developing countries, see the analysis by NGOs such as GRAIN 2003; MSF 2003; and Oxfam 2002, 2004a, 2004b. GRAIN has argued, for example, that "the European Union is aggressively forcing developing countries to adopt the strictest intellectual property rules on seeds that are possible." See GRAIN 2003.

broader economic issues important to a given developing country.[18] For many developing countries, foreign policy imperatives spur them to pursue bilateral trade agreements, despite potential economic or social costs, because the existence of such agreements is considered a valuable symbol of cooperation and consolidates relationships with valuable political allies. Because developing countries are very much in need of trade and other benefits, such as development assistance, they are vulnerable to developed countries' efforts to make assistance contingent on agreeing to strengthened IP protection, including TRIPS-plus IP standards and enforcement. Multinational corporations with strong interests in higher IP protection in developing countries also undertake a variety of activities to pressure developing countries, including lobbying national officials, legal challenges in national courts, and calling on their own developed country governments to pressure developing countries.

While economic pressures can explain the incidence of TRIPS-plus reforms in many developing countries, references to coercive pressures from powerful, developed countries and multinationals does not adequately explain a good deal of the variation we see in the nature of IP reforms in developing countries, including, for example, why certain countries do make use of some flexibilities in international IP laws and others do not.

A close review of the evidence suggests that, in spite of unbalanced power relations, developing country governments have some capacity to shape their responses to international pressures. The clearest evidence to support this argument is that the terms of TRIPS-plus free trade agreements (FTAs) vary. A nuanced assessment of the role of economic power reveals that the economic and strategic interests of the United States and European Union vary by country, and also that the distinctive character of national politics in developing countries affects their capacities to filter external pressures. Among developing countries, those with the greatest access to expertise, the most effective internal coordination, and powerful domestic constituencies in favor of TRIPS flexibilities have sometimes been, at the margin, able to alter the terms of their TRIPS-plus deals and to balance the impact of pro-IP pressures. While the United States has tried to ratchet up the IP commitments it secured in each successive FTA, the most technically competent governments, such as Chile, have negotiated marginally better deals for themselves than those with less capacity, such as Morocco. The engagement of interest groups, both in favor of and opposed to stronger IP protection, had impacts on the terms of TRIPS-plus deals that countries accepted. In countries where the poorest segments of society were better represented by lobbyists and in parliamentary fora where trade policy issues were debated, the trade deals and IP concessions that governments were willing to make differed

18. This definition draws from the description of compulsory power provided by Barnett and Duvall 2005.

from those where trade-related decision-making was driven by forceful market-access lobbies. In countries where constituencies concerned about the public interest implications of TRIPS-plus measures were vocal or where powerful, local commercial interests were at stake, legislatures were sometimes able to push the government to resist or walk away from proposed TRIPS-plus FTAs (e.g., Bolivia, Ecuador). In South Africa, the combination of relatively strong local expertise on IP issues and requirements on the government to consult with national legislative bodies, interest groups, and experts in order to negotiate, ratify, and implement foreign agreements, meant that South Africa was not able to *quietly* propose, consider, or enact changes to IP policies without public debate. This in turn lent the government strength to resist discussion of IP in its bilateral trade negotiations with the United States.

To explain IP reforms, one also needs to look beyond *economic* expressions of power to consider the more subtle, indirect ways that force and influence are exercised in the global economy. Most notably, pressure was also exercised through ideational vehicles—those related to the power of ideas. There are many vehicles through which ideational power can be expressed, including media campaigns, research, and epistemic communities of like-minded experts, as well as technical assistance, training and advice. Capacity building is a particularly potent vehicle for ideational pressure, particularly when combined with significant financial resources.[19]

A range of multilateral institutions is engaged in the provision of IP-related technical assistance and capacity building, including the World Trade Organization (WTO), the World Health Organization (WHO), the Joint United Nations Programme on HIV/AIDS (UNAIDS), the United Nations Conference on Trade and Development (UNCTAD), the United Nations Development Program (UNDP), and the World Customs Union (WCU). WIPO is, however, the single largest provider of IP-related advice, training, and capacity building to developing countries. Together, these activities make WIPO a powerful player in national IP politics across the developing world. Bilateral aid agencies, developed country patent offices, industry associations, individual corporations, and civil society groups are also involved. Among these donors, perspectives and priorities often differ significantly.

In many instances, IP-related capacity building is explicitly designed to promote the adoption of TRIPS-plus laws and enforcement measures, and to discourage the use of TRIPS flexibilities. For WIPO, WTO, and most developed countries, the goals of assistance are to ensure compliance with TRIPS and to promote stronger enforcement of IP laws. By contrast, the goal of technical assistance provided by the WHO, UNCTAD, and UNAIDS is to promote developing countries' awareness and use of the TRIPS flexibilities with an eye toward advancing public policy goals, such as public health or industrial development.

19. See Deere 2008.

The WHO, for example, provides information and advice to governments through seminars and meetings regarding the patent situation of key essential medicines and their options and responsibilities under TRIPS.

II. WIPO'S RELEVANCE TO IP POLITICS IN DEVELOPING COUNTRIES

WIPO has a critical relevance to national IP politics in developing countries and to the prospects for development-oriented IP policies and reforms, most notably through its capacity building activities. To understand the extent of WIPO's influence at the national level, a brief review of several core institutional characteristics of this institution is required, especially its relationships with member governments and non-government constituencies, financing, technical authority, and distinctive internal culture.

The WIPO Secretariat, like most international bureaucracies, insists upon the member-driven nature of its work. In WIPO documents, there is consistent reference to a work plan defined by *members*, defending the rules to which *members* have committed, and facilitating the efforts of *members* to meet their treaty commitments.[20] In practice, the responsiveness of intergovernmental organizations (IGOs) to particular member states, or groups of member states, varies over time. Similary WIPO is sometimes partially or completely captured by particular member states hoping to harness its institutional capacities, resources, or processes to serve as conduits for their interests.[21] Like other bureaucracies, the WIPO secretariat and its staff have also advance organizational goals and priorities that are sometimes independent of the preferences of member states, such as the expansion of a particular department, increasing the number of ratitications of a particular new treaty, or the completion of a new treaty that would bolster the organizations relevance. A core source of this capacity is the authority from its reputation as a leading source of IP expertise and through its status as a UN organization.[22]

WIPO's responsiveness to its entire membership is further compromised by its distinctive relationship with international business. Although WIPO's budget and program is approved by member states, the primary source of the Secretariat's

20. The role of international civil servants in international organizations and their influence on policy debates has been taken up elsewhere by Yi-Chong and Weller 2002, and Barnett and Finnemore 1999.

21. This point is made by Barnett and Duvall in their discussion of institutional power and IGOs as a vehicle for the indirect expression of the interests of powerful states. See Barnett and Duvall 2005.

22. The fact that staff of international organizations may sometimes promote the perception that they possess rational-legal and expert authority has been explored extensively in the scholarly literature. See, for example, Barnett and Finnemore 2004: 23–25.

funds is private-sector users, mostly multinational corporations, of the global IP system that WIPO administers. In general, more than 90 percent of WIPO's annual income comes from fees collected for services it provides to IP right-holders. Only the small remaining portion comes from member state contributions.[23] The WIPO Secretariat openly affirms the status of private IP right-holders as organization's core non-government constituency.[24] In 1988, the WIPO director general established an Industry Advisory Commission (IAC) to ensure that "the voice of the market sector is heard and that the organization is responsive to its needs."[25] Although its formal role is advisory only, the director general emphasized that this group was designed to ensure "a direct input of industry into the policy-making process in WIPO."[26] Over 90 percent of the NGOs accredited as permanent observers to its work are, in reality, business associations of IP holders and related industries.

The WIPO Secretariat openly declares its purpose as one of advocating stronger IP protection in developing countries.[27] Through research, outreach, and raising awareness, WIPO works to influence the terms of IP debates by asserting the links between stronger IP protection and economic development.[28] WIPO publications systematically, for instance, link stronger IP protection to modernization, innovation, growth in foreign direct investment, and technology transfer.[29] At the national level, the WIPO Secretariat is actively involved in promoting an *IP culture* that recognizes and endorses the importance of the IP system.[30]

---

23. Through the Patent Cooperation Treaty (PCT), WIPO provides a unified procedure for filing patent applications to protect inventions internationally. WIPO also collects fees for the dispute resolution services (mediation and arbitration) that it offers to individuals or enterprises seeking to avoid litigation. See Gurry 1999.

24. Ibid.

25. See the report of the first meeting of the IAC in WIPO 1999a.

26. See press release regarding the first meeting of the IAC; see WIPO 1999b.

27. Irrespective of the particular interests or preferences of members or advocates of an IGO at a specific time, the concept of "path dependence" alerts us to the ways in which a core set of ideas can dominate an international bureaucracy over many years. See, for example, Arthur 1989 and 1994.

28. The notion that international organizations may act as *agents* in their own right in international policy debates has been explored most recently by Barnett and Finnemore 2004. The nature of international bureaucracies and the role of their staff in global politics has, however, long attracted the attention of international-relations scholars. See, for example, Weiss 1975, Langrod 1963, and Cox and Jacobson 1973.

29. See Drahos 1996.

30. Article 3 of the WIPO Convention sets out the objectives of WIPO as administrative cooperation among the various international agreements it oversees, and promotion of the "the protection of intellectual property throughout the world through cooperation among states, and, where appropriate, in collaboration with any other international organization." In addition, the substantive functions set out in Article 4 of the Convention are to "promote the development of measures designed to facilitate the efficient protection

In 2003, for example, the preface of a flagship publication by WIPO's director general aimed at policymakers and companies worldwide, entitled *Intellectual Property—A Power Tool for Economic Growth,* proclaimed its "definite perspective—that IP is good."[31] Not surprisingly, it is common for representatives of national IP offices to echo this perspective. In 1999, the head of Burkina Faso's IP office defended TRIPS-plus reforms in the Francophone Africa region, stating that countries "must make the necessary arrangements and adjustments, because globalisation is here. We cannot afford to marginalise ourselves."[32] Similarly, a senior official in Benin's IP office argued that: "Africa must create 'trust' that it can protect intellectual property rights. . ."[33] Notably, part of the motivation on the part of the original champions of the WIPO Development Agenda was to counter the influence in developing countries of what they described as a hegemonic discourse in favor of stronger IP protection.[34]

WIPO's impact on IP decision-making in developing countries is not limited to promoting a pro-IP discourse and culture. Through capacity building, it also directly influences the content and timing of legislative reforms. These activities support and reinforce political dynamics that favor strong IP protection and the limited use of the flexibilities available in international IP laws.[35]

From 1996 to 2007, WIPO's contribution to IP-related technical assistance in developing countries increased dramatically, from around US$25 million to more than US$60 million per year. WIPO's capacity building activities include legislative and policy advice related to the implementation of international IP agreements; training and human resource development (courses, seminars, workshops, etc.); administrative and IT support (including automation and

---

of intellectual property throughout the world and to harmonise national legislations in the field"; to "encourage the conclusion of international agreements designed to promote the protection of intellectual property"; and to assemble and disseminate information concerning the protection of intellectual property, carry out and promote studies in this field, and publish the results of such studies.

31. See Idris 2002. Such statements have prompted critics to allege that WIPO is acting "not as a servant of the whole international community but as an institution with its own agenda." See Musungu and Dutfield 2003: 11. For a discussion of WIPO's evolution, see May 2006b.

32. See Ngangoue and Oeudraogo 1999.

33. Ibid.

34. Interview with Ahmed Abdel Latif, February 2007, former Egyptian TRIPS and WIPO delegate.

35. The scale and nature of IP-related capacity building for IP reforms in developing countries has attracted critical attention from several scholars. The following scholars each note the bias of technical assistance from WIPO and developed countries in favor of a compliance-driven approach to TRIPS and of strengthened IP protection in general: Matthews 2005, Matthews and Munoz-Tellez 2006, and May 2004. Several NGOs have also published critical reviews. See Bellmann and Vivas-Eugui 2004, Kostecki 2005, Musungu 2003, and Pengelly 2005.

computerization); and institutional support for enforcement. WIPO also supports the infrastructure and salary costs associated with IP administration, training of IP professionals, participation of developing country IP officials in international meetings, and the provision of resources for enforcement. In 1996, WIPO forged a formal agreement with the WTO Secretariat to work together on matters of technical assistance related to TRIPS. As part of this effort, the heads of both organizations introduced two joint, technical-cooperation agreements. The first, launched in 1998, was to help developing countries meet the January 1, 2000 deadline for conforming to the TRIPS Agreement. The second, in 2001, was a similar program to help least developed countries with their original January 1, 2006 deadline later extended to mid-2013 and to make use of IP protection for their economic, social, and cultural development.

The superior scale of WIPO's resources for capacity building relative to those available in the national budgets of developing countries lends the agency tremendous influence on the nature of the particular reforms undertaken. As noted above, WIPO's status as a UN agency endows its capacity building activities with a legitimacy not enjoyed by bilateral aid agencies or industry consultants; many developing country officials assume that WIPO's advice is neutral, which in turn eases their acceptance of WIPO's advice and assistance, even on controversial IP matters.[36] In practice, however, WIPO's capacity building is not neutral with respect to the nature of domestic IP reforms, but promotes a pro-IP perspective. It frequently downplays the importance of flexibilities available in international IP treaties that might benefit developing countries. Moreover, WIPO's technical assistance offers a narrow, legalistic approach to IP reforms, neglecting a broader public policy perspective on the competing goals and options for IP policies and laws. By its own account, WIPO's capacity building advances IP-centric objectives: to promote legislative reforms to ensure compliance with TRIPS commitments, higher IP standards, greater efficiency of IP administration, and more effective enforcement.

In WIPO's key interlocutors at the national level are national offices for industrial property and copyright. In many countries, WIPO is their core source of institutional support, particularly for training opportunities. Whereas IGOs such as UNCTAD, WHO, and FAO work to build the IP capacity of other parts of national government, the bulk of WIPO's assistance is directed toward national IP offices. Given that national IP offices enjoy considerable autonomy within national governments, WIPO's emphasis on strengthening and concentrating expertise in these offices serves to bolster their authority in the national reform process. Through its special relationship with IP offices, the WIPO Secretariat maintains a conduit for its own influence on national IP law and practice.

Countries with the lowest technical capacity on IP, such as those in Africa, are particularly vulnerable to pro-IP capacity building. Low capacity for coordination,

---

36. See Kostecki 2005, MSF 2003, May 2004, and Musungu 2003.

even where political will is present, heightens the vulnerability of governments to WIPO's efforts to "fill the capacity gap". Even in national IP offices with relatively strong capacity, the consistent supply of training, advice, and capacity building from international donors serves to reinforce the dominance of pro-IP technocrats in national IP decision-making and debates. The Philippines, where the Intellectual Property Office (IPO) has some 300 professional staff, provides a case in point. A 2005 study on IP-related capacity building in the Philippines notes that the "purely compliance-driven nature of the assistance converged with IPO's statutory mandate and orientation to strengthen the administration of the IP system; that is, the technical assistance only reinforced the compliance agenda of the IPO."[37] The study highlights that the national IP office is by far the dominant recipient of WIPO's capacity building and is also the agency most active in pushing for higher standards of IP protection and enforcement. In 2000, for example, the Philippine IPO announced that its vision was "to be an active player in the IP global community," thus "projecting itself as part of an international network of IP offices that share a common objective: advancing IP protection."[38] Other national agencies relevant to IP policymaking in the philippines, such as the Department of Science and Technology, received no assistance for their work.

Similarly, a study of Thailand highlights the dominance of WIPO as the core provider of capacity building and finds that most technical assistance on legislative matters "appears to be designed to further the development of IP rights."[39] The senior official in Thailand's IP office has observed that the bulk of donor resources to Thailand focus on IP enforcement, whereas Thailand's national priorities are to better manage IP through, for example, more strategic approaches to licensing technologies and commercializing new inventions.[40]

WIPO's relationship with IP offices is forged and maintained through a combination of material enticements and socialization.[41] Access to training, seminars, and international conferences provides attractive incentives for many developing country IP officials to advance the agenda of donors in their countries. Training and repeated attendance at seminars are also tools through which developing

37. See Villaneuva 2005.

38. See Andersen 2006a.

39. In a series of interviews conducted by Jakkrit Kuanpoth, a Thai law professor, leading officials from the Thai Department of Intellectual Property expressed doubts that the emphasis of donors on policing and law enforcement would actually reduce IP infringement, arguing that "raising public awareness may be a better strategy," as well as helping the country make sustainable use of IP: "If the public sees the benefits from IP, which they can receive from commercialization using IP, this will lead them to have concern for IP protection and thus less IP infringements." Kuanpoth 2005.

40. Ms. Wiboonluck Ruamrak, Deputy Director-General, Thai Department of Intellectual Property, cited in Kuanpoth 2005.

41. The importance of socialization as a mechanism through which power is exercised is explored by Ikenberry and Kupchan 1990.

country policymakers are advised and persuaded to adopt the ideas, assumptions, and policy preferences of their donors, and to espouse the benefits of stronger IP protection.[42] In the context of weak oversight of many IP offices, and the limited salaries and professional prospects in many developing countries, WIPO's influence is sometimes personal as well as institutional.[43] Access to training and international conferences can be personal opportunities to build career prospects and to supplement salaries with sizeable per diems. Some developing-country officials have also worked part time as consultants for WIPO and receive promises of future jobs in exchange for cooperation in promoting particular perspectives back home or in WIPO meetings.

The provision of legislative advice to decision makers responsible for drafting national IP laws is a further vehicle through which WIPO affects the national political process and advances particular approaches to IP reform. WIPO uses a series of model laws to guide its advice to developing countries; countries can consult these as guidelines or adopt them *off the shelf*. Legal reviews of these model laws reveal that they fail to draw full attention to the flexibilities and options available to developing countries with respect to TRIPS implementation.[44] WIPO also provides targeted legal advice to countries on matters of TRIPS interpretation, provides feedback on proposed laws, and assists with legal drafting of laws. This assistance can have a significant influence on national perceptions and understanding of the political and legal options available and on the decisions governments ultimately take. In the Philippines, for example, WIPO provided legal advice to the patent office regarding the implementation of TRIPS and WIPO's model laws were used as the basis for legislation on integrated circuits. In addition, WIPO provided seminars "to orient the IPO and other stakeholders on new IP conventions to which the Philippines is not yet a party," which in turn "paved the way" for the IPO to successfully lobby the Philippines Congress for the ratification of the WIPO Patent Cooperation Treaty in 2001 and the WIPO Internet Treaties in 2002.

As the scale of WIPO's capacity building has grown, so has the scope of its activities in developing countries and its channels for influencing domestic politics. In some countries, WIPO provides financial support for public outreach

42. The idea that particular assumptions, beliefs, and worldviews come to dominate international organizations over time has been presented in the literature for many years. The influence of pro-market economists on the policy advice of the World Bank has been the subject of detailed analysis. See, for example, Standing 2000 and Wade 2002 on the influence of pro-market economists on the World Bank, and Kindleberger 1955 and Ramsay 1984 on the influence of economists in international organizations.

43. This observation draws from personal interviews with a range of developing-country delegates to WIPO and long-term observers of WIPO, including its former and current staff.

44. See May 2004 and Consumers International 2006.

on IP issues, as well as for the creation of interest groups of IP *users*. Parliaments are also an important focus of WIPO's outreach efforts; in many countries, WIPO organizes seminars on IP and TRIPS for members of national legislatures. Further, WIPO has supported the travel of parliamentarians to WIPO and has arranged for these to meet with selected industry interest groups, such as the International Federation of Pharmaceutical Manufacturers Associations (IFPLIA) and Pfizer in Geneva.

In recent years, WIPO has faced complaints of biased, low-quality technical assistance, and conflicts of interest in its choice of providers.[45] Critics have drawn attention to inadequate oversight of the recruitment of IP technical assistance providers (sometimes resulting in the appointment of unqualified or underqualified, staff and consultants), and also to the practice of hiring former government and industry officials as both WIPO staff and providers of technical assistance. The revolving door, so to speak, between industry and WIPO puts industry-friendly experts in positions with influence on decision-making on regulatory issues. A second revolving door spins officials from national IP offices and developing country government delegations toward WIPO, either as staff members or consultants, from where they can exercise considerable influence over national governments.

III. CONCLUSIONS: MAKING THE DEVELOPMENT AGENDA REAL

This chapter has shown that, among developing countries, considerable variations exist in the political process and organization of IP decision-making. In order to advance a development agenda at WIPO and, ultimately, development-oriented IP policies at the national level, greater consideration must be given to how IP decision-making occurs in developing countries and to the role of WIPO in that process. This chapter suggests a particular need for more critical assessment of the role of national IP offices in domestic IP decision-making processes, especially in guiding the implementation of international agreements and as the key national interlocutors with WIPO and the core recipients of its technical advice and capacity building. Deeper political analysis will also help identify the obstacles to more development-oriented IP laws and policies, and the political strategies that would enable progress in that direction.

While a detailed exploration of the links between national approaches to IP decision-making and the development orientation of IP reforms was beyond the scope of this chapter, the analysis offered here already suggests several conclusions about the kinds of politics and processes likely to enable development-oriented IP reforms. First, the prospects for such reforms are highest where countries

45. See New 2005a, 2005b, and 2006.

have a public policy framework through which implementation of international IP obligations is approached. Second, coordination within national governments is critical to ensure that IP policies and laws are designed and implemented in ways that support development goals, particularly in the areas of innovation, public health, education, and technological development. This kind of interagency coordination would also promote stronger oversight of national IP offices. Third, decision-making processes that draw on national expertise within and beyond government, especially through consultation with industry and NGOs, are more likely to generate legal and policy proposals that address national development goals. Although national governments do not have the ability to control the presence or absence of international power pressures, including those from WIPO, their performance in each of these three areas, combined with political will, can help them to manage how external pressures impact the decisions they make.

At the international level, this paper has reinforced the importance of making WIPO's capacity-building more demand-driven and development-oriented and of broadening the scope of the organization's work away from its narrow focus on stronger IP protection. Moreover, it has emphasized the importance of the national politics of IP reform to making the Development Agenda real on the ground in developing countries. If the Development Agenda can indeed counter the pro-IP orientation of international negotiations at WIPO and its capacity-building, this will also help enable improvements in the development orientation of national IP policies, laws, institutions, and practices.

REFERENCES

Abbott, F. 2003. Trade Diplomacy: The Rule of Law and the Problem of Asymmetric Risks in TRIPS. *Occasional Paper #13*. Geneva: Quaker United Nations Office (QUNO).

Abdel Latif, A. 2005. *Developing Country Coordination in International Intellectual Property Standard-Setting*. Geneva: South Centre.

Andersen, R. 2006a. Explaining Compliance with Intellectual Property Commitments: The Case of Agrobiodiversity. Paper presented at the *47th Annual Convention of the International Studies Association*. San Diego, CA: 22–25 March.

Andersen, R. 2006b. *Governing Agrobiodiversity: Plant Genetics and Developing Countries*. Aldershot: Ashgate.

Arthur, W. 1989. Competing Technologies, Increasing Returns, and Lock-in by Historical Events. *Economic Journal*, 99: 116–31.

Arthur, W. 1994. *Increasing Returns and Path Dependence in the Economy*. Ann Arbor: University of Michigan Press.

Barnett, M., and R. Duvall. 2005. Power in Global Governance. In M. Barnett, and R. Duvall, eds. *Power in Global Governance*. Cambridge: Cambridge University Press, 1–32.

Barnett, M., and M. Finnemore. 1999. The Politics, Power and Pathologies of International Organizations. *International Organization*, 53, 4: 699–732.

Barnett, M. 2004. *Rules for the World: International Organizations in Global Politics.* Ithaca: Cornell University Press.

Beier, F., and G. Schicker. 1996. *From GATT to TRIPS: The Agreement on Trade Related Aspects of Intellectual Property Rights.* Studies in Industrial Property and Copyright Law. New York: Weinheim.

Bellmann, C., and C. Vivas-Eugui. 2004. Towards Development-Oriented Technical Assistance in Intellectual Property Policymaking. Paper presented at *Reflections on IPR Technical Assistance to Developing Countries and Transition Economies.* Burnham Beeches, UK: 15–17 September.

CIPR. 2002. *Integrating Intellectual Property Rights and Development Policy.* London: Commission on Intellectual Property Rights.

Consumers International. 2006. *Copyright and Access to Knowledge: Policy Recommendations on Flexibilities in Copyright Law.* Kuala Lumpur: Consumers International Asia Pacific Office.

Correa, C. 2000. *Intellectual Property Rights, the WTO and Developing Countries: The TRIPS Agreement and Policy Options.* Penang, Malaysia: Third World Network.

Correa, C. 2004a. Bilateral Investment Agreements: Agents of New Global Standards for the Protection of Intellectual Property Rights? *GRAIN Briefing Note,* August. Barcelona: Genetic Resources Action International (GRAIN).

Correa, C. 2004b. Bilateralism in Intellectual Property: Defeating the WTO System for Access to Medicines. *Case Western Reserve Journal of International Law,* 36, 1: 79–96.

Correa, C. 2007. *Trade-Related Aspects of Intellectual Property Rights: A Commentary on the TRIPS Agreement.* Oxford: Oxford University Press.

Cox, R., and H. Jacobson. 1973. *The Anatomy of Influence: Decision Making in International Organizations.* New Haven: Yale University Press.

Das, K. 2003. The Domestic Politics of TRIPS: Pharmaceutical Interests, Public Health, and NGO Influence in India. Paper prepared for the research project on *Linking the WTO to the Poverty-Reduction Agenda* as part of a DFID-funded globalization and poverty research program. Gujarat Institute of Development Research, Ahmedabad (India).

Deere, C. 2008. *The Implementation Game: The TRIPS Agreement and the Global Politics of Intellectual Property Reform in Developing Countries.* Oxford: Oxford University Press.

Drahos, P. 1995. Global Property Rights in Information: The Story of TRIPS at the GATT. *Prometheus,* 13, 1: 6–19.

Drahos, P. 1996. *A Philosophy of Intellectual Property.* Hants, UK: Dartmouth Publishing Co. Ltd.

Drahos, P. 1997. States and Intellectual Property: The Past, the Present and the Future. In D. Saunders, and B. Sherman, eds. *From Berne to Geneva: Recent Developments in International Copyrights and Neighbouring Rights.* Nathan, Queensland: Australian Key Centre for Culture and Media Policy, 47–70.

Drahos, P. 2001. Negotiating Intellectual Property Rights: Between Coercion and Dialogue. Paper presented at *International Seminar on Intellectual Property and Development: What Future for the WTO TRIPS Agreement?* Sponsored by Oxfam, Brussels: 20 March.

Drahos, P. 2002. Developing Countries and International Intellectual Property Standard Setting. *Journal of World Intellectual Property,* 5, 5: 765–89.

Drahos, P. 2003. *Expanding Intellectual Property's Empire: The Role of FTAs.* Canberra: Research School of Social Sciences, Australian National University.

Drahos, P. 2005. Securing the Future of Intellectual Property: Intellectual Property Owners and Their Nodally Coordinated Enforcement Pyramid. *Case Western Reserve Journal of International Law*, 36: 53–79.

Drahos, P. 2007. Society, Social Contract and the Patent Office. Paper presented at *10th Annual Niro Scavone Haller and Niro Distinguished Lecture, DePaul University College of Law*. Chicago: 15 March.

Dutfield, G. 2000. *Intellectual Property Rights, Trade and Biodiversity*. London: Earthscan.

Endeshaw, A. 2005. Intellectual Property Enforcement in Asia: A Reality Check. *International Journal of Law and Information Technology*, 13, 3: 378–412.

Gervais, D. 1998. *The TRIPS Agreement: Drafting History and Analysis*. London: Sweet and Maxwell.

GRAIN. 2003. TRIPS-'Plus' Must Stop: The European Union Caught in Blatant Contradictions. Genetic Resources Action International (GRAIN) March. Available at http://www.bilaterals.org/IMG/doc/TRIPS_PLUS_Mar03_fin.doc.

Gurry, F. 1999. The Dispute Resolution Service of the World Intellectual Property Organization. *Journal of International Economic Law*, 2, 2: 385–98.

Idris, K. 2002. *Intellectual Property: A Power Tool for Economic Growth*. Geneva: World Intellectual Property Organization (WIPO).

Ikenberry, J., and C. Kupchan. 1990. Socialisation and Hegemonic Power. *International Organization*, 44, 5: 283–315.

Kindleberger, C. 1955. Economists in International Organizations. *International Organization*, 9, 3: 340–53.

Knapp, I. 2000. The Software Piracy Battle in Latin America: Should the United States Pursue its Aggressive Bilateral Trade Policy Despite the Multilateral TRIPS Enforcement Framework? *University of Pennsylvania Journal of International Economic Law*, 21, 1: 173–210.

Kostecki, M. 2005. Intellectual Property and Economic Development: What Technical Assistance to Redress the Balance in Favour of Developing Nations? *Issue Paper #14*, March. Geneva: International Centre for Trade and Sustainable Development (ICTSD).

Kuanpoth, J. 2005. Intellectual Property-Related Technical Assistance, Cooperation and Capacity Building: The Thailand Experience. Paper presented at *IP-related Technical Cooperation for Developing Countries*, hosted by ICTSD, Geneva: 12–13 June.

Langrod, G. 1963. *The International Civil Service: Its Origins, Its Nature, Its Evolution*. New York: Oceana Publications.

Li, H. 2006. Piracy, Prejudice and Profit: A Perspective from US-China Intellectual Property Rights Disputes. *The Journal of World Intellectual Property*, 9, 6: 727–46.

Matthews, D. 2002. *Globalising Intellectual Property Rights: The TRIPS Agreement*. London: Routledge.

Matthews, D. 2005. TRIPS Flexibilities and Access to Medicines in Developing Countries: The Problem with Technical Assistance and Free Trade Agreements. *European Intellectual Property Review*, 27, 11: 420–27.

Matthews, D., and V. Munoz-Tellez. 2006. Bilateral Technical Assistance and TRIPS: The United States, Japan and the European Communities in Comparative Perspective. *Journal of World Intellectual Property*, 9, 6: 629–53.

May, C. 2004. Capacity Building and the (Re)Production of Intellectual Property Rights. *Third World Quarterly*, 25, 5: 821–37.

May, C. 2006a. Escaping the TRIPS Trap: The Political Economy of Free and Open Software in Africa. *Political Studies*, 54, 1: 123–46.

May, C. 2006b. *The World Intellectual Property Organization: Resurgence and the Development Agenda*. Oxford: Routledge.

Mertha, A. 2005. *The Politics of Piracy: Intellectual Property in Contemporary China*. Ithaca: Cornell University Press.

Mertha, A., and R. Pahre. 2005. Patently Misleading: Partial Implementation and Bargaining Leverage in Sino-American Negotiations on Intellectual Property Rights. *International Organization*, 59: 695–729.

MSF. 2003. *Doha Derailed—Technical 'Assistance': A Case of Malpractice?* Paris: Médecins Sans Frontières (MSF).

Musungu, S. 2003. Designing Development-Oriented Intellectual Property Technical Assistance Programmes. Paper presented at *Second Bellagio Series of Dialogues on Intellectual Property and Sustainable Development*, sponsored by the UN Conference on Trade and Development and International Centre for Trade and Sustainable Development. Bellagio, Italy: 30 October–2 November.

Musungu, S., and G. Dutfield. 2003. *Multilateral Agreements and a TRIPS-plus World: The World Intellectual Property Organisation. Issues paper #3*, Geneva/Ottawa: Quaker United Nations Office (QUNO) and Quaker International Affairs Program (QIAP).

New, W. 2005a. Debate Heats Up Over WIPO Development Agenda. *Intellectual Property Watch*, 1 April. Available at http://www.ip-watch.org/weblog/wp-trackback.php/39.

New, W. 2005b. Reform Debate Trips up WIPO Development Aid Meeting. *Intellectual Property Watch*, 15 April. Available at http://www.ip-watch.org/weblog/wp-trackback.php/45.

New, W. 2006. Group B+ Draft Patent Harmonisation Treaty Emerges. *Intellectual Property Watch*, 7 November. Available at http://www.ip-watch.org/weblog/wp-trackback.php/.

New, W. 2007. WIPO Launches New Agenda on IP and Development. *Intellectual Property Watch*, 29 September.

Ngangoue, N., and B. Oeudraogo. 1999. Small Farmers Seed Rights Up for Grabs? La protection des inventions s'étend aux variétés végétales. *Interpress News Service*, 5 March.

Oxfam. 2002. U.S. Bullying on Drugs Patents: One Year After Doha. *Oxfam Briefing Paper #33*, November. Oxford: Oxfam International.

Oxfam. 2004a. Comparison of Five US FTAs. *Oxfam Briefing Note #2*, June. Oxford: Oxfam International.

Oxfam. 2004b. Free Trade Agreement between the USA and Thailand Threatens Access to HIV/AIDS treatment. Oxford: Oxfam.

Pengelly, T. 2005. Technical Assistance for the Formulation and Implementation of Intellectual Property Policy in Developing Countries and Transition Economies. *UNCTAD-ICTSD Project on Intellectual Property Rights & Sustainable Development Series: Issue Paper #11*, June. Geneva: International Centre for Trade and Sustainable Development.

Ramanna, A. 2005. Shifts in India's Policy on Intellectual Property: The Role of Ideas, Coercion and Changing Interests. In P. Drahos, and U. Suthersanen, eds. *Death of a Patent System*. Witney: Lawtext Press, 150–174.

Ramsay, R. 1984. UNCTAD's Failure: The Rich Get Richer. *International Organization*, 38, 2: 387–97.

Ryan, M. 1998. *Knowledge Diplomacy: Global Competition and the Politics of Intellectual Property*. Washington, DC: Brookings Institution Press.

Sell, S. 1995. Intellectual Property Protection and Antitrust in the Developing World: Crisis, Coercion, and Choice. *International Organization*, 49, 2: 315–49.

Sell, S. 1998. *Power and Ideas: North-South Politics of Intellectual Property and Antitrust*. SUNY series in global politics. Albany: State University of New York Press.

Sell, S. 2002. TRIPS and the Access to Medicines Campaign. Paper presented at *Access to Medicines for the Developing World: Facilitation or Hindrance?* Sponsored by the University of Wisconsin Law School, Madison: 9–10 March.

Sell, S. 2003a. Competing Knowledge Networks: The Quest for Global Governance in Intellectual Property. Paper presented at *SSRC Workshop: Intellectual Property, Markets, and Cultural Flows*. New York: 24–25 October.

Sell, S. 2003b. *Private Power, Public Law: The Globalisation of Intellectual Property Rights*. Cambridge: Cambridge University Press.

Sell, S. 2006. Books, Drugs, and Seeds: The Politics of Access. Paper presented at the *47th Annual Convention of the International Studies Association*. San Diego, CA: 22–25 March.

Sell, S., and A. Prakash. 2004. Using Ideas Strategically: The Contest between Business and NGO Networks in Intellectual Property Rights. *International Studies Quarterly*, 48, 1: 143–75.

Shadlen, K. 2006. The New Politics of Intellectual Property in the Developing World. Paper presented at the *47th Annual Convention of the International Studies Association*, San Diego, CA: 22–25 March.

Shadlen, K., A. Schrank, and M. Kurtz. 2005. The Political Economy of Intellectual Property Protection: The Case of Software. *International Studies Quarterly*, 49, 1: 45–71.

Standing, G. 2000. Brave New Words? A Critique of Stiglitz's World Bank rethink. *Development and Change*, 31, 4: 737–764.

Stewart, T. 1993. *The GATT Uruguay Round: A Negotiating History, 1986–1992*. Boston: Kluwer Law and Taxation Publishers.

UNCTAD. 1996. *The TRIPS Agreement and Developing Countries*. Geneva: United Nations Conference on Trade and Development (UNTAD).

UNCTAD–ICTSD. 2005. *Resource Book on TRIPS and Development*. Cambridge: Cambridge University Press.

UNDP. 2003. *Making Global Trade Work for People*. London: United Nations Development Program/Earthscan.

Villaneuva, S. 2005. Intellectual Property-Related Technical Assistance: The Philippine Experience. Paper presented at *Dialogue on IP-Related Technical Assistance*. Sponsored by International Centre for Trade and Sustainable Development (ICTSD). Geneva: 12–13 June.

Wade, R. 2002. US Hegemony and the World Bank: The fight over people and ideas. *Review of International Political Economy*, 9, 2: 215–43.

Watal, J. 2001. *Intellectual Property Rights in the WTO and Developing Countries*. The Hague: Kluwer Law International.

Weiss, T. 1975. *International Bureaucracy: An Analysis of the Operation of Functional and Global International Secretariats*. Lexington, MA: D.C. Heath and Company.

WIPO. 1999a. Industry Advisory Commission Report of the Inaugural Meeting, February 4–5. *WIPO Document WO/GA/24/6/Annex 1*, Geneva: WIPO.

WIPO. 1999b. WIPO and Private Sector Forge New Relationship: Industry Advisory Committee Wraps up Inaugural Meeting. *WIPO Press Release PR/99/156*, 5 February.

Wolfhard, E. 1991. International Trade in Intellectual Property: The Emerging GATT Regime. *University of Toronto Faculty Law Review*, 49, 1: 106–51.

Yi-Chong, X. and P. Weller. 2002. International Civil Servants and Multilateral Trade Negotiations. Paper presented at *Jubilee Conference of the Australasian Political Studies Association*. Sponsored by the Australian National University. Canberra: October.

PART THREE

THE DEVELOPMENT AGENDA: CAUTIONARY NOTES FROM TWO DIRECTIONS

6. HISTORY LESSONS FOR THE WIPO DEVELOPMENT AGENDA

RUTH L. OKEDIJI*

I. INTRODUCTION

Momentous events in the history of the international intellectual property (IP) system have rarely been noted, much less celebrated, in the broader international community with such force as has been the case[1] with the WIPO Development Agenda.[2] In part, this could be attributed to a tacit *lex*

* William L. Prosser Professor of Law & Solly Robins Distinguished Research Fellow, University of Minnesota Law School.

1. *See, e.g.*, *Intellectual Property: The Cost of Ideas*, ECONOMIST, Nov. 13, 2004, at 94, 2004 WLNR 10895995; *WIPO to Focus Harder on Helping Developing Nations*, WASH. INTERNET DAILY, June 19, 2007, 2007 WLNR 11705655; Ben Wallis, *The Politics and Ideology of Intellectual Property*, CONSUMER POL'Y REV., May 1, 2006, at 117, 2006 WLNR 11879185.

2. *See* World Intellectual Property Organization (WIPO), General Assembly, Proposal by Argentina and Brazil for the Establishment of a Development Agenda for WIPO, WIPO Doc. WO/GA/31/11, August 27, 2004, available at http://www.wipo.int/documents/en/document/govbody/wo_gb_ga/pdf/wo_ga_31_11.pdf (last visited April 20, 2008) [here after Development Agenda Proposal]; WIPO, Proposal to Establish a Development Agenda for WIPO: An Elaboration of Issues Raised in Document WO/GA/31/11, WIPO Doc. IIM/1/4, April 6, 2005, available at http://www.wipo.int/meetings/en/doc_details.jsp?doc_id=42376 (last visited April 20, 2008); WIPO, Proposal by Morocco on Behalf of the African Group Entitled The African Proposal for the Establishment of a Development

specialis[3] treatment of the IP system, which for many years insulated the relationship between IP and social welfare from intellectual scrutiny, policy collaboration, and strategic coordination with other international regimes. Despite a number of formal relationships between the World Intellectual Property Organization (WIPO) and other international organizations, particularly the United Nations (UN),[4] the fact remains that the development of IP norms has occurred in relative isolation from other international law regimes.[5] This situation was unalterably

---

Agenda for WIPO, WIPO Doc. IIM/3/2, July 18, 2005, available at http://www.wipo.int/meetings/en/doc_details.jsp?doc_id=47470 (last visited April 20, 2008).

3. Analysis of possible applications of the lex specialis maxim to IP deserves considerable attention well beyond the scope of this chapter. Briefly, in international law, the lex specialis principle refers to special (or specific) law that emerges as an exception to a general law or standard. It is usually understood as a rule of interpretation to ascertain legal hierarchy or to resolve conflict between regimes. An important question with regard to lex specialis is what makes a rule (or treaty) specific/special or general. *See generally* United Nations (UN) International Law Commission, Study Group on Fragmentation of International Law, Study on the Function and Scope of the Lex Specialis Rule and the Question of "Self-Contained Regimes," Preliminary Report by Martti Koskenniemi, Chairman of the Study Group of the ILC, May 7, 2004, UN Doc. ILC(LVI)/SG/FIL/CRD. IP could be "special" in many regards, including, for example, the technical nature of the subject matter relative to most other public law regimes or its peculiar focus on creating incentives for private action which is highly unusual in a realm largely concerned with the activities of public actors. Of course, justifications for global IP rules could also represent a general international standard from which special derogations emerge; for example, by viewing human rights obligations as exceptions to IP. *See* UN International Law Commission, Study Group on Fragmentation of International Law, Fragmentation of International Law, at 3, available at http://untreaty.un.org/ilc/sessions/55/fragmentation_outline.pdf (last visited April 20, 2008) (noting a decision by the European Court of Human Rights treating human rights as an exception to general law "justified because of the special properties of the subject matter."). Lex specialis may apply to determine the relationship between two provisions of a single treaty; between provisions in two different treaties; between a treaty and non-treaty rule; or between two non-treaty standards. *See generally* General Assembly, Report of the International Law Commission, 56th Sess., UN Doc. A/59/10, ¶¶ 304–13 (2004), available at http://untreaty.un.org/ilc/reports/2004/2004report.htm (last visited April 20, 2008).

4. *See* Agreement between the United Nations and the World Intellectual Property Organization, Dec. 17, 1974, available at http://www.wipo.int/treaties/en/agreement/index.html (last visited April 20, 2008). *See also* Agreement between the World Intellectual Property Organization and the World Trade Organization, Dec. 22, 1995, 35 I.L.M. 754 (1996), available at http://www.wipo.int/treaties/en/agreement/trtdocs_wo030.html (last visited April 20, 2008).

5. Autonomous lawmaking in specialized fields detached from a coherent, unifying framework has increasingly become characteristic of the globalized world system and has in recent times become the subject of extensive academic commentary and a seminal report by the UN International Law Commission. *See* General Assembly, Report of the Study Group of the International Law Commission on Fragmentation of International

transformed in 1994 by the allocation of power to the World Trade Organization (WTO) to enforce minimum global IP standards pursuant to the Agreement on Trade-Related Aspects of Intellectual Property Rights (TRIPS Agreement).[6]

The IP-trade linkage reflected in the WTO TRIPS Agreement quickly became a stage for a fervent global debate, in which old and new claims regarding the causal effects of IP on a variety of human welfare concerns were relentlessly and purposefully advanced, ultimately with some important successes.[7] Outside the expansive infrastructure of the WTO system, demands for IP accountability to other international law regimes made by non-governmental organizations (NGOs),

---

Law: Difficulties Arising from the Diversification and Expansion of International Law, U.N. GAOR, 55th Sess., Supp. No. 10, at 237, UN Doc. A/CN.4/L.628 (2002) [hereafter Report on Fragmentation]. Examples of some notable academic contributions include, inter alia, PAUL SCHIFF BERMAN, THE GLOBALIZATION OF INTERNATIONAL LAW (2005); Andreas Fischer-Lescano & Gunther Teubner, *Regime-Collisions: The Vain Search for Legal Unity in the Fragmentation of Global Law*, 25 MICH. J. INT'L L. 999 (2004). *See also generally* Symposium on Diversity or Cacophony?: New Sources of Norms in International Law, 25 MICH. J. INT'L L. 845 (2004); Symposium on the Proliferation of International Tribunals: Piecing Together the Puzzle, 31 N.Y.U. J. INT'L L. & POL. 919 (1999).

6. Agreement on Trade-Related Aspects of Intellectual Property Rights, Marrakesh Agreement Establishing the World Trade Organization, Annex 1C, Apr. 15, 1994, in WORLD TRADE ORGANIZATION, THE LEGAL TEXTS: THE RESULTS OF THE URUGUAY ROUND OF MULTILATERAL TRADE NEGOTIATIONS 321 (1999) [hereafter TRIPS Agreement], available at http://www.wto.org/english/tratop_e/trips_e/t_agmo_e.htm (last visited April 20, 2008).

7. The most notable success is the 2001 Doha Declaration on the TRIPS Agreement and Public Health. *See* Doha WTO Ministerial 2001, Declaration on the TRIPS Agreement and Public Health, Nov. 14, 2001, WTO Doc. WT/MIN(01)/DEC/2, 41 I.L.M. 755 (2002), available at http://www.wto.org/English/thewto_e/minist_e/min01_e/mindecl_trips_e.htm (last visited April 20, 2008); Decision of General Council of 30 Aug. 2003, Implementation of Paragraph 6 of the Doha Declaration on the TRIPS Agreement and Public Health, September 1, 2003, WTO Doc. WT/L/540, 43 I.L.M. 509 (2004), available at http://www.wto.org/english/tratop_e/trips_e/implem_para6_e.htM (last visited April 20, 2008). In addition, a number of allowances have been made for developing and least developed countries. For example, since 2004, the implementation of the TRIPS Agreement has been extended, and the application of some provisions suspended. Articles 27–34 of the TRIPS Agreement became generally operational for developing countries on January 1, 2000. *See* TRIPS Agreement, *supra* note 6, art. 65.2. However, developing countries that did not previously allow product patents on pharmaceutical and agricultural chemical products were given another five years to cover them, subject to a "mailbox" provision for patents arising in the meantime. *See* TRIPS Agreement, *supra* note 6, arts 65.4, 70.8–70.9 (mailbox and minimum exclusive marketing rights). Least developed countries (LDCs) are entitled to further extensions of TRIPS implementation, up to 2013 for TRIPS on the whole and 2016 for those provisions dealing with matters of public health, including patent protection for pharmaceuticals.

inter-governmental organizations[8] (IGOs), and networks of transnational pressure groups rapidly gained currency as both matters of policy and collective action.[9] The WIPO Development Agenda can, in many respects, be viewed as one outcome of these demands, nesting a substantive call for global IP reform within a framework that, at a minimum, requires an historic shift from an institutional emphasis on rote extensions of IP laws in developing countries (DCs) to evaluations of how IP might actually effect development gains in the majority of WIPO Member States.[10] The Agenda is widely regarded as an important milestone in the framework of an organization that historically has viewed development as an inevitable, rather than directed, incidence of IP regulation. It is not yet clear (and many are skeptical) that the values, coalitions, and strategies that ensured the successful conclusion of the Development Agenda will resonate sufficiently deeply within WIPO's infrastructure to bring about substantive outcomes measurable by, among other things, re-oriented IP norm-setting activity reflective of development aspirations. Yet by purposively directing scrutiny to the methodology and content of the relationship between other international law regimes and the activities of WIPO, the Development Agenda has, at a minimum, occasioned reexamination of the unsettled relationship between IP protection and development goals.

In this chapter, I explicitly treat development as a pseudonym for a complex network of benefits associated with economic growth and human social capital. The integral role of technical change in national growth prospects requires that

---

8. *See, e.g.*, UN Sub-Commission on the Promotion and Protection of Human Rights, Intellectual Property Rights and Human Rights, Res. 2000/7, 52nd Sess., UN Doc. E/CN.4/Sub.2/RES/2000/7 (August 17, 2000) [hereinafter UN Human Rights Sub-Commission, Intellectual Property Rights and Human Rights]; Convention on Biological Diversity (CBD), The Convention on Biological Diversity and the Agreement on Trade-Related Intellectual Property Rights (TRIPS): Relationships and Synergies, Conference of the Members to the Convention on Biological Diversity, November 4-15 1996, UN Doc. UNEP/CBD/COP/3/23, available at http://www.cbd.int/doc/meetings/cop/cop-03/official/cop-03-23-en.doc (last visited April 20, 2008). *See also* L. R. Helfer, *Human Rights and Intellectual Property: Conflict or Coexistence?*, 5 Minn. Intell, Prop. Rev. 47 (2003), available at http://mipr.umn.edu/archive/v5n1/Helfer.pdf (last visited April 20, 2008); L. R. Helfer, *Toward a Human Rights Framework for Intellectual Property*, 40 U. C. Davis L. Rev. 971 (2007); P. K. Yu, *Reconceptualizing Intellectual Property Interests in a Human Rights Framework*, 40 U.C. Davis L. Rev. 1039 (2007).

9. *See* Amy Kapczynski, *The Emerging Access to Knowledge Movement and the New Politics of Intellectual Property Law*, 117 YALE L.J. 804 (2008); Ellen't Hoen, *TRIPS, Pharmaceutical Patents, and Access to Essential Medicines: A Long Way from Seattle to Doha*, 3 CHI. J. INT'L L. 27 (2002); L. R. Helfer, *Regime Shifting: The TRIPS Agreement and the New Dynamics of International Intellectual Property Lawmaking*, 29 Yale J. Int'l L. 1 (2004).

10. Of the 184 WIPO Member States, 124 are either developing or least-developed countries. *See* WIPO, Member States, available at http://www.wipo.int/members/en/ (last visited April 20, 2008).

the nature and causes of technology production remain critical considerations for the WIPO Development Agenda, specifically the relationship between IP protection and technology creation. In addition, the pervasiveness of digital networks and the great expectations of information-leveraged development gains[11] have explicitly associated IP regulation with opportunities for socio-cultural and political development through limitations and exceptions to proprietary rights. Such doctrinal limits are, for example, directed at precluding encroachment on fundamental minimum freedoms (e.g., the fair use doctrine), maintaining a competitive equilibrium in the market (e.g., the idea/expression dichotomy and compulsory licensing), promoting innovation (e.g., blocking patents, scope of patentable subject matter, the idea/expression dichotomy), and safeguarding certain consumer protection interests.[12] Further, the regulation of digital content through para-copyright agreements such as the WIPO Copyright Treaty[13] (WCT) or private law mechanisms sourced in contract or tort law[14] affect opportunities for participation in governance processes, both local and national, that are facilitated by information communication technologies (ICTs).[15] Finally, the adequate

---

11. *See, e.g.*, Margaret Chon, *Intellectual Property from Below: Copyright and the Capability for Education*, 40 U.C. Davis L. Rev., 803, 840-41 (2007); Ruth L. Okediji, Development in the Information Age: Issues in the Regulation of Intellectual Property Rights, Computer Software and Electronic Commerce, UNCTAD-ICTSD Project on IPRs and Sustainable Development, Issue Paper No. 9, May 2004, available at http://www.iprsonline.org/unctadictsd/docs/CS_Okediji.pdf (last visited April 20, 2008); Murray Gibbs, Special and Differential Treatment in the Context of Globalization, Note presented to the G15 Symposium on Special and Differential Treatment in the WTO Agreements, New Delhi, 10 December 1998, 11–12, available at http://www.wto.org/english/tratop_e/devel_e/semo1_e/gibbs_e.doc (last visited April 23, 2008).

12. *See, e.g.*, Ruth L. Okediji, *Securing Intellectual Property Objectives: New Approaches to Human Rights Considerations*, in Margot E. Salomon, Arne Tostensen and Wouter Vandenhole (eds.), Casting the Net Wider: Human Rights, Development and New Duty-Bearers (Intersentia, 2007); Helfer, *Toward a Human Rights Framework for Intellectual Property, supra* note 8; Yu, *Reconceptualizing Intellectual Property Interests in a Human Rights Framework, supra* note 8.

13. WIPO Copyright Treaty, Dec. 20, 1996, S. Treaty Doc. No. 105-17, 36 I.L.M. 65 [hereafter WCT], available at http://www.wipo.int/treaties/en/ip/wct/trtdocs_wo033.html (last visited April 20, 2008).

14. *See generally* Graeme B. Dinwoodie, *Private Ordering and the Creation of International Copyright Norms: The Role of Public Structuring*, 160 J. Institutional & Theoretical Econ. 161, 173–74 (2004); Carlos Correa, *Fair Use in the Digital Era*, 33(5) Int'l Rev. Ind. Prop. & Copyright L. 570 (2002); Jerome H. Reichman, Graeme Dinwoodie & Pamela Samuelson, *A Reverse Notice and Takedown Regime to Enable Public Interest Uses of Technically Protected Copyrighted Works*, 22 Berkeley J. L. & Tech. 981 (2007).

15. David Held and Anthony McGrew, *Political Globalization: Trends and Choices*, in Providing Global Public Goods (Inge Kaul et al. eds., 2003) 185, 187 ("new communications systems create new experiences, new modes of understanding, and new frames of political reference independent of direct contact with particular peoples, issues or events").

supply of global public goods is threatened by the "privatization" of domestic public goods taking place in the European Union and the United States through the agency of IP law.[16] These factors, and many more, establish the need for a critical evaluation of how the WIPO Development Agenda, and indeed WIPO itself, will occupy this new transborder political, economic, and social space.

I explore the technology-related focus of the IP–development linkage, outlining WIPO's role in the initial development paradigm which prevailed from 1964 to 2004, when a proposal for a Development Agenda was first submitted.[17] I then examine the WIPO Development Agenda in light of this history, identifying possible paradigm shifts discernible both in the structure of the Agenda and in preliminary considerations regarding its implementation. Finally, I suggest a number of ways to interpret the WIPO Development Agenda and reflect briefly on how these different 'faces' of the Agenda might inform WIPO's institutional role in responding to a spectrum of development interests in an era of rapid technological transformation.

II. SITUATING DEVELOPMENT IN WIPO'S PAST

A. A Brief History of Development at WIPO

As an organizational matter, the WIPO Development Agenda represents a distinct moment in the life of WIPO, whose central preoccupation—and indeed its very design—has traditionally been structured around the advancement and harmonization of IP rights.[18] This is not to say, however, that "development"

---

16. *See, e.g.*, Keith E. Maskus and Jerome H. Reichman, *The Globalization of Private Knowledge Goods and the Privatization of Global Public Goods*, in INTERNATIONAL PUBLIC GOODS & TRANSFER OF TECHNOLOGY UNDER A GLOBALIZED INTELLECTUAL PROPERTY REGIME (Keith Maskus and Jerome Reichman eds., 2005); M. Abbott and Jerome H. Reichman, *The Doha Round's Public Health Legacy: Strategies for the Production and Diffusion of Patented Medicines Under the Amended TRIPS Provisions*, 10(4) J. INT'L ECON. L. 921 (2007); *see also* Stephen M. McJohn, *Fair Use and Privatization in Copyright*, 35 SAN DIEGO L. REV. 61 (1998); Charles R. McManis, *The Privatization (or "Shrink-Wrapping") of American Copyright Law*, 87(1) CAL. L. REV. 173 (1999).

17. *See* Development Agenda Proposal, *supra* note 2; WIPO General Assembly, Thirty-First (15th Extraordinary) Session, Report, October 5, 2004, WIPO Doc. WO/GA/31/15, available at http://www.wipo.int/documents/en/document/govbody/wo_gb_ga/pdf/wo_ga_31_15.pdf (last visited April 20, 2008). This original proposal submitted on behalf of the so-called "Friends of Development" was joined by 12 other Member States: Bolivia, Cuba, the Dominican Republic, Ecuador, Egypt, Iran, Kenya, Peru, Sierra Leone, South Africa, Tanzania, and Venezuela.

18. *See* Convention Establishing the World Intellectual Property Organization, 848 U.N.T.S. 3 (July 14, 1967), available at www.wipo.int/treaties/en/convention/trtdocs_wo029.html (last visited April 20, 2008). The Preamble to the Convention expresses the desire to ". . . encourage creative activity, to promote the protection of intellectual property

concerns related to economic challenges facing countries of the global South have not been an important part of WIPO's operations. To the contrary, WIPO distinguished itself beginning in the mid-20th century as an institution crucial to the coordinated efforts, led by the UN, to address problems relating to the integration of developing countries into the international economic system. As early as the 1950s, applied science and technological knowledge had assumed a central role in institutional deliberations within the UN system regarding principal elements of a multilateral framework for addressing the challenges of underdevelopment in the global South.[19] The significant political impetus and normative credibility associated with the IP internationalization program and related technical assistance activities characteristic of WIPO's work throughout much of the 1970s and 1980s took place as an explicit response to the identified priority of technology acquisition as a primary tool in economic development. During this period, the principal objective was expanding membership of WIPO-administered treaties,[20] not only to neutralize incipient threats to the international IP system from developing countries but, more importantly, to establish WIPO as the exclusive forum with the competency and jurisdiction to oversee the development concerns associated with technology acquisition.

The transformation of WIPO into a primary actor in global IP lawmaking with respect to *substantive* development issues was a political feat accomplished, interestingly enough, with the facility of developing countries, whose early initiative in questioning the welfare gains of the IP system forced a compromise resolution in the UN. A draft resolution initiated by Brazil before the UN General Assembly in 1961 called, inter alia, for a study on the effects of domestic and foreign patents on the economies of developing countries and for an analysis of patent legislation in developing countries in light of development objectives. Concerned about the implications of the Brazilian draft resolution, WIPO (then called the United International Bureau for the Protection of Intellectual Property [known

---

throughout the world." *See* id., pmbl. ¶2. *See also* id., art. 3(1) (setting forth the normative objective of WIPO as "[promotion of] protection of intellectual property throughout the world through cooperation among States and, where appropriate, in collaboration with any other international organization").

19. *See* G.A. Res. 1429 (XIV), U.N. GAOR, 14th Sess., Supp. 16 at 15, U.N. Doc. A/4354 (Dec. 5, 1959) (directed at increasing the international exchange of knowledge and experience in the field of applied science and technology).

20. This effort concerned primarily norm-setting global treaties of which the major ones are the Paris Convention for the Protection of Industrial Property, Mar. 20, 1883, 21 U.S.T. 1583, 828 U.N.T.S. 305 (revised July 14, 1967) [hereinafter Paris Convention], available at http://www.wipo.int/treaties/en/ip/paris/trtdocs_wo020.html (last visited April 20, 2008), and the Berne Convention for the Protection of Literary and Artistic Works, Sept. 9, 1886, 25 U.S.T. 1341, 828 U.N.T.S. 221 (last revised July 24, 1971) [hereinafter Berne Convention], available at www.wipo.int/treaties/en/ip/berne/trtdocs_wo001.html (last visited April 20, 2008).

by its French acronym, BIRPI]) encouraged intervention by the International Chamber of Commerce (ICC),[21] which submitted a statement to the UN Secretary General with a view to "defend the patent system" and correct "inaccuracies" which underlay the Brazilian "point of view" regarding adverse effects of the patent system for developing countries.[22] The ICC statement, relying on generalized assumptions about the propriety of IP protection and issued without any formal study or empirical basis,[23] recited the prosperity of industrialized countries attributable "to a large extent" to the patent system as a means to rebut the Brazilian proposal.[24] It urged developing countries to embrace the system in order to encourage foreign investment, stimulate local innovation, and facilitate the transfer of know-how and technological information.[25] In an eminently strategic act, the ICC statement identified the Paris Convention for the Protection of Industrial Property[26] as "[t]he most advanced and equitable system of international patent rights, taking account of public interest in the use and working of foreigners' patents. . . ."[27]

Simultaneously, the WIPO Director sent a letter to the UN Secretary General offering WIPO's services with respect to the proposed draft resolution as a specialized institution solely engaged in the development of principles for the international protection of industrial property.[28] Although the timeline of events suggests that the ICC and WIPO interventions may not have been significant formal influences in the ultimate UN Resolution[29] that emerged, it seems clear that the convergence of technical expertise, sole jurisdiction, and substantive oversight over the primary IP treaties in force at the time empowered WIPO's mission and lent its work important legitimacy with respect to the application of IP rights in the cause of development. A collage of UN resolutions,[30] starting

---

21. For a summary record of the ICC's deliberations and the ensuing statement, see INDUS. PROP. (Vol. 1) at 38 (1962).

22. Id. at 38.

23. In fact, the only comprehensive study of this period examining the effects of patent protection on the development prospects of developing States concluded that strong international patent norms in fact run contrary to the development interests of these countries. *See* EDITH PENROSE, THE ECONOMICS OF THE INTERNATIONAL PATENT SYSTEM (1951) (criticizing the international patent system, particularly its application to developing countries).

24. INDUS. PROP., *supra* note 21 at 39.

25. INDUS. PROP., *supra* note 21 at 39.

26. Paris Convention, *supra* note 20.

27. INDUS. PROP., *supra* note 21 at 39.

28. INDUS. PROP., *supra* note 21 at 40.

29. G.A. Res. 1429 (XIV), U.N. GAOR, 14th Sess., Supp. 16 at 15, U.N. Doc. A/4354 (Dec. 5, 1959).

30. *See, e.g.*, UN General Assembly Resolution 1995 (XIX), Dec. 30, 1964; Economic and Social Council Resolution 1454 (XLVII), August 8, 1969; Economic and Social Council Resolution 1544 (XLIX, July 30, 1970. *See also* General Principles to Govern

with the draft one originated by Brazil in 1961,[31] symbiotically addressed "access to knowledge," patent protection, and economic development in the global South. Between 1961 and 1974, strong emphasis was placed in a variety of fora on technology transfer and IP rights, such that these were key components of a collaborative work program between the UN and WIPO, formalized by a working agreement concluded in 1964.[32] In response to a UN-commissioned study, WIPO more explicitly sought to interpose itself in shaping the nature and substance of the UN's approach to IP. WIPO's preliminary reactions to the issues expressed in the study identified concerns raised with respect to the capacity of developing countries to utilize domestic patent systems, the integration of limitations on patent rights, and the availability of compulsory licensing and monitoring of license agreements—all activities already taking place within WIPO's jurisdiction.[33] More tellingly, with respect to a question regarding holding an international conference on the problems associated with patents, WIPO responded that such a conference "would not seem to serve any useful purpose," but that if such a conference were to take place, it "should utilize the existing machinery of the International Union for the Protection of Industrial Property." It concluded that:

> On the whole, it would seem to follow from the U.N. Report that the problems that underdeveloped countries may have in connection with patents for inventions are mainly problems which can be solved by appropriate legislative and administrative measures. Since these measures are of a rather special technical nature, it seems to be the natural solution that under-developed countries should draw on the experience of BIRPI, the only intergovernmental body specialized in patent questions. . . .[34]

The success of WIPO's cooption of the UN initiatives was starkly manifest in the formal working agreement established between WIPO and the UN just seven months after issuance of the UN Report on patents. The Agreement opened up institutional space for WIPO to become involved at every level of the UN's work on IP;[35] this was reflected in later resolutions by UN agencies explicitly referencing cooperation with BIRPI and/or noting WIPO treaties as dominant frameworks for addressing the questions of development. In its efforts to install itself as the

---

International Trade Relations and Trade Policies Conducive to Development, UN Conference on Trade and Development (1964).

31. G.A. Res. 1713 (XVI), U.N. GAOR, 16th Sess., Supp. No. 17 at 20, U.N. Doc. A/5100 (Dec. 19, 1961).

32. Indus. Prop. (Vol. 3) at 207 (1964).

33. Indus. Prop., *supra* note 32, at 62.

34. Indus. Prop., *supra* note 32, at 63.

35. *See, e.g.*, Cooperation between the United Nations and BIRPI on Patents: 1966, Indus. Prop. (Vol. 6) at 46 (1967) (describing WIPO's presence at multiple UN events related to industrial property).

sole arbiter for the regulation of global IP norms, WIPO's activities assumed a particular orientation toward development—consistent with prevailing international development theory at the time—emphasizing IP protection as an indispensable element of national economic growth policy in a period dominated by the neoclassical model of economic growth that identified technological change as a primary source of economic development.[36] As a result, WIPO's (and vicariously the UN's) early IP "development" agenda emphasized the link between increase in foreign investment, enhanced industrialization potential, and technology transfer on one hand and the establishment of strong domestic IP regulatory frameworks on the other.

Today, the importance of general purpose technologies and the significance of technical change in the process of economic growth are hardly contestable. It is no secret, however, that the technology-centered postcolonial environment in which WIPO's early "development" work thrived was a failure for both developed countries, which invested in processes and institutions that spawned development projects, and for developing countries, which hoped to benefit from them.[37] Indeed, the interrelated goals and aspirations that generally define development—i.e., social goals, such as poverty reduction and gender equality; political goals, such as stable democratic governments; economic goals, such as sustainable increases in levels of GDP, strong domestic markets, and gains in technological progress; and

36. Robert M. Solow, *Technical Change and the Aggregate Production Function*, 39 REV. OF ECON. & STATISTICS 312 (1957). Of course, Schumpeter had earlier identified innovation as a source of change in the production function, highlighting innovation, credit, and profit maximization in a theory of economic development in which innovating firms occupied a central role. *See* J.A. SCHUMPETER, BUSINESS CYCLES, chaps. 3 & 4 (1939).

37. There has been extensive criticism of development theory, practice, and ideology particularly in fields such as anthropology and law. A leading body of work by anthropologist Arturo Escobar has influenced a generation of international law scholarship that applies methodologies of postmodern critical discourse to conclude that development as an idea and a practice has been a failure. *See, e.g.*, Ruth E. Gordon and Jon H. Sylvester, *Deconstructing Development*, 22 WIS. INT'L L.J. 1 (2004); Ruth Gordon, *Saving Failed States: Sometimes a Neocolonialist Notion*, 12 AM. U. J. INT'L L. & POL'Y 903 (1997). Other critiques of development often come to similar conclusions, regardless of the theoretical framework within which the examination occurs. The important work of Professor David Trubek on the law and development discourse is a leading example. But this is not to say that development has not been successful in all places at all times. For example, the dynamic growth of East Asian economies in the late 1980s and'90s clearly reflects development successes although most economists attribute this to factors other than technological progress. *See, e.g.*, Paul Krugman, *The Myth of Asia's Miracle*, 73(6) FOREIGN AFFAIRS, at 62 (1994); Gregory N. Mankiw, *The Growth of Nations*,1 BROOKINGS PAPERS ON ECON. ACTIVITY 275 (1995). Further, although improvements in most indicators of economic development have been limited, they nevertheless are evident throughout many developing countries.

legal goals, such as the protection of civil liberties and human rights—have yet to be realized in the vast majority of the world.[38]

Low rates of domestic innovation and foreign investment in many developing and least-developed countries (LDCs), their domestic IP laws notwithstanding, have underscored the complexity of economic development processes and the peripheral role of IP legislation in light of prevailing macroeconomic conditions.[39] Even as far back as 1961, studies on the effects of patent protection on development had urged caution, balance, and a healthy use of limitations and government regulations as levers to mediate access to technology by developing countries.[40] As has been noted by commentators today, foreign investments as well as local innovative activities involve long-term decisions not dependent singularly on the design of national IP frameworks, but rather on the overall economic and regulatory environment within a particular country or region.[41]

---

38. Indeed, one need look no further for evidence of the ongoing pursuit of core development goals than the UN Millennium Development Goals, which reflect several of the fundamental concerns that animated President Harry Truman's Point IV Program (poverty, economic malaise, prevalent disease), which most scholars pinpoint as the origin of the development movement. *See* UN, The UN Millennium Development Goals, available at http://www.un.org/millenniumgoals/(last visited April 20, 2008).

39. *See* Keith E. Maskus, *Intellectual Property Rights and Economic Development*, 32 Case W. Res. J. Int'l L. 471, 472 (2000).

40. The first major report on the effect of patents on technology transfer to developing countries was concluded under the auspices of the UN in 1961. The Report, requested by the Generally Assembly through Resolution 1713 (XVI) of 1961 which expressed the need for the international patent system to be applied in a way "as to take fully into account the special needs and requirements of the economic development of under-developed countries," examined in detail the institutional handicaps faced by developing countries in the implementation of domestic patent legislation as well as the role of technology transfer in stimulating domestic innovation and development. The fundamental problem to be resolved by the international system, according to the Report, is "the one-sided relationship under which the possession of know-how and capital resources are so unequally distributed." Among the chief concerns to be addressed in relation to development interests of DCs and LDCs, the Report identified, most importantly, (1) the need to facilitate institutional capacity of developing countries to regulate the patent system for the public interest and (2) the elimination of unduly restrictive features of licensing agreements which diminish the ability of local firms to acquire and disseminate patented innovations in domestic markets. Similar to the Development Agenda, the Report, noting the "legitimate interest [of developing and least-developed countries] in preventing excessive exploitation of their one-sided technological and financial dependence," called on the governments of developed States and the international community as whole to assist DCs and LDCs by adopting policies aimed at facilitating technology transfer. *See* UN, The Role of Patents in the Transfer of Technology to Under-Developed Countries, UN Doc. E/C.5/52/Rev.1 (February 14, 1964).

41. World Bank, World Development Report 2005: A Better Investment Climate for Everyone (2004); Bernard M. Hoekman, Keith Maskus, & Kamal Saggi, *Transfer of*

Moreover, market responsiveness to a given IP regime is country-, region-, and even sector-specific, presenting the danger that the uniformity inherent in any given multilateral IP consensus may not necessarily cohere with the particular cultural context in a country and thus may impede rather than stimulate innovative endeavors.[42]

Ultimately, the reasons for sustained underdevelopment are varied, exceedingly complex, and plainly irreducible to a single or manageable set of legal or economic prescriptions. Nevertheless, it is clear that technology plays a causal role in economic growth, and, accordingly, the importance of innovation for productivity and wealth generation has significant methodological implications for the implementation of the WIPO Development Agenda.

B. IP as Development: From the UN NIEO to the WIPO Development Agenda

For much of the post–World War II period, scholars from a variety of disciplines focused significant attention on the socio-cultural structure of colonialism,[43] analyzing its multivariate effects on the productive capacity of former colonies in relation to world markets. Consistent with prevailing economic growth theory[44] and the interests of the industrialized North, the international framework adopted a rigid commitment to the inevitability of technology transfer as a central means of fostering development in the newly independent countries of the South.[45] Enmeshed in this global project of technology transfer were complex assumptions about the *process* of technology production—namely that private production and

---

Technology to Developing Countries: Unilateral and Multilateral Policy Options, 33 WORLD DEVELOPMENT 1587 (2005) (noting that international technology transfer is predominantly affected by national policies).

42. *See, e.g.*, James Boyle, *A Manifesto on WIPO and the Future of Intellectual Property*, 2004 DUKE L. & TECH. REV. 9 (2004) (criticizing a one-size-fits-all IP system). *See also* W. Keller, *Absorptive Capacity: On the Creation and Acquisition of Technology in Development*, 49 J. OF DEV. ECON. 199 (1996) (noting that access to foreign technology alone does not increase growth rates in developing countries); Hoekman et. al., *Transfer of Technology to Developing Countries: Unilateral and Multilateral Policy Options, supra* note 41, at 1592 (citing studies that suggest that in poor countries, patents do not expand FDI flows; and the poorest countries are unlikely to benefit from strong IP rights).

43. For an excellent overview of contributions from various fields, see VERNON W. RUTTAN, SOCIAL SCIENCE KNOWLEDGE AND ECONOMIC DEVELOPMENT: AN INSTITUTIONAL DESIGN PERSPECTIVE (2003).

44. *See* Robert M. Solow, *A Contribution to the Theory of Economic Growth*, 70 QUARTERLY J. ECON. GROWTH 65 (1956). *See also supra* note 36.

45. The Draft Code of Conduct on Transfer of Technology is a leading example of the commitment by international organizations to technology transfer as a key component of promoting development. *See generally* INTERNATIONAL TRANSFER OF TECHNOLOGY: THE ORIGINS AND AFTERMATH OF THE UNITED NATIONS NEGOTIATIONS ON A DRAFT CODE OF CONDUCT (S. Patel et al., eds., 2001); W. FIKENTSCHER, THE DRAFT INTERNATIONAL CODE OF CONDUCT ON THE TRANSFER OF TECHNOLOGY (1980). *See also* infra note 64.

ownership of technology was an indispensable element of innovation[46]—and presumptions about the *efficacy* of technology transfer, namely that technology generated in foreign markets would invariably add value to and facilitate the growth process in developing countries.[47] These two cardinal features dominated the global institutional framework under the auspices of the UN, which in 1974 adopted a Declaration on the Establishment of a New International Economic Order (NIEO)[48] founded in part on the principle of "*giving* developing countries access to the achievements of modern science and technology and promoting the transfer of technology."[49] Here, then, was the first structured articulation of an "access to knowledge" (A2K) principle reflecting development aspirations and projecting strategies for fulfillment implicitly linked to the design of the IP system.

Broadly, the NIEO principles acknowledged political rights of self-determination for developing countries[50] and then imposed obligations on developed countries to provide economic and technological support to them.[51] Accompanying the NIEO Declaration was a plan of action detailing modalities of implementation on a wide range of issues directly linked to addressing the objectives articulated in the Declaration.[52] Within this plan, five specific action points were identified regarding technology transfer: (1) to develop an international code of conduct

46. A WIPO publication aimed at "students in the developing countries of Asia and the Pacific, who are most affected by the unavailability of suitable teaching literature on intellectual property" states that a patent "constitutes an incentive for inventiveness and innovative activity [and] also creates a favorable climate for the transfer of technology. . . ." *See* WIPO, Background Reading Material on Intellectual Property, at 28, WIPO Doc. 659(E) (1988). *See also generally* WIPO, The Role of Industrial Property in Economic Development, WIPO Doc. WIPO/IP/ACC/86/5 (1997).

47. Pedro Roffe, *Comment I, Technology Transfer on the International Agenda*, in International Public Goods & Transfer of Technology Under a Globalized Intellectual Property Regime, *supra* note 16, at 257–58 (noting that many elements necessary for the successful transfer of technology were not considered in the global debate that dominated the 1970s).

48. Declaration on the Establishment of a New International Economic Order, G.A. Res. 3201, U.N. GAOR, 6th Special Sess., Supp. No. 1, UN Doc. A/9559 (May 1, 1974) [hereinafter NIEO Declaration], available at http://www.un-documents.net/s6r3201.htm (last visited April 20, 2008); *see also* Charter of Economic Rights and Duties of States, adopted by G.A. Res. 3281, 29 U.N. GAOR, Supp. (No. 31) 50, UN Doc. A/9631 (1974), available at http://www.vilp.de/Enpdf/e162.pdf (last visited April 20, 2008).

49. NIEO Declaration, *supra* note 48, para. 4(p) [emphasis added].

50. *See* NIEO Declaration, *supra* note 48, paras. 4(a), (d), (e).

51. *See* NIEO Declaration, *supra* note 48, paras. 4(k)–(t).

52. *See* General Assembly, Resolution 3202 (S-VI)—Programme of Action on the Establishment of a New International Economic Order, May 1, 1974, UN Doc. A/RES/S-6/3202, available at http://www.un-documents.net/s6r3202.htm (last visited April 20, 2008) [hereinafter NIEO Programme of Action].

governing technology transfer;[53] (2) to give access on improved terms to modern technology and to adapt the technology to developing countries;[54] (3) to increase levels of assistance from developed to developing countries in research and development (R&D) programs and in the creation of indigenous technologies;[55] (4) to tailor commercial practices that govern technology transfer to the specific environments of developing countries while also preventing the abuse of rights by owners;[56] and (5) to promote international cooperation in R&D in the exploitation, conservation, and utilization of natural resources and energy.[57]

Like the principles themselves, each action plan was structured around the idea of dependency on developed countries to source the technology needs of developing countries. No basis was identified for determining how countries and/or private firms could or should implement these goals. Instead, however, the private realm of proprietary rights was highlighted within the UN, which noted that global patent protection had "contributed to technical research and, therefore to international and national industrial progress"[58] and that such private rights could not be forcibly directed in aid of development.[59] The General Assembly entrusted its considerations of the role of patents in development to WIPO.[60] The assumption that there existed no legal or strategic alternatives for addressing the technology needs of developing countries occasioned a reliance on the private rules of IP protection as a limitation on what governments should do to ensure access to technology across geographical borders. By requiring developed countries to facilitate access to technology by developing countries, the NIEO fortuitously buttressed the legitimacy of the global IP system as a rational justification to aid fulfillment of the NIEO's development agenda, reinforcing the demand for global IP rules and constraining the power of developing countries to act outside of the IP paradigm.

In contrast to the modern A2K movement,[61] the rudimentary vision of access to knowledge articulated in the NIEO and its associated instruments[62] explicitly conceded the efficacy of the proprietary nature of technology and thus sought

53. Id., § IV(a).
54. Id., § IV(b).
55. Id., § IV(c).
56. Id., § IV(d).
57. Id., § IV(e).
58. G.A. Res. 1713 (XVI), *supra* note 31.
59. This latter point was made by some developed countries in response to the principle adopted by the UN Conference on Trade and Development which provided that scientific achievements and technological developments be made accessible under favorable conditions to developing countries. *See* MILAN BULAJIC, PRINCIPLES OF INTERNATIONAL DEVELOPMENT LAW 99 (1986).
60. Id. at 92–93.
61. *See* Kapczynski, *supra* note 9, at 821–39.
62. *See generally* BULAJIC, *supra* note 59.

not to transform the established rules of IP regulation, but rather to restructure the relationships among States by articulating a legal framework in which considerations of power in determining the prospects of States to negotiate terms of participation in the global economy would be less dominant.[63] However, by situating technology at the heart of the development process, protecting the system of technology production invariably became a necessary and central preoccupation of development assistance and support managed through a network of international organizations, including WIPO. The failed negotiations over the Draft Code of Conduct for Technology Transfer[64] was an epiphenomenon linked to much deeper unresolved challenges of how legal doctrines of sovereignty and equality could logically find meaning in a global market in which the productive capacity of most developing countries was viewed as being dependent on economic and political support from the developed world.

Yet historical accounts of dense innovation periods suggest that innovation strategically occurred outside of the patent system. In environments or sectors where "learning by doing" represented greater efficiencies in communicating new skills, or where technical change required collaborative applications of specialized knowledge, patents were not considered ideal investments. Thus, through the late 18th century in England, for example, agricultural innovations were rarely patented; this was also the case in the mining industry.[65] Both sectors, although significant in size, were nevertheless enhanced by innovations without being governed by patenting activity.[66] The point is that patents represent particular incentives for agents to capture or hold a share of the market only in particularized contexts. For example, IP protection appears to impact economic growth more positively in relatively open markets when competitive frameworks are sufficient to stimulate successive innovation.[67] These recent findings are consistent with historical patterns suggesting that patents were sought more often in highly capitalized and geographically concentrated sectors and in areas where competition could be cabined through a monopoly grant. In areas where market entry was sufficiently difficult due to the structure of the market or industry (e.g., strict requirements for apprenticeships in commercial brewing in the early

63. The NIEO Declaration noted political, social, and technological disparity between the industrialized countries and developing countries and then listed 20 principles to address these concerns. *See* NIEO Declaration, *supra* n. 48, paras. 1–4.

64. The United Nations Conference on an International Code of Conduct on the Transfer of Technology, Draft International Code of Conduct on the Transfer of Technology (1985 version), UN Doc. TD/CODE TOT/47, available at http://stdev.unctad.org/compendium/documents/TD.CODE.doc (last visited April 20, 2008).

65. Christine MacLeod, Inventing the Industrial Revolution: The English Patent System, 1660–1800, 98–102 (1988).

66. Id. *See also generally* id., chapter 6.

67. David M. Gould & William C. Gruben, *The Role of Intellectual Property Rights in Economic Growth*, 48 J. Dev. Econ. 323 (1996).

18th century in England combined with significant capital requirements), patenting was not an inevitable strategy to protect investments in innovation.[68] In short, proprietary interests are only one particular form of incentive for innovation and, increasingly, such property-like entitlements are giving way to contracts and other private arrangements as alternative forms of protection, with serious implications for the public interest and access to technology.

C. Back to the Future? "Access to Knowledge" in the NIEO and the WIPO Development Agenda

It is now well established that the NIEO agenda failed both as an organizing principle of international economic relations and as a pragmatic set of projects around which growth in developing countries could be structured. For sure, IP regulation is only a small piece of the larger failure of the development movement of the 1970s. Nevertheless, the centrality of IP to the national aspirations of developing countries and the social aspirations of citizens in both developed and developing countries still require serious attention to new considerations that govern the international IP system.

In evaluating the NIEO within the context of the WIPO Development Agenda, striking similarities are immediately evident. Like the NIEO, the Development Agenda is framed as a regime of special and differential (S&D) treatment for DCs and LDCs. Initiated by developing countries, with Brazil again at the lead, the proposal for a WIPO Development Agenda challenges the passive orthodoxy that positive welfare gains are inexorably a byproduct of IP protection. Like the Brazil-initiated resolution almost half a century ago, the various proposals focus squarely on the core IP treaties administered by WIPO and the absence of any explicit identification of how IP rights can and will complement the objectives of other international regimes or foster the goals of the global public order with respect to improving the lives of millions around the world. Finally, the WIPO Development Agenda challenges the constitutional context of WIPO's institutional isolationism, requiring the Organization to meaningfully integrate the objectives of IP protection with the rights which serve as means to those ends.

Although the political similarities between the NIEO and the Development Agenda are powerful reflections of a deeply pathological process in the construction of IP relations between developed and developing countries, the Development Agenda in my opinion does far more to retool the basic levers of the IP system.

Historical patterns of IP regulation in the global economy depict a pervasive divide between developed and developing countries. In this schema, proposals for new norm-setting activities originate from developed countries—which presumptively

68. MacLeod, Inventing the Industrial Revolution: The English Patent System, *supra* note 65, at 108–19. *See also* Trotter Hardy, *Property (and Copyright) in Cyberspace*, 1996 U. Chi. Legal F. 217, 220–28 (discussing a similar issue in the context of copyright law where state of the art limitations affect the desirability/need for entitlement-like protection).

benefit from the new rules—and are resisted by developing countries, which view new norm-setting activities as attempts to impede opportunities for their domestic firms and citizens to benefit from new innovations by raising the costs of access. This classic representation of the political economy of global IP relations is in reality a caricature of a complex set of political and economic conditions, in which coalitions of self-interested transnational private parties whose influence over domestic governments[69] has been strategically parlayed on the multilateral stage, have overtaken the global IP lawmaking process. The interest in expansive IP rights has been leveraged as much to overcome the consequences of increased competition from newly industrializing countries such as Brazil, India, and China, as to override constitutional constraints on national IP lawmaking by appealing to a hierarchical privilege enjoyed by international law.[70]

New modes of technology production; sharply decreased returns on investment in technology as a result of cheap imitation costs; shifts in production centers aimed to exploit low labor costs; and differentiated regulatory standards in areas such as the environment, tax, and competition law have upset the traditional North–South representation of stakes in the global IP system, transforming conventional State-centered concerns to consumer-based expectations regarding the content and scope of IP law. In this new economy, the beneficiaries of the WIPO Development Agenda are not political units of States as such, but instead an uncontained, widespread, and vastly diverse consumer base, including firms adopting technological platforms based on Open Source, Internet Service Providers (ISPs), and other content providers whose business strategies often require the ability to work seamlessly across national borders, and individual users whose participation in networked social spaces encourages and facilitates the economic value of creativity in the information age.[71] If the WIPO Development Agenda is viewed not merely as a series of activities but rather as a coordinated

69. *See* Ruth L. Okediji, *Public Welfare and the Role of the WTO: Reconsidering the TRIPS Agreement*, 17 Emory Int'l L. Rev. 819 (2003); Susan Sell, Private Power, Public Law: The Globalization of Intellectual Property Rights (2003).

70. *See generally* Ruth L. Okediji, *Toward an International Fair Use Doctrine*, 39 Colum. J. Transnat'l L. 75, 136–51 (2000); Pamela Samuelson, *The U.S. Digital Agenda at WIPO*, 37 Va. J. Int'l L. 369, 373–74 (1997).

71. *See, e.g.*, Thomas Rogers & Andrew Szamosszegi, Fair Use in the U.S. Economy: Economic Contribution of Industries Relying on Fair Use, a study prepared for the Computer & Communications Industry Association (2007), available at http://www.ccianet.org/artmanager/uploads/1/FairUseStudy-Sep12.pdf (last visited April 20, 2008) (concluding that in 2006 the "fair use industries"—a diverse group including, among others, computer and peripheral equipment manufacturers, audio and video equipment manufacturers, Internet publishers, ISPs, Web search companies, and electronic shopping companies—generated revenues of $4.5 trillion, value added of $2.2 trillion, a payroll of $1.2 trillion, and exports of $194 billion. As such, the fair use industries accounted for 16.6% of the U.S. current dollar GDP and 18.3% of U.S. economic growth).

call to restructure the traditional IP paradigm to reflect new economic and social realities related to ICTs, the beneficiaries of this prospective legal change are not only historically disadvantaged nations but indeed the global public. It is imperative that developed countries recognize their own immediate and direct stake in the success of the Development Agenda. Unlike the technology transfer provisions of the NIEO, the sole beneficiaries of which were developing countries of the postcolonial South, developed countries cannot simply be mere passive suppliers of knowledge goods under the Development Agenda. Instead, they must be engaged in the substantive work of restructuring the international IP system to be less dominated by the proprietary interests of a few in the interests of the welfare benefits made possible by enhanced competition and less barriers to entry for potential new participants in the transnational innovation system.

A defining characteristic of the WIPO Development Agenda is its demand on the doctrinal space of the current IP system. Unlike the NIEO, the Development Agenda pivots on the central question of how IP doctrines are developed internationally to fill a space that has traditionally been occupied by States. By contextualizing the call for a Development Agenda as one in which norm-setting exercises must reflect utilitarian values, the Agenda must be understood as a bold effort to overcome systemic market failures in the interactions between developed and developing countries over the terms of global IP protection and the importance of admitting new perspectives from non-state actors to be more effectively represented in norm-setting activities. In effect, although the Agenda does reflect S&D treatment principles, it takes an "S&D-plus" approach by purporting to transform the political basis for differentiating between the effects of IP in developed and developing countries into one in which the normative oeuvre of WIPO's activities can be represented as a foundational aspect of ensuring that benefits of IP protection can be equally accessed by all members of the global system.

To this end, as an administrative matter, the WIPO Development Agenda cannot be structured as an adjunct to WIPO's so-called "main" work of promoting the protection of IP through rights-promoting activities, with minimal consideration of other normative elements of the IP system or of the recognized linkages between the global IP framework and other trade-related regimes. Indeed, reading the proposal for a WIPO Development Agenda as an integral part of the Agenda itself precludes such structural marginalization. Further, the activities formally adopted by the Agenda should not be viewed as discrete windows in which "development" projects aimed singularly at assisting developing countries take place, but rather—given the ways in which globalization has transformed the landscape of interests affected by IP and in light of emerging forms of scientific and creative collaboration—the challenge of the Development Agenda is for a new understanding and reformulation of WIPO's charter and operational processes. Both have been used in the recent past to excuse the bureaucracy from engaging in norm-setting activities that explore ways to balance competing interests between owners and users, as well as the development potential of new innovation platforms such as Open Source.[72] Relying on procedural form, WIPO successfully avoided engaging such new opportunities and evoked its governance rules to insulate it from pressure to do so.[73] WIPO's activities under the Development Agenda must not be structured as a specialized and fixed "development" mandate aimed at a discrete set of state actors, but rather as a broad context which demands constant attention to and evaluation of the overall costs associated with particular global IP norms, combined with openness toward emerging models of innovation.

Moreover, as the Development Agenda proposal states,[74] WIPO's operations should reflect the important ramifications of the relationship between the global regulation of IP and relevant IP-related regimes and feature a framework for the collaboration of the Organization with relevant international bodies facilitative of the Agenda's objectives. For example, as noted by commentators, the relationship between WIPO and the UN should in the future translate into a balanced approach toward global IP regulation.[75] Yet given the mutations of the UN-WIPO collaboration under the NIEO and similar initiatives, it is important to be mindful that inter-regime collaboration will not lead, ineluctably, to a better-mediated IP regulatory system. Indeed, in some cases, inter-institutional collaboration could serve simply to reinforce the ascendancy of private interests in global markets. Nevertheless, the moral force of the Development Agenda undoubtedly does provide a window of opportunity for overcoming the historical failure of WIPO's inter-regime initiatives, and unlike the NIEO, may result in retaining the participation of other IGOs in the process of global IP policymaking.

III. IP AND THE FUTURE OF DEVELOPMENT: THE SEVERAL POSSIBLE FACES OF THE WIPO DEVELOPMENT AGENDA

The role of the Development Agenda in economic growth depends largely on determinations of what the Agenda represents, which in turn will determine how it might be leveraged. Is the Agenda a political statement accompanied by a series of programs for implementation much like the NIEO? Or is it a negotiated

---

72. On Open Source, see generally GLYN MOODY, REBEL CODE (2001); STEVEN WEBER, THE SUCCESS OF OPEN SOURCE (2004); Eric von Hippel & Georg von Krogh, *Open Source Software and the "Private-Collective" Innovation Model: Issues for Organization Science*, 14 ORG. SCI. 209 (2003).

73. *See* Boyle, *A Manifesto on WIPO and the Future of Intellectual Property*, *supra* note 42.

74. *See* Development Agenda Proposal, *supra* note 2.

75. *See, e.g.*, Boyle, *A Manifesto on WIPO and the Future of Intellectual Property*, *supra* note 42; Margaret Chon, *Intellectual Property and the Development Divide*, 27 CARDOZO L. REV. 2821 (2006).

series of guiding principles to assist WIPO in rendering more meaningful service to the majority of its Member States?

Formally, the Agenda is an operational program in WIPO within which a set of 45 recommendations,[76] set forth as prescriptive guidelines, explicitly integrate concerns most commonly expressed by DCs and LDCs into WIPO's work program and activities. Organized in six clusters, the recommendations address: (1) the nature and quality of WIPO's technical assistance programs;[77] (2) norm-setting activities reflective of flexibilities, public policy concerns, and the importance of the public domain; (3) technology transfer and ICTs; (4) assessments by WIPO of its development activities, including the impact of IP on development concerns; (5) matters of institutional cooperation with other IGOs, in particular to promote openness and transparency in WIPO's activities; and (6) a general provision for WIPO to carry out its activities with a view to fostering a dynamic balance between the objectives of IP regulation and the means by which those objectives are accomplished.[78]

Politically, the Agenda represents the startling effect of collaborative networks and transborder coalitions of non-state actors on a hierarchical bureaucratic institution long considered the primary domain of powerful private actors whose interests were protected by the major developed countries. That an explicit affront on the rights-centered focus of WIPO's constitution should succeed even on paper was rightly regarded as a landmark achievement by a network of actors whose penetration of and influence on WIPO's core functions has long been stymied by procedural rules directed at insulating the institution from external pressures. As a strategic matter, then, the Agenda is an official opening of WIPO's ideological space in which concrete actions can be tabled for inclusion in the global agenda. At a minimum, the Agenda is an instrument for legitimizing demands for particular activities that may otherwise be deemed inconsistent with WIPO's traditional functions. The Agenda imports new obligations to attend specifically to the costs and effects of particular activities on DCs and LDCs, and by so doing, to consider alternative narratives of the innovation process. However, given WIPO's rigid adherence to rights protection, how might the Development Agenda disrupt the Organization's sense of its global mandate

76. WIPO, The 45 Agreed Recommendations under the WIPO Development Agenda, available at http://www.wipo.int/ip-development/en/agenda/cdip_recommendations.html (last visited April 22, 2008).

77. The focus on the quality of WIPO's technical assistance programs and on a balanced approach toward global IP policymaking is indeed a key feature that distinguishes the Development Agenda from the NIEO Declaration. On the relevance of technical assistance for development, see Sisule F. Musungu, *Towards a Development Oriented IPR Agenda: TRIPS-plus, Technical Assistance and Technology Transfer*, ICTSD/UNCTAD Bellagio Series of Dialogues, September, 2003.

78. *See* id.

and how might this disruption be rationalized broadly in the international setting given the multiplicity of actors involved in global IP lawmaking? There are several possible faces of the Development Agenda which I briefly describe below.

A. WIPO's Constitutional Amendment

Despite the intensity of global political organization focused on an array of IP issues, WIPO remains the premier international institution for IP norm-setting. Accordingly, the Development Agenda could be interpreted as a constitutional amendment, transforming the Organization's character as an administrative entity governing only in the interest of stronger rights into an agency responsible for developing norms that effectuate IP's exceptional commitment to the advancement of the public interest. The Development Agenda thus makes WIPO accountable to the public, and not just its Member States, for positively demonstrating ways in which its activities broadly reflect, support, and improve technology innovation, diffusion, and welfare promotion.

B. Ensuring WIPO's Future Relevance

Complementing the constitutional amendment theory, the Development Agenda could be viewed as an explicit expansion of WIPO's mandate necessary for ensuring that the Organization remains relevant in the future. Such expansion could result in WIPO's involvement in initiating new means of promoting rewards for innovation, while also facilitating new approaches to dealing with barriers to access to new technologies. This would require a methodological shift; the characteristic response of proposing and crafting treaties to address new problems as a dominant form of lawmaking cannot be sustained in a digital environment, where rapid advances in technology far outpace the cumbersome process of international policymaking. WIPO must become more agile and adept in responding to novel issues that arise in global technology markets and in addressing new patterns of IP use that may require incremental resolutions more amenable to soft-law mechanisms.[79] The Development Agenda is an important opportunity for WIPO to overcome a path-dependency, which binds its operational model to hard-law outcomes, and to instead retool its procedures to strengthen its ability to embrace and use the vast range of modern international law instruments,[80] many of which have important advantages over the

79. *See, e.g.*, P. Bernt Hugenholtz & Ruth L. Okediji, Conceiving an International Instrument on Limitations and Exceptions to Copyright, a study sponsored by the Open Society Institute (2008), at 44–46, 49, available at http://www.ivir.nl/publicaties/hugenholtz/finalreport2008.pdf (last visited April 13, 2008).

80. *See, e.g.*, Pierre Marie Dupuy, *The Impact of Legal Instruments Adopted by UNESCO on General International Law*, in ABDUL K. YUSUF (ed.), STANDARD-SETTING IN UNESCO,

traditional treaty model and, even in the softest of soft-law incarnations, have far ranging positive effects in fostering compliance with global norms.[81]

C. A Call for Strategic Integration and Coherence in IP Administration

Third, the Development Agenda could be viewed as a call for the development of a global IP policy that coheres more meaningfully with other international law regimes. This would involve more deliberate interaction between WIPO and the larger international community, including NGOs, as well as a sustained focus on understanding the depth and impact of linkages between IP protection and global concerns such as the environment or public health. But this argument is not just about the importance of IP norms reflecting and accommodating social welfare values, whether intrinsic to IP such as privacy and freedom of speech, or extrinsic to it such as using human rights as a buffer against the impact of strong global IP rights.[82] All these functions of coherence are undoubtedly relevant in evaluations of how human welfare goals could be advanced in an integrated world economy. Rather, one of the cardinal lessons from the NIEO is the implausibility that a single issue—no matter how central to the stimulation of economic development (such as technological progress)—can fully address the spectrum of challenges created by the production and consumption patterns of an insatiable global consumer base. Scholars increasingly point to the inadequacies (and inefficiencies) of a uniform IP system[83] and there is already some evidence that in more mature IP systems, regulatory agencies do in fact differentiate between fields of innovation in the application of presumptively uniform standards.[84]

This view of the Development Agenda as a call for strategic coherence would insist on reexamination of the costs of applying minimum rights to all IP-related areas in light of the relative importance of some fields, such as agriculture for example, for global welfare. Developing specialized rules for countries has been a forte of the global IP system for many decades;[85] surely, it would not be impossible to

---

VOLUME I: NORMATIVE ACTION IN EDUCATION, SCIENCE AND CULTURE, ESSAYS IN COMMEMORATION OF THE SIXTIETH ANNIVERSARY OF UNESCO, 351–63 (2007).

81. *See* id.; *see also* Hugenholtz & Okediji, Conceiving an International Instrument on Limitations and Exceptions to Copyright, *supra* note 79, at 44–46.

82. *See* Okediji, *Securing Intellectual Property Objectives: New Approaches to Human Rights Considerations, supra* note 12.

83. Hoekman et al., *Transfer of Technology to Developing Countries: Unilateral and Multilateral Policy Options, supra* note 41, at 1594 (citing studies that emphasize a freedom to experiment with regulatory policies as important to DCs and LDCs and noting that "detailed international policy harmonization is inappropriate").

84. *See, e.g.*, Dan L. Burk & Mark A. Lemley, *Is Patent Law Technology-Specific?*, 17 BERKELEY TECH. L.J. 1155 (2002).

85. *See, e.g.*, Mihály Ficsor, *The WIPO "Internet Treaties:" The United States as the Driver; The United States as the Main Source of Obstruction—As Seen by an Antirevolutionary Central European*, 6 J. MARSHALL REV. INTELL. PROP. L. 17, 29 (2006).

develop new specialized rules to manage the balance between incentives and access for particular areas of technology to promote the production of public goods. The strongest appeal for interpreting the Development Agenda as a directive for integrated IP norm-setting is that a decrease in the supply of global public goods imposes costs far beyond the IP system to the very components of the production process on which the global economy most tenuously rests. Perhaps developed countries' ultimate acquiescence to the Development Agenda reflects a preliminary concession to the political, social, and economic costs of IP transactions that simultaneously discourage market entry for new participants and undermine the ability to address basic human needs.

IV. THE WIPO DEVELOPMENT AGENDA AS A CUMULATIVE REFLECTION ON INSTITUTIONAL COMMITMENT

The absence of development gains from WIPO's past norm-setting activities and the blatant failure of development-oriented treaty provisions negotiated within WIPO (e.g., the Berne Appendix),[86] coupled with an orchestrated (if diplomatic) resistance to new models of collaborative innovation such as Open Source frameworks,[87] have reinforced perceptions that WIPO possesses neither the political capacity nor the institutional commitment to embrace the major task of shaping the global IP system to facilitate access to the transformative power of technology and knowledge. Reinterpreting WIPO's charter in light of the Development

86. *See, e.g.*, Ruth L. Okediji, The International Copyright System: Limitations, Exceptions and Public Interest Considerations for Developing Countries, UNCTAD-ICTSD Project on IPRs and Sustainable Development T 13–14 (March 2006), at 15–16, available at http://www.unctad.org/en/docs/iteipc200610_en.pdf (last visited April 20, 2008) (providing an overview of the Berne Appendix and discussing its failure to facilitate developing country access to needed copyrighted materials).

87. For an overview of the Open Source movement, *see, e.g.*, MOODY, REBEL CODE, *supra* note 72; WEBER, THE SUCCESS OF OPEN SOURCE *supra* note 72; von Hippel & von Krogh, *Open Source Software and the "Private-Collective" Innovation Model: Issues for Organization Science*, *supra* note 72. *See also* Kenneth J. Rodriguez, *Closing the Door on Open Source: Can the General Public License Save Linux and Other Open Source Software?*, 5 J. HIGH TECH. L. 403, 404 (2005); Carina Dennis, *Biologists Launch "Open-Source Movement,"* 431 NATURE 494 (2004); Josh Lerner & Jean Tirole, *The Scope of Open Source Licensing* (Nat'l Bureau of Econ. Research, Working Paper No. 9363, 2002), available at http://www.nber.org/papers/w9363 (last visited April 13, 2008); Thomas Goetz, *Open Source Everywhere*, WIRED, November 2003, available at http://www.wired.com/wired/archive/11.11/opensource.html (last visited April 20, 2008); Stephen M. Maurer, Arti Rai, & Andrej Sali, *Finding Cures for Tropical Diseases: Is Open Source an Answer?*, 1 PLOS MED. 183 (2004), available at http://www.tropicaldisease.org/documents/MauRaiSal_PLOS2004.pdf (last visited April 20, 2008); Kapczynski, *supra* note 9, at 830–32.

Agenda offers new opportunities—and new risks—in experimenting with a new transnational social space.

Digital networks and information technologies that characterize the new digital age have altered greatly the structural limitations to access to foreign technology by developing countries that were prevalent in the industrial era by virtue of limitations imposed by the state of the technical art. Geographical distances that affected the transfer of associated knowledge necessary to effectively utilize machines and tools are today less pertinent to the capacity of the developing world to appropriate foreign technology. Instead, information networks have greatly increased the scope and rate of diffusion of newly generated technical information to the developing world; concerns of adaptability and suitability of new technology to effectively address problems in the developing world are less applicable with respect to many knowledge-mediated products pervasive in global markets today. Moreover, new forms of collaborative innovation likely resonate more consistently with cultural endowments in many developing countries, potentially signaling a future in which firms in those countries will have unprecedented opportunities to participate in global technology markets as both suppliers and buyers. Finally, the rapid pace of technical change in the digital era, combined with the ease of copying and communicating across national boundaries, has vastly shortened technological lead time that allowed firms in developed countries to exploit proprietary privileges associated with the IP system.

All these factors (and more) combined have dramatically increased the pressure on the global IP system, supported by bilateral and regional trade agreements in which stronger legal entitlements have become the indispensable tools to sustain lead time and to enlarge the prospects for maximum returns to investment in innovation. In other words, just as technological developments have made it easier to facilitate increases in the global knowledge base, and as globalization has deepened the economic interdependence of markets, maximalist IP regulation seeks to reintroduce the inefficiencies of the industrial age to constrain the great possibilities of the digital age with its promise of welfare gains for all countries, not just developing ones. Indeed, the increased skepticism over arguments that maximum IP protection is a prerequisite for advancing global welfare must be transformed into rigorous examination of empirical economic data, which not only suggests that increasingly strong IP rights impede innovation but also portends the widespread adverse effect of maximum rights on the provision of global public goods. It is certainly no secret that the often overstated claims of innovating firms about the costs of innovation and the costs of piracy mask the larger costs associated with decreases in competition and an overall reduction in innovation as a result of restrictions on downstream users of technology. In this environment, the WIPO Development Agenda is more than just a call for reform of the global IP system in favor of a particular group of countries. Instead, it may very well be a clarion call for a reevaluation of the knowledge economy and a new and different role for IP in the production of knowledge in a global economy.

V. CONCLUSION

Utilitarian justifications for IP are traditionally associated with common law jurisdictions, but it is now clear that IP protection in the global arena explicitly links multilateral protection with the promise of development. In other words, IP rights are a means to promote and accomplish social and economic ends. The preamble to the TRIPS Agreement reflects this unbroken relationship between development goals and IP protection by recognizing that "the protection and enforcement of intellectual property rights should contribute to the promotion of technological innovation and to the transfer and dissemination of technology."[88] In short, whether explicitly or implicitly, IP regulation has featured prominently as an integral part of development thought, practice, and policy for well over three decades, but with far less agreement or strategic plan for precisely how IP might deliver on these promises. The WIPO Development Agenda may be an important step to fill this historic vacuum.

To learn from and overcome the failures of the NIEO, the WIPO Development Agenda must be more than a work program, a series of activities that "assist" underdeveloped members of the international community to appreciate in the abstract the value of IP protection, and more than a method for identifying discrete success stories about how IP has benefited particular segments of a handful of developing States. Rather, the WIPO Development Agenda must be understood and implemented as a transformative instrument calling for innovative reform in an environment energized by the promise of technology-enabled human development that could benefit disparate regions around the world.

The WIPO Development Agenda is clearly much more that the sum of its 45 recommendations. Fundamentally, it is a charter that supplements the WIPO Convention and reconstitutes the narrow conception of what it means to "promote the protection of intellectual property" with a substantive vision that includes the integration of IP into a broader investigation of how social welfare is best secured and advanced in the global regulatory space.

---

88. TRIPS Agreement, *supra* note 6, pmbl. *See also* id., art. 7 ("The protection and enforcement of intellectual property rights should contribute to the promotion of technological innovation and to the transfer and dissemination of technology, to the mutual advantage of producers and users of technological knowledge and in a manner conducive to social and economic welfare, and to a balance of rights and obligations.").

7. THE WIPO DEVELOPMENT AGENDA
A Cautionary Note

KEITH E. MASKUS*

I. INTRODUCTION

Among the specialized UN agencies, the World Intellectual Property Organization (WIPO) has had a unique recent history. Prior to the conclusion of the Agreement on Trade-Related Aspects of Intellectual Property Rights (TRIPS) at the World Trade Organization in 1995, WIPO was a quiet backwater. It was charged mainly with facilitating the negotiation of international conventions, publishing some data serials, and maintaining a repository of information on laws governing intellectual property rights (IPR) in its member countries.

Its other function was to provide expertise, through the promulgation of "model laws," to national governments considering reforms in their IPR systems. These model laws invariably were based heavily on advanced systems found in the industrialized countries, especially in Western Europe. The laws were sold as pristine embodiments of the best legal scholarship, and it was considered best just to accept them, unquestioningly. The professional lawyers at WIPO could hardly be faulted for this attitude, for it was equally common in the intellectual property (IP) agencies of national governments and private practitioners of the time, not to mention law schools. This notion, that the "law of intellectual property is supreme" and economic analysis of its provisions is beside the point—or even harmful—holds considerable sway even today.

When I first wrote about economic aspects of patent reforms in 1990, there were just a few dedicated economists who considered IPR as a subject in great need of rigorous theoretical and empirical analysis *as an aspect of globalization and development*. Virtually no one had paid attention to this issue prior to then, and our initial efforts were met with bemusement or disdain. Here is a good example. In negotiating

* Contact: Keith E. Maskus, Department of Economics, UCB 256, University of Colorado, Boulder CO 80309-0256. Telephone 303-492-7588; fax 303-492-8969; email maskus@colorado.edu.

TRIPS, the *demandeurs* from the United States and the European Union consistently made strong claims that stronger and more harmonized IPR systems in the world would expand international trade by reducing the costs of trade. But how could they know this? There was no systematic evidence on this point—not even good economic theory. In 1995, I published, with a colleague, the first serious empirical study of this question.[1] This paper was the foundation for what is now a deep and sophisticated empirical literature relating IPR policies around the world to flows of trade, investment, licensing, and knowledge. And yet true believers do not think the evidence compelling, simply because IPR regulations stem from "sound legal principles," and their economic implications are beside the point.

In any event, WIPO has been hit by a train since TRIPS was concluded. Policymakers, non-governmental organizations, the media, and even many legal scholars have awakened to the fact that IP regulations have rather fundamental implications for the processes of economic development. The relative inability of the WTO process to move forward in the Doha Round means that it has not served as a sensible forum for advocating global reforms. WIPO, however, has been forced to come to grips with the question of its relevance as a purveyor of stronger global laws at a time when much of the developing world wants serious attention paid to fitting IPR into overall development policies. The greatest, but by no means only, expression of this sea change in attitudes is the push to include a "Development Agenda" in WIPO's philosophy and operations.

It is a difficult match to make. To introduce a development-regarding philosophy into an institution that had paid attention only to bureaucratic lawmaking is naturally uncomfortable. WIPO is short on economic expertise, and serious analysis of IPR and development is tough under the best of circumstances. The agency increasingly will find itself straddling the middle ground between two masters: national advocates of strong harmonization (e.g., the United States) and countries that prefer slower approaches to raising technology protection. For WIPO to emerge from this tussle a professional institution with considerable expertise and knowledge is to be hoped for but perhaps not to be expected.

In this chapter, I elaborate on these potential problems by discussing whether a serious commitment to the "Development Agenda" may overwhelm WIPO and considering the international costs of such an outcome.

II. THE "DEVELOPMENT AGENDA"

The TRIPS Agreement committed all WTO member nations to implement and enforce substantive minimum standards of protection in a nearly comprehensive

1. Keith E. Maskus and Mohan Penubarti, "How Trade-Related are Intellectual Property Rights?" *Journal of International Economics*, vol. 39, nos. 3–4 (November 1995): 227–248.

range of IPR, including patents, copyrights, trademarks, designs, plant varieties, and other elements.[2] Adopted in 1995, with differentiated phase-in periods for developing countries, TRIPS invoked virtually immediate critical comment. An early and influential statement came from the United Nations Conference on Trade and Development (UNCTAD), which pointed out that IPR standards were traditionally the purview of individual countries and naturally varied by level of economic development.[3] That report also spelled out a number of "flexibilities" in IPR permitted by TRIPS and called on developing countries to take advantage of them. Even more influential was the report by the U.K. Commission on Intellectual Property Rights.[4] Besides taking a strongly skeptical view of the potential for TRIPS standards to encourage economic development, that document encouraged developing countries to pursue flexible and minimalist implementation of required regulations. Continuing in this vein, an influential recent article called for a moratorium on additional global-standards setting so that poor nations could adopt suitable policies and even experiment with more competitive regulations than those envisioned by TRIPS.[5]

Such commentaries exemplify what has become a torrent of criticism of a strongly protective global IPR regime.[6] Such criticism has accelerated in response to the dubious policy of the United States to demand so-called "TRIPS-plus" standards in its bilateral regional trade agreements. That approach offered marginal gains in access to the U.S. market in return for, among other things, rigorous protection of patents and data confidentiality in pharmaceuticals, biotechnology products, and agricultural chemicals. A number of poor countries accepted such demands in order to achieve an overall trade agreement, but domestic opposition by health professionals and NGOs contributed sufficiently to a pushback in attitudes such that the U.S. Trade Representative's office has essentially abandoned this aspect of its trade policy.

The most prominent articulation of this pushback is the "Development Agenda" at WIPO, as originally set out by the governments of Brazil and Argentina in 2004.

---

2. Keith E. Maskus, *Intellectual Property Rights in the Global Economy* (Washington, DC: Institute for International Economics, 2000); Jayashree Watal, *Intellectual Property Rights in the WTO and Developing Countries* (The Hague: Kluwer Law International, 2001).

3. United Nations Conference on Trade and Development, *The TRIPS Agreement and Developing Countries* (Geneva: UNCTAD, 1996).

4. UK Commission on Intellectual Property Rights, *Integrating Intellectual Property Rights and Development Policy* (London: Commission on Intellectual Property Rights, 2002). See also International Center for Sustainable Development, *Intellectual Property Rights: Implications for Development* (Geneva: ICTSD, 2003).

5. Keith E. Maskus and Jerome H. Reichman, "The Globalization of Private Knowledge Goods and the Privatization of Global Public Goods," *Journal of International Economic Law*, vol. 7, no. 2 (2004): 279–320.

6. See, for example, Joseph E. Stiglitz and Andrew Charlton, *Fair Trade for All: How Trade Can Promote Development* (Oxford: Oxford University Press, 2005).

Over the ensuing two years, multiple delegations at WIPO advanced a comprehensive set of proposals for moving the institution sharply in the direction of advocating and facilitating a flexible, development-regarding approach to IPR. Ultimately, 111 proposals were put forward, covering such disparate elements as a global treaty ensuring free access to knowledge generated by public subsidies to research, policy interventions to encourage international technology transfer, greater sovereignty in pursuing public health objectives as regards pharmaceutical patents, and means of reducing the "digital divide" in access to Internet-mediated information and services. These ideas reflected not just the policy preferences of the 15 countries making up the "Group of Friends of Development" but also the hard advocacy of many academics and numerous NGOs, including the Consumer Project on Technology, the South Center, and the Electronic Frontier Foundation.

A number of these proposals were sufficiently sweeping that they would have radically altered the global IP landscape. For example, the concept of free access to publicly generated knowledge, which I have helped advocate in some forms,[7] is unlikely to find agreement in the United States, the European Union, and other places that generate that knowledge, sometimes at high cost, and would be reluctant to share it freely. Also unacceptable to U.S. and EU policymakers would be a WIPO policy supporting unfettered use of compulsory licensing in medicines, particularly in middle-income countries, or a global endorsement of widespread free access to digital goods under some concept of international fair use. Thus, it was predictable that, during negotiations in 2006 and 2007, the scope of the original Development Agenda would be substantially whittled down. Indeed, as of June 2007 the discussions had limited the Agenda to 45 draft proposals in five clusters, which will be taken up for further deliberation in 2008 by the newly created WIPO Committee on Development and IP.

A detailed description of these remaining proposals would take up too much space in this chapter, but a brief categorization and discussion is useful.[8] The first cluster relates to WIPO's technical assistance and capacity-building efforts. These proposals largely had been conceived originally as a means of pushing WIPO toward encouraging adoption of minimally protective standards and full use of TRIPS flexibilities. However, under pressure from U.S. negotiators, the emphasis was shifted from such encouragement's emanating from WIPO toward a "demand-driven and transparent" program of technical assistance, putting the onus on client countries to ask for specific help. Still, current language recognizes that developing countries have "special needs" in the IPR area, and

7. John H. Barton and Keith E. Maskus, "Economic Perspectives on a Multilateral Agreement on Open Access to Basic Science and Technology." In Simon J. Evenett and Bernard M. Hoekman, eds., *Economic Development and Multilateral Trade Cooperation* (Palgrave/MacMillan and World Bank, 2006): 349–68.

8. Annex A and Annex B—WIPO Development Agenda, 2007.

that advice should vary across levels of development. Particularly notable in this regard is that WIPO would "promote measures to help countries deal with IP-related anti-competitive practices . . . in order to better understand the interface between intellectual property rights and competition policies." This emphasis would be new for WIPO's technical-assistance activities. Further, member states would be assisted in making national IP institutions more efficient and achieving a "fair balance between IP protection and the public interest." If such emphases were truly integrated into the agency's work program, its technical assistance would undergo a sea change in attitudes toward the importance of development-sensitive IP policy.

The second cluster relates to norm-setting, policy flexibilities, and the public domain. Here, the primary language is vague, again referring to the need for member-driven consideration of norms, a balance of costs and benefits, and an emphasis on the importance of preserving the public domain. Not much can be read into any negotiating intentions here, setting the stage for wide-ranging deliberations in 2008 and beyond.

A third cluster addresses technology transfer, information technologies, and access to knowledge, perhaps the areas of greatest promise as seen by the original *demandeurs* of the Development Agenda. Yet here the language is the most diluted, leaving no indication that a multilateral agreement on open access to knowledge might be envisioned in later negotiations. Rather, the provisions suggest exploring means of using "IP-related policies and initiatives" to promote the transfer of technology and an exhortation to developed nations to urge their research and scientific institutions "to enhance cooperation and exchange with research and development institutions in developing countries." These, and further provisions, actually stop short of the language on technology transfer found in Articles 7 and 66.2 of TRIPS on the need for technology transfer. Thus, the Development Agenda is not likely to spark much global policy reform on access to information, differential prices for knowledge, or other key aspects of technology diffusion.

The remaining two clusters deal with the need for evaluation and institutional improvements in IP. One proposal calls on WIPO to undertake new studies of the "economic, social and cultural impact" of IP systems in member states, an analytical task the agency is not well equipped to perform. Another suggests that WIPO enhance the ability of civil society organizations to participate in the agency's activities, a task that professionals in the WIPO secretariat likely would find inconvenient or even daunting.

III. SOME CAUTIONARY NOTES

All things considered, I believe the Development Agenda could support important and desirable reforms in the emphases and activities of what has been an excessively hidebound and insular UN agency. Further, it could provide a forum within which governments can officially recognize that IP policies potentially have significant impacts on development and need to be varied across national levels of per capita income and technological attainment. In that way, the Development Agenda could break the "one size fits all" logjam that characterizes the TRIPS Agreement and the approach to IPR endorsed by the WTO. It could also mobilize more resources for technical assistance and the improvement of institutions in poor countries to allow them to benefit from their own IP systems. Thus, further negotiations to clarify, and even strengthen, the Agenda will be valuable.

Nevertheless, it is advisable to issue a few words of caution about some potentially damaging, if unintended, consequences of implementing a Development Agenda at WIPO. If the new agenda were to enact a sharp revision of the global IP regime that significantly undercut standards and expectations in TRIPS, for example, technology-intensive multinational firms might pull back from their increasing engagement with developing countries. In this section, I identify two areas in which prudence would call for negotiators to consider such consequences carefully.

A. Technology Transfer: The Need for Markets

The use of TRIPS "flexibilities" refers largely to restrictions on IP eligibility and scope in areas of central concern for public health and nutrition. Thus, for example, governments may be advised to avoid extending patent eligibility to computer programs, recognize relatively narrow claims in pharmaceutical product patents, retain rights to compulsory licensing, remain open to parallel imports of medicines and new seed varieties, limit the periods during which confidential clinical-trials test data are protected, and recognize a legitimate research use in patented biotechnological goods and protected plant varieties.[9] As a matter of social policy, it is hard to argue against the need for ensuring such policy space.

However, one clear motivation for pushing the Development Agenda is the notion that unconstrained policy setting in IPR can be an effective form of industrial policy. It is often noted that the United States, Japan, and Korea developed extensive manufacturing prowess without erecting strong patent regimes or protecting foreign technological secrets.[10] Further, for years China has attracted

---

9. An extensive discussion of such policies may be found in Chapter 5 of World Bank, *Global Economic Prospects and the Developing Countries 2002: Making Trade Work for the World's Poor* (Washington, DC: World Bank, 2001).

10. Linsu Kim, "Technology Transfer and Intellectual Property Rights: Lessons from Korea's Experience," International Centre for Trade and Sustainable Development (Geneva: ICTSD, 2002), Working paper, supra note 4; Joseph E. Stiglitz and Andrew Charlton, *Fair Trade for All: How Trade Can Promote Development* (Oxford: Oxford University Press, 2005).

a disproportionate share of trade and foreign direct investment, with their implicit inward transfers of technology, without adequately enforcing patents or discouraging industrial espionage.[11] To patent foreign materials that may be made available cheaply through imitation, reverse engineering, or forced licensing seems questionable from a development standpoint.

There is considerable truth in such claims. Throughout the 19th century, the United States was widely condemned by policymakers in Europe for its tolerance of patent infringement and its unwillingness to protect foreign copyrights.[12] The Japanese patent system in place from the 1950s through the late 1980s encouraged the filing of huge numbers of single claims on narrow innovative improvements while publishing patent applications prior to their grant. Moreover, public policy favored extensive licensing arrangements among domestic competitors and required licensing of international technologies on favorable terms. This system clearly favored widespread diffusion of new technological information into the economy and has been shown to be a factor in Japan's productivity growth.[13] Korean manufacturing firms took considerable advantage of mature technologies that could be adapted to their needs in labor-intensive sectors in the 1970s and 1980s, permitting them a base from which to build global firms in ensuing years through investments in capital and innovation.[14]

In light of such histories, it is difficult to argue against permitting unrestrained sovereignty in IPR policy for developing countries. However, those histories are context-specific, referring to large countries with growing markets, high savings and investment rates, reasonably competent public administrations, and considerable investments in human capital and industrial infrastructure. These characteristics may not yet exist adequately in many developing economies today, suggesting that an aggressive policy of weak IPR may do little to improve domestic innovation or encourage technology transfer.

More fundamentally, the nature of international competition has shifted considerably from the times in which the United States, Japan, and Korea industrialized. Engagement with the globalized economy, in which technology is

---

11. Keith E. Maskus, "Intellectual Property Rights in the WTO Accession Package: Assessing China's Reforms." In Deepak Bhattasali, Shantong Li, and William J. Martin, eds., *China and the WTO: Accession, Policy Reform, and Poverty Reduction Strategies* (Oxford: Oxford University Press, 2004): 49–68.

12. B. Zorina Khan, "Intellectual Property and Economic Development: Lessons from American and European History," Background paper, U.K. Commission on Intellectual Property Rights (London, 2002).

13. Janusz Ordover, "A Patent System for both Innovation and Exclusion," *Journal of Economic Perspectives*, Vol. 5 (1991): 43–60; Keith E. Maskus and Christine McDaniel, "Impacts of the Japanese Patent System on Productivity Growth," *Japan and the World Economy*, Vol. 11, no. 4 (November 1999): 557–74.

14. Kim, supra note 10.

traded through extensive vertical supply chains and FDI, requires openness, transparency, skill development, and related factors.[15]

In this context, the role of IPR is complex and multifaceted.[16] Although a full discussion is beyond the scope of this chapter, a few observations are relevant for the discussion here. To begin, available evidence suggests that investments in innovative activities by domestic enterprises, whether measured by R&D expenditures or patent applications, do not rise appreciably for a lengthy time period after the implementation of more rigorous IPR, particularly patent rules. Robust innovation depends on a host of factors, including the nature of competition, economic growth, skill endowments, and national innovation policies. Countries that adopt more restrictive patents in the hope of generating additional domestic innovation may be frustrated if they do not pay equal attention to these other structural factors. As has often been noted, IPR should be treated as a component of an overall economic development strategy.[17] Neither adopting strong patents nor resorting to significant policy flexibility is likely to be effective without investments in complementary activities.

It is not surprising that the medium-term responsiveness of domestic innovation to IPR reforms is small, because throughout history the pressure for reforms has come largely from foreign countries or firms seeking greater protection of their ability to exploit technologies through trade and direct investment.[18] To simplify, the impacts of patent reforms are twofold: multinational enterprises gain greater market power to sell technologies and products at higher markups but also become more confident in their ability to protect proprietary information, inducing more technology transfer. The principal question for policymakers, then, is whether adopting strong and non-discriminatory patent rules, as envisioned by TRIPS, will generate greater costs through foreign monopolization or greater benefits through inward technology flows, learning, and spillovers.

This is a difficult question to answer, and ideological approaches to it are generally unhelpful for policymakers. However, my reading of the available evidence suggests that the following observations are important to keep in mind.

---

15. A review of the determinants of international technology transfer may be found in Bernard M. Hoekman, Keith E. Maskus, and Kamal Saggi, "Transfer of Technology to Developing Countries: Unilateral and Multilateral Policy Options," World Bank Policy Research Paper 3332, *World Development*, vol. 33, no. 10 (October 2005): 1587–1602. An excellent treatment of FDI in this context is Bruce A. Blonigen, "A Review of the Empirical Literature on FDI Determinants," (Cambridge, MA: *NBER Working Paper No.* 11299) (2005).

16. For a review, consult Walter G. Park, "Intellectual Property Rights and International Innovation," in Keith E. Maskus, ed., *Intellectual Property, Growth and Trade* (Amsterdam: Elsevier North-Holland, 2008).

17. Keith E. Maskus, *Intellectual Property Rights in the Global Economy* (Washington, DC: Institute for International Economics, 2000).

18. Joshua Lerner, "Patent Protection and Innovation over 150 Years" (Cambridge, MA: National Bureau of Economic Research, 2002), Working Paper No. 8977.

First, imports of capital goods and high-technology products respond positively to patent strength, however measured, among middle-income and larger developing countries. Such imports are important sources of technical information and learning. Second, multinational enterprises are more likely to transfer proprietary information to local affiliates or partners that are themselves engaged in adaptive R&D, suggesting that policies to encourage domestic innovation are complementary to inducing inward technology flows. Third, the volume of licensing transactions in advanced technologies seems to be sensitive to domestic IPR policies, indicating that concerns about market power are secondary.[19] Fourth, all of these findings are conditional on other economic and policy variables, as noted above. The elasticity of FDI with respect to patents seems to rise with the abundance of local human capital, for example. Fifth, in the poorest countries there seems to be little impact at all of IPR reforms on technology transfers, though this may be more a result of the absence of other factors affecting the business climate than of the strength of technology protection.

A final observation is that, as countries improve their IPR regulations, particularly with respect to patents and trade secrets, the costs of achieving effective transfer of proprietary technologies is reduced.[20] One positive outcome is the emergence of efficient technology brokers in specific industries, such as industrial chemicals and the life sciences that can bring together multinational firms and potential partners in developing countries that may have been overlooked under prior policy systems. In short, policy reforms in IPR can support the development of markets for technology, short-circuiting the need for expensive reverse engineering.[21]

One reasonable interpretation of this evidence is that the net gains from adopting global IPR standards tend to rise (or net costs to fall) with income levels, manufacturing capacity, and human capital endowments. In this regard, sustaining flexibility in standards and their application is an appropriate basic policy stance for the poorer developing economies. At the same time, transparency and certainty in policy are significant factors in attracting FDI and other forms of technology transfer. Thus, governments might be advised to couple their adoption of "TRIPS flexibilities" with greater investments in transparent enforcement activities and judicial procedures to ensure that the IPR levels on

---

19. Lee Branstetter, Raymond Fisman, and C. Fritz Foley. "Do Stronger Intellectual Property Rights Increase International Technology Transfer? Empirical Evidence from US Firm-Level Panel Data." *Quarterly Journal of Economics*, vol. 121, no. 1 (2006): 321–49.

20. Guifang Yang and Keith E. Maskus, "Intellectual Property Rights, Licensing, and Innovation in an Endogenous Product Cycle Model," *Journal of International Economics*, vol. 53, no. 1 (February 2001): 169–87.

21. For a lengthy discussion and analysis, see Ashish Arora, Andrea Fosfuri, and Alfonso Gambardella, *Markets for Technology: The Economics of Innovation and Corporate Strategy* (Cambridge, MA: MIT Press, 2001).

offer are actually protected. Ultimately, however, the IPR regime itself is not likely to have much effect unless it is complemented with other policies ensuring robust competition and innovation possibilities. Put simply, governments should not view IPR flexibilities as a substitute for sound development policy.

B. Linkages to Developed-Country Policy Preferences

Firms headquartered in the United States, the European Union, Japan and other developed economies view the global IPR regime as a means of defending their technologies from rapid leakage to industrial competitors. An agreement by those countries to sign on to the WIPO Development Agenda must be seen as a concession, for which compensation will be demanded. Thus, a second area in which advocates of using IPR policy sovereignty to support industrial policies must be wary is in accommodating the pushback.

This pushback is already evident in demands by U.S. negotiators that the Development Agenda be tied to significant global harmonization of patent policies. The dimensions of such harmonization remain unclear at this time. A benign approach, which could generate real benefits through lower costs of registering innovations, would be an agreement for patent authorities essentially to mutually recognize the outcomes of patent examination procedures at key patent offices in the United States, Europe, Japan, Australia, China, Brazil, and elsewhere. A single application through the Patent Cooperation Treaty at WIPO, with examination in one of these offices taking effect in other designated countries, subject to local opposition procedures as needed, could generate global efficiencies. The key here, however, is that each national office would sustain its own patent regulations.

The United States prefers a far stronger approach to harmonization. Its preferred policy would be to negotiate a WIPO treaty under which each major patent office would largely harmonize its eligibility rules, examination procedures, approaches to claim construction, and processes for third-party registration of prior art. A treaty of this kind would erect a high-level global equalization that would exceed the minimum standards in TRIPS and essentially overturn the Development Agenda.[22]

As deliberations on the Development Agenda go forward, other forms of pushback may emerge. For example, both the United States and the European Union have expressed strong interests in achieving global consensus on the need for robust IPR enforcement procedures and activities. An international pact on minimum enforcement investments, which would go beyond what is required in TRIPS, may be one outcome.

---

22. This approach has been under way for some years in the currently stalled negotiations to establish at WIPO a Substantive Patent Law Treaty. A critical analysis of U.S. policy is in Keith E. Maskus, *Reforming U.S. Patent Policy: Getting the Incentives Right*, Council Special Report no. 19 (New York: Council on Foreign Relations, 2006).

Whether such pushback agreements on harmonization and enforcement would harm or benefit particular developing countries is a complex question deserving close analysis. The main point here, however, is that caution is advised in pushing forward with a Development Agenda that significantly would unwind the protection for technologies established by TRIPS, lest it result in more rigorous protection through less direct means.

IV. CONCLUDING REMARKS

Viewed through the prism of realist politics and economics, the cautions raised here may not be much to worry about. For one thing, negotiations to this point already have diminished the more radical proposals of the original Development Agenda to the level of vague statements about the needs for more technology transfer and policy space. The likelihood that such statements ultimately will end up in a multilateral commitment to permit extensive use of flexible IPR regulations is limited, at best. For another, WIPO itself is a weak institution in relation to the WTO, which facilitates TRIPS. Language in a WIPO agreement that would seem to encourage norm-setting that frustrates the intent of TRIPS is not likely to have much meaning. Finally, as discussed above, many developing countries need to invest strongly in complementary development policies that are more important than IPR reforms. Failure to fit IPR into broader development strategies significantly reduces the gains that can be had from policy flexibility.

Nonetheless, a WIPO agreement would have some force in terms of giving countries some legal cover for their IPR policies. It may also be effective in improving the nature of technical assistance and policy guidance for poor nations. Finally, if its ultimate effect is to permit the intelligent use of policy choices in a transparent and enforceable manner, a Development Agenda could do much to link countries into the global technological economy while safeguarding legal means for ensuring public health and nutritional needs.

Still, the potential for a significant policy pushback cannot be discounted. In this regard, the circumstances surrounding the WIPO Development Agenda are reminiscent of the negotiations in the 1980s, at the United Nations, on a so-called New International Economic Order (NIEO). A central plank of those proposals would have permitted countries to eliminate patents in an effort to gain free access to global technologies, erect intrusive policies to force technology transfer under zero or low royalty rates, and pursue punitive antitrust policies against perceived market-power abuses by international firms.[23] Unsurprisingly,

23. See Susan K. Sell, *Power and Ideas: North-South Politics of Intellectual Property and Antitrust* (Albany: State University of New York Press, 1995).

such firms reacted negatively, and government negotiators from developed countries abandoned the negotiations. Arguably, however, these discussions sparked interest in the United States in strengthening global IPR protection, a factor that ultimately led to TRIPS. Enthusiasts of the WIPO Development Agenda may wish to think twice about whether achieving it could push the interests of global IPR *demandeurs* into new and uncharted territories.

PART FOUR

INTELLECTUAL PROPERTY AND DEVELOPMENT: A COMPARATIVE ANALYSIS

8. WHAT DIRECTION IS THE WIND BLOWING? Protection of DRM in China

HONG XUE*

Wild spirit, which art moving everywhere;
Destroyer and preserver; hear, oh, hear!
—"Ode to the West Wind" by Percy Bysshe Shelley

I. INTRODUCTION

Shelley's masterpiece depicts the tremendous power of the Wind from the West.[1] But famous Chinese poet Xu Zhimo, who had studied in England in the 1920s, was much confused by the direction of the wind. Xu divulged, "I don't know which direction the wind is blowing."[2] If Xu were not a romantic poet but an intellectual property scholar, his question would be very absurd. In international political circles, anyone with basic knowledge of intellectual property law knows that the West Wind is sweeping through the world. Namely, the

* Associate Professor, Faculty of Law of the University of Hong Kong and Fellow, Information Society Project, Yale Law School. Email: hongxueipr@gmail.com. My hearty thanks to Prof. Neil W. Netanel for his insightful comments and enlightenment. I especially benefited from his paper, Neil W. Netanel, "Why Has Copyright Expanded? Analysis and Critique," in Fiona Macmillan, ed., *New Directions in Copyright Law* (London: Edward Elgar, forthcoming 2008).

1. Percy Bysshe Shelley, "Ode to the West Wind," in Harry Buxton Forman, ed., *The Poetical Works of Percy Bysshe Shelley* (London: Reeves & Turner, 1880).

2. Xu Zhimo (1897–1931), "I Don't Know Which Direction the Wind Is Blowing," in Han Shishan, ed., *The Works of Xu Zhimo* (Tianjin: Tianjin People's Publisher, 2005). It's a very popular love poem that exhibits Xu's trademark romantic style. An excerpt follows:

I don't know,
Which direction the wind is blowing—
I am in a dream,
Dimness is the glory of the dream.

developed countries are leading the trend toward greater intellectual property protections and are aggressively pushing the developing countries to follow.

Under the power of the West Wind, what is the developing countries' response? Because the World Trade Organization (WTO) linked intellectual property obligations to the chains of trade, developing countries are unlikely to forcefully resist the developed countries' demands regarding such protections. The interesting question, then, is precisely *how* the developing countries choose to follow the West Wind. Do they follow blindly or thoughtfully, thoroughly or superficially, indiscriminately or selectively? These questions are hardly ever examined and answered from the perspective of the developing countries. We can see that a dozen developing countries being "watched" by the United State Trade Representative (USTR) under the "Special 301" designation are busy making new laws and taking new enforcement measures.[3] Obviously, they are following the West Wind to avoid trade sanctions, but how far do they really go? Why are they making one choice over another?

This chapter uses the example of China—the largest developing country—to illustrate how a developing country reacts to the West Wind vis-à-vis legislation. The study of the legal protection of digital-rights management (DRM) in China shows that Chinese lawmakers are overwhelmed by the demands of the West.

This essay demonstrates that developing countries are internally surrendering to, as well as externally pressured by, the West Wind. Under the power of the West Wind, the developing countries are educated to believe that the West is the Way, by default: They should not only proceed along its prescribed path but should even go further than the West. As a result, the developing countries are losing, step by step, their internal capacity for normative innovation. This essay shows that only if the developing countries stop blindly following the West Wind will they be able to establish intellectual property systems that comport with their domestic situations as well as international norms.

---

3. Section 301 is the statutory means by which the United States asserts its international trade rights, including its rights under World Trade Organization agreements. In particular, the "Special 301" provisions of the Trade Act of 1974 allow the USTR to identify trading partners that deny adequate and effective protection of the intellectual property of, or fair and equitable market access to, U.S. artists and industries reliant upon intellectual property protection. Under Section 306 of the Trade Act, the USTR monitors a country's compliance with bilateral intellectual property agreements that are the basis for resolving an investigation under Section 301. USTR may apply sanctions if a country fails to satisfactorily implement an agreement. *See* the USTR, "2006 Special 301 Report," available at http://www.ustr.gov/Document_Library/Reports_Publications/2005/2005_Special_301/Section_Index.html (last visited October 10, 2006).

II. CHINA'S INTERNET COPYRIGHT REGULATIONS

On May 18, 2006, the Chinese State Council enacted the "Regulations for Protection of the Right of Communication via the Information Network" (hereafter "China's Internet Copyright Regulations").[4] As the State Council explains, China's Internet Copyright Regulations serve primarily to implement the two WIPO Internet Treaties[5] that China ratified in 2006 and to protect the right of communication over information networks.[6] Almost half of the provisions concern protections against the circumvention of technological measures that underlie digital-rights management (DRM) systems.[7]

It is very easy to discover the similarities in DRM protection between China's Internet Copyright Regulations and the United States Digital Millennium Copyright Act (DMCA). Apart from the structure and format, they share similar substance and expression. Even the Legislative Office of the State Council, which was responsible for drafting the regulations, acknowledges that the regulations

---

4. The Regulations entered into force on July 1, 2006. The USTR translates the title as the "Regulations on the Protection of Copyright over Information Networks." Although it makes sense when considering the contents of the Regulations, it is by no means an accurate translation of the title. *See* the USTR, "2006 Report to Congress on China's WTO Compliance," available at http://www.ustr.gov/assets/Document_Library/Reports_Publications/2006/asset_upload_file688_10223.pdf.

5. The "WIPO Internet Treaties" are the WIPO Copyright Treaty (adopted Dec. 20, 1996, 36 I.L.M. 65) and the WIPO Performances and Phonograms Treaty (adopted Dec. 20, 1996, 36 I.L.M. 76).

6. Under China's Constitution, the State Council is the Central People's Government, which is the highest organ of State executive power, as well as the highest State administration office. Article 58 of the Copyright Law requires the State Council to establish the Regulations for the right of communication via information networks. *See* "Interview with the Legislative Office of the State Council," May 29, 2006, published on the website of the Central People's Government of the People's Republic of China and available at http://www.gov.cn/zwhd/2006-05/29/content_294127.htm. On December 29, 2006, the Standing Committee of the 10th National People's Congress (NPC) approved the proposal on joining the two WIPO Internet Treaties. The NPC Standing Committee also makes statements that these two WIPO treaties will not apply to the Hong Kong Special Administrative Region's government or the Macao Special Administrative Region before the central government makes further decisions. *See* "China formally ratified the two Internet Treaties," December 30, 2006, from Xinhua Net, available at http://news.xinhuanet.com/politics/2006-12/29/content_5548001.htm. On June 9, 2007, China formally became a member state of the two WIPO Internet Treaties. *See* the contracting parties of the WCT, available at http://www.wipo.int/treaties/en/ShowResults.jsp?lang=en&treaty_id=16; and the contracting parties of the WPPT, available at http://www.wipo.int/treaties/en/ShowResults.jsp?lang=en&treaty_id=20.

7. Rights-management information is another important part of DRM. China's Internet Copyright Regulations do establish a protection system for it (Article 5), but this thesis focuses on technological measures only.

are built on "foreign advanced experience."[8] Comparison of the new regulations and the DMCA is an interesting tour of discovery that reveals the triumph of the West Wind.

A. Definition

China's Internet Copyright Regulations provide a very lengthy and ambiguous definition of "technological measures." Any measures purporting to prevent or restrict access to a work or to the public communication of a work without the permission of the rights owner fall into this category.[9]

That very long provision (a true mouthful) sounds nothing like everyday Chinese. It must have its origin somewhere in a foreign language. What might be the source? The two WIPO Internet Treaties do not contain any definition of "technological measures," and the DMCA merely defines the meaning of "circumvention" of a technological measure, not "technological measure" itself.[10] Interestingly, the 2001 European Union "Directive on the Harmonization of Certain Aspects of Copyright and Related Rights in the Information Society" (the EU Copyright Directive) does define "technological measures."[11] When compared with both the DMCA and the EU Copyright Directive, the definition in China's Internet Copyright Regulations seems like an awkward mixture. It largely borrows EU wording, yet it follows the spirit of the DMCA by emphasizing the rights owners' right to use technological measures to control access and copying. American observers have widely criticized the DMCA for going far beyond the WIPO Internet Treaties' requirements and enabling rights owners to use technological controls to greatly extend their copyright monopoly.[12] China's Internet Copyright Regulations show that Chinese lawmakers are deaf to that criticism.

Given that China's Internet Copyright Regulations, as their title indicates, serve to implement communication via the information network stipulated in the Copyright Law, one would assume that the legal protection for the technological

---

8. *See* "The Interview with the Legislative Office of the State Council," May 29, 2006, published on the website of the Central People's Government of the People's Republic of China and available at http://www.gov.cn/zwhd/2006-05/29/content_294127.htm.

9. *See* China's Internet Copyright Regulations, Article 26. "Technological measures" refer to "any effective technologies, devices or components purporting to prevent or restrict the browsing or appreciation of a work, performance, or sound or video recording without the permission of the right owner or the provision of the work, performance, or sound or video recording to the public via the information network without the permission of the right owner."

10. *See* Digital Millennium Copyright Act of 1998, 217 U.S.C. § 1201 (1998).

11. *See* the EU Copyright Directive, Article 6.

12. *See*, e.g., Julie E. Cohen, "WIPO Copyright Treaty Implementation in the United States: Will Fair Use Survive?" 21 *European Intellectual Property Review* 236 (1999); Neil W. Netanel, "Why Has Copyright Expanded? Analysis and Critique," *in* Fiona Macmillan, ed., *New Directions in Copyright Law* (London: Edward Elgar, forthcoming 2008).

measures granted by the Regulations applies only to the online environment.[13] However, the definition of "technological measures" seems to imply that these measures are subject to protection offline as well as on.[14] The provisions call for legislative or judicial interpretation. The USTR, meanwhile, has already complained that "a number of gaps remain to be filled for China to meet the challenges of Internet piracy and fully implement the WIPO Internet Treaties."[15]

The use of DRM has not been limited to producers of cultural works. Manufacturers have begun to use technological measures to prevent competition in the aftermarket for spare parts and other related goods and services, ranging from garage-door openers to ink cartridges. The technology typically involves software code on interoperating parts that must effect a "handshake" in order for the parts to work with one another. In the United States, manufacturers have met little success in suing competitors who mimic the handshake for a violation of the DMCA.[16]

At the beginning of 2007, a similar case was decided in China.[17] A manufacturer of micro-engraving machines designed a special data-output format to ensure that its micro-engraving software could operate only on its own machines. The defendant developed a program to circumvent the plaintiff's special data-output format in order to make the plaintiff's software operable on other manufacturers' machines. The court ruled for the defendant, finding that the defendant's program affected only the data files generated during the computer operation, which had no function of controlling access or copying of the plaintiff's software. In the court's decision, a technological measure that served for the purpose of tie-in sales of the software and hardware, rather than for copyright protection, was not protectable. This decision alerts enforcement bodies of the potential side effects of protections of technological measures themselves. The court applied the

---

13. *See* China's Internet Copyright Regulations, Article 4: "for the purpose of protection of the right of communication via the information network, a right owner may adopt a technological measure." The provision is puzzling. Apart from this exclusive right, a rights owner's other rights (such as the reproduction right) may also need the protection of the technological measure.

14. China's Internet Copyright Regulations, Article 26, addresses both measures that prevent or restrict sharing a work with the public via the Internet and measures that prevent or restrict browsing or other access to a work.

15. "2006 Report to Congress on China's WTO Compliance." The report is available at http://www.ustr.gov/assets/Document_Library/Reports_Publications/2006/asset_upload_file688_10223.pdf.

16. *See, e.g., Chamberlain Group Inc. v. Skylink Technologies Inc.*, 381 F.3d 1178 (Fed. Cir. 2004), Sup. Ct. No. 04-997, cert. denied (U.S. Mar. 21, 2005); *Storage Technology Corp. v. Custom Hardware Engineering & Consulting, Inc.*, 421 F.3d 1307 (Fed. Cir. 2005); *Lexmark Int'l, Inc. v. Static Control Components, Inc.*, 387 F.3d 522 (6th Cir. 2004).

17. *See Jindiao Company v. Naikai Company*, Shanghai First Intermediate People's Court, *dismissed*; Shanghai High People's Court, *affirmed* (January 11, 2007).

Internet Copyright Regulations to consider the eligibility for protection of a technological measure that is applied in an offline environment. The decision thus implies that offline as well as online technological measures are protected under the Internet Copyright Regulations.

B. Scope of Protection

The WIPO Internet Treaties require only that member states "provide adequate legal protection and effective legal remedies against the circumvention of effective technological measures,"[18] leaving considerable room for domestic interpretations of legal adequacy and effectiveness. Although the DMCA purports to implement the Treaties, it actually goes far beyond what the Treaties require. The DMCA prohibits not just circumvention itself, but also the manufacture and distribution of devices "primarily designed or produced" for circumventing technological controls or that are marketed with the knowledge that they will be used for circumvention.[19] The DMCA also prohibits the circumvention of measures designed to control *access* to copyrighted works, even though the Treaties only require protection against circumvention of technological measures used by authors "in connection with the exercise of their [copyrights]."[20] Neither the Treaties nor, until the DMCA, U.S. copyright law gave copyright holders a right to control access.[21]

The United States, pushed by its strong copyright industry, has been skillful at requiring its trading partners to bring their intellectual property laws up to U.S. standards by leveraging trade through both multilateral and bilateral regimes.[22] It is no wonder that the DMCA model that protects against both circumvention acts and devices, as well as against circumvention of access and copy controls, seems to have become the standard answer to the "legal adequacy" required by the Treaties.[23]

Apparently, China's Internet Copyright Regulations follow the DMCA model by defining technological measures to include controls over browsing and

---

18. WIPO Copyright Treaty, Article 11 (adopted Dec. 20, 1996, *International Legal Materials* 36, 65).

19. 17 U.S.C. § 1201(a)(2); 1201(b). In fact, the DMCA prohibits the act of circumvention for access controls, not use controls.

20. Jane Ginsburg proffers a number of possible arguments that WIPO Article 11 could be interpreted to require protection against circumvention of access control. None are derived from the text or negotiating history of Article 11. J. C. Ginsburg, "Achieving Balance in International Copyright Law," *Columbia Journal of Law and the Arts* 26, 201 (2003), 213–14.

21. *See* Netanel, *supra* note 1.

22. *See* Netanel, *supra* note 1; A. Chander, "Exporting DMCA Lockouts," *Cleveland State Law Review* 54 (2006), 205.

23. *See* Digital Millennium Copyright Act of 1998, 217 U.S.C. § 1201(a)(b); the EU Copyright Directive, Article 6.

appreciating a work, not just providing the work to the public, and by prohibiting the following acts, unless stipulated by any law or regulation otherwise:

1. Intentionally bypassing or circumventing the technological measures
2. Intentionally manufacturing, importing, or providing to the public any device or component that is primarily used to bypass or circumvent technological measures
3. Intentionally providing the technological services allowing others to bypass or circumvent the technological measures.[24]

An eye-catching difference from the DMCA is that China's Internet Copyright Regulations cite no distinction between the measures for access control and the measures for copy control.[25] However, China's lawmakers may not comprehend that this non-distinction will seriously impair the public's ability to make fair use of the works. (I address this issue more fully below.)

With respect to legal remedies, China's Internet Copyright Regulations provide for civil remedies as well as administrative sanctions against actual acts of circumvention, but merely administrative sanctions against the manufacture or supply of circumvention devices or services.[26]

An act of circumvention is subject to civil liabilities, such as injunctions and damages, depending on the level of severity of the infraction's consequences.[27] If the circumvention also impairs the public interest, such as by resulting in rampant piracy of a work and disrupting the market, it is also subject to administrative sanctions in the form of administrative injunction, confiscation of illegal gains, and a fine up to RMB Yuan 100,000 (approximately US$12,800). In serious circumstances, the facilities or computers that are primarily used to provide network services may also be confiscated.[28]

In the case of manufacturing or supplying a circumvention device or service, the manufacturer or supplier shall be subject to an administrative warning, confiscation of the illegal gains, and confiscation of the devices or components that are primarily used to bypass or circumvent the technological measures. In serious circumstances, the computers primarily used to provide the offending network services may be confiscated, and/or a fine up to RMB Yuan 100,000 (approximately US$12,800) may be imposed.[29]

---

24. *See* China's Internet Copyright Regulations, Article 4.

25. Even the EU Copyright Directive mentions the distinction between the access control measures and the copy-control measures. *See* the EU Copyright Directive, Article 6.

26. *See* China's Internet Copyright Regulations, Articles 18 and 19.

27. The forms of civil remedies are described in the General Principles of the Civil Law, Article 134. Apart from injunctions and damages, the other common forms of remedies against torts include elimination of ill effects and public apologies.

28. *See* China's Internet Copyright Regulations, Article 18.

29. *See* China's Internet Copyright Regulations, Article 19.

When an act of circumvention is conducted via a network, the network service provider shall not be liable for providing access to the actor, provided that the service provider neither knows of, nor is directly involved in, the act.[30]

If China's Internet Copyright Regulations intentionally omit a civil remedy against supplying circumventing devices or services, it means that the civil remedy has been precluded in these circumstances. Thus, apart from suing the person who has allegedly engaged in the direct act of bypass or circumvention, a rights owner who suspects that a device or service is primarily used for circumvention may not sue the device or service provider in a civil proceeding. Instead, the rights owner must complain to the copyright administration, allowing the authority to investigate and then determine whether to impose administrative sanctions against the provider.[31] Given that administrative enforcement has always been equally important as, if not more important than, judicial enforcement in China, the Internet Copyright Regulations' new arrangement will by no means weaken the protection for technological measures. Indeed, because of the prolonged and costly nature of judicial proceedings, copyright administrative enforcement is gaining popularity among the international copyright industry. Because the Internet Treaties allow the member state to define what the "effective" legal remedies are, the solution given by China's Internet Copyright Regulations is not inconsistent with those laws.

Like the DMCA,[32] China's Internet Copyright Regulations make reference to criminal offences and penalties, but the Regulations' wording is quite ambiguous. They provide merely that any act that constitutes a crime shall be subject to penalties in accordance with the law.[33] In the Chinese legal hierarchy, only the state legislature—the National People's Congress (NPC) and its Standing Committee—has the power to enact legislation on crimes and penalties.[34] China's Internet Copyright Regulations were enacted by the State Council, not the NPC. Accordingly, the Regulations cannot describe any *ultra vires* rules on crimes or penalties; they can only provide for the enforcement of existing criminal laws.[35] Because the criminal law does not make acts of circumvention of technological

30. The Internet Copyright Regulations, like the DMCA, set out a list of safe harbors, assisted with a notice-and-takedown mechanism, to shield the network service providers from infringement liability.

31. Under China's Copyright Law, the National Copyright Administration of China (NCAC) is the highest office for copyright administrative enforcement. NCAC and copyright administrations in 31 provinces comprise the copyright administration system.

32. *See* Digital Millennium Copyright Act of 1998, 217 U.S.C. § 1204, § 1205.

33. *See* China's Internet Copyright Regulations, Articles 18 and 19.

34. *See* China's Lawmaking Law (effective July 1, 2000), Article 8.

35. The Chinese criminal laws refer to the Criminal Code and its supplements, for instance, the Decision of the Standing Committee of NPC Regarding the Safeguarding of Internet Security (adopted Dec. 28, 2000).

measures a "crime against intellectual property rights,"[36] China's Internet Copyright Regulations have no way to criminalize them.[37]

C. Exceptions

Article 12 of China's Internet Copyright Regulations provides very limited exceptions to the protection of technological measures. These include exceptions for teaching and scientific research, visually impaired people, law enforcement, and security testing.

But the exceptions are subject to two common conditions: (1) not providing any circumventing technology, device, or component to anybody else and (2) not infringing any other rights enjoyed by the rights owner.[38] The latter requirement may impact the limitations and exceptions to copyright and related rights provided in the Regulations.[39] The former is even more problematic as its language is quite ambiguous. It could mean that a circumventor, apart from doing what is permitted by the Regulations, shall not disseminate any circumventing technology, device, or component to anybody else. But it is still questionable whether any technology, device, or component for circumvention may be provided to the circumventor in the first place. If any technology, device, or component for circumvention is excluded from the scope of exceptions, then any circumventor could only do the circumvention through self-help. If so, the application of circumvention in even the permitted circumstances would be dependent on the circumventor's sole technical ability.

It is noteworthy that the Internet Copyright Regulations' list of exceptions is much shorter than that of the DMCA.[40] China's State Council filtered out from the DMCA list the exception for nonprofit libraries and archives (Section 1201(d)), reverse engineering (Section 1201(f)), protection of minors (Section 1201(h)), and personal privacy (Section 1201(i)). Some of these, such as the exceptions for protection of minors or personal privacy, might have been omitted because of their unimportance to or incompatibility with the Chinese legal system.[41] But some

---

36. The Criminal Code contains a section on the "Crime against Intellectual Property Rights" (Articles 213–220).

37. China has substantially strengthened criminal punishments against intellectual property infringements in response to U.S. trade pressure. It is now unclear whether the National People's Congress or its Standing Committee will add a new crime on circumvention acts or devices in the Chinese Criminal Law. If the USTR's pressure mounts, such action may well be taken.

38. *See* China's Internet Copyright Regulations, Article 12.

39. *See* China's Internet Copyright Regulations, Articles 6 and 7.

40. *See* Digital Millennium Copyright Act of 1998, 217 U.S.C. § 1201(a)(1)(B)–(E), § 1201 (d)–(j).

41. China has yet to develop a national privacy-protection law. Protection of personal information relies on scattered local or ministerial rules. It is unlikely that privacy protection would be considered in copyright regulation. Protection of minors is enabled under

omissions have serious consequences. Without an exception for nonprofit libraries and archives, for example, those entities' information-collection processes and dissemination abilities will be severely impaired. Even where a library or archive is otherwise permitted to provide a work online or to make a digital copy,[42] the Regulations do not permit it to bypass or circumvent a technological measure that controls access to or making copies of the work. This means that legitimate "fair use" can be excluded through applying technological measures.[43] Likewise, reverse engineering is important to technological innovation and market competition, and its legitimacy has just been confirmed by China's Supreme People's Court.[44] However, given its omission from the Regulations' list of exceptions, reverse engineering can be effectively barred by deploying a technical "lock."

In addition, those exceptions that are included in the Regulations are so narrow to be of little practical effectiveness. Teaching and research are not excepted unless the content that is subject to the technological protection measure is "only accessible via the information network."[45] The exception for the blind is subject to the same restriction.[46] Even the DMCA does not set such restrictive preconditions. If an exception is warranted for a given act of circumvention, the exception should

---

the "Law for Protection of Juveniles" (effective January 1, 1992) and, thus, is rarely addressed by any other law.

42. *See* China's Internet Copyright Regulations, Article 7.

43. Given that "fair use" has a specific meaning in the U.S. Copyright Act, the paper uses "excepted use" to refer to the free use of copyright works and other subject matter permitted by Chinese copyright law.

44. The Supreme People's Court published the "Interpretations on the Several Issues Regarding Application of Law in the Trials of Unfair Competition Civil Cases" on January 12, 2007. The Interpretations, effective February 1, 2007, affirm that acquiring another's trade secret through independent research and development or reverse engineering is not deemed an act of unfair competition. Reverse engineering is defined as the act of disassembling, measuring, or analyzing through technical means a product obtained through public channels so as to acquire relevant technical information of the product. But whether reverse engineering can be legitimately defended under the Copyright Law is still a question. The Regulations on Computer Software Protection (effective January 1, 2002), which provide the implementing rules for software copyright, do not give out a clear answer but contain a provision that seems peripherally relevant to this issue. It permits a user to install, display, transmit, or store a piece of software for the purposes of studying or researching the design ideas or principles embodied therein, without permission from, and without payment of remuneration to, the software copyright owner (Article 17). This provision is actually copied from Article 5(3) ("exceptions to the restricted acts") of the 1999 EU Directive on the legal protection of computer programs. But Article 5(3) can by no means substitute Article 6 ("decompilation") of the Directive.

45. *See* China's Internet Copyright Regulations, Article 12.

46. Ibid.

not depend on the media type through which the content is available or be subject to an extraordinary burden of proof.[47]

Like the DMCA, China's Internet Copyright Regulations make exceptions to the protection of technological measures (Article 12) independent of the excepted use of copyrighted works and other subject matter in the network environment (Articles 6, 7).[48] The relationship between the two sets of exceptions is very worrisome. Since the two sets of exceptions are not in conjunction, no circumvention is permitted unless covered by Article 12, irrespective of whether the circumvention is necessary for the excepted use under Article 6 or Article 7. So, once a technological measure is applied, the excepted use under Article 6 or 7 may be precluded, unless the use happens to overlap with what is listed in Article 12, such as classroom teaching and scientific research, governmental use, and use by the blind. Moreover, even these overlapping circumstances could be ruled out by Article 12 because of its additional restrictions. Both Article 12 and Article 6 except classroom teaching, scientific research, and use by the blind. However, circumvention is additionally restricted by Article 12 to content that is accessible only via the information network. Unless this additional requirement is met, circumvention for the purpose of classroom teaching, scientific research, and assisting the blind is still prohibited.

Consequently, the legal protection for technological measures becomes an insurmountable barrier to the people's freedom to use works. Such a consequence may not have been contemplated by the lawmakers, but it will be acutely felt in enforcement. The theoretical question left here is whether the rights owners may preclude the statutory exceptions and limitations through technical barriers. They may, to some extent, achieve the same goal through contractual arrangement.[49]

Apart from allowing technological measures to prevent legitimate excepted uses, China's Internet Copyright Regulations oblige users availing themselves of excepted uses to take technological measures to prevent any impermissible access or copying.[50] Such obligation, though very considerate to the rights

---

47. Given that cross-media use is so widespread, it will be extremely difficult for any circumventor to prove that a work is only accessible through an information network. It's puzzling why such a precondition would have been set. Probably, this is a reiteration that the legal protection for technological measures is only limited to "online" measures. (*See* China's Internet Copyright Regulations, Article 4.)

48. Under Articles 6 and 7 of China's Internet Copyright Regulations, the limitations and exceptions to copyright and related rights cover quotations, news reporting, classroom teaching, scientific research, governmental use, translation for minority nationalities, use for the blind, media use, communication of public speech, and library use.

49. *See* W. R. Cornish and David Llewelyn, *Intellectual Property: Patents, Copyrights, Trademarks and Allied Rights*, 5th edition (London: Sweet & Maxwell, 2005), pp. 808–09.

50. *See* China's Internet Copyright Regulations, Article 10 (4). The users under non-voluntary licensing schemes stipulated in Articles 8 and 9 are also obliged to take such measures.

owners, increases the users' burden in making use of the works as permitted by the Regulations.

Ironically, an ordinary user may be better off under the DMCA, despite all its chilling effects on fair use. Under the DMCA, the legal protection of copy-control measures is distinct from that of access-control measures. With respect to copy-control measures, the act of circumvention in itself is not prohibited. Thus, the distinction opens a small door to ensure that the public may continue to make fair use of copyrighted works through copying.[51] But under China's Internet Copyright Regulations, even such a door is closed.

Anti-circumvention has been controversial since the first day it was introduced into the legal system. Although the DMCA and parallel laws in other countries have not devised any satisfactory solutions to avoid problems, these laws at least purport to diminish negative impacts. The DMCA, for instance, establishes an administrative rule-making proceeding to evaluate the impact of anti-access control measures.[52] Likewise, the EU Copyright Directive requires the member states to promote voluntary measures taken by rights owners to accommodate achieving the objectives of certain exceptions or limitations provided for in national law.[53] Although these mechanisms may not be appropriate or effective, they show the awareness that the anti-circumvention should apply without prejudice to public policy and social justice. Unfortunately, China's Internet Copyright Regulations totally ignore this fundamental concern. They do so, even though the officials who drafted the Internet Copyright Regulations claim a "balance of interests" as one of the priorities of the legislation.[54]

---

51. *See* Digital Millennium Copyright Act of 1998, 217 U.S.C. § 1201. But the DMCA prohibits the act of circumventing a technological measure in order to gain access, which still affects the way software engineers, computer scientists, and computer security specialists do their work.

52. *See* the Digital Millennium Copyright Act of 1998, 217 U.S.C. § 1201(a)(1)(B)–(E). The purpose is to create an exception for users of a work in a particular class of works if users are, or are likely to be, adversely affected by virtue of the prohibition in making noninfringing uses. *See* also the U.S. Copyright Office, the "Rulemaking on Exemptions from Prohibition on Circumvention of Technological Measures that Control Access to Copyrighted Works," available at http://www.copyright.gov/1201/anticirc.html.

53. *See* the EU Copyright Directive, Article 6(4). In the absence of such voluntary measures or agreements within a reasonable period of time, member states should take appropriate measures to ensure that rights owners provide beneficiaries of such exceptions or limitations with appropriate means of benefiting from them, by modifying an implemented technological measure or by other means.

54. *See* "The Interview with the Legislative Office of the State Council," May 29, 2006, published on the website of the Central People's Government of the People's Republic of China, available at http://www.gov.cn/zwhd/2006-05/29/content_294127.htm.

III. CONCLUSION

The Chinese version of the DMCA opens us to the prevailing West Wind. It shows the "wild spirit" is indeed "moving everywhere." U.S. trade pressure and the international intellectual property–protection regime are the drivers behind this new addition to Chinese intellectual property law. But what concerns us more is that Chinese lawmakers seem to have been overwhelmed by U.S. standards. They expressly stated that the Internet Copyright Regulations are built on "foreign advanced experience." namely the DMCA. They even created a few DMCA "plus" norms, apparently believing that more copyright protection is better copyright protection.

China's experience with using the DMCA as a model demonstrates that developing countries require legislative, as well as technological, know-how and innovation capacity. When a developing country's intellectual property norms become either a copycat, or a poor imitation, of those in the developed countries, those norms can hardly serve the harmonious social and economic development of that country. Indeed, such legislation will serve to consolidate the developed countries' competitive advantage, and, consequently, to widen the development gap between the North and the South.

The former paramount Chinese leader, Mao Zedong, made a well-known statement during the Cold War: "If the East Wind does not prevail over the West Wind, then the West Wind will prevail over the East Wind." [55] At least in the arena of international intellectual property law, the West Wind is still prevailing. Could the international political-economic weather change, allowing the "East Wind" to prevail? Perhaps, but developing countries will have a very long way to go. At present, the developing countries' priority should be to stand up to the West Wind and build capacity for domestic norm-setting domestically, and then gradually expand those capacities internationally.

---

55. This saying was used in *A Dream of Red Mansions* (a Chinese classic novel) and is well known. The former paramount leader of China, Chairman Mao Zedong, borrowed the saying for his famous statement, "The East Wind prevails over the West Wind." *See* "Chairman Mao's remarks to Chinese students in Moscow" (November 17, 1957), at http://news.sohu.com/20051128/n227613496.shtml. Mao said, "There are two winds in the world, the East Wind and the West Wind . . . I think the characteristic of the current situation is that the East Wind prevails over the West Wind."

9. ARE NATIONAL PATENT LAWS THE BLOSSOMING RAINS?

Evidence fron Domestic Innovation, Technology Transfers, and International Trade Post Patent Implementations in the Period 1978–2002

YI QIAN*

I. INTRODUCTION

The rationale for patent protection is that patentees who gain exclusive marketing rights to their innovations can reap the benefits, and recoup the costs, of their research and development (R&D) investments; such a policy creates the incentive to innovate. The actual effect of intellectual property rights (IPRs) on innovation, however, remains one of the most controversial questions in the economics of technology.[1] National patent policies have also been advocated to developing countries as a means of attracting foreign direct investment and technology transfers. Although the World Trade Organization's (WTO) Trade-Related

---

* I would like to give my special thanks to Professors Richard Caves, Donald Rubin, Josh Lerner, and Richard Cooper for their constant advice and encouragement; to Drs. Arvind Subramanian, Jayashree Watal, Gary Haufbauer, and Keith Maskus for their advice and references at early stages of my research; to Professors Andrei Shleifer, Paul Beamish, and Dr. Fritz Foley for providing data. Many thanks also go to Professors Neil Netanel and Robert Spich for organizing the IPR symposium at UCLA and to the participants' comments, which stimulated new idea developments in this paper. I am also grateful to Neil for editing this book and for his comments on this chapter.

1. Please see Jaffe 2000 for a detailed review on the vast literature.

Aspects of Intellectual Property Rights[2] (TRIPS) negotiations were successfully concluded in late 1993, the question of whether national intellectual property rights protections are beneficial to developing countries still provokes heated debate. Does such legislation stimulate enough innovation and technology transfer to justify the economic, political, and social costs associated with patent-law implementation and enforcement?

In a global patenting environment, national patent-law implementation in developing countries could bring domestic welfare gains if the new laws stimulate more domestic innovation and attract more effective foreign direct investment (FDI), bringing, in turn, advanced technology and technical know-how. This paper studies the effects of new implementation of a nation's pharmaceutical patent policy on technology transfer and international trade and synthesizes in the effect estimates on innovation outcomes in Qian (2007). The analyses cover a sample of 92 countries from 1978 to 2002, including annual observations for a set of country covariates, as in Qian (2007). Here, technology transfer is primarily proxied by FDI establishments—the subsidiaries established by multinational corporations (MNCs) in the country of interest. Imports are sometimes considered a means of technology transfer, too, if importers are able to reverse engineer the imported products and learn from them, or if the imported equipment can impart advanced techniques. An innovation is typically a new chemical entity that satisfies the regulatory agency's efficacy and efficiency requirements, or "a molecular manipulation of a known drug that yields significant benefits" (Taggart 1993, p. 14). Qian (2007) uses three alternative estimates to measure innovations: U.S. patents awarded to a particular country of origin, R&D expenditures by a country's pharmaceutical industry, and the country's pharmaceutical exports. I summarize the findings from that paper and draw out implications jointly with the new results obtained in the current study.

This study adopts the methodological innovations in Qian (2007): that is, panel analyses of patent effects on matched country pairs. First, fixed-effects regressions on matched country pairs control more thoroughly for observed country characteristics. Second, non-parametric matching methods easily accommodate a large number of control covariates; this, in turn, enables the succeeding estimation to control for many observable country characteristics that are correlated with a country's innovative potential and patent implementation.[3] Combining these two procedures may reduce biases in the patent effect estimate. The main findings in Qian (2007) are that, in the group of sampled countries, the implementation of patent laws alone does not promptly stimulate domestic innovation. However, national patent laws in combination with high levels of development, education, and economic freedom do have a positive effect on innovation. Qian (2007) also provides some of the first empirical support for the theory that the relationship between

---

2. Intellectual property rights are a category of law that generally include patents, copyrights, trademarks, geographical indications, industrial designs, utility models, plant-breeder rights, integrated-circuits rights, and trade secrets.

3. A country legally implements patent protection for a particular sector.

innovation and the strength of intellectual property rights is an "inverted U" shape (Gallini 1992, Cadot and Lippman 1995, Horwitz and Lai 1996). In particular, an optimal level of intellectual property rights strength appears to exist, above which additional strengthening measures actually tend to discourage innovation.

This companion study finds that U.S. and Japanese FDI establishments in the pharmaceutical industry did not increase significantly in countries where new national pharmaceutical patent laws were implemented, using the same dataset as collected in Qian (2007). The interaction effects between patent implementation, education attainment, and economic freedom are again found to be positively related to increases in FDI establishments a year after the patent reforms. Imports expanded over years. Coupled with the finding that pharmaceutical exports did not increase significantly after patent reform (Qian 2007), the results on imports imply that the terms of trade worsened after the countries implemented new patent laws, mirroring the findings in Scherer and Weisburst (1995).

Countries at various stages of development began to implement or extend their national intellectual property rights protections[4] since the 1980s, some voluntarily and others under pressure. The United States pressed developing countries' to implement patents not only through direct bilateral trade threats[5] but also through indirect multilateral pressure, particularly by bringing intellectual property rights to the agenda of the Uruguay Round negotiations of the WTO. The impact of patent protection on innovation and technology transfer is, therefore, an important policy question—one that is especially pertinent for developing countries. However, only a few studies have been done for non–Organization for Economic Cooperation and Development (OECD) countries (Lerner 2000, Branstetter et al. 2006, Qian 2007), mainly because of the difficulty in collecting data. Furthermore, some previous studies of intellectual property rights in developing countries tested their effects on innovation or technology transfers for the whole economy. This is potentially problematic because patent protection may have different effects in different industries. For instance, surveying 650 U.S. firms, Levin et al. (1986) found patenting important mainly in the pharmaceutical industry, where copying is easy.

A few empirical studies have tested the effect of patent protection on countries' pharmaceutical innovation or technology transfer, with inconclusive results. Pazderka (1999), the Patented Medicines Prices Review Board (PMPRB 1997), and

4. At least 40 developing countries lacked pharmaceutical-product patent protection as of the late 1980s (Siebeck et al. 1990). By the end of 1999, however, only 16 WTO member countries excluded pharmaceuticals from national patent protection (Scherer and Watal 2000).

5. The U.S. Congress enacted legislation in 1988 that required the U.S. trade representative to annually identify such countries in the "Priority Watch List" of the "Super-301" trade report and to take unilateral trade sanctions against those countries not assisting in the protection of U.S. patent rights. These threats were credible. One example is the increasing U.S. tariff on Brazilian imports in 1989 in retaliation for Brazil's copying of patented drugs (Lanjouw and Cockburn 2000). Similarly, the threat of U.S. trade action, rather than internal factors, pushed forward South Korea's decision to strengthen its intellectual property rights (McFetridge 1997, p. 3).

McFetridge (1997) each found a statistically significant increase in pharmaceutical R&D expenditure after the tightening of Canadian pharmaceutical patent protection in 1987.[6] In contrast, Scherer and Weisburst (1995) showed that the Italian pharmaceutical patent legislation of 1978 did not increase R&D expenditures. Instead, it seemed to have worsened Italy's terms of trade. Challu (1995) also demonstrated a decline in new chemical entities introduced in Italy after patent protection.

These inconsistent and inconclusive results provide little consensus on the general effects of augmenting national patent protection. Because we cannot observe counterfactual outcomes of patent protection, international comparisons provide valuable leverage for analysis. There have been some cross-country studies related to IPR. To name a few, Maskus and Penubarti (1995) found IPR had a strong positive effect on imports, and Smith (1999 and 2001) reported results that are consistent with IPR's encouragement of U.S. exports. Maskus and Eby-Konan (1994) found no effect of IPR on FDI. Maskus (1998) reported regressions that are consistent with a positive effect of IPR on FDI, but only for more developed countries. Branstetter, Fisman, and Foley (2006) found positive impacts of IPR on FDI using unique panel data of U.S. multinational corporations. Yang and Maskus (2001) examined the impact of IPR on technology licensing. Although these studies are very interesting, results are again pooled across sectors, with the exception of the Branstetter et al. study, which controlled for firm fixed effects. The passage of national pharmaceutical patent laws in a group of countries in the 1980s and 1990s creates a natural experiment to test the economic impact of patent protection.

The remainder of the paper is structured as follows: Section II introduces a graphical approach to illustrate the theories and policy issues. For technically inclined readers, section III describes the study design and briefly motivates the choice of data and methodology employed. The model is laid out in section IV. Section V presents the main empirical findings. Discussions and policy implications are addressed in section VI. Finally, section VII summarizes the main approach and results, and makes recommendations for future studies. Practitioners can feel free to skim through section II and focus on the results and discussion in sections V–VII.

II. ECONOMIC THEORIES ON IPR

Faith in patent systems is related to Schumpeter's (1942) revolutionary idea that large-scale firms with monopoly power can be a superior market structure to

6. Nonetheless, all these studies point out that the dramatic increase in the R&D-spending growth rate is also attributable to the commitment of expanding R&D by PMAC member companies in order to facilitate the passage of Canadian patent legislation. This commitment to raise their R&D-to-sales ratio to 10% by 1996 was satisfied in 1993, and the rate of growth in R&D spending in these companies slowed substantially in the period from 1994 to 1997 (McFetridge 1996).

perfect competition. The practical effects of patent protection on innovation, however, have been controversial. It has been argued that patent systems are irrelevant for appropriating returns on investment in an era where product life cycles are shorter than patent processing times. Patents may even be counterproductive, incurring additional application costs, and promoting litigation, defensive behavior, and wasteful invention around patents[7] (Jaffe and Lerner 2004). Patent laws could also block spillover effects in sequential innovations, where each innovation is built upon its predecessors, by fostering high licensing fees and races for licensing (Scotchmer and Green 1990). Although the negative correlation between tightening IPR and innovation was found empirically in Bessen and Maskin (1999) and in Sakakibara and Branstetter (1999), it was not supported in Kortum and Lerner (1998). The hypothesis of whether patent protection stimulates innovation deserves continuing attention.

Although a series of surveys conducted in the United States (Taylor and Silberston 1973, Mansfield et al. 1981, Levin et al. 1987) and Switzerland (Harabi 1997) uniformly established the importance of patents for pharmaceutical innovations relative to other industries, it is not clear how much patent protection is optimal. One could argue that sufficient incentives to innovate are already ensured through well-established patent systems in the major markets, such as the U.S. and European markets, and that additional patent laws in developing countries might not stimulate much more innovation, given their limited capacity to innovate domestically. Counter-arguments propose that additional pharmaceutical patent laws provide a favorable local environment for domestic inventors with firsthand knowledge of country-specific diseases. A four-phase diagram,[8] shown in the appendix of this chapter, illustrates the static and dynamic welfare changes. The four figures represent four different phases of a particular pharmaceutical process or product supply associated with the national patent legislation change: Phase One prior to national patent implementation, Phase Two when static impacts immediately follow the national patent legislation, Phase Three when possible dynamic developments are felt after patent legislation, and Phase Four when the particular patent has expired.

For simplicity, linear demand and supply relationships are assumed. It helps to concentrate first on cost-reducing innovations,[9] which seem to represent the

7. "Inventing around a patent" occurs when imitators attempt to avoid patent-protection and licensing rules by making small modifications on the original innovation. The disclosure of technical details required in granting a patent helps this activity.

8. Subramanian (1991) motivates the development of this set of graphs. As in the original Schumpeterian model, this set of graphs directly depicts the process innovation, but the economic implications apply similarly for product innovations.

9. Such innovations include the development of new drugs that are less costly to produce or more effective than the existing drugs used in therapy: In both cases, innovations improve consumer surplus.

majority of pharmaceutical innovations. A discussion of the case where there is no existing medicine in Phase One will follow later in this section. In Phase One, P_w is the world monopoly price of a foreign patented drug, and P_d is the domestic competitive price of its generic equivalent drug. Domestic consumers alone purchase the drug at price P_d and enjoy their surplus triangle AB_1C_1. The domestic-producer surplus is zero, assuming a perfectly competitive industry with many imitators.[10] (See Figure 1 in the appendix.)

In Phase Two, domestic imitative production is prohibited, and the foreign innovator charges a monopoly price at P_w[11] (Figure 2). Consumer surplus shrinks to AB_2C_2, foreign innovators receive monopoly revenue of $B_1DC_2B_2$, and the regulation creates a deadweight loss of DC_2C_1.

These costs in Phase Two may be worthwhile if the national patent legislation stimulates innovation in Phase Three. Consider two types of innovations according to their degree of ingenuity. A major innovation is represented by the lower-cost supply curve S_2 in Figure 3a. If the new cost of production as a result of innovation is lowered enough that the monopoly price of the new drug is below the Phase One domestic price P_d, then consumers would gain a surplus of AB_3C_3. This is greater than the Phase One consumer surplus AB_1C_1, and certainly greater than the Phase Two consumer surplus AB_2C_2. If the new innovation is originated by a national, producer surplus of $B_3C_3EB_4$ is added to the total welfare of the country. Otherwise, monopoly rents go to the foreign inventor and are not captured by the country. In either case, there is a deadweight loss C_3EC_4 associated with the monopoly supply. With a small innovation, represented by a higher Phase Three supply curve in Figure 3b, the resulting consumer surplus is greater than that in Phase Two, but less than that in Phase One.

In Phase Four, when the patent expires, the drug invented in Phase Three is widely produced and marketed at price P_d' in Figure 4a (or 4b). The consumer surplus increases to AB_4C_4 (or $AB_4'\,C_4'$). Compare Phase Four with Phase One: The consumers now enjoy a larger quantity of new drugs at a lower price as a result of the innovation.

As the graphs clearly show, whether or not a country benefits from adopting national patent legislation depends on the dynamic impact of the patent privilege. If the patent legislation stimulates innovation, consumers can realize more surpluses in Phase Four. The welfare of the country may even rise as early as Phase Three, depending on the degree of the innovation (how low the new supply curve lies) and the innovation's origin. If the new innovation in Phase Three is originated by a

10. This assumption is practically applicable in many developing countries. For instance, Lanjouw (1998) accounts for the competitiveness in the Indian pharmaceutical industry, where different imitators line up to reverse engineer and sell their products.

11. For convenience, I assume that patent protection leads to a perfect monopoly. This does not have to be the case in practice, such as in case of licensing, but it serves to highlight the extreme case.

national, then producer surplus of $B_3C_3EB_4$ is added to the total welfare of the country. If the new innovation is originated by a foreigner, the country could still benefit as long as the technology was transferred to the home country at a relatively low cost: for instance, technology transfers via foreign inventors' (frequently employees of MNCs) imparting knowledge and skills to the national employees in the subsidiaries established by the MNCs in a country. Alternatively, the country could acquire the new innovation through licensing or importing. This, however, is usually associated with large amount of rent pocketed by the foreign inventor. In the foreign monopoly with no technology-transfer case, the surplus is not captured by the country.

Multi-country theoretical models predict that more national patent protection in developing countries may not add much to R&D investment incentives, given the high level of patent protection in the developed world (Chin and Grossman 1990, Deardorff 1992, and Helpman 1993). If so, then developing countries are better off without national patent protection, which will allow them to free-ride off innovations generated elsewhere. In the graph, this could be shown as movement directly from Phase One to Four without any potential loss in the other two phases. Notably, this will also shorten the technology diffusion time for the country. The domestic imitators will bring the new innovation into the domestic market at price P_d shortly after the innovation is developed without having to wait until patent expiration (typically 20 years, according to the TRIPS agreement).

The importance of domestic patent protection for pharmaceuticals in developing countries is least controversial in special cases where the targeted diseases are only found in the home country. Consider an illness for which no medicines are currently available: There is no consumer surplus in the country at all in Phase One. The lack of demand elsewhere makes foreign patent laws irrelevant. Without a national patent system to block imitations, inventors are not likely to invest in developing a new medicine unless through altruism or through government-funded projects.[12]

Of course, even a developing country's national patent might not provide enough market incentive for innovators to devote research resources to the country's specific disease. This implies that a group of countries with similar therapeutic needs should implement patent laws together. The Pharmaceutical Research and Manufacturing Association of America (PHARMA) advanced that view during the TRIPS negotiations, and it is formalized mathematically by Diwan and Rodrik (1991). Yet there is no evidence so far that the research investments or innovations in tropical disease drugs have increased significantly

12. Trouiller and Olliaro (1999) provide some figures: "... of the 1,223 new molecular entities sold worldwide during 1975–96, less than 1% were destined for tropical diseases." Most of these drugs are generated either from "incidental discoveries in veterinary medicine or from molecules discovered by governmental or academic institutions" (p. 1).

following a group of developing countries' implementation of TRIPS-compliant national patent laws (Lanjouw and Cockburn 2000).[13]

The costs of patent implementation for developing countries are clearly identified in the literature. They range from the capture of national patent monopoly rights mainly by foreigners (Lanjouw 1998, Maskus 2000) to the legal administration and litigation costs that a national patent system entails (UNCTAD 1996, Love 2001). At the same time, previous research fails to reach consistent conclusions regarding the innovation gain that countries may derive from the implementation of national patent systems. (Challu [1995], Scherer and Weisburst [1995], and Lanjouw and Cockburn [2000] contrast with Pazderka [1999], the PMPRB [1997], and McFetridge [1996].) The present study controls for national pre-patent (Phase One) characteristics that are relevant for patent implementation and innovative potential, and tests whether domestic patent laws have stimulated domestic pharmaceutical innovations and technology transfer, primarily foreign direct investment, in Phase Three.

III. STUDY DESIGN AND DATA

Had national patent systems been implemented as exogenous shocks, the effects of patent protection on innovation and technology transfers could be tested simply by comparison of mean innovation and FDI levels between the patent and non-patent countries. This ideal randomization faces severe practical limitations. In fact, individual countries make the decisions as to whether to have national patent laws. The country characteristics may affect the innovation, FDI, and trade outcomes, as well as the decision of national patent implementation. Qian (2007) and this companion study apply a statistical matching method to form country pairs where patent treatment can be considered randomly assigned within each pair. Limited space does not permit full discussion here; please see Qian (2007) for details. I define treatment as the implementation of new, national pharmaceutical patent law, and control as no change of patent law. A dummy variable "PAT" is constructed to indicate the patent treatment. Two control groups ("PAT" = 0) are defined in order to make the most use of the sample size available and to check the robustness of results. One control group consists of countries that never had patent protection for pharmaceuticals up until the reference period, and the other control group consists of countries that had patent protection even before the reference period. The treated group ("PAT" = 1) consists of the countries that implemented new pharmaceutical patent laws during the reference period. Table 9.1 lists the specific years the sampled countries started to implement new pharmaceutical patent protection.

---

13. One reason might be that the impacts were not yet felt by the year 2000, when their research was conducted. I am working on a project to investigate the impacts of TRIPS-compliant, national patent laws on various disease categories.

TABLE 9.1 TIMELINES OF NATIONAL PATENT IMPLEMENTATIONS

Year of Patent Laws	New Patent Countries
Period 1	**(1978–82)**
1983	Denmark
Period 2	**(1983–85)**
1986	Taiwan
1987	Canada
1986	Korea
1987	Austria
Period 3	**(1986–90)**
1993	Brazil
1991	Chile
1991	China
1992	Spain
1995	Finland
1992	Greece
1992	Hungary
1992–93	Indonesia
1991	Mexico
1992	Norway
1992	Portugal
1992–93	Thailand
Period 4	**(1991–95)**
1996	Bolivia
1996	Colombia
1997	Ghana
1996	Iceland
1996	Peru
1996 or 1997	Turkey
1997	Romania
1996	Ecuador
1996	Venezuela

Most of the new-patent countries had some degree of protection for pharmaceutical processes before they formally introduced national patents for pharmaceutical products in the corresponding periods. The only exceptions are Brazil, China, Chile, Korea, Indonesia, Mexico, Peru, Romania, Taiwan, Thailand, and Turkey.[14]

14. This information is obtained by cross-referencing Lerner (2000) Table 1, his listed source documents, and the WIPO (1992) document.

An indicator variable "PATMOD" is constructed to distinguish countries that started implementing pharmaceutical patent law anew (PATMOD = 0) from those that modified their patent laws to protect pharmaceutical products as well as processes (PATMOD = 1).

The study design called for an extensive effort to gather suitable data, and Qian (2007) collected data from various international databases and different countries' Yearbooks. This companion study gathered more U.K. FDI data and international trade data to merge with the original database in order to test the impacts of patent laws on technology transfers.[15] However, because the other FDI data I have are the number of U.S. and Japanese FDI subsidiaries in each country, they are not compatible with the U.K. data. I thus carry out analyses on them separately and sum the U.S. and Japanese FDI establishments to test the patenting effects on aggregated FDI. As will be discussed in detail later, the results across various specifications are robust. The dataset described in Qian (2007) already includes trade data from the World Trade Analyzer by Statistics Canada. I now obtain the total pharmaceutical imports each country purchased annually worldwide from the new NBER database by Feenstra and Lipsey (2005). I transform some of the variables logarithmically.

IV. METHODOLOGY

The same two-stage procedure as proposed by Qian (2007) is executed in this study. Please refer to Qian (2007) for the methodology details and the list of matched countries. The formal regression model is estimated on the two groups of matched pairs (Set 1: non-patent and new-patent pairs, and Set 2: always-patent and new-patent pairs) separately:

$$\mathbf{RESPONSE}_{ij(t+n)} = \beta_0 + \beta_1 * \mathbf{PAT}_{ij} + \beta_2 * \mathbf{PATMOD}_{ij} + \beta_3 * \mathbf{INTERACT}_{ij} + \beta_4 * \mathbf{COVARIATES}_{ij} + \beta_5 * \mathbf{D}_t + \beta_6 * \mathbf{RESPONSE}_{ijt} + \varepsilon_i \quad (1)$$

where β_0 consists of the pair specific-effects. That is, $\beta_0 = \alpha_1 * D_1 + \alpha_2 * D_2 + \ldots + \alpha_m * D_m = \Sigma_{j=1}^{m} \alpha_j * D_j$. D_j is the indicator variable for pair j, which takes on value 1 if the observation belongs to pair j, and 0 otherwise. PAT_{ij} is the dummy indicator of whether the country j in pair i changed pharmaceutical product patent laws or not.[16] All the countries in the control group (that have not experienced law change

15. I obtained the amount of FDI the United Kingdom poured into different countries in the sampled period from the various U.K. Yearbooks. Only the FDI host countries that are listed in the Yearbooks were included.

16. Pharmaceutical-patent laws are quite separate from other patent laws. Empirically, the probability that a country has a change in drug patents at the same time as other areas is less than 5%. This study is of pharmaceutical patents, not patents generally, and one does not necessarily suggest anything regarding the other.

during the period under examination) had process patents. $\text{RESPONSE}_{ij(t+n)}$ is the outcome variable of each country *j* of pair *i* in the reduced sample in period (or year) $t + n$ (*n* years after patent implementation). A similar definition applies to RESPONSE_{ijt} for period (or year) *t*. In Qian (2007), the outcome variable was the increase in the U.S. patent awards after the new patent implementation, the R&D expenditure in pharmaceuticals, and the pharmaceutical exports, respectively, in separate specifications. In this companion study, I use the FDI measures (from the United States, Japan, and the United Kingdom, first separately, and then the sum of U.S. and Japanese subsidiaries) as the outcome variable. When testing the impacts of patents on imports, I specify the outcome to be the total value of pharmaceutical imports of each country in the year of examination.

D_t stands for the five dummy variables for each of the periods (e.g., D_t takes on value 1 if pair *i* is matched when examining the period 1978–1983, and the other four period dummies for pair *i* have a value of 0). PAT and PATMOD are as defined in section III (see also Table 9.2 in section V.B). INTERACT and control variables are specified in Qian (2007). The regression residual is denoted by ε_i.

V. RESULTS

A. Patenting Effects on Innovations: Summarizing Results from Qian (2007)

The citation-weighted U.S. patent awards and pharmaceutical exports can be considered estimates of innovation outputs, whereas R&D expenditures provide an estimate of innovation inputs. Different regression specifications yield the same result: There is insufficient statistical evidence to conclude that pharmaceutical-patent implementation by itself has generally stimulated R&D incentives.

Although national patent laws alone were not found to stimulate domestic innovations, Qian (2007) discovered some conditional importance of the pharmaceutical-patent implementations. In particular, a more developed country with pharmaceutical patents is likely to have more R&D incentives compared to a similarly developed country without patents or to a less developed country with patents. Similarly, patent-law implementations are associated with higher levels of domestic innovations in countries with higher educational attainment or economic freedom.

It is interesting to note that the positive interaction effect of paten t policy and the economic freedom index are especially pronounced in the OECD subsample. Qian (2007) suggested the possibility that in a highly integrated market, such as that formed by the OECD countries, the national patent law could complement a member country's open-market access and favorable domestic investment policies to attract FDI and other forms of foreign-technology transfers. The results presented in the next section lend support to this explanation. National patent laws could also help domestic companies in assimilating these inbound technology transfers through patent disclosures. Economic freedom can also help countries with new patent systems leverage their emerging national intellectual property advantages by facilitating exports. Qian (2007) additionally

TABLE 9.2 IMPACTS OF NATIONAL PATENT LAWS ON LOG FDI AND IMPORT VALUES

	Dependent Variable: *Log* FDI, forwarded by 1 year				Dependent Variable: *Log* Imports, forwarded by 1 year	
Covariates	No Patent and New Patent Countries		Always Patent and New Patent Countries		No Patent and New Patent	Always Patent and New Patent
PAT Implementation	.01 (.92)	.33 (.23)	−.03 (.11)	.31 (.18)	.80** (.40)	.95** (.30)
PAT**log* GDPpcPPP		.20 (.60)		.68 (.69)		
PAT**log* Freedom		2.19** (.79)		2.93** (1.06)		
PAT**log* Education		.42* (.22)		.62** (.29)		
PAT**log* IPR score		1.35* (.75)		.30 (.36)		
PAT*Price Control		.73 (.98)		.13 (.47)		
Log GDP per capita PPP	.46 (1.27)	.69 (1.33)	.24 (.62)	.10 (.64)	1.08*** (.45)	1.74*** (.36)
Log Economic Freedom	6.45** (2.39)	1.28* (.67)	1.45** (.38)	.11 (.32)	.44 (1.00)	.39 (.78)
Log Education	1.57** (.78)	2.90 (2.74)	1.59* (.91)	3.21** (1.32)	1.58 (.85)	.17 (.77)
Log IPR Score	2.15 (1.69)	−.79 (1.83)	−.57 (.81)	−1.25 (.89)	.69 (.57)	−.75 (.50)
Log IPR square	.68 (1.34)		.51 (.90)		.34 (.48)	−.51 (.39)
Price Control	−.18 (1.23)	1.11 (4.54)	.78 (1.79)	−.92 (2.20)	−.03 (.45)	−.37 (.38)
Log Innovative Potential	4.02 (2.16)	2.09 (1.65)	2.68 (1.79)	1.66 (1.80)	.32* (.18)	.81*** (.14)
Log Labor	2.8*** (.64)	.59 (1.52)	.97 (.63)	.38 (.74)	.17 (.23)	.16 (.19)
Log Pharmaceutical Exports to the U.S.	1.21** (.58)	.76 (.24)	.86 (.56)	.13 (.12)		

Pair (Year) Fixed Effects	Y	Y	Y	Y	Y	Y
# of Obs.	52	52	52	52	52	52
R–square	.72	.79	.62	.68	.72	.86

Regression results from different regression specifications are tabulated in different columns. The dependent variable of each specification is listed in each column header. FDI is the sum of all the pharmaceutical FDI from U.S. and Japanese establishments in the year of specification. Total import values of a country are from the NBER Trade Database (Feenstra et al. 2001). The PAT Implementation dummy equals 1 in the years starting from domestic patent implementation identified in Table 1. The PATMOD dummy equals 1 if the country had pharmaceutical-process patents prior to patent implementation, as listed in section III. Macro data are obtained from World Trade Analyzer, *WDI*, and UNIDO *Industrial Property Statistics*. The economic-freedom index includes trade and tax policies and other regulatory and economic freedom proxies. It is constructed by the Fraser Institute, legal families from La Porta *et al.* (1996), and the education proxy from Barro and Lee (2000). The price-control dummy equals 1 if a country has a pharmaceutical price-control policy and is drawn from Danzon (1997) and Economic Intelligence Unit Reports. The numbers of subsidiaries of U.S. and Japanese MNE are provided by Prof. Fritz Foley and Paul Beamish. I constructed the "innovative potential" categorical variable using the data from the USPTO. It equals 6 if the U.S. patent awards (in all industries except the pharmaceuticals in a year) surpass 1,000, 5 if patent count is < 1,000 but > 100, 4 if it is < 100 but > 6, 3 if it is < 6 and > 1, and 1 if there are no patent awards. "PAT * X" refers to the interaction variable of PAT dummy and the covariate X, where X is the log of GDP per capita PPP, economic-freedom index, education, or IPR index, or the price-control dummy.]Heteroskedasticity-consistent standard errors that correct for clustering at the pair level appear in parentheses (10% statistical significance is marked with *, 5% statistical significance with ** and 1% statistical significance with ***).

analyzed the patenting effects on the R&D scientists, technicians, and engineers (RSE) for the 10 OECD countries with available data on pharmaceutical RSE, and the results corroborate those on R&D expenditures.

Qian (2007) provides empirical evidence that the relationship between patent strength and innovation adopts an "inverted U" shape. Most OECD countries had pharmaceutical process patents before they introduced product patents; it is likely that a country's process innovations were effectively protected if its initial national IPR protection is strong. Additional product patents, then, may not stimulate innovation, as Scherer (1977) and Kumar (1996) also seem to suggest.[17] In fact, the strengthening of patent protection may block domestic initiatives to engage in "imitative" innovations, whereas "ingenious" innovation may not come easily and quickly. This leads to an overall decline in domestic R&D activities in the short run. Figure 1 in Qian (2007) provides a visual check of the innovation trends across countries of different IPR strengths.

As a side note, Qian (2007) provides some evidence for a negative association between a country's price-control policy and its innovation outcomes. The interaction variable between pharmaceutical patent law and price-control policy also takes a negative coefficient. This finding is in agreement with those of others (Grabowski and Vernon 1992, Danzon 1997) that price-control policy tends to impair domestic innovation, evinced by the fewer patents obtained in the United States and by lower levels of R&D.

B. Patenting Effects on FDI

Table 9.2 lists the regression estimates of the patenting effects on FDI, as measured with the sum of the pharmaceutical FDI establishments by U.S. and Japanese subsidiaries in the home country where a national pharmaceutical-patent law was newly implemented. The statistically insignificant coefficients on the patent-implementation variable again exhibit null effects when patent policy alone is switched. However, patent implementation in combination with a freer economy (for instance, having more favorable domestic tax and regulatory regimes and more open trade policies) and with reasonable human capital in the host country does seem to attract FDI establishments, as evinced by the significantly positive

17. Scherer (1977) finds no clear relationship between the strength of intellectual property protection and the number of new drugs introduced per dollar of GDP (p. 39). Among his pieces of evidence is the fact that Switzerland and Denmark had the highest new drug-to-GDP ratio during 1940–75, when they protected only pharmaceutical processes. The United States and Belgium, where both processes and products are protected, ranked third and fourth. Italy ranked 13th, although it had no pharmaceutical protection then. Canada only protected processes and had compulsory licensing during 1969–75, and ranked 15th (p. 38). Scherer's result is corroborated in Kumar (1996) for the food and chemicals industries. Kumar finds that the R&D intensity of majority-owned affiliates of U.S. multinationals is no higher in countries that grant both product and process patents than it is in countries where only process patents are granted.

coefficients on the interaction variables. (The patent-implementation dummy interacted with the economic-freedom index and with education attainment—see columns 3 and 5 in Table 9.2, respectively.) This empirically confirms the conjecture in Qian (2007) that the national patent law could complement a member country's open-market access and favorable domestic investment policies to attract FDI. Branstetter *et al.* (2006) additionally finds positive impacts of IPR reforms on FDI by using a unique and confidential dataset from the Bureau of Economic Analyses. Their data on FDI is admittedly better than the establishment data I have because the detailed, firm-level data enable them to see royalty payments from U.S. MNCs to subsidiaries in various countries. Patent reforms could have stimulated R&D expenditures and transfers in the MNCs subsidiaries in the host countries, even if the number of FDI subsidiaries did not increase.

Education levels are predicted to be positively correlated with FDIs, statistically significant at the 5 percent level. This speaks to the strong attraction of human capital for FDI. CEOs of several top, international companies (e.g., GE, P&G, and Unilever) recently stated on Chinese television that they had established multiple subsidiaries in China more to benefit from China's wealth of talented, innovative people than to save on labor costs. It is perhaps not coincidental that MNCs' research laboratories have proliferated in countries like China and India as these countries have developed and improved their national education attainments.

I used FDI at two, three, and up to six years after national patent implementation as alternative response-variable specifications, and the results remain robust. The gist of the findings also did not change when I analyzed the U.S. and Japanese FDI establishments and U.K. FDI expenditures separately.

C. Patenting Effects on Imports

As displayed in columns 6 and 7 of Table 9.2, the sampled countries absorbed more pharmaceutical imports after the implementation of national pharmaceutical-patent laws for the first time. This hints at the possibility that foreign producers are more willing to sell their products to these countries knowing that the new patent laws will guard against imitations in these importer countries.

The welfare implications of import increases are harder to fathom from the data at hand. On one hand, imports are sometimes considered a channel of technology transfer because the imports are products that importers lack or need, and importers can learn from reverse engineering them. Even if the new patent laws prohibit copycats, the laws certainly do not prohibit making use of imported equipments or learning from imported products. On the other hand, the increase in imports and insignificant change in exports in the pharmaceutical industry after patent reforms could imply a deterioration of terms of trade, a finding that was also concluded in the Italian IP study by Scherer and Weisburst (1995).

A country's purchasing power, openness, and pharmaceutical-industry size are naturally positively correlated with the import values as well, reflected by the positive and significant coefficients on the GDP per capita PPP, economic freedom, and pharmaceutical-industry employment variables.

VI. DISCUSSION

The empirical findings that national patent protection alone does not lead to a positive jump in innovation, as estimated by U.S. patent awards, R&D expenditures, and pharmaceutical exports, is hardly surprising. Some developing countries have always had patent protection, yet, domestically, they do not have innovative potential and rely heavily on imports. For instance, patent-application data from the EPO and awards data from the USPTO show that French West Africa never applied for or obtained any pharmaceutical patent from these two offices during 1978–2000, despite its well-established national patent laws. Reports reveal that the top 10 MNCs control 35 percent of the $297 billion in gross sales of the global pharmaceuticals industry generated in 1998 (Human Development Report 1999). These top companies are responsible for the major pharmaceutical innovations. The top 27 pharmaceutical companies ranked by R&D spending in U.S. dollars for 1998 are mostly concentrated in Britain, Germany, Japan, Switzerland, and the United States (Industrial Research Institute 2000).

It is also possible that the lack of a statistically significant increase in U.S. patent awards and FDI after national patent legislation is linked to data limitations, most of which are discussed in detail in Qian (2007) and in Section V.B. In addition, the pharmaceutical industry-level FDI data I was able to obtain are limited to those from the United States, Japan, and the United Kingdom. To the extent that these three countries' FDI expenditures are the major components of total FDI from North America, Asia, and Europe, and under the assumption that the changing pattern of FDI from other nationalities most likely parallels that of the data at hand, the results presented here at least provide a glimpse of the patenting effects on FDI. We do need to be careful not to overgeneralize the findings, however, especially in light of research findings elsewhere that support a positive relationship between patenting and FDI using other datasets (Branstetter et al. 2006).

Concerns regarding institutional details may also have slowed down the impacts of national patent implementations. The TRIPS agreements were not reached until the final moments of the Uruguay Round negotiation, and innovators may have been uncertain about the future of patent protection. The aforementioned difficulty faced by developing countries in training legal personnel and enforcing their domestic patent laws can also add to innovators' hesitation to engage in R&D activities there. UNCTAD (1996) estimates the administrative compliance costs with TRIPS agreements for a number of developing countries to far exceed US$1 million. Patent implementation may, in fact, divert the resources that could have been employed in R&D activities. Even with a reported median cost of U.S. patent litigation of $1.2 million per side (*New York Times*, December 27, 1998), the quality of U.S. patent examination is not ensured. "According to a study by Lemley and Allison, of patents litigated to judgment [between 1989 and 1996], 54 percent were found to be valid and 46 percent invalid" (Love 2001). The technical know-how required of legal personnel is an unrealistic expectation for developing countries at this stage, and the lack of it could lead to misjudgments with serious impacts on the domestic market. For example, Bristol-Myers Squibb (BMS), an American drug company, was able to obtain patents for formulation claims of DDL, a drug for HIV/AIDS, in Thailand even though BMS is not the inventor of DDL. BMS used this patent to block generic DDL pill production in Thailand (Love 2001). If innovators doubt that the domestic legal system could make good judgments, the incentives to innovate, or to extend FDI and technology transfers, could be dampened.

Patent laws may affect innovation in dimensions other than raising its absolute number, in particular, changing the direction of innovative activity (Moser 2003). Nevertheless, the findings in Qian (2007) and this companion piece have important policy implications. They vindicate Maskus's (2000) argument that "expectations that stronger IPRs alone will bring technical change and growth are likely to be frustrated" (p. 199). Countries with different degrees of development, general intellectual property strength, and economic freedom have varying innovative responses to changes in national patent law, as evidenced by domestic pharmaceutical R&D levels and by the number of drug patents obtained in the United States. Most of these country characteristics indeed go hand in hand with each other. Kumar (1996) finds a positive relationship between the R&D intensity of U.S. affiliates and the strength of the country's intellectual property rights—in developed countries, but not in developing ones.

In that vein, many developed countries, including the United Kingdom, Germany, and Switzerland, had opposed national patent legislation when they were technology importers (Chang 2001). These countries took advantage of the freely accessible foreign technologies during their industrialization process. Evenson (1990) argues that countries have no interest in strong intellectual property rights until they become significant technology exporters. WTO advocates may argue that the TRIPS agreements already allow for adjustment time, because developing countries had a grace period of five years and the least-developed countries had ten years. However, it is unlikely to see developing countries transform from mere "technology importers" to even moderate "technology exporters" within this short timeframe. It is thus highly recommended that, prior to implementing TRIPS-compliant patent laws, developing countries should focus on improving their overall development levels, establishing solid technological infrastructure, and lubricating market transactions. The capacity of national patent protection to stimulate domestic innovations and inbound technology transfers appears to be contingent on these other factors.

Furthermore, it may be important for developing countries to have a discriminatory national patent system to help domestic companies flatten their learning curves and gradually learn to innovate. According to the welfare analyses in section II, national patenting could bring welfare gains to a country if innovation is stimulated and, particularly, if the innovation is originated by nationals. Previous research shows that, in many cases, domestic patent law mainly benefits foreign innovators, because producer surplus is captured mostly by foreigners (Lanjouw 1998, McFetridge 1996). Therefore, it might generally be in developing countries' interests to grant patents only to nationals and not to foreigners.

Granted, if patent laws in developing countries could help stimulate innovations that target nation- or region-specific diseases, then the optimal strategy for developing countries might be to grant patents to all innovators, including nationals and foreigners. But this would apply only to the region-specific underdeveloped drugs in question. After all, why not tackle the source of the problem by targeting just the drugs that are most urgently in need of development?

Although economically sound, these discriminatory policies are unlikely to be implemented because of the WTO norms of nondiscrimination and reciprocity. To borrow Schiff's (1971) phrase in this context, regarding the desirability and feasibility of a unilateral discriminatory patent policy, "economically, the answer is yes . . . [but] politically, the answer is no" (p. 26). It is perhaps an encouraging sign that the recent Doha Act resulting from WIPO negotiations acknowledges individual needs of different countries, although the Doha Declaration and Article 31*bis* added to TRIPS to reflect the Declaration are far more limited than is suggested here.

VII. CONCLUSIONS

After controlling for a list of country- and industry-level variables that are likely to affect innovative potentials and technology transfer, there is no statistically significant relationship between national pharmaceutical-patent protection and innovation or FDI establishments. However, the interactions of national patent-law implementation with development level, educational attainment, and economic freedom, respectively, are shown to have a positive relationship with domestic R&D expenditures and domestic pharmaceutical-patent awards in the United States after national patent implementation. Furthermore, there appears to be an optimal level of intellectual property rights regulation, above which further enhancement of protection is actually associated with a decline in innovative activities in developed, as well as developing, countries (Qian 2007). National patent protections in combination with economic freedom and higher education levels are also positively related to increases in U.S. and Japanese MNC subsidiaries and British FDI. Imports increased with unclear welfare implications. In short, for countries that have relatively low levels of development and market freedom, the net domestic welfare change as a result of patent protection is clear: rent transfers to foreigners immediately follow the national patent legislation (Figure 2), and any benefits from additional innovation depend ultimately on the country's macroeconomic factors and require a substantial time-discount (Figures 3a and b).

Although this study yields interesting results, more research should follow on this topic. Qian (2008) examined the IPR enforcements and the impacts of counterfeits, the flipside of IPR. Rigorous investigation of the impacts of TRIPS-compliance patent-law implementations on the global incentives to innovate new drugs for different disease types and on developing countries' access to drugs are all important questions to address.

APPENDIX

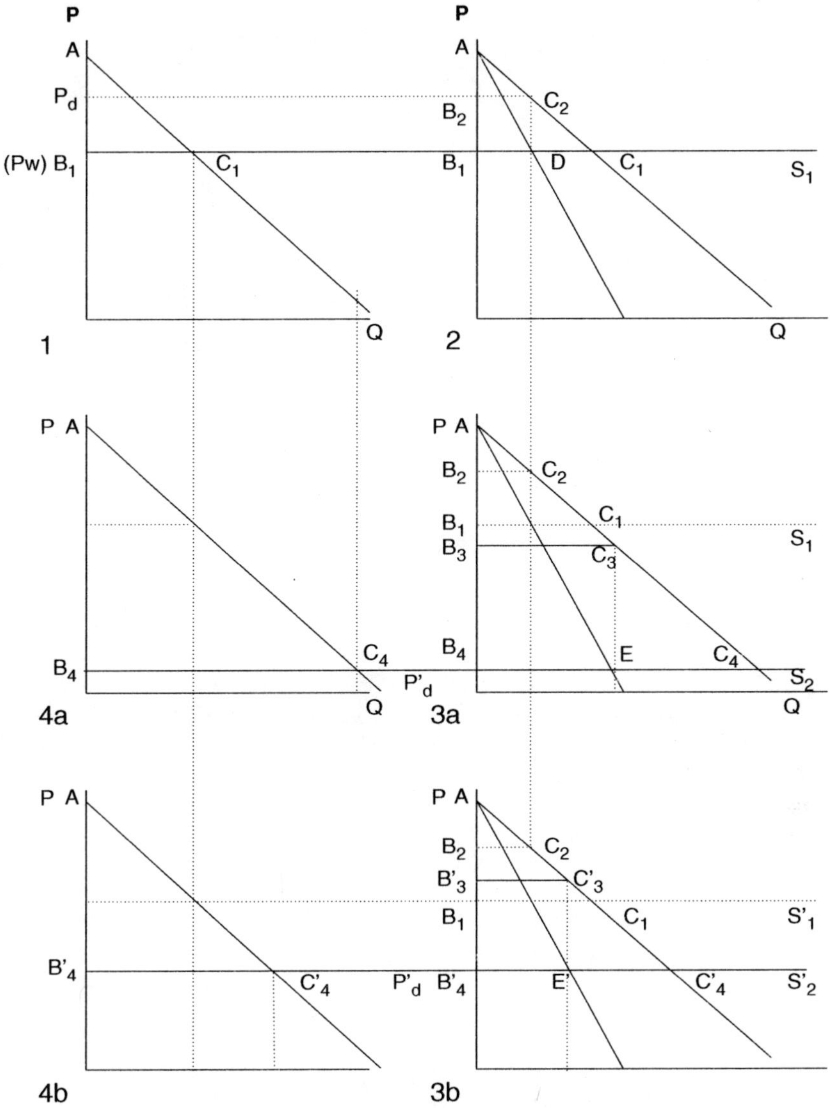

FIGURE 1 PHASE ONE:BEFORE NATIONAL PATENT LEGISLATION.

FIGURE 2 PHASE TWO: IMMEDIATE CONSEQUENCE OF PATENT LAW.

FIGURE 3A PHASE THREE: DYNAMIC IMPACT OF PATENT LAW: MAJOR INNOVATION.

FIGURE 3B PHASE THREE: DYNAMIC IMPACT OF PATENT LAW: SMALL INNOVATION.

FIGURE 4A PHASE FOUR: AFTER A PATENT EXPIRES.

FIGURE 4B PHASE FOUR: AFTER A PATENT EXPIRES.

REFERENCES

Barro, Robert and Jong-Wha Lee (2000) "International Data on Educational Attainment Updates and Implications." NBER working papers, W7911.

Bessen, James, and Eric Manskin. 2000. Sequential Innovation, Patents, and Imitation. Working Paper No. 00-01, Department of Economics, Massachusetts Institute of Technology.

Branstetter, Lee, Raymond Fisman, and Fritz Foley. 2006. "Do Stronger Intellectual Property Rights Increase International Technology Transfer?" *Quarterly Journal of Economics* 121:1, 321–349.

Cadot, Olivier, and Steven Lippman. 1995. Barriers to Imitation and the Incentive to Innovate. Working Paper No. 434, Western Management Science Institute; University of California, Los Angeles.

Challu, Pablo, M. 1995. "Effects of Monopolistic Patenting of Medicine in Italy since 1978." *International Journal of Technology Management* 10, 237–51.

Chin, Judith, and Gene Grossman. 1990. Intellectual Property Rights and North-South Trade. In Ronald W. Jones and Anne O. Krueger, eds. *The Political Economy of International Trade: Essays in Honor of Robert E. Baldwin*. Cambridge, MA: Basil Blackwell, pp. 90–107.

Cochran, W. G., and S. Paul Chambers. 1965. "The Planning of Observational Studies of Human Populations." *Journal of the Royal Statistical Society, Series A (General)*, 128: 2, 234–66.

Danzon, Patricia. 1997. *Pharmaceutical Price Regulation*. Washington DC: American Enterprise Institute.

Deardorff, Alan. 1992. "Welfare Effects of Global Patent Protection." *Economeica*, 59, 36–51.

Diwan, Isaac, and Dani Rodrik. 1991. "Patents, Appropriate Technology, and North-South Trade." *Journal of International Economics*, 30, 27–48.

Evenson, Robert E. 1990. Survey of Empirical Studies. In Wolfgang E. Siebeck, ed. *Strengthening Protection of Intellectual Property in Developing Countries: A Survey of the Literature*. Washington, DC: The World Bank Discussion Paper No.112.

Evenson, Robert E. 1990a. Intellectual Property Rights, RandD, Inventions, Technology Purchase. In Robert E. Evenson and Gustav Ranis, eds. *Science and Technology: Lessons for Development Policy*. Boulder, CO: Westview Press, pp. 325–55.

Evenson, Robert E. 1990b. Piracy in Economic Development: An International Comparative Study. In Robert E. Evenson and Gustav Ranis, eds. *Science and Technology: Lessons for Development Policy*. Boulder, CO: Westview Press, pp. 325–55.

Feenstra, R.C., R.E. Lipsey, H. Deng, A.C. Ma, and H. Mo. 2005. *World Trade Flows: 1962–2000*. NBER Working Paper 11040.

Gallini, Nancy. 1992. "Patent Policy and Costly Imitation." *Rand Journal of Economics*, 23, 52–63.

Gnanadesikan, R. 1977. *Methods for Statistical Data Analysis of Multivariate Observations*, Second Edition. New York: John Wiley & Sons.

Grabowski, Henry G., and John M. Vernon. 1992. "Brand Loyalty, Entry, and Price Competition in Pharmaceuticals after the 1984 Drug Act." *Journal of Law and Economics*. 35: 2, 331–50.

Griliches, Zvi. 1984. *R&D, Patents, and Productivity*. Chicago: The University of Chicago Press.

Ha-Joon, Chang. 2001. Intellectual Property Rights and Economic Development—Historical Lessons and Emerging Issues. In United Nations Development Programme, ed. *Human Development Report Background Papers.* New York: Human Development Report Office.

Harabi, Najib. 1997. "Appropriability of Technical Innovations: An Empirical Analysis." *Research Policy* 24: 6, 981–92.

Heckman, J. J., H. Ichimura, J. Simith, and P. Todd. 1996. "Sources of Selection Bias in Evaluating Social Programs: An Interpretation of Conventional Measures and Evidence on the Effectiveness of Matching as a Program Evaluation Method." *Proceeding of the National Academy of Sciences of the United States of America,* 93, 13,416–13,420.

Helpman, Elhanan. 1993. "Innovation, Imitation, and Intellectual Property Rights." *Econometrica,* 61, 1247–80.

Industrial Research Institute, Inc. 2000. "R&D Spending Patterns of Global Firms: Part 1 of 7." *Research Technology Management,* 43: 5, 40–56.

Jaffe, Adam. 2000. "The U.S. Patent System in Transition: Policy Innovation and the Innovation Process." *Research Policy,* 29, 531–57.

Jaffe, Adam, and Josh Lerner. 2004. *Innovation and Its Discontents: How Our Broken Patent System Is Endangering Innovation and Progress and What to Do About It.* Princeton, NJ: Princeton University Press.

Kaufer, Erich. 1989. *The Economics of the Patent System.* New York: Harwood Academic Publishers.

Kortum, Samuel, and Josh Lerner. 1998. "Stronger Protection or Technological Revolution: What Is Behind the Recent Surge in Patenting?" *Carnegie-Rochester Conference Series on Public Policy,* 48, 247–304.

Kumar, Nagesh. 1996. "Intellectual Property Protection, Market Orientation and Location of Overseas R&D Activities by Multinational Enterprises." *World Development,* 24, 673–88.

La Porta, Rafael, Florencio Lopez-de-Silanes, Andrei Shleifer, and Robert Vishney (1996). "Law and Finance." NBER Working Paper, W5661.

Lanjouw, Jean, and Iain Cockburn. 2000. Do Patents Matter? Empirical Evidence after GATT. NBER Working Paper W7495.

Lanjouw, Jean. 1998. The Introduction of Pharmaceutical Product Patents in India: Heartless Exploitation of the Poor and Suffering? NBER Working Paper W6366.

Lanjouw, J., A. Pakes, and J. Putnam. 1996. How to Count Patents and Value Intellectual Property: Uses of Patent Renewal and Application Data. NBER Working Paper W5741.

Lerner, Josh. 2000a. 150 Years of Patent Office Practice. NBER Working Paper W7477.

Lerner, Josh. 2000b. 150 Years of Patent Protection. NBER Working Paper W7478.

Levin Richard, Alvin Klevorick, Richard Nelson, and Sidney Winter., 1987. Appropriating the Returns from Industrial Research and Development. *Brookings Papers on Economic Activity,* 3, 783–820.

Love, James. 2001. Access to Medicine and Compliance with the WTO TRIPS Accord: Models for State Practice in Developing Countries. Paper for the United Nations Development Programme Consumer Project on Technology. Available online at http://www.cptech.org.

Mansfield, Edwin, Mark Schwartz, and Samuel Wagner. 1981. "Imitation Costs and Patents: An Empirical Study." *The Economic Journal,* 91, 907–18, December 1981.

Maskus, Keith. 1998. "The International Regulation of Intellectual Property." *Weltwirtschaftliches Archiv*, 134, 186–208.

Maskus, Keith. 2000. *Intellectual Property Rights in the Global Economy*. Washington, DC: Institute for International Economics.

Maskus, Keith, and D. Eby-Konan. 1994. Trade-Related Intellectual Property Rights: Issues and Exploratory Results. In Alan Deardorff and Robert M. Stern, eds. *Analytical and Negotiating Issues in the Global Trading System*. Ann Arbor, MI: University of Michigan Press.

Maskus, Keith, and M. Penubarti. 1995. "How Trade-Related Are Intellectual Property Rights?" *Journal of International Economics*, 39, 227–48.

McFetridge, Donald G. 1996. *Intellectual Property, Technology Diffusion and Growth*. Mimeo. Ottawa: Carleton University.

Moser, Petra. 2003. How Do Patent Laws Influence Innovation? Evidence from Nineteenth-Century World Fairs. NBER Working Paper 9909.

Nelson, Richard R. 1990. On Technological Capabilities and Their Acquisition. In Robert E. Evenson and Gustav Ranis, eds. *Science and Technology: Lessons for Development Policy*. Boulder, CO: Westview Press, pp. 71–80.

Park, Walter G. 2000. International Patenting, Patent Rights, and Technology Gaps. American University Manuscript, March 2000.

Patented Medicines Prices Review Board. 1997. A Comparison of Pharmaceutical Research and Development Spending in Selected Countries. Paper presented at the Canadian Economics Association Annual Meetings, St. John's, Newfoundland, June 6–8.

Pazderka, Bohumir. 1999. "Patent Protection and Pharmaceutical R&D Spending in Canada." *Canadian Public Policy*, 25: 1, 29–46.

Qian, Yi. 2007. "Do National Patent Laws Stimulate Domestic Innovation in a Global Patenting Environment?—A Cross-Country Analysis of Pharmaceutical Patent Protection: 1978–2002." *Review of Economics and Statistics*, 89: 3, 436–53.

Qian, Yi. 2008. Impacts of Entry by Counterfeiters. forthcoming at the Quarterly Journal of Economics, November, 2008, MIT Press.

Sakakibara, Mariko, and Lee Branstetter. 1999. Do Stronger Patents Induce More Innovation? Evidence from the 1988 Japanese Patent Law Reforms. NBER Working Paper 7066.

Scherer, F. M. 1977. The Economic Effects of Compulsory Patent Licensing. New York: New York University Graduate School for Business Administration.

Scherer, F. M., and Jayashree Watal. 2000. Post-TRIPS Options for Access to Patented Medicines in Developing Countries. Center of International Development Manuscript, December 2000.

Scherer, F. M., and S. Weisburst. 1995. "Economic Effects of Strengthening Pharmaceutical Patent Protection in Italy." *International Review of Industrial Property and Copyright Law*, 26, 1009–24.

Schiff, Eric. 1971. *Industrialization without National Patents*. Princeton, NJ: Princeton University Press.

Scotchmer, Suzanne, and Jerry Green. 1990. "Novelty and Disclosure in Patent Law." *Rand Journal of Economics*, 21, 131–46.

Schumpeter, Joseph. 1942. *Capitalism, Socialism, and Democracy*. New York: Harper & Brothers Publishers.

Siebeck, Wolfgang E., ed., with Robert E. Evenson, William Lessor, and Carlos A. Primo Braga. 1990. *Strengthening Protection of Intellectual Property in Developing Countries: A Survey of the Literature*. Washington, DC: World Bank Discussion Papers No. 112.

Smith, Pamela J. 1999. "Are Weak Patent Rights a Barrier to U.S. Exports?" *Journal of International Economics*, 48, 151–77.

Smith, P. 2001. "How Do Foreign Patent Rights Affect U.S. Exports, Affiliate Sales, and Licenses?" *Journal of International Economics*, 55, 411–39.

Subramanian, Arvind. 1991. "The International Economics of Intellectual Property Right Protection: A Welfare-Theoretic Trade Policy Analysis." *World Development*,19: 8, 945–56.

Taggart, James. 1993. *The World Pharmaceutical Industry*. London: Routledge.

Taylor, C., and Z. Silberston. 1973. *The Economic Impact of the Patent System*. Cambridge: Cambridge University Press.

Trouiller, Patrice, and Piero Olliaro. 1999. "Drug Development Output: What Proportion for Tropical Diseases?" *The Lancet*, 354, July 10.

UNCTAD. 1996. *The TRIPs Agreement and Developing Countries*. Geneva: United Nations Conference on Trade and Development.

United Nations Development Programme. 1999. *Human Development Report*. New York: Oxford University Press.

Yang, G., and Keith Maskus. 2001. "Intellectual Property Rights and Licensing: An Econometric Investigation." *Weltwirtschaftliches Archiv*, 137, 58–79.

10. HISTORICAL PERSPECTIVES ON PATENT SYSTEMS IN ECONOMIC DEVELOPMENT

B. ZORINA KHAN AND KENNETH L. SOKOLOFF

I. INTRODUCTION

Growth rates in per capita income vary enormously across countries, and an objective of the development agenda is to ensure that overall convergence is toward higher standards of living. Integral to this objective is the design of institutions to encourage private actors to undertake investments that are conducive to improvements in social welfare. Technological change has likewise long been realized to make a fundamental contribution to prospects for economic and social progress. It is, therefore, hardly surprising that a long history of public policies and laws crafted to stimulate would-be inventors, innovators, and investors has contributed to the advancement and diffusion of technological knowledge. A further task of analysts who wish to explain the sources of cross-country variation in national income is to understand why there is persistence over time in outcomes, and here it is clear that a historical approach is not only appropriate, but required. This chapter therefore assesses the evolution of institutions toward inventions across countries over the past two centuries, highlights the extent to which such institutions have been customized to suit the needs of social and economic circumstances, and discusses potential implications for policies toward today's developing countries and their institutions.

Over the critical period since the late eighteenth century, evidence has accumulated to indicate that ongoing technological progress is feasible, is capable of altering the fates of nations, and responds to material incentives. Consequently, the early industrializers' appreciation of the potential importance of technology policies grew over this era.[1] A wide variety of schemes were introduced and

1. Especially after the landmark British Crystal Palace Exhibition of 1851, there was a continued fascination with inventive property, including whether patent systems were

debated at one time or another, including subsidies, state investments, prizes and honorific awards, public buyouts, and permanent monopolies. By the end of the nineteenth century, patent systems had emerged as the dominant method by which national governments promoted the growth of intellectual capital in invention. An institution that had been rather obscure a century before had come to be regarded as a virtual necessity for any country with plans to industrialize or modernize.

Despite the consensus about the importance of patent laws and their implementation, important differences existed across countries in terms of how intellectual property institutions were structured; these differences remained evident even after a series of international conventions held in the 1870s and 1880s strove to obtain more uniformity. Many scholars have suggested that this historical experience offers a valuable opportunity to study the effects of differences in patent systems but have paid limited attention to determining the sources of these differences and to the issue of whether there were systematic patterns in the institutions countries chose to adopt. The issues are related because, if the particular choice of patent system is a function of a society's potential or actual inventive activity, then the estimation of the impact of a patent system is far from straightforward. Given the limited knowledge of what the historical record was, and the significance of whether patent institutions were exogenous or endogenous, this chapter will focus on the crucial patterns in the evolution of patent systems over the nineteenth century and will present evidence to support the notion that their characteristics were not exogenously determined. These conclusions bear on any assessment of the efficacy of the current regime of intellectual property rights, which has to a large extent removed such flexibility and self-determination from the portfolio of choices that today's developing economies confront.

In the first section, we discuss the evolution over time and the implications of several salient differences among the patent systems of the three leading industrial nations. As we detail below, Britain, France, and the United States were early leaders in industrialization and in establishing formal property rights in new technological information. Instead of adopting the precedent set by European standards, the United States crafted a unique approach for the design of its patent rules and standards, incorporating principles that assured broad and equal stakes in intellectual property rights to all of society. The framers of the system were confident that relatively equal access to resources and the potential for returns would ultimately generate greater economic development; as Stanley Engerman and Kenneth Sokoloff have shown in a variety of contexts, those expectations

desirable for all countries, how they should be designed, and (for individuals) how to make money from them. See Machlup and Penrose (1950) for an excellent account of one part of the debate.

were soon realized.[2] The intellectual property institutions in the United States allowed authors and inventors, regardless of their status or background, the opportunity to obtain and exploit rights to their creativity. This system also took direct, positive action to help inventors exploit their output and facilitated the development of an extensive market in patents and patented technologies. In return, American institutions required prompt disclosure and facilitated access to the additions to the stock of knowledge, so as to promote social progress in the forms of learning and additional technological change.

The second section focuses on the diffusion of patent institutions to the rest of the world, identifies systematic patterns in the characteristics of the systems countries adopted, and considers the sources of these regularities. It is, perhaps, not entirely surprising that, as patent systems spread and were revised, across the world, the great majority of countries (with several prominent exceptions, such as Germany and parts of Scandinavia) followed the Anglo-French approach. Many imposed restrictions to an even greater degree, with higher fees and more attention to working requirements. It could well be argued that "follower countries" adopted such institutions because they were better suited to their circumstances and, thus, more likely to promote their economic growth (or, at least, the objectives of influential interest groups). Follower countries were acutely aware that the bulk of new technologies was being generated abroad and may have wanted to focus their patent systems' incentives on encouraging the importation of inventions rather than on stimulating domestic invention. Alternatively, policymakers in these countries may have held that only inventors of very important inventions—whose status would be reflected in the inventor's willingness to pay high fees—deserved patent rights, or that inventors who sought patent protection (especially in cases where they were typically foreigners) might reasonably be required to share their rents with the government treasury.

The final sections conclude with a discussion of whether the relatively poor follower countries (today's developing economies) are better off under the current intellectual property rights regime. In the international sphere, in part because of active lobbying by the United States, patent systems have proliferated among the newly developing countries, but their structures and objectives have not been entirely aligned with the fundamental principles of American intellectual property rights. We find it telling that, in the earlier era through the end of the nineteenth century, when follower countries had greater leeway in choosing their patent institutions, most did not offer much in the way of access to patent rights to the great majority of their populations. We emphasize that policy measures can only be effective if based on a realization that intellectual property systems in

2. Engerman and Sokoloff (2002). William Easterly (2000) provides a theoretical model that shows how non-inclusive groups will tend to underinvest in human capital and infrastructure when there is leakage to another group and also presents evidence that supports the Engerman and Sokoloff hypothesis.

developing countries are part of a network of institutions that tend to replicate and perpetuate initial conditions. At the same time, harmonization, by restricting the menu of choices that face developing countries today, is likely to impose further constraints on the development agenda.

II. PATENT INSTITUTIONS IN THE MAJOR INDUSTRIAL NATIONS

At the beginning of the eighteenth century, Britain and a number of other European countries possessed vast empires that spanned the globe, and the American colonies simply comprised yet another entity subject to their dominion. The twentieth century, however, became known as "the American century" because of the rapid rise of the United States as the world's foremost industrial power. Academic debates have centered on the reasons for this trajectory, in part to inform policy and in part to discern the lessons that history might hold for today's developing societies. A number of influential scholars have pointed to the influence of intellectual property institutions as a factor in explaining the historical growth paths of these economies.[3] As Figure 10.1 readily shows, even without adjusting for population, the scale of patenting in the United States equaled or exceeded the entire sum of patents filed in the major European countries. It is not coincidental that European scholars have been skeptical of the beneficent effects of patent systems, whereas those who are more sanguine have tended to be students of the American experience.[4]

A. British Patent System

Britain, the first industrial nation, introduced a patent system in 1624 that has been in continuous operation for a longer period than any other in the world.[5] The Statute of Monopolies offered a grant of a patent for 14 years for "the sole making or working of any manner of new manufacture within this realm to the first and true inventor . . ."[6] The "first and true inventor" was broadly interpreted

---

3. Notably, Douglass C. North (1981) and Nathan Rosenberg and L. E. Birdzell, Jr. (1986). For an influential Japanese Commission in the nineteenth century: "We have looked about us to see what nations are the greatest so we can be like them. We asked ourselves 'What is it that makes the United States such a great nation?' and we have investigated and found that it was patents and we will have patents" (cited in Khan 2005).

4. "There is no evidence that it was institutional changes providing better rewards for innovators in the industrial era that unleashed mankind's creative potential" (Clark, 2003); see also Mokyr (1990). However, a number of U.S. scholars recently have criticized the modern American patent system, drawing on both theory and practice (Jaffe and Lerner, 2004; Stiglitz, 2006).

5. The standard references for the early British patent system are Boehm and Silberston (1967), Dutton (1984), and Macleod (1988). See also Khan (2005).

6. 21 Jac I C 3, 1623, Sec. 6.

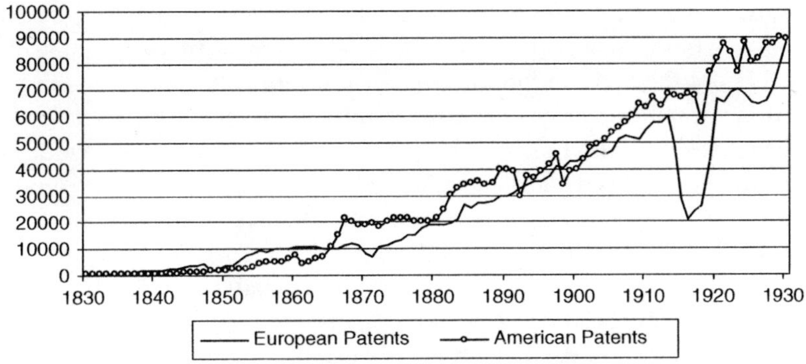

FIGURE 10.1 PATENT APPLICATIONS FOR FRANCE, BRITAIN, NETHERLANDS, GERMANY, BELGIUM, AND SPAIN COMPARED TO APPLICATIONS FOR THE UNITED STATES, 1830–1930.

Source: Federico, P. J., "Historical Patent Statistics: 1791–1961." *Journal of the Patent Office Society* 46 (Feb. 1964): pp. 89–171.

to include importers of inventions that had been created abroad, and patent agents frequently applied for patents under their own names on behalf of inventors from overseas. Certain salient features of the British patent system reflected its origins in royal privilege well into the nineteenth century. In effect, the British system advantaged groups that had more wealth, or access to private information and capital, by favoring inventors of more capital-intensive devices as opposed to smaller, incremental inventions in labor-intensive industries. Despite a series of changes in the laws (including major reforms in 1852 and 1883), these patterns characterized patenting and trade in technological information in Britain until well into the twentieth century.

Before 1852, inventors who wished to obtain protection throughout the Realm had to contend with the prohibitive bureaucracy of three separate patent systems and pay fees that ranged from £100 (four times per capita income at mid-century) for an English patent to £300 for patent rights that extended to Ireland and Scotland.[7] Potential patentees were well advised to incur additional charges in order to obtain the help of a patent agent who could aid in negotiating the numerous steps and offices required in pursuit of the application in London. The cumbersome process of patent applications (variously described as "medieval" and "fantastical") afforded ample material for satire, but obviously imposed severe

7. The complexity of the system is evident in the fact that nobody seems to have had a clear idea of the specific costs, and estimates ranged from £274 to £350. These charges should be compared to the mid-century per capita income of roughly £25 in England.

constraints on the impecunious inventor who wished to obtain protection for his discovery.[8] The complicated system also inhibited the diffusion of information and made it difficult, if not prohibitive, for inventors outside of London to conduct patent searches. However, it created substantial rents for a select class who had incentives to attempt to block prospects for reform, so it is not coincidental that the staunchest defenders of the unreformed patent system included employees of the patent applications bureaucracy, patent agents, and lawyers.

The defects of the British system led to numerous investigations and calls for institutional reform, especially after 1829. The Crystal Palace Exhibition in 1851 contributed to the official recognition of the need for legislation to meet some of these longstanding criticisms. In 1852 the patent laws were revised in the first major adjustment of the system in two centuries.[9] The patent application process was rationalized in one patent office, and fees were adjusted. A renewal system was adopted, so patentees initially paid £25 and later installments of £50 (after three years) and £100 (after seven years) to maintain the patent for a full term of 14 years. Provision was made for the printing and publication of the patent records. The 1852 reforms undoubtedly instituted improvements over the former opaque procedures. Nevertheless, the system retained many of the former features that had implied that patents were in effect viewed as privileges rather than merited rights and only temporarily abated expressions of dissatisfaction.

The state of the common law regarding patents, which was confused and prejudicial to the appropriation of returns, comprised an inefficiency that endured until the end of the nineteenth century. For instance, British patents were granted for inventions that were novel and useful, and courts did not hesitate to enforce both of these conditions. Utility under the patent law was regarded as unrelated to the commercial success of the patented invention.[10] Moreover, nineteenth-century courts held that if part of an invention had value, whereas

8. For instance, Jeremy Bentham, who favored the granting of patents, noted: "A new idea presents itself to some workman or artist. . . . He goes, with a joyful heart, to the public office to ask for his patent. But what does he encounter? Clerks, lawyers, and officers of state, who reap beforehand the fruits of his industry. This privilege is not given, but is, in fact *sold* for from £100 to £200—sums greater than he ever possessed in his life. He finds himself caught in a snare which the law, or rather extortion which has obtained the force of the law, has spread for the industrious inventor. It is a tax levied upon ingenuity, and no man can set bounds to the value of the services it may have lost to the nation." From the *Works of Jeremy Bentham*, cited in Moureen Coulter, *Property in Ideas*, p. 76.

9. The 1852 law did not apply to British colonies, which were able to adopt legislation suited to their individual circumstances.

10. According to *Badische Anilin und Soda Fabrik v. Levinstein*, 4 RPC 462, 466: "I do not think that it is a correct test of utility to enquire whether the invented product was at the time of the patent likely to be in commercial demand or capable of being produced at a cost which would make it a profitable venture."

part had no value, the entire patent was deemed to be void.[11] The question of utility was decided by judges and juries who tended to be hostile toward grants they viewed as unwarranted monopolies, which led to arbitrary decisions.[12] Because the legal system was unpredictable, patent rights could not be regarded as settled unless the patent had been contested in court with a favorable outcome.[13]

Other constraints on the market for inventions related to policies toward assignments. Ever vigilant to protect an unsuspecting public from fraudulent financial schemes on the scale of the South Sea Bubble, ownership of patent rights was limited to five investors (later extended to twelve). Nevertheless, the law did not offer any relief to the purchaser of an invalid or worthless patent, so potential purchasers were well advised to engage in extensive searches before entering into contracts.[14] When coupled with the lack of assurance inherent in a registration system, the purchase of a patent right involved a substantive amount of risk and high transactions costs—all indicative of a speculative instrument. It is, therefore, not surprising that the market for assignments and licenses seems to have been somewhat limited: even in the year after the 1852 reforms, only 273 assignments were recorded as the law required.[15]

In 1883 new legislation introduced procedures that were somewhat simpler. The fees fell to £4 for the initial term of four years and the remaining £150 could be paid in annual increments.[16] For the first time, applications could be forwarded to the Patent Office through the post office. This statute introduced opposition proceedings, which enabled interested parties to contest the proposed

---

11. *United Horsenail Co v. Stewart*, 2 RPC 132.

12. For instance, Justice Grove instructed the jury in *Young v. Rosenthal*, 1 RPC 41 that if the invention "is not as good as those existing before, or no better than those existing before in any particular point, then you would say it is not useful."

13. According to an editorial in 1862, "there can be no doubt that a large amount of property is bound up in patent rights, and that the utmost uncertainty exists as to the legal value of that property" (*Newton's London Journal*, cited in Coulter, p. 140).

14. The case law on licenses was more convoluted. See for instance *Lawes v. Purser*, 6 Ell and Bl 930, in which a licensee refused to continue payments on the grounds that the patent was void. It was held that the licensee could not make such a defense as long as the contract for the invalid patent had been executed without fraud.

15. See the first report of the Commissioner of Patents, 1853. The patent agency of Munn & Co. noted that: "From January 1, 1865 to the 1st of December, the whole number of applications for patents to the British Patent Office will not have exceeded three thousand. Within the same period the applications made by Munn & Co. to the United States Patent Office number at least three thousand five hundred; thus showing that our professional business considerably exceeds the entire business of the British Patent Office." *Scientific American* 13 (23 Dec. 1865): 415.

16. Despite the relatively low number of patents granted in England, between 1852 and 1880 the patent office had made a profit of over £2 million (*Report of the Commissioners of Patents for 1880*).

patent within two months of the filing of the patent specifications.[17] Compulsory licenses were introduced in 1883 (and strengthened in 1919 as "Licences of Right") for fear that foreign inventors might injure British industry by refusing to grant other manufacturers the right to use their patent. In 1907 patentees who manufactured abroad were required to also make the patented product in Britain.

It is worth noting that a number of the proposals for change were explicitly drawn from the American system, including lower fees and examinations for novelty. The 1852 patent reform bills had included calls for an examination system, but this was amended in the House of Commons, and the measure was not included in the final version. Opponents were allegedly reluctant to vest examiners with the necessary discretionary power, and pragmatics pointed to the shortage of a cadre of officials with the required expertise. The 1883 act provided for the employment of "examiners," but their activity was limited to ensuring that the material was patentable and properly described. Indeed, it was not until 1905 that the British system included an examination for novelty, and, even then, the process was not as stringent as that in other countries.

Changes in the British patent system were, in part, motivated by the realization that England's early industrial and technological supremacy was threatened by the United States and by other nations in Europe. The debate about patent rights in this period was far ranging, and (like today) explicitly linked questions of trade, comparative advantage, and intellectual property. Proposals extended from the creation of a national fund to reward inventors, through the abolition of any property rights in inventions; however, policies that had emerged from this era of activism were far from optimal. Legal advances in the nineteenth century were piecemeal and inadequate, consisting, as they did, of compromises between those with vested interests in maintaining rents under the former system, inventors of limited means who stood to benefit from changes, and manufacturers and politicians who wished to deter short-run foreign competition—even if at high costs in the long run.

B. French Patent System

The early French policies toward inventions and innovations in the eighteenth century are worth a close examination because they were based on an extensive array of rewards and incentives, and they illustrate the relative benefits and costs of alternative routes to statutory granting of patent rights.[18] During this period, inventors or introducers of inventions could benefit from medals, titles, and pensions that sometimes extended to spouses and offspring; loans (some interest-free); prizes and

17. The patent would be refused if the idea had been stolen, if it had previously been patented in Britain, or if the patent specification was different from the description in the provisional patent. See 46 and 47 Vic C 57, 1883.

18. Excellent assessments of such issues during the Enlightenment include Liliane Hilaire-Perez (2000).

lump-sum grants, bounties, or subsidies for production; exemptions from taxes; or monopoly grants in the form of exclusive privileges. Exclusive rights could extend to a specific region or throughout the entire kingdom, and their term varied from five years to perpetuity. This flexibility came at a cost, for such awards, prizes, and privileges could be arbitrary and based on non-economic criteria.[19] Correspondence and records from the eighteenth century provide numerous examples of awards to undistinguished inventions that were made based on court connections.[20] At the other end of the spectrum, large sums were awarded to the "deserving" on the basis of age or family need.[21] Members of the scientific community who examined applications were not necessarily qualified to assess their potential commercial value. Even if the privileges were commercially successful, active trade in these rights was inhibited because official permission had to be obtained first. Moreover, the administrative and opportunity costs of such a system were nontrivial on the part of both supplicants and the state bureaucracy.

This complex network of state policies toward inventors and their inventions was replaced after the outbreak of the French Revolution. The French patent system of 1791 declared that it comprised a major break with the past and proclaimed the natural rights of inventors, but in many ways the system resembled that of its neighbor across the channel. Throughout the nineteenth century, one detects patterns and consequences of the French policies toward inventors that are reminiscent of the former system of privileges owing only to a select group of society. Although the legal rhetoric implied that the primary intent of the legislation was to recognize the natural rights of inventors, the actual clauses led to results that were different from these proclamations and reflected former mercantilist policies. Until 1844, patents were voided if the inventor attempted to obtain a patent from another country for the same invention, in order to prevent the international diffusion of French technologies. In order to qualify for a patent of importation, the applicant

19. A law of October 16, 1791, created the Bureau of Consultation of Arts and the Trades, which consisted of 30 members drawn from various academies. They were to examine and report on the inventions, making recommendations about the rewards to offer to inventors. In 1797 this committee was replaced by the National Institute of the Sciences and Arts. The Minister of the Interior was also authorized to propose to the National Assembly any major discoveries which had been made either in France or imported to France "particulièrement lorsque ces découvertes feront dues à des travaux pénibles, ou à voyages longs et périlleux." [Sec. V of Law of 1791]. Under this law Coste d'Arnobat received 5,000 livres on the 29th of December for the importation of rhubarb into France. Archives Nationales, Files in F/12/2424. "Encouragement donné aux artistes et aux inventeurs de 1786 à 1793."

20. Archives Nationales, Files in F12/992, No. 239 (Oct. 1781). M. le Chevalier de Gruyère requested a privilege for the manufacture of a vegetable-based cosmetic rouge. He was willing to pay 1.2 million livres for the grant. His application was supported by influential women at court.

21. Archives Nationales, Files in 12/992, No. 3376.

had to have obtained practical knowledge of how the item worked through personal risk and effort, although he was not obliged to prove that the invention had been patented elsewhere nor to even state its country of origin.

Access to property rights in invention was limited by high fees, and France relied on a registration system that left the sorting of claims about priority, novelty, and general validity to the courts. The lack of a third-party assessment that examination systems provide raised the transaction costs in trading patent rights, likely hampering the growth of a market for patented technologies. The statutes placed another limit on the rights of inventors in the form of working requirements because "it would be injurious to society at large, to allow any one individual to cramp the efforts and attempts of more industrious inventors by obtaining a patent upon which he did not intend to work."[22] Patentees, therefore, had to put the invention into practice within two years from the initial grant or face a tribunal, which had the power to repeal the patent unless the patentee could point to unforeseen events that had prevented his complying with the provisions of the law.

The outlook for the evolution of an extensive market in technological knowledge (if not the impetus to further invention, as well) was further clouded by the significant obstacles that hindered those who wished to consult the specifications of previously granted patents. The French patent statutes included a statement regarding the right of the public to view patent specifications, which echoed the "bargain" theory of patents that underlay American and British grants. In return for the limited monopoly right, the patentee was expected to describe the invention in such terms that a workman skilled in the arts could replicate the invention, and this information was expected to be made public. However, since no provision was made for the publication or distribution of these descriptions, in effect, the statutory clause was a dead letter. At least until 1902, specifications were only available in manuscript form in the office in which they had originally been lodged, and printed information was limited to brief titles in patent indexes.[23] The attempt to obtain information was also inhibited by restrictions placed on access: viewers had to state their motives; foreigners had to be assisted by French attorneys; and no extract from the manuscript could be copied until the patent had expired.

The state remained involved in the discretionary promotion of invention and innovation through policies beyond the granting of patents. In the first place, the patent statutes did not limit their offer of potential appropriation of returns only to property rights vested in patents. If the inventor of a discovery could prove its utility, it was possible to make a gift of the invention to the nation in exchange for an award from funds that were set aside for the encouragement of enterprise.

22. Perpigna (1852), p. 29.

23. The law of 1844 only allowed for the publication of the full text of patents that were judged to be important.

Second, panels of eminent scientists and industrialists, belonging to institutions such as the Société d'encouragement pour l'industrie nationale, distributed a number of medals each year to stimulate new discoveries in areas they considered to be worth pursuing, and they also rewarded patents to "deserving" inventors and manufacturers. Third, the award of assistance and pensions to supplicant inventors and their families continued well into the nineteenth century. As a result, inventors had an incentive to direct their attention to rent-seeking activities in place of, or in addition to, productive efforts to commercialize their discoveries.[24]

Similarly, patent assignments were filed in the office of the prefect for the district, but, because there was no central source of information, it was difficult to trace the records for specific inventions. Like patents themselves, assignments and licenses were issued with a caveat emptor clause. This was partially the result of the nature of patent property under a registration system and partially the outcome of the uncertainties of legal jurisprudence in this area. The case law suggested that the burden of proof of validity was on the purchaser of a patent in the case of *vices apparents* such as a lack of novelty. The purchaser could be protected if the exchange involved *vices cachés* (hidden flaws); however, it was not evident which specific circumstances would qualify, and the jurisprudence contained conflicting decisions. The patentee was advised to draw up a contract explicitly stating what was implicit, and also stating that the trade was conducted without any guarantees. For both parties, the risk and uncertainties associated with the exchange reduced the net expected benefits from trade.

The basic principles of the modern French patent system were evident in the early French statutes and were retained through later revisions. Because France during the *ancien régime* was likely the first country to introduce systematic examinations of applications for privileges, it is somewhat ironic that commentators point to the retention of registration without prior examination as the defining feature of the "French system."[25] In 1910 fees remained high, although

24. *Archives Nationales,* Files in F/12/1025 (1816). The "privilege mentality" could be detected in the records for Felix Lemaistre of Paris, who invented a shoe that could be made in one piece without sewing and tried to get the state to purchase the invention. His file includes a letter from the Under-Secretary of State rejecting Lemaistre's proposal to have the government take over the invention. "C'est à vous à gérer dans vos seuls intérêts l'exploitation de votre découverte ou à quelques speculateurs particuliers qui puissent y associer par des avances de fonds." Lemaistre sold the rights in October of the following year to a firm in Paris.

25. In 1968 a partial examination system was adopted that was similar to the early British reforms along these lines, because it did not include a search for novelty but merely a test for accordance with the law: "[il] se situe à mi-chemin entre la libre délivrance et l'examen préalable. . . . en effet, l'administration n'avait pas les moyens de pratiquer un tel examen" (Marcellin, Yves. *La Procédure Franaise de Délivrance des Brevets d'Invention.* p. 21, Editions Cédat, Rosny-Sous-Bois). The changes were made to give value to patents and to protect the interests of third parties. It was only in 1978 that an examination for novelty was introduced.

somewhat lower in real terms, at 100 francs per year. When a patent was assigned, the annual fees for its entire term had to be paid in advance. Working requirements were still in place, and patentees were not allowed to satisfy the requirement by importing the article—even if the patentee had manufactured it in another European country. However, the requirement was waived if the patentee could persuade the tribunal that the patent was not worked because of unavoidable circumstances. The list of acceptable reasons that could be presented to the courts to justify inaction included a lack of capital, political or commercial crises, the availability of superior inventions that rendered the patent unprofitable, high prices of raw materials, or competition from infringers. Thus, with a modicum of ingenuity, this particular restriction could be evaded, but the time costs and uncertainty could not be avoided.

C. American Patent System

The third major model for patent institutions was that of the United States. From the introduction of the first federal intellectual property laws in 1790, the United States made a sharp and deliberate break from Old World precedent. Its system stood out as offering strong incentives for invention, across all segments of the population and for an extensive range of technologies. The U.S. system provided for relatively widespread opportunities to obtain patents and universal public access to databases with patent specifications. Both the patent rules and the legal system encouraged extensive trade in patented technologies. Another significant divergence from the Old World approach was the explicit rejection of constraints on the rights of legitimate patents in the form of working requirements or provision for compulsory licensing. These were viewed as an unwarranted infringement on productive inputs into economic progress because the disincentives to inventors were held to outweigh any potential benefits to industry or the public.

The primary feature of the "American system" is that all applications are subject to an examination for conformity with the laws and for novelty.[26] The examination system that was set in place in 1836 enabled early reviews of the basic validity of the patent grant, and, by reducing uncertainty about its asset value, facilitated enforcement of rights and trade in patented technologies. The French and English had

26. Although the statutes proposed to grant patents for "new and useful" inventions, in practice the utility claim was never enforced. Courts declared that it was up to the market, not to administrators, to determine what was useful. In the 1817 case *Lowell v. Lewis*, 15 F Cas 1018, Joseph Story charged the jury that the utility of the invention "is a circumstance very material to the interest of the patentee, but of no importance to the public. If it is not extensively useful, it will silently sink into contempt and disregard." It was, thus, the role of the market, rather than the courts, to determine the ultimate success of the patent. This policy was continued by the patent office, which also did not attempt to gauge the social or technical value of an invention, deciding conflicting claims predominantly on the basis of novelty.

opposed examination, in part because they were reluctant to create positions of power that could be abused by office holders, but the characteristic U.S. response to such potential problems was to institute a transparent policy of checks and balances. Employees of the patent office were not permitted to obtain patent rights. In order to constrain the ability of examiners to engage in arbitrary actions, the applicant was given the right to file a "bill in equity" to contest the decisions of the patent office, and the further ability to appeal decisions to the Supreme Court of the United States.

The American patent system, likewise, stands out in its insistence on affordable fees. The legislature debated the question of appropriate fees, and the first patent law in 1790 set the rate at the minimal sum of $3.70, plus copy costs. In 1793 the fees were increased to $30 and were maintained at this level until 1861, when they were raised to $35 (at a time when the average per capita income was approximately $128 in the country as a whole and $180 in the inventive Northeast region). The term was changed from 14 years (with the possibility of an extension) to 17 years (with no extensions). The 1869 Report of the Commissioner of Patents compared the $35 fee for a U.S. patent to the significantly higher charges in European countries such as Britain, France, Russia ($450), Belgium ($420), and Austria ($350), among others. The Commissioner speculated that both the private and social costs of patenting were lower in a system of impartial specialized examiners than under a system where similar services were performed on a fee-per-service basis by private solicitors. He pointed out that, in the United States, the fees were not intended to exact a price for the patent privilege—the disclosure of information was the price of the patent property right. Rather, these fees were imposed merely to cover the administrative expenses of the patent office.[27] As policymakers intended, the much lower costs of obtaining patents in the United States, as compared to other industrial nations, extended the opportunity to gain property rights in invention to a broader spectrum of the population. In other work, we have shown that artisans and people from other rather ordinary occupations accounted for a markedly larger share of patentees in the United States than in Britain during the early nineteenth century.[28]

The basic parameters of the U.S. patent system were, thus, transparent and predictable, in itself an aid to those who wished to obtain patent rights. In addition, American legislators were concerned with ensuring that information about the stock of patented knowledge was readily available and diffused rapidly, and

27. Report, 1869, pp. 4–9.

28. In work focusing on the period before the Civil War, we found that not only were the occupations reflective of a broad cross-section of the U.S. population, but that the level of formal schooling was equally inclusive. See Khan and Sokoloff (1993, 1998, 2004) and Khan (2005, 2007).

took pragmatic steps to facilitate the process.[29] As early as 1805, Congress stipulated that the Secretary of State should publish an annual list of patents granted the preceding year and, after 1832, also required the publication in newspapers of notices regarding expired patents. The patent office functioned as an extension station for knowledge, a source of centralized information on the state of the arts. However, Congress was also concerned with the question of providing decentralized access to patent materials in outlying areas. Legislators debated policies such as how to ensure that copies of specifications and models would be publicly available in each state. The patent office maintained repositories throughout the country, where inventors could forward their patent models at the expense of the office. Rural inventors could apply for patents without significant obstacles because applications could be submitted by mail free of postage.

American laws employed the language of the English statute in granting patents to "the first and true inventor." Nevertheless, unlike in England, the phrase was used literally: to grant patents for inventions that were original in the world, not simply within U.S. borders. Unlike many other countries of the world, patents for imported discoveries were never permitted. American patent laws provided strong protection for citizens of the United States but varied over time in their treatment of foreign inventors. The earliest statutes of 1793, 1800, and 1832 restricted patent property to citizens or to residents who declared that they intended to become citizens (although it should be noted that, even in the earliest years, foreigners frequently were successful in their petitions to Congress to gain American patents). As such, although an American could not appropriate patent rights to a foreign invention, he could freely use the idea without any need to bear licensing or similar costs that would otherwise have been due if the inventor had been able to obtain a patent in this country. In 1836, the stipulations on citizenship or residency were removed but were replaced with discriminatory patent fees that owed to a policy of reciprocity for the higher fees in other countries: generally, foreigners could obtain a patent in the United States for a fee of $300—or $500 if they were British. After 1861, patent rights (with the exception of caveats) were available to all applicants on the same basis without regard to nationality. During the proceedings to celebrate the centenary of the

29. When a fire destroyed the patent office records in 1836, Congress appropriated $100,000 for the restoration of the patent records up to that date. See the Act of 1837, Section 4. As early as 1828, the office freely distributed circulars with information about the law relating to patents and on how to apply for a patent. These ad hoc circulars became more extensive and were subsequently entitled the "Rules of Practice," formalized by the Act of 1870. After 1870, the patent office began to publish weekly information on granted patents in the form of the *Official Gazette*. By 1891, more than 3,000 copies of the *Gazette* were being distributed each week without charge to libraries, depositories, or members of Congress, and a further 3,000 copies were circulated to subscribers for a nominal fee of $5 per year.

U.S. patent system, this liberality was noted as one of its essential features and, indeed, was acknowledged throughout the world. Nevertheless, this "generosity" had hardly any real implications in an environment in which few foreign technologists were competitive with domestic U.S. inventors, as gauged by the low percentage of patents claimed by nonresident patentees until well into the twentieth century.

The American patent system was based on the presumption that social welfare coincided with the individual welfare of inventors. Accordingly, legislators emphatically rejected restrictions on the rights of American inventors.[30] Another very important feature of the U.S. system was its extraordinarily favorable rules toward trade in patent rights. From the special provision made in the 1790 law for keeping a registry of all assignments onward, it is clear that the framers of the system expected and desired an extensive market in patents to develop. On one hand, assignments provide a straightforward index of the effectiveness of the American system, because trade in inventions would hardly proliferate if patent rights were uncertain or worthless. But the market in patents that the extensive volume of assignments reflects is, in fact, far more significant. In defining a tradable asset, the system enhanced the potential private and social returns all the more by enabling patentees to extract income from their ideas by selling them off to a party better positioned for commercial exploitation. This division of labor helped creative individuals specialize in their comparative advantage.

As seen in Figure 10.2, it is apparent that the volume of trade in U.S. patents was much higher than that in British patents, and the contrast is the more remarkable because the British figures include licenses together with assignments.[31] It is difficult to explain the difference without relying primarily on the role of the examination system in providing some validation to patents, and thus decreasing the transaction costs of market exchange. The patent system also encouraged trade in technology by requiring immediate public disclosure of the

---

30. The 1832 and 1836 laws stipulated that foreigners had to exploit their patented invention within 18 months, but these clauses seem to have been interpreted by the courts in a fairly liberal fashion. *See Tatham et al. v. Lowber et al.*, 23 F Cas 721, April 21, 1847. In any case, such provisions proved to be quite transient and were not included in subsequent legislation. Working requirements or compulsory licenses were regarded as unwarranted infringements of the rights of "meritorious inventors" and as being incompatible with the philosophy of U.S. patent grants. Patentees were not required to pay annuities to maintain their property; there were no opposition proceedings; and, once granted, a patent could not be revoked unless there was evidence of fraud.

31. The law required that assignments be reported to the patent office within three months in order for them to be legally binding. If one estimates the volume of assignments over the late nineteenth century from the reports of the fees the patent office collected from registering assignments and compares the ratios of annual estimated totals to the ratios of the reported number of assignments and licenses to patents in Britain, one can gauge the relative volume of trade in patents to the number of patents in the two countries.

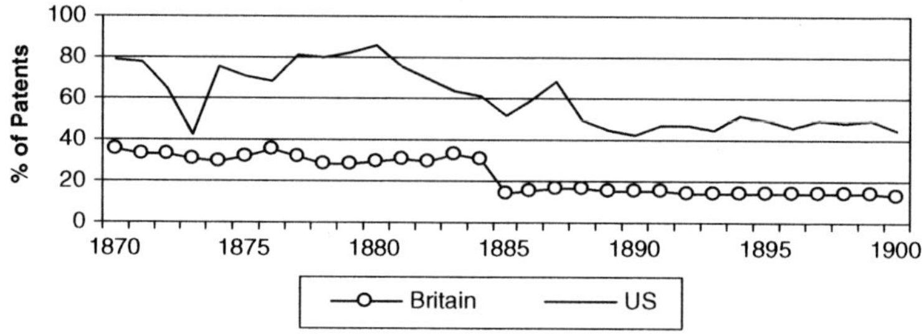

FIGURE 10.2 MARKET FOR INVENTIONS IN BRITAIN AND THE UNITED STATES, 1870–1900.

Sources: United States: *Annual Report of the Commissioner of Patents*, various years. Because the number of words per assignment fell significantly over time, the trend is biased downward. The figure reports the ratio of assignments in the given year to the number of patents in that year. Britain: The series represents all assignments and licenses as a fraction of total patents sealed in that year. *Annual Report of the Commissioners/Comptroller General of Patents*, various years.

specifications of patents and by helping to disseminate this information broadly. As mentioned above, early in the nineteenth century, the Patent Office began to regularly publish descriptions of patent grants and maintained offices throughout the country where models of recently patented inventions could be displayed and examined. Public knowledge about new patents and developments in technology was likewise spread by the growing legions of patent agents or lawyers who materialized soon after the 1836 law, especially in major cities and other localities where rates of patenting were high. Over time, intermediation in this market for technology grew ever more articulated in a process not unlike the evolution of financial intermediaries. As the extent of the market for technology expanded over the course of the nineteenth century, creative individuals with a comparative advantage in technology appear to have increasingly specialized in inventive activity. This tendency was likely reinforced by the increasing importance to inventors of specialized technical knowledge as technology became more complex.

Overall, the patent system played a larger role in the processes of technological change in the United States than it did in Britain or France. The much lower cost of obtaining a patent in the United States attracted a broader spectrum of the population to pursue property rights protection, especially during the first three-quarters of the century when individuals with very modest education levels were still represented among even the most prominent of great inventors. Of perhaps even more importance over the longer term, the patent system was crucial in facilitating markets in technological knowledge by defining legally enforceable rights in intellectual capital. At least judging from the experience of the

United States, the greater ease of effecting transactions involving technological knowledge could and did encourage creative individuals to invest in invention-augmenting human capital to raise their productivity at invention. Not only did the most productive inventors of the late nineteenth century specialize at invention and rely extensively on the market to extract their returns, but inventors in the geographic areas with the highest rates of inventive activity were more likely to trade in patent rights. The operations of this market for technology thus seem likely to have raised the level of inventive activity (and patenting), both through increasing the return to such investment and by increasing the productivity of resources allocated toward invention.

III. FOLLOWER COUNTRIES AND PATENT INSTITUTIONS

Tracing back at least as far as Alexander Gerschenkron, scholars of long-term economic development have wondered whether follower countries naturally evolve, if not benefit, from a systematically different set of institutions than do early industrializers. Gerschenkron's analysis, in particular, focused on capital-market institutions, but some of his insights might well apply to the question of what sort of intellectual property institutions follower countries might evolve.[32] As with financial capital, follower countries might have had difficulty mobilizing all forms of capital (including social and intellectual capital) to invest in inventive activity and, thus, be expected to be more oriented toward developing institutions that would mobilize technological knowledge from foreign sources. As societies decided to establish or revise their patent institutions, they were able to draw from the example and experiences of the three leading industrial nations of the early nineteenth century, each of which was also a pioneer in formulating innovations in public policy toward technology. However, the nations that came after Britain, the United States, and France modified existing institutions to fit their own particular needs. They adopted patent systems that were very much focused on securing, or adjusting to, flows of technology from abroad, especially technological knowledge that was embodied in actual production.

Table 10.1 categorizes the salient features of patent laws and systems in these countries, which clearly exhibit significant diversity. The Spanish experience during the nineteenth century is instructive, because this country lagged well behind the early industrializers. Per capita rates of patenting in Spain were lower than in other major European countries, and foreigners filed the majority of patented inventions; thus, the transfer of foreign technology was a major concern in the political economy of Spain. This dependence on foreign technologies

32. Gerschenkron (1976) explicitly identified the ability to draw on the technologies developed in those countries that had industrialized earlier as one of the greatest advantages for follower countries.

TABLE 10.1 DESCRIPTIVE CHARACTERISTICS OF PATENT SYSTEMS

	Examination System	Working Requirements or Compulsory Licenses	Patents for Importation or Introduction	Cost
EUROPE				
Austria				
1871	—	Y	Y	$$
1899	Y	Y	N	$$$$
Belgium				
1848	N	Y	Y	$$$
1871	N	Y	Y	$$$
1899	N	Y	N	$$
Denmark				
1871	—	Y	—	$$
1899	Y	Y	N	$$
France				
1848	N	Y	Y	$$$
1871	N	Y	—	$$$
1899	N	Y	N	$$$
Germany				
1891	Y	Y	N	$$$$
1899	Y	Y	N	$$$$
Great Britain				
1848	N	N	Y	$$$$
1871	N	Y	Y	$$$$
1899	N	Y	N	$$$$
Italy				
1871	N	Y	Y	$$
1891	N	Y	Y	$$$
1899	N	Y	Y	$$$
Norway				
1871	—	Y	—	$$
1899	Y	Y	N	$$
Portugal				
1848	N	Y	Y	$
1899	N	Y	Y	$

	Examination System	Working Requirements or Compulsory Licenses	Patents for Importation or Introduction	Cost
Prussia				
1871	Y	Y	N	$$
Russia				
1848	—	Y	Y	$$$$
1871	—	Y	Y	$$$$
1899	Y	Y	Y	$$$$
Spain				
1848	N	Y	Y	$$$
1871	N	Y	Y	$$$
1899	N	Y	Y	$$
Sweden				
1848	—	Y	Y	—
1871	—	Y	—	$$
1899	Y	Y	N	$$
SOUTH AND CENTRAL AMERICA				
Argentina				
1891	N	Y	Y	$$$$
Brazil				
1871	N	Y	Y	$$$
1891	N	Y	—	$$$$
1899	N	Y	N	$$$$
Br. Guiana				
1891	N	N	—	$$$$
Br. Honduras				
1891	N	N	—	$$$$
Chile				
1891	N	Y	—	$$$
Colombia				
1891	N	Y	—	$$$
Cuba				
1871	N	Y	Y	$$$
Ecuador				
1891	N	Y	Y	$$

	Examination System	Working Requirements or Compulsory Licenses	Patents for Importation or Introduction	Cost
Guatemala				
1891	N	Y	Y	$$$
Mexico				
1871	N	Y	N	$$$$
1899	N	N	N	$$$$
Peru				
1891	N	Y	N	$$$$
Uruguay				
1891	N	Y	—	$$$$
Venezuela				
1891	N	Y	N	$$$$
OTHERS				
Barbados				
1891	N	Y	—	$$$
Canada				
1871	—	Y	N	$
1899	Y	Y	N	$
Fiji				
1891	N	N	—	$$
Hawaii				
1891	Y*	N	Y	$$
India				
1891	N	Y	—	$$$$
Jamaica				
1891	N	Y	—	$$$
Japan				
1899	Y	Y	N	$$
Liberia				
1891	Y*	Y	—	$$$
Mauritius				
1891	N	N	N	$$
New South Wales				
1891	N	N	N	$

	Examination System	Working Requirements or Compulsory Licenses	Patents for Importation or Introduction	Cost
New Zealand				
1891	N	Y	N	$$
South Africa				
1891	N	N	—	$$$
United States				
1848	Y	N	N	$
1899	Y	N	N	$

* Although this country officially had an examination system, its patent office does not appear to have carried out a serious examination of applications for novelty or utility. The code for cost pertains to the estimated cost in current $US for a patent taken to a term of 15 years. In those countries where the maximum term is less than 15, the cost is for a patent of that term. $ = ≤$100; $$ = >$100 but ≤$250; $$$ = >$250 but ≤$400; $$$$ = >$400.
Sources: 1848: John Kingsley and Joseph Piesson, *Laws and Practice of All Nations and Governments Relating to Patents of Inventions* (New Yourk: Kingsley and Piesson, 1848).
1871: *United States and International Patent Office Manual* (New York: Fitch and Co., 1871)
1891: *Epitome of the World's Patent Laws and Statstics* (New York: The British and European Patent Agency, 1891).
1899: Arthur Greeley, *Foreign Patent and Trademark Laws* (Washington, DC: John Byrne and Co., 1899).

was reflected in the structure of the Spanish patent system, which permitted patents of introduction or grants to entrepreneurs who wished to produce foreign technologies that were new to Spain, with no requirement of claims to being the true inventor. Patentees were required to work the patent within one year, and the rather high proportion of about a quarter of patents granted between 1826 and 1878 were actually implemented. Because patents of introduction had a brief term, they encouraged the production of items with greater expected profits and a quick payback period, after which monopoly rights expired, and the country could benefit from diffusion.

One of the features that stands out from the table is that, with only a few exceptions, nearly all these societies were like Spain in maintaining working requirements (or, in a few cases, compulsory licensing) as a central component of their patent systems. Similarly, the great majority of follower countries had provisions for so-called patents of importation, whereby one who was the first to introduce a new, foreign technology to the country (regardless of whether he or she were the inventor) could obtain a property right (typically lasting until the original foreign patent on the technology expired). This was disallowed late in the century after international patent conventions—under pressure from the United States—urged countries to adopt the principle that original inventors alone had the right to a patent. Even then, many countries specified that the first applicant for a patent would be presumed to be the inventor, and only the actual inventor would have legal standing to have the patent voided.

It might be further noted that the influence of colonial heritage is not nearly as powerful as one might have expected. There was, for example, enormous diversity in the characteristics of the patent systems of the British colonies. The quite different institutional path of the more developed follower countries is also of much relevance for studying whether the selection of patent system characteristics was exogenous or endogenous. Germany had very high fees for obtaining patents that were of interest to foreigners but also offered "petty patents" that were considerably more accessible to local residents. Japan emerged from the Meiji era as a follower nation that deliberately designed institutions to emulate those of the most advanced industrial countries. The influence of the German laws were evident in subsequent Japanese reforms in 1909 (petty patents for minor inventions were protected) and 1921 (protection was removed from chemical products, work-for-hire doctrines were adopted, and an opposition procedure was introduced). However, even in its earliest statute, differences existed that reflected Japanese priorities: patents were not granted to foreigners; protection could not be obtained for fashion, food products, or medicines; patents that were not worked within three years could be revoked; and severe remedies were imposed for infringement, including penal servitude. Subsequent legislation also permitted the state to revoke a patent grant on payment of appropriate compensation if it were deemed to be in the public interest. Medicines, food, and chemical products could not be patented, but protection could be obtained for processes relating to their manufacture.

It might be argued that follower countries that are particularly underdeveloped have no interest in maintaining a patent system, because the native population would not be very likely to make new contributions to technological knowledge. It is traditional to point to Switzerland (up to 1888) and the Netherlands (1869–1912) as models for progress without patents, but in our view, these examples do not have much general significance beyond their unique circumstances. For instance, in Switzerland, the scale of output and markets were quite limited; much of Swiss industry generated few incentives for invention; and most of the items at which Swiss manufacturers excelled, such as handmade watches, chocolates, and food products, were not susceptible to technological improvements warranting patent protection. Export-oriented inventors were likely to have been more concerned about patent protection in the important overseas markets, rather than at home. Once technical changes began to render artisanal methods obsolete in products with mass markets, the Swiss endogenously adopted patent laws because of falling competitiveness in their key industrial sectors.

What was the impact of the introduction of patent protection in Switzerland? Foreign inventors could obtain patents in the United States regardless of the state of patent legislation in their native land, so we can approach this question tangentially by examining the patterns of patenting in the United States by Swiss residents before and after the 1888 reforms. After the introduction of its own domestic system, the rate of Swiss patenting in the United States immediately increased relative to the previous era. Moreover, the introduction of Swiss patent laws also affected the direction of inventions that Swiss residents patented in the United States. After the passage of the law, such patents covered a much broader range of inventions, including gas generators, textile machines, explosives, turbines, paints and dyes, drawing instruments, and lamps, and the relative importance of watches and music boxes immediately fell. Thus, the evidence on Switzerland suggests that the introduction of patent rights was accompanied by changes in the rate and direction of inventive activity. In short, although the Swiss experience is often cited as proof of the redundancy of patent protection, the limitations of this special case should be taken into account.

In the case of more typical developing countries, one could justify the implementation of an effective patent system if it were necessary to make substantial investments to import technologies from abroad or if the cooperation or assistance of the original inventor were an important factor for diffusion and later upgrades. To the extent that capital-intensive technologies were more likely than labor-intensive technologies to satisfy either of these criteria, another striking feature of the characteristics of patent systems in follower countries might make sense. As Table 10.1 shows, many of the follower countries (especially those that were less developed) assessed very high fees for patents, at rates that are all the more remarkable for the relatively low per capita incomes prevailing there. Indeed, many Central and South American countries were distinguished for having fees for patent protection that were among the highest in the world, and the pattern holds across quite a range of national institutional heritages (Brazil, British Honduras, and Peru, for example). The logic is that high fees might not be such a disincentive to investing in a country with high patenting costs if the application of the technology required a major outlay for the actual investment in plant; the marginal increment of the cost of the patent would be relatively insignificant for the potential investor (especially given that even the high fees of the late nineteenth century might not seem so lofty to the foreigners who predominated among the patentees—see Table 10.2). Of course, another possible explanation for the high fees is that they helped insulate businessmen with considerable resources from competition. Given that onerous patent fees were typical in Central and South America, where inequality in wealth and political influence was extreme as compared to, say, Spain and Portugal (which also had rather low per capita incomes), this hypothesis is perhaps worth further investigation.

TABLE 10.2 PROPORTION OF PATENTS AWARDED TO FOREIGN RESIDENTS, C. 1900

Australia	1905	37.8*
Austria	1894	60.4
	1898	67.2
	1902	77.0
Belgium	1901	78.4
Brazil	1896	44.5
Canada	1893	78.3
	1903	86.0
Denmark	1903	69.2
France	1906	52.5
	1911	51.9
Germany	1895	33.2
	1900	36.9
	1905	34.5
Hungary	1895	80.7
	1900	78.4
	1905	72.7
India	1899	69.9*
Italy	1904	64.4
Luxembourg	1907	98.3
Mexico	1904	57.6
New Zealand	1898	65.9
Norway	1907	77.8
Portugal	1907	86.3
Russia	1898	82.8
	1908	74.8
Sweden	1894	56.9
Tunisia	1904	68.0
Turkey	1909	94.1
U.K.	1901	53.2
U.S.A.	1901	13.3

* Based on the proportion of patent applications submitted by foreign residents.
Source: World Intellectual Property Rights Organization, *100 Years Protection of Industrial Property: Statistics*. Geneva, 1983.

Such differences, whether or not advisable, were gradually eliminated or moderated as international conventions, with overarching goals of pursuing uniform international patent laws, proliferated. International gatherings tended to reflect the objectives of the convenors, rather than real attempts to reach compromise solutions that would reflect the needs and wishes of all participants: the United States was the most prolific patenting nation in the world; many of the major American enterprises owed their success to patents and were expanding into international markets; and the U.S. patent system was recognized as the most successful. It is therefore not surprising that, despite resistance from other nations, patent harmonization implied convergence toward the American model.

IV. HISTORY LESSONS FOR PATENTS AND POLICY IN THE TWENTY-FIRST CENTURY

The historical comparison of patent systems supports the claim that intellectual property institutions over the past two centuries were largely endogenous. In other words, the evidence suggests that the types of patent systems adopted were systematically related to factors associated with the potential for inventive activity or economic development more generally. Although the major question of whether the type of patent institutions a country evolves are good for social welfare (as opposed to generating narrow benefits for a politically influential group) remains open, this finding has at least three implications. First, that patent rules vary with context implies that the harmonization of intellectual property regimes across countries at different levels of economic development may impose significant costs on some countries. Second, constraints that are imposed in one policy arena (namely, intellectual property rights) may have countervailing or unintended consequences in other unconstrained areas (such as competition policies, taxes, trade practices or tariffs, or contract laws). Third, scholars who try to relate patterns of invention in a country to the characteristics of that country's patent systems should adjust for the likelihood of endogeneity between the two variables.

Endogenous growth models encouragingly suggest that technological change is not exogenous but can be induced through effective policies, and proposals to bridge this divide have become a global priority. We believe that any effective discussion of the desirable and feasible elements of appropriate intellectual property institutions needs to incorporate the lessons of history. To that effect, we now present some of the preliminary conclusions that can be drawn from the historical record. Such conclusions are based on the premise that, for all their flaws, the market-orientation of effective patent institutions comprises the most productive means of inducing technological and social progress. Although some researchers have recommended the use of non-market policy instruments such as state grants and prizes, the abundant evidence from France during the Age of Enlightenment and from developing countries today illustrates the inefficiencies and corruption that are likely to accompany their use.

Generally, the experience in Europe and America underlines that successful policies assure access to property rights and to the returns from individual efforts to all members of society. In practical terms, this translates into policies that encourage widespread participation, such as affordable fees and the adherence to predictable rules and procedures. Perhaps even more important are effective mechanisms to disseminate and manage information. An examination system worked well for the United States because, from the earliest decades, it was fortunate to possess high stocks of information and human capital; for other countries, an opposition system effectively economized on these relatively scarce resources. Today much is made of the benefits of information on the Internet, but the reality is that such sources are likely to be of little use to the majority of the population in developing countries, and the commitment of public organizations to the supposedly elementary aspects of provision and diffusion may play a much more productive role in the democratization of innovation.

Corporate interest groups in the twentieth century successfully lobbied to prohibit discriminatory enforcement that varied across sectors or products, but the historical record demonstrates that, except for the United States, the majority of countries adopted different levels of protection for vital industries, such as drugs, foodstuffs, and national security. A further distinction was made between different types of patent grants, such as the two-tiered system that Germany introduced in the nineteenth century. German patent rules distinguished between the high-value/high-cost grant of a full patent that is likely to be dominated by multinationals and a lower-value/low-cost model with a shorter term. The cost of administration was low because, unlike regular patents, petty patents were not subject to an initial examination. In both Germany and Japan, they proved to be an effective way of allowing residents to participate in the patent system and created an incentive for the commercialization of follow-on inventions. Thus, today's developing countries might similarly create incentives for domestic ingenuity, as well as diffusion, through a two-tiered system that allows weaker property rights for incremental inventions with a shorter term.

A significant part of the value of any property right derives from its enforcement. The legal system comprises an important aspect of an intellectual property regime, implying that changes in IPR rules must occur in tandem with developments in the courts, the judiciary, the legal system, and society in general. To other countries that wish to emulate the success of the United States in patenting, the prescription necessarily includes similar attention to legal institutions. For developing countries with a much inferior stock of legal resources, in practical terms, this is likely to require a long-term evolutionary process of building legal capital, providing at least one reason to suggest that policies to strengthen intellectual property rights are unlikely to succeed instantly. In terms of a more rule-oriented level of enforcement, from the very beginning of the movement toward international harmonization of patent laws, deep divisions have occurred regarding the extent to which restrictions should be placed on the rights of patentees, including stipulations about working requirements and compulsory licenses. The United States has consistently opposed these mechanisms—and for good reason, because such legal expropriation tends to be arbitrarily applied and is associated with significant disincentives for invention.

A final aspect of this discussion relates to the cultural context of intellectual property rights regimes. The United States created institutions that accorded well with the needs of an economic and political democracy based on a belief in individual rights and an entrepreneurial, free-market orientation. However, such institutions may function less effectively in societies with alternative values, such as states that are not liberal democracies or indigenous communities in which additions to knowledge and innovations are regarded as public goods. Scholars of China, in particular, fault the attempt to dictate Western intellectual property precepts to a country where Confucian philosophy and traditional values still prevail. At the very least, attempts to institute such Western-style intellectual property regimes should begin with an understanding that effective reforms may require fundamental social and cultural changes that are unlikely to occur overnight, even with the strongest of political wills on the part of developing countries.

In sum, the quest for harmonization in intellectual property rights has resulted in a "race to the top," directed by the efforts and self-interest of the countries that have had the strongest property rights. In the international sphere, the preferences and interests of the United States have been to replicate its domestic policies toward patent holders, which have been the most liberal in the world. Some of the changes in the American and European intellectual property regimes assessed in this study, such as the introduction of the examination of patent applications, implemented what might be thought of as technical improvements. However, others, such as product exemptions and the use of compulsory licenses, involved adaptations that seem related to the stage of a country's economic development. This analysis of the evolution of intellectual property regimes in Europe and the United States raises questions about the desirability of applying the same system to all places at all times. Indeed, the major lesson that one derives from this aspect of the economic history of Europe and America is that intellectual property rights best promoted the progress of science and arts when they evolved in tandem with other institutions and in accordance with the needs and interests of social and economic development in each nation. As Thomas Jefferson long ago pointed out, perhaps one of the most crucial elements of achieving growth is to ensure that institutions are sufficiently flexible in responding to the needs of a developing society.

REFERENCES

British Parliamentary Papers. 1968. 2 Reports from Select Committees on the Law Relative to Patents for Inventions, 1829–72. Shannon: Irish University Press.

Clark, Gregory. 2003. The Great Escape: The Industrial Revolution in Theory and in History. Working Paper.

Coulter, Moureen. 1991. *Property in Ideas.* Kirksville, MO: Thomas Jefferson University Press at Northeast Missouri State University.

Crosland, Maurice, and Antonio Galvez. 1989. The Emergence of Research Grants within the Prize System of the French Academy of Sciences, 1795–1914. *Social Studies of Science* 19 (1): 71–100.

Dutton, Harold I. 1984. *The Patent System and Inventive Activity during the Industrial Revolution, 1750–1852.* Manchester, UK: Manchester University Press.

Easterly, William. May 2000. The Middle Class Consensus and Economic Development. World Bank Policy Research Working Paper No. 2346.

Engerman, Stanley L., and Kenneth L. Sokoloff. 2002. Factor Endowments, Inequality, and Paths of Development among New World Economies. *Economia* 3 (Fall): 41–102.

Federico, P. J. 1964. Historical Patent Statistics: 1791–1961. *Journal of the Patent Office Society* 46 (Feb. 1964): 89–171.

Gerschenkron, Alexander. 1976. *Economic Backwardness in Historical Perspective.* Cambridge, MA: Belknap Press.

Hilaire-Perez, Liliane. 2000. *L'invention technique au siècle des Lumières.* Paris: Albin Michel.

Jaffe, Adam, and Josh Lerner. 2004. Innovation and Its Discontents: How Our Broken Patent System is Endangering Innovation and Progress, and What to Do About It. Princeton, NJ: Princeton University Press.

Johnson, James, and J. Henry Johnson. 1890. *The Patentee's Manual: A Treatise on the Law and Practice of Patents for Inventions.* London: Longmans, Green & Co.

Khan, B. Zorina. 2005. The Democratization of Invention: Patents and Copyrights in American Economic Development, 1790–1920. New York: Cambridge University Press.

Khan, B. Zorina. 2007. Science and Technology in the British Industrial Revolution: Evidence from Great Inventors, 1750–1930. Working Paper.

Khan, B. Zorina, and Kenneth L. Sokoloff. 1993. Schemes of Practical Utility. *Journal of Economic History* 53 (2): 289–307.

Khan, B. Zorina, and Kenneth L. Sokoloff. 1998. Two Paths to Industrial Development and Technological Change. In Maxine Berg, Kristine Bruland, eds., *Technological Revolutions in Europe, 1760–1860.* Cheltenham: Edward Elgar, 292–313.

Khan, B. Zorina, and Kenneth L. Sokoloff. 2001. The Early Development of Intellectual Property Institutions in the United States. *Journal of Economic Perspectives* 15 (3): 233–246.

Khan, B. Zorina, and Kenneth L. Sokoloff. 2004. Institutions and Democratic Invention in 19th Century America. *American Economic Review* 94 (2): 395–401.

Kremer, Michael. 1998. Patent Buyouts: A Mechanism for Encouraging Innovation. *Quarterly Journal of Economics* 113 (4): 1137–67.

Lamoreaux, Naomi R., and Kenneth L. Sokoloff. 1996. Long-Term Change in the Organization of Inventive Activity. *Proceedings of the National Academy of Sciences* 93 (Nov.): 12,686–12,692.

Machlup, Fritz, and Edith Penrose. 1950. The Patent Controversy in the 19th Century. *Journal of Economic History* 10 (Mar.): 1–29.

MacLeod, Christine. 1988. *Inventing the Industrial Revolution.* Cambridge: Cambridge University Press.

MacLeod, Roy M. 1971. Of Medals and Men: A Reward System in Victorian Science, 1826–1914. *Notes and Records of the Royal Society of London* 26 (1): 81–105.

Marcellin, Yves. 1983. *La Procédure Française de Délivrance des Brevets d'Invention.* Editions Cédat, Rosny-Sous-Bois.

Maurer, Stephen M., and Suzanne Scotchmer. 2004. Procuring Knowledge. In Gary Libecap, ed., *Intellectual Property and Entrepreneurship: Advances in the Study of Entrepreneurship, Innovation and Growth* 15: 1–31.

Mokyr, Joel. 1990. *The Lever of Riches: Technological Creativity and Economic Progress.* Oxford: Oxford University Press.

Murphy, Kevin M., Andrei Shleifer, and Robert W. Vishny. 1991. The Allocation of Talent: Implications for Growth. *Quarterly Journal of Economics* 106 (2): 503–30.

North, Douglass C. 1981. *Structure and Change in Economic History.* New York: W. W. Norton & Company.

Perpigna, Antoine. 1852. *The French Law and Practice of Patents for Inventions, Improvements, and Importations.* Philadelphia: J. S. Littell.

Rosenberg, Nathan, and L. E. Birdzell, Jr. 1986. *How the West Grew Rich: The Economic Transformation of the Industrial World.* New York: Basic Books.

Shavell, Steven, Tanguy van Ypersele. 2001. Rewards versus Intellectual Property Rights. *Journal of Law and Economics* 44 (2): 525–47.

Sobel, Dava. 1995. *Longitude: the True Story of a Lone Genius Who Solved the Greatest Scientific Problem of His Time.* New York: Penguin Books.

Sokoloff, Kenneth L. 1988. Inventive Activity in Early Industrial America: Evidence from Patent Records, 1790–1846. *Journal of Economic History* 48 (4): 813–50.

Sokoloff, Kenneth L., and Stanley L. Engerman. 2000. Institutions, Factor Endowments, and Paths of Development in the New World. *Journal of Economic Perspectives* 14 (Summer): 217–32.

Sokoloff, Kenneth L. 1992. Invention, Innovation, and Manufacturing Productivity Growth during the Antebellum Period. In Robert Gallman, and John Wallis, eds., *The Standard of Living in Early 19th Century America.* Chicago: University of Chicago Press.

Sokoloff, Kenneth L., and B. Zorina Khan. 1990. The Democratization of Invention during Early Industrialization: Evidence from the United States, 1790–1846. *Journal of Economic History* 50 (June): 363–78.

Stiglitz, Joseph. December 2006. Scrooge and Intellectual Property Rights. *British Medical Journal* 333 (7582): 1279–80.

PART FIVE

ACCESS TO MEDICINE

11. EXPANDING PATENT RIGHTS IN PHARMACEUTICALS
The Linkage between Patents and Drug Registration

CARLOS M. CORREA

I. INTRODUCTION

Patents confer a set of exclusive rights that, depending on the particular situation of the relevant market, creates considerable power to determine prices and other sale conditions.[1] Article 28.1 of the TRIPS Agreement provides that a product patent shall confer on its owner the following exclusive rights: "to prevent third parties not having the owner's consent from the acts of: making, using, offering for sale, selling, or importing for these purposes that product." "Offering for sale" includes acts performed with the intent of selling patented products.[2] Correctly interpreted, in accordance with the method prescribed by articles 31 and 32 of the Vienna Convention on the Law of the Treaties, "offering for sale" does not include preparatory acts that may eventually lead to the offer for sale and ultimately to the sale of a patented product, such as those necessary to obtain regulatory approval for marketing a drug (or agrochemical product).

Nonetheless, in some countries, provisions stretch the patent owner's exclusive rights by allowing him or her to block the regulatory approval of marketing for the competing pharmaceutical "generic" products. Such provisions create a "linkage" between patent protection and drug-marketing approval, despite the fact that the objectives of these two areas of regulation differ completely. Whereas patent protection aims at rewarding new and inventive contributions to the state

---

1. However, in the United States and other developed countries, the law does not presume that patents per se create market power in the antitrust context. *See*, for example, *Antitrust Guidelines for the Licensing of Intellectual Property* (para. 2.0[b]), available at http://www.usdoj.gov/atr/public/guidelines/0558.htm.

2. *See* Carlos Correa, *Trade Related Aspects of Intellectual property Rights. A Commentary on the TRIPS Agreement* 297 (Oxford Univ. Press, 2007).

of the art, drug-approval regulations seek to ensure that only drugs with proven efficacy and safety are commercialized.

The U.S. Trade Representative (USTR) has championed the adoption of "linkage" provisions in the context of free-trade agreements (FTAs), signed with several developed and developing countries,[3] and threatens unilateral sanctions under Special Section 301 of the U.S. Trade Act of 1974 against those countries that do not implement some form of drug-patent/registration linkage.[4] Ironically, the modality of "linkage" imposed on developing countries by the USTR is more restrictive than that applied in the United States itself.[5]

The USTR and the U.S. pharmaceutical industry's justification for seeking linkage provisions is the prevention of the infringement that may occur if generic versions of a patented product are approved for commercialization.[6] This argument overlooks the fact that most patents do not cover the drugs, as such, but different forms thereof, including pharmaceutical formulations and combinations, and that the role of drug regulatory agencies is to protect public health, not to take part in private disputes about intellectual property protection. The development implications of linkage provisions may be substantial, as they may unduly restrain generic competition that reduces drug prices and increases access to medicines.

---

3. The United States has negotiated bilateral and regional free-trade agreements (FTAs) with more than 20 countries. Some of these agreements have already been ratified by the U.S. Congress: United States–Jordan free-trade agreement, signed at Washington, D.C., October 24, 2000, and entered into force December 17, 2001 (Jordan FTA); United States–Chile free-trade agreement, signed at Miami, June 6, 2003, and entered into force January 1, 2004 (Chile FTA). United States–Singapore free-trade agreement, signed at Washington, D.C., May 6, 2003, and entered into force January 1, 2004 (Singapore FTA); United States–Morocco free-trade agreement, signed at Washington, D.C., June 15, 2004, and entered into force on July 1, 2005 (Morocco FTA); United States–Dominican Republic–Central America free-trade agreement, signed at Washington, D.C., May 28, 2004, and August 5, 2004 (parties: Costa Rica, Dominican Republic, El Salvador, Guatemala, Honduras, Nicaragua, and the United States [DR-CAFTA]). The United States also signed FTAs with Peru, Colombia, Panama, and South Korea.

4. *See 2007 Special 301 Report*, available at http://www.ustr.gov/assets/Document_Library/Reports_Publications/2007/2007_Special_301_Review/asset_upload_file230_11122.pdf. One of the Report's arguments to include Argentina, Chile, and Egypt on the "Priority Watch List" is the alleged lack of "an effective coordination system" between their health and patent authorities to prevent the issuance of marketing approvals for patent-infringing pharmaceutical products (p. 25).

5. *See* Fredrick M. Abbott, *Intellectual Property Provisions of Bilateral and Regional Trade Agreements in Light of U.S. Federal Law* 10-11 (Issue Paper No. 12, UNCTAD-ICTSD, 2006).

6. The pharmaceutical industry strongly influences USTR policies. The USTR Advisory Board IFAC-3 (which has provided advice on the IPRs chapters of FTAs) is composed of representatives, inter alia, from the International Intellectual Property Alliance; The Gorlin Group; Pfizer, Inc.; Eli Lilly and Company; Pharmaceutical Research and Manufacturers (PhRMA); Biotechnology Industry Organization; International AntiCounterfeiting Coalition; and Intellectual Property Owners Association.

This chapter briefly examines, first, the characteristics of the "linkage" systems applied in the United States and Canada, which essentially rely on the judicial activity of the patent owner. Second, it describes the administrative linkage established under FTAs and promoted by the United States in developing countries. Third, some of the implications of the system are reviewed.

II. JUDICIAL LINKAGE

A. United States

In the United States, the linkage system is based on limited intervention by the Food and Drug Administration (FDA) and the judicial resolution of any disputes arising from the marketing approval of a generic product. In accordance with U.S. law, the applicant shall file with a new-drug application (NDA):

> . . . the patent number and the expiration date of any patent which claims the drug for which the applicant submitted the application or which claims a method of using such drug and with respect to which a claim of patent infringement could reasonably be asserted if a person not licensed by the owner engaged in the manufacture, use, or sale of the drug. If an application is filed under this subsection for a drug and a patent which claims such drug or a method of using such drug is issued after the filing date but before approval of the application, the applicant shall amend the application to include the information required by the preceding sentence (Section 505 of the Federal Food, Drug, and Cosmetic Act).

Similarly, within 30 days after the date of approval of its application or supplement, the applicant shall submit a form for each patent that claims the drug substance (active ingredient), drug product (formulation and composition), or approved method of use.[7]

The patents are listed in the so-called "Orange Book,"[8] including information on the coverage and expiration date of the patents. Patents that must be reported to the FDA include those covering drug substances (active ingredients), drug products (formulations and compositions), and method-of-use patents (which claim indications or other conditions of use of a pending or approved application).[9] Product-by-process patents in which the product claimed is novel must also be reported.

In cases where a patent claims a polymorph that is the same as the active ingredient described in the approved or pending application, the NDA applicant

---

7. *See* Section 314.53 of the Code of Federal Regulations, Title 21, Food and Drugs, Part 314 (hereinafter "21 CFR").

8. An electronic version of the Orange Book is available on the FDA website at http://www.fda.gov/cder/ob/.

9. 21 CFR § 314.53 (c)(2)(i)(O)(1–2); § 314.53(c)(2)(ii)(P)(1–3).

or holder must certify that test data demonstrate that a drug product containing the polymorph will perform the same as the drug product described in the new-drug application.[10] This requirement was introduced in 2003 in order to ensure that only relevant polymorphs are listed in the Orange Book,[11] thereby avoiding the abuse of the rules based on the alleged infringement of polymorph patents.

Information about patents relating to the relevant drugs must be completed under penalty of perjury.[12] The regulations do not seem to require that the patents listed in the Orange Book must necessarily belong to the NDA applicant or holder.

Process patents, patents claiming packaging metabolites, and intermediates are not covered. Information on these patents need not be submitted to the FDA.[13] Thus, these patents cannot be invoked to block the approval of generic products.

In accordance with 21 CFR § 314.53, the FDA should only rely on the information submitted by the NDA applicant or holder, but the FDA will not list or publish patent information if the patent declaration is incomplete or indicates the patent is not eligible for listing. It is unclear whether the FDA is bound to review the declared patents to determine their eligibility, or whether it entirely relies on the received declaration. The latter seems to be the approach actually followed.

In *Alphapharm PTY v. Tommy G. Thompson* (Secretary of Health and Human Services) (DDC 2004) (CA 03-2269), the District Court in Washington, D.C., ruled—in agreement with the Federal Circuit, the Fourth Circuit, and a District Court in Maryland—that the listing of patents in the Orange Book by the FDA is merely "a ministerial act" and that the Hatch-Waxman Act does not require the FDA "to police the listing process by analyzing whether the patents listed by NDA (New Drug Application) applicants actually claim the subject drugs or applicable methods of using those drugs."[14]

The FDA's reluctance to assume, on the grounds that it lacks the resources and the expertise to review patents, an affirmative role in determining whether a

10. There is no obligation, however, to submit these test data to the FDA or to demonstrate that they have been developed by the NDA applicant or holder.

11. *See* Mark Pohl, "Orange Book Patent Listing: The Rationale and Economic Impact of the New Rule," 1 *Journal of Generic Medicines* 224 (issue 3, 2004).

12. 21 CFR § 314.53 (c)(2)(i)(Q). If the applicant believes there are no relevant patents that claim the drug substance (active ingredient), drug product (formulation or composition), or method(s) of use for which the applicant has received approval, and with respect to which a claim of patent infringement could reasonably be asserted if a person not licensed by the owner of the patent engaged in the manufacture, use, or sale of the drug product, the applicant will verify this information in the appropriate forms.

13. 21 CFR § 314.53. Instead, patents covering drug-delivery systems for particular drugs should be listed in the Orange Book.

14. *See* Mark Chael, "Court: FDA's Role is Not to Analyze Patent Claims," 2004, available at http://www.patentlyo.com/patent/2004/08/court_fdas_role.html (collected online Aug 3, 2007).

patent covers an approved drug-product's formulation, composition, or use, leaves any patent disputes under the direct responsibility of the patent owner and the alleged infringer. This is in sharp contrast to the administrative linkage that the USTR has forced partners in FTAs to accept,[15] as examined below.

When an application is submitted to the FDA for a generic drug, the applicant must provide a certification with respect to each patent that claims the drug indicating that, in the opinion of the applicant and to the best of his or her knowledge, relevant patent information has not been filed, the patent has expired, the use will take place as of the date on which the patent will expire, or the patent is invalid or will not be infringed by the manufacture, use, or sale of the new drug for which the application is submitted.[16]

The patent owner is subsequently notified by the FDA about the generics application. He or she can file an infringement suit against the applicant in federal court with an important procedural advantage: an automatic stay of up to 30 months is granted for FDA approval of the generic product until the court determines whether or not the patent is valid and infringed. At the same time, the law aims at balancing the advantages conferred to the patent owner by establishing an incentive for generic firms to challenge the validity of pharmaceutical patents listed in the Orange Book: the first company that succeeds is granted a 180-day period of marketing exclusivity.[17]

As mentioned, product pharmaceutical patents may cover a wide range of subject matter.[18] New chemical entities, the development of which shows a declining trend since the 1990s, account for a small fraction of the thousands of drug-related patents obtained every year, [19] including pharmaceutical formulations and compositions, combinations of known products, optical isomers, active metabolites, salts, ethers and esters of known substances, and polymorphs.[20]

Patents listed in the Orange Book have often been aggressively used to threaten competitors or to bring them into costly litigation, although low-quality patents may be invalidated totally or partially if subjected to strict scrutiny. A U.S. FTC study found that for nearly 75 percent of the drugs covered by the

---

15. FTA negotiations have been essentially asymmetric. U.S. counterparts lacked bargaining power to resist U.S. demands for higher protection for pharmaceuticals. USTR made explicit that the acceptance of such conditions were a sine qua non for the signature of an FTA.

16. 21 USC §355(b).

17. 21 USC §355(j)(5)(B)(iv)(I).

18. *See*, for example, Carlos M. Correa, *Trends in Drug Patenting: Case Studies* (Corregidor, 2001).

19. *See* Report of the Commission on Innovation, Intellectual Property and Public Health (CIPIH), available at http://www.who.int/intellectualproperty/documents/thereport/ENPublicHealthReport.pdf.

20. *See*, for example, Attila Mándi, Protection and Challenge of Pharmaceutical Patents, 1 *J Generic Med* 1 (2003).

study, brand-name companies initiated patent-infringement litigation against the first generic applicant.[21] A judicial determination had been made (at the time of conclusion of the study) for 53 out of 75 drug products. A court resolved the patent-infringement claims for 30 drug products. Generic applicants prevailed 73 percent of the time. Settlements were reached in 38 percent of the instances. Nine of these settlements obliged the brand-name company to pay a certain amount of money to the generic applicant. In seven cases the brand-name company licensed the generic applicant to use the patents for the brand-name drug product prior to patent expiration, and in two cases the settlements allowed the generic applicant to market the brand-name drug product as a generic product, under the brand-name company's own marketing approval. In 18 instances, a court held that the brand-name company's patents were either invalid or not infringed.[22]

In addition, litigation took place against the second generic applicant in cases in which the first generic applicant settled its patent-infringement litigation. Out of a total of twenty drug products with first generic settlements, nine drug products involved litigation with the second generic applicant. In four cases, a settlement was also reached with the second generic applicant; in three cases, the second generic applicant won the patent-infringement suit; brand-name companies only prevailed in one infringement suit.[23]

The use of legislative provisions and loopholes in the drug-registration system has been one of various ways that pharmaceutical firms have sought to artificially extend the monopolization of their drugs.[24] In 2002, in response to the findings of the Federal Trade Commission regarding the abuses of the Orange Book system (listing of patents on secondary technical developments, including polymorphs, and multiple requests of automatic stays) President Bush announced modifications to the system. He stated,

> The FTC . . . discovered that some brand-name drug manufacturers may have manipulated the law to delay the approval of competing generic drugs. When a drug patent is about to expire, one method some companies use is to file a brand-new patent based on a minor feature, such as the color of the pill bottle or a specific combination of ingredients unrelated to the drug's effectiveness. . . . In the meantime, the lower-cost generic drug is shut out of the market. . . . This is not how Congress intended the law to work. Today, I'm taking action

21. The brand-name company generally sued all generic applicants if the drug product had annual sales larger than $500 million in the year the first generic applicant filed its marketing approval. *See* Federal Trade Commission, *Generic Drug Entry Prior to Patent Expiration* 18 (FTC Study, July 2002), available at htpp://www.ftc.gov.

22. *See* id., pp. 17–18.

23. Id.

24. Lara J. Glasgow, Stretching the Limits of Intellectual Property Rights: Has the Pharmaceutical Industry Gone Too Far? 2 *IDEA The Journal of Law and Technology* 227–58 (2002).

to close the loopholes, to promote fair competition and to reduce the cost of prescription drugs in America. . . . These steps we take today will not undermine patent protection. Instead, we are enforcing the original intent of a good law. Our message to brand name manufacturers is clear: You deserve the fair rewards of your research and development; you do not have the right to keep generic drugs off the market for frivolous reasons.[25]

In 2003 the FTC condemned in one case the misuse of the drug-registration regime and practices aimed at deceiving the U.S. patent office to unduly obtain patent protection:

> Through Bristol's [Bristol-Myers Squibb] decade-long pattern of alleged anticompetitive acts, Bristol avoided competition by abusing federal regulations in order to block generic entry; deceived the U.S. Patent and Trademark Office (PTO) to obtain unwarranted patent protection; paid a would-be generic rival over $70 million not to bring any competing products to market; and filed baseless patent-infringement lawsuits to deter entry by generics.[26]

The FTC reported that Bristol:

> . . . has settled charges that it engaged in a series of anticompetitive acts over the past decade to obstruct the entry of low-price generic competition for three of Bristol's widely-used pharmaceutical products: two anti-cancer drugs, Taxol and Platinol, and the anti-anxiety agent BuSpar. According to the FTC's complaint, Bristol's illegal conduct protected nearly $2 billion in annual sales at a high cost to cancer patients and other consumers, who—being denied access to lower-cost alternatives—were forced to overpay by hundreds of millions of dollars for important and often life-saving medications.[27]

As a result of the amendment to the linkage system in 2003, as mentioned, NDA applicants or holders were obligated to certify the availability of test data demonstrating that a drug product containing the polymorph will perform the same as the drug product described in the NDA. In addition, the automatic stay can only be requested once for the same drug.

B. Canada

In accordance with the Candian "Patented Medicines (Notice of Compliance) Regulations" (PM[NOC] Regulations), as amended October 5, 2006, patents that

---

25. *See* President Takes Action to Lower Prescription Drug Prices (Press release, the White House, Oct. 22, 2002), available at http://www.whitehouse.gov/news/releases/2002/10/20021021-2.html.

26. *See* FTC Charges Bristol-Myers Squibb with Pattern of Abusing Government Processes to Stifle Generic Drug Competition (Press release, Federal Trade Commission, Mar. 7, 2003), available at http://www.ftc.gov/opa/2003/03/bms.htm.

27. Id.

may be listed on the Patent Register for the purposes of the linkage provisions include those claiming a medicinal ingredient, formulation, dosage form,[28] or indication for which drug regulatory approval is sought. Patents over particular forms (including polymorphs) of a medicinal ingredient, such as salts, esters, enantiomers, or solvates, cannot be listed. The 2006 reform limited the type of patents eligible for registration but not the number of patents that may be listed for the same drug. It has not excluded the possibility of "evergreening" patents[29] to delay or block generic competition.[30]

Unlike the case of the FDA, in order to have a patent listed on the Patent Register, the Ministry of Health reviews the patent and decides whether it is "relevant" and should be added to the Register. In order for a patent to be added to the Register and be protected under the PM(NOC) Regulations, the following conditions must be met: the patent application must have been filed prior to the date of the submission for drug approval, and the patent must be submitted for listing at the time an application for the notice of compliance is filed—or within 30 days of issuance of the patent if granted after that date.

Listing of a patent on the Patent Register provides a clear procedural advantage to the patent owner:

> . . . when marketing approval is sought for a generic drug through comparison to an innovative product for which there is a listed patent, the generic drug manufacturer must either accept that the marketing approval cannot be issued until expiry of the listed patent or serve the manufacturer of the innovative product with a "notice of allegation." The notice must specify why the listed patent should not prevent the generic drug from coming to market as soon as marketing approval is obtained. The PM(NOC) Regulations permit the manufacturer of the innovative drug to commence legal proceedings in response to the notice of allegation. The proceedings trigger an automatic stay of marketing approval for the generic product for up to 24 months.[31]

The Canadian generics industry has strongly criticized the automatic stay and its abuse by patent owners. (See Box 1.)

---

28. A claim for a dosage form is defined as a claim for a delivery system for a medicinal ingredient or formulation that includes that medicinal ingredient or formulation.

29. "Evergreening" is generally used to refer to patents on minor modifications to existing products generally applied for as part of a deliberate strategy to delay generic competition.

30. For instance, Eli Lilly Canada, Inc., listed a patent (No. 2380087) covering a particulate form (at least 90% of the particles with a size of less than about 40 microns) for Tadalafil. See http://cpe0013211b4c6d-cm0014e88ee7a4.cpe.net.cable.rogers.com/patent/english/record_results.cfm?din_number=02296888&patent_number=2380087&term=02296888; and http://patents1.ic.gc.ca/claims?patent_number=2380087&language=.

31. Torys LLP., http://www.mondaq.com/article.asp?articleid=43458 (collected online August 3, 2007).

Box 1 Automatic Stay in Canada: A Critical View

The automatic 24-month injunction under the Patented Medicines (Notice of Compliance) Regulations of Canada's *Patent Act* allows brand-name pharmaceutical companies to prolong their market monopolies by simply alleging patent infringement against generic manufacturers. This differs from patent dispute resolution in *any other* industry in Canada.

The Regulations, as they stand, mean that no generic drug can be approved by Health Canada until any claim of alleged patent infringement is decided in court. The Regulations withhold Health Canada approval not when a patent is actually shown to be infringed, but when the brand-name company says it might be.

Clearly, this provides an enormous financial incentive to the brand-name companies to allege patent infringement, regardless of the possible outcome of the litigation. The merits of the patent-infringement suit have no effect upon the injunction: a completely meritless suit enjoys the same 24-month stay as a meritorious one.

Brand-name companies strategically list a number of additional patents on a single drug in order to prolong the litigation under the regulations and keep competition off the market. This practice is called "evergreening" or "layering."

Even when the generic manufacturer wins (which has happened in 80 percent of the cases since the last amendments to the Regulations in 1998), the generic drug is still kept off the market through lengthy and costly litigation—often for years past the expiration of the original patent.

Abuse of the regulations is now routine. Since they came into force in 1993, more than 220 court cases have been started under the regulations, each triggering the automatic 24-month injunction. The Supreme Court of Canada has described the regulations as "draconian" in their effect on the generics industry.

Source: Submission—*High Quality, Affordable Medicines for Canadians and the World*, by the Canadian Drug Manufacturers Association, available at http://innovation.gc.ca/gol/innovation/site.nsf/en/in02270.html.

One important implication of a court-based system, as applied in the United States and Canada, is that the patent owner is liable for any actions he or she takes on the basis of existing rules to prevent the registration of competing generic drugs. It is the patent owner who must eventually file an infringement suit against the generic company and bear the corresponding liability.

III. ADMINISTRATIVE LINKAGE

In the FTAs that the United States signed with a number of developed and developing countries, however, the United States aggressively sought a linkage system based on the direct intervention of the national health authority, as illustrated by the DR-CAFTA provisions on the matter. Article 15.10.2 of the DR-CAFTA provides that:

> Where a Party permits, as a condition of approving the marketing of a pharmaceutical product, persons, other than the person originally submitting safety or efficacy information, to rely on evidence or information concerning the safety and efficacy of a product that was previously approved, such as evidence of prior marketing approval in the territory of a Party or in another country, that Party:
>
> (a) shall implement measures in its marketing approval process to prevent such other persons from marketing a product covered by a patent claiming the previously approved product or its approved use during the term of that patent, unless by consent or acquiescence of the patent owner; and
>
> (b) shall provide that the patent owner shall be informed of the request and the identity of any such other person who requests approval to enter the market during the term of a patent identified as claiming the approved product or its approved use.[32]

Whereas the DR-CAFTA linkage provisions leave parties some room to limit the intervention of the administrative authority and require judicial intervention to eventually suspend procedures for the approval of a generic product, there are two important differences from the U.S. system.

First, the U.S. implementation bill passed by Congress established the conditions for entry into force of the Agreement (Sec. 101):

> At such time as the President determines that countries . . . have taken measures necessary to comply with the provisions of the Agreement that are to take effect on the date on which the Agreement enters into force with respect to those countries that provide for the Agreement to enter into force for them.[33]

This permitted the USTR to carry out a "certification" process that gave it a further opportunity to influence the implementing legislation of the DR-CAFTA. In fact, the linkage (and other) FTAs' rules were implemented in some of the parties more restrictively than in the DR-CAFTA itself. Drug regulatory authorities

32. Id. at art. 15.10.2.

33. Dominican Republic–Central American–United States Free Trade Agreement Implementation Act, Public Law 109-53, 109th Congress, 1st Session (2005).

have been obligated to deny the marketing approval of a generic product if a patent related thereto is in force. In the case of the U.S.-Colombia FTA, moreover, a "side letter" to the treaty relating to article 16.10.3 specifies that each party must adopt measures to prevent the approval of a pharmaceutical product while a patent is in force in its territory.[34]

Second, unlike the U.S. and Canadian regulations reviewed above, DR-CAFTA and other FTAs do not distinguish which patents may be invoked under the linkage provisions and which may not. Given the vast proliferation of product pharmaceutical patents on marginal developments, as mentioned above, this is clearly an unfair situation. Should, under the vague formulation of the DR-CAFTA ("a patent claiming the product"), marketing approval be denied if there were, for instance, a patent over a particular salt of a drug that is in the public domain? If so, the linkage would widely and unduly exclude generic competition until all patents around a product had expired.

As a result of its FTA with the United States, Australia also implemented a linkage system. However, a mid-course was adopted that did not follow either the U.S. Orange Book, or the more stringent regime developed under the DR-CAFTA and other FTAs signed with developing countries.

In accordance with Article 17.10.4 of the U.S.-Australia FTA (AUSFTA), Australia was required to provide measures in its marketing-approval process to prevent a person from entering the market with a generic version of a patented medicine before a patent covering that product had expired. The AUSFTA Implementation Act 2004 amended the Therapeutic Goods Act 1989 (TGA) and provided that an applicant seeking to include therapeutic goods in the Australian Register of Therapeutic Goods (ARTG) must provide one of two certificates. The applicant must certify, in good faith, either:

a) that he or she does not propose to market the therapeutic good in a way or circumstances that would involve an infringement of a patent covering the product; or
b) that he or she intends to market a generic version of a patented product before the patent expires because he or she believes the patent is invalid and has notified the patent owner of his or her application to include the therapeutic good in the ARTG.

A person is guilty of an offense if the person gives the TGA a certificate that is false or misleading. Interestingly, amendments were also made to the TGA imposing penalties and damages on patent owners if they take unreasonable

34. The U.S. legislation, as described above, does not comply with this requirement. An amendment to the U.S. law with that purpose is very unlikely. FTAs are in reality only nominally bilateral. *See* Carlos M. Correa, Bilateralism in Intellectual Property: Defeating the WHO System for Access to Medicines, 1 *Case Western Reserve Journal of International Law* 36 (Winter 2004).

legal action against generics (Section 26C). A patent owner must also notify the attorney-general of the commonwealth, state, or territory before it can apply for an interlocutory injunction against a generic who has notified the patent owner of its intention to enter the market before the end of the patent.[35]

A comparison of the U.S., Canadian, and Australian linkage provisions with those implemented under the DR-CAFTA and other FTAs shows that the United States has ironically imposed on poor developing countries more stringent conditions than those applied at home and in other developed countries.[36] Moreover, it must be noted that the patent-registration linkage is not required—for good reasons—in the European Union, where there is complete independence between intellectual property protection and registration. Health authorities have no legal capacity to look into IPR issues and deny approval to an application that conforms to the relevant technical standards, even if there were an infringement of IPRs. This is simply not their business.

The viability of an administrative linkage has been questioned even in the United States. In the already mentioned decision in *Alphapharm PTY Limited v. Tommy G. Thompson*, the court reasoned that substantive patent analysis is beyond the expertise of the FDA and is a function it is not mandated to perform. Rather, substantive patent analysis is better left with the U.S. Patent and Trademark Office. The function of the FDA, on the other hand, is to assure the safety and availability of useful pharmaceutical compounds. The laws and regulations that govern the FDA, in particular those laws and regulations that govern the listing of patents in the Orange Book, "commit the resolution of disputes between ANDA (Abbreviated New Drug Application) applicants and patent holders regarding the validity or correctness of the listed patent information to actions between ANDA applicants and patent holders, rather than to FDA action."[37]

The administrative linkage creates an almost absolute presumption of validity for pharmaceutical patents. Paradoxically, the U.S. FTC has held that the circumstances under which a patent is granted "suggest that an overly strong presumption of a patent's validity is inappropriate" and that it "does not seem sensible to treat an issued patent as though it had met some higher standard of patentability."[38] A bill was introduced to the U.S. Congress in April 2007 for the

35. *See* http://www.health.gov.au/internet/wcms/publishing.nsf/Content/health-ausfta.

36. Although the U.S.-Chile FTA also contains linkage provisions, the government has refused to give the drug-approval authority the competence to suspend or reject applications of generic products. It has only mandated the publication on a Web page of such applications, thereby allowing the patent owners to initiate legal proceedings if they so wish. The USTR has placed Chile on the Special Section 301 Priority list, arguing lack of appropriate drug-registration patent protection. *See 2007 Special 301 Report* (cited in note 4).

37. *See* Chael (cited in note 15).

38. U.S. Federal Trade Commission, To Promote Innovation: The Proper Balance of Competition and Patent Law and Policy, 8, 10 (Oct 2003), available at http://www.ftc.gov/os/2003/10/innovationrpt.pdf.

reform of various aspects of the patent law aiming at improving patent quality,[39] including a reduction in the threshold to obtain the invalidation of a patent.[40]

In fact, given the shortcomings in the examination procedures for the granting of a patent, the presumption of validity should be limited to compliance with formal procedures rather than to substance. An interesting precedent has been provided by the Delhi High Court in deciding two appeals against interim orders in patent infringement suits filed by Bilcare Limited (*Bilcare v. Amritdhara*, pending before the High Court of Delhi, and *Bilcare v. Associated Capsules & Supreme Industries*, pending before the Delhi District Court-Tis Hazari). The court stated that, for the purpose of temporary injunction, a patent will be presumed valid only if the patent is sufficiently old (more than six years) and has been worked, but not when it is a new one. The court also stated that it is settled law that in an action for infringement of a patent, an injunction would not be granted where the validity of the patent itself has been questioned and a revocation petition has been filed.[41]

The linkage provisions are not only incompatible with the essentially fragile presumption of validity of patents. More fundamentally, they run counter to the internationally recognized rights of states, as enshrined in the Doha Declaration on the TRIPS Agreement and Public Health[42] to implement intellectual property in a manner consistent with the protection of public health.[43] Moreover, by significantly delaying marketing approval for generic drugs, linkage provisions may limit states' actions aimed at progressively realizing the human right to health, as required by the International Covenant of Economic, Social, and Cultural Rights.[44]

---

39. *See* Patrick Leahy et al., The Patent Reform Act of 2007, available at http://leahy.senate.gov/press/200704/041807a.html.

40. Only a "preponderance of the evidence" and not "a clear and convincing evidence" standard would be required to rebut the presumption of validity of a patent.

41. *See* http://spicyipindia.blogspot.com/2007/05/bilcare-decisions-by-delhi-high-court.html (collected online August 3, 2007).

42. Adopted at the Fourth WTO Ministerial Conference (November 9–14, 2001).

43. The Doha Declaration recognized the "gravity" of the public health problems afflicting many developing and least-developed countries (LDCs), especially—but not limited to—those resulting from HIV/AIDS, tuberculosis, malaria, and other epidemics, and recognized that the TRIPS Agreement can and should be interpreted and implemented in a manner supportive of WTO members' right to protect public health and, in particular, to promote access to medicines for all (para. 4).

44. *See*, for example, Xavier Seuba, On the Right to Health as a Human Right, Human Rights and Intellectual Property Rights, in Carlos M. Correa and Abdulqawi A. Yusuf, eds., *Intellectual Property and International Trade: The TRIPS Agreement* (Kluwer, 2d ed. forthcoming); Yaël R. Hazan and Philippe Chastonay, eds., *Santé et droits de l'homme* (CMS, 2004); Alicia E. Yamin, Not Just a Tragedy: Access to Medications as a Right under International Law, 21 *Boston University International Law Journal 325*. *See also* Phillipe Cullet, Patents and Medicines: The Relationship between TRIPS and the Human Right to Health, 79:1 *International Affairs* 139 (2003).

The administrative linkage, as implemented under the DR-CAFTA and other FTAs, can make illusory the granting of compulsory licenses and non-commercial government use—because generic companies that wish to produce and distribute under a compulsory license would be unable to get approval to market their generic products. It may also neutralize the use of the "Bolar exception," which allows firms to initiate procedures for generic-drug approval before the expiration of the relevant patents. Moreover, the linkage transfers the liability for rejection of applications by generic companies onto the states themselves, thereby freeing patent owners from any liability in case the patents are invalid or non-infringed. National health authorities become enforcing agents of the private rights of the patent owners.

The negative effects on public health of the administrative linkage provisions adopted in the FTAs with Peru and Panama (similar to those in DR-CAFTA), and the excessive burden put on states' regulatory agencies, were recognized in the bipartisan agreement reached in June 2007 between the Republican and Democratic parties in the U.S. Congress. Both parties agreed to amend the public health–related provisions of the FTAs signed by the U.S. government with Peru and Panama.

The bipartisan agreement has already led to the revision of the U.S. FTA with Peru. (See Box 2.)

Box 2 Linkage Under the Revised U.S.-Peru FTA

Article 16.10.3. Each Party shall provide:

(a) procedures, such as judicial or administrative proceedings, and remedies, such as preliminary injunctions or equivalent effective provisional measures, for the expeditious adjudication of disputes concerning the validity or infringement of a patent with respect to patent claims that cover an approved pharmaceutical product or its approved method of use;
(b) a transparent system to provide notice to a patent holder that another person is seeking to market an approved pharmaceutical product during the term of a patent covering the product or its approved method of use; and
(c) sufficient time and opportunity for a patent holder to seek, prior to the marketing of an allegedly infringing product, available remedies for an infringing product.

4. Where a Party permits, as a condition of approving the marketing of a pharmaceutical product, persons, other than the person originally submitting safety or efficacy information, to rely on evidence of safety or efficacy information of a product that was previously approved, such as evidence of prior marketing

approval in the territory of the Party or in another territory, the Party may implement the provisions of paragraph 3 by:

(a) implementing measures in its marketing approval process to prevent such other persons from marketing a product covered by a patent claiming the product or its approved method of use during the term of that patent, unless by consent or acquiescence of the patent owner;[45] and

(b) providing that the patent owner shall be informed of the identity of any such other person who requests marketing approval to enter the market during the term of a patent identified to the approving authority as covering that product;

provided that the Party also provides:

(c) an expeditious administrative or judicial procedure in which the person requesting marketing approval can challenge the validity or applicability of the identified patent; and

(d) effective rewards for a successful challenge of the validity or applicability of the patent.*

* A Party may comply with clause (d) by providing a period of marketing exclusivity for the first applicant to successfully challenge the validity or applicability of the patent.

Although the revised text still constitutes a TRIPS-plus provision, it substantially moderates the impact of the linkage provisions. It does not establish a straight administrative linkage but the obligation to provide for "procedures or remedies" for the expeditious adjudication of disputes concerning the validity or infringement of a patent, with respect to patent claims that cover an approved pharmaceutical product or its method of use. This requirement may be fulfilled by the general enforcement rules provided for under the TRIPS Agreement, notably Article 50,[46] upon request filed by the patent owner. Interestingly, the text refers to both patent validity and infringement, thereby implying that the

45. For greater certainty, the Parties recognize that this provision does not imply that the marketing-approval authority should make patent-validity or -infringement determinations.

46. A significant risk, however, is the abuse of provisional injunctions, as experienced in some developing countries. *See*, for example, Carlos M. Correa, TRIPS and TRIPS-plus Protection and Impacts in Latin America, in Daniel Gervais, ed., *Intellectual Property, Trade and Development Strategies to Optimize Economic Development in a TRIPS Plus Era* (Oxford Univ. Press, 2007).

generic companies should also be given the opportunity to "expeditiously" establish the invalidity of an invoked patent.

The revised text permits Peru to eventually fulfill its obligation, for example, by posting information about drug registration on a Web page. With this information, the patent owner may seek relief in courts in cases of infringement as he or she sees fit. It is to be noted that the obligation is to publish an "approved pharmaceutical product." Hence, it is not mandatory to make available data on applications for marketing approval. In addition, there is no automatic stay, as there is in the United States and Canada.

Finally, and in line with U.S. legislation, the revised text provides for a market advantage to the company that successfully challenges the validity or applicability of a patent, by means of 180 days of exclusivity.

IV. CONCLUSIONS

The linkage system is clearly a TRIPS-plus obligation. Under its extreme modality, it creates a new exclusive right (the right to prevent marketing approval of a pharmaceutical product) nonexistent under Article 28 of the TRIPS Agreement and national patent laws. It also creates a strong presumption of validity of pharmaceutical product patents that health authorities are neither empowered nor have the capacity to assess. In numerous cases, however, patents—often acquired deliberately to block genuine competition—are invalid or not infringed by generic versions of an approved drug.

The patent-registration administrative linkage, as provided for in some FTAs, ignores that patents are private rights, as stated in the preamble to the TRIPS Agreement, and that whether or not a given product infringes a patent is a legal matter entirely separate from the technical issues concerning safety and efficacy of drugs. It transfers to the states the liability for any improper allegation of a patent (invalid or nor infringed), as it is the regulatory authority that is bound to prevent the marketing of a generic drug.

The DR-CAFTA and other FTAs show how far the U.S. administration, influenced by the pharmaceutical industry, had gone in imposing obligations that clearly exceed those applied in the United States and other developed countries.[47] Recent developments in the U.S. Congress corrected, as discussed above, some of these excesses in relation to the FTAs with Panama and Peru. It would be a matter of basic fairness to extend at least the same treatment to other countries that have previously signed FTAs.

---

47. This is not, in fact, the only case in which FTAs have gone beyond the U.S. legislation. Other examples can be found, for instance, with the extension of the patent term and data exclusivity.

However, the linkage provisions, even as reformed by the U.S. Congress, impose obligations that go beyond the requirements internationally agreed upon under the TRIPS Agreement.[48] The best way to serve the public interest and, particularly, to protect public health is to keep patent protection and drug approval fully independent from one another.

---

48. The extent to which the privileged treatment accorded to pharmaceutical patents under linkage provisions is consistent with the non-discrimination clause of the TRIPS Agreement is an issue that requires further investigation. Article 27.1 of the TRIPS Agreement stipulates that patent rights shall be available and enjoyable without "discrimination as to the field of technology." Curiously enough, U.S. FTAs only partially reproduce article 27.1 of the TRIPS Agreement. They omit the non-discrimination clause provided therein.

12. IS PRODUCT PATENT PROTECTION NECESSARY TO SPUR INNOVATION IN DEVELOPING COUNTRIES?

R&D by Indian Pharmaceutical Companies After TRIPS

SUDIP CHAUDHURI*

I. INTRODUCTION

The principal economic rationale for granting patents is that it will stimulate investment for research for innovation. Yet, even if this supposition generally holds true,[1] strong patent protection has traditionally been seen as unnecessary until relatively late in a country's development process (Siebeck 1990, p. 1). The developing countries are net users, not net developers, of research and development (R&D)-intensive products. Penrose (1951) and some later studies, including Vaitsos (1972) and Greer (1973), have argued that developing countries lose by

* Revised version of the presentation at the Conference on "Intellectual Property and Developing Countries: The WIPO Development Agenda," University of California, Los Angeles, March 11–12, 2007. This research has been funded by the Economic and Social Research Council under the ESRC Non-Governmental Public Action Programme. The author thanks Neil Netanel for detailed comments, suggestions, and editorial inputs that have significantly improved the paper. The author also thanks the other conference participants and acknowledges the useful discussions with Sunil Mani and the other members of the ESRC research project team: M. M. Mackintosh, Meri Koivusalo, and Phares Mujinja. Usual disclaimers apply.

1. The positive impact of patents on R&D is being increasingly questioned, and alternatives are being discussed. (See Baker 2004 for a review of some of the proposals.)

granting patent protection. For such countries, these studies contend, the costs of patent protection actually outweigh the benefits. The developing countries suffer from higher prices resulting from patent monopolies, whereas the benefits of technological progress that are supposed to follow from patent protection take place in the developed countries, not in developing countries.

Despite these doubts—and despite the lack of empirical evidence that the net benefits are indeed positive (Primo Braga 1990, p. 87)—the 1994 Agreement on Trade Related Aspects of Intellectual Property Rights (TRIPS) requires all World Trade Organization member countries to provide product patent protection for all products, including pharmaceuticals, within a specified timeframe. Moreover, the United States has used bilateral Free Trade Agreements to promote a "TRIPS-plus" agenda, requiring developing countries to provide patent protection that exceeds the TRIPS minimum standards (Roffe and Spennemann 2006). Concurrently, an attempt is also being made within the World Intellectual Property Organization (WIPO) to upgrade and harmonize patent standards.

But has the situation changed in recent years to justify stronger patent protection in developing countries? Maskus (2000) contests the traditional view that developing countries do not gain technologically from stronger intellectual property rights (IPRs), such as patents. He argues, in fact, that inadequate protection may stifle technological change even at low levels of economic development (p. 147). But a study on Japan by Sakakibara and Branstetter (2001) did not find that stronger patent protection has resulted in more innovation. Moreover, after a review of several other empirical studies, Branstetter (2004) concluded that there is little empirical evidence that stronger IPRs stimulate local innovation. Conversely, a study on China by Maskus, Dougherty, and Mertha (2005) suggests that there may be a positive relationship between stronger IPRs and development.

I take up the debate empirically with respect to the Indian pharmaceutical industry. As I have shown elsewhere, the abolition of product patent protection in 1972 was one of the major factors that contributed to the remarkable growth of the pharmaceutical industry in India (Chaudhuri 2005b). Today, India has one of the most advanced pharmaceutical industries among developing countries. With the introduction of the mailbox facility from January 1, 1995, to receive and hold product patent applications[2] and the reintroduction of full-fledged product patent protection in pharmaceuticals from January 1, 2005, in line with TRIPS, the legal framework is similar to that before 1972.

In the underdeveloped pharmaceutical industry before 1972, the capacity to conduct R&D was limited. But has the situation changed following the rapid growth of the industry since the 1970s? What has been the nature of R&D activities and

2. Such applications could be taken up for granting patents not before January 1, 2005. But Exclusive Marketing Rights (EMRs) could be obtained for the application if (1) a patent were granted in some other WTO member country, and (2) the application were not rejected in the country as not being an invention.

innovation in the Indian pharmaceutical industry? Does India's experience support the claims of the multinational corporations (MNCs) and their followers that strong patent protection is needed in India for R&D and innovation?[3] During the TRIPS negotiations, it was specifically claimed that TRIPS-compliant patent protection would prompt developing-country companies to conduct more R&D for the development of new drugs more suited to local needs.[4] Have those claims been borne out in India? In this paper, I will canvass such questions to cast some light on the relationship between product patents, R&D, and innovation in developing countries.

II. R&D: QUANTITATIVE AND QUALITATIVE CHANGES

Traditionally, the Indian pharmaceutical industry spent very little on R&D. In the early 1990s, its R&D expenditures amounted to only about 1.5 percent of sales (Grace 2004, p. 37). Even larger companies, such as Ranbaxy and Dr. Reddy's Laboratories, spent only 2 to 3 percent of their sales on R&D in 1992–93.[5] Since then, however, and particularly since the early 2000s, there has been a substantial increase in research spending in a segment of the industry. Table 12.1 reflects the R&D expenditures for two sets of companies: (1) 28 major R&D spenders, and (2) the remaining 81 companies of the 109 for which R&D data have been reported in the database.[6] For the latter group, R&D expenditures as a percentage of sales continue to fluctuate around 1 percent. Indeed, in 2005–06, that proportion was only 1.2 percent. But for the group of 28 major spenders, R&D expenditures increased steadily from 1.78 percent of sales in 1992–93 to 3.86 percent in 2001–02, and then sharply to 7.83 percent in 2004–05 and 8.79 percent in 2005–06 (Table 12.1).

---

3. Such claims have resurfaced after an Indian court rejected Novartis's challenge of India's patent law. (See, for example, the editorial in the *Wall Street Journal*, "Drug Patents in India," August 14, 2007.) Section 3(d) of India's Patents Act, which Novartis challenged, provides for the conditional grant of patents for modifications of existing chemical entities (see below).

4. See Velasquez and Boulet 1999, p. 37, for a reference to such views.

5. Prowess database, Centre for Monitoring Indian Economy, Mumbai (CMIE). It provides company-level data culled from company annual reports and other sources. Since 1992–93, R&D-expenditure data are available for a sizable number of companies from this database. In 1992–93, R&D expenditures were only 1.1% of sales for a sample of 47 companies considered by the Prowess database.

6. My sample of 28 pharmaceutical companies (see Table 12.2) includes each of the 27 largest R&D spenders in 2005–06, each with R&D expenditures above Rs 100 million for the year. I have also added to the sample Natco (R&D expenditures Rs 74.3 million), which is a major DMF filer in the United States, the focus of my discussion in Section IV below.

TABLE 12.1 R&D EXPENDITURES BY THE INDIAN PHARMACEUTICAL INDUSTRY

	Major Spenders: Number of Firms	Major Spenders: R&D Exp. as % of Sales	Other Firms: Number of Firms	Other Firms: R&D Exp. as % of Sales
1992–93	7	1.78	40	0.86
1994–95	14	2.42	64	1.15
1995–96	13	2.98	74	1.42
1996–97	16	2.80	73	1.23
1997–98	15	3.06	66	0.94
1998–99	15	3.10	71	0.86
1999–2000	18	3.17	70	0.94
2000–01	21	3.88	68	1.16
2001–02	24	3.86	74	1.33
2002–03	25	4.72	72	1.18
2003–04	28	5.79	81	1.23
2004–05	28	7.83	73	1.40
2005–06	28	8.79	65	1.20

Source: Prowess database, Centre for Monitoring Indian Economy, Mumbai. All companies in the drugs and pharmaceutical industry that reported positive R&D have been considered here.
Column 2 shows the number of major spenders for which data are available from the aforementioned source. For the list of major spenders, see Table 12.2.

In this paper, I focus on this more dynamic segment of the Indian pharmaceutical industry for which R&D expenditures have substantially increased. Ranbaxy is the largest R&D spender in the Indian pharmaceutical industry. In 1994–95, when TRIPS came into effect, it spent Rs 365.8 million on R&D (4.61 percent of its sales).[7] Initially the increase was moderate with R&D expenditures reaching 5.5 percent of sales in 2002–03, but they subsequently shot up to 9.35 percent in 2004–05 and 17.21 percent in 2005–06 with an expenditure of Rs 6,339.3 million. For Dr. Reddy's, the second largest R&D spender, expenditures increased steadily and sharply from Rs 39.8 million (2.01 percent of sales) in 1994–95 to Rs 2,977.9 million (17.12 percent) in 2004–05. The following year, the company's R&D expenditures declined to Rs 2,539.5 million, but it still constituted 10.85 percent of sales. Among the other major spenders, between

7. The source of R&D and sales data reported in this paragraph is the Prowess database, CMIE.

1994–95 and 2005–06, R&D expenditures have increased for Sun from 4.05 percent to 11.93 percent, for Torrent from 2.68 percent to 11.74 percent, and for USV from 0.73 percent to 10.74 percent of sales. For nine companies, the proportion of R&D expenditures exceeds 10 percent of sales in 2005–06 (Table 12.2). The larger Indian pharmaceutical companies are among the largest investors in R&D among all industries combined in India. Four of the top five R&D spenders in corporate India are pharmaceutical companies: Ranbaxy, Dr. Reddy's Laboratories, Sun, and Cipla. (The only non-pharmaceutical company is second-ranked Tata Motors, which spends about 2.3 percent of its sales on R&D.) Ten of the top twenty Indian R&D spenders in India are pharmaceutical companies (*Business World*, 25 December 2006).

The objectives of R&D conducted by Indian companies can be broadly classified as follows:

- Development of new chemical entities (NCEs)
- Modification of existing chemical entities to develop new formulations, compositions, combinations (also known as incrementally modified drugs)
- Development of generics (that is, development of processes for manufacturing active pharmaceutical ingredients [APIs] and development of formulations to satisfy quality and regulatory requirements for marketing patent-expired drugs).[8]

A remarkable feature of pharmaceutical R&D in India is that about 11 companies are involved in NCE R&D. In Section III, I will focus on the status and the implications of that activity. I will discuss how Indian companies still lack the necessary skills and the funds to carry out such R&D independently, and how they are partnering with the MNCs and other companies from developed countries. The R&D partnering agreements have typically given the developed-country partner commercial rights in designated developed-country markets and stipulated that it must pay royalties to Indian companies in the event the product is successful. The Indian company, in turn, holds the commercial rights in remaining countries, including India.

If the product developed under a partnering agreement is successful, the Indian company will typically earn significantly more from the Indian market than during the pre-TRIPS era when India had no product patent protection. Not unexpectedly, therefore, patenting activity has gone up sharply after India started accepting patent applications under the mailbox facility after TRIPS (Mueller 2006, pp. 158–61).

8. The companies get a handsome benefit of weighted deduction of 150% for expenditures relating to in-house R&D for income tax purposes (Mani 2006). This could be one of the factors explaining the rapid rise in R&D expenditures.

TABLE 12.2 R&D EXPENDITURES OF MAJOR INDIAN PHARMACEUTICAL COMPANIES

Company	R&D Exp. 2004–05 in Rs Millions	R&D Exp. as % of Sales 2004–05	R&D Exp. 2005–06 in Rs Millions	R&D Exp. as % of Sales 2005–06	R&D Exp. 2005–06 In US$ Millions
Ranbaxy Laboratories Ltd.	3,996.6	9.35	6,393.3	17.21	144.40
Dr. Reddy's Laboratories Ltd.	2,977.9	17.12	2,539.5	10.85	57.36
Sun Pharmaceutical Ind. Ltd.	1,159.8	11.09	1,614.9	11.93	36.48
Cipla Ltd.	983.8	4.10	1,554	5.01	35.10
Cadila Healthcare Ltd.	1,032	8.96	1,187	8.87	26.81
Lupin Ltd.	836.1	6.86	1,080.2	6.29	24.40
Nicholas Piramal India Ltd.	1,084.4	8.29	911.5	6.04	20.59
Torrent Pharmaceuticals Ltd.	673.2	12.46	873.6	11.74	19.73
Wockhardt Ltd.	692.8	7.86	810.8	8.73	18.31
Aurobindo Pharma Ltd.	543.1	4.67	770.1	5.22	17.39
USV Ltd.	269.3	5.24	624.6	10.74	14.11
Orchid Chemicals & Pharmaceuticals Ltd.	522.1	7.57	613.6	6.95	13.86
Matrix Laboratories Ltd.	272	4.09	599	7.48	13.53
Panacea Biotec Ltd.	199.5	5.82	490.2	8.87	11.07
Glenmark Pharmaceuticals Ltd.	486.8	9.04	466.9	7.52	10.55
Ind-Swift Laboratories Ltd.	286.5	12.51	458.6	14.18	10.36
Strides Arcolab Ltd.	168.8	6.90	401.9	12.13	9.08
Biocon Ltd.	240.9	3.49	400.8	5.48	9.05

Ipca Laboratories Ltd.	335.9	4.58	378.8	4.62	8.56
Dabur Pharma Ltd.	215	9.12	268.9	9.94	6.07
Alembic Ltd.	311.2	5.44	266.7	4.00	6.02
Shasun Chemicals & Drugs Ltd.	308.2	9.27	263.6	7.14	5.95
Dishman Pharmaceuticals & Chemicals Ltd.	39.7	2.49	245.1	11.18	5.54
Unichem Laboratories Ltd.	153.9	3.64	123.2	2.58	2.78
J B Chemicals & Pharmaceuticals Ltd.	66.1	1.75	121.8	2.53	2.75
Bharat Serums & Vaccines Ltd.	93.6	10.23	114	11.67	2.57
Divi's Laboratories Ltd.	94.6	2.58	100.6	2.55	2.27
Natco Pharma Ltd.	52.2	3.04	74.3	4.30	1.68
TOTAL	18,096	7.83	23,747.5	8.79	536.38

Source: Prowess database, Centre for Monitoring Indian Economy, Mumbai.

Figures in rupees have been converted to U.S. dollars by using the average exchange rates for the revelant financial years obtained from the Reserve Bank of India, *Handbook of Statistics on Indian Economy* (accessed at http://www.rbi.org.in).

However, TRIPS has made no difference to the product patent regimes of developed countries. Such countries already recognized product patents before TRIPS. Thus, even in the absence of TRIPS, Indian companies would earn royalties on drugs developed in India but marketed and patented in developed countries. And because developed country markets are much larger and more lucrative than the Indian market, Indian companies would have the incentive to do NCE R&D for such pharmaceutical products even in the absence of TRIPS.

In contrast, when developing country markets matter—as in the case of neglected diseases—Indian companies are hardly involved in developing drugs. We find in Section III that, contrary to what was claimed during the TRIPS negotiations, the product patent regime has not prompted Indian companies to devote more resources to developing drugs for neglected diseases that exclusively or predominantly affect developing countries.

NCE R&D is not yet a significant part of R&D activities of Indian companies—it constitutes less than a quarter of total R&D expenditures by the major companies.[9] It should be noted that most of the large R&D spenders are not involved in NCE R&D. Cipla, for example, is not yet involved in NCE R&D, but it is the fourth largest spender, and its R&D expenditures increased by more than 50 percent in 2005–06 (Table 12.2).

Pharmaceutical R&D conducted by Indian companies has been primarily related to generics and incrementally modified drugs. I will discuss in Section IV how significant R&D efforts are being directed toward developing processes and products to get regulatory approvals for entry and growth in patent-expired generic markets in developed countries. This has nothing to do with TRIPS. It is the result of an increasing export orientation of Indian pharmaceutical companies and diversification to the regulated markets, particularly to the United States. The United States is already the largest export market for India, and most Indian companies are trying to enter and grow there. The focus of Section IV, accordingly, will be on the United States.

Most of the Indian exporters in the United States operate in the commodity generics market, where entry barriers and prices are low. In Section IV, we will also discuss how, in order to move up the value chain, some Indian companies in the United States are targeting value-added generics in different ways: by challenging patents and developing non-infringing processes and by being the first,

9. Ranbaxy, Dr. Reddy's Laboratories, and Cadila Healthcare spend about one-third of their R&D budgets on NCE R&D (Singh 2006, p. 198; Dr. Reddy's Laboratories *Annual Report, 2005–06*, p. 75; Cadila Healthcare, Investor Presentation, October 2006 (available at the company website at http://www.zyduscadila.com.)) Assuming that other Indian pharmaceutical companies involved in NCE R&D maintain a similar proportion (and this may be an overestimate for the smaller companies), total R&D expenditures for NCE were about Rs 5,531 million in India in 2005–06. This constitutes only 23% of total R&D expenditures by the 28 major companies.

or among the first few, to enter the generics market and enjoy higher profit margins. They are also trying to modify existing drugs and develop new formulations. Patenting activity by Indian companies in the United States has accordingly gone up sharply. TRIPS permits them to simultaneously hold patents for these formulations in India and profit from them if and when these innovations are commercialized. But even in the absence of TRIPS, the companies would still be interested in undertaking such innovative activities because of the promise of much higher returns from the United States.

III. R&D FOR NEW DRUG DEVELOPMENT

The Indian private sector began investing in R&D for new chemical entities when TRIPS came into effect in the mid-1990s.[10] R&D investments were initiated by Dr. Reddy's Laboratories, followed by Ranbaxy Laboratories. Since then nine other companies—Sun, Cadila Healthcare, Lupin, Nicholas Piramal, Dabur Pharma, Torrent, Wockhardt, Orchid, and Glenmark—have also joined in.[11] As mentioned above, and as can be seen from Table 12.2, these 11 companies are among the major pharmaceutical R&D spenders.[12] Together, they invested Rs 16,760.2 million (10.9 percent of their sales) in R&D in 2005–06. The amount increased by 22.5 percent from Rs 13,676.7 million in 2004–05 (calculated from Table 12.2). The increase is impressive, but it still pales in comparison to what the MNCs spend on R&D. The 11 Indian companies together spent $379 million in 2005–06. Pfizer alone spent $7,440 million (*Pharmaceutical Executive*, May 2006).

It is important to note that none of these companies is engaged in the entire process of drug development. The reason is simple: Indian pharmaceutical companies are not yet ready for a start-to-finish model in NCE research because they do not yet have all the skills and the funds required to develop a drug and market it.[13] The model that the Indian companies have adopted, rather, is to develop new molecules up to a certain stage and then license out to partners from developed

---

10. In the Indian private sector, Sarabhai Research Centre was the first to be set up in the 1960s for developing new drugs, but it was wound up in the 1980s.

11. Among the large Indian companies, a notable absentee is Cipla.

12. Few other companies have also initiated or are in the process of initiating new drug-discovery R&D. Panacea Biotec has announced that it is setting up a new center for such R&D (see http://www.panacea-biotec.com, accessed July 28, 2007). Biocon is involved in R&D for development of novel biotherapeutics (*Annual Report, 2006-07*). Suven Life Sciences has diversified from contract research to collaborative research. It has started collaboration with Eli Lilly in 2006 for pre-clinical molecule R&D (see http://www.suven.com, accessed July 28, 2007). Similarly Dr. R. Barbhaiya, ex-chief of Ranbaxy R&D, has set up Advinus Therapeutics in collaboration with the Tata group. It is involved in new drug-discovery services (www.advinus.com, accessed July 28, 2007).

13. See Chaudhuri 2005a, section V; and Chaudhuri 2005b, chapter 5.

countries, primarily to MNCs. There has been a marriage of interests. It is the development of biotechnology companies that has encouraged specialization according to stages of the drug-development process. The MNCs seek and contract out specific activities (Nwaka and Ridley 2003, p. 920). As the NCE pipeline of the MNCs has begun drying up, they, in fact, have intensified efforts to license promising compounds developed by others. In fact most of the major MNCs have opened compound-acquisition departments in their companies. There are also specialized companies, which keep track of promising compounds, maintain libraries, catalogue them, and offer them for sale to prospective clients.[14]

Even at the pre-clinical stage, Indian companies are not engaged with all levels of R&D. Indian companies are not involved in the basic research of target identification for new drugs. They rely on the basic research of others and adopt an approach called "analogue research." This entails working on certain pre-identified targets for specific diseases to develop molecules that alter the target's mechanism in the diseased person.[15] But even this requires medicinal chemistry and biology skills that are still scarce in the Indian pharmaceutical industry. In the pre-TRIPS era, Indian pharmaceutical-industry scientists primarily acquired and developed the organic chemistry skills required for process development. The Indian companies are filling up this gap primarily by hiring Indian scientists who worked in MNC laboratories in India and abroad, and in the Indian public sector laboratories.[16]

Dr. Reddy's commenced drug-discovery R&D in 1993. It filed for its first U.S. patent in 1995 for an anti-diabetic compound. This was out-licensed to Novo Nordisk in 1997. It developed two more anti-diabetic compounds and out-licensed these to Novo Nordisk in 1998 and to Novartis in 2001. The deal with Novartis involved upfront and milestone payments up to $55 million, depending on progress, and the company received $5 million to start with in 2002–03. These deals were major news and generated tremendous optimism, luring other smaller companies into new-drug R&D. Of them, Glenmark has struck the best licensing deals.[17]

---

14. Personal discussion with B. Gopalan, then with Glenmark Research Centre, Navi Mumbai, February 11, 2005.

15. Glenmark Pharmaceuticals Ltd. *Annual Report, 2003–04.*

16. In the pre-TRIPS regime, too, some R&D for new-drug development was undertaken in India primarily by Central Drug Research Institute (CDRI) (public sector), Ciba Geigy, Hoechst, and Boots (all MNCs). As a result of these efforts, not many drugs have come to the market, but it generated skills: see Chaudhuri 2005a.

17. Glenmark has developed a compound for the treatment of asthma/COPD and entered into a licensing agreement with Forest Laboratories of the United States. Forest has paid the former an upfront amount of $10 million on signing the agreement and, depending on development and commercialization of the product, other milestone payments will follow, totaling $190 million. In addition, Glenmark will get "mid-teens"

The initial optimism is reflected in what the chairman of Dr. Reddy's Laboratories said in its *Annual Report 2002–03* after signing the Novartis licensing agreement:

> When we started our drug discovery program in 1993, industry pundits viewed it with skepticism. This ambition, they said, would not be within the reach of an Indian company. The challenge was to prove them wrong. And in this last decade, we have done just that.[18]

However, Ranbaxy and Dr. Reddy's, the two Indian companies that have invested most heavily in R&D (Table 12.2) and served as prime advocates for new-drug R&D in India, have each suffered several setbacks. Novo Nordisk and Novartis discontinued further development of the three compounds in-licensed from Dr. Reddy's. Similarly, Schwartz Pharma discontinued the clinical trials of a compound licensed from Ranbaxy. No success at the clinical-trial stage has yet been reported from the much publicized Ranbaxy-GlaxoSmithKline (GSK) R&D collaboration.[19] Given that drug development did not progress as anticipated, the prospect of huge licensing revenue through milestone and other payments failed to materialize.

What the Indian companies initially did not understand is that although their objectives are to earn license fees and royalties from successful commercialization, the MNCs do not necessarily aim to develop the in-licensed compounds for commercialization. In fact, where the compound may compete with the MNC's existing or planned products, the MNC's objective may actually be to "kill" the compound.

Indian companies are now aware of this potential conflict. In some cases, they are attempting to develop drugs further themselves, despite the lack of interest on the part of the MNCs who initially licensed them. Torrent, for example, entered into an agreement with Novartis in 2002 for the development of the

---

royalty from Forest on net sales of the product in North America, if the product is commercialized.

18. Similarly, the chairman said in the company's *Annual Report, 2000–01* that "Our achievements in drug discovery are testimony to our belief that there is little correlation between innovation and size," and in its *Annual Report 2001–02* that, "Even today, I am often inundated by various 'facts and figures.' . . . Our response to such data has been that in the area of discovery research we cannot be a prisoner of averages. The test of successful R&D driven pharmaceutical company should be its ability to consistently beat these so-called averages. Your Company exemplifies this tenet."

19. Unlike the other product-specific licensing deals, the second largest MNC in the world, GSK, and the largest pharmaceutical company in India, Ranbaxy, announced in October 2003 that they have entered into an R&D-collaboration agreement covering a wide range of therapeutic areas. The agreement has been revised and the scope was enlarged in February 2006. (See press releases on the company website at http://www.ranbaxy.com.)

AGE breaker compound for the treatment of heart disease and diabetes. In 2004, the compound was out-licensed to Novartis. The agreement was terminated in 2005 when Novartis decided not to proceed further with the compound. Torrent is now trying to develop it on its own and explore other options. Torrent received only $500,000 initially, and then $3 million, from Novartis.[20] This was too small an amount for a large MNC such as Novartis to have any stake in the project.

The later the stage at which a compound is licensed out, the higher the license revenues. The licensor is also in a better position to select the licensee to ensure that the licensee is actually interested in developing the drug for commercializing, so that the licensor can hope to earn royalties. But Indian companies face the predicament that unilaterally developing a drug to that later stage entails considerable cost and risk.

Dr. Reddy's has suffered several similar setbacks. As a result, that company's R&D expenditures even declined by about 15 percent in 2005–06 (Table 12.2). Dr. Reddy's has now started rethinking its strategies. Rather than licensing out the molecules to MNCs, Dr. Reddy's is experimenting with a number of alternative business models. One such is joint development and sharing of costs with smaller, specialized research companies, such as Rheoscience and ClinTec. Dr. Reddy's entered into an agreement with the former in September 2005 to co-develop an anti-diabetic compound (DRF 2593) and with the latter in September 2006 to co-develop an anti-cancer compound (DRF 1042). Dr. Reddy's has also sought to minimize the risk in R&D investment by setting up a separate drug-development company with equity investment from two leading venture capital companies in India: Citicorp Venture Capital and ICICI Venture Fund. Dr. Reddy's transferred to the new company four NCEs it had already developed. The new company will be responsible for the clinical development and out-licensing, co-development, or joint commercialization of those NCEs. Currently three of these NCEs are undergoing clinical trials (Table 12.3).[21]

No NCE developed by Indian companies has yet been approved for marketing in any country. But as Table 12.3 shows, at the end of 2006–07, 25 NCEs developed by Indian companies were at various stages of clinical trials. Dr. Reddy's has five NCEs under clinical trials; followed by Lupin with four; and Cadila Healthcare, Glenmark, and Nicholas Piramal with three each. Ranbaxy, the largest pharmaceutical company in India (and the largest R&D spender), has only two NCEs under clinical trials.

20. "Novartis Acquires Rights in Torrent's AGE Compound," press release October 31, 2002, and "Torrent Licenses AGE Compound to Novartis," press release July 29, 2004, Torrent Pharmaceuticals Ltd. (Accessed at http://www.torrent-india.com.)

21. Similarly, Sun Pharmaceuticals has de-merged the company and set up a new company to exclusively deal with NCE R&D, the investment requirements, risk profile, and skill sets for which are different (Sun Pharmaceuticals *Annual Report 2005–06*, p. 5).

TABLE 12.3 NCES UNDER CLINICAL TRIALS, INDIAN PHARMACEUTICAL COMPANIES AS OF 2006–07

Company	NCE	Indication	Development Stage
Cadila Healthcare	ZY11	Anti-inflammation, pain	Phase I
Cadila Healthcare	ZYH2	Diabetes	Phase I
Cadila Healthcare	ZYH1	Dyslipidemia	Phase II
Dabur	DRF 7295	Anti-cancer	Phase II
Dr. Reddy's Labs	DRF2593	Diabetes	Phase II completed (partner Rheoscience, Denmark)
Dr. Reddy's Labs	DRL11605	Obesity	Phase I (assigned to Perlecen)
Dr. Reddy's Labs	RUS3108	Atherosclerosis	Phase I (assigned to Perlecen)
Dr. Reddy's Labs	DRF10945	Dyslipidemia	Phase II (assigned to Perlecen)
Dr. Reddy's Labs	DRF1042	Anti-cancer	Phase II (partner Clintec International, United Kingdom)
Glenmark	GRC8200	Diabetes	Phase II
Glenmark	GRC6211	Osteoarthritis, pain	Phase I
Glenmark	GRC3886	Asthma/COPD	Phase II
Lupin	LL3348 (herbal)	Anti-psoriasis	Phase II
Lupin	LL4858	Anti-TB	Phase I
Lupin	LL2011	Anti-migraine	Phase II completed
Lupin	LL4218	Anti-psoriasis	Phase I completed
Nicholas Piramal	P276	Anti-cancer	Phase II
Nicholas Piramal	PP04 (herbal)	Anti-fungal	Phase II
Nicholas Piramal	PP05 (herbal)	Arthritis	Phase II
Orchid	BLX1002	Diabetes	Phase II
Ranbaxy Labs	RBx9841	Urological disorders	Phase I
Ranbaxy Labs (jointly with MMV)	RBx11160	Antimalarial	Phase II (in India, Thailand, and Africa)
Sun Pharmaceutical Industries	NCE	Anti-allergy	Phase II (in the United States independently with a CRO)
Wockhardt	WCK771	MRSA, resistant infection	Phase II
Wockhardt	WCK1152	Respiratory infections	Phase I

Source: Company annual reports and websites, accessed February 2007.

As Table 12.3 further shows, the NCEs being developed by the Indian companies are related primarily to "global diseases," such as diabetes, cancer, heart diseases, asthma, and obesity. These are the diseases that offer much larger and more lucrative markets in developed countries (though they are also prevalent in developing countries). The "neglected diseases," which primarily (or exclusively) affect the developing countries and promise much smaller financial returns are absent from the list, except for malaria and TB. In both these cases, public-sector or philanthropic funding is involved. Ranbaxy is participating in an international project sponsored and funded by the Medicines for Malaria Venture (MMV), a public-private partnership, to develop a synthetic anti-malarial drug. Lupin is involved in developing an anti-TB drug in partnership with some publicly funded research institutions in India (CIPIH 2006, p. 101). The trend toward R&D for drugs for global diseases is unlikely to change in the future. A survey on the R&D plans of Indian companies found that only about 10 percent of R&D funds are aimed at diseases principally affecting developing countries (CIPIH 2006, p. 101).

In short, the anticipated benefit of TRIPS, that the product patent incentive will prompt local companies to put resources into developing drugs more suited to developing countries, has not materialized.

IV. R&D FOR EXPORTS TO THE U.S. MARKET

The growth in exports is one of the most outstanding features of the pharmaceutical industry in India. Exports were negligible in the product patent regime before the 1970s. Exports started picking up in the 1970s after the amendment of the Patents Act. Initially, growth was modest, but it accelerated in the 1980s. Exports have grown particularly rapidly since the mid-1990s. Exports have increased at an annual compound rate of 21.4 percent from $698.7 million in 1995–96 to $4,874 million in 2005–06.[22] The export market is larger than the domestic market for a number of Indian pharmaceutical companies—for example, for Ranbaxy, 60 percent of sales; for Dr. Reddy's Laboratories, 51 percent; for Orchid, 70 percent; for Divi's, 85 percent; and for Shasun, 66 percent (Table 12.4). Most of the major R&D spenders (Table 12.2) are also major exporters (Table 12.4). The top six exporters account for one-third of India's total pharmaceutical exports (calculated from Table 12.4).

The export market can be broadly divided between regulated markets and unregulated markets. In the regulated markets, regulatory barriers exist in the sense that exporters are required to follow an elaborate registration—and, in some countries, inspection—procedure to satisfy the drug-control authorities about the efficacy and safety of medicines. Such requirements are absent or are

22. Updated Table 2.5 of Chaudhuri 2005b, p. 45.

TABLE 12.4 EXPORT INTENSITY OF MAJOR INDIAN PHARMACEUTICAL COMPANIES, 2005–06

Company	Exports in Rs Millions	Exports as % of Sales	Exports as % of Total Exports of India
Ranbaxy Laboratories Ltd.	22,243.4	59.89	10.31
Cipla Ltd.	15,136.4	48.77	7.01
Dr. Reddy's Laboratories Ltd.	11,966.6	51.11	5.55
Aurobindo Pharma Ltd.	8,163.3	55.32	3.78
Lupin Ltd.	7,611.0	44.32	3.53
Orchid Chemicals, & Pharmaceuticals Ltd.	6,210.1	70.32	2.88
Matrix Laboratories Ltd.	3,902.7	49.50	1.81
Ipca Laboratories Ltd.	3,857.7	47.02	1.79
Sun Pharmaceutical Inds. Ltd.	3,652.1	26.97	1.69
Biocon Ltd.	3,577.2	49.10	1.66
Divi's Laboratories Ltd.	3,348.0	84.91	1.55
Wockhardt Ltd.	3,201.7	34.49	1.48
Strides Arcolab Ltd.	2,624.1	79.22	1.22
Shasun Chemicals & Drugs Ltd.	2,452.8	66.41	1.14
J B Chemicals & Pharmaceuticals Ltd.	2,447.1	50.87	1.13
Nicholas Piramal India Ltd.	2,201.5	14.59	1.02
Cadila Healthcare Ltd.	2,073.0	15.48	0.96
Ind-Swift Laboratories Ltd.	1,507.1	46.60	0.70
Unimark Remedies Ltd.	1,468.2	44.39	0.68
Dishman Pharmaceuticals & Chemicals Ltd.	1,431.6	65.31	0.66
Glenmark Pharmaceuticals Ltd.	1,408.1	22.68	0.65
Torrent Pharmaceuticals Ltd.	1,344.2	18.06	0.62
Alembic Ltd.	1,192.5	17.91	0.55
Dabur Pharma Ltd.	1,158.5	42.84	0.54
Ajanta Pharma Ltd.	1,116.3	52.56	0.52
Claris Lifesciences Ltd.	1,039.0	36.47	0.48
Neuland Laboratories Ltd.	1,037.5	60.80	0.48
Total	117,371.7	44.93	54.39

Source: Prowess database, Centre for Monitoring Indian Economy, Mumbai.
These are the 27 largest Indian exporters in 2005–06 for which data have been reported. Each of these companies exported more than Rs 100 million in 2005–06. Only one MNC (Aventis Pharma) is a major exporter from India, exporting Rs 2,222 million (24.9% of its sales).

not as elaborate in the unregulated markets. The stricter the regulations, the higher are the entry barriers and, accordingly, the prices.

The regulated markets include countries in North America and Western Europe, as well as the nations of Japan, Australia, and New Zealand.[23] The Indian pharmaceutical industry has increasingly exported to the regulated markets. These markets accounted for about 41 percent of India's total exports in 2005–06. The United States is now India's largest export partner, making up 14.2 percent of India's total pharmaceutical exports.[24] Larger Indian companies, in particular, increasingly focus on the United States and other regulated markets (CIPIH 2006, p. 101). The United States is already Ranbaxy's largest market, with a 28 percent share of its global sales of $1,178 million. India is the second largest, with a 20 percent share (Ranbaxy *Annual Report 2005*, p. 7).

In this section, I focus on the United States and show how Indian companies must, and are, conducting significant R&D in order to enter and grow in the U.S. generics market.

A. R&D for DMFs and ANDAs

To get marketing approval for a patent-expired drug, generics companies are required to satisfy the quality and regulatory standards of the country.

To sell Active Pharmaceutical Ingredients (APIs) in the United States, manufacturers are required to file a Drug Master File (DMF) with the U.S. Food and Drug Administration (FDA) for each such API. A DMF is a confidential document containing information on the manufacturing facility and processes used in the manufacture, packaging, and storage of an API. DMFs are kept on file and are reviewed when a pharmaceutical manufacturer files an Abbreviated New Drug Application (ANDA). The latter is required for getting approval to market a formulation. Manufacturing facilities and processes, and the standards employed, must be approved. Generics companies are required to undertake various types of studies (e.g., bioequivalence studies) and to generate data and submit dossiers to the U.S. FDA. Marketing approval is granted after various types of review by the U.S. FDA, including a chemistry review, a bioequivalence review, and a plant inspection.

The filing of DMFs and submission of ANDAs involve R&D efforts. The development of processes for manufacturing APIs and the product development of formulations, process validation, bioequivalence testing, and generation of other data required for DMFs and ANDAs for getting international regulatory

23. I have considered as regulated markets all the OECD countries except the recent members (Czech Republic, Korea, Mexico, Poland, and Hungary).

24. Calculated from export data compiled by the Directorate General of Commercial Intelligence & Statistics and obtained from CMIE India Trades database.

approvals are specifically mentioned as areas in which R&D is undertaken by the companies active in the regulated markets.[25]

B. DMFs and ANDAs by Indian Companies

Indian companies are now a dominant source of APIs for the U.S. market, either as direct suppliers to U.S. generics companies or for processing the APIs in India and exporting formulations to the United States (Hoffman 2005, p. 9). Indian pharmaceutical companies started filing DMFs in the United States around the 1980s, but until the late 1990s, only a few DMFs were filed (the most being eight DMFs filed in 1993). Since then, the rate of filing has accelerated. The number of DMFs filed by Indian companies increased from 17 in 1997 to 33 in 2000, 65 in 2002, 195 in 2004, and 300 in 2006.[26] In relative terms, DMFs filed from India as a percentage of total DMFs filed with the U.S. FDA increased steadily from 18.3 percent in 2001 to 44 percent in 2006 (CRIS INFAC 2006, p. A-16). Between January 2001 and March 2006, India has been by far the most prominent country in terms of DMFs filed, way ahead of second-ranked China (CRIS INFAC 2006, p. A-17). India has displaced some of the traditional Italian and Spanish API suppliers (Hoffman 2005, p. 9). Aurobindo and Dr. Reddy's have filed more than 100 DMFs each as of 2006–2007. As can be seen from Table 12.5, some other major Indian companies also have individually filed a large number of DMFs.

Until recently only a few Indian companies, particularly Ranbaxy and Dr. Reddy's Laboratories, had ANDAs in their own names. Some, such as Cipla, that also exported formulations had the ANDAs in the names of their marketing partners in the United States. The situation has dramatically changed over the last few years. From 161 ANDAs filed by only four companies—Ranbaxy, Dr. Reddy's Laboratories, Wockhardt, and Lupin—in the last quarter of 2003, the number has gone up to 701 ANDAs filed by 17 companies by the second quarter of 2007 (Table 12.5). ANDA approvals by India as a percentage of total approvals have gone up sharply, from about 7 percent in 2001 to 21 percent in 2006 (CRIS INFAC 2006, p. A-8). India now has 75 manufacturing plants approved by the U.S. FDA. This is the highest number of U.S. FDA–approved plants outside the United States. Italy has 55 plants, China has 27, and Spain has 25 plants approved (Ernst & Young n.d., p. 13).

---

25. See, for example, Dr. Reddy's Laboratories *Annual Report, 2005–06*, p. 85; Ranbaxy *Annual Report, 2005*, p. 46. Mani (2006) has suggested that DMFs and ANDAs also should be used as indicators of research output of Indian pharmaceutical companies.

26. Information on DMFs has been obtained from the website of the U.S. FDA at http://www.fda.gov/cder/dmf/. For APIs/intermediates to be manufactured in a location outside the United States, FDA mentions the country. The data on DMFs for India have been compiled for all the DMFs for which India has been mentioned as the country.

TABLE 12.5 R&D OUTPUT OF MAJOR INDIAN PHARMACEUTICAL COMPANIES AS OF 2006–07

Company	Number of DMFs	Number of ANDAs	Number of Patents Issued in United States
Aurobindo Pharma Ltd.	105	70	9
Dr. Reddy's Laboratories Ltd.	103	84	73
Cipla Ltd.	88	4	3
Matrix Laboratories Ltd.	80		
Ranbaxy Laboratories Ltd.	77	204	79
Cadila Healthcare Ltd.	73	50	3
Lupin Ltd.	55	49	17
Sun Pharmaceutical Ind. Ltd.	53	78	8
Orchid Chemicals & Pharmaceuticals Ltd.	44	36	21
Hetero Drugs Ltd.	35		5
Wockhardt Ltd.	35	51	13
Divi's Laboratories Ltd.	29		1
Glenmark Pharmaceuticals Ltd.	26	29	5
Neuland Laboratories Ltd.	25		
Ipca Laboratories Ltd.	24	1	1
USV Ltd.	19		8
Jubilant Organosys Ltd.	19	18	3
Shasun Chemicals and Drugs Ltd.	17		1
Cadila Pharmaceuticals Ltd.	17		2
Biocon India Ltd.	16		6
Alembic Ltd.	16		5
Wanbury Ltd.	15		
Natco Pharma Ltd.	13	2	1
Sekhsaria Chemicals Ltd.	11		1
Ind Swift Laboratories Ltd.	10		1
Unichem Laboratories Ltd.	8	2	
Nicholas Piramal India Ltd.	6		3
Unique Chemicals	6	10	2
Torrent Pharmaceuticals Ltd.	5	9	2
Dabur India Ltd.	5	4	37
Panacea Biotec			13

Sources: (i) For DMF, see http://www.fda.gov/cder/dmf/. (Retrieved on July 15, 2007—list updated until May 15, 2007; (ii) For ANDAs, Electronic Orange Book, accessed July 10, 2007, from http://www.fda.gov (searced by applicant holder for both prescription and OTC drug products); (iii) for patent data, see http://www.uspto.gov, accessed July 24, 2007 (searched issued patents by assignee name).

Sun Pharmaceuticals includes Caraco; Dr. Reddy's Laboratories includes Dr. Reddy's Research Foundation; Dabur India includes Dabur Research Foundation.

C. R&D for Value-Added Generics

R&D is required not only for developing the product to get regulatory approvals as described above. R&D is also required to ensure that the products do not infringe on any existing patents. An innovator company usually does not obtain a patent only on the active ingredient (NCE) involved in a new drug. Other secondary patents relating to the same NCE which can be obtained are for new formulations and compositions, such as new dosage forms or routes of administration; new salts, esters, and so forth of existing ingredients (that is, chemical derivatives of existing active ingredients); new uses to treat health problems; and new processes for manufacturing active ingredients. These secondary patents are obtained later and, hence, typically expire after the basic patent on the NCE expires. Thus, by taking such patents, the innovator companies can delay the entry of generics, as, for example, in the case of the anti-depressant drug paroxetine. The basic NCE patent expired in the mid-1990s, but GlaxoSmithKline could delay the entry of generics by obtaining several secondary patents (Hutchins 2003, pp. 67–68). Studies have shown that the innovator companies use patenting as a matter of strategy to maintain their market dominance.[27] In fact, with a number of drugs scheduled to go off-patent, they have intensified their efforts in recent years to extend the period of patent protection and protect the sales of their branded drugs (Mandi 2003, p. 3).

Thus, it is not enough to just file DMFs and ANDAs. Generics companies must be sure not to infringe on the secondary patents in API processes and formulation products. In fact, the generics companies that can challenge the secondary patents of the originator companies and own their own patents can reap huge benefits, as I will discuss below.

Most of the Indian companies operate in the commodity generics, where regulatory barriers are, practically speaking, the only entry barriers. These markets are characterized by intense competition among a large number of companies, and by low prices and profit margins. Indian companies, in fact, compete a lot among themselves. The success of one Indian company in a field often induces the entry of other Indian companies into the same field (Chaudhuri 2005b, pp. 198–201). A few Indian companies have lately started targeting these value-added segments in different ways. Apart from DMFs and ANDAs, patenting is increasingly becoming important for generics companies desiring to move up the value chain.

D. Challenging Patents

The U.S. FDA provides for two types of applications: the New Drug Application (NDA) for seeking permission to market a new drug, and the ANDA for seeking

27. See, for example, Federal Trade Commission 2002, which did a detailed study on patents and generics entry into the United States.

to market a generic drug. When the NDA is filed (for any drug product other than biologicals and vaccines, for which the system is different), the applicant must also provide the FDA with certain information regarding the patents relating to the drug product for which permission is sought. When an ANDA is filed, the application must contain a certification with respect to the patents so listed in what is known as the Orange Book. There are four certification options. One of these is Para IV application for which the generic company certifies that the patent is invalid or will not be infringed on by the generic drug for which the ANDA applicant seeks approval.[28] Para IV certification is relevant because even when the patent on the active ingredient (NCE) expires, there can be secondary patents on formulations and on methods of use, which may still be valid. In almost all Para IV ANDA cases, the generics applicant is sued by the patent holder (Federal Trade Commission 2002). If the generics company successfully contests such a patent case and obtains a Para IV ANDA, it gets market exclusivity for 180 days. During this period, no other generics company is permitted to enter the market.

Any successful first to file Para IV ANDA can bring immense returns to the company, as the experience of Dr. Reddy's Laboratories shows. Dr. Reddy's was the first Indian company to get the 180-day exclusivity for marketing fluoxetine (Eli Lilly's Prozac) 40mg capsule in August 2001.[29]

Dr. Reddy's Laboratories and Ranbaxy are the two Indian companies that have been very active in challenging patents in order to be the first to enter the generics market.[30] These two companies have been the first to file Para IV ANDAs in several cases, but—except for the 180-day exclusivity obtained by Dr. Reddy's as mentioned above and one by Ranbaxy in June 2006 for simvastatin, 80 mg (Merck's Zocor)[31]—they have not yet tasted any success (*Business World*, 15 May 2006). Patent litigation is a high risk–high gain strategy. A failure means the loss of several years of hard labor and huge legal expenses. It is no wonder that other Indian companies are not involved in product patent challenges (Chaudhuri 2005b, pp. 205–06).

---

28. The other certifications, known as Para I, II, and III, respectively, are (1) the required patent information has not been filed; (2) the patent has expired; and (3) the patent has not yet expired, and approval is sought after patent expiration.

29. The total sales of generics of Dr. Reddy's increased from Rs 304 million in 2000–01 to Rs 4,066 million in 2001–02, driven largely by the success of Fluoxetine 40mg, which contributed 81% of total generics sales. About half of Dr. Reddy's operating profits in 2001–02 came from this product alone—see Dr. Reddy's Laboratories Ltd. *Annual Report, 2001–02.*

30. Another way in which a generics company can be the first to enter is to directly challenge the existing patents as Ranbaxy did in the case of cefuroxime axetil (Chaudhuri 2005b, p. 204).

31. Ranbaxy *Annual Report, 2006.*

E. Non-Infringing Processes

Process patents are not required to be listed by the originator companies with the U.S. FDA, and, hence, when a generics company applies for an ANDA, no certification is required for such patents. But originator companies usually have patents for a large number of processes. In fact, the proportion of process patents among all the secondary patents is now higher than before. Originator companies have been relying to a significant extent on process patents to delay generics entry (Leighton 2007). In such cases, a generics player which can develop a non-infringing process and enter the market can earn a higher price and margin. Matrix Laboratories of India, for example was the first company to develop a non-infringing process for manufacturing citalopram. With restricted competition it was able to reap huge benefits—sales of the product were Rs 5,600 million until 2005–06.[32] Another commercially successful example is the cefotaxime process developed by Lupin.[33] Because of entry barriers, the returns on such bulk drug activities can be significantly higher than those in conventional formulations with a number of competitors.

F. Novel Drug-Delivery Systems (NDDS)

Several Indian companies are increasingly focusing on R&D for modifications of existing drugs. The idea is to develop new formulations, get patents on them, and sell at a higher price. The new formulations include novel drug-delivery systems (NDDS), such as developing a controlled- or extended-release formulation of existing oral therapies to reduce side effects or increase patient compliance; developing alternative delivery routes, including oral as opposed to injectables, to increase patient convenience and compliance; and enhancing purification of the product to reduce dosing and side effects (Datamonitor 2001, p. 37).

Commercially, the most successful example is that of the NDDS developed by Ranbaxy for ciprofloxacin, whereby patients are required to take the drug once a day against the twice-a-day dosage earlier. It took out a patent and licensed it to Bayer, the innovator of the drug. The latter put the new dosage form on the market after approval from the U.S. FDA. Ranbaxy receives royalty on the sales of the product, though the patent on the original molecule has expired (Singh 2006, pp. 195–96).

Developing NDDS products is now a thrust area for most of the larger Indian companies, and they are increasing R&D resources to it. Companies not yet involved in NCE R&D, such as Cipla, Alembic, and JB Chemicals & Pharmaceuticals, have been involved in R&D for NDDS. In the parliamentary debate preceding the amendment of India's patent law to fulfill the TRIPS requirement, a demand was raised that product patenting in pharmaceuticals

---

32. Matrix Laboratories Ltd. *Annual Report, 2005–06.*
33. Lupin, Ltd. *Annual Report, 2002–03.*

may be restricted to NCEs only. The Mashelkar Committee (2006) was set up by the Government of India to look into it. Ranbaxy argued in its submission to this committee that NDDS products are less expensive and have lower gestation periods. Indian companies, which have fewer resources than the MNCs, are, in fact, better placed to benefit from patenting NDDS than patenting NCEs. And hence, Ranbaxy argued, India must permit patenting of NDDS. But in view of the fact that Indian companies are increasingly eyeing the Western markets where NDDS patents are recognized, the Indian companies would continue to invest in R&D for NDDS to move up the value chain even if such patents were not permissible in India. In fact, as Cipla has argued, such patenting abroad is required also for defensive reasons: If Indian companies do not patent, others will and may, thus, block Indian companies from the pertinent market (Mueller 2006, p. 59).

G. Patenting by Indian Companies in the United States

Not unexpectedly, efforts of Indian companies to move up the value chain have been accompanied by increasing patenting in the United States, as the information provided by the United States Patent and Trademark Office (USPTO) shows.

Patenting by major Indian pharmaceutical R&D spenders (listed in Table 12.2) started in the United States in the 1990s. In 1990 Ranbaxy obtained two patents.[34] Since then, and particularly since the late 1990s, there has been an increasing trend. Before 1995, only seven patents were obtained, all of them by Ranbaxy. Thereafter, for the 12 major Indian patentees in the United States, the number increased from 40 patents during 1995–99 to 174 during 2000–05. Big companies, such as Dr. Reddy's and Lupin, started patenting in the late 1990s. Others, such as Sun, Wockhardt, and Aurobindo, did so in the early 2000s (Table 12.6). As of July 2007, 32 Indian pharmaceutical companies have obtained 312 patents in United States. The big three are Ranbaxy (79 patents), Dr. Reddy's Laboratories (73), and Dabur (37). In the next group are Orchid (21), Lupin (17), and Wockhardt (13). Others have fewer than 10 patents each. Among the major exporters who are not major patentees are Cipla (only 3 patents in the United States), and Ipca (1) (see Table 12.5).[35] India has emerged as a major pharmaceutical patentee among the foremost developing countries. India has long had a much

34. Company-wise and year-wise patent data obtained from "Patenting by Geographical Region (State and Country), Breakout by Organization: Count of 1969–2005 Utility Patents Grants by Calendar Year of Grant," accessed at http://www.uspto.gov on June 21, 2007. The list includes all organizations (first name assignees) with five or more patents.

35. The number of Cipla's published patent applications not yet issued in the United States is, however, 14. Moreover, the number of patents filed in the United States is far lower than what Indian companies do worldwide. In 2006 alone, Cipla had 49 patent applications published worldwide. (See the European Patent Office website: http://ep.espacenet.com.) See also Li 2007.

TABLE 12.6 PATENTING BY INDIAN PHARMACEUTICAL COMPANIES IN THE UNITED STATES

First Name Assignee	Before 1989	1990–94	1995–99	2000–05	Total
Ranbaxy Laboratories Ltd.	0	7	13	45	65
Dr. Reddy's Laboratories Ltd.	0	0	10	33	43
Dabur India Ltd.	0	0	1	27	28
Orchid Chemicals & Pharmaceuticals Ltd.	0	0	0	18	18
Panacea Biotec Ltd.	0	0	6	8	14
Lupin Ltd.	0	0	9	3	12
Torrent Pharmaceuticals Ltd.	0	0	0	8	8
USV Ltd.	0	0	1	7	8
Biocon India Ltd.	0	0	0	7	7
Wockhardt Ltd.	0	0	0	7	7
Aurobindo Pharma Ltd.	0	0	0	6	6
Sun Pharmaceutical Industries Ltd.	0	0	0	5	5
Total	0	7	40	174	221

Source: Company and year patent data obtained from "Patenting by Geographical Region (State and Country), Breakout by Organization: Count of 1969–2005 Utility Patents Grants by Calendar Year of Grant." Accessed at http://www.uspto.gov (retrieved June 21,2007). The list includes all organizations with five or more patents. Some discrepancies have been observed between this source and patent data obtained from direct search (Table 12.5). The numbers of patents granted to Panacea Biotec and Biocon, for example, are 13 and 6, respectively, in Table 12.5.
Dr. Reddy's Laboratories includes Dr. Reddy's Research Foundation; Dabur India includes Dabur Research Foundation.

higher number of pharmaceutical patents in the United States than have China, South Africa, or Brazil, but the gap has widened in recent times. Between 2001 and 2005, India obtained 572 patents, but China obtained only 134, Brazil 32, and South Africa 30 (see Table 12.7).

Details are not available from the USPTO about the classification of the patents granted—to what extent the patents are for NCEs, modifications of NCEs, and the development of generics. But information provided by Ranbaxy to the Mashelkar Committee (2006, pp. 18–19) suggests that patents have been obtained in the United States primarily for generics. Of the 59 patents granted to Ranbaxy in the United States, 38 are for new processes, and just 21 are for new products: 8 patents for NCEs and 13 for modifications of NCEs.[36] For most of the

36. The period to which these patents refer has not been mentioned.

TABLE 12.7 PHARMACEUTICAL PATENTING IN THE UNITED STATES BY INDIA, CHINA, BRAZIL, AND SOUTH AFRICA

Country	Before 1995	1995–2000	2001–2005	Total
India	161	189	572	922
Brazil	20	19	32	71
South Africa	59	37	30	126
China	30	60	134	224
Total	270	305	768	1,343

Source: "Patenting In Technology Classes Breakout by Geographic Origin (State and Country): Count of 1963–2005 Utility Patent Grants, by Calendar Year of Grant with Patent Counts Based on Primary Patent Classification." Accessed at http://www.uspto.gov on June 21, 2007. I have considered Class 424, Drug, Bio-Affecting and Body Treating Compositions (includes Class 514), and Class 532 Organic Compounds (includes Classes 532–70).

other Indian pharmaceutical patentees in the United States that are less involved in new-drug R&D, the proportion of product patents is lower.

V. CONCLUSIONS

R&D expenditure has dramatically increased for a segment of the Indian pharmaceutical industry since around the mid-1990s when TRIPS came into effect. It is not only that the amount of R&D expenditure has gone up: The structure of R&D activities of the Indian companies has changed. Whereas in the past they were primarily engaged in development of new processes for manufacturing drugs, now they are also involved in R&D for NCEs and modifications of existing drugs to develop new formulations and compositions. Patenting by the Indian pharmaceutical companies has also gone up significantly.

The large Indian pharmaceutical companies, which are the major R&D spenders in the country, have been focusing on the larger and more lucrative developed-country markets, particularly that of the United States. In that regard, the primary incentive to invest in R&D, whether for NCEs, modifications, or the development of generics, has not been the new TRIPS-compliant product patent regime in India but the product patent regime in developed countries that was in place well before TRIPS. TRIPS may have accelerated the trend toward such R&D because of the anticipated shrinkage of domestic opportunities. But in the absence of TRIPS, such R&D activities would still have been undertaken. With the larger domestic operations, Indian companies, in fact, would have had access to larger resources and would have been better placed to undertake such R&D.

If we focus on the outcome of R&D rather than on the incentives for R&D, we find that even after TRIPS, India's proficiency continues to be in process development. Although R&D activities have diversified, Indian pharmaceutical firms have yet to prove their competence in innovating new products. No NCE has yet been developed. There have been several setbacks, and the partnership model has not always worked properly. There has been no significant success in new formulations either, except for the once-a-day formulation developed by Ranbaxy for Cipro. What Indian companies have really demonstrated is the ability to develop generics for the regulated (and other) markets—an ability that they acquired and improved during the pre-TRIPS period (Chaudhuri 2005b).

Accordingly, as our case study shows, little has changed to dispute the traditional wisdom that developing countries should not grant product patent protection. In the absence of TRIPS-compliant protection, the impact on R&D for developing-country firms is unlikely to be negative because developed countries have such protection anyway, and these countries have the largest markets for new drugs. Moreover, there will be significant positive outcomes: generics companies from developing countries, such as India, will not be forbidden from developing processes for the new drugs innovated abroad or from manufacturing and supplying these at low prices locally and to other developing-country markets (as in the case of anti-retroviral drugs [ARVs] for HIV/AIDS). The price charged by the originator company for the triple combination—stavudine + lamivudine + nevirapine—exceeded $10,000 per person per year: this was far beyond the reach of most people in developing countries. Access to ARVs improved substantially after competition from Indian generics companies reduced the price dramatically. By June 2007, the combination was available at less than $100 from India (MSF 2007, p. 6).[37]

But is it not unfair for developing countries to withhold product patent protection while enjoying the fruits of such protection in developed countries? As Challu (1991) and Chang (2001) have shown, most developed countries adopted pharmaceutical-product patent protection only after they had reached a high degree of economic development. Thus, it is actually morally and historically unfair to deny the developing countries the privileges that developed countries enjoyed at comparable stages in their development.

REFERENCES

Baker, Dean. 2004. Financing Drug Research: What Are the Issues? Issue Brief. Washington, DC: Center for Economic and Policy Research.

Branstetter, Lee G. 2004. Do Stronger Patents Induce More Local Innovation? *Journal of International Economic Law* 7(2): pp. 359–70.

Challu, Pablo. 1991. The Consequences of Pharmaceutical Product Patenting. *World Competition: Law and Economics Review* 15(2) pp. 65–126.

37. These ARVs, being pre-1995 drugs, are not required to be patented in India under TRIPS.

Chang, Ha-Joon. 2001. Intellectual Property Rights and Economic Development: Historical Lessons and Emerging Issues. *Journal of Human Development* 2(2) pp. 287–309.
Chaudhuri, Sudip. 2005a. R&D for Development of New Drugs for Neglected Diseases: How Can India Contribute? A study prepared for the World Health Organization Commission on Intellectual Property Rights Innovation and Public Health.
Chaudhuri, Sudip. 2005b. *The WTO and India's Pharmaceuticals Industry: Patent Protection TRIPS and Developing Countries.* New Delhi: Oxford University Press.
CIPIH. 2006. Public Health Innovation and Intellectual Property Rights. *Report of the Commission on Intellectual Property Rights, Innovation and Public Health.*
CRIS INFAC. 2006. Pharmaceutical Annual Review.
Datamonitor. 2001. The Generics Industry in 2005: A New Threat to Pharmaceutical. Available at http://www.datamonitor.com. (Retrieved online September 6, 2007, registration required.)
Ernst & Young. n.d. India: Pharmaceuticals. A report prepared for India Brand Equity Foundation.
U.S. Federal Trade Commission. 2002. Generic Drug Entry Prior to Patent Expiration: An FTC Study. Available at http://www.ftc.gov/os/2002/07/genericdrugstudy.pdf. (Retrieved online September 6, 2007.)
Grace, Cheri. 2004. *The Effect of Changing Intellectual Property on Pharmaceutical Industry Prospects in India and China: Considerations for Access to Medicines.* London: DFID Health Systems Resource Centre.
Greer, Douglas F. 1973. The Case Against Patent Systems in Less-Developed Countries. *The Journal of International Law and Economics,* 8: pp. 223–66.
Hoffman, Jean. 2005. Generics Growth in the USA and the EU: The Role of India. *Journal of Generic Medicines,* 3(1): pp. 7–19.
Hutchins, Mike. 2003. Extending the Monopoly—How "Secondary Patents" Can Be Used to Delay or Prevent Generic Competition upon Expiry of the Basic Patent. *Journal of Generic Medicines,* 1(1): pp. 57–71.
Leighton, Howard. 2007. The Changing Face of Patents in Generic Pharmaceutical Development: Facts and Figures. *Journal of Generic Medicines,* 4(2): pp. 154–57.
Li, Xuan. 2007. Higher Standards of Patent Protection and Pharmaceutical Industry—A Comparative Study on China and India. Presentation on at the South Centre Side Event at the WIPO, PCDA. Geneva, June 12.
Mandi, Attila. 2003. Protection and Challenge of Pharmaceutical Patents. *Journal of Generic Medicines,* 1(1): pp. 72–81.
Mani, Sunil. 2006. The Sectoral System of Innovation of Indian Pharmaceutical Industry. Working Paper No 382, Trivandrum: Centre for Development Studies.
Mashelkar Committee. 2006. Report of the Technical Expert Group on Patent Law Issues. Arranged by Government of India, Ministry of Commerce and Industry with R. A. Mashelkar as Chairman.
Maskus, Keith E. 2000. *Intellectual Property Rights in the Global Economy.* Washington, DC: Institute of International Economics.
Maskus, Keith E. Sean M. Dougherty, and Andrew Mertha. 2005. Intellectual Property Rights and Economic Development in China. In Carsten Fink, and Keith E. Maskus, eds. *Intellectual Property and Development: Lessons from Recent Economic Research.* New York: The World Bank and Oxford University Press: pp. 295–331.
MSF. July 2007. Untangling the Web of Price Reductions: A Pricing Guide for the Purchase of ARVs for Developing Countries, 10th edition. Available at http://www.accessmed-msf.org/documents/Untangling10.pdf. (Retrieved online September 6, 2007).

Mueller, Janice M. 2006. The Tiger Awakens: The Tumultuous Transformation of India's Patent System and the Rise of Indian Pharmaceutical Innovation. University of Pittsburgh School of Law Working Paper Series, Paper 43.

Nwaka, Solomon, and Robert G. Ridley. November 2003. Virtual Drug Discovery and Development for Neglected Diseases through Public-Private Partnerships. *Nature Reviews*, 2: pp. 919–28.

Penrose, Edith Tilton. 1951. *The Economics of the International Patent System*. Baltimore: The Johns Hopkins University Press.

Primo Braga, Carlos. 1990. The Developing Country Case For and Against Intellectual Property Protection. In Wolfgang E. Siebeck, ed. *Strengthening Protection of Intellectual Property in Developing Countries: A Survey of the Literature*. World Bank Discussion Paper. Washington, DC: The World Bank.

Roffe, Pedro, and Christoph, Spennemann. 2006. The Impact of FTAs on Public Health Policies and TRIPS Flexibilities. *International Journal of Intellectual Property Management*, 1(1–2): pp. 75–93.

Sakakibara, Mariko, and Lee Branstetter. 2001. Do Stronger Patents Induce More Innovation? Evidence from the 1988 Japanese Patent Reforms. *The Rand Journal of Economics*, Spring: pp. 77–100.

Siebeck, Wolfgang E. 1990. Introduction. In Siebeck Wolfgang E., ed. *Strengthening Protection of Intellectual Property in Developing Countries: A Survey of the Literature*. World Bank Discussion Paper. Washington, DC: The World Bank.

Singh, Malvinder Mohan. 2006. Will India Become the Global Centre for Pharmaceutical Research & Development? *Journal of Generic Medicines*, 3(3): pp. 194–200.

Vaitsos, Constantine. 1970. Patents Revisited: Their Function in Developing Countries. *Journal of Development Studies*, 9(1): pp. 71–97.

Velasquez, German, and Pascale Boulet, 1999. Globalization and Access to Drugs: Perspectives on the WTO/TRIPS Agreement. *Health Economics and Drugs*, DAP Series No. 7 (Revis,ed), Geneva: World Health Organization.

13. IPRs AND TECHNOLOGICAL DEVELOPMENT IN PHARMACEUTICALS

Who Is Patenting What in Brazil After TRIPS?

FRANCESCO LAFORGIA, FABIO MONTOBBIO, AND LUIGI ORSENIGO*

I. INTRODUCTION

The adoption of the TRIPS Agreement—and, more generally, the global tendency to strengthen intellectual property rights—has raised a heated debate regarding the relationships between stronger intellectual property rights (IPRs) regimes, innovation, and development. After years of stagnation, the economic analysis of the patent system is experiencing a substantial revival. Interestingly, most of the new contributions to the literature are of an empirical nature. Indeed, the economic theory of patents was often deemed to be inconclusive by many economists, given that radically different results could be obtained by slight changes in even ancillary assumptions. Above all, the empirical evidence was so flimsy that it was hard to discriminate against alternative conclusions.

The debate has been particularly virulent with respect to the pharmaceuticals industry. Indeed, this sector brings the trade-offs and issues involved in patent theory to their extreme consequences. Pharmaceuticals is one of the few industries in which patents are unambiguously recognized as being key instruments for privately appropriating the economic benefits of innovation and, therefore, serving as an important incentive for innovation. In this sector, competition is largely based on innovation, and basic science is becoming increasingly crucial for the

* The authors would like to thank Neil Netanel, Claudia Chamas, and Grid Thoma for their helpful comments and suggestions.

discovery and development of new products. The pharmaceuticals industry also has many of the characteristics usually associated with "strategic" industries. It is a high-growth and skill-intensive sector, which provides products that are in themselves associated with further growth: Health is a major engine of growth, and growth is associated with higher health standards. The pharmaceuticals industry also occupies an extremely socially sensitive sector: large parts of the population increasingly perceive health care as a fundamental human right. The very definition of what a just society should look like increasingly involves references to health care. For developing countries in particular, health has become a major issue, magnified by the tragedies of pandemics such as HIV/AIDS. Thus, it should come as no surprise that TRIPS—of which the pharmaceuticals industry was a firm supporter—has ignited raging controversies regarding the desirability of property rights in drugs, both between developed and developing countries and within rich countries.

An analysis of the relationships between IPRs, innovation, and growth in the context of pharmaceuticals is made even more difficult and irksome because of the intricate relationships between health and growth, especially for developing countries. Moreover, the pharmaceuticals industry itself is undergoing deep and unforeseeable transformations.

In this paper, we try to provide an introduction to some of the most salient aspects of the debate, reviewing the relevant theoretical issues and, above all, the sparse empirical evidence available. The main thrust of our argument is as follows:

- There are, indeed, profound trade-offs between the incentives to innovate and ensuring public access to medicines for which no obvious and simple solutions exist.
- The effects of strengthening the patent regime depend on a wide variety of conditions in any given country: institutions (antitrust, patent offices, etc.); capabilities; modes of competition; the specific nature of patent laws themselves and court interpretations (scope, novelty, etc.). In the specific case of pharmaceuticals, other complementary institutions play a key role, as do such factors as price controls; health systems, in general; basic research, and so forth.
- Both economic theory and the evidence increasingly suggest that the strengthening of IPR regimes in developing countries is likely to impose upon them a series of negative consequences that probably outweigh any comparable benefits gained from the more robust regime.
- The IPR system governing pharmaceuticals has become increasingly dysfunctional—even in countries like the United States. The efficacy and desirability of extending strong IPR protection in the rest of the world raises very legitimate doubts.

We also emphasize that, despite increased knowledge on the subject, little is known about the relationships between IPRs, innovation, and growth, especially as developing countries are concerned. Thus, theoretical development and especially new empirical evidence are badly needed.

In this vein, we report on very preliminary research addressing the patenting activities in Brazil using domestic patent data, rather than—as is customary—international (that is, U.S. or European) patents. A first look at these data suggests, indeed, that domestic patents reveal somewhat different and relevant insights into the nature and patterns of innovation in developing countries. In particular, we show that the adoption of TRIPS had a great impact on the number of patent applications in Brazil, and that, after 1996, there was a great inflow of nonresident patents. Importantly, the impact of TRIPS is heterogeneous across different technological fields. In particular, the number of pharmaceuticals patent applications started increasing in 2000, at least three years after the number of patents in other fields, and has kept increasing thereafter.

II. PHARMACEUTICALS: BACKGROUND

Ever since its inception, the pharmaceuticals industry has been dominated by a stable core of large, globalized, innovative firms based in a few countries: the United States, the United Kingdom, Switzerland, Germany, Japan, and France. However, this sector is highly competitive. Concentration is very low as compared to other research and development (R&D)- and marketing-intensive industries, mainly because the market is composed of several independent submarkets (for example, tranquilizers are not substitutes for cardiovascular drugs), economies of scale are not very strong, and innovations tend not to build on preceding work. Discovering and successfully developing a new drug remains a highly uncertain activity, and firms find it difficult to use the knowledge accumulated in developing one product for developing a truly different one. Today, after substantial mergers and acquisitions in the industry, the largest pharmaceuticals company controls a market share lower than 10 percent of the world market. In the United States, the market share of the top five and the top ten firms are, respectively, less than 36 percent and around 60 percent. Moreover, the industry comprises many other types of firms competing and, in some cases collaborating, with the major corporations: small, domestic firms involved in adaptation, manufacturing, or marketing; biotech firms mainly active in the early stages of the research and development process; and producers of generics.

Pharmaceuticals have been systematically characterized by little entry and turbulence: the biotechnology revolution and the diffusion of generics constitute major changes in this respect, but nevertheless, most of the biotech companies do not compete directly on the final-product market, whereas the generics segment is already undergoing a process of consolidation. Schumpeterian competition is, however, a distinct feature of this industry. Firms compete first by trying to discover and develop new drugs. The process is highly costly and risky, and only a very small number of molecules actually reach the market. Innovators, thanks to patent protection, enjoy high profits after the introduction of a new, successful drug. But quite early, innovative products become exposed to competition from imitators, which provide patented variants of the original drug. After patent expiration, generics enter the market, in some cases substantially eroding the profits of the original innovator.

Finally, the industry is characterized by strong information asymmetries: consumers are typically unable to properly evaluate the quality of a drug before taking it. The prescribing doctor decides which drugs to use, but even doctors often do not know all the properties of a drug, especially a new drug for which much of the available information is provided by the company itself. Given the value users may attribute to the product, especially in extreme cases, demand price elasticity tends to be low. Moreover, most consumers are insured (privately or publicly) against at least a part of the cost of prescription drugs, so they are only partially interested in drug prices. The prescribing physicians are, likewise, not completely sensitive to prices, both because they will not pay for the prescribed drugs and because professional norms make them more attentive to the safety and therapeutic value of medicines than to their prices.

The industry has undergone deep transformations in the past 25 years. First, the data gleaned via the veritable molecular-biology revolution has substantially changed the relevant knowledge base and drug research procedures. Chemical analysis and molecular synthesis based on randomized trials now inform the drug-discovery process. Today, it is guided by the understanding of the intrinsic biological bases of diseases, drugs, and cures. Second, the organization of the industry and of individual firms is profoundly changing through the entry of specialized "biotechnology companies," and, more generally, through processes of partial vertical disintegration spanning not only pre-clinical research but also clinical trials. Thus, drug discovery and development now rely on a dense web of interactions between universities, biotech companies, hospitals, firms, organizing trials, and so forth, although large corporations still maintain key positions as integrators of the whole process (Orsenigo et al. 2001).

However, the new opportunities promised by the new technologies do not appear to have materialized. Between 1978 and 2003, research "productivity," measured by the number of patents per dollar of R&D expenditure, in fact, fell: R&D expenditures increased tenfold, whereas patenting output increased only sevenfold (Nightingale and Martin 2004). This data is further corroborated by the number of New Chemical Entities (NCE, a much more demanding measure of innovative activity than is patent assignation) approved by the FDA in the United States between 1983 and 2003. Some increase was displayed until the mid 1990s, followed by a sharp decline in the years since. In 2002, U.S. R&D expenditures in pharmaceuticals were 30 times greater than in the early 1980s, whereas roughly the same number of drugs were approved annually. At the same time, marketing expenditures also increased substantially, reaching more than one-third of sales (Orsenigo et al. 2006).

To some extent, the productivity paradox in pharmaceuticals can be attributed to more demanding regulation. Over time, the regulatory system for product approval has become more stringent, before and after product approval, increasing the cost and the time for launching a new drug on the market.[1] In addition, cost-containment policies have put pressures on the price of drugs in many countries and, with considerable differences across countries, have stimulated the diffusion of generics. The generics industry is growing and is already undergoing a consolidation phase.

It is important to emphasize, though, that the opening and growth of the generics market has also changed the geography of the industry. As in other industries, entry of new companies and new countries occurs in lower value-added segments of the industry and/or in specific niche markets. Indeed, countries like India, Israel, Thailand, and Brazil have been able to develop lively domestic industries in this segment, and some of the firms in these nations have acquired significant positions in the world market. An Israeli company is now among the 20 largest pharmaceuticals corporations worldwide in terms of sales, and there is more than one Indian company among the top 50.

III. STRENGTHENING IPR REGIMES AND TRIPS

A further important change in the industry is linked to the progressive tightening of the IPR regime. In the United States, in particular, various actions and court decisions have introduced reforms essentially aimed at saving the cost and time linked to patent procedures, extending patent duration for some classes of products, and encouraging "non-profit research institutions" to patent and market technologies developed with public funding. Moreover, a series of court cases in the mid-1990s overturned previous practices, granting patents on upstream research and significantly extending patents' scopes, even to cases where the practical application of the patented invention had not been clearly demonstrated. Just to recall a few important steps in this direction, in 1980, the Bayh-Dole act was introduced, which greatly facilitated the patenting and licensing of the results of publicly funded research; in the same year, the U.S. Supreme Court ruled in favor of granting patent protection to living organisms (*Diamond v. Chakrabarty*). These two decisions practically gave birth to the biotechnology industry. In 1982 the Court of Appeals for the Federal Circuit (CAFC) was created. As a result, the whole "inventing system" became more homogeneous (Adelman 1987). Moreover, the CAFC strongly supported the "equivalents doctrine," through which inventors were protected not only from imitative products and processes, but also from

1. However, in more recent years, regulations have become more relaxed and approval times have been shortened (as a result of the Prescription Drug User Fee Act in 1992 and the FDA Modernization Act in 1997).

those substantially similar (or similar in their results), although outside the *literal patent's scope*. Also, the Court strongly encouraged significant compensation for all the damages stemming from the violation of patent protection. In subsequent years, a number of patents were granted establishing the right for very broad claims (Merges and Nelson 1994). Finally, a one-year grace period was introduced for filing a patent after the publication of the invention.

Last, the adoption of TRIPS in 1994 extended and sought to homogenize patent protection in all countries participating in the WTO. Subsequent bilateral agreements even strengthened the TRIPS provisions.

IV. PATENTS AS AN INCENTIVE TO INNOVATE

The debate sparked by TRIPS—and by developments in the United States—touches on a mind-boggling series of difficult questions. In sum, they address the following issues:

- What would be the effects of stronger IPRs on domestic, innovative pharmaceutical-development activities in the southern hemisphere?
- What would be the effects of stronger IPRs on innovative pharmaceutical-development activities in the northern hemisphere?
- Would stronger patent protections induce higher levels of Foreign Direct Investment (FDI) and, thereby, higher rates of R&D and innovation in the southern hemisphere?
- What are the effects on drug prices and public access to drugs?
- How can the negative effects of stronger patent protections be offset? In particular, are price discrimination and parallel trade viable solutions for granting access to drugs at lower prices in poorer countries?
- Are alternative mechanisms for incentivizing and funding research possible and viable?

To introduce discussion on these issues, it might be worthwhile to go back to the basics.

The first, fundamental motivation for patents is that they provide an incentive for private agents to engage in innovative activities. Thus, theory predicts that stronger IPRs should increase the propensity for R&D and, therefore, for innovation. Yet, neither the theoretical nor the empirical literature clearly shows how big this incentive is or should be. Results depend critically on a series of variables, some of which are extremely hard to measure. For example, effects depend on the curvature of the innovation function and/or the probability distribution of innovating for any given dollar spent in R&D (the space of innovative opportunities); on the composition of the population of potential and actual innovators (Baumol 1990, Murphy et al. 1991), and, in particular, on their technological competencies; on the cost structure of R&D; on the costs of imitation with respect to the costs of innovation; on the actual patterns of imitation (how much does imitation erode innovators' profits?); and, of course, on the specifics of the R&D decision-making process.

Moreover, stronger patent protection might actually hinder technological progress. This is the case whenever incentives for innovation under a monopoly are lower than in more competitive markets. Earlier, theoretical literature suggested that the threat of a new firm entering the market would "force" the incumbent monopolist to have a high rate of innovation (Arrow 1962, Dasgupta and Stiglitz 1980a and 1981, Gilbert and Newbery 1982). But then it was recognized that, given the "sunk cost" nature of research expenditures, an incumbent could deter competitive entry with only a limited amount of research, so that innovation under a monopoly could be substantially lower than with more competition (Dasgupta and Stiglitz 1981 and 1982, Dasgupta et al. 1982, Farrell et al. 2003). Even more important, strong patent protection can significantly slow technological progress when innovation is sequential or cumulative—that is, when it builds on previous innovations (Scotchmer 1991, Merges and Nelson 1994, Bessen and Maskin 2000). Strategic use of patents and litigation costs further deters innovation. Finally, strong patents can distort the direction, in addition to the rate, of innovation. To the extent that patents imply higher prices, research will be focused on diseases with patients who are typically rich enough to pay for prescriptions, and, more generally, on patentable cures and treatments (excluding, for example, nutrition, exercise, environment, etc.). Moreover, to the extent that firms engage in patent races (winner takes all), duplication of effort may occur.

The empirical evidence on these issues is surprisingly thin. A few studies have tried to measure the impact of patent protection on innovation in pharmaceuticals. Scherer (2001) finds evidence of cyclical co-movement in pharmaceutical-industry gross margins and R&D outlays. Schankerman (1988) estimates the value of patent rights using data on patent renewal rates and fees for France and computes the equivalent cash subsidy to R&D, obtaining a value of only 4 percent. However, this result might depend on the fact that, in France, drug prices are very low. Indeed, a similar exercise for Germany yields a value of 15.2 percent (Lanjouw 1998b). These studies focus on the impact of patents on R&D or on innovation as measured by patents themselves. Arora et al. (2005) uses survey data to estimate the so-called patent premium—that is, the proportional, incremental increase in the value of an innovation that is realized by patenting it. A value of the premium less than 1 would, therefore, imply a loss. Results indicate an expected patent premium around 1.3 in biotechnology and 1.05 for drugs. However, these values increase considerably—to 2.45 and 2.3, respectively—if the patent premium is computed conditionally on having actually patented the innovation. These results imply that a 10 percent increase in patent premium increases R&D by 10.6 percent in biotech and by 8.9 percent in drugs, corresponding to an equivalent subsidy rate equal to 22 percent.

Moreover, a 10 percent increase in patent premium increases patent applications by 14.3 percent in biotech and by 12.5 percent in drugs. These results are broadly in line with the findings by Acemoglu and Linn (2004), who estimate that, in pharmaceuticals, a 1 percent increase in the size of the market for pharmaceuticals products raises the number of new drugs by 4 to 6 percent, implying an elasticity of innovations to R&D ranging from 0.8 to 0.85.

These results confirm that patent protection is important in pharmaceuticals, but said results refer to highly developed countries and do not consider the effects of changes in the strength of the patenting regimes. Moreover, critics maintain that the degree of innovativeness of the pharmaceuticals industry might be overstated, because only a few of the new drugs are really innovative—many only introduce minor modifications (for example, in terms of dosage) to existing products.

In this respect, it is important to recall that, throughout the history of pharmaceuticals, the scope and efficacy of patent protection has varied significantly over time and across countries. The United States has provided relatively strong patent protection in pharmaceuticals. Yet many other European countries—including Germany, France, Italy, Japan, Sweden, and Switzerland—traditionally did not offer protection for pharmaceuticals products: only process technologies could be patented. France introduced product patents in 1960; Germany in 1968; Japan in 1976; Switzerland in 1977; Italy, Netherlands, and Sweden in 1978; and Canada and Denmark in 1983. In many cases, as in Japan and Italy (and possibly France), the absence of product patent protection induced firms to avoid product R&D and to concentrate instead on finding novel processes for making existing molecules. In these countries, the development of "me, too" drugs, or inventing around and getting licenses from other companies, became the main research activity.

In other cases (primarily Germany and Switzerland, but also Denmark and Sweden), the absence of product patent protection did not seem to produce such negative effects. Similarly, the reforms of patent laws do not appear to have had a visible and significant impact on the innovative capabilities of industries such as the Italian or Japanese pharmaceuticals industries. If anything, it has been argued that according patent protection to pharmaceuticals products might have had a negative effect, further weakening national industries mainly composed of generic producers (Scherer and Weisburst 1995).

Conversely, in India, pharmaceuticals product patents were abolished in 1970. After this reform, tremendous growth in the domestic generics industry was observed. India became an exporter of bulk drugs and final therapeutics, providing them to many parts of the developing and developed world at lower costs. Almost all the empirical studies on the Indian case agree that a weaker intellectual protection system encouraged the development of indigenous technological capabilities and catching up (see, among others, Lanjouw 1998a, Kumar 1998 and 2002, Ramani and Maria 2005, Chaudhuri2005).

The effects of TRIPS-compliant patent protection[2] on the Indian industry are not clear yet. However, the available evidence suggests that, indeed, a few Indian companies are trying to enter the club of innovative firms, raising their R&D intensity significantly with mixed results thus far. On the other hand, although evidence does not yet show any dramatic shake-out of local producers of generics, most analysts seem to agree that a substantial restructuring is bound to occur. In the best scenarios, most local generics-producing firms would become intermediate-product manufacturers or service providers to larger foreign companies or would continue as generics producers but with much higher costs linked to access to licenses, litigation, and so forth.

These insights are confirmed by other, more recent studies on the effects of strengthening patent protection on innovation. Theoretical analysis suggests that when patents are already strong, increasing patent protection further may actually depress the level of innovation (Gallini 1992, Cadot and Lippman 1995, Horowitz and Lai 2006). Similarly, in countries lagging behind the technological frontier and with low per capita income, stronger patent protection has little effect on the rate of innovation (Deardorff 1992, Helpman 1993, Lall 2003).

Empirically, various studies have confirmed these predictions. Examples include studies of the broadening of the scope of Japanese patents (Sakakibara and Branstetter 2001), the establishment of the Court of Appeals for the Federal Circuit in the United States (Kortum and Lerner 1998, Hall and Ziedonis 2001), and statistical analyses of episodes of strengthening IPR over a 150-year period (Lerner 2005). Moser (2003) examines data constructed from the catalogues of two 19th-century world fairs: the Crystal Palace Exhibition in London (1851) and the Centennial Exhibition in Philadelphia (1876). She also finds no evidence that patent laws increased overall levels of innovative activity but strong evidence that patent systems influenced the *distribution* of innovative activity across industries—that is, the direction of innovative activity.[3]

In sum, there are strong reasons to doubt that strengthening IPRs in developing countries would have a positive impact on domestic innovative activities. Such effect presumes sufficient scientific and technological capabilities, access to knowledge and active participation in research networks, and large domestic markets and/or the ability to export. If anything, stronger IPRs might possibly make life more difficult for local brands and generics producers, especially

---

2. India signed the Uruguay round of GATT in 1994, but it availed itself of the complete term of the transition period (i.e., 10 years), which was accorded to developing countries to set up a TRIPS-compliant IPR system.

3. In this respect, it has sometimes been argued that stronger IPRs in developing countries could introduce incentives for developing drugs for local diseases—for example, malaria. However, there seems to be no evidence that this is, or could actually be, the case. Decisions concerning the direction of innovative activities would still be influenced by considerations of profitability, by both local and foreign innovators.

if data-exclusivity agreements and patentability for second-use provisions are enforced.

It is even harder to evaluate the effect on R&D and innovation in companies located in rich countries. This will depend on how big the increase in sales and profits might be (which depends also on the resulting price increase), on how much of that will be translated into higher R&D, and on the elasticity of innovation to R&D.

V. PATENTS AS INCENTIVES TO COMMERCIALIZE INNOVATIONS

One finds less skepticism toward the effects of IPRs on innovation when a second set of arguments concerning the role of patents is advocated—namely, that patents disclose information. In the absence of patents, innovations are much more likely to remain secret. Moreover, patents may induce the commercialization of innovation and the development of markets for technology (Arora et al. 2004, Lamoreaux and Sokoloff 1999, Kahn and Sokoloff 1998). The establishment of property rights on research outcomes facilitates the economic exploitation of such knowledge (in the absence of patents, firms would not invest in R&D based on new discoveries because anyone could have access to it) and allows an "ordered" path of exploitation of such knowledge, avoiding the wasteful duplication of effort. The Bayh-Dole Act is clearly based on these assumptions, and the boom in biotech companies (often founded by university scientists) is typically cited as an example of the positive effects of the "new" IPR regime on the commercial exploitation of basic scientific research.

In sum, one finds less skepticism when patents are conceived not so much as an incentive to innovate but as a mechanism for creating markets for technologies. Several objections, however, have been raised against this argument. First, this incentive is not needed in the case of publicly funded scientific research: the invention has already been paid for (by the public), and it has already been realized. Moreover, the argument in favor of the imposition of property rights on otherwise open science rests on a series of specific assumptions about the mechanisms of generation and economic exploitation of knowledge that, as argued by Mazzoleni and Nelson (1998), makes it very hard to accept that argument, in general. In particular, the argument for patenting implies that no further mechanisms of protection are available in the development process.

Indeed, broad patents on basic inventions might hinder further innovation, especially if licenses are given on exclusive terms or at very high prices. First, bringing science into the "market" is likely to distort incentives away from basic research and into specific practical areas that promise commercial rewards. Second, science "*proceeds most effectively and cumulatively when those who do science are part of a community where open publication and access to research results is the norm, and rewards are tied to recognized contributions to the communal scientific effort*" (Nelson 2004). But widening the scope of discoveries allowed to be kept as proprietary runs precisely against this principle. Other sources of worry relate to the "anticommons problem" (Heller and Eisenberg 1998), which concerns the possibility that the extension of patents into research tools will limit innovation as a result of numerous property-rights claims to the separate building blocks of some product or line of research.

In this case, the evidence is mixed. First, various studies have shown that the Bayh-Dole Act did not give birth to technology transfer from university to industry and that the surge in university patents and licenses predates Bayh-Dole (Mowery et al. 2001). Rather, university patenting seems to be triggered by new technological opportunities (biotechnology, software, etc.) and from improvements in the management of the innovative processes (Kortum and Lerner 1998). Moreover, patents are just one instrument of technology transfer, nor are they the most important one (Cohen et al. 2002, Agrawal and Henderson 2002). Second, there is contrasting evidence that university scientists may shift their focus from basic to applied research. Indeed, much of the research conducted in universities is located in the so-called Pasteur's quadrant (i.e., it is at the same time basic and use-inspired [Stokes 1997]), and, if anything, the evidence seems to indicate strong correlations between patenting and publishing (Agrawal and Henderson 2002, Azoulay et al. 2004, Geuna and Nesta 2006, Breschi et al. 2005). Walsh et al. (2003), in a survey of biomedical researchers in universities and private companies, find no major delays or abandonment of projects as a result of transaction costs, but some evidence of increasing obstacles and delays in securing material transfer agreements for research purposes. Other studies, however, find evidence for a quantitatively modest, but statistically significant, anticommons effect (Murray and Stern 2006) and document solid evidence on publication restrictions for sponsored research in the life sciences (Thursby and Thursby 2003 and 2006).

In the case of developing countries, stronger IPRs might hinder the development of domestic scientific capabilities if royalties on basic research tools are too expensive. However, for these countries, the argument that well-defined IPRs may contribute to the development of markets for technologies and to the commercialization of inventions has a further facet: they could attract foreign direct investment (FDI) and, possibly, related R&D. This argument has some empirical support (Maskus 2001), particularly as it concerns clinical trials and market-development activities. Yet it is also widely recognized that IPRs are only one of the motivations leading to FDI. Other considerations—the availability of local skills, research infrastructures and capabilities, and demand characteristics, as well as other institutional and legal preconditions—are usually more important.[4]

4. A counter-argument is that increased foreign direct investment might produce a crowding-out effect on skilled labor and local researchers for domestic companies.

VI. IMPACT ON PRICES

The obvious cost of stronger IPRs is higher prices. In turn, the impact on prices depends on a series of variables, such as market structure before and after the new patent regime (including the number of domestic and foreign firms, the nature of competition, the ease of market entry and exit, quality differentiation among products, openness to trade, and wholesale and retail distribution mechanisms); demand elasticity; and pricing regulations and competition policies (in particular as it concerns parallel imports and sole distributorship laws [Maskus 2001, Nogues 1993]).

Once again, it is very difficult to evaluate, in general, the effects of TRIPS on drug prices. Scarcity of data and the extreme difficulties in computing comparable price indexes (Danzon 1997, Danzon and Kim 1998) prevent systematic analysis. Clearly, such effect will be different across countries. The evidence surveyed by Maskus (2001) suggests, however, a substantial impact. Price increases after the introduction of patents were estimated by Watal (2000) and Fink (2000) to range from 50 percent to 200 percent in India, whereas Baker and Chatani (2002) suggest that the average increase in price for pharmaceuticals as a result of patent protection is probably close to 400 percent. More specific analyses of specific drugs report that, in Brazil, free-market versions of AIDS drugs were available at $200 as opposed to $10,000 a year for patent-protected versions (Coriat et al. 2006).

Two issues deserve specific attention. First, price regulations certainly have a large role to play in limiting price increases. However, patent holders may choose not to supply the local market at the regulated prices. Moreover, when price regulations are based on "cost-plus" formulae, firms are encouraged to set high transfer prices on imported ingredients, leading to potentially higher prices (Lanjouw 1998a). Conversely, when prices are defined on the basis of reference indices of prices in other markets, firms have an incentive to bargain for the highest possible prices in the low-price economies in order to gain a higher set of global reference prices (Maskus 2001).

Second, price discrimination is often considered as a possible counterbalance to unaffordable drug prices in poor countries. However, this implies banning parallel imports, an important source of low-price drugs in many countries (and a source of exports for producers in developing countries). Further, price discrimination is often viewed as anticompetitive because it allows firms to set prices according to market power in each country. Indeed, Maskus (2001) shows that prices are often higher in developing nations than would be expected under a simple price-discrimination equilibrium and, indeed, are at times higher than in the rich nations.

VII. THE TRIPS AGREEMENT AND PATENTING ACTIVITY: THE CASE OF BRAZIL

Given the complexity of the relationship between the strength of IPR protection and innovative activities (and access to medicines), it is increasingly important to be able to collect reliable and disaggregated patent data from national patent offices in developing countries. In this section, we focus in particular on the Brazilian case and show some preliminary evidence.

A. Data Analysis

Typically, international patent databases (the European Patent Office [EPO] and the U.S. Patent and Trademark Office [USPTO]) have been used to assess the technological activity and specialization of developing countries (Montobbio and Rampa 2005, Huang and Miozzo 2004) because they allow for international comparability (Pavitt 1988). Because patenting abroad is expensive, patents at the EPO and USPTO should also have the highest perceived economic value by applicants and inventors. However the use of EPO and USPTO patents is not particularly appropriate for the analysis of the economic impact of IPR reinforcement in developing countries—in this case, Brazil.

In the first place, the analysis of international patenting activity can only be based on patents whose applicant or inventor is Brazilian. In principle, one could argue that, if reinforced IPRs in Brazil really constituted an incentive to perform more R&D, this would be observed in patenting activity abroad. Still, the analysis of patenting activity by foreign companies in Brazil would remain out of the picture. Second, a small number of Brazilian (owned or invented) EPO and USPTO patents exist, relative to the overall economic and technological activity of the country (Montobbio 2007, FAPESP 2005, Albuquerque 2000). Brazilian patents numbered 1,715 at the USPTO from 1968 to 2001 and 1,244 at the EPO from 1978 to 2001. Thus, Brazilian firms (in particular, the small and medium ones) do not patent systematically abroad, and international patents provide only a partial view of the nation's inventive activities. International patents mainly reflect the activities of exporters, and, in many cases, they are the results of technological cooperation between Brazilian and U.S. or EU inventors. In fact, the important Brazilian actors involved in international patenting are mainly U.S. and German companies with a foreign address, or their foreign subsidiaries with a Brazilian address. The main Brazilian patenting company is Petrobras, with patents in a set of heterogeneous sectors of economic activity (oil, glass, electric, metals, and machinery).

In particular, in the pharmaceuticals sector between 1975 and 2001, 190 USPTO patents document Brazilian inventions with widely dispersed ownership. Only one-third of the applicants have a Brazilian address, and the top patentees are (excluding 57 patents that are "individually owned") Johnson & Johnson (10), Fond. Osvaldo Cruz (5), and St. Jude Medical (4).[5]

5. Consistent with what is observed above, it can be noted that most of the 10 patents by Johnson & Johnson are related to a specific project and reflect the activity of a specific team of inventors on different types of sanitary napkins and absorbent articles. Finally, it can be noted that 19 USPTO patents with a Brazilian inventor are owned by U.S. universities or medical schools.

Thus, analysis of the data from the national patent offices is more appropriate if the research question concerns the effects of strengthening patent protection within a country. Domestic data provide a much more accurate description of the nature of patenting activity in a developing country, and they allow for investigating the impact in changes in legislation. Typically, these data are very hard to obtain, coverage is partial, and not all the information contained in a patent is available. We provide here an introductory picture of the patenting activity at the domestic patent office in Brazil, using the PATSTAT database.[6] The database contains 442,070 patent applications between 1972 and 2006; 342,453 patents are from firms and other institutions, and 62,162 are from individual applicants (but 37,445 patents' applicants are not identified).[7] Moreover, the database contains 155,871 applicants, including 47,037 individuals. Among the 110,008 applicants with an address (most of them are companies), 68,176 are from Brazil (i.e., 62 percent). However the share of patents of Brazilian applicants of those with an address is only 41 percent.

B. Findings

Inspection of these data suggests a number of findings.

1. The number of patents increased rapidly after 1996. Figure 13.1 shows the total number of patent applications at INPI[8] between 1974 and 2004 from PATSTAT and from the official data provided by INPI through WIPO.[9] The coverage of the PATSTAT database is good, and, particularly in recent years, the numbers of patents in the two databases are very similar. In the PATSTAT database, the total number of patents remained stable between 1974 and 1991; it declined sharply between 1992 and 1996; it increased significantly after 1996.

In fact, between 1996 and 2001, we observe a fourfold increase in the number of patents. The new Industrial Property Law 9.279/96 was approved in 1996 and, in accordance with the TRIPS, introduced patent protection for pharmaceuticals, biotechnological products, and chemical products and processes that were excluded from patentability in the previous 1971 IP code. At the same time, data also show a declining trend between 2001 and 2003. This may suggest that the impact of the legislative change is temporary, even if there is another sharp increase in 2004.

2. The sectoral composition of patenting activity does not vary substantially, except for the increased weight of chemicals and pharmaceuticals after 2002. This aggregate trend covers a heterogeneous sectoral dynamic. Figure 13.2 shows

---

6. PATSTAT is the OECD and EPO Worldwide Patent Statistical Database.

7. The dataset also contain utility-model applications.

8. The law of creation of the INPI (Instituto National de Propriedad Industrial) was approved in 1970, and the law on industrial property is 5,772, on December 1971.

9. The PATSTAT database provides the publication date of the patent; for WIPO data, see http://www.wipo.int/ipstats/fr/statistics/patents/.

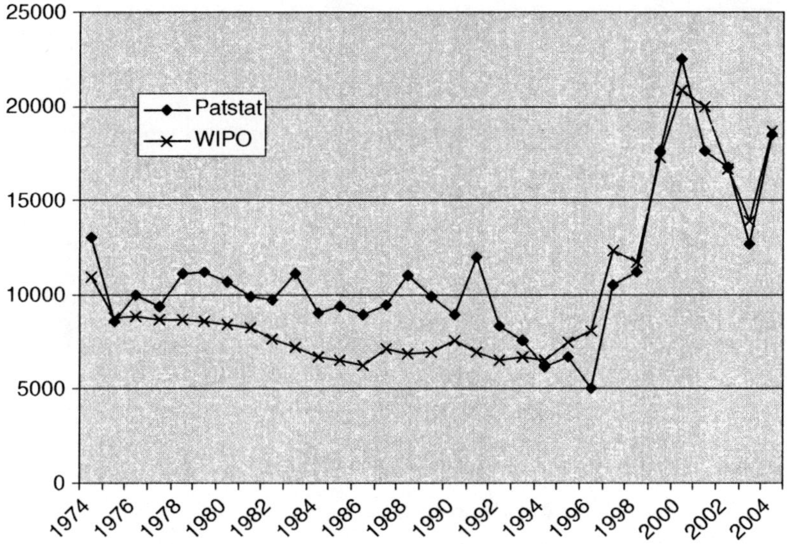

FIGURE 13.1 NUMBER OF PATENT APPLICATIONS IN BRAZIL.
Source: Our elaboration on PATSTAT data.

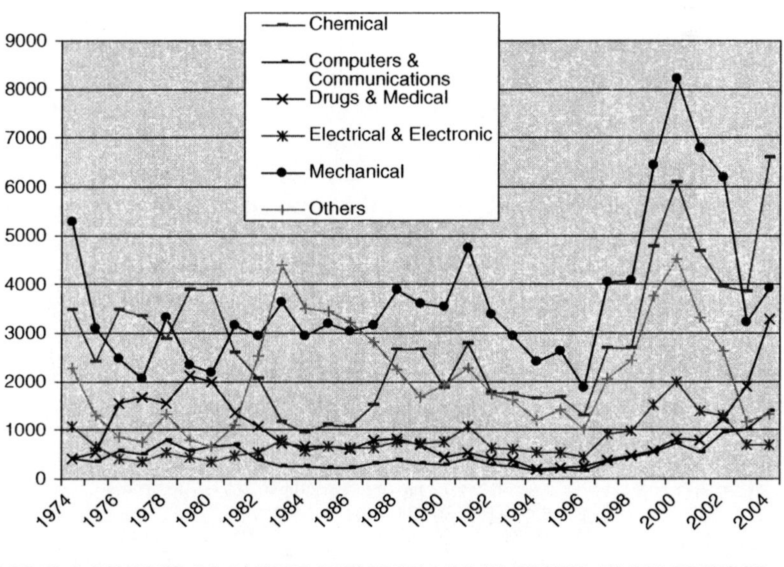

FIGURE 13.2 NUMBER OF PATENT APPLICATIONS IN BRAZIL IN SIX SECTORS.
Source: Our elaboration on PATSTAT data.

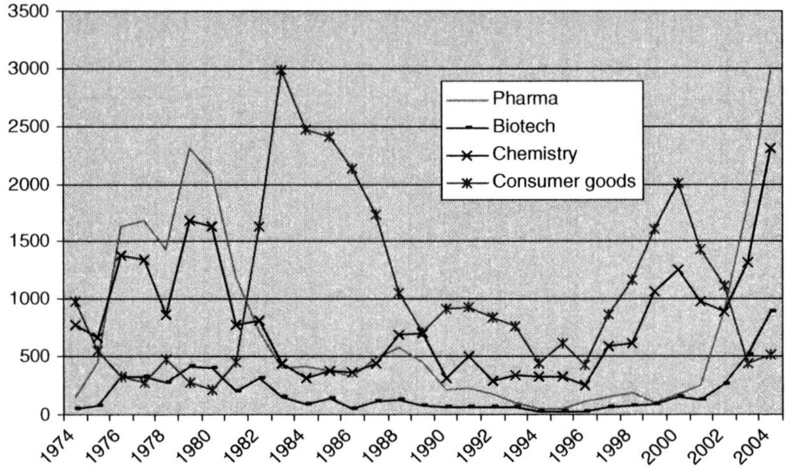

FIGURE 13.3 NUMBER OF PATENT APPLICATIONS IN BRAZIL IN FOUR TECHNOLOGICAL CLASSES.
Source: Our elaboration on patstat data.

the breakdown by six broad sectors; Figure 13.3 shows a more detailed picture of four smaller technological fields.[10] In Brazil, 40 percent of all patents come from the mechanical sector. This share was substantially constant until 2002. Patents in all sectors increased proportionally after 1996, with the exception of a sharp increase in patenting activity in the chemical and pharmaceuticals sectors between 2002 and 2004. In particular, in the pharmaceuticals sector in 2004, the number of patent applications is more than four times as big as the 2001 figure (from 778 to 3,271).[11] However, this trend reflects, in all likelihood, that pharmaceuticals were not patentable (nor were products, nor processes) from 1971 to 1996. Thus, this increase is likely mainly the result of the extension of foreign patents.

Some other relevant facts emerge from these figures. First, there was substantial patenting activity in Brazil between 1974 and 1979 in the pharmaceuticals field. Questions arise: what types of technological activities does this indicate? Which are the main economic actors? Second, throughout the 1990s, very few patents in pharmaceuticals were granted, with only 30 patents in 1994.

3. **Nonresident patents increased much faster than resident patents.** Figure 13.4 shows that the increase in the number of patents between 1996 and 2000 was mainly the result of patent applications filed by nonresidents, with a more than threefold

10. The different IPC classes have been reaggregated into economic sectors and technological fields following OECD (1994). The sectoral classification is available from the authors upon request.

11. We define pharmaceutical patents as all the patents corresponding to the class named "pharmaceuticals and cosmetics" of the classification OST30. The IPC four-digit codes corresponding to such class are A61K and A61P.

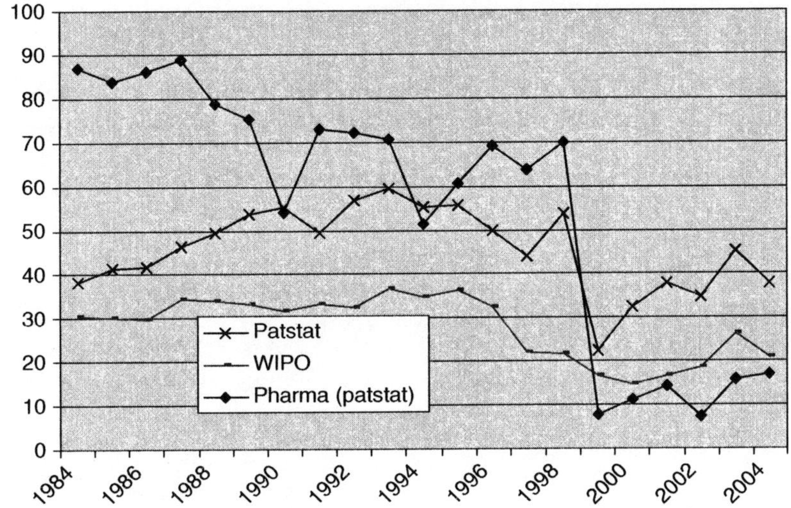

FIGURE 13.4 RESIDENT SHARE OF TOTAL PATENTS.
Source: Our elaboration on PATSTAT data.

increase (from 5,446 in 1996 to 17,741 in 2000, according to WIPO). In the same period, patents by residents increased by 50 percent. After 1999, according to the PATSTAT database (and after 2000, according to WIPO), the ratio of resident patents to total patents started rising again. Note that in the PATSTAT databases, on average, the percentage of resident patents is lower. This is probably because we do not have the addresses for all the applicants. Overall, these data show that there was a massive inflow of patent applications after the introduction of the law 9.279. Many of these applications were probably patents already filed abroad and extended to Brazil.

Moreover, Figure 13.4 shows a sudden drop in the share of patents applied for by Brazilian residents, particularly in pharmaceuticals. As pharmaceuticals patents grew rapidly after 2000, the shares of patent applications from Brazilian residents dropped from 66 percent between 1993 and 1998 to 15 percent from 1999 to 2004.

Finally, Table 13.1 shows that all the top pharmaceuticals companies are multinational, foreign-owned corporations. After 2001, the top five companies accounted for more than one-fifth of the total number of patents in the pharmaceuticals sector, and the top 10 companies accounted for 27 percent of pharmaceuticals patents.[12] In particular L'Oreal, Astrazeneca, and the group Pfizer-Pharmacia have 19 percent of all pharmaceuticals patents in Brazil.

12. However, it is important to note that the number of firms increased substantially with the number of patents. From 1993 to 1996, the pharmaceutical sector comprised 249 patents and 114 patenting firms (2.18 patents per firm); from 2001 to 2004, the sector comprised 4,583 patents and 848 firms (5.4 patents per firm). Moreover, in the sub-periods

TABLE 13.1 TOP 10 PATENTING PHARMACEUTICAL COMPANIES IN BRAZIL IN THREE SUB-PERIODS

	1993–1996	Country	Patents	% of total patents
1	L'OREAL	FR	34	13.65
2	PFIZER	US	13	5.22
3	GLAXO	GB	12	4.82
4	ASTRAZENECA	SE	7	2.81
5	GRUNENTHAL	DE	7	2.81
6	BAYER	DE	7	2.81
7	NOVARTIS	CH	6	2.41
8	BRISTOL-MYERS SQUIBB	US	6	2.41
9	AVON PRODUCTS	US	6	2.41
10	EMISPHERE TECHNOLOGIES	US	5	2.01
	TOTAL PATENTS IN THE SUB-PERIOD		249	100
	TOTAL FIRMS IN THE SUB-PERIOD		114	
	1997–2000			
1	L'OREAL	FR	26	5.46
2	COLGATE PALMOLIVE	US	20	4.20
3	NOVARTIS	CH	18	3.78
4	HOFFMANN LA ROCHE	DE	18	3.78
5	ASTRAZENECA	SE	13	2.73
6	GRUNENTHAL	DE	11	2.31
7	HOECHST	DE	10	2.10
8	NIPPON SHINYAKU	JP	9	1.89
9	EISAI CO	JP	7	1.47
10	HENKEL	DE	7	1.47
	TOTAL PATENTS IN THE SUB-PERIOD		476	100
	TOTAL FIRMS IN THE SUB-PERIOD		224	
	2001–2004			
1	PFIZER	US	358	7.81
2	L'OREAL	FR	297	6.48
3	ASTRAZENECA	SE	178	3.88
4	BASF	DE	71	1.55
5	HOFFMANN-LA ROCHE	DE	69	1.51

	2001–2004			
6	ELI LILLY	US	60	1.31
7	AVENTIS	DE	60	1.31
8	JOHNSON & JOHNSON	US	53	1.16
9	PHARMACIA	US	50	1.09
10	NOVARTIS	CH	48	1.05
	TOTAL PATENTS IN THE SUB-PERIOD		4583	100
	TOTAL FIRMS IN THE SUB-PERIOD		848	

Source: Our elaboration on PATSTAT data.

4. **The increase in the number of pharmaceuticals patent applications lags other sectors' by at least three years. The number of pharmaceuticals patents granted is still very low.** The substantial take-off of pharmaceuticals and biotech patents took place in 2000. These numbers refer, however, to patent applications, and not to granted patents. The number of patents granted is still very low.[13] These observations are probably the outcome of some specific features of the process through which TRIPS was implemented in Brazil, in particular as it concerns pharmaceuticals.

First, according to the Brazilian Government, article 65(2) of TRIPS is applicable to Brazil as a developing country, and, therefore, the transitional period of four years (which ended in 2000) may have created uncertainty about the validity of some pharmaceuticals patents. Moreover, the highly disputed 1999 Provisional Measure 2014—transformed into law 10.196 in 2001—conditionally grants pharmaceuticals patents on ANVISA's approval (Agência Nacional de Vigilância Sanitária[14]) and rejects applications for some substances, matters, and products

1997 to 2000 and 2001 to 2004, no decline in the concentration rate occurred even though the number of companies was almost four times higher.

13. See, for example, INPI statistics on www.inpi.gov.br or EFPIA (2004). According to EFPIA (2004), Brazil has only issued 428 non-pipeline and 628 pipeline pharmaceuticals patents between 2000 and 2004. Unfortunately, we do not have data on the number of patents granted in different sectors.

14. The National Health Surveillance Agency (ANVISA), established in 1999, is an independent and financially autonomous regulatory agency that exercises sanitary control over production and marketing of products and services subject to sanitary surveillance (http://www.anvisa.gov.br).

related to pharmaceuticals inventions that lack pipeline protection.[15] In general, since the ratification of TRIPS, Brazil has imposed relatively more restrictions on pharmaceutical-related patents than have other countries. This particularly concerns the issues of compulsory licensing; high fees and obligations for pipeline applications; international exhaustion and parallel imports; and a permissive attitude toward actions intended exclusively to produce information, data, and test results by unauthorized parties (e.g., Provisional Measure 2014 claims that these actions, aimed to obtain marketing approval for a patented pharmaceuticals product, are not considered infringement of the patent). Thus, the data suggest that the inflow of foreign pharmaceuticals patents was delayed until 2000 by the actions of Brazilian authorities who sought to soften the actual strength of patent protection in this sector.

VIII. CONCLUSION

The available evidence, including Brazilian patent data, although difficult to assess, would seem to suggest that the links between patent protection and innovative performance are less direct than is usually assumed, even in the pharmaceuticals sector and especially in the short-to-medium run. Strong patent laws do, indeed, confer an advantage to innovators in the pharmaceuticals industry, but they may not be enough to promote innovation in contexts where innovative capabilities are low or missing altogether.

In particular, our preliminary analysis of Brazilian data suggests that the adoption of TRIPS had a substantial positive impact on the number of patent applications in Brazil. However, the great majority of these new patent applications have come from nonresidents, most likely as extensions of foreign patents. Thus, it is too early to assess whether this substantial increase in (foreign) patents is the result of pipeline patents under the TRIPS mailbox provision, or whether it will become a permanent characteristic of patenting activity in Brazil.

Second, the impact of TRIPS is heterogeneous across different technological fields. In general, the introduction of TRIPS does not seem to have changed the pattern of technological specialization in Brazil, with one major exception: the growth of the share of the chemical and pharmaceuticals patents, especially after the year 2000—three years *after* the upsurge of patenting in other fields. After

15. A pipeline protection is available as an "extension" of the patent granted in some other country. Any Brazilian patent granted on such a pipeline application must be identical to the foreign patent on which it is based and will expire on the same date as that foreign patent. No patents shall be issued, however, for inventions (a) that were already commercialized in any market by the holder or with his or her consent, (b) that were already worked by third parties in Brazil, or (c) that any third party in Brazil has been engaged in serious and effective undertakings with a view to start working the invention.

2000, pharmaceuticals patents continued to grow, and five big, foreign industrial groups have accounted for more than one-fifth of all the pharmaceuticals patents after 2001.

These data also show that domestic patent statistics are very sensitive to changes in the legislation and administrative procedures of the national patent office. Still, they provide a crucial source of information for evaluating the impact of TRIPS and for appreciating how relative specific national provisions may expand or reduce effective patent protection.

REFERENCES

Acemoglu, Daron, and Joshua Linn. 2004. Market Size in Innovation: Theory and Evidence from the Pharmaceutical Industry. *Quarterly Journal of Economics* 119(3): 1049–90.

Adelman, Martin J. 1987. The New World of Patents Created by the Court of Appeals for the Federal Circuit. *University of Michigan Journal of Law Reform* 20: 979–1007.

Agrawal, Ajay, and Rebecca M. Henderson. 2002. Putting Patents in Context: Exploring Knowledge Transfer from MIT. *Management Science* 48: 44–60.

Albuquerque, Eduardo. 2000. Domestic Patents and Developing Countries: Argument for Their Study and Data from Brazil (1980–1995). *Research Policy* 29: 1047–60.

Arora, Ashish, Andrea Fosfuri, and Alfonso Gambardella. 2001. *Markets for Technology: The Economics of Innovation and Corporate Strategy*. Cambridge, MA: MIT Press.

Arora, Ashish, Marco Ceccagnoli, and Wesley M. Cohen. 2005. R&D and the Patent Premium. *NBER Working Paper Series*, No. 9431.

Arrow, Kenneth J. 1962. Economic Welfare and the Allocation of Resource for Invention. In Richard R. Nelson, ed., *The Rate and Direction of Inventive Activity: Economic and Social Factors*. Princeton: Princeton University Press for the NBER.

Azoulay, Pierre, Waverly Ding, and Toby Stuart. July 23, 2004. The Effect of Academic Patenting on (Public) Research Output. *Academic Science and Entrepreneurship: Dual Engines of Growth?* NBER Summer Institute. Cambridge, MA.

Baker, Dean, and Noriko Chatani. August 7, 2007. Promoting Good Ideas on Drugs: Are Patents the Best Way? Center for Economic and Policy Research; http://www.cepr.net/documents/publications/Promoting_Good_Ideas_on_Drugs.pdf.

Baumol, William J. 1990. Entrepreneurship: Productive, Unproductive and Destructive. *The Journal of Political Economy* 98(5): 893–921.

Bessen, James, and Erik Maskin.2000. Sequential Innovation, Patents, and Imitation. Institute of Technology Massachusetts, Department of Economics. Working Paper No. 00-01.

Breschi, Stefano, Francesco Lissoni, and Fabio Montobbio. 2005. From Publishing to Patenting: Do Productive Scientists Turn Into Academic Inventors? *Revue d'Economie Industrielle* 110(2): 75–102.

Cadot, Oliver, and Steven A. Lippman.1995. Barriers to Imitation and the Incentive to Innovate. Western Management Science Institute, University of California at Los Angeles. Working Paper No. 434.

Chaudhuri, Sudip. 2005. *The WTO and India's Pharmaceutical Industry. Patent Protection, TRIPS and Developing Countries* Oxford: New Delhi: Oxford University Press.

Cohen, Wesley M., Richard R. Nelson, and John P. Walsh. 2002. Links and Impacts: The Influence of Public Research on Industrial R&D. *Management Science* 48: 1–23.

Coriat, Benjamin, Fabienne Orsi, and Cristina d'Almeida. 2006. TRIPS and the International Public Health Controversies: Issues and Challenges. *Industrial and Corporate Change* 15(6): 1033–62.

Danzon, Patricia M. 1997. *Pharmaceutical Price Regulation: National Policies versus Global Interests.* Washington, DC: American Enterprise Institute Press.

Danzon, Patricia M., and Jeong Kim. 1998. International Price Comparisons for Pharmaceuticals: Measurement and Policy Issues. *Pharmacoeconomics* 14: 115–28.

Dasgupta, Partha, and Joseph E. Stiglitz. 1980a. Uncertainty, Industrial Structure, and the Speed of R&D. *Bell Journal of Economics* 11(1): 1–28.

Dasgupta, Partha, and Joseph E. Stiglitz. 1981. Entry, Innovation, Exit: Toward a Dynamic Theory of Oligopolistic Industrial Structure. *European Economic Review* 15(2): 137–58.

Dasgupta, Partha, Richard J. Gilbert, and Joseph E. Stiglitz. 1982. Invention and Innovation under Alternative Market Structures: The Case of Natural Resources. *Review of Economic Studies* 49(4): 567–82.

Deardorff, Alan V. 1992. Welfare Benefits of Global Patent Protection. *Economica* 59(233): 35–51.

FAPESP—The State of São Paulo Research Foundation.2005. Patenting Activity in Brazil and Abroad. In *Science, Technology & Innovation Indicators in the State of São Paulo/Brazil 2004*, Chapter 6 (Coordinator, Eduardo Albuquerque).

Farrell, Joseph, Richard J. Gilbert, and Michael L. Katz. 2003. Market Structure, Organizational Structure, and R&D Diversity. In Richard Arnott et al., eds., *Economics for an Imperfect World—Essays in Honor of Joseph E. Stiglitz*. Cambridge, MA: MIT Press, 195–220.

Fink, Carsten.2000. How Stronger Patent Protection in India Might Affect the Behavior of Transnational Pharmaceutical Industries. Policy Research Paper, The World Bank, no. 2352.

Gallini, Nancy T. 1992. Patent Policy and Costly Imitation. *Rand Journal of Economics* 23: 52–63.

Gallini, Nancy T. 2002. The Economics of Patents: Lessons from Recent U.S. Patent Reform. *Journal of Economic Perspectives* 16: 131–54.

Geuna, Aldo, and Lionel Nesta. 2006. University Patenting and Its Effects on Academic Research: The Emerging European Evidence. *Research Policy* 35(6): 790–807

Gilbert, Richard J., and David M. G. Newbery. 1982. Preemptive Patenting and the Persistence of Monopoly. *American Economic Review* 72(3): 514–26.

Grabowski, Henry, and John M. Vernon. 2000. Effective Patent Life in Pharmaceuticals. *International Journal of Technology Management* 19: 98–120.

Hall, Bronwyn H., and Rosemarie Ham Ziedonis. 2001. The Patent Paradox Revisited: An Empirical Study of Patenting in the U.S. Semiconductor Industry, 1979–1995. *Rand Journal of Economics* 32: 101–28.

Heller, Michael H., and Rebecca S. Eisenberg. 1998. Can Patents Deter Innovation? The Anticommons in Biomedical Research. *Science* 280: 698–701.

Helpman, Elhanan. 1993. Innovation, Imitation, and Intellectual Property Rights. *Econometrica* 61(6): 1247–80.

Henderson, Rebecca, Luigi Orsenigo, and Gary P. Pisano. 1998. The Pharmaceutical Industry and the Revolution in Molecular Biology: Exploring the Interactions between Scientific, Institutional and Organizational Change. In D. Mowery and R. Nelson, eds., *The Sources of Industrial Advantages*. Cambridge, MA: Cambridge University Press.

Horowitz, Andrew W., and Edwin L. C. Lai. 1996. Patent Length and the Rate of Innovation. *International Economic Review* 37: 785–801.

Huang, Hsin-Ting, and Marcela Miozzo. 2004. Patterns of Technological Specialisation in Latin American and East Asian Countries: An Analysis of Patents and Trade Flows. *Economics Innovation New Technology* 13(7): 615–53.

Jaffe, Adam B. 2000. The U.S. Patent System in Transition: Policy Innovation and the Innovation Process. *Research Policy* 29(4–5): 531–57.

Jaffe, Adam B., and Josh Lerner. 2004. *Innovation and Its Discontents: How Our Broken Patent System is Endangering Innovation and Progress, and What to Do about It*. Princeton: Princeton University Press.

Khan, B. Zorina, and Kenneth L.Sokoloff. 1998. Patent Institutions, Industrial Organization and Early Technological Change: Britain and the United States 1790–1850. In Maxine Berg, and Kristine Bruland, eds., *Technological Revolutions in Europe: Historical Perspectives*. Cheltenham, U.K.: Edward Elgar.

Kortum, Samuel, and Josh Lerner. 1998. Stronger Protection or Technological Revolution: What is Behind the Recent Surge in Patenting? *Carnegie-Rochester Conference Series on Public Policy* 48: 247–304.

Kumar, Nagesh. 1998. Technology Generation and Transfers in the World Economy: Recent Trends and Prospects for Developing Countries. In N. Kumar et al., eds., *Globalization, Foreign Direct Investment and Technology Transfer: Impacts on and the Prospects for Developing Countries*. London and New York: Routledge.

Kumar, Nagesh.2002. Intellectual Property Rights, Technology and Economic Development: Experiences of Asian Countries. Paper Prepared for the Commission of Intellectual Property Rights (CIPR). London.

Lall, Sanjaya. 2003. Indicators of the Relative Importance of IPRs in Developing Countries. *Research Policy* 32: 1657–80.

Lamoreaux, Naomi R., and Kenneth L. Sokoloff.1999. Inventive Activity and the Market for Technology in the United States, 1840–1920. *NBER Working Papers Series*, No. 7107.

Lanjouw, Jean O.1998a. The Introduction of Pharmaceutical product Patents in India: Heartless Exploitation of the Poor and Suffering? *NBER Working Papers Series*, No. 6366.

Lanjouw, Jean O. 1998b. Patent Protection in the Shadow of Infringement: Simulation Estimations of Patent Value. *The Review of Economic Studies* 65: 671–710.

Lerner, Josh. 2002. 150 Years of Patent Protection. *American Economic Review* 92(2): 221–25.

Levin, Richard C., Alvin K. Klevorick, Richard R. Nelson, and Sidney G. Winter. 1987. Appropriating the Returns from Industrial Research and Development. *Brookings Papers on Economic Activity* (3): 783–820.

Lichtenberg, Frank R., and Tomas J. Philipson. 2002. The Dual Effects of Intellectual Property Regulations: Within—and Between—Patent Competition in the U.S. Pharmaceuticals Industry. *The Journal of Law and Economics* 45: 643–72.

Maskus, Keith. 2000. Lessons from Studying the International Economics of Intellectual Property Rights. *Vanderbilt Law Review* 53: 2219–39.

Maskus, Keith.2001. Parallel Imports in Pharmaceuticals: Implications for Competition and Prices in Developing Countries. *Final Report to World Intellectual Property Organization.*

Mazzoleni, Roberto, and Richard R. Nelson. 2000. Economic Theories about the Benefits and Costs of Patents. *Journal of Economic Issues* 32: 1031–52.

Merges, Robert P., and Richard R. Nelson. 1994. On Limiting or Encouraging Rivalry in Technical Progress: The Effect of Patent Scope Decisions. *Journal of Economic Behavior and Organization* 25: 1–24.

Montobbio, Fabio.2007. Patenting Activity in Latin American and Caribbean Countries. In World Intellectual Property Organization (WIPO)—Economic Commission for Latin America and the Caribbean (ECLAC)—Study on Intellectual Property Management in Open Economies: A Strategic Vision for Latin America, http://eco.uninsubria.it/webdocenti/fmontobbio/cv/Montobbio2006wipo_draft.pdf.

Montobbio, Fabio, and Fancesco Rampa. 2005. The Impact of Technology and Structural Change on Export Performance in Developing Countries. *World Development* 33(4): 527–47.

Moser, Petra.2005. How Do Patent Laws Influence Innovation? Evidence for 19th Century World Fairs. *NBER Working Papers Series*, No. 9909.

Mowery, David C., Richard R. Nelson, Bhaven N. Sampat, and Arvids Ziedonis. 2001. The Growth of Patenting and Licensing by U.S. Universities: An Assessment of the Effects of the Bayh-Dole Act of 1980. *Research Policy* 30: 99–119.

Murphy, Kevin M., Andrei Shleifer, and Robert W. Vishny. 1991. The Allocation of Talent: Implications for Growth. *The Quarterly Journal of Economics* 106(2): 503–30.

Murray, Fiona, and Scott Stern. Do Formal Intellectual Property Rights Hinder the Free Flow of Scientific Knowledge? An Empirical Test of the Anti-Commons Hypothesis. *Journal of Economic Behavior & Organization*, forthcoming.

Nightingale, Paul, and Paul Martin. 2004. The Myth of the Biotech Revolution. *Trends in Biotechnology* 22(11): 564–69.

Nogues, Julio J. 1993. Social Costs and Benefits of Introducing Patent Protection for Pharmaceutical Drugs in Developing Countries. *The Developing Economies* 31: 24–53.

Nordhaus, William D. 1969. *Invention Growth, and Welfare: A Theoretical Treatment of Technological Change.* Cambridge, MA: MIT Press.

OECD.1994. The Measurement of Scientific and Technological Activities. Using Patent Data as Science and Technology Indicators—Patent Manual. *OECD.* Paris.

Orsenigo, Luigi, Fabio Pammolli, and Massimo Riccaboni. 2001. Technological Change and the Dynamics of Networks of Collaborative Relations. The Case of the Biopharmaceutical Industry. *Research Policy* 30: 485–508.

Orsenigo, Luigi, Mariana **Mazzucato** and Giovanni Dosi. 2006. The Dynamics of Knowledge Accumulation, Regulation and Appropriability in the Pharma-Biotech Sector: Policy Issues. In Giovanni Dosi, and Mariana **Mazzucato**, eds., *Knowledge Accumulation and Industry Evolution: The Case of Pharma-Biotech.* Cambridge, MA: Cambridge University Press.

Pavitt, Keith. 1988. Uses and Abuses of Patent Statistics. In A. F. J. Van Raan, ed., *Handbook of Quantitative Studies of Science and Technology.* Amsterdam: Elsevier Science Publishers.

Ramani, Shyama V., and Augustin Maria.2005. TRIPS: Its Possible Impact on Biotech Segment of the Indian Pharmaceutical Industry. *EPW Special Articles* February 12–18: 675–83.

Sakakibara, Mariko, and Lee Branstetter. 2001. Do Stronger Patents Induce More Innovation? Evidence from the 1988 Japanese Patent Law Reforms. *Rand Journal of Economics* 32: 77–100.

Schankerman, Mark. 1998. How Valuable is Patent Protection? Estimates by Technology Field. *Rand Journal of Economics* 29(1): 77–107.

Scherer, F. M. 2001. The Link between Gross Profitability and Pharmaceutical R&D Spending. *Health Affairs* 20(5).

Scherer, F. M., and Sandy Weisburst. 1995. Economic Effects of Strengthening Pharmaceutical Patent Protection in Italy. *International Review of Industrial Property and Copyright Law* 6: 1009–24.

Scotchmer, Suzanne. 1991. Standing on the Shoulders of Giants: Cumulative Research and the Patent Law. *Journal of Economic Perspectives* 5(1): 29–41.

Stokes, Donald. 1997. *Pasteur's Quadrant: Basic Science and Technological Innovation.* Washington, DC: The Brookings Institution.

Thursby, Jerry G., and Marie C. Thursby.2003. University Licensing under Bayh-Dole: What Are the Issues and Evidence? Emory University Working Paper.

Thursby, Jerry G., Anne Fuller, and Marie C. Thursby.2007. *U.S.* Faculty Patenting: Inside and Outside the University. *NBER Working Paper Series*, No. 13256.

Walsh, John P., Wesley M. Cohen, and Ashish Arora. 2003. Patenting and Licensing of Research Tools and Biomedical Innovation. In S. Merrill and M. Meyers, eds., *Innovation in a Knowledge-Based Economy*. Washington, DC: National Academies Press.

Watal, Jayashree. 2000. Pharmaceutical Patents, Prices and Welfare Losses: A Simulation Study of Policy Options for India under the WTO TRIPS Agreement. *The World Economy* 23: 733–52.

PART SIX

CULTURAL INDUSTRIES

14. THE PRODUCTION OF KNOWLEDGE, INNOVATION, AND IP IN DEVELOPING COUNTRIES
Creative Industries and the Development Agenda

DIANA V. BARROWCLOUGH*

I. INTRODUCTION

This paper views the WIPO Development Agenda and intellectual property rights (IPR) debate through the lens of interlinked activities that make up the "creative industries" economic sector. Its practical and empirical approach is prompted by the recent boom in production and trade of creative industries by developing countries. It contributes to the debate on how to encourage and reward innovators and investors alike, in order to enable broad public access to a diverse range of ideas and knowledge. The creative industries make up one of the newest, fastest growing, and most dynamic sectors of global services trade and are a key element in the new "knowledge economy." A significant role is emerging for developing countries, and IP issues are among the important areas where policy attention is required.

This new, high-value sector of the global knowledge economy is capturing policy attention in developed countries in a way that was unimaginable just 10 years ago, and developing countries are waking up to its potential. Some developing countries already find that the sector offers more economic potential than traditional activities; moreover, they have some important sources of comparative advantage.

* Diana Barrowclough is an economist at the United Nations Conference for Trade and Development. She has a long-held interest in the economics of the creative industries. This paper is written in her personal capacity and is not to be taken as the official view of UNCTAD or its member states. This paper builds upon and expands Barrowclough and Kozul-Wright (2007). It has benefited from comments by colleagues at the UCLA conference on the Development Agenda, June 2007, and the World Music Council annual meeting in Beijing, October 2007. The author also thanks Carolyn Deere for her improving suggestions. Any errors remain the author's own.

However, succeeding in these markets does not happen automatically: a well-established framework of enabling policies is essential to counteract the sector's many sources of market failure, externalities, and public goods. IP-related issues are not the only challenges, but they are important and lie at the heart of any country's aspirations to earn export revenues and to create sustainable employment in the sector.

In terms of the IP and Development Agenda issues discussed in this volume, this chapter is concerned with copyright rather than with the industrial rights or patents that have, for obvious reasons, dominated most of the debate. Also, rather than focusing on the role of developing countries as the *consumers* of IP goods and services, the paper focuses on their role as *producers*. This gives a different perspective to the relative costs and benefits of the current IP framework. Moreover, the paper finds that institutions matter as much as standards: it is irrelevant to talk about "weak" or "strong" IP regulations if the institutional capacity to enforce them is lacking.

More generally, the profound technological changes occurring with information and communications technologies (ICTs), digitalization, and the Internet require a rethinking of the meaning of "copyright." When it is possible to download a video or a song in a matter of seconds, it seems outdated to think about copyright in terms of meaning "the right to copy." More useful nowadays, when seemingly everyone can costlessly copy, is to think about how creators can be paid for their innovation and creativity and how investors can be rewarded for their risk. How are livelihoods to be earned? How to ensure broad and far-reaching access? What balance between public and private domains will most benefit a country, and how should it be achieved? This sets up creative industries as a concrete example of the more general debate taking place thanks to the Development Agenda and the new emphasis being given to development by its proponents. The various merits and dismerits of proprietary systems vis-à-vis other mechanisms, including competitions, rewards, or even patronage (whether it be financed through the state or through wealthy *angels*) can be explored in this context.

However, other factors are important also, as IP issues do not emerge out of a vacuum. Two related and broader issues are therefore also examined. The first is the role of industrial policy related to knowledge accumulation and the production of tradable goods and services that embody knowledge and creativity. From this perspective, IP is an important means to an end, but it is not the end in itself. Policies geared toward boosting innovation and knowledge are as important as, or more important than, policies geared solely toward capturing or liberating IP. Second, there is a distinction between having creative ideas and getting them into tradable and marketable form: that is, the link between invention and innovation—or, in this case specifically, between *culture* and *commerce*. From this perspective, the output of knowledge and creativity embodies more than just "IP content": it includes social relations, communication, and other elements that can be overshadowed when IP is discussed in purist terms.

The paper is structured as follows. Section II defines industries composing the "creative industries." Section III identifies the pertinent aspects of the IP and

Development Agenda debate. Section IV describes some recent trends in the creative-industry trade, showing why the sector has become of such interest to developed and developing countries alike, and where the IP issues arise. Section V describes why the sector has grown so fast, and why these trends are likely to continue. Section VI identifies some of the key policy issues with respect to creative industries, IP, and the Development Agenda. Section VII concludes.

II. DEFINING CREATIVE INDUSTRIES

What is included in the term "creative industries" can be contentious. This paper uses a narrow definition that suits its industrial focus, restricting itself to the subset of tangible and intangible activities that can be produced and traded in large scale through the market, and which are embodied as *intellectual property*.[1]

The concept therefore includes both "core" and "periphery"[2] activities such as film, music, television, advertising, design, publishing, software, and computer services, for example, but it excludes textiles, handicrafts, and other creative activities that are traditionally thought of in a developing-country context. Barrowclough and Kozul-Wright (2007) concentrate on core activities in the audio-visuals sector of film, television, and music. The reason for this is to highlight industrial domains, not cottage or artisanal activities. So, it is not about culture, per se, but about industrial production and consumption that has a cultural, creative, and essentially IP-producing manifestation. This concept of "creative industries" links ancient and traditional skills of creativity and communication with the latest IT technologies and, moreover, with a liberalized global economy that is increasingly open to international investment and trade.

III. CREATIVE INDUSTRIES AND IP: CATEGORIES, CONVENTIONS, AND HOT TOPICS

From an economic perspective, IPRs can be usefully classified into two broad categories (Ozgen 2007). Industrial IPRs include patents, trademarks, and utility

1. Other definitions have been used since the concept was formulated by the U.K. Creative Industries Taskforce in the 1980s, and there is still no standard classification system used today. Britain's DCMS definition included art and antique markets; UNESCO publications have included the manufacturing of television sets as well as the production of television programs. UNCTAD is currently working on classification and measurement and will report this in 2008.

2. Florida first introduced the terms "core" and "periphery," and more recent definitions reflect the purpose of the user (e.g., WIPO definitions in terms of their implications for copyright: "core," "independent," "partial," and "non-dedicated").

models (see Table 14.1). Copyright IPRs include "real copyright" (relating to literary, musical, dramatic, visual, and applied arts, etc.), and also neighboring rights, software rights, and databases.

Most of the debate in the Development Agenda has focused—for obvious reasons—on the first category, and on developing countries as *consumers* of IP-products. In the industrial IPR category, some research and development (R&D) and other IP-producing activities are taking place in developing countries, in pharmaceuticals and computer software, and, of course, activities related to "traditional knowledge" continue, but the number of developing countries actively engaged in industrial IP revenue-earning activities is still rather small. The most attention has been directed toward consumption—that is, to the high cost burdens imposed on developing-country consumers by the IP-royalties and licenses associated with the purchases of lifesaving pharmaceuticals or on imports of the computer software and technologies need to help developing countries shift to modern, industrial production. This has contributed to an ongoing debate about special and preferential treatment, exclusions and dispensations, compulsory licensing, and so forth. In the broader perspective, it has led to a profound questioning of the impact of proprietary rights systems upon creativity, knowledge transfer, and innovation. This has been most evident in the movement for a reformed WIPO Development Agenda, discussed in this book.

However, when focusing on the second category, copyright, many more opportunities arise for developing countries to act as the *producers*, as well as consumers, of IP. This role has attracted much less international policy attention, even though it may be just as important for long-term economic development and a sustainable path out of poverty and dependency. Authoritative studies on the history, scale, and role of copyright include Okediji (2003, 2006), Towse (2001), Landes (1989), Reese (2001), and Romer (2002), but the perspective is usually that of developing countries as IP consumers. It is not clear what the implications of this reverse perspective will be, and new research questions need to be addressed.

For example, it has been argued that, at certain stages of development, weak levels of IPR protection are more likely to stimulate economic development and poverty alleviation than are strong ones (see UNCTAD-ICTSD 2003, Chang 2002). This is always assumed to refer to patents, and the relationship may be less likely to hold when the IP in question is copyright.

In terms of the legal conventions, the main framework agreements include the Berne Convention for the Protection of Literary and Artistic Works; the International Convention for the Protection of Performers, Producers of Phonograms and Broadcasting Organizations (Rome convention); the Agreement on Trade Related Aspects of Intellectual Property Rights (TRIPS); the WIPO Copyright Treaty (WCT) of 1996; and the WIPO Performances and Phonograms Treaty (WPPT) of 1996. Developing countries are most highly represented in the TRIPS convention (with

TABLE 14.1 MAIN CATEGORIES OF IP

IP Form	What It Is; Application in the Case of Creative Industries
1. INDUSTRIAL IPRS	
Trademarks for goods and services	A sign or combination of signs that distinguishes one's goods or services from those of others. This can include a musical signature, as well as brand name, etc.
Collective marks and certification marks	A mark indicating that products/services are certified or can be distinguished from those of competitors. Have been used in some countries to promote traditional indigenous arts: Harris Tweed; Toi Iho Maori art.
Geographical indications and appellations of origin	Sign that indicates goods have a specific geographical origin (e.g., champagne, Roquefort cheese, Aboriginal art, Inuit sculpture).
Industrial designs	Sets out and protects the visual design—shape, colors, form, or layout—of a product (e.g., car design, furniture, architecture).
Utility models and patents	Legal certificate giving an inventor exclusive rights to prevent others from producing, using, selling, or importing an invention for a fixed period. To qualify for patenting, invention should be useful, novel, and non-obvious (or involve an inventive step). Creative industry examples could include the invention of the ipod, cell-phone billing technologies.
Trade secrets, confidential business information	In many countries, trade secrets and confidential information are protected by common law and not by patent, as this would require disclosing the secret information. The recipe for Coca-Cola is a frequently used example. This category does not typically arise in the creative industries.

IP Form	What It Is; Application in the Case of Creative Industries
Plant breeders rights	A form of patent for new plant varieties that prevents others from producing or reproducing the plants, or buying or selling them. This right has caused many controversies in developing countries, but the category is not applicable in the case of creative industries.
2. COPYRIGHT IPRS	
Copyright and related rights * Real copyright * Neighboring rights * Software * Sui generis database rights	Copyright gives the copyright holder legal protection for literary works, dramatic and musical works, artistic works, maps and technical drawings, photographic works, motion pictures and sound recordings, and computer programs and databases. Legal protection governs the expression of the ideas, not the ideas themselves. Moral rights can give the author the legal right to be identified on his or her work, even if the copyright has been transferred to another owner. Neighboring rights relate live performances, and sound and broadcasting (television and radio) recordings.

151 countries in total having signed up), and the debate associated with TRIPS and the Development Agenda has highlighted attention to the general tightening of copyright restrictions that has been occurring under other conventions, but with less visibility. Issues such as the gradually lengthening timespan of copyright protection (from 50 to 70 years in a number of countries) gathered more attention as the TRIPS debate widened its focus and its participation.

Much attention in the debate has gone to the discussion of "piracy," or "unauthorised use": in music, for example, in the context of virtually free digital downloading. In the context of developing countries as producers of creative goods and services, the concern relates to how creators and investors can be reimbursed. Numerous propositions have been floated, including bulk payment of limitless downloads, for example, but more recently researchers are seeking more nuanced approaches. Some hope that the same technology that has made copyright a more or less historical construct will also hold some of the answers—for example, a pilot scheme currently starting in Ghana aims to use cell phone technology as a means of simultaneously downloading music and extracting payment. This takes the issue away from how to establish IP ownership and collect its rents, and more toward business-model issues of marketing, distribution, and communication between consumer and producer. For example, when the variety of products available is so vast, and the branding and marketing role of gatekeeper labels has gone, how are consumers to find what they want? Technology may step into these shoes, for example by finding a way to organize "metadata" (type of music, name of singer, name of composer, derivative of X, etc.) so that consumers can search through the products and services that are available in order to find what they want.

Serious policy challenges therefore exist both in the IP element of creative industries and in the economic characteristics of the activities themselves—with or without the IP dimension. Succeeding in global creative-industries markets requires a great deal of supporting public policies and private investment and productive capacity, and most developing countries have yet to put in place the kind of enabling environment that exists in the developed countries. This includes responding to the market failures and public-good elements of the sector that have long been seen as justifying government intervention in developed countries. Moreover, it includes supporting the move to new digital technology that is needed; otherwise, developing countries will be even further removed from the new opportunities that are opening up for them.

There are also important tensions that exist in the marriage of culture and the market that will need to be resolved. These are manifested in core IP challenges to which a better policy response is needed. For example, a domestic IP regime is needed that will stimulate local creativity and investment and reward artists with real returns, while at the same time ensuring access and affordability to consumers. What would this look like? It is not only a question of the rules and regulations of the game, but also of how they are implemented. It is not sufficient for developing countries to designate a collector of revenues if those revenues are not properly collected and subsequently disbursed to its national performers and creative producers. This can also impact the way in which the public sector plays its supporting role. Most public agencies cannot rely on tax revenues alone for this job and many will ask for a share of the royalties that are created—but what should be the agency's share of IP-related returns, vis-à-vis that of the original creator?

IV. KEY TRENDS IN THE GLOBAL CREATIVE-INDUSTRIES TRADE

IP issues are gathering attention in this sector because of the extraordinary scale and scope of global trade in recent years. That scale and scope present new challenges for developing countries, in terms of receiving payment for the creative products they export and in terms of payments they must make for what they import.

Data are limited, but in the United Kingdom it has been estimated that the creative industries accounted for 8 percent of gross value added in 2006 (compared to 4% in 1997). The sector grew by an average of 5 percent per annum over the period—compared to only 3 percent for the economy as a whole—and accounted for 4 percent of total exports (Holden 2007). Similarly, World Bank estimates have placed the global value of the creative industries at between 7 and 10 percent of GDP, and industry forecasts typically predict growth rates of up to 10 to 20 percent per annum. Other estimates vary depending on how the sector is defined, but, even taking a fairly narrow definition of "entertainment and media" (including only film, music, television, and publishing), it appears significant: some $1.2 trillion in 2005, according to Price Waterhouse Cooper (Table 14.2). It is obvious why this is of growing interest to developed and developing countries alike.

The employment potential may also be attractive because the sector is much more interlinked and cross-cutting than some (e.g., extractive industries). In the United Kingdom, for example, the sector has been estimated to employ 1.3 million people; in India, the film industry alone has been estimated to employ, directly and indirectly, as many as 5 million people.

At present, the shares of these global markets are still very uneven, and even those developing countries that are participating reasonably actively (India,

TABLE 14.2 GLOBAL MARKET VALUE FOR SELECTED CREATIVE INDUSTRIES (IN $ MILLIONS)

	2001	2005	2010 (Estimated)
Films	64,169	80,473	104,060
Television distribution	109,953	154,351	230,282
Television networks	127,048	164,222	226,577
Recorded music	39,008	37,123	47,927
Videogames	20,631	27,054	46,462
Magazine publishing	92,758	98,453	117,585
Newspaper publishing	167,775	178,760	208,129
Book publishing	103,419	112,953	130,533
Sports	68,427	86,298	120,900
Internet advertising	65,617	144,513	265,561
Business information	71,112	78,022	101,226
Total	929,917	1,162,222	1,599,242

Source: Derived from Pricewaterhouse Coopers LLP (2006).

South Africa, Brazil, and some other Latin American countries) have a long way to go before they capture a significant share. However, the widespread diffusion of new technologies is helping to make the distribution of global market shares much more fluid. The data on developing country trade in these activities is at best patchy, but on the basis of the limited data available on the COMTRADE database, the indications hint to a potential new balancing of global trade (Table 14.3). Global audiovisual imports from developing countries accounted for only 5 percent of total world imports in 1989, but by 2004, the latest year for which data are currently available, this had increased to 12 percent. By comparison, the share accounted for by the United States fell from 35 percent of the total to only 20 percent. Some developing countries (notably Africa and Latin America), have, in recent years, seen their share of the world audiovisuals market decrease, but for a number of others, exports have grown at a pace far exceeding that of exports of goods and services in general. (This includes, but is not restricted to, China, India, and Brazil.) In part, this reflects the fact that the baseline is low, but the

TABLE 14.3 WORLD IMPORTS OF AUDIOVISUALS, FROM SOURCE COUNTRIES AND REGIONS (1989–2004) (DESCENDING SIZE)

World Imports From	1989 ($ m)	2004 ($ m)	Rate of Change 1989–2004		
			Change by a Factor of	% Change	% Change in all Imports*
World	6,105	24,973	4.1	309	200
Developed world	5,793	21,825	3.8	277	153
Europe	3,429	15,897	4.6	363	184
North America	2,158	4,974	2.3	130	139
United Kingdom	625	2,002	3.2	220	128
Developing world	293	2,953	10.1	905.6	320
Developing Asia, including	412	3,304	8	701.5	269
India	30	265	8.7	774.6	368
Malaysia	6.3	58	9.3	826	405
Latin America, including	39	410	10.4	942.3	264
Brazil	3.7	20	5.4	437.4	180
Africa	3.9	12	3.1	207	192

Source: Barrowclough and Kozul-Wright (2007), derived from COMTRADE database.
* "All imports" includes all agriculture, all manufacturing, and so forth, in addition to a/v imports.

remarkable point is that, for some areas of the world, the share of global audiovisuals trade that is attributed to developing countries is rising fast.[3]

The evidence also suggests, unexpectedly, that trade in these new and dynamic sectors has been no more volatile than trade of all goods and services, in general.

V. WHY THE SECTOR HAS GROWN SO RAPIDLY

The rapid growth of the sector stems from a multiplicity of ongoing and self-reinforcing supply and demand factors, which, in turn, are related to trends of structural change in the global economy.

First, the creative industries have risen along with the general rise of the service economy that has characterized globalization in the last few decades. International trade in services more than quadrupled since the 1980s, and creative industries have been affected by this, in the way that a rising tide can lift all boats. Related to this, much of the growth in services trade has come on the back of a massive increase in investment in information and communication technologies; the link to many creative industries reflects the fact that they are, to a large extent, ICT-based and have contributed to, and benefited from, the convergence of complementary technologies and the emergence of digital and multimedia technology. Digitalization, with its dramatic reduction of production costs, lead times, and other forms of barriers to entry, has created a real opportunity for smaller producers and for latecomers. These forms of technological "creative destruction," to use the Shumpeterian phrase that described a period of similar technological burst at the turn of the nineteenth century, may be a concern for the established majors, but for newcomers to the sector they can be seen as an opportunity rather than a threat. The new peer-to-peer distribution mechanisms, for example, may offer new entrants new ways of gaining access to global markets—if they have the right copyright and collection mechanisms in place.

A second feature contributing to the boom has been the opening up of markets, stemming from the deregulation of national cultural and media policy frameworks experienced by most countries from the 1990s onward. Markets that were previously closed have been opened, creating new incentives to boost production and trade, coupled with an increase in private-sector investment as many governments have sought to maximize their national broadcasters' abilities to earn market revenues, rather than rely on private finance. In some developed countries, including New Zealand, for example, this contributed to the creation of new, independent

3. The rise in so-called "World Music," for example, is a special part of this. World Music was estimated to account for 1% of the total global music market of around $40 billion annually (Collins 2000) and is probably rising, and African music is estimated to make up about 50% of the World Music genre (Penna et al. 2003). The definition of World Music is music that is roughly ethnic, traditional, or indigenous, and so it is a subset of the entire global music market in which performers from developing countries can and do participate.

production sectors that had not existed before. In India, as a special case, it led to a formalization of the film industry that has helped to access increased finance, to improve production standards, and to widen the market. On the other hand, liberalization also brought with it threats to nascent domestic industries through the effect of low-cost, low-risk imported film, music, and television products.

Demand-side effects have also been significant and will most likely become more so in the next decade. The growing affluence of many developing, as well as developed, countries is leading to an increase in purchases of income-elastic goods such as film and music, which were once luxuries but which are now increasingly part of the household shopping basket. The rise of new, young, middle-class consumers in China, India, and South Africa is one of the most visible examples, coupled with growing diaspora and "world music" markets in developed countries. Reinforcing this shift are the falling prices of many CI products, such as CDs and DVDs; the rise of the Internet and other usage has further contributed to the demand for audiovisual content. This surge in demand offers opportunities to new producers with fresh and original ideas.

These various supply-and-demand influences feed into the natural imperative to trade that exists in any economic activity that is marked by features such as economies of scale. When unit costs are either the same or falling as the scale of production, distribution, or marketing rises, producers aim to spread their costs over larger markets—moving from being domestic producers to global ones. These markets rely on novelty and increasingly fast production cycles, adding to the power of scale. In the past, this was a barrier to new entrants, such as developing and small countries, not least because the supply response led to highly concentrated, oligopolistic market structures. However, new technologies are creating possibilities for small and nimble firms to enter global markets as never before by offering highly niched services. The new income streams related to digital music are just one example. Whereas physical sales of recorded music have been on a declining trend since 2002, sales of digital content have been rising, and it is estimated that revenue streams from digital platforms will account for one-quarter of all music revenues within a few years. Mobile telephony is increasingly seen as holding the key—evidenced by the fact that, in the EU, 12 percent of households accessing the Internet do so through mobile phones.[4] In countries that are newer to the technology, the uptake is even faster: in Latvia, the figure is as high as 67 percent. New research is taking place on the way that these cycles of technological change can be seen as offering opportunities, as well as costs.[5]

The less regulated markets, the more open trading system, and the ceaseless oxygen of technological change have implied not only more competition but a different kind of competition. It is based more on knowledge and information, product quality and originality, speed of delivery and customization. Some have argued

4. UNCTAD 2007, Information Economy Report.

5. Z. Kozul-Wright and P. Jenner 2007.

that the human "software" of originality and experience is worth at least as much as, and perhaps more than, the "hardware" that is embodied in physical plants or facilities. This can be an important incentive for developing countries, but it is also a problem because it is not easy to ensure that a labor force has the necessary skills without having the opportunity to nurture and exercise them in the first place.

VI. POLICY IMPLICATIONS

As with the ICT sector in general, being left out of this market matters—not least because of the role that the creative industries play in the global knowledge economy. Skills developed in creative industries tend to be generic (i.e., readily directed or transferable to other high value-added activities). Over the last two decades, most developing countries have lost their share in terms of high value-added and service exports and have become increasingly dependent upon exports of commodities. It is not only about technology and enterprise development; it is also that they lack the complementary services needed to develop with regard to these new and dynamic activities. Failing to participate in the creative industries–boom is part of the "falling behind" phenomenon described by earlier UNCTAD reports (see UNCTAD's Least Developed Countries Report 2004, 2006; Trade and Development Reports from various years).

Second, the growing global trade in creative industries means that if developing countries do not produce their own films, music, and other creative products, they will increasingly find themselves importing them. This is, of course, not without some benefit, in the sense that consumers are offered international products previously unavailable, and at low prices. However, increased dependence on cultural imports is likely to have an adverse impact on domestic production and domestic "voice." A steady decrease in domestic film production, for example, has been noted in many African and Latin American countries (UNESCO 2006).

This new, industrial and global trade perspective puts a different twist onto traditional public-goods arguments that have historically been used to support domestic production and consumption of creative products such as music, film, and the arts. Such traditional arguments about market failure, merit goods, and externalities are intrinsic to our approach, but there are now additional arguments based more on industrial policy, trade policy, and global diversity.

For example, the industry structure is typically very heterogeneous, characterized by a small number of "major" firms alongside a mass of tiny, often precarious, enterprises. There is a great deal of part-time or self-employment, usually on a project-by-project basis. Most learning is conducted on the job, and workers flip in and out of employment, often supplementing their creative-industry work with work in other, more conventional, activities. This leads to arguments for industrial policies to boost small firms, or human resources policies to strengthen employment and skills transfer.

Another marked characteristic is that creative-industry clusters frequently emerge. This leads to a policy focus on "creative cities" or other spatial organizations as policymakers attempt to understand the complex and shifting networks of collaboration and competition that occur between highly mobile firms, investors, and creative individuals who travel from one location to another in search of opportunities. More formal collaborations increasingly take place, both at the inter-firm level and between countries through the signing of bilateral co-production agreements, adding to the challenges of policymakers eager to find the particular entry point at which they should focus their interventions. Finally, at the corporate level, strategies focus on protecting economic rent, especially copyright, but also through other ways of organizing the value chain, such as control of the distribution network. The sector is, therefore, very different from traditional forms of economic activity.

Another characteristic is the intrinsic Schumpeterian pattern of "creative destruction." As I have described before, what appears to be a threat can also be an opportunity—especially for the newcomers to the scene who are not yet entrenched and tied into existing technologies, structures, and business models. This heterogeneity and diversity preempt a uniform industrial structure—and a uniform policy prescription. No "one-size-fits-all" policy tool exists because what is needed in each country is very different. Some common obstacles and challenges typically arise, mostly in developing countries but also in many developed ones.

A. What Can Governments Do?

The main challenge today is to create the kind of "enabling environment," at a low cost, that will help the creative industries sector to flourish. Throughout the 1960s and 1970s, most of the activities that came under the creative-industries rubric in developing countries were marked by strong state involvement—as in many developed countries. Today that is very rarely the case (with the exception of a few ASEAN countries), and now most developing countries lack either specialized or general polices to develop the sector. This reflects a more general lack of an enabling environment in the economy that has limited the growth of the majority of non-Asian countries over the last two decades, with the LDCs in particular falling further behind. Reflecting this, there is now a growing interest in industrial policy in the developing world, which goes far wider than the creative industries but which shares many features in common.

Policy attention in five main areas will facilitate the more equal participation of developing countries in the rapidly growing global creative-industries economy. These include

i) raising the level and nature of domestic capabilities and capacities;
ii) mobilizing investment (foreign as well as domestic);
iii) determining how best to promote innovation;

iv) providing infrastructure to support the linkages between the various cross-cutting creative activities; and
v) supporting social, educational, and economic institutions to foster creativity.

Rather than present the exhaustive list of actual mechanisms that are used in developed and developing countries (see Barrowclough and Kozul-Wright 2007), these many policy strands can be drawn together under loose titles such as "the development-oriented state" or "'public entrepreneurship." These terms mean that a positive, enabling role can be envisioned for government to help promote markets and to harness the benefits of markets where possible, but it is also recognized that there are some critical activities for which markets will fail or are not appropriate. This does not mean, for example, the wholesale subsidization of large-scale public cultural schemes, and it goes beyond fine-tuning and adjusting copyright or getting the IPR system right—to take just a few topical examples. It includes a host of policy measures that will help create an environment that will promote the cycle of resource mobilization and capital accumulation (including human capital, as well as physical capital), boost domestic demand and overcome supply constraints, help with enterprise development and provide support for innovation, and stimulate the kinds of structural and technological changes that will promote creative industries, in general, and music in particular.

Traditional and important interpretations of this role would include, for example, measures in support of a basic musical education in schools or of the domestic music publications industry, which would nurture appreciation, capabilities, and capacities in the broad field relating to music: a more entrepreneurial role would also extend to investment in the teaching of high-tech applications related to digitalization and multimedia convergence, because entry costs are high, and the market may underestimate, or not understand, the longer term value. The state is not seen as a patron in this view but as a facilitator. Other entrepreneurial and market-oriented policies would include promoting creative-industries clusters by financing, or providing the financing for, those public-good elements of infrastructure that the private sector will not itself provide—not the least of which include financing the move to digitalization and other new technologies. This may include establishing special agencies to help SMEs or even promoting the establishment of technology banks for bigger music or film projects, helping to lower capital costs by mechanisms designed to reduce risk and transactions costs, or pooling finances, for example.

Attention may need to be given to the value chain to determine exactly where public intervention can be used to greatest effect: to help new and unknown talent to get a first hearing, for example, or to help talent that has already made a name for itself at home find opportunities to reach a global audience. Even though the new technologies relating to digitalization and the Internet offer potential benefits to developing-country musicians in terms of lowering production costs and bypassing entrenched distribution networks, they will still need help, for example, with branding and gaining access to markets; otherwise, their voices will stand little chance of reaching potential listeners in global markets. The new metadata standards will help, for example, if they lead to the development of filtering mechanisms that guide consumers to new tracks out of the 30 million titles currently estimated to be available online, but there will also be an important role for an intermediary to help unknown artists create a "profile" that will enable them to be found by search engines.

Similarly, national and regional trade and competition policies need to be aligned to achieve a balance between the beneficial effects of both competition and coordination. The role can also include designing appropriate incentives for innovation and systems of remuneration that can stimulate local creativity and investment and reward artists with real returns, while at the same time ensuring access and affordability to consumers. The Internet and the ability to download millions of songs in a fraction of a second has changed the business model completely, and national and international policy attention needs to be focused onto how to develop entirely new mechanisms of payment for artists, while still ensuring that cultural funds are available for new and local musicians. The challenge is not only about which systems are in place but also *how they are managed*.

Another message is that the particular, required enabling policies and the role this implies for the state, will vary from country to country. It may depend on which resources and skills are already available in the markets, including the activities of philanthropists and *angels*, and the nature of the opportunities and obstacles presented by local and international conditions. No "one-size-fits-all" model exists, and a great deal can be learned from the various experiments many developed countries have used or are currently using.

VII. CONCLUSION

The creative industries sector is one of the most rapidly growing and dynamic sectors of the global economy. In addition to its long-recognized intrinsic traditional and cultural value, a new appreciation of the possible contributions of this sector to a more general development path of economic diversification, trade, and, ultimately, growth is blooming.

This will not, however, happen automatically. Most developed countries have a variety of measures and institutions in place that promote and enhance domestic production, and developing countries will need to give this attention, too. Positive policy responses are needed to face internal obstacles relating to poorly developed capacity as well as to face the international ones.

The new developments in digital technologies that are creating a headache for the established *majors* in the industry can have the opposite effect in developing countries because they lower the costs of entry and shake up the system, making it easier for newcomers to grab a foothold. The challenge is how to use these opportunities in a way that can create revenue. Experimental advances in the use of mobile telephony for downloading and paying for music is one example of the way new and innovative business models can create opportunities for newcomers, including those in developing countries. Imaginative policies will still be needed to enable new voices to cut through the cacophony of choices available. However, even if the appropriate marketing and business models are in place, countries also must attend to the collecting side of the equation. Implementing a system of payment properly is as important as designing a new one.

The task has other potential pitfalls that do not exist in more conventional industrial sectors. Caution is needed to walk the difficult line between culture and commerce, to avoid an outcome in which efforts to enhance and boost creative-industry production somehow devalue and undermine the authenticity and integrity of a country's output. Music or films designed to appeal to all markets, rather than to express an authentic voice, may fail to find acclaim in any market.

This facet poses particular challenges for policymakers in terms of, for example, deciding which aspects of an industry or which projects to support, and which to leave to their own devices. Most developed countries that support their domestic film and music industries, for example, continue to flounder with the definition of "success" in terms of policy interventions. Should they finance films or musical productions that provide moderate pleasure for large audiences, or should they focus their support on productions that are highly appreciated by a few? It is unclear whether new business models that could potentially allow price discrimination rather than single or bulk pricing will make a difference here. Another question concerns whether governments should support the provision of critical high-tech infrastructure that can be applied to a number of different industries, or whether they should continue the tradition of focusing on sectors defined instead by their outputs, such as the film industry or the music sector. The effective use of public support will be particularly important in developing countries, where the sums to invest will be small, and many needs will be competing for the public purse. In addition, the notion of support for an industry in its infancy implies that, one day, support will be removed, making a clearly defined exit strategy important.

These questions are important, because being left out of the global creative industries sector matters in important ways. First, the skills involved in creative industries are generic and can readily be applied to other important sectors of the knowledge economy, including but not restricted to ICTs. Failing to invest in these activities means that countries will be less able to compete in other, related ones. Over the last two decades, many developing and least-developed countries have lost out in terms of high value-added and service exports, as they lack infrastructure, skills, and complementary services to produce, market, and distribute them. Failing to participate in the global creative industries sector is part of this "falling behind" phenomenon.

Second, being left out matters to the extent that countries that do not produce any of their own films, music, or other creative products will find themselves of necessity relying on imported ones. This is not without benefit, in the sense that consumers are offered previously unavailable international products at low prices. But if this occurs in the absence of a thriving, domestic creative industries sector, countries may not only miss out on valuable export opportunities, but they may also lose the distinctive voice that comes from hearing their own songs and seeing their own stories. Consumers in the global marketplace also face a narrower range of music or films from which to choose, meaning that we are losing the global public good of cultural diversity and choice.

REFERENCES

Andersen, B., Z. Kozul-Wright, & R. Kozul-Wright. 2000. Copyrights, Competition and Development: The Case of the Music Industry, *UNCTAD Discussion Papers* 145, United Nations Conference on Trade and Development, Geneva.

Barrowclough, D., and Z. Kozul-Wright, eds. 2007. *Voice, Choice and Economic Growth: Creative Industries and Developing Countries.* UK: Routledge, pp. 3–37.

Barrowclough, D. 2007. Knowledge, Human Capital and FDI in Developing Countries: Recent Trends from an Endogenous Growth Theory Perspective. In Arestis et al., eds. *Economic Growth: New Directions in Theory and Policy.* UK: Edward Elgar, pp. 238–259.

Barrowclough, D. 1998. Public Television Quasi-markets in New Zealand and the United Kingdom. In W. Bartlett et al., eds. *A Revolution in Social Policy: Lessons from the Development of Quasi-markets in the 1990s.* UK: The Policy Press.

Barrowclough, D. 2001. *Spilling Over and Crowding Out: Public/Private Sector Convergence and Competition in the Provision of Public Goods.* CESifo Working Paper No 569, Centre for Economic studies and IFO Institute for Economic Research, Germany.

Baumol, W. J., and W. G. Bowen. 1969. Performing Arts, the Economic Dilemma. *Journal of Research in Music Education* 17(1), Reading, Spring, pp. 170–172.

Baumol, W., and H. Baumol. 1984. The Mass Media and the Cost Disease. In W. S. Hendon, D. V. Shaw, and N. K. Grant, eds. *The Economics of Cultural Industries.* Akron, OH: Association for Cultural Economics, pp. 109–123.

Boyle, J. 2004. A Manifesto on WIPO and the Future of Intellectual Property. *iBRIEF/International, Duke Law and Technology Review, 0009.*

Caves, R. 2000. *Contracts between Art and Commerce.* Cambridge, MA: Harvard University Press.

CIPR, Commission on Intellectual Property Rights. 2002. Integrating IPRs and Development Policy. London, September 2002, C/O DFID.

Chang, H. J. 2002. *Kicking Away the Ladder: Development Strategy in Historical Perspective.* London: Anthem Press.

Coase, R. H. 1966. The Economics of Broadcasting and Government Policy. *American Economic Review* 65 (2), May, pp 440–447.

Collins, J. 2000. *World Music World-Wide Sale, unpublished paper, presented at workshop* "Developing the Music Industry in Africa," World Bank and the Policy Sciences Centre Inc., Washington, D.C. June 2000.

DCMS (Department of Culture, Media and Sport). 1988. Creative Industries Mapping Document. London: DCMS.
DCMS (Department of Culture, Media and Sport). 2003. Creative Industries Mapping Document. London: DCMS.
European Commission. 2007. Interactive Content and Convergence: Implications for the Information Society. Brussels: European Commission.
Falvey, R., N. Foster, and D. Greenaway. 2004. Intellectual Property Rights and Economic Growth. Internationalisation of Economic Policy Research Paper No. 2004/12.
Florida, R. 2002. *The Rise of the Creative Class and How It's Transforming Work, Leisure, Community and Everyday Life*. New York: Basic Books.
Gana, R. 1995. Has Creativity Died in the Third World? Some Implications of the Internationalization of Intellectual Property. *Denver Journal International Law and Policy* 24, p. 109.
Garrison, C. 2006. Exceptions to Patent Rights in Developing Countries. UNCTAD-ICTSD Project on IPRs and Sustainable Development, Issue Paper No. 17.
Hirschman, A. 1970. *Exit, Voice and Loyalty*. Cambridge, MA: Harvard University Press.
Holden, J. 2007. *Publicly-funded Culture and the Creative Industries*. London: Arts Council England.
Holzl, W. 2005. *Entrepreneurship, Entry and Exit in Creative Industries: An Exploratory Survey*, Vienna: WIFO, Mimeo.
Howkins, J. 2001. *The Creative Economy*. London: Penguin Books.
Jassawalla, A. R., and H. C. Sashittal. 2002. Cultures That Support Product-Innovation Processes. *Academy of Management Executive* 16(3), pp. 42–54.
Jeffcutt, P., and A. C. Pratt. 2002. Managing Creativity in the Cultural Industries. *Creativity and Innovation Management* 11(4), pp. 225–233.
Johansson, F. 2004. *The Medici Effect*. Cambridge, MA: The Harvard Business School Press.
John-Steiner, V. 2000. *Creative Collaboration*. New York: Oxford University Press.
Johnson, W. 2005. Creative Pricing in Markets for Intellectual Property. *Review of Economic Research on Copyright Issues* 2(1), pp. 5–10.
Katz, J. 2006. Tecnologia de la Informacion y la Comunicación e Industrias Culturales. Una Perspectiva Latinoamericana. CEPAL, UN, LC/W.92, Santiago de Chile.
Kamoche, K. N., M. P. Cunha, and J. V. Cunha, eds. 2002. *Organizational Improvisation*. London: Routledge.
Kern, P. 2006. The Future Digital Economy. Presentation to the OECD, January 31, 2006.
Kozul-Wright, R. and P. Rayment. 2004. Globalization Reloaded: An UNCTAD Perspective. UNCTAD Discussion Paper, No. 167, Geneva, UNCTAD/OSG/DP/2004/1.
Kozul-Wright, Z., and P. Jenner. 2007. Creative Destruction in the Music Industry and the Copyright. Dynamics of Institutions and Markets in Europe (DIME) Working Papers on Intellectual Property Rights (IPR). Birkbeck College, University of London.
Kozul-Wright, Z., and L. Stanbury. 1998. Becoming a Globally Competitive Player: The Case of the Music Industry in Jamaica. *UNCTAD Discussion Papers* 138, United Nations Conference on Trade and Development.
Landes, W., and R. Posner. 1989. An Economic Analysis of Copyright Law. *The Journal of Legal Studies* 18(2), June, pp. 325–363.
Landry, C. 2000. *The Creative City*, London: Earthscan.

Livingstone, L. P., L. E. Palich, and G. R. Carini. 2002. Promoting Creativity through the Logic of Contradiction. *Journal of Organizational Behaviour* 23, pp. 321–326.

Lubart, T. I. 1999. Creativity Across Cultures. In R. J. Sternberg, ed., *Handbook of Creativity*. Cambridge, UK: Cambridge University Press, pp. 339–350.

Maskus, K., and J. Reichman. 2005. *International Public Goods and Transfer of Technology under a Globalised Property Regime*, Cambridge, UK: Cambridge University Press.

Moglen, E. Freeing the Mind: Free Software and the Death of Proprietary Culture. Keynote address, Technology and Law Conference, University of Maine, Portland, Maine: June 29, 2003.

Nemeth, C. J., M. Personnaz, B. Personnaz, and J. A. Goncalo. 2003. The Liberating Role of Conflict in Group Creativity: A Cross Cultural Study. *Institute of Industrial Relations*, University of California Berkeley, Paper 090-03.

Netzer, D. 2004. The Subsidized Muse: The Government and the Arts in Western Europe and the United States. *Journal of Cultural Economics*.

Okediji, R. L. 2003. The International Relations of Intellectual Property: Narratives of Developing Country Participation in the Global Intellectual Property System.

Okediji, R. L. 2006. The International Copyright System: Limitations, Exceptions and Public Interest Considerations for Developing Countries. UNCTAD/ITCSD Project on IPRs and Sustainable development, Issues paper No. 15, Geneva.

Ozgen, B. 2007. Copyright and Related Rights: An Overview of the Set of Rights and Their Application. Paper presented at the World Forum on Music, Beijing, October.

Paulus, P. B., and B. A. Nijstad, eds. 2003. *Group Creativity: Innovation through Collaboration*. Oxford: Oxford University Press.

Peacock, A. 1986. Making Sense of Broadcasting Finance. Reprinted in R. Towse, ed. 1997. *Cultural Economics: The Arts, the Heritage and the Media Industries*, volume 1. Cheltenham, UK: Edward Elgar Publishing Inc.

Penna, F. J., M. Thorman, and M. Finger. 2003. The Africa Music Project. In J. Michael and P. Schuler, eds., *Poor People's Knowledge: Promoting Intellectual Property in Developing Countries*. Oxford, UK: Oxford University Press.

Pricewaterhouse Coopers. 2006. Global Entertainment and Media Outlook 2006–2010. London.

Reese, R. A. 2001. Copyright and Internet Music Transmissions: Existing Law, Major Controversies, Possible Solutions. *Miami Law Review* 55, p. 237.

Romer, P. 2002, When Should We Use Intellectual Property Rights? *The American Economic Review* 92(2), 1 May, pp. 213–216.

Siwek, S. 2004. Copyright Industries in the US Economy. Report prepared for IIPA, International Intellectual Property Alliance, Washington, D.C.

Throsby, D. 2001. *Economics and Culture*. Cambridge, UK: Cambridge University Press.

Tschmuck, P. 2003. How Creative Are the Creative Industries? *Journal of Arts Management, Law and Society* 33(2), pp. 127–142.

Tomlinson, J. 1994. A Phenomenology of Globalization? Giddens on Global Modernity. *European Journal of Communication* 9(2), pp. 149–172.

Towse, R. 2000. *Economic Aspects of Limitations and Exceptions to Copyright: A Seminar Report*. Rotterdam: Erasmus University.

Towse, R. 2001. Creativity, Incentive and Reward: An Economic Analysis of Copyright and the Information Age. Cheltenham: Edward Elgar Publishing.

Towse, R. 2005. Alan Peacock and Cultural Economics. *The Economic Journal* 115, June, pp. F262–F276.

UNCTAD. 2001. Intellectual Property Rights and Development. Policy Discussion Paper.

UNCTAD. 2004a. Creative Industries and Development. 11th Session, Sao Paulo, Geneva.
UNCTAD. 2004b. Creative Industries and Development. TD (XI) BP/13, June 4, 2004. Background document prepared for UNCTAD XI, Sao Paulo, Brazil.
UNCTAD. The Least Developed Countries Report. New York and Geneva: UN. Various years.
UNCTAD. 2006. Developing Productive Capacities. The Least Developed Countries Report. New York and Geneva: UN.
UNCTAD-ICTSD. 2003. Intellectual Property Rights: Implications for Development.
UNESCO. October 2005. Convention on the Protection and Promotion of the Diversity of Cultural Expressions, Paris.
UNESCO. 2006a. Trends in Audio-Visual Markets, Regional Perspectives from the South. Paris.
UNESCO. 2006b. International Flows of Selected Cultural Goods and Services, 1994–2003. Paris: Institute of Statistics.
UNIDO. 2005. International Comparison of National Policy Instruments and Innovation Systems for Technology Development, Vienna.
Wassall, G., and N. Alper. 1992. Towards a Unified Theory of the Determinants of Earnings of Artists. In R. L. Towse, ed. *Cultural Economics.* Berlin: Springer Verlag.
World Bank. 2001. Intellectual Property: Balancing Incentives with Competitive Access. *Global Economic Prospects.* Washington, DC., pp. 129–150.
World Bank. 2006. *World Development Indicators.* Washington, DC: World Bank.
Wu, W. February 2005. Dynamic Cities and Creative Clusters. World Bank Policy Research Working paper 3509. Washington, DC: World Bank.

15. ARAB MUSICONOMICS, CULTURE, COPYRIGHT, AND THE COMMONS

NAGLA RIZK*

I. INTRODUCTION

The past few years have witnessed a vibrant debate over the structure, operation, and, indeed, survival of the music industry. This was ignited by the massive advances in digital technologies and the expansion in music downloads and peer-to-peer music-file sharing. Such developments call for taking another look at the currently prevailing structures and business models of the industry. Of utmost relevance in this context is the role of intellectual property (IP) systems in resolving issues related to music access, production, distribution, and compensation of music creators.

This paper is an attempt to look at these issues within the Arab context. Specifically, the paper takes a closer look at the Arab music industry in light of

* This paper is based on a presentation at the UCLA conference on "Intellectual Property and Developing Countries: The WIPO Development Agenda" March 2007. I am grateful to UCLA Law School for the invitation and to Neil Netanel for his support. Financial support for this research was provided by the American University in Cairo. Thanks are due to Maggie Riad, May Fayez, and Amira El Marsafawy for their valuable assistance, to Madiha el Safty, and Lina Attalah for their constructive comments, and last but not least, to my interviewees without whom this paper would not have come to life. Special thanks to Ousso for disclosing what would have otherwise been classified information.

the region's sociocultural, economic, political, and legal realities. The paper sheds light on the current practices and value chains for commercial and underground musicians, with the objective of examining the role that copyright plays—or does not play—in this context.

At the heart of this work is the belief that IP regimes and business models should not be imposed from the top, but rather should emanate from the base, addressing the special needs and unique circumstances of respective countries or regions. In the paper, I argue that there exists a de facto commons for Arab music and propose that suitable IP regimes and alternative business models be devised to accommodate the region's special characteristics. Inherent in this work is the belief in music as a component of knowledge, which is in itself an integral component of sustainable human development (Figure 15.1). As such, IP systems are seen as tools to promote access and contribution to this component of human knowledge. The fact remains that music, and correspondingly knowledge, cannot be understood apart from the cultural context in which it operates.

The focus of this paper is on two major groups: the popular (henceforth, "pop") stars and the underground musicians, with the latter defined as alternative bands that are out of the mainstream, sometimes also known as "independent musicians." Given the lack of published data on the Arab music industry, this research is primarily based on interviews with a wide range of people reflecting a broad spectrum of interests: musicians, producers, distributors, lawyers, agents, NGOs, and government officials. Most of the information is collected firsthand and includes a good deal of anecdotal evidence; all is released with the approval of the interviewees. The paper is the first attempt to study these issues in the Arab region and is the start of long-term research project that will delve into this subject in more detail. The paper should be read in that spirit.

Although the paper refers to Arab music broadly, the bulk of the field research has been done in Egypt, which has rightly been termed "the Hollywood of the East." Egypt has always attracted Arab musicians, partly because of the size of its market, the history of its business, and the presence of the region's best recording

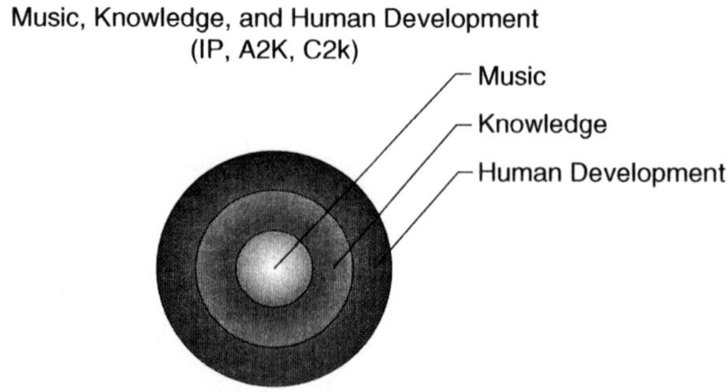

FIGURE 15.1 MUSIC, KNOWLEDGE, AND HUMAN DEVELOPMENT.

studios and technical personnel. Whenever relevant and feasible, the data cover other Arab musicians, as well.

The paper is constructed as follows. Following the introduction, section II is a summary of the recent past and present market structures, players, and value chains for the two groups of music makers under study. In section III, I review the context: the sociocultural, economic, political, and legal framework. This context, I argue in section IV, has brought about models of disseminating Arabic music—both pop and underground—that can be described as a de facto commons. Within such platforms, Arab music creators and users are brought closer together officially, unofficially, and sometimes illegally, and copyrighted recordings play a marginal role. In section V, I conclude that wider access models for Arab music should be acknowledged and accommodated through flexible IP systems and novel business models that maximize access for users and reward the music creator rather than the middleman—namely the label.

II. PLAYERS ON THE MUSIC SCENE: THEN AND NOW

At present, the Arab music market is an oligopoly, with four major labels dominating the market: Rotana, Alam El Phan, Melody, and, to a lesser extent, Mirage. There are no published figures on the exact shares of pop versus independent players in the Arab music market. Rough estimates based on interviews reveal that four major labels represent almost 85 percent of the market for Arabic. Rotana (www.rotana.net) is owned by Prince Al Waleed Ibn Talal and has signed with more than 100 pop stars. Some 20 smaller labels take up 13 percent of the market, and the remaining 2 percent is made up of alternative and underground musicians (various interviews) (see Figure 15.2). There are around 50 such underground bands in Egypt, and many others in Lebanon, Morocco, Algeria, and Tunisia (Ousso interview). In the next part, I trace the birth and growth of the nascent pop scene and the underground bands in the region, with an emphasis on Egypt.

A. Pop Stars: Commercial Music

Pop stars dominate the commercial music scene. The current state of commercial music can be traced back to the start of the 1980s, when the shorter, "lighter" style of singing came to overshadow the classical genre of longer songs and to dominate the market, which it has done ever since. These songs were literally called "the light song" *("al-'oghneya al khafifa")* and/or "the youth song" *("al oghneya al shababeya")*.

In the 1980s, three major labels prevailed: Sawt el Hobb, Alam El Phan, and Mirage (Ousso, Salama interviews). Major labels produced albums (on cassette tapes at the time) for the pop stars, each producing for one or two famous stars at the most. The typical value chain started with the singer approaching the big

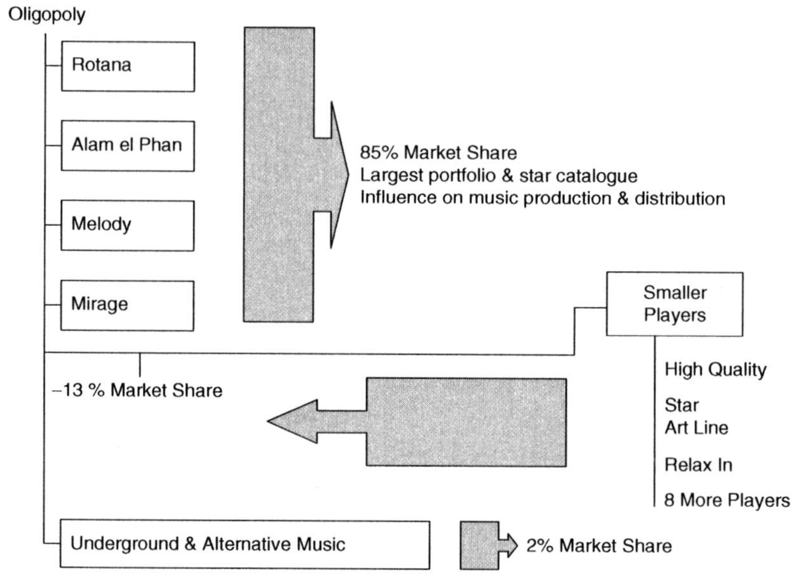

FIGURE 15.2 THE ARAB MUSIC MARKET.

label, mostly through personal contacts. The label would then arrange for three major players: the lyricist, melody composer, and music arranger. Then the label would arrange for studio time in which a sound engineer would be involved in recording and mixing the songs. A series of permits would then be required for selling and exchange (*"bei' wa tadawul"*), censorship (*"riqaba"*), the syndicate of musicians *("neqabat al mosiqueyeen")*, and standards and classifications (*"mosannafat"*) (see Figure 15.3). In reality, one or more of these may have been skipped, through bribery if necessary. The final step would be the production of tapes, which would sell for L.E. 5 (equivalent to $4 at the time), against a pirated version that sold for L.E. 1 (equivalent to 80 cents at the time) (Ousso interview). This trend continued well into the 1990s, with compact discs (CDs) being produced—and pirated—alongside the already popular tapes.

The year 2001 witnessed a turning point for Arab commercial music: the genesis of satellite television. The interest in pop stars shifted almost instantaneously from the album to the music video, commonly known as the "video clip." This brought a natural shift in the players and the value chain for commercial music. The four previous players remained (lyricist, melody composer, arranger, and sound engineer), but they were now joined by others: the video-clip director, the executive producer (*"modeer intag"*), and, most important, the agent (*"simsar"*), who initiated the whole "project" (see Figure 15.3). These represented a "gang" that would go around looking for young, good-looking men and women, and lure them into becoming video-clip stars (Ousso interview).

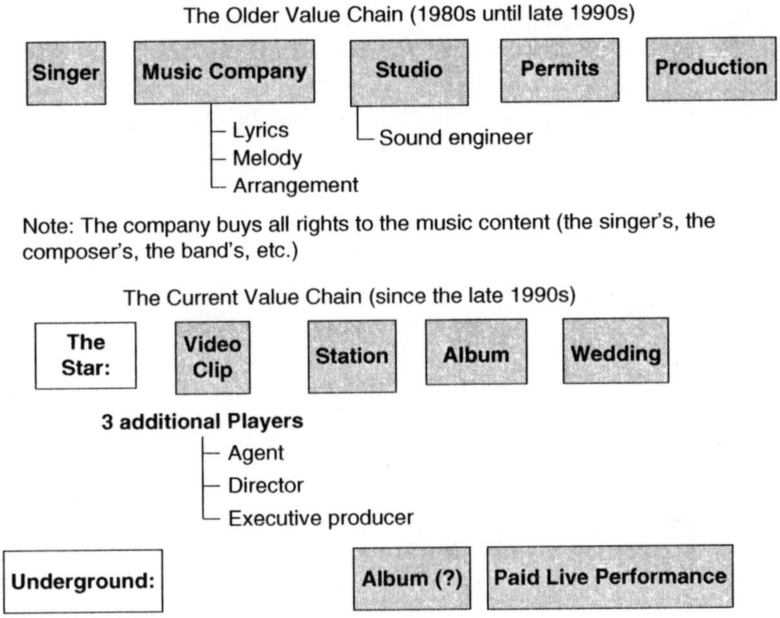

FIGURE 15.3 CHANGE IN VALUE CHAINS, 1980S TO PRESENT.

Good looks have become sufficient for a star to be born, with less emphasis being placed on genuine singing talent, partly thanks to voice makeover technologies. As one BBC commentator summarized the situation, "stars used to make video clips, now video clips make stars" (Sharp 2005). The term "new look" is often cited in the press, written ad-verbatim in Arabic letters, as either a promotional technique or to refer to a singer's comeback. This becomes particularly interesting as seen against a background of a general move to a more conservative culture in Arab societies.

These developments have greatly reduced performers' need for a physical recording studio. The video clip has taken over as the ultimate venue for singers to be known, especially with television being an integral part of everyday life for almost everyone, and shared access being the norm. This has changed the role of the production company, and the giant labels have had to adapt. Alam El Phan started its own TV station, Mazzika; Mirage became a distributor; Sawt el Hobb closed down. A new television channel, Melody, also started at this time and is said to be outdoing the rest in its sensationalism in the type of female and male pop singers it features (Ousso interview).

A major breakthrough for commercial music and the video-clip world was the emergence of the giant Rotana and its television network in 2003. Rotana swept the market, took over most of the pop stars in the region, became a partner in the Mazzika satellite television channel and created its own channels (Ousso interview). There are currently four different music-television channels owned by Rotana.

Contracts signed by Rotana are literally called "monopoly" contracts "*'Aqd Ihtikar,*" which, in practice, means exclusivity, whereby the label owns all rights to the music. Sometimes singers will get a percentage of the revenues, the size of which will depend on the contract and the clout of the star. Others may agree on a lump sum paid upon signing the contract. The upfront lump sum is usually the pattern with major stars to avoid administrative hassles (El Kashef interview). In one instance, a top singer was paid $5 million upon the signing of his three-year contract, in return for waiving his rights to royalties, as well as his obligations to pay a percentage of live-concert revenues to the label.

Since then, the video clip has become the most important outlet for presenting and promoting Arab pop singers. Normally, the channel would buy the video clip from the producing label or directly from the "gang." The "gangs" have thrived and continue to fish for new "singers" to feed the chain. Some labels demand that the video clip be broadcast exclusively on the channel they own (Ousso interview). Unlike the singer, the lyricist and songwriter are supposed to receive copyright royalties from video-clip broadcasts. These are presumably channeled through the Association of Lyricists and Songwriters as the TV channels pay an annual lump sum on all broadcasts at the end of the year (El Kashef interview).

Against this, live parties have continued as a well-rooted tradition, providing an important venue for pop stars. Live parties expanded considerably in the last 10 years, given the boom in development of holiday resorts along the northern coast of Egypt and the Red Sea. Beach concerts thrived and continued to attract audiences from all over the country, as well as visitors from around the region, especially the Gulf countries. Marina beach resort, in particular, became a hot spot for Arab pop singers, where parties attracted thousands of fans. Similarly, Sharm El Sheikh on the Red Sea started to attract Arab singers in frequently held concerts all year round. Hotels continued as major outlets for live parties, hosting Arab pop stars and attracting audiences from Egypt and other Arab holiday makers.

Between the video clips and the thriving party scene, new pop stars are continuously emerging. Competition is more visible, and demand is still strong. Amidst weddings and live parties at hotels, beaches, and elsewhere, pop stars are able to charge exorbitant rates for appearances despite the greater competition, generally (see Table 15.1).

Given these developments, the value chain has changed into a straightforward sequence from the video clip on the satellite channel to the production of the album and, eventually, to the live parties and weddings (Ousso interview) (see Figure 15.3). Once the pop singer has signed the contract with the label, any significant additional financial gain for him or her will come from the live party. Singers do not receive royalties from the video clips, and, in the few cases in which revenue sharing is contracted, receive only negligible royalties from sales of CDs and tapes. Lyricists and songwriters supposedly receive royalties from

TABLE 15.1 STAR RATES FOR WEDDING PERFORMANCES

Singers (Names Withheld)	Earnings Per Wedding (in $US)
Most Paid Stars	
Top Lebanese Pop Singer (female)	40,000
Top Egyptian Pop Star (male)	35,880*
Top Lebanese Pop Star (male)	25,000
Lowest Paid Star	
Less Popular Egyptian Singer	877*

*Calculated at the exchange rate of 5.7 EGP/$. Compare to annual per capita income of Egypt: $1350 (source: World Bank 2007).
Source: Salah Salem, Banquet Manager, Cairo Sheraton Hotel.

broadcasts of video clips. In practice, however, the norm in the Arab music world has been agreements involving upfront, lump-sum payments, whether with musicians or with songwriters and lyricists (El Kashef interview).

B. Underground Musicians: An Alternative Voice

Alongside this trend, the underground music movement started in Egypt and elsewhere in the region in the early 1990s. Performing outside the mainstream commercial channels, these groups provided an alternative voice and were often associated with social rebellion and political dissent. Some prefer to be called "alternative," emphasizing that this highlights the new voice, in addition to, or perhaps, instead of, simply referring to their operating outside the mainstream (Refaat, Salama interviews). Others prefer the term "independent," referring to their being free from all strings, business or political (Samy interview).

It is not surprising to find that the timid, but gradually developing, underground music movement was dealt a severe blow in the late 1990s. A harsh clampdown restricted underground musicians, based on claims of engagement in group festivities involving satanic worship and, in some cases, homosexual activities. Although the latter is merely a social taboo, the former is a crime punishable by law. This took place in Egypt in 1997, in Lebanon around the same time, and in Morocco later in 2003 (Al-Zubaidi 2006 and Tarbush 2007).

Underground music survived, nonetheless, and festivals were eventually held in different Arab countries. In Morocco, the Boulevard des Jeunes Musiciens continues to be a haven through which underground bands from the region promote their music. After the 2003 incident dubbed "Affair of the 14 Satanists," strong support was afforded to musicians by civil society generally, and social and political activism began to accompany the Boulevard performances (Al Zubaidi and Zine 2006).

In the case of Egypt, few musicians survived the much more dramatic "satanic" trauma, as most underground musicians were jailed, and the rest were subjected to strong family pressures. Egyptian underground bands received a shot in the arm in 2001, however, when two new outlets opened: the Cairo Jazz Club and Sakiet El Sawy Al Thaqafeyya (commonly referred to as "El Sakia"). The former is a bar frequented by music lovers and usually offers an outlet for the better-quality underground bands. Musicians get paid L.E. 200 (equivalent to $35) per head per performance (Ousso interview). The Club is still relatively elitist, attracting clientele from upper-class Cairo circles.

Literally translated as "cultural wheel," the second venue, El Sakia, is a particularly interesting case, especially because it was built on the site of a garbage dump under a flyover by the Nile. It has offered an outlet for *all* underground musicians, with an arrangement of splitting concert proceeds directly with performers. For most bands, the split was 50%–50%; in the case of established bands, performers got 75 percent of the proceeds (Adel, Ousso interviews). El Sakia has provided a haven of access for underground musicians and music lovers alike. Tickets are inexpensive, ranging from L.E. 10 to L.E. 25, very roughly the equivalent of $2 to $5. With two separate theaters, El Sakia often runs two concerts a day, and crowds are often seen gathering on the streets awaiting the doors' opening. According to Hussein Samy, musician and initiator of Kawalees Masr Free CD Initiative, the owner of El Sakia announced that the venue had hosted 750 music concerts in 2006, most of which were performed by underground bands (Samy interview).

These two venues opened a whole new world for underground bands. At the beginning there were only four bands: al Hob Walsalam, Eftikasat, Nagham Masry, and Wust el Balad. Today, there are more than 50 (Ousso interview). Thanks to these outlets, live performances have become the bread and butter of these bands, especially given the lack of interest from the giant labels. As with pop stars, underground musicians view live performances as their principal source of revenue.

Unlike pop stars, the production of an album is out of reach for many underground musicians (see Figure 15.3). The production of a CD is sought as a symbol of recognition—a social validation of creativity—rather than as a potential source of substantive financial return. At present, only a handful of underground bands in Egypt have produced CDs, with most relying entirely on live performances at the Jazz Club, El Sakia, and a few more outlets and private parties for remuneration from their work.

III. THE FRAMEWORK: SOCIOCULTURAL, ECONOMIC, POLITICAL, AND LEGAL REALITIES

For different reasons, live performances are the ultimate target for both pop stars and underground musicians, even if the gap in the rates charged is huge. Live performances align very well with the sociocultural, economic, political, and legal realities. In this section, I provide a brief overview of this framework.

A. The Sociocultural Framework

The Arab region comprises a unique sociocultural heritage that is the outcome of a long and rich tribal history. It is a society of close collectivity based on kinship solidarity, a group culture characterized by limited individuality and numerous group festivities featuring live performances. A moderate climate further encourages outdoor festivities and group celebrations.

Traditional culture carries on in the prominent place live performances continue to enjoy in Arab society. In Egypt, good summer weather encourages frequent and popular beach parties where pop singers, and sometimes underground bands, perform. Live concerts in major hotels are also frequent, especially in festive times and during holiday seasons when tourists come from neighboring Arab Gulf countries. Hotels compete for the pop stars; the choice of star is a sign of prestige.

Underground bands, too, earn from live performances, albeit less lavishly. It is worth noting that peer collaboration is evident among members of underground bands. They will often back each other up and help in paid concerts, regardless of the financial return. There is an interesting and noticeable spirit of group support among such bands, a firm solidarity that the writer of these lines witnessed firsthand backstage. There is also an active network of communication between underground musicians from different countries in the region (Salem, Salama, Ousso interviews).

Then there are the wedding parties. In Arab culture, marriage is the only sanctioned relationship between a man and a woman; it is the sole form for couples living together. Anything else is not only a social taboo: it is illegal. Marriage is expected of young people of a certain age, and arranged marriages are not uncommon. Within this framework, the wedding party becomes a highlight of the parents' lives, and the choice of a wedding singer is a most important status symbol. The small stratum of the upper class tends to make an excessively lavish show of its wealth in the form of extravagant weddings. This flagrant display of luxury is especially seen among families with newly acquired wealth. Families may live in debt, if only to ensure that their sons and daughters have a properly prestigious wedding. Pop stars are usually at the center of this choice, and are naturally in high demand.

Arabs' cultural predilection to pay generously for live-music performances contrasts sharply with the widespread cultural acceptance of making and sharing copies of music cassettes and CDs. The Arab culture is also a deeply rooted gift culture. Music recordings, among other items, are warmly exchanged and generously shared. It may be socially unacceptable to refuse a request to copy an admired CD. Copyright concerns pale in such contexts. Indeed, copyright may actually be disruptive to social norms.

B. The Simple Economics

The live-performance market for pop stars is indeed interesting. Demand is strong and inelastic, and supply is offered by the pop star acting as a monopolist in his/her own right. The pop star charges exorbitant rates for weddings, and these are multiplied by two to three times for live concerts or private parties. There is a price for "superstardom": talent is not replaceable, nor is it additive (Connolly and Krueger 2005). The market then settles at an oddly high equilibrium price for each pop star. For weddings, the rate ranges from the equivalent of almost US$36,000 for the top Egyptian singer to the equivalent of almost $900 for the lowest-paid singer (see Table 15.1). Lebanese singers charge between $25,000 and $40,000, in addition to expenses for travel and accommodation for themselves and their accompanying musicians (Salem interview).

Given the considerable revenue that top singers earn from live performances, the major record labels have recently pushed singers to agree to recording-contract provisions that give them a share of singers' live-performance proceeds. Even when singers acquiesce to labels' demands, such provisions are more easily enforced in the case of concerts than weddings. Weddings are informally contracted, with artists wanting to cash in on the wedding proceeds in return for their effort. There have been disputes between artists and labels on this particular issue.

Artists' earnings from live performances are compared to two figures. First, they contrast sharply with the annual gross per capita income for Egypt, which stands at $1350 (see Table 15.1). The pop star makes almost 30 times the annual per capita gross national income for Egypt in *less than two hours* performing at one wedding. The ratio is more striking when measured for the public party, for which the singer charges two to three times the wedding rate.

I next compare earnings from live performances to singers' earnings from the sale of copyrighted recordings, namely tapes and CDs. In undertaking this exercise, my objective was to estimate the relative importance for the musician of the copyrighted item, as opposed to the live performance. The major challenge faced in attempting to undertake this comparison was the lack of information on sales of musical units, proceeds from royalties, and receipts of major labels from the live performance. This challenge was overcome in two ways. The pop star whose case I cover (and whose name I withhold) had signed a deal with the major label whereby a lump sum of $5 million was paid at the signing of the contract, with all rights and obligations waived. His annual earnings from copyrighted items were thus calculated by dividing the lump sum of $5 million over three years, giving an annual earning of $1.67 million a year. I then compared this figure with his earnings out of live parties and weddings, which I estimate based on the frequency and rates charged (Salem, Ousso interviews). With this in mind, a simple calculation shows that the sum of his earnings from live performances is 4.5 times that coming from the sale of copyrighted recordings (see Table 15.2).

As mentioned earlier, this singer received a lump-sum payment upon signing the contract in lieu of a percentage of sales. Other pop stars may sign to receive percentages of sales, a good part of which escapes the collection chain in

TABLE 15.2 EARNING DIFFERENTIALS (GUESSTIMATES)

Singers	Annual Earnings (in US$)	Ratio (Performances/Sale of Copyrighted Items)
Commercial Music (Egyptian Superstar, name withheld)		
Cassettes/CDs	1,666,667	4.5
Performances	7,578,947*	
Alternative Music (Eftikasat band)		
Cassettes/CDs	351	13.2
Performances	4632	

* Calculated at the exchange rate of 5.7 EGP/$.
Source: Calculated based on information from Salah Salem, banquet manager at the Cairo Sheraton, and Ousso, Eftikasat leader.

most cases. The latter is partly the result of a lack of proper accounting mechanisms, as well as inaccurate reporting on the part of vendors (Ousso interview). Although not formally studied, I expect these artists' earnings out of copyrighted recordings to be quite modest. Even with their rate for live performances being lower than the singer under study, I still expect their earnings ratio of live performances to copyrighted items to be much higher given the negligible proceeds from copyrighted sales.

After undertaking this exercise, I came across a similar calculation undertaken for the top 35 pop stars in the United States (Connolly and Krueger, Table 1.1, p. 71). In this case, the authors use data published in *Rolling Stone* magazine on the stars' earnings in 2002. The ratio of live-performance earnings to copyrighted items came out as 7.5 on average (Connolly and Krueger 2005), even higher than that of star performers in Egypt.

In the case of underground bands, I attempted a similar exercise based on the leading band with accurate information from its lead musician (Ousso interview). This band produced one CD as the winners of a competition organized by an NGO (Al-Mawrid Al-Thaqafi). They usually perform in the main outlets already mentioned (Cairo Jazz Club and El Sakia). With the help of the band leader, I estimated their annual earnings out of live concerts at $4632 as opposed to their annual earnings from the CD ($351). Their ratio stood at 13.2 (see Table 15.2).

It is to be noted that this band is one of the few underground bands that have had a CD produced. It is often the case that earnings from copyrighted recordings stand at absolutely zero, and hence the band's livelihood depends solely on live performances. One may philosophically argue that for zero earnings from

TABLE 15.3 2004 REGIONAL COMPARISON—PRODUCTION OF MUSIC UNITS

	Unit* Change (From 2004 to 2005)
World	−0.4%
North America	2.6%
Europe	−1.6%
EU	−3.1%
Asia	−3.7%
Latin America	9.2%
Australasia	−5.8%
Middle East	−13.3%

* Units include music cassettes, CDs, and DVDs.
Source: IFPI 2005.

copyrighted recordings, the ratio of live performance to copyrighted items earnings is indeed infinity for underground musicians.

Given the above, one concludes that live performances weigh more heavily in Arab musicians' earnings than do revenues from sales of music recordings. In the few cases in which musicians sign for revenue sharing, this claim is made stronger by the fact that sound-recording production has generally declined (see Table 15.3), with no similar signs for the live-music scene. This raises questions as to the role that copyright plays—or, indeed, does not play—in the Arab music industry.

C. The Legal Realities

The legal framework for copyright protection is officially established in almost all Arab countries. Intellectual property laws are there, and protection of creative works is quite often clearly stated (El Sherif interview). In practice, however, high rates of piracy prevail (see Table 15.4).

Arabic music is widely pirated over the Internet. A knowledgeable observer has estimated that in 2005 there were more than 500 pirate music sites in the Middle East. In Egypt alone, pirated music is an industry worth $12 million, representing the earnings of pirated music sales (Barakat 2007).

Piracy is more obvious in the case of physical recordings. Copied tapes and CDs are often seen in kiosks on the sidewalks of Egypt. In the 1980s, a pirated tape was sold at 20 percent of the price of a licensed copy. Today, a pirated CD is sold at less than 10 percent of the price of the licensed recording.

Perhaps, as in some other parts of the world, the seriousness of piracy in Egypt may pale in comparison to crimes with more visible victims. The generous and pervasive gift culture lessens the immediate association of music piracy with outright theft. At the law-enforcement level, music pirates may be viewed as

TABLE 15.4 DOMESTIC MUSIC PIRACY LEVELS (SELECTED ARAB COUNTRIES)

Over 50%	25%–50%	10%–25%	Less Than 10%
Egypt	Kuwait	Bahrain	UAE
	Lebanon	Oman	
	Saudi Arabia	Qatar	

Source: IFPI 2002.

trivial offenders when compared to, say, political dissidents, especially at times when political stability is in jeopardy.

Moreover, law-enforcement officials receive a modest monthly pay. It is not difficult to believe claims of bribes paid in return for some officials' "understanding." Indeed, one cannot study law enforcement in the music industry, or in any other industry for that matter, in isolation from general development indicators, especially poverty. If one adds the perception of music as a "light" field—a luxury—then it is not difficult to understand the poor man's perception that "no one is hurt" by the prevalence of pirated CDs. Copyright gets an all-new meaning in this context.

Corruption may sometimes extend to checks for permits and syndicate membership cards that are supposedly required of every music performer. One interviewee confirmed that the law enforcer sent to check on performers' syndicate cards is regularly offered L.E. 100 to turn a blind eye to their absence. This figure is equivalent to less than $20, yet it represents roughly two-thirds of his monthly pay. Collectors, too, are said to pocket some of the proceeds of sales of CDs and tapes, causing leakage in the collection chain (Ousso interview). Musicians are harmed by such leakage, given that they receive only a percentage of such proceeds to start with.

Weak institutional structures aggravate the situation. Lack of proper documentation and checks and balances creates loopholes. Lawsuits take too long to settle; faith in "the system" is generally limited. Procedures for revenue collection and royalty compensation are cumbersome and unrealistic (Adel, El kashef, Ousso, Refaat interviews).

In short, although the legal system has been formally laid out, capacity development for IP enforcement has been generally modest. This further shrinks the already limited financial return to musicians on their creativity from copyrighted items. There is, therefore, a need for devising simpler IP systems that take into consideration such shortcomings, especially the region's weak institutional structures.

D. The Political Dimension

The political stance toward the two groups of musicians is interestingly different. On one hand, Arabic pop music is encouraged and welcomed by the authorities.

Given the questionable quality of some of the pop music and the lyrics used, one cannot help being reminded of the "feelies" of Huxley's *Brave New World.* In Huxley's world, leaders support the "feelies," which present a form of entertainment meant to distract the masses and provide them with a false and sensual sense of "happiness." In the Arab world, one wonders if such music is similarly encouraged as a weapon of mass distraction.

In one instance in Egypt, a famous pop singer's case of evading military service (a major crime in Egypt) was dealt with lightly, to the relief of the masses of young fans. This case was placed in sharp contrast to imprisoned political dissidents and outspoken Internet bloggers. The pop singer has been released and has continued performing with a vengeance.

On the other hand, a portion of underground music seems to have received the cold shoulder, if not frowns, from the authorities. The lyrics express the suffering of the layman, and the singers are often considered socially rebellious and politically daring. In Morocco, the Boulevard des Jeunes Musiciens has become a venue for NGOs and other associations to promote social and political issues, such as AIDS prevention and mobilization against international-trade inequalities. The Moroccan underground mélange of rock and Moroccan *gnawa* is described as "far from political correctness" and is "classified as the music of the 'marginalized youth' challenging the adult world" (Al Zubaidi 2006).

There are several examples of underground music in the spotlight. In Lebanon, underground musicians are subject to censorship, especially if they "cross the mainstream media," which is "only possible" when the artist has the good looks and "the good connections—or a name" (Tarboush 2007). One Lebanese singer is cited as having fit those criteria and having produced "controversial" video clips criticizing Syria and the Lebanese government. These were broadcast on Lebanese satellite-television channels and did create a buzz (Tarbush 2007). In Algeria, underground musicians suffer severe censorship. The authorities take especially severe measures against those singing in the Berber language. In 1998, a Berber singer was assassinated (Al-Zubaidi 2006). In Egypt a censor is occasionally sent to the underground bands' performances (Ousso interview). In one instance, the theater (Genaina Theater) was actually closed without prior notice the day of the concert after the authorities learned of the content of the lyrics to be sung. In that case, theater supporters demonstrated in the streets, singing the very same songs at Tahrir Square at the heart of Cairo. The theater was reopened a few months later.

A fair number of Arab underground bands have been targeted for serving as conduits of political expression. Arabic pop stars, on the other hand, are favored because they serve as means to distract the masses. This extra layer of favoritism poses an additional challenge for underground musicians over and above what they already face from the labels. For underground musicians, the copyrighted recording is far from reach (because of the labels), and the live performance is monitored, even if distantly (by the authorities). As underground musicians strive to be heard, their agenda and motivations do not include copyright as a high-priority concern.

E. Summary

The previous analysis presents a scenario whereby direct monetary appropriation to the musician out of copyrighted recordings is quite modest. Whether the musician gets a percentage of the sales or a lump sum, what reaches him/her after the collection chain—given leakage, piracy, and the decline in music production—ends up being relatively negligible. The primary source of earnings for musicians is the live performance, which flourishes thanks to the region's social and cultural heritage. Whether pop or underground, the musician will always seek the live performance, through which he or she will receive a direct return on creativity. In this context, copyrighted recordings and video clips mainly serve as reputation promoters or marketing devices.

IV. THE CURRENT PLATFORM: A DE FACTO COMMONS

Given the above realities, "the commons" seems to be a more suitable platform for providing Arabic music. In this section, I take this point further by examining the current practices of some Arab pop stars and underground musicians in this respect. The main hypothesis is that there actually exists an informal, and sometimes illegal, commons in a system where significant monetary appropriation to musicians comes mostly from live performances—mainly weddings and public parties.

A. Pop Stars

In this part, I select four of the top Arab singers and examine the extent to which they present their material via the world of the commons. Ragheb Alama, for example, is a top Lebanese singer who is nicknamed "King of the Stage," and for good reason. A top live performer, Mr. Alama makes his video clips freely downloadable from his official website (www.ragheb-alama.com). People can also send the clips as e-cards, which clearly widens the circulation of the clips through an obvious networking effect. Given the rate the singer charges for performing at weddings, it is perfectly understandable that such clips are used purely as marketing devices to promote his songs.

Two top Lebanese singers, Nancy Ajram and Alissa, also make their music freely downloadable from their official websites (www.nancyajramonline.com and www.alissa-lebanon.com, respectively). Both singers provide their video clips online. They are among the most expensive Arab live performers.

In addition to such official venues of music availability, some top pop singers reportedly have no objection to their music's being illegally exchanged and downloaded on the Internet. This becomes understandable as the marketing benefits from such practices strongly outweigh the minimal "damage" that such downloads may impose on the musicians. The net effect is positive, at least in the short run.

On the Internet, there is a myriad of websites that offer free downloads of Arab pop music, but to my knowledge, the only legal one in Egypt is Mazika.com[1] (www.mazika.com). Bought by one of the major Internet providers (Link.net), Mazika.com offers music for free to Link.net subscribers and for a small price to others. The price is L.E. 1.50 per song (roughly equivalent to 30 cents); payment is made using prepaid debit cards. The company has signed contracts with major labels, as well as with individual musicians, in which case the proceeds are split and the artist receives 50 percent of the sale price (Sobhy interview).

B. Underground Musicians

There have been various forms of de facto commons already taking place, whereby underground musicians offer their music to the public without much concern for copyright. The most visible are free street festivals that are held to promote the bands. In Morocco, for example, the Boulevard des Jeunes Musiciens attracts musicians from all over the country, among which are musicians of the Moroccan mélange of rock and *gnawa* which is described as being "based on the free copy to fill the void of diffusion, on creativity when it comes to recording facilities, performance arenas, and new modes of creation, and on cultural mix" (Al-Zubaidi 2006). The initial and primary goal of the festival is "to provide a venue for young alternative Moroccan bands, especially for those that lack commercial support." The festival includes a competition for young bands in which the winner "is awarded a monetary prize that allows them to realize a particular musical project." The Boulevard also offers music workshops, providing young bands with exposure to more experienced musicians (Al Zubaidi 2006).

Another particularly interesting case is the Save Our Souls (SOS) festival held in Cairo (www.sosmusicfestival.com). A free, full-day concert of underground bands, SOS takes place bi-monthly with the sole purpose of promoting music. The SOS organizers have created a website, which serves as a venue of interactive communication among underground music lovers in the country and the region. In line with that regional scope, the organizers also plan to involve underground bands from Morocco and Lebanon in future SOS festivals (Ousso interview). They are also exploring means of providing the bands' music for free and legal downloading on the Internet to fans of underground Arab music the world over.

The festival is free, but invitations are provided based on answers to a questionnaire posted on the website. This is meant to "to guarantee the access to only the right crowd, who want to be there for the music and the good time, and to prevent any misbehavior." The purpose of SOS, then, is to provide bands with access to a large audience and to attract the interest of the media and the entertainment industry in general (see www.sosmusicfestival.com/node/1).

---

1. Mazika.com is different from Mazzika satellite channel.

These models are comparable to Brazil's *tecnobrega*, which is often cited as an example of street music that thrives "outside the realm of traditional copyright" (Open Business 2005). In Brazil, the live *tecnobrega* parties are "used as a method of marketing events." Held every weekend, "the parties are advertised by the distribution of the music itself" (Open Business 2005). *Tecnobrega* music owes its expansion and popularity to the free, live scene, a model of free street music which is aligned with the Brazilian culture, much like live-music performance resonates in Arab culture.

Another example of free music offered to promote underground bands is provided by Kawalees Masr (literally meaning "Backstage Egypt"). This is an initiative to provide a bi-monthly free CD with a compilation of songs of independent musicians. Kawalees Masr team is also involved in preparing an annual festival in Alexandria (Independent Music Festival). The team member I interviewed also enthusiastically discussed plans to provide Arabic music within social networking sites, a vehicle that would be most suitable for the culture of young people in the region (Samy interview).

Another alternative model providing Arabic music is given by 100copies (www.100copies.com), which is an independent label that promotes musicians with flexible licensing schemes. The producer's idea was to limit quantities to 100 copies per album, which provides an interestingly conscious violation of the expected economies of scale given the zero marginal cost of reproducing endless digital copies of an information good. Nevertheless, the producer argued that the objective has been to make the bands known and not to reap abnormal profits. He further indicated his interest in working out an arrangement with the musicians by means of which all music would be freely accessed on the 100copies website, perhaps through radio streaming. He is in full accordance that there should be a "fair return" to music creators, rather than having the bulk of revenues eaten up as huge rents by a big label (Refaat interview).

Another initiative encouraging wider access and contribution to the music scene has been taken up by an NGO, Al-Mawred Al-Thaqafy (literally meaning "Cultural Resource"). With funding from several sponsors, including the Open Society Institute, Al Mawrid provides support to Arab musicians, mostly underground, to perform and produce outside the mainstream, commercial scene. Among their many activities, they produce and distribute free CDs with compilations of musicians from different Arab countries. They also receive proposals via a competition for Arab bands, resulting in grants for musicians to produce their own CD and own full copyright.

Recently there has been another interesting initiative to promote commons-based Arab content on the Internet. The Arab Commons project aims at promoting the creative commons and encouraging Arab intellectuals and artists to release their works under flexible copyright terms (see www.arabcommons.org). Such calls provide suitable platforms for Arab content and could very well serve to host commons initiatives for Arab music.

The above are examples of alternative platforms through which underground Arabic music is being offered for consumption outside the mainstream. Rather than protect their creations to reap direct monetary gains, these musicians offer their music, often for free, with the primary objective of being known and recognized. These musicians are quite relaxed about copyright; it is not a priority on their agenda.

V. CONCLUSION: THE ROLE OF COPYRIGHT

Based on the analysis here, I conclude that wider access models already prevail for pop and underground Arab music, officially and unofficially, and sometimes illegally. This is more aligned with the cultural, economic, and legal realities of the region. Effective channels of music dissemination are live performances, the Internet, and pirated recordings. Copyrighted recordings and video clips are used as marketing or reputation-making devices. Direct-value appropriation from copyrighted material is marginal. One therefore questions the role that copyright plays, or does not play, in this context.

Given the above, I argue for acknowledging and formalizing the de facto Arab commons through flexible IP systems and alternative business models that emanate from the base rather than being imposed from the top. The IP system would thus serve as a tool to promote access and contribution to music content through novel business models that are more suited to the Arab context and that reward music creators rather than middlemen.

Historically there has been one model and little choice for music creators. The giant label appropriates huge rents over the labor of the musicians, a model that is blessed by the official IP system. In today's world, there are, and should be, other alternatives, partly thanks to technological developments. The transformation of the role of the middleman has been a natural development in the digital economy. It is time that the music industry experiences this as one venue to restore the inequality in the distribution of power. More justice can be afforded to music creators as technology brings them into closer proximity with their audiences, in physical or virtual terms.

One suggestion in this regard is a subscription-based model that incorporates social networking, virtual gift giving, and virtual party holding. Such a format would be highly suitable for Arab culture. The experiment of Mazika.com is worth further study as a possible best practice.

VI. A FINAL WORD

As an experience good, music is a special and significant component of knowledge content, which is, in turn, an integral component of sustainable human development. The situation of Arab music must be understood in the context of the specific nature of the culture at the social, economic, and political levels. Within this, an intellectual property regime should not be an end in itself, but rather a tool to promote *access* and *contribution* to knowledge content—music, in this case. Widening access benefits consumers and enriches their experience. Promoting contribution encourages new talent and benefits current musicians, rewarding the creators rather than the middlemen. The call for formalizing the commons, whereby music creators hold full rights to their creativity, is made in this spirit.

REFERENCES

Abdallah, Mohamad. Al-Mawred Al-Thaqafy Cultural Center. Personal Interview, Cairo, January 23, 2007.

"About SOS Music." Available at http://www.sosmusicfestival.com/node/1. (Collected online June 25, 2007.)

Adel, Hany. Lead singer of Wust el Balad. Personal Interview, Cairo, February 15, 2007.

Ajram, Nancy. Official Website. Available at http://www.nancyajramonline.com. (Collected online June 25, 2007.)

Alama, Ragheb. Official Website. Available at: http://www.ragheb-alama.com. (Collected online June 25, 2007.)

Al-A'sar, Marwa. "Make Way for Experimental Oriental Sounds." *The Daily Star Egypt*, October 9, 2006. Available at http://www.dailystaregypt.com/article.aspx?ArticleID=3527. (Collected online June 25, 2007.)

Alexa Statistics. "Top Sites in Egypt." Available at http://www.alexa.com/site/ds/top_sites?cc=EG&ts_mode=country&lang=none. (Collected online June 25, 2007.)

Alissa, Official Website. Available at http://www.alissa-lebanon.com. (Collected online June 25, 2007.)

Al-Mawred Al-Thaqafy. Available at http://www.mawred.org/genainatheatre.htm. (Collected online June 25, 2007.)

Al-Zubaidi, Laila. 2006. Moroccan Youth between Rock and Gnawa, Shouting for Change. *Qantara.de Dialogue with the Islamic World*. Available at http://www.qantara.de/webcom/show_article.php/_c-587/_nr-24/i.html?PHPSESSID=5. (Collected online June 25, 2007.)

Al-Zubaidi, Laila, and Reda Zine. 2006. "Undermarocked?" *Norient*, July 20, 2006. Available at http://norient.com/html/show_article.php?ID=87. (Collected online June 25, 2007.)

"The Arab Commons Initiative." Available at http://www.arabcommons.org. (Collected online June 25, 2006.)

Arab Music Downloads Online. Available at http://www.6arab.com. (Collected online June 25, 2007.)

Backstage Egypt *("Kawalees Masr")*. Official Website. Available at http://www.backstage-egypt.com. (Collected online June 25, 2007.)

Barakat, Islam, Content Acquisition Manager, LinkdotNet, and previous Product Manager, Mazika.com. Personal Interview, Cairo, October 22, 2007.

Barakat, Islam. 2007. On Internet Music Piracy. Presentation made at the Conference on Intellectual Property and Development in the Digital Age, Cairo, May 29, 2007.

Bollier, David. 2006. The Rise of Tecno-Brega, or How to Build Markets on Top of Social Commons. September 18, 2006. Available at http://onthecommons.org/node/977/print. (Collected online June 25, 2007.)

Connolly, Marie, and Alan B. Krueger. April 2005. Rockonomics: The Economics of Popular Music. National Bureau of Economic Research Working Paper No. 11282. Available at http://www.nber.org/papers/w11282. (Collected online October 30, 2007.)

Diab, Amr. Official Website. Available at http://www.amrdiabworld.com. (Collected online June 25, 2007.)

El-Jesri, Manal. 2005. Ahmed El-Maghraby. *Egypt Today*, January, Volume 26 Issue 01, available at http://www.egypttoday.com/article.aspx?ArticleID=3355. (Collected online June 25, 2007.)

Elliot, Julie. Middle Eastern Music—An Introduction. Available at http://www.shira.net. (Collected online June 25, 2007.)

El Kashef, Tarek. Veteran Music Producer. Telephone Interview, Cairo, October 29, 2007.

El Maghraby, Ahmad. Founder of Makan Cultural Center. Personal Interview, Cairo, January 31, 2007.

El Sherif, Omar. President of Court of Appeal, National Telecommunication Regulatory Authorities. Personal Interview, February 12, 2007.

Ezzat, Dina. 2007. Intellects for Sale. *Al-Ahram Weekly*, February 10, 2007, Issue No. 831. Available at http://weekly.ahram.org.eg/2007/831/feature.htm. (Collected online June 25, 2007.)

Fayez, Salah. Egyptian Syndicate of Musicians. Personal Interview, Cairo, January 25, 2007.

Fischer, William. 2004. Introduction and Chapter 6. *Promises to Keep: Technology, Law, and the Future of Entertainment*. Stanford University Press. Available at http://www.tfisher.org/PTK.htm. (Collected online June 25, 2007.)

Harabi, Najib. 2004. Copyright-Based Industries in Selected Arab Countries. Study supported and published by the World Intellectual Property Organization (WIPO), Geneva. Available at http://www.gdnet.org/fulltext/harabi.pdf. (Collected online June 24, 2007.)

Huxley. Aldous. 1969. *Brave New World*. New York: Harper and Row.

International Intellectual Property Alliance (IIPA). 2006. IIPA 2004–2005 Estimated Trade Losses Due to Copyright Piracy, Middle East/Africa. Available at http://www.iipa.com/pdf/IIPA%202006%20Table%20of%20Estimated%20Trade%20Losses%20and%20Piracy%20Levels%20for%202005%20ME-AFRICA%20FINAL%20091806.pdf. (Collected online June 25, 2007.)

Intellectual Property Rights in the Middle East/Arabia. Available at http://www.bustpatents.com/forarab.htm. (Collected online June 26, 2007.)

International Federation of Phonographic Industries (IFPI). 2007. *Digital Music Report 2007*. Available at http://www.ifpi.org/content/library/digital-music-report-2007.pdf. (Collected online June 25, 2007.)

International Federation of Phonographic Industries (IFPI). 2006. *Digital Music Report 2006*. Available at http://www.mipi.com.au/documents/piracy-report2006.pdf. (Collected online June 25, 2007.)

International Federation of Phonographic Industries (IFPI). 2005. *The Recording Industry World Sales 2005*. Available at http://www.ifpi.org.uk/content/library/worldsales2004.pdf. (Collected online June 25, 2007.)

International Federation of Phonographic Industries (IFPI). 2003. IFPI's Regional Committee Meeting in Dubai Joins Local Music Industry to Step up Anti-Piracy Efforts. October. Available at www.ifpi.org/content/section_news/20031000.html. (Collected online June 25, 2007.)

International Federation of Phonographic Industries (IFPI). 2003. Police Seize 2 Million Tapes in Egypt's Biggest Ever Piracy Raid. IFPI, July 2, 2003. Available at http://www.ifpi.org/content/section_news/20030707.html. (Collected online June 25, 2007.)

International Federation of Phonographic Industries (IFPI). 2002. *IFPI Piracy Report 2002*. Available at http://www.ifpi.org/content/library/piracy2002.pdf. (Collected online June 25, 2007.)

Iskander, Sherif. *Google's Regional Manager of Middle East and North Africa*. Personal Interview, Cairo, February 22, 2007.

Maher, Sameh Adel. Owner of Mirage Music Company. Personal Interview, Cairo, January 31, 2007.

Mazika.com. Official Website. Available at http://www.mazika.com. (Collected online June 26, 2007.)

Mischiatti, Alessandro. Marketing Manager of Mazzika TV station. Personal Interview, Cairo, January 23, 2007.

Netanel, Neil. 2003. Impose a Noncommercial Use Levy to Allow Peer-to-Peer File Sharing. Law and Economics Working Paper No. 009, December 2003. *Harvard Journal of Law & Technology* Volume 17 Number 1, Fall.

OpenBusiness. 2005. Tecnobrega Shows Off an Open Business Model. September 26. Available at http://www.openbusiness.cc/2006/09/06/tecnobrega-shows-off-an-open-business-model. (Collected online June 26, 2007.)

Ousso (Mohamed Lotfy). Organizer of SOS Music Festival and lead musician in bands Eftikasat and Nagham Masry. Personal Interview, Cairo, February 25, 2007.

Refaat, Mahmoud. Musician and owner of 100copies label. Personal Interview, Cairo, February 27, 2007.

Rotana. Official Website. Available at http://www.rotana.net. (Collected online April 4, 2007.)

Samy, Hussein. Sound engineer and partner in Kawalees Masr Free CD Initiative. Personal Interview, Cairo, April 3, 2007.

Salama, Fathy. Grammy-award winner. Personal Interview, Cairo, February 02, 2007.

Salem, Salah. Banquet Manager. Cairo Sheraton Hotel. Telephone Interview, Cairo, January 1, 2007.

Sharp, Heather. 2006. Sexy Stars Push Limits in Egypt. *BBC News*, Cairo, September. Available at http://blogs.albawaba.com/geminimay_no/40744/2006/09/08/63551-shocking_but_true.

Sobhy, Samer. Portal Development Executive, Mazzika.com. Telephone Interview, Cairo, June 25, 2007.

Tarbush, Suzanne. 2007. Lebanese underground music groups are highlighted at the Freemuse conference in Istanbul.*Al Hayat*, February 1, 2007. Available at http://thetanjara.blogspot.com/2007_02_01_archive.html. (Collected online June 25, 2007.)

Tawileh, Anas. Arab Commons Initiator. Official Website. Available at http://www.arabcommons.com. Email interviews, February 22–27, 2007.

Tarifeh, Hanadi. 2006. New Year, New Commons. *Icommons*, September 18. Available at http://icommons.org/2007/01/15/new-year-new-commons. (Collected online June 25, 2007.)

World Bank. 2007. Egypt Data Profile Based on World Development Indicators. Available at http://devdata.worldbank.org/external/CPProfile.asp?PTYPE=CP&CCODE=EGY. (Collected online October 30, 2007.)

16. TRADING COPYRIGHT
Global Pressure on Local Culture

MICHAEL D. BIRNHACK*

I. INTRODUCTION

The meeting point of global intellectual property (IP) norms and local culture produces an unsettled process of glocalization.[1] The global and the local might merge, but they often conflict, and their intersection then mirrors another clash: that between trade and culture. This chapter argues that the global copyright regime

* Senior Lecturer, Faculty of Law, Tel-Aviv University. Thanks to Eyal Benvenisti, Daniel Gervais, Neil Netanel, Guy Pessach, Lior Zemer, participants at the conference on Intellectual Property and Developing Countries: The WIPO Development Agenda (UCLA Law School, March 2007), and participants at the conference on Exploring the Boundaries of IP Law (IDC, June 2007) for helpful comments. Thanks to Yoav Lifshitz for able research assistance. All websites were last visited on July 25, 2008.

1. The term "glocalization" emerged in sociology and is used in various ways. Here, the term is used as "the interpenetration of the global and the local resulting in unique outcomes in different geographic areas." See George Ritzer, *The Globalization of Nothing* 73 (Sage Publications, 2004).

(G©) should be evaluated against the backdrop of a complex set of local factors that form each country's cultural field, instead of being based on an exclusive legal or economic inspection. The main factors to be considered are the legal system of a country taken as a whole, its economy, its unique cultural features, and its political situation. No less important is the dynamic interaction of these factors. G© should be evaluated not only by studying the law in books, but also by exploring the law in action.

This chapter outlines the G© regime in political terms and describes it as a spiral, an expanding net of laws. It then outlines a general framework of the glocal gap in a particular context. After setting the stage, I describe the various factors that form the cultural field and trace the political dynamics of global IP pressures. Especially, I describe a process of *foreign leverage*, in which local interest groups turn to global players to pressure the local government. The case of Israel serves as an illustration of the general framework. Israel is defined as a high-income developing country. It has a shaky international political status, but it does enjoy the close support of the United States. Israel has a robust local culture but struggles to maintain its uniqueness in the face of external powers. Thus, Israel is not a typical "southern" country; rather, it is caught between the North and the South. The conclusion is rather dim: whereas copyright used to be about science, culture, education, and the flourishing of humankind, it has become a matter of trade, safeguarding the flourishing of some, but not all.

II. THE GLOCAL IP GAP

This part offers a framework for the evaluation of a country's situation vis-à-vis the current global IP order. I begin with presenting the regime and then turn to the local cultural field. Such an evaluation should take into account a combination of (at least) several factors: copyright law, the local legal system taken as a whole, economics, particular cultural needs, and the (internal and international) political situation of a country. The differences between the global regime and the local field reflect the *glocal IP gap*.

The purpose here is threefold. First, I wish to offer a toolkit with which to assess a country's readiness to join the global regime. Better assessments can prevent hasty political decisions, later invariably described as ignorance, as some have characterized the Southern countries' joining the World Trade Organization (WTO) and the Agreement on Trade Related Aspects of Intellectual Property Rights (TRIPS).[2] Second, on a normative level, the proposed framework advocates

---

2. Agreement on Trade-Related Aspects of Intellectual Property Rights, Apr. 15, 1994, Marrakesh Agreement Establishing the World Trade Organization, Annex 1C, 33 I.L.M. 1125 (1994). Peter Yu observes that the story of TRIPS is usually told in one of four narratives: a bargain narrative, a coercion narrative, an ignorance narrative, and a self-interest narrative.

that we should consider a "big picture" instead of singular economic or legal measurements, to which the cultural field is often reduced. Comparing the copyright act of a country to the G© regime is the typical measure of legal compliance, as applied by the WTO or by the United States in its unilateral reviews. But such reductionism ignores local needs. The proposed framework warns against treating copyright as a mundane matter of trade, as it is often treated under the new G© regime. Once copyright is equated to bananas or online gambling, one should not wonder that traditional knowledge is left behind or that access to knowledge is neglected.[3] Third, on a theoretical level, the proposed framework attempts to take a close look at the actual mechanism of globalization and zoom in on the intersection of the global and the local. The proposed glocal IP yardstick reflects a more complex reality. It reflects the uniqueness of each country[4] and enables better calibration of the global regime.[5] It is then for each country to decide for itself whether it wishes to give up its own local needs for the benefits of the global regime.

A. Global Copyright Regime[6]

Up until the mid-1990s, national copyright systems around the world were governed by the rather loose framework of the Berne Convention for the

---

Yu argues that none of these narratives is complete, but each provides valuable insights into TRIPS. Peter K. Yu, *The First Ten Years of the TRIPS Agreement: TRIPS and Its Discontents*, 10 *Marq. Intell. Prop. L. Rev.* 369 (2006).

3. A trade dispute under the auspices of the World Trade Organization (WTO) between Ecuador and the EU over quotas of bananas almost resulted in a remedy in the copyright sector. See Panel Report *European Communities—Regime for the Importation, Sale and Distribution of Bananas—Recourse to Article 21.5 by Ecuador*, WT/DS27/RWECU (Apr. 12, 1999), which found that the EU had violated its commitments under the WTO. See WTO, *Overview of the State-of-Play of WTO Disputes* (July 13, 2001), available at http://www.wto.int/english/tratop_e/dispu_e/stplay_e.doc. Eventually, Ecuador did not pursue this remedy. For discussion, see Marco Bronckers and Naboth van den Broek, *Financial Compensation in the WTO, 8 J. Int'l Econ. L. 101*, 105 (2005). Similarly, following their successful challenge of the American ban on Americans' Internet gambling, the nation of Antigua and Barbuda asked the WTO to permit its citizens to violate IP laws, in case the United States does not comply with the ruling. See Gary Rivlin, "Gambling Dispute with a Tiny Country Puts U.S. in a Bind," *New York Times*, Aug. 23, 2007, available at http://tinyurl.com/6qldnh.

4. See, similarly, Carsten Fink and Keith E. Maskus, "Why We Study Intellectual Property Rights and What Have We Learned," in Carsten Fink and Keith E. Maskus, eds., *Intellectual Property and Development: Lessons from Recent Economic Research* 1, 2, 13 (World Bank & Oxford University Press, 2005).

5. Daniel Gervais in his chapter in this book discusses the need for calibration. I expand it to cover also cultural calibration.

6. This section partially builds on and updates previous work, Michael D. Birnhack, "Global Copyright, Local Speech," 24 *Cardozo Arts & Ent. L.J.* 491, 505–17 (2006).

Protection of Artistic and Literary Works (1886). The establishment of the WTO with TRIPS marked a significant change. The Berne Convention established minimum standards and some benefits for the countries that joined. However, not all countries became members, and there was no effective threat or a lucrative bonus for those who did join, but for a broad geographical coverage: the Convention includes a principle of national treatment, according to which member states are obliged to provide foreign nationals an equal level of protection to that provided to their own citizens. The United States, for example, joined Berne only in 1989; up until then, it had only been a member of the Universal Copyright Convention (UCC).[7] The Berne Convention is now incorporated by reference into the TRIPS Agreement.[8]

TRIPS is the baseline of the current phase of G©. It is now accompanied by a competing multilateral treaty, the World Intellectual Property Organization (WIPO) Copyright Treaty of 1996 (WCT), and by a set of bilateral agreements (mostly in the form of Free Trade Agreements [FTAs]) mainly between the United States and its trading partners, and the European Union and its trading partners. The United States and, recently, the European Union have also undertaken unilateral measures. The combination of the three layers—the multilateral, bilateral, and unilateral—results in an expanding spiral net, which forms the G© regime.[9]

The Berne Convention has been administered by WIPO since the 1967.[10] However, WIPO's "one nation, one vote" system has given developing countries the power to block the initiatives of industrialized nations.[11] Those nations and industries that wanted more protection (i.e., an expansion of the copyright bundle of rights, stronger protection, greater compliance, and better enforcement) have

---

7. Universal Copyright Convention, Sept. 6, 1952, 6.3 U.S.T. 2731, *revised* July 24, 1971, 25.2 UST 1341. Currently, 100 countries are party to the UCC, 64 of which have ratified the Paris Amendment. The UCC is administered by the United Nations Educational, Scientific, and Cultural Organization (UNESCO). Available at http://erc.unesco.org/cp/convention.asp?KO=15381&language=E.

8. TRIPS, art. 9(1).

9. Ruth Okediji suggests that we understand TRIPS as a "regime." Her analysis is based on a "regime theory," derived from international-relations theory and international law. See Ruth Okediji, "TRIPS Dispute Settlement and the Sources of (International) Copyright Law," 49 *J. Copyright Soc'y U.S.A.* 585, 597 (2001).

10. Prior to WIPO, the Berne Convention was administered by the United International Bureau for the Protection of Intellectual Property (better known as BIRPI, which is the French acronym). See WIPO's short history, available at http://www.wipo.int/treaties/en/general.

11. See Michael P. Ryan, *Knowledge Diplomacy: Global Competition and the Politics of Intellectual Property* 91, 104–13 (Brookings Institution Press, 1998); Peter Drahos, "Negotiating Intellectual Property Rights: Between Coercion and Dialogue," in Peter Drahos and Ruth Mayne, eds., *Global Intellectual Property Rights: Knowledge, Access and Development* 161, 166 (Palgrave, 2002).

had to turn to other forums.[12] The Uruguay Round of Trade Negotiations provided such a forum.[13] The initiative to include intellectual property issues within the framework of trade came from a group of industry leaders: the Advisory Committee on Trade Negotiation (ACTN), which persuaded the United States Trade Representative (USTR) to do so.[14] The United States applied political pressure against objecting developing countries in a process described by one scholar as no less than "bully[ing]."[15] In the TRIPS negotiations, developed countries applied a strategy of "linkage bargain diplomacy," in which they tied unrelated issues together and refused to break up the package: a developing country had an all-or-nothing choice.[16] In the case of TRIPS, the linkage was between IP and trade of goods, such as agricultural products and textiles. This "negotiation" strategy led to the inclusion of TRIPS in the framework of the WTO.

TRIPS now binds the 153 members of the WTO.[17] It includes several layers. The first is the requirement of minimum standards of protection by the incorporation of the Berne Convention, as supplemented in 1971, which ensures some commonality among member states.[18] The second layer adds new kinds of works to be protected and expands the bundle of rights beyond those guaranteed by the

---

12. See Laurence R. Helfer, "Regime Shifting: The TRIPS Agreement and New Dynamics of International Intellectual Property Lawmaking," 29 Yale J. Int'l L. 1, 20–21 (2004).

13. See Ryan, *Knowledge Diplomacy*, supra note 11, at 104-13. For a documentation of the shift from GATT to TRIPS, see Daniel Gervais, *The TRIPS Agreement: Drafting History and Analysis*, 10–26 (Sweet and Maxwell 2d ed., 2003).

14. See Ryan, *Knowledge Diplomacy*, supra note 11, at 105; Peter Drahos & John Braithwaite, *Information Feudalism: Who Owns the Knowledge Economy?* 114–20 (The New Press, 2002).

15. See Ryan, *Knowledge Diplomacy*, supra note 11, at 108. Drahos also documents the use by the United States of bilateral means to convince objecting countries to accept TRIPS, especially in the case of Brazil. Drahos, *Negotiating Intellectual Property Rights*, supra note 11, at 170–71.

16. Ryan, *Knowledge Diplomacy*, supra note 11, at 92.

17. See *Understanding the WTO: The Organization, Members and Observers*, WTO (Dec. 11, 2005), available at http://www.wto.org/english/thewto_e/whatis_e/tif_e/org6_e.htm, for a current list of WTO members. TRIPS set three dates for complying: 1996 for the developed countries, 2000 for the developing countries, and 2006 for the less developed countries, later to be extended to 2013, and to 2016 regarding provisions on pharmaceutical patents, as decided in the Doha Ministerial Declaration on the TRIPS agreement and Public Health. WTO, Ministerial Conference, WT/MIN(01)/DEC/2, (Nov. 20, 2001), available at http://www.wto.org/english/thewto_e/minist_e/min01_e/mindecl_trips_e.pdf.

18. One of TRIPS's novelties was the introduction of the "Most Favored Nation" (MFN) treatment in the context of IP. TRIPS, art. 4. See also 4 Melville B. Nimmer & David Nimmer, *Nimmer on Copyright* §18.06[A][1][b] (Matthew-Bender). This principle requires that *all* nationals of all WTO members should enjoy the same legal treatment. See Gervais, *The TRIPS Agreement*, supra note 13, at 104–10.

Berne Convention. For example, TRIPS requires protection for computer programs and grants the right of commercial rental for computer programs and sound recordings.[19] The third layer is enforcement.[20] TRIPS requires member countries to provide copyright owners with civil and administrative procedures to enforce their rights, as well as criminal penalties for violations of those rights. In practice, this requirement means that countries need to allocate resources and change their spending priorities according to external interests. Indeed, IP police units have been established worldwide.[21] A fourth layer is the WTO's dispute-settlement system, which is a central pillar of the multilateral trade system.[22] The dispute-settlement system creates one resolution mechanism for violations of any WTO agreement, including TRIPS. The authority to decide trade disputes lies with the WTO Dispute Settlement Body (DSB), which is the WTO's General Council.

---

19. TRIPS, arts. 10 (computer programs), 11 (rental rights).

20. TRIPS, pt. III. Gervais reports that the enforcement provisions of TRIPS were "drafted on the basis of concerns expressed by industry experts and other interested parties." Gervais, *The TRIPS Agreement*, supra note 13, at 69.

21. See, e.g., "Global Congress/Interpol Latin America Regional Forum on Combating Counterfeiting and Piracy," *The Rio Declaration* §§ 3, 4, 6, 7 (June 14, 2005), available at http://www.ccapcongress.net/archives/Regional/Files/Rio%20Declaration%20Final.doc; Interpol, Intellectual Property (IP) Crime, available at: http://www.interpol.int/Public/FinancialCrime/IntellectualProperty/Default.asp. This interference occurs despite article 41(5) of TRIPS, which declares that "[n]othing in this Part creates any obligation with respect to the distribution of resources as between enforcement of intellectual property rights and the enforcement of law in general." The reason for the redistribution of resources is the bilateral commitments and unilateral measures that require enforcement beyond TRIPS. See, e.g., art.15.11(3) of the United States–Morocco Free Trade Agreement, June 15, 2004, KAV 7206 (stating that "[t]he Parties understand that a decision that a Party makes on the distribution of enforcement resources shall not excuse that Party from complying with this Chapter"), available at http://www.ustr.gov/Trade_Agreements/Bilateral/Morocco_FTA/FInal_Text/Section_Index.html; Art. 17.11(2) of the United States–Chile Free Trade Agreement, June 6, 2003, KAV 6375, echoes TRIPS art. 41(5) but adds that "[t]he distribution of resources for the enforcement of intellectual property rights shall not excuse a Party from compliance with the provisions of this Article," available at http://www.ustr.gov/Trade_Agreements/Bilateral/Chile_FTA/Final_Texts/Section_Index.html. FTAs that are pending for Congressional approval or for implementation apply somewhat different language. See, e.g., United States–Peru FTA, art. 16.11, which echoes TRIPS, but adds (art. 16.11[4]) that "The Parties understand that a decision that a Party makes on the distribution of enforcement resources shall not be a reason for not complying with the provisions of this Chapter." Available at http://www.ustr.gov/Trade_Agreements/Bilateral/Peru_TPA/Final_Texts/Section_Index.html.

22. WTO, *Understanding on Rules and Procedures Governing the Settlement of Disputes*, at art. 3(2), (Apr. 15, 1994) available at http://www.wto.int/english/docs_e/legal_e/28-dsu_e.htm; WTO, Marrakesh Declaration of 15 April 1994, 1869 U.N.T.S. 401, 33 I.L.M. 1125 (1994), available at http://www.wto.int/english/docs_e/legal_e/marrakesh_decl_e.htm. Article 64 of TRIPS subjects it to the DSU.

In practice, the disputes are decided by special panels, which make recommendations to the DSB. A panel's recommendation is accepted, unless there is a consensus against it. Thus, the panels enjoy tremendous power.[23] A panel thus decides whether the "defendant" state provides adequate intellectual property protection. Upon a finding of noncompliance, the panel may authorize the complaining state to levy trade sanctions against the non-complying state. This layer renders TRIPS far more effective than any previous IP treaty.

For most Northern countries, the glocal IP gap is negligible. This is no wonder, as the global IP regime was designed according to their already existing laws, which in turn already reflected their local legal systems, cultures, economies, and international political power. For example, TRIPS incorporated the Berne Convention but left out the commitment to protect moral rights, which the United States has not expressly implemented, but for a minor exception.[24] In other cases, the Northern countries are simply strong enough to get away with their obligations.[25] This is illustrated in the case of the U.S. Fairness in Music Licensing Act (FIMLA).[26] FIMLA exempts small businesses, such as restaurants and bars, from liability when they play the radio or television in their public venue. A WTO panel found that the U.S. violates its TRIPS commitments,[27] but Congress has yet to take any step to amend the act, choosing instead to authorize annual monetary compensation to the aggrieved parties.

Southern countries, however, face a much wider glocal IP gap. The new IP laws, which they have enacted at the instruction of the global IP agents, do not suit their legal systems or their economic conditions and do not answer to their unique cultural needs. They are not strong enough to bring about changes. From a cultural viewpoint, the Development Agenda recently adopted by WIPO is best understood as a cry of despair from some of the stronger Southern countries, facing an almost unbridgeable glocal IP gap.[28]

WIPO, perhaps fearing that TRIPS would render it irrelevant, and perhaps driven by powerful industries, initiated amendments to the Berne Convention, which culminated in the "Internet Treaties" of 1996, the WCT, and the WIPO Performances

23. See arts. 16, 17(14).

24. See TRIPS, art. 9(1) and 17 U.S.C. §106A, respectively.

25. See Ruth Okediji, "TRIPS Dispute Settlement," supra note 9, at 634 (arguing that stronger countries are able to "bargain down" their TRIPS obligations).

26. As codified in 17 U.S.C. §110(5)(B).

27. Panel Report, *United States—Section 110(5) of the US Copyright Act*, WT/DS160/R (June 15, 2000). For an analysis of the decision, see Jo Oliver, "Copyright in the WTO: The Panel Decision on the Three Step Test," 25 *Colum. J. L. & Arts* 119 (2002).

28. In September 2007, WIPO's General Assembly adopted the Development Agenda, which originated in a proposal by Argentina and Brazil, submitted in 2004. For the proposal, see http://www.wipo.int/documents/en/document/govbody/wo_gb_ga/pdf/wo_ga_31_11.pdf. The stated goal of the proposal is to "ensure, in all countries, that the costs do not outweigh the benefits of IP protection." Id. at 2.

and Phonograms Treaty (WPPT).[29] Like TRIPS, the WCT incorporates the Berne Convention and further expands both the subject matter of copyright law and the accompanying bundle of rights. But the WCT expansions go beyond TRIPS. Most notably, Article 11 requires contracting countries to provide "adequate legal protection . . . against the circumvention of effective technological measures," or, in other words, to provide anti-circumvention rules as a protection for Technological Protection Measures (TPMs).[30] Currently, the WCT includes 65 members.[31]

TRIPS served a baseline for an additional layer of G©, in the form of a series of bilateral agreements, mostly FTAs. These bilateral agreements resulted in a "TRIPS-plus" regime,[32] through a process of global "ratcheting up."[33] Examples are that parties to the FTA should provide authors the exclusive right to make their works available to the public[34] and should enact anti-circumvention rules.[35] These two obligations are required by the WCT but not by TRIPS.[36] Australia and Morocco, for example, committed, in their FTAs with the United States, to enact anti-circumvention statutes, even though at the time they had not ratified the WCT.[37] The bilateral layer builds on the multilateral layer and should be understood as a deliberate strategy.[38]

29. WCT: WIPO Copyright Treaty, Dec. 20, 1996, 36 I.L.M. 65 (1997), at art. 1(1), available at http://www.wipo.int/treaties/en/ip/wct/trtdocs_wo033.html. More precisely, the WCT is a "special agreement" within the meaning of article 20 of the Berne Convention. See art. 1(1). WPPT: Dec. 20, 1996, 36 I.L.M. 76 (1997). Here I focus on the WCT.

30. This section of the WCT served American content industries to convince Congress to enact the anti-circumvention rules in the Digital Millennium Copyright Act of 1998, 17 U.S.C. §§ 1201–05 (2006).

31. See WIPO, *Contracting Parties: WCT*, available at http://www.wipo.int/treaties/en/ShowResults.jsp?lang=en&treaty_id=16.

32. Peter Yu suggests that we distinguish between various kinds of provisions, such as TRIPS-plus and TRIPS-extra. See Peter K. Yu, "The International Enclosure Movement," 82 *Ind. L.J.* 827 (2007).

33. See Peter Drahos, "Securing the Future of Intellectual Property: Intellectual Property Owners and Their Nodally Coordinated Enforcement Pyramid," 36 *Case W. Res. J. Int'l L.* 53, 55 (2004) (describing the process in which bilateral agreements ratchet up the level of intellectual property protection).

34. See U.S.-Chile FTA, art. 17.5(3); U.S.-Australia Free Trade Agreement, May 18, 2004, 43 I.L.M. 1248, art. 17.4(2); U.S.-Bahrain Free Trade Agreement Sept. 14, 2004, 44 I.L.M. 544, art. 14.4(2); U.S.-Morocco FTA, art. 15.5(3).

35. See U.S.-Chile FTA, art. 17.7(5); U.S.-Australia FTA, art. 17.4(7); U.S.-Bahrain FTA, art. 14.4(7); U.S.-Morocco FTA, art. 15.5(8).

36. See WCT, art. 6 (regarding making works available), art. 11 (regarding anti-circumvention rules).

37. See U.S.-Australia FTA, art. 17.4(7); U.S.-Morocco FTA, art. 15.5(8). Australia joined the WCT in 2007. Morocco is required, under the FTA, to ratify the WCT, but had not yet done so at the time of writing.

38. See Eyal Benvenisti and George W. Downs, "The Empire's New Clothes: Political Economy and the Fragmentation of International Law," 60 *Stan. L. Rev.* 595 (2007).

Unilateral measures provide a powerful means to expand IP rights. One such measure is found in the European Union, in the form of the Trade Barrier Regulation of 1994, which enables private entities to complain to the European Commission about third countries' breach of their commitments under international trade treaties.[39] However, this mechanism is not a pure unilateral measure, as it channels the private complaints to WTO's dispute resolution procedure.

The most influential unilateral measure is found in section 301 of the U.S. Trade Act of 1974, as amended.[40] The Act empowers the USTR to examine the level of protection afforded to American-owned intellectual property in countries with which the United States has trade relations. Following a 1988 amendment,[41] the USTR publishes an annual report on intellectual property, in a process called "Special 301."[42] Countries are placed on one of several lists: Priority Foreign Country (PFC), Priority Watch List (PWL), and Watch List (WL). Classification as a PFC, the worst category, might result in trade sanctions, although this has not yet happened. Classification in any list is likely to result in heavy political pressure. The Trade Act was amended in 1994 to enable the USTR to reach a finding that a country's IP protection is inadequate, even if the country is TRIPS-compliant.[43] This is a powerful TRIPS-plus mechanism. Following a European challenge, a WTO panel found that section 301 does not violate the WTO dispute-settlement system per se, but that it must be

39. See Council Regulation 3286/94 of 22 December 1994 laying down community procedures in the field of the common commercial policy in order to ensure the exercise of the community's rights under international trade rules, in particular those established under the auspices of the World Trade Organization, available at http://ec.europa.eu/trade/issues/respectrules/tbr/legis/adgrego6a.htm. For detailed discussion, see Marco Bronckers and Natalie McNelis, "The EU Trade Barriers Regulation Comes of Age," 35(4) *J. of World Trade* 427 (2001); Stephen Woolcock, "European Union Trade Policy: Domestic Institutions and Systematic Factors," in Dominic Kelly and Wyn Grant, eds., *The Politics of International Trade in the Twenty-First Century* 234, 242–43 (Palgrave, 2005).

40. Trade Act of 1974, Pub. L. 93-618, 88 Stat. 2041 (1975) (codified as amended at 19 U.S.C. §§2411–2420, 2242).

41. Omnibus Trade and Competitiveness Act of 1988, Pub. L. 100-418, 102 Stat. 1107.

42. See 19 U.S.C. §2242.

43. See Pub. L. 103-465, 108 Stat. 4939, amending 19 U.S.C. §2411(d)(3), which states in subsection (A) that "An act, policy, or practice is unreasonable if the act, policy, or practice, while not necessarily in violation of, or inconsistent with, the international legal rights of the United States, is otherwise unfair and inequitable," and in subsection (B) defines "fair and inequitable" to include "provision of adequate and effective protection of intellectual property rights notwithstanding the fact that the foreign country may be in compliance with the specific obligations of the Agreement on Trade-Related Aspects of Intellectual Property Rights" (19 U.S.C. §2411(d)(3)(B)(i)(II)).

applied in accordance therewith.[44] Later on, we shall take a close look at the 301 process.[45]

Thus, G© is a complex web of interrelated layers of international law. Unlike the elaborate philosophical understanding of copyright law in the United States or Continental European countries, G© is devoid of theory, reflecting instead an ideology of trade, or more precisely, free trade.[46]

B. The Local Field of Cultural Production[47]

Lawyers tend to evaluate social fields according to their regulatory scheme. We can compare a country's copyright law to the G© requirements, to determine, for example, whether a country is TRIPS-compliant or whether it provides anti-circumvention rules according to the WCT. However, the law reveals only part of the picture.

Several factors compose a country's cultural field, other than the copyright act itself: the legal system as a whole, the economic status of the country, its unique cultural features, and its internal and external politics. These are broad categories which can subsume other considerations, such as a country's history or educational system. In order to be able to evaluate a country's cultural field, it is insufficient to look at the law alone, or at the economy alone, or to isolate any other single factor, for that matter.

Accordingly, we should undertake a complex, multi-factor, holistic analysis of a country in order to be able to evaluate its copyright status. We should search for the aforementioned factors and study them carefully. Furthermore, we should attempt an even more ambitious task and search for the many relationships between these factors. How did a country's political situation affect its choice of a regulatory scheme? Which role did the economy play in adopting the copyright act? How did cultural needs factor in? What was the interaction between the economy and the culture? Another complicating element is that none of these factors, let alone their interactions, is static. To the contrary, the overall picture is in a state of continuous change. This is a complex task, but it is worth pursuing, as it will enable decision-makers, both within the country and at the global level, to better adjust policies and ease friction at the glocal meeting point. It also fits

44. See Panel Report, *United States—Sections 301–310 of the Trade Act of 1974*, WT/DS152/R (Dec. 22, 1999); Lina M. Montén, "The Inconsistency between Section 301 and TRIPS: Counterproductive with Respect to the Future of International Protection of Intellectual Property Rights?" 9 *Marq. Intell. Prop. L. Rev.* 387 (2005).

45. See part III.B.2 infra.

46. For a view that celebrates copyright as trade, see Joseph Strauss, "The Impact of the New World Order on Economic Development: The Role of the Intellectual Property Rights System," 15 *Eur. Rev.* 47 (2007).

47. The term is derived from Pierre Bourdieu, *The Field of Cultural Production* (Columbia University Press, 1993).

the Development Agenda neatly. Let us look briefly into the main factors of the proposed framework.

1. **The Legal System** The copyright law should be located on the broader map of the local legal system of a country. Other fields of law might address certain aspects of the copyright regime or affect them, by either expanding or decreasing the scope of IP protection. For example, contract law can determine which transactions can or cannot be done with copyrighted works.[48] Employment law might affect allocation rules of the copyright of works made within the context of the workplace.[49] Antitrust law might limit the freedom of copyright owners to perform certain activities or affect the collective management of rights.[50] Another central field in this legal map is free speech.[51] The non-copyright legal landscape can either be a substitute for some of the G© requirements[52] or render existing copyright rules less effective.

Furthermore, the power of the judiciary vis-à-vis the legislature needs to be addressed. In some jurisdictions, courts enjoy a wide leeway in interpreting legislation, whereas in others they carefully follow the legislative text, to the extent that it is clear enough. Recall, for example, the introduction of the fair use

---

48. See, e.g., in Germany, where a detailed regime of contracts relating to copyright is adjunct to the copyright act. See Act on Strengthening the Contractual Position of Authors and Performers of March 22, 2002. For discussion, see Reto M. Hilty and Alexander Peukert, "'Equitable Remuneration' in Copyright Law: The Amended German Copyright Act as a Trap for the Entertainment Industry in the U.S.?" 22 *Cardozo Arts & Ent. L.J.* 401, 416–21 (2004); Gerhard Schricker, "Efforts for a Better Law on Copyright Contracts in Germany—A Never-Ending Story?" 35 *IIC* 850 (2004).

49. To the extent that courts deciding copyright disputes search for guidance in employment law or agency law, for example, in determining whether an author is an employee or an independent contractor. See, e.g., Community for Creative Non-Violence v. Reid, 490 U.S. 730 (1989); Robert A. Kreiss, "Scope of Employment and Being an Employee under the Work-Made-for-Hire Provision of the Copyright Law: Applying the Common-Law Agency Tests," 40 *U. Kan. L. Rev.* 119 (1991).

50. See Ariel Katz, "The Potential Demise of another Natural Monopoly: Rethinking the Collective Administration of Performing Rights," 2(2) *J. of Competition L. & Econ.* 245 (2006).

51. For discussion of the copyright–speech relationship, see Michael D. Birnhack, "Freedom of Speech," Chapter 19E, *Nimmer on Copyright* (2007) (in the U.S. context); Michael D. Birnhack, "Acknowledging the Conflict between Copyright Law and Freedom of Expression under the Human Rights Act," *Ent. L. Rev.* 24 (2003) (in the UK); Michael D. Birnhack, "Copyrighting Speech: A Trans-Atlantic View," in Paul Torremans, ed., *Copyright and Human Rights* 37 (Kluwer Law International, 2004) (comparing the United States and Europe).

52. Thus, for example, the United States was of the opinion that no changes in American law were required following its adherence to the Berne Convention because of "adequate practical equivalents." See discussion in Jane C. Ginsburg and John M. Kernochan, "One Hundred and Two Years Later: The United States Joins the Berne Convention," 13 *Colum. VLA J. of L. & the Arts* 1 (1988), esp. at 27–31.

defense into American law in *Folsom v. Marsh*, in 1841,[53] to be incorporated in the statute 135 years later.[54] The central role of the originality requirement, declared by the Supreme Court in its 1991 case of *Feist Publications, Inc. v. Rural Telephone Service Company, Inc.*, to be the sine qua non of copyright law, is yet another example of the power of the judiciary.[55] A related matter to be studied is the constitutional setting. The constitution creates and limits the judiciary's power to interpret a law in general and the copyright law in particular.[56] This is true of many constitutions, not only the U.S. Constitution, which is explicit about the issue of copyright.[57]

Another important element is a country's prevailing theory of copyright law. There are several competing philosophies of copyright, ranging from a Hegelian, personality-based theory that emphasizes the importance of the relationship between an author and her work, to a labor theory, emphasizing the time, effort, and, more generally, the labor, invested by an author, to an instrumental, incentive-based theory.[58] In many cases the different theories lead to the same conclusion, creating no need to choose among them. In some instances, however, they dictate contradictory results. Moral rights, for example, are justified mostly under a personality-based theory—hardly so under an economic-based, incentive theory.[59]

When we evaluate the impact of G© on a country, we should be aware of a country's choice of copyright theory, to the extent that it has so chosen. In some cases, the G© regime is imposed onto existing copyright law in a country that may have a preference for one philosophical justification, resulting in a theoretical mixture or conflict.

2. **Economics** The economic status of a country is the main criterion in the familiar globalization scale of developed, developing, and least developed countries (LDCs). The group at the bottom end of the scale is determined by the United Nations, which publishes an authoritative list, based on three criteria: low income, a capital status (which in turn is based on a composite Human Assets Index that takes into account nutrition, mortality among children, education,

---

53. 9F. Cas. 342, 344 (C.C.D. Mass. 1841).

54. 17 U.S.C. §107.

55. 499 U.S. 340, 345 (1991).

56. The constitutional limits extend both to the courts' power vis-à-vis Congress and their power to interpret the copyright clause. For both strands, see Eldred v. Ashcroft, 537 U.S. 186 (2003).

57. U.S. Const. art. 1, §8 cl.8.

58. For theories of copyright law, see Edwin C. Hettinger, "Justifying Intellectual Property," 18 *Phil. & Pub. Aff.* 31 (1989); Justin Hughes, "The Philosophy of Intellectual Property," 77 *Geo. L.J.* 287 (1988).

59. See Roberta Rosenthal Kwall, "Inspiration and Innovation: The Intrinsic Dimension of the Artistic Soul," 81 *Notre Dame L. Rev.* 1945 (2006).

and adult literacy), and an economic-vulnerability criterion.[60] Currently, there are 50 countries on this list.[61] There is no authoritative list of the members at the top-end of the globalization scale, and the conventional classification is based on combining membership in the Organization for Economic Cooperation and Development (OECD) with the data provided by the World Bank. The latter, not surprisingly, classifies countries according to economic indices, namely the Gross National Income (GNI) per capita. It lists 27 high-income countries.[62] The rest of the countries constitute the developing countries. The World Bank offers an internal classification, based on economic criteria.[63]

The globalization scale is carried into the realm of global IP through the WTO, which relies on the UN's LDC list but enables each remaining country to choose for itself its status as a developed or developing country.[64] The choice is important, as the LDCs have been given longer transition periods for implementing TRIPS.[65]

To better evaluate the copyright field, the macroeconomic data about the size and strength of an economy is an important background, but it does not provide the entire picture. The cultural market should be examined as well, both in terms of its components and of the market as a whole. Such a study should be conducted on a per-industry basis: publishing, music, motion picture, software, etc.[66] Each of the industries has a unique structure and features. For example, the authors' (including all kinds of artists and producers of creative works) bargaining power vis-à-vis the relevant industries is important. Independent musicians have a different position in their negotiations with the producer than do architects, who negotiate directly with clients. Another example is the role of language in each of these industries. Print is extensively language-based and

60. See The Criteria for the Identification of the LDCs, available at http://www.un.org/special-rep/ohrlls/ldc/ldc%20criteria.htm, and criticism at Wolfgang Sachs, *"Neo-Development: Global Ecological Management,"* in Jerry Mander and Edward Goldsmith, eds., *The Case Against the Global Economy and for a Turn Toward the Local* 239–41 (Sierra Club Books, 1996).

61. Available at http://www.un.org/special-rep/ohrlls/ldc/list.htm.

62. The World Bank's list is available at http://tinyurl.com/ane6m; the OECD's list is available at http://tinyurl.com/2jksv.

63. The World Bank divides the developing and developed countries into "low income economies" (49 countries); lower-middle income countries (54), upper-middle income economies (41), and high-income economies (65). See The World Bank, Data & Statistics, Country Groups by Income, available at http://tinyurl.com/2agxhp.

64. See WTO, *Who Are the Developing Countries in the WTO?*, http://www.wto.org/english/tratop_e/devel_e/d1who_e.htm.

65. See supra note 17.

66. The sub-discipline of cultural economics provides such research. See Ruth Towse, "Introduction," in Ruth Towse, ed., *A Handbook of Cultural Economics* 1 (Edward Elgar, 2003), and other contributions therein.

corresponds to the level of literacy in a country. Music is less language-dependent and, hence, might thrive despite low literacy rates. Thus, the import/export balance of cultural products should also be evaluated, and the participants should be identified.[67] Per-industry studies might teach us about the players in the field, their interests, and the level of efficiency (and the possible deficiencies) of each particular market. Such particularized study might slightly ease the rather blunt "one-size-fits-all" approach of copyright law, which is not sensitive to the differences between various kinds of authors in different fields.

3. **Culture** Culture is a fuzzy term, and measuring it is an elusive task. UNESCO's Convention on the Protection and Promotion of the Diversity of Cultural Expressions, which took effect in March 2007, can provide a good starting point for devising a measure of local cultural concerns.[68] Unlike the economic studies, there is no one yardstick that fits all cultures. Some countries devote much attention and effort to preserving and enhancing at least some aspects of their culture, such as language, heritage, or traditional knowledge. Demographics, language, history, and sociology all play a role here. Official cultural policies are yet another important source: Which sectors does a government wish to promote? How does it perceive the needs of the local community/ies? An additional relevant factor is the tradition of free speech,[69] which often reflects a country's history, as well as the current sociopolitical issues with which it struggles and which are central to a nation's communal life. Having a detailed picture of the local cultural field, including its players, achievements, mix of interests, needs, and weaknesses, will enable a better-tailored implementation of G© and perhaps reduce cultural costs.

4. **Politics** Politics is yet another fuzzy term. Understanding the political situation of a country will better explain the commitments it has undertaken and those it has avoided, while enabling us to evaluate the present and future pressures that the country is likely to face. Relevant facts are a country's ability to bargain down its international commitments[70] and its relative political power on

67. Ed Baker examines the relationship between a policy of global free trade and cultural products and argues that the latter should not be subject to the former. See C. Edwin Baker, "An Economic Critique of Free Trade in Media Products," 78 *N.C. L. Rev.* 1357 (2000). He distinguishes between cultural products that have universal content and those that have domestic content and observes that the universal products often include action, violence, and sex, as these things have universal appeal. See id., at 1384 and 1397. He further argues that the cultural products with high levels of universal content and little domestic content will marginalize or replace domestic products. See at 1396.

68. Available at http://tinyurl.com/2h9swz. For the relationship between the Convention and the global IP regime, see Laurence R. Helfer, "Toward A Human Rights Framework for Intellectual Property," 40 *U.C. Davis L. Rev.* 971, 1001–1007 (2007).

69. See Birnhack, "Global Copyright," supra note 6, at 530–36.

70. See Okediji, supra note 9.

a bilateral scale vis-à-vis its trade partners. One can assume that the discussions between the USTR and Canada or members of the European Union differ greatly from the nature of the discussions between each of these parties and a developing country or an LDC. The relative power of a country is even more acute in the unilateral layer. A possible American threat to impose economic sanctions on a country because of its position in the "Special 301" report affects the Ukraine differently than it affects China or Canada, for example.

C. The Glocal Situation

Each of the local factors outlined above, and taken together, interacts with the G© regime. The result is the meeting of global law with local legal system/economics/culture/politics. The glocal situation can be a rosy picture of a productive joint venture and the convergence of local and global interests, but it can also be a battle zone, where mighty forces collide or where one mighty party crushes a weaker party.

It is crucial to identify the hidden costs of the G© regime. The costs can be financial and direct, such as an external requirement to devote more resources to establish IP law enforcement units,[71] or indirect, in cases where adhering to global standards means that a country needs to allocate more money to providing updated books to maintain its level of education, as copying of books is no longer acceptable, or, if no funds are allocated, the quality of education is likely to deteriorate.[72] The money might remain within the country's borders, facilitating the growth of a local print industry, but it can also find its way to foreign hands, thus affecting macroeconomic figures. G© can also have a non-monetary impact. For example, G© requirements may undermine local culture by fostering a steady importation of foreign movies, mostly those produced in Hollywood, to the detriment of a local movie industry. This may run counter to tradition in some countries, whereas in others it might offer a welcome change.[73]

---

71. See, e.g., Denis Borges Barbosa, *Counting Ten for TRIPs: Author Rights and Access to Information—A Cockroach's View of Encroachment*, available at http://ssrn.com/abstract=842564 (stating that in Brazil, "[s]pecial courts and special forces were created to pursue [IP enforcement], even though the increase of budgetary and personal resources was not proportionately extended to other pressing needs, like fighting drug-related crime").

72. See, e.g., a comment about Indonesian students, in Simon Butt, "Intellectual Property in Indonesia: A Problematic Legal Transplant," 24 *E.I.P.R.* 429, 432 (2002), and about a student protest in Brazil, following changes in copyright law that restricted copying in educational books, in Ronaldo Lemos, "From Legal Commons to Social Commons: Brazil and the Cultural Industries in the 21st Century," 15–17, Working Paper Centre for Brazilian Studies CBS-80-07 (2007), available at http://www.brazil.ox.ac.uk/workingpapers/R.%20Lemos80.pdf.

73. See Keith Acheson, "Globalization," in *A Handbook of Cultural Economics*, supra note 66, at 248.

III. CASE STUDY: ISRAEL

This section applies the general framework presented above to Israel. The case study reflects how a country can be caught in the spiral net of the G© regime. This is not to say that Israel does not have its own economic and cultural interests in expanding copyright protection. It does.[74] Rather, the emphasis here is on understanding the complexity of the picture, recognizing the glocal gap, and allowing for a better understanding of the process. I begin by discussing the four main factors and then explore the glocal process (i.e., how the global regime is applied to a local setting), with a focus on the unilateral process. Here, we observe an interesting pattern in which local industries use their foreign affiliates as an external source of leverage on the Israeli government.

A. The Cultural Field

1. **The Legal System** Current Israeli copyright is a multi-layered legislation, reflecting the legal history of the country. Under the Ottoman regime, which lasted for four centuries until 1917, no official copyright law was in place. In 1924, the British who ruled then-Palestine under a United Nations Mandate implemented two main statutes: the first is the 1911 Copyright Act.[75] Whereas in other legal fields the British implemented Ordinances, the 1911 Act was the very English Act which was in force in England, with some minor modifications. The Act was supplemented with the Copyright Ordinance of 1924.[76] The Act and the Ordinance enjoy the same legal status and should be read together. Both were absorbed into Israeli law in 1948, upon the establishment of the state. Unlike most other British Mandatory legislation, the authoritative language of the statutes till this day is the English version.[77] In 1953, the 1911 Act was given a Hebrew name.[78] Until then, the Hebrew title of the Act was the phonetic spelling of the English word "copyright." The 1953 amendment opted for the phrase *Zchuyot Yotsrim*, which means authors' rights. This was a first tilt toward the Continental understanding of copyright as law of authors' rights.

The Israeli parliament, the Knesset, amended the statutes over the years: protecting computer programs as literary works (1988), defining criminal acts (1981, 1988, 2002), adding statutory damages (1981), and providing an exemption for

---

74. Applying the classification offered by Daniel Gervais in his chapter, Israel's benefits from innovation outweigh the rent seeking extracted by industrialized countries through the TRIPS regime.

75. See Copyright Act of 1911, 3 Hukey Eretz Israel 2475.

76. See Copyright Ordinance of 1924, 1 Hukey Eretz Israel 389.

77. Other than the colonial symbolism of the foreign language, the English origin is far better than the Hebrew translation. The Hebrew version, for example, omitted the word "original" in the first section of the act. It took a Supreme Court decision to state that the originality requirement is valid in Israeli copyright law. See CA 360/83 Strosky Ltd. v. Vitman Ice-cream Ltd., 40(3) P.D. 340, 346 (1985) [Hebrew].

78. See Copyright Act (Amendment) of 1953, LSI 38.

private use, accompanied with a levy system and governmental compensation to copyright owners (1996). An important amendment added moral rights to the bundle of rights (1981), reflecting another tilt, this time not only symbolic, as was the 1953 amendment, toward the Continental understanding.[79]

The Knesset recently passed a new copyright act, which came into force in May 2008.[80] The new act is mostly a restatement of the old statutes in up-to-date language, with several important additions: the addition of a general derivative right and the right to make available a work, an explicit reference to temporary copying, and some other changes. The act also marked a shift from the English fair-dealing defense to the American fair-use defense. Interestingly, it does not include anti-circumvention rules.[81]

On the multilateral layer of the global front, Israel joined the Berne Convention in 1950, and in 2003, following an agreement with the European Communities, it adhered to the Paris Act.[82] Israel has also been a member of the UCC since 1955. Israel joined the WTO in 1995 and opted for the status of a developing country, which allowed it a five-year grace period to update its IP laws. It did so in December 1999.[83] In the copyright realm, Israel's TRIPS implementation legislation clarified that the protection to computer programs extends both to source code and object code, added a rental right for computer programs, and codified courts' prior holdings that ideas, concepts, mathematical terms, facts, and news of the day are unprotected subject matter. The TRIPS amendments also included some minor modifications in the area of remedies. Israel has not ratified or implemented the WCT.[84] Thus, Israel has undertaken no international obligation to enact—and has not enacted—anti-circumvention rules.

On the bilateral level, Israel has been committed to protecting U.S. works since 1948.[85] In 1985 the United States and Israel signed an FTA, the first-ever

---

79. See chronologically, Copyright Act (Amendment) of 1981, LSI 300; Copyright Act (Amendment) of 1988, LSI 171; Copyright Act (Amendment) of 1996, LSI 244; Copyright Act (Amendment) of 2002, LSI 4.

80. See Copyright Act of 2007, LSI 34.

81. The Ministry of Justice published a "call for comments" on the matter in February 2007 and, after a review, has decided not to include anti-circumvention rules within the new act.

82. See http://www.wipo.int/treaties/en/Remarks.jsp?cnty_id=972C. The Paris Act added an appendix to the Berne Convention, which provides developing countries with the option to expand the exceptions to the right of reproduction and translation. See *WIPO Intellectual Property Handbook: Policy, Law, and Use* (2d ed., Geneva, 2004), at §§5.186–5.193, 5.201, 5.205 (pp. 265–68), available at http://www.wipo.int/about-ip/en/iprm/pdf/ch5.pdf#berne.

83. See Act to Amend Intellectual Property Laws (Adjustment to the TRIPS Agreement) of 1999, LSI 44.

84. See http://www.wipo.int/treaties/en/Remarks.jsp?cnty_id=1514C.

85. See Copyright Decree (United States), KT 365 (1953), which instructs that the decree is effective retroactively.

FTA of the United States, which includes a general statement reaffirming the countries' mutual obligations in the field of IP[86] but is otherwise far from resembling the highly detailed IP sections found in recent FTAs of the United States with its trade partners.[87] Israel is also committed to an "association agreement" with the European Communities which came into force in 2000. That agreement requires that IP be protected "in accordance with the highest international standards."[88]

On the unilateral level, Israel has been subject to routine reviews of the USTR and has not fared well on section 301 reports. This layer will be discussed later.[89]

In short, Israel's copyright legislation has an English basis with some important Continental additions and an international/global influence. For its part, Israel's judiciary has been deeply influenced, first by English, and subsequently by American, case law.[90] Thus, for example, whereas early interpretations of the requirement of originality turned to British case law, newer cases explicitly adopted the rule and spirit of *Feist*.[91] An interesting example of imposing U.S. law onto U.K. law is the fair-dealing exception. The 1911 Act provided that "any fair dealing with any work for the purposes of private study, research, criticism, review or newspaper summary" shall not constitute an infringement.[92] Israeli courts interpreted the exception to cover only uses that fall within the five enumerated purposes, deemed to be a "closed" list, although the Supreme Court was willing to interpret the five purposes quite broadly (e.g., so that "criticism"

---

86. See art. 14 of the United States–Israel Free Trade Agreement, Apr. 22, 1985, 25 I.L.M. 653, available at http://tcc.export.gov/Trade_Agreements/All_Trade_Agreements/exp_005439.asp (stating that "The Parties reaffirm their obligations under bilateral and multilateral agreements relating to intellectual property rights, including industrial property rights, in effect between the Parties. Accordingly, nationals and companies of each Party shall continue to be accorded national and most favored nation treatment with respect to obtaining, maintaining and enforcing patents of invention, with respect to obtaining and enforcing copyrights, and with respect to rights in trademarks, service marks, trade names, trade labels, and industrial property of all kinds").

87. The Israeli government is currently (as of March 2008) reviewing the FTA to assess whether it would like to initiate negotiations for a new FTA with the United States.

88. See art. 39 of the Euro-Mediterranean Agreement, OJ L147/3 (2000), available at http://www.moital.gov.il/NR/old_res/F116E87E_F0ED_413D_93DA_ABA0C9D44E56.files/agreem.doc.

89. See infra, part III.B.2.

90. Courts reduced their citations to English law and increased citations to American law. See Yoram Shachar, Ron Harris, and Meron Gross, "Citation Practices of the Supreme Court, Quantitative Analysis," 27 *Mishpatim* 119, 157 (1996) [Hebrew].

91. See CA 513/89 Interlego A/S v. Exin-Lines Bros. SA 48(4) P.D. 133, 166 (1994) [Hebrew].

92. See s. 2(1) of the 1911 Copyright Act.

includes also positive evaluations and parodies).[93] However, the Court also inserted into the English fair-dealing exception the four American fair-use factors, requiring that an excepted use must both fall within an enumerated fair-dealing category and pass muster under the fair-use test.[94] The result was the worst of each model: the rigidity of the English fair dealing version, which at least had relative predictability, was supplemented with the open-ended elements of American fair use. Thus, the exception was not flexible enough to include uses such as teaching or reverse engineering, and it was difficult to rely on it ex ante, as it is applied on a case-by-case basis. The new copyright act shifts to the fair-use defense and abandons the fair-dealing approach.

An important characteristic of Israeli law is the relative power of the judiciary vis-à-vis the legislature. Courts, acting within a common-law tradition, do not shy away from interpreting statutes broadly, turning to comparative sources, declaring new causes of action, and the like. Courts do not see themselves bound by black-letter legislation. Rather, courts search for a statute's purpose. This is found not only in the text and original intent of the legislators, but often within theoretical analyses.[95] In the realm of copyright, perhaps because of the multi-layered character of the law, courts have declared that the overarching philosophy of Israeli copyright law is the Anglo-American tradition, and more specifically incentive-based theory.[96] However, this declaration is not always applied consistently. Some cases clearly tend toward a Continental, author-centric view of copyright law.[97]

As noted in the previous section, the copyright act should be located within the legal system as a whole. Several other statutes should be mentioned here. Antirust law, for example, has been applied to the collective societies of authors and music producers.[98] Labor law has affected the definition of an employee

---

93. See CA 2687/92 Geva v. Walt Disney Inc. 48(1) P.D. 251 (1993) [Hebrew].

94. See Geva, id.

95. See Aharon Barak, *Purposive Interpretation in Law* (Princeton University Press, 2005). For the transformation of Israeli law see Menachem Mautner, *The Decline of Formalism and the Rise of Values in Israeli Law* (1995) [Hebrew].

96. See Interlego; CA 326/00 City of Holon v. N.M.C. Music Ltd. 57(3) P.D. 658 (2003) [Hebrew].

97. The most recent example is found in the Dead Sea Scrolls case, in which the Supreme Court determined that a researcher who deciphered an ancient scroll was entitled to the copyright in the deciphered text. See CA 2790, 2811/93 Eisenman v. Qimron, 54(3) P.D. 817 (2000) [Hebrew] (an unofficial translation is available at http://www.tau.ac.il/law/members/birnhack/DSStransaltion.pdf); Michael D. Birnhack, "The Dead Sea Scrolls Case: Who Is an Author?" 23 *E.I.P.R.* 128 (2001); David Nimmer, "The Dead Sea Scrolls: Authorship and Originality," 38 *Houston L. Rev.* 1 (2001).

98. See Determination of the General Director of the Israeli Antitrust Authority re Acum (Society of Authors, Composers, and Music Publishers in Israel) as a monopoly (March 2004); A"T 3574/00 Israeli Recording Industry Association v. The Director General of the Israeli Antitrust Authority (Jerusalem District Court, 2004).

within the context of the work-made-for-hire doctrine.[99] The Unjust Enrichment Act provides an additional legal avenue to copyright owners, if some threshold is met.[100]

Another important element is the constitutional setting. Israel has a series of Basic Laws, which are of constitutional magnitude and are interpreted to allow judicial review. These include, inter alia, the constitutional protection of private property.[101] In one of its opinions, albeit an intermediate decision authored by one Justice alone, the Supreme Court has stated that copyright, as a branch of intellectual property, should be considered "property" for the purposes of constitutional law.[102] This controversial statement has been applied by lower courts to strengthen copyright protection in several cases, with the result that injunctions are considered a prime remedy.

In sum, Israeli copyright law is by and large TRIPS-compliant, and a technical legal comparison of Israel's copyright law to its international commitments would indicate that Israel's glocal IP gap is negligible. Those interested in greater protection complain about insufficiencies in Israeli copyright law, but they tend to focus on the language of the Copyright Act and Ordinance, ignoring liberal judicial interpretation and other aspects of the surrounding legal environment.

2. Economics: Heading North Here are some figures:[103] Israel is classified by the World Bank as a high-income developing country. With $142.5 billion GDP (2007),[104] the Gross National Income (GNI) per capita is $19,890 (2006). With a population of 7.2 million (2008), it is a small economy. After a recession during 2001–02, the economy is steadily growing at rates of 5 (2006)[105] and 6

---

99. Compare CA 571/68 Yanai v. Mansfeld, 23(1) P.D. 501 (1969) [Hebrew] (applying a "control test") to CC 2184/90 (Tel Aviv District Court) Haaretz v. Bugss, (unpublished opinion) (1996) [Hebrew] (applying the "integration test").

100. See the decision by the Supreme Court in L.C.A. 5768/94 A.Sh.I.R Import, Export & Distribution v. Forum Accessories and Consumer Products Ltd., 52(4) P.D. 289 (1998) [Hebrew] (finding that plaintiffs who cannot sue under an IP cause of action may nevertheless assert that their rights under the Unjust Enrichment Act, 1979).

101. See art. 3 of Basic Law: Human Dignity and Liberty.

102. See C.A. 6141/02 Acu"m v. I.D.F. Radio, 57(2) P.D. 625 (2003) [Hebrew].

103. The data is drawn from several sources: Israel Central Bureau of Statistics (CBS), 58 Statistical Abstract of Israel 2007, available at http://www1.cbs.gov.il/reader/shnatone-new_site.htm (hereafter: CBS 2007); WTO Trade Policy Review, Report by the Secretariat, WT/TPR/S/157 (Dec. 22, 2005), available at http://www.wto.org/english/tratop_e/tpr_e/s157-0_e.doc (hereafter: WTO TPR); The World Bank, Israel Data Profile, available at http://devdata.worldbank.org/external/CPProfile.asp?PTYPE=CP&CCODE=ISR; The Israel Export and International Cooperation Institute, Trade Overview—Summary Report 2006, available at http://www.export.gov.il/_Uploads/15362israel.pdf.

104. CBS 2007, table 28.6 available at http://www1.cbs.gov.il/shnaton58/download/st28_06.xls.

105. CBS 2006, available at http://www.cbs.gov.il/dafdefet_02/indictb1h_07.pdf.

(2007) percent.[106] A WTO report, issued in 2005, notes that, in proportion to GDP, Israel ranks first worldwide in its investment in research and development, second in quality of education, and third in entrepreneurship.[107] The economy has shifted from manufacturing toward high-technology goods and services. Unemployment stands at 7.3 percent (2007) and is declining. The government is continuously privatizing various government-owned companies. The bottom line is that the economy receives good grades from foreign observers, and the May 2007 invitation to open discussions for joining the OECD is an indication that the country is climbing up the globalization scale.[108]

The trade relationship of Israel and the United States is of particular interest here. In 2006, 38 percent of Israel's exports were directed to the United States, and 12 percent of its imports came from the United States.[109]

Judged on this data, Israel would be classified as a "Northern" country, and proponents of free trade would argue that G© perfectly fits that country. However, Israel's partial embrace of the global copyright regime has imposed some costs. These are unquantifiable and are thus excluded from the statistics. But they are significant nonetheless. They are cultural costs.

3. Culture: A Trade Deficiency Measuring cultural needs is a most difficult task, and developing such measurements is much needed. As for Israel, we can deduce several cultural policies, reflected in various legal measures. Prime among these are preserving the multicultural nature of the country. Israel has a large non-Jewish minority, mostly of Muslims and members of other religious groups.[110] Within the Jewish population, there are various ethnic groups, roughly divided into Ashkenazim and Sephardim, each further divided into sub-ethnicities. Each group wishes to maintain its unique heritage, and, thus, we witness many non-governmental organizations devoted to this cause, with some governmental support. For example, there are various statutory bodies whose task is to assist in preserving the heritage of ethnic groups and preserving the Jewish dialects Yiddish and Ladino.[111] The place of the Hebrew language is also a national cultural policy.

---

106. CBS 2007, Expenditure on the Gross Domestic Product and the Uses of Resources, available at http://www.cbs.gov.il/hodaot2008n/08_08_030t1.pdf.

107. WTO TPR, at vii.

108. See OECD Council Resolution on Enlargement and Enhanced Engagement, May 16, 2007, available at http://www.oecd.org/document/7/0,3343,en_2649_201185_38604487_1_1_1_1,00.html.

109. See Ministry of Trade and Labor, Trade Relations Israel-U.S. (2006), available at http://www.moital.gov.il/NR/exeres/23F8E96E-9E88-4F03-A74C-A1B8DFADC302.htm [Hebrew].

110. For demographic statistics, see CBS 2007, table 2.2.

111. See, e.g., Council for Preserving the Heritage of Sephardi and Eastern Jewish Communities Act of 2002, LSI 92; National Authority for the Heritage of Buchara Judaism Act of 2007, LSI 101; Authority for the Heritage of Libya Judaism Act of 2007, LSI 105; Center for Druze Heritage in Israel Act of 2007, LSI 324; National Authority for Yiddish

There is a constant and apparent increase in the use of other languages, mostly English in commercial settings, such as firms' names and signs. Responding to this cultural globalization, several local municipalities require that signs at least include Hebrew.[112]

Promoting local culture, including the arts, movie productions, music, and literature, is a recurrent theme in Israeli cultural policy and is evident in several kinds of incentives. Prizes and awards of both governmental authorities and private bodies are routine in all creative fields. Direct regulation is also applied. For instance, cable broadcasters are required to meet a minimum quota of local productions.[113]

Another feature is a negative "cultural trade balance." There are cultural and political barriers on exporting Israeli culture, whereas much foreign material easily enters the country. For a local author, moviemaker, or musician, the potential market is, first and foremost, the local, Hebrew-speaking, rather small Israeli market. Translating books and movies is possible, of course: Several Israeli authors have gained worldwide reputations, a few Israeli movies have been successful abroad, and some local musicians have become well known outside of Israel. But these are the tip of the iceberg. Most authors do not cross the geographical borders or the cultural barriers. At the same time, however, foreign books, movies, and music easily find their way into Israel, translated or in their original language, particularly English and Russian, through various distribution channels. Thus, the local author competes not only with her fellow Israeli authors, but with many foreign authors.[114] Technological changes enable even easier importation and distribution of foreign material, whereas language remains a barrier to exporting locally created materials.

The result of the negative cultural balance is apparent in the continuous Americanization of local culture.[115] Israeli youth imitate the dancing styles they see on MTV, watch the same television series as American youth, wear and use the same brands, eat the same kinds of fast food, and use the same gadgets. The movie industry provides an interesting example of this process and of the attempt to protect and promote local cultural production.

Culture Act of 1996, LSI 182; National Authority for Ladino Culture Act of 1996, LSI 185.

112. See, e.g., s. 32 of the Jerusalem Bylaw (Signs) of 1980, KT 1026; s. 27 of the Haifa Bylaws (Signs) of 1995, KT 130.

113. See s. 6E1 of the Telecommunications Act (Telephony and Broadcasting) of 1982, LSI 218, as amended.

114. This, of course, might be beneficial to local readers, but at the cost of promoting local culture.

115. For discussion of the Americanization of Israeli culture, see Uri Ram, *The Globalization of Israel: McWorld in Tel Aviv, Jihad in Jerusalem* (2005) [Hebrew], esp. chapter 4. See also Yuval Elizur, *Israel's Global Challenge* (2005) [Hebrew].

The total number of full-length films screened in Israel declined since the early 1980s from an average of 243 a year, to 180 in 2000, but in 2004 there was a substantial increase (228 films).[116] Whereas in the early 1980s, movies screened in Israel came from a diverse range of origins, the picture in the early 2000s is less diverse and more American, though changes to local law have had a substantial impact as of 2004. During the five-year period of 1980–84, a total of 1,217 films were screened in Israeli movie theaters. Of these, 573 were made in the United States (47%); 314 in Europe (25.8%); 136 in Asia (11.1%); 72 in Israel (5.9%); 62 in Africa (mostly Egypt) (5.1%); 20 in Australia (1.64%); 10 in Canada (0.8%); and 8 in Central and South America (0.65%); the remaining 22 (1.8%) were co-produced.

Over the 1980s and 1990s, we observed first a decline in the number of movies (from an average of 243 in the first half of the 1980s to 180 in 2000); second, a small decline of Israeli films down to only 9 movies in 2000 (5% of the total of 180); third, a steady increase in the share of U.S. films (130 in 2000, accounting for 72.2%);[117] fourth, the complete disappearance of Canadian, Central and South American, and African films; and fifth, a substantial decline of European movies (29 in 2000, accounting for 16.1%).[118]

The next available data relates to 2004 and indicates a change: 27 Israeli films were produced (11.8%). The number of U.S. films slightly declined (120), accounting for only 52.6 percent of the market, and the share of European films (48) rose once again (21%).[119] These changes can be attributed to the enactment of the Film Act of 1999,[120] which created a new budgetary mechanism to support local Israeli productions. The funding is collected from royalties paid by broadcasters to the state.[121]

These changes over the past 25 years can be attributed to various factors, such as changing technologies, namely, the rise of video in the 1980s and DVD in the late 1990s; the rise of Internet use in the mid-1990s; the expansion of cable and satellite television, which enable those with specific demands to find foreign

---

116. See CBS 2007, table 9.3.

117. Hollywood movies dominate many foreign markets. See for example the case of Brazil, as reported in Lemos, *From Legal Commons to Social Commons,* supra note 72, at 18–22.

118. Within the European category, diversity has also shrunk. Whereas in the early 1980s, films came from 14 countries, mostly Italy, the United Kingdom, Germany, and France, in 2006 films from only 6 European countries were screened in Israel, mostly from France and the United Kingdom.

119. The figures for 2006 indicate some changes. There was an increase in the total number of films (248), out of which, 22 were Israeli; 139 were made in the United States; 42 were made in Europe; and the rest were from Canada (2), Asia (7), and Australia (3). Additionally, 27 were co-productions.

120. 1999 LSI 53.

121. See s. 11 of the Film Act, 1999.

movies in these media rather than in cinemas; changes in the global movie industry; changes in the structure of the local distribution industry and patterns in ownership of movie theaters;[122] and changes in the Israeli population (patterns of language and the large Russian immigration in the 1990s, although the demand for content in Russian was supplied by cable television and Internet content). These are all plausible speculations to explain the changes, and there are probably more. In any case, it is clear that American movies still dominate the Israeli market.[123]

This section pointed to a small subset of local cultural needs and does not purport to be comprehensive. However, one lesson can be drawn: Free trade in content and cultural goods has asymmetrical effects. It enables foreign culture not only to enter but also to dominate the local market. A small market with unique culture(s) and language can hardly withstand the mighty powers of the global economy. Cultural diversity has been discussed in various international forums, especially UNESCO, often facing American opposition,[124] but that debate has yet to be tied to copyright policies. The cultural cost is not reflected in a technical legal comparison or an economic study.

4. Politics Israel's political status vis-à-vis its trade partners, especially the United States and the European Union, heavily influences the structure and content of local copyright law. This section emphasizes the external politics; the following part explores an interesting pattern, in which local industries turn to foreign nodes of power to affect the Israeli government.

Examining the external political scene, we should bear in mind Israel's complex geo-political situation. Israel has no diplomatic ties with most Arab countries (with the notable exceptions of Egypt and Jordan) and no diplomatic ties

122. According to a report of the Knesset Research Department, in 2004 there were between 60 and 70 movie theaters in Israel with a total of 315 screens. The report notes the trend to increase the number of screens per theater, which is similar to the trend elsewhere (in the United States, for example, as noted in the report, the number of theaters dropped from 7,151 in 1995 to 5,658 in 2003, whereas the number of screens increased from 26,958 in 1995 to 35,499 in 2003.) The market is highly concentrated, with 77% of the screens operated by two nationwide groups, and the remaining 23% operated by four smaller companies. See Rita Yankelevich, Report on the Movie Theater Market and Cinema Prices, Oct. 19, 2004, available at http://www.knesset.gov.il/mmm/data/docs/m00951.doc [Hebrew].

123. In addition, some of the factors mentioned might also enhance American cultural products, as American films are also available on video and DVD, and via cable television and, of course, the Internet.

124. See supra note 68. For discussion of cultural diversity, see Rosemary J. Coombe, "Protecting Cultural Industries to Promote Cultural Diversity: Dilemmas for International Policy-Making Posed by the Recognition of Traditional Knowledge," in Keith Maskus and Jerome Reichman, eds., *International Public Goods and Transfer of Technology Under a Globalized Intellectual Property Regime*, 559 (Cambridge University Press, 2005).

with some Muslim countries (such as Indonesia). The Arab boycott on Israel and on firms that do business with Israel has somewhat eroded over the years, but it still has some effect.[125] On the other hand, Israel is a close ally of the United States. The export of Israeli goods to the United States has a crucial meaning for the Israeli economy. American political support is also apparent in the strong military ties between the countries. Furthermore, politics and economics converge. Since Israel's independence, the United States has provided it with a total of $153.8 billion in economic and military financial aid,[126] and Israel has been the top recipient of U.S. aid for the past three decades.[127] The second largest recipient, Egypt, received about half this amount.[128] These close political, economic, and military ties mean that Israel is dependent on the United States in many respects. Hence, when Uncle Sam asks Israel to amend its IP laws or support his global cultural policies, the request is one that Jerusalem is hardly in a position to decline.[129]

To illustrate this point, it is interesting to follow comments by the American ambassador to Israel, Richard H. Jones. In several public speeches, the ambassador emphasized the close ties of the two countries, but he also mentioned "rough edges" in the economic relationship, providing IP as an example, while urging Israel to adopt "world class patent and copyright laws." He noted that "there are still some gaps in Israel's regime for protecting IPR."[130] The ambassador also commented on the then-pending copyright bill, noting that it "also contains clauses of great concern to America."[131] In yet another speech, the Ambassador again said that "the United States and Israel must work together to

---

125. See Bureau of Industry and Security, Office of Anti-boycott Compliance, Department of Commerce, available at http://www.bis.doc.gov/complianceandenforcement/antiboycottcompliance.htm; Gil Feiler, *From Boycott to Economic Cooperation: The Political Economy of the Arab Boycott of Israel* (Routledge, 1998).

126. See "U.S. Overseas Loans and Grants" (Greenbook), available at http://tinyurl.com/63jvlq (select "Israel" and then reports).

127. In 2005 the total aid reached $2.684 billion (cf. Egypt—$1.541 billion), $2.2 billion out of which were military aid. The peak of U.S. financial aid was in 2000, when the total aid reached $4.243 billion (cf. Egypt in 2000: $2.32 billion). See id.

128. See Curt Tarnoff, and Larry Nowels, Report for Congress, "Foreign Aid: An Introductory Overview of U.S. Programs and Policy" (2001), available at http://fpc.state.gov/documents/organization/45939.pdf.

129. For example, Israel was the only country to join the United States in its opposition to the Convention on the Protection and Promotion of the Diversity of Cultural Expressions 2005.

130. Ambassador Richard H. Jones, speech in the Israel-America Chamber of Commerce, Annual Gala—Presentation of Awards, Nov. 10, 2005, available at http://israel.usembassy.gov/publish/mission/amb/111005b.html.

131. Ambassador Richard H. Jones, Reception Prepared Remarks, *Ethics, Education and IPR Curriculum Program*, Sept. 5, 2006, available at http://israel.usembassy.gov/publish/mission/amb/050906.html.

resolve lingering irritants such as insufficient protection for U.S. intellectual property."[132] These diplomatic statements are followed by less diplomatic deeds.[133]

Another element that should be taken into consideration on the external political level is that Israel is currently undergoing a review of the OECD. Although the OECD has not traditionally been a central player in the IP field, it has increased its involvement in this field in recent years; this might have further effects on copyright law.[134]

The political scene means that free trade dominates the making of copyright law, at the expense of local cultural, educational, and related interests—and perhaps also local economic policies.

B. Foreign Leverage

This subsection traces the political process regarding Israel's adaptation to G© and identifies a pattern of *foreign leverage* in which local players who have not (yet?) captured the local government turn to their foreign affiliates, who in turn have (already) captured their governments. The foreign government then acts through one of the several avenues provided by the G© regime to pressure the local government. I begin with general patterns and then address the Israeli context.

1. **Patterns of Political Pressure** The interrelated structure of the G© regime—of the multilateral, bilateral, and unilateral layers—defines the playground. The rule of the game is politics and power, the tool is copyright, and the goals are government capture and rent-seeking. The players are the international and foreign enforcers of the corresponding layers (WTO, WIPO, USTR), the local government, and foreign and local interest groups. The last are composed of copyright owners (content industries), intermediaries (broadcasters, ISPs), and authors of all kinds (whether owners or not). My focus is on the local players. The content industries (foreign or local) are usually well organized, politically sophisticated, and deeply involved in the legislative work related to their interests.[135] Users, on the other hand, are usually unorganized—with the exception of libraries, universities, and those players who are both copyright owners and users, such as the media.

This asymmetry of power between content industries and users is also found in Israel. Not all groups are equally powerful. Some of the Israeli industries represent foreign copyright owners and distributors and, hence, are a mixture of

---

132. Ambassador Richard H. Jones, Amcham Awards Dinner Remarks, Nov. 21, 2006, available at http://israel.usembassy.gov/publish/mission/amb/112106.html.

133. See infra, text to note 157.

134. See *Compendium of OECD Work on Intellectual Property (IP) (2007)*, available at http://www.oecd.org/dataoecd/60/61/34305040.pdf; OECD, Project on Counterfeiting and Piracy, available at http://www.oecd.org/sti/counterfeiting.

135. See Jessica Litman, *Digital Copyright: Protecting Intellectual Property on the Internet*, 129 (Prometheus Books, 2001).

local and foreign interests. These include Business Software Alliance (BSA)–Israel,[136] International Federation of the Phonographic Industry (IFPI)–Israel,[137] and the Israel Anti-Piracy Organization (ALIS), a branch of the Motion Picture Association of America (MPAA).[138] These groups gained more in the current legislative process of the new copyright act than did local industries that do not represent foreign interests, such as the Book Publishers' Association of Israel, which, though it is a member of the International Publishers' Association, represents only Israeli publishers.[139] For example, the publishers' main legislative objective was to limit the exceptions that would allow universities to use works for teaching. The publishers objected to the inclusion of "teaching" as a statutory example of a fair-use activity but failed to convince the Knesset Economics Committee.[140] In marked contrast, lobbyists representing foreign and domestic software-industry companies achieved several legislative victories, including a provision that makes the user's right to make a backup of a computer program subject to the user's obligation to destroy the backup once it is no longer needed, in order to prevent its sale.[141] However, even the more powerful industries have not achieved their entire legislative wish list. Anti-circumvention rules, for example, were left out of the 2007 Copyright Act, despite the music industries' attempts to add it during the Knesset discussions. The Ministry of Justice served as a public buffer and managed to withstand the industries' pressure.

However, where the local interest groups are not powerful enough and cannot capture the Israeli legislature, they occasionally seek an external avenue to bypass the local government and overcome their relative weakness. I suggest that we acknowledge several political avenues that are open to local interest groups to achieve their political goals. This is not a comprehensive list.

One pattern is the capture of the local government by interested parties. Political scientists, economists, and legal scholars have described the internal mechanisms of political power, in which interested parties de facto control the political process, under the heading of public-choice theory.[142] We need not delve

136. Business Software Alliance. See http://www.bsa.org.il/.

137. International Federation of the Phonographic Industry. See IFPI Israel: http://www.ifpi.co.il/mainEN.asp?name=about.

138. See ALIS, Anti-Piracy Organization: http://www.alis-il.com/site/index.asp?depart_id=38334&lat=en-uk.

139. See http://www.tbpai.co.il/(and the members list, available at: http://www.tbpai.co.il/hotzaot/hotzaotlistEng.asp).

140. See Protocol 148 of the Economics Committee of the Knesset, of January 2, 2007, available at http://knesset.gov.il/protocols/data/html/kalkala/2007-01-02.html [Hebrew].

141 See Protocol 141 of the Economics Committee of the Knesset, of December 26, 2006, available at http://knesset.gov.il/protocols/data/html/kalkala/2006-12-27-01.html [Hebrew].

142. For discussion, see Daniel A. Farber and Philip P. Frickey, *Law and Public Choice—A Critical Introduction* (University of Chicago Press, 1991).

into this phenomenon or assess its normative aspects. Suffice it to note that the phenomenon exists. The cultural industries have been particularly successful in using this political method, as Jessica Litman has extensively researched in the American context.[143] The structure is simple:

Local Player → Local Government

A second political process, as described by Eyal Benvenisti (though not in the copyright context), is that of local interest groups exiting their local boundaries and turning to international forums to bypass their local governments and become players in the global field.[144] Once the local player becomes a multinational corporation or organization, it is no longer bound by the local government, or it might have a stronger standing when dealing with the state. The structure is:

Local Player → International Player → Local Government

A third pattern is when a local player turns to international bodies to put pressure on its own government. Unlike the previous pattern, in the current pattern, the local player remains local. If successful, the international bodies serve as a source of external leverage over the local government. In the case of copyright law, the structure of G© enabled some American content industries to shift their targets according to the possibilities. Pamela Samuelson described the "copyright grab," in which the content industries approached the U.S. Congress and WIPO simultaneously, advocating a digital agenda (later to become the WCT and the DMCA).[145] The structure here is:

Local Player → International Body → Local Government

The fourth process, *foreign leverage*, is a variation of the previous patterns. The local players do not become international players (unlike the "exit" pattern) and do not turn directly to international bodies (unlike the "grab" pattern). Rather, they turn to their foreign affiliates, who have captured their respective governments. The foreign government then places pressure on the local government. From the viewpoint of the local players, the foreign players (affiliates, government, and international bodies) serve as a political Archimedes fulcrum to bring political change at home.[146] The process is then:

Local Industry → Foreign Affiliate → Foreign Government → Local Government

143. See Litman, *Digital Copyright*, supra note 135.

144. See Eyal Benvenisti, "Exit and Voice in the Age of Globalization," 98 *Mich. L. Rev.* 167 (1999).

145. See Pamela Samuelson, *The Copyright Grab, Wired* 4.01 (1996), available at http://www.wired.com/wired/archive/4.01/white.paper_pr.html.

146. Archimedes is credited with saying, "Give me a fulcrum, and I will move the Earth."

2. From a Wish List to a Watch List[147] In the Israeli case, the local players are the various content and cultural industries, some represent only foreign copyright owners (e.g., the BSA), and some represent a mixture of foreign and local players (e.g., ALIS, representing the MPAA, Israeli video producers, Israeli distributors and, cinema owners, and IFPI, representing both local and foreign music labels). The foreign affiliates are the international organizations such as BSA, MPA, IFPI, and the International Intellectual Property Alliance (IIPA). The most relevant foreign government is the United States. The "Special 301" process serves as the basis for the foreign leverage.[148]

Under the U.S. Trade Act, any party may petition the USTR to conduct an investigation to determine whether a country should be placed on the watch list for possible, eventual trade sanctions.[149] Intellectual property industries are all too happy to request USTR investigations and, indeed, to effectively conduct those investigations on the USTR's behalf.[150] As one scholar noted, the USTR lacks the resources to conduct its own research in each of the surveyed countries; it is also rather weak within the federal government. Hence, it heavily relies on American firms doing business outside the United States.[151] A prominent player here is the IIPA, a coalition of U.S. copyright-based industries, consisting of the publishing, software (business and entertainment), television, motion picture, and recording and music industries, and representing some 1,900 companies. In the IIPA's own words, it "works closely" with the USTR.[152]

The IIPA provides highly detailed reviews to the USTR, presenting concrete recommendations. It is highly instructive to read the USTR's annual reports and recommendations in tandem with the IIPA's. The USTR's Special 301 Reports do not explicitly cite the IIPA reports (though "U.S. industry" was cited in the 2004 and 2005 reports), but they do address issues raised in the IIPA reports, echoing its complaints and occasionally its language.

In that vein, a close reading of the IIPA and USTR reports on Israel for the years 2000–2007 carries some interesting lessons for Israel's glocal IP situation. I first survey the reports on a per-issue basis and then draw some lessons.[153]

---

147. The author of this phrase is Howard Poliner of the Israeli Ministry of Justice.

148. See supra Part II.A.

149. 19 U.S.C. §2412.

150. See Drahos, *Negotiating Intellectual Property*, supra note 11, at 173; Drahos and Braithwaite, supra note 14, at 90–99. The content industries are not alone in capturing the regulators. Pharmaceutical companies have tremendous power over these governmental agencies.

151. See Duncan Matthews, *Globalising Intellectual Property: The Trips Agreement* 25–27 (Routledge, 2002); Ryan, *Knowledge Diplomacy*, supra note 11, at 80.

152. See IIPA Fact Sheet, available at http://www.iipa.com/pdf/IIPA%20Fact%20Sheet%2009212006.pdf.

153. For the USTR reports, see USTR 2001 Special 301 Report http://usembassymalaysia.org.my/pdf/301.pdf and reports for the years 2002–2007, available at http://www.

The main issues addressed in the IIPA and USTR's reports are (1) piracy, (2) enforcement, (3) sound recordings, and (4) the then-pending copyright bill.

(1) Piracy: In 2001, the USTR report on Israel noted a drop in illicit, commercial-scale production of optical media but condemned Israel for pirated music and video and for software piracy, describing the country as "an enormous transshipment network for pirated versions of Russian-Language software." Interestingly, the IIPA report for that year (published before the USTR report), complained of "[a] transshipment network" for pirated software in Russian.

In 2002 the IIPA report first addressed "end-user piracy." The USTR 2002 report echoed that complaint, citing Israel's "lack of clear definition for end-user piracy of business software as a crime." The complaint was repeated in subsequent IIPA and USTR reports (2002–2004, 2008).

The IIPA provides specific estimates of losses to U.S. industry as a result of Israeli piracy. The IIPA estimates were $164.3 million (2001), $159.4 million (2002), $112.1 million (2003), $106 million (2004), $107.4 million (2005), and $129 million (2006). The USTR regularly relies on those estimates, without actually citing the IIPA numbers. The methodology of the IIPA's reports is somewhat of a mystery. For example, it contains claims such as "it is now known that 10 percent of the 'legitimate' [video] stores contain illegal product" (2001),[154] but it does not explain how this is known. The 2004 USTR report cited U.S. industry, stating that "U.S. industry notes that the persistence of a significant level of piracy suggests that additional enforcement resources may be needed." The 2005 USTR report once again cited the U.S. industry's claims about the persistence of a significant level of piracy of CDs and DVDs.

(2) Enforcement: The USTR has noted improved copyright enforcement in Israel's public sector (2001 and since). It has also announced that it is closely following the operations of Israel's IP police unit, noting improvement in police enforcement (2001) but complaining that the unit is too small and underfunded (2001)—albeit with "notable progress" (2002, 2003) including enforcement against "Internet piracy" (2004). These fine-tuned findings precisely mirror the IIPA's findings for those years. The 2002 amendment to Israel's Copyright Ordinance, increasing criminal penalties, was commended (IIPA 2002, USTR 2002, USTR 2003). The IIPA and USTR also both critically assess Israel's judiciary. The IIPA has expressed disappointment with criminal verdicts and civil-damage awards (2001) in particular cases. It has also complained about procedural hurdles in the law-enforcement system (2002). The USTR, in turn, has noted that convictions are rare and penalties insufficient to pose a deterrent (2001). It has also cited Israel for court procedural delays and inadequate civil remedies (2002).

---

ustr.gov/Trade_Sectors/Intellectual_Property/Section_Index.html; the IIPA reports are available at: http://www.iipa.com/special301.html.

154. IIPA 2001 Report, at 123.

(3) Sound Recordings: In 2002, the IIPA report first raised the issue of copyright protection for U.S. sound recordings, noting that the Israeli government had issued a legal opinion "that payment for the broadcasting and public performance of U.S. sound recordings is no longer necessary." The complaint was echoed in the USTR 2002 and 2003 reports, citing Israel's bilateral commitments. In 2005, the IIPA noted that the concerns regarding protection of sound recordings had been allayed, following an Israeli court decision which assured that the foreign works do enjoy protection in Israel. The USTR 2005 report noted that Israel had provided written assurances that it would continue to provide national treatment for U.S. sound recordings, but the issue was once again raised in the 2006 reports from the IIPA and USTR, this time with reference to the then-pending copyright bill.[155]

(4) Copyright Legislation: In 2002, the USTR report directly addressed the Knesset, encouraging it to enact stronger IP laws. The IIPA 2004 report assessed the draft of the copyright bill circulated earlier in that year, complaining that it did not implement the WCT anti-circumvention rules. The IIPA 2005 report similarly raised concerns about "overly broad exceptions" found in the bill. The IIPA 2006 report then went into great detail on many issues contained in the bill. It even commented on specific language of the proposed legislation, recommending that the Knesset strike out some words and insert others. It stated, indeed, regarding the proposed section on temporary copying, that "the wording and explanation is awkward and may give rise to confusion."[156] These concerns were repeated in the IIPA 2007 report. The USTR mentioned that it is monitoring the pending bill (2006, 2007), but unlike the IIPA, it did not go into detail.

However, in addition to its public reports and occasional diplomatic speeches, the USTR has less visible political channels at its disposal. It was actively involved in the legislative process taking place in the Knesset, though this involvement remained behind the scenes. The USTR closely monitored the bill and parliamentary discussions, and expressed its concerns to the Israeli Ministry of Justice in an unofficial letter of comments and video conversations.[157]

155. IFPI raised the issue in the Knesset Economics Committee, both by the Israeli IFPI branch and by a representative of IFPI's headquarters in London who attended the discussions. See Protocol 167 of the Economics Committee of the Knesset, of January 23, 2007, available at http://knesset.gov.il/protocols/data/html/kalkala/2007-01-23.html [Hebrew]. The first IIPA report after the new Copyright Act was enacted in 2007, the 2008 report, again referred to this topic, arguing that the legal protection for foreign phonograms producers, excluding American producers, is seriously weakened.

156. IIPA 2006 Report, at 93.

157. Interviews with senior sources at the Ministry of Justice. The only public evidence of these comments and conversations is a letter sent by the Ministry of Justice to the Economics Committee of the Knesset on February 11, 2007, regarding section 45 of the Copyright Bill. The letter states in the opening, "Following a comment we have received from the U.S. government," and then continues to explain a change of wording in that section.

These comments do not have any binding legal force, but they are taken very seriously by the local government.

Comparing the IIPA and the USTR reports carries some lessons:

1. The concerns raised by the IIPA are repeatedly echoed in the USTR's reports. Almost all issues raised by the IIPA found their way into the USTR reports, and occasionally, the similarity of the language is striking.
2. The IIPA has close familiarity with the local industries' copyright-infringement activities (referred to as "piracy" in all reports), even down to the level of naming specific shops where infringing material is sold. The reports also reveal familiarity with various aspects of the domestic copyright field, including law enforcement efforts and legislative proposals. The USTR reports do not indicate such close familiarity, though they are highly condensed (one to three paragraphs).
3. The IIPA reports heavily rely on information provided by local Israeli industries and do not shy away from including estimates, asserting facts, and presenting demands in firm tones. The USTR has not quoted the specific estimates but has reflected them, citing "U.S. industry."

The methods the IIPA uses to gather the data upon which the USTR then relies deserve attention. Consider, for example, the IIPA figures for losses as a result of "piracy" suffered by the motion picture industry that appeared in its 2007 report. The IIPA explicitly cited its source, ALIS, the Israeli enforcement arm of the MPAA (which represents also Israeli distributors and theater owners).[158] ALIS, in turn, provides some figures about the Israeli market for motion pictures on its website.[159] It states that the level of piracy in the motion picture industry reaches about 40 percent, that the direct damages to movie theaters are an annual NIS 80 million (about $19.4 million, Sept. 2007), and that there has been a decline of 2.5 million viewings at cinemas between 2001 (10.8 million) and 2005 (8.37 million).[160] The ALIS figures and, hence, the IIPA report suggest a causal connection between piracy and the decline of cinema viewings. ALIS's methodology is straightforward: The decline in viewing is multiplied by

158. The IIPA explains its methodology in calculating losses. See Appendix B to the 2007 IIPA Report, available at http://www.iipa.com/pdf/2007spec301methodology.pdf. The methodology of ALIS does not seem to fit that of the IIPA. ALIS actively searches for copyright infringements, complains to the police, initiates legal proceedings, and conducts raids.

159. See ALIS Website [Hebrew], at http://www.alis-il.com/38334/ללכי. The figures appear in a report published by the Federation of Israeli Chambers of Commerce. See Intellectual Property Report, 2006, available at http://www.chamber.org.il/_Uploads/18441report.DOC.

160. Id., at 33.

the cost of a ticket, and the result is considered a loss.[161] However, that causal connection is highly dubious: One can postulate many other possible explanations about the decline of cinema viewings in Israel, including similar, pre-Internet worldwide trends;[162] Israel's security situation, which has periodically led many Israelis to stay at home (especially in 2000–2002); the economic recession during 2001–2003; the rise of legal substitutes to movies, such as more television options and Internet entertainment; and the rising costs of movies.[163] The example of the alleged piracy in the motion picture market illustrates how the estimates of an industry group turn into the claims of the local coalition of IP businesses and find their way to the IIPA to be subsequently echoed by the USTR (though in a general form, without citing the figures).[164]

4. The USTR has not always followed the advice of the IIPA. In 2000, the IIPA recommended that Israel be placed on the Priority Foreign Country watch list (PFC),[165] and in 2003 and 2004 that Israel be placed on the Priority Watch List (PWL), which is one step below the PFC in the U.S. Trade Act's hierarchy: namely, the threat of economic retaliation is lower by one degree. The USTR declined to follow those recommendations, opting for the slightly less problematic Watch List (WL) instead. In 2005 the IIPA recommended that Israel be included on the WL. The USTR once again declined to follow the IIPA's recommendation, but this time, it was the USTR that took the harsher position by including Israel on the PWL. These differences are most probably explained by the fact that the USTR designation reflects its patent, as well as copyright, law review.[166]

---

161. As explained to me by Mr. Yizhak Cohen, the CEO of ALIS. Telephone interview, Aug. 12, 2007.

162. See Sam Cameron, "Cinema," in *A Handbook of Cultural Economics*, supra note 66, at 114.

163. Mr. Cohen firmly believes that the decline is almost entirely attributed to piracy. Supra note 161. The calculation should also be doubted because not all tickets cost the maximum price (senior citizens pay less), and no expenses are deducted. For the structural changes in the local motion picture industry and the prices of tickets, see the Knesset Research Report, supra note 122.

164. The Israeli Chambers of Commerce maintains ties with the IIPA but has not sent the figures directly to the IIPA, as explained to me by Ms. Shlomit Weishoff of the ICC, telephone interview, Aug. 12, 2007. The data is available, however, on the Chambers' website.

165. IIPA Press Release, "IIPA Asks USTR to Designate Israel and Ukraine as Special 301 'Priority Foreign Countries' in April 2000" (Feb. 18, 2000), available at http://www.iipa.com/pressreleases/2000_Feb18_301.PDF. It described Israel as overwhelmed by piracy and as a center for international piracy.

166. The patent field requires a separate study. Suffice it to mention that Teva Pharmaceutical Industries Ltd., currently the leading generic firm in the world, is located

Furthermore, the USTR has not expressly echoed all the IIPA's concerns. For example, in its reports, the USTR did not delve into the details of the pending copyright legislation. However, as mentioned, it did share its views with the Israeli government through other channels.

5. Neither the IIPA nor the USTR reports discuss local cultural needs. There is no discussion of the local situation, such as urgent and pressing security needs that require a different priority for law-enforcement efforts in the country, with the exception of some understanding in the IIPA's 2001 and 2002 reports. The analysis of the copyright law does not go beyond the direct copyright statutes. The constitutional setting, the interpretive method of Israeli courts, adjunct statutes such as the Unjust Enrichment Act, and similar avenues that either strengthen the power of the copyright owners or that would have shed light on what seemed to the IIPA to be "awkward" are not mentioned. No cultural needs are discussed. The IIPA and the USTR reports focus exclusively on the language of the copyright statutes, figures of enforcement, data on convictions, and estimates of copyright-industry losses. There is no reference to the broader legal, economic, or cultural landscape.

A troubling example is the IIPA's comments on the proposed fair-use exception in the then-pending copyright bill. The bill proposed a shift from the English fair-dealing defense to the American fair-use defense. The IIPA (2006) acknowledged that the proposed defense adopts the American model, but then commented, "We are very concerned that the result of this change is that considerable case law interpretation in Israel on 'fair dealing' may be thrown out in favor of as yet undeveloped factors in Section 19(b). . . . There is a significant risk that in Israel the adoption of these factors at this time might be viewed by the community as a free ticket to copy."[167] This is yet another example of the danger of interpreting a foreign legal system by isolating one section and detaching it from its legal underpinnings. Israeli courts routinely turn to U.S. case law and adopt many of its rules. In interpreting the current fair-dealing exception, the Israeli Supreme Court turned to the U.S. Copyright Act and applied its famous four fair-use considerations.[168] Section 19(b) of the new 2007 Copyright Act incorporated the already existing

---

in Israel. Teva plays a central role in the country's economy. PhRMA, the Pharmaceuticals Research and Manufacturers of America, has consistently recommended to the USTR that Israel remain on the PWL. Furthermore, in 2006, PhRMA urged the United States to oppose Israel's candidacy for OECD membership, a call that was not followed. See PhRMA "Special 301" Submission for 2005 (2006), available at http://members.phrma.org/international/PhRMA_2005_Special_301.pdf.

167. IIPA 2006 Report, at 95. The IIPA repeated its concerns also in the 2008 report, after the enactment of the 2007 Act. See IIPA 2008 Report, at 224–25.

168. See the Geva case, supra note 93.

practice and shifts from the closed list of fair uses to an open list. Israeli courts are likely to enhance their references to American case law.

The reports reveal that the sources of the IIPA are, to a great extent, the local Israeli industries. Comparing the IIPA to the USTR reports reveals the relative capturing of the latter by the former. Thus, the industries' wish list turns into a Watch List. The watch list is then converted into political power. Although no sanctions have been imposed through the process, the political pressure is immense, especially once we recall the close political and financial relationship between Washington and Jerusalem. As mentioned above, the USTR closely followed the current legislative process and delivered its views to the Ministry of Justice in an unequivocal and direct manner.[169]

IV. CONCLUSION

This chapter locates the current debates on the copyright regime within a general framework that juxtaposes the global regime with local interests. I suggested that in order to fully understand the meaning of the G© regime for each country, we need to engage in a multifactor, sociocultural, economic, and political study of the country, as well as its legal system, as a whole. The meeting of the global and the local, the "glocal" situation, indicates the gap between a country's needs and the global regime imposed onto it. I then applied that framework to the case of Israel, which is not a member of the South, but also is not (yet?) a member of the North. Despite promising economic figures, the cultural and political analyses better explain some of the developments in Israeli law. I have focused on the political process of the "Special 301" review conducted by the USTR. This discussion reveals several patterns of political pressure, such as direct external pressure (e.g., foreign industries channel their power to their foreign governments, which then turn to the local government) and a pattern of *foreign leverage*, in which some local cultural industries attempt to influence the local government from the outside by turning to their foreign affiliates, which in turn mobilize their (foreign) governments, to pressure Israel.

169. See supra note 157.

PART SEVEN

INDUSTRY STRUCTURE, INNOVATION, AND ACCESS

17. ANTITRUST, PATENTS, AND DEVELOPING NATIONS

JOHN H. BARTON*

*George E. Osborne Professor of Law, Emeritus, Stanford Law School, Stanford, CA, 94305, jbarton@stanford.edu. I want to thank the participants in the UCLA Conference on Intellectual Property and Developing Countries: The WIPO Development Agenda, as well as Mark Lemley and Robin Feldman, for their comments and insights. The mistakes are, of course, mine.

INTRODUCTION

In the developed world, antitrust policy has traditionally been a foil to intellectual property (IP). There are now serious concerns that the world's IP system, including both rules created by national legislation and those created by international agreements, is stronger than is in the economic interests of developing nations. A stronger antitrust law might be a valuable response.

This article, therefore, examines the actions that developing nations might take in the antitrust area, looking both at national legislation and at international arrangements. It attempts to develop approaches that reflect sound economic analysis and explores how to pursue such approaches consistently with current law in the area.[1] The article concentrates on patents but considers copyright law where that law affects technological innovation, as in the case of software. The article does not explore other areas of antitrust law, such as the general treatment of cartels. Also, it differs radically from the study carried out by the U.K. Commission on Intellectual Property Rights,[2] which noted the possible role of antitrust law but did not explore it in depth because antitrust law proved less relevant to the poorest nations than did the basic access issues explored in that analysis. Nor, except in passing, does the article consider compulsory licensing based on broad principles, such as those included in TRIPS Article 31[3] or the Doha Declaration.[4]

The article avoids emphasizing specific technical doctrines, emphasizing instead the various economic standards that permeate antitrust practice. It considers three important contexts: the response to a (generally foreign) monopolist, the response to a (generally primarily foreign) global oligopoly or cartel, and the management of relations between a major (generally foreign) firm and a local licensee.

---

1. For solid summary and background, see the Executive Summary of Organisation for Economic Cooperation and Development, *Competition Policy and Intellectual Property Rights*, OECD Committee on Competition Law and Policy, CAFFE/CLP(98) 18 (1998), and the report, U.S. Department of Justice and Federal Trade Commission, *Antitrust Enforcement and Intellectual Property Rights: Promoting Innovation and Competition* (April 2007).

2. *Intellectual Property Rights and Development Policy* (London, September 2002).

3. Agreement on Trade-Related Aspects of Intellectual Property Rights, 1869 UNTS 299, 33 ILM 1197 (1994).

4. World Trade Organization, Doha Declaration on the TRIPS Agreement and Public Health, WT/MIN(1)/DEC/1, 41 ILM 746 (2001).

I. MONOPOLIST AND COMPULSORY LICENSING UNDER ANTITRUST PRINCIPLES

The first typical pattern is that in which a nation is confronted with a global monopolist that uses IP in a way that may hinder the development of the nation's economy or industry. This section explores the economic issues in conjunction with the standards that a developing nation may legitimately employ to address them, building on the principles of European Union law, in which the issue is treated as one of abuse of a dominant position under § 82 of the Treaty of Rome (as amended) (abuse of a dominant position), and of U.S. law, in which it is sometimes treated as one of monopolization under § 2 of the Sherman Act (15 U.S.C. § 2) and sometimes under a common-law doctrine of patent abuse.[5]

A. The Economics

There is a basic tension between IP goals and antitrust goals. The point of most IP rights is to provide market exclusivity in order to permit an inventor to invest in developing a product or process with some confidence that there will be a greater-than-competitive return down the road through which to recoup the research and development costs. In contrast, the goal of antitrust is to ensure that prices will be as competitive as possible. Clearly, these goals are in conflict. Furthermore, there is no bright line for choosing between the goals in the face of a practice by an IP holder that appears to increase the holder's return. Such practices may increase the incentive to innovate at the same time that they raise the price.

This fundamental tension between IP and antitrust goals requires a balance between the two goals of improving consumer welfare through lower immediate prices or, alternatively, through improved products later. A developing nation might reasonably have a shorter time horizon (i.e., a higher discount rate) than a developed nation. The balance is, in some sense, arbitrary, and it is certainly hard to mark precisely—no one could reasonably argue that a patent term is a year too short or too long. In light of this fact, the wisest thing for developing nations to do may often be to choose the most liberal of the legally available standards.

B. Antitrust-Based Restrictions

1. Patent Misuse Based on Fraud or Absence of a Patent There are several contexts in which antitrust principles permit the overriding of a patent. The first

---

5. For a solid presentation and evaluation of U.S. practice in the area, see Herbert J. Hovenkamp, Mark D. Janis, and Mark A. Lemley, "Unilateral Refusals to License in the U.S.," Working Paper No. 303 (Stanford Law School, John M. Olin Program in Law and Economics, 2005), available at http://papers.ssrn.com/sol3/papers.cfm?abstract_id=703161. (Collected online August 2, 2007.)

and most broadly accepted is when the patent has been acquired fraudulently.[6] There is a similar principle applying to sham litigation. In such cases, there has been no innovation to reward. It is also obvious, although this is perhaps more a matter of patent law than of antitrust law, and the issue is not one of fraud, that a product cannot be restricted in a nation in which no patent is in force. This means that a nation can reject restrictions—in its own market—based on patents that its law does not recognize. For example, it is almost certainly consistent with TRIPS to reject patents on business methods, on basic scientific principles, and on some of the minor improvements that have been used to "evergreen" drugs. If a nation's laws do not grant patents on such inventions, then the nation is free to allow a firm to produce the corresponding product within the nation, regardless of any objection by the patent holder. By the same token, it is reasonably an antitrust offense to try to enforce a patent on a plant variety that has been taken from a nation and that fails to satisfy normal patent or plant breeders' rights novelty rules.

2. **Tying** The second clearly legitimate basis for antitrust law to override a patent includes certain cases of tying. Many times, a patent holder will attempt to control a market additional to the one covered by the patent. Thus, a patent holder might license a patent only on condition that a particular related product is bought from it. The classic example was a patent on a machine that uses salt—and the patent holder insisted that its salt be used.[7] Among the leading current examples are the *Microsoft* cases in the United States[8] and Europe.[9] In general, among the arguments in these cases is that Microsoft has "tied" or bundled the purchase of a new product (a browser in the U.S. cases and a media player in the EU cases) to the purchase of its basic Windows operating system. The feared result is that the company leverages its strong market position in the operating-system market (in this case, gained from the network power of Windows, rather than from IP) into a position that restricts competition in the browser or media-player market. As a matter of underlying economics, network-based market power, such as that of Microsoft, must be allowed because of the enormous benefit to society that its operating-system standard provides, just as a patent-based market power must be allowed to encourage innovation. But a firm that benefits from such market power should not be able to use that power in a way that forecloses competition in other markets or makes it impossible to challenge its market position at times of technological change. In the U.S. *Microsoft* cases, a change of this nature occurred when personal computers went from local operation to Internet connection, and the development of browsers threatened the firm's position.

---

6. *Walker Process Equipment v. Food Machinery and Chemical Corp.*, 382 U.S. 172 (1965).

7. *Morton Salt v. G.S. Suppiger, Inc.*, 314 US 488 (1942). The case has been at least in part overruled by *Illinois Tool Works v. Independent Ink*, 126 S Ct 1281 (2006).

8. *United States v. Microsoft*, 253 F 3d 34 (DC Cir 2001). Note that this decision rejected the tying arguments that had succeeded at trial.

9. Case No. COMP/37.792 Microsoft of 24.3.2004.

In some contexts, there is a reasonable argument that such "tying" provides the licensor with a way to legitimately price discriminate between those who use its product heavily and those who use it lightly. An example is a requirement that the purchasers of a patented copying machine use toner cartridges provided by the licensor—the prices will be arranged so that a significant portion of the licensor's profits comes from the toner cartridges, and the heavy user will thus pay more than light users. This is economically beneficial, for the copier becomes available to more users. There is an antitrust case currently in litigation in China that raises this issue—the suit is against Sony for designing a digital camera "to shut down when competing batteries are installed."[10] As an economic matter, China should probably not win that litigation.

Although laws differ from nation to nation in this context, and the economic argument allowing price discrimination is not always accepted, the typical antitrust principle is to regard tying in an IP context as *sometimes* an improper extension of the licensor's IP rights. There is usually a "rule of reason" standard requiring economic analysis, rather than a "per se" analysis that finds liability from the fact of tying alone. A typical rule of reason standard for antitrust violation is that there be tying, that there be substantial market power in the tying product, and that there be harm to competition as a result of the tying.[11] For developing nations that may be a target of tying practices, the key examples arise when tying becomes a way to raise a technology cost or leads to a monopoly in a market separate from that covered by a patent.

To consider a contemporary example of great relevance to developing nations, there was recent U.S. appellate litigation over agricultural biotechnology company Monsanto's legal arrangements to ensure that users of its patented genetically modified corn also used its herbicide even though the herbicide was no longer on patent. The arrangements were upheld, but a dissent regarded the arrangements as constituting illegal tying.[12] It would not seem unreasonable for a developing nation to adopt the dissenting position, thus reducing the effective cost of the technology, although also reducing the inventor's incentives to develop or apply it.

3. Accumulation of Patents A third broadly accepted basis is that it may be an antitrust offense for a firm having a dominant position to protect its monopoly by purchasing patent rights that a competitor might use to enter its market. It is, of course, legitimate for a firm to develop a strong patent position based on its own research. The problem arises when the firm acquires patent rights from potential competitors.

10. Jesse W. Markham, *China Court Hears Antitrust Suit Against Sony*, Morrison & Foerster (January 22, 2007).

11. See, for a slightly different version, European Commission, DG Competition, *DG Competition discussion paper on the application of Article 82 of the Treaty to exclusionary abuses* (December 2005). As an example, consider *Windsurfing v. Commission*, [1986] ECR 611.

12. *Monsanto Co v. Scruggs*, No 04-1532, slip op at 729 (CAFC, August16, 2006).

4. Refusal to License One of the most contentions issues in IP/antitrust law is whether a unilateral refusal to license should ever be regarded as an antitrust offense. In the United States, a patent holder can refuse to license—this is, in general, part of the legally intended effect of a patent.[13] Even though there is an "essential facility" principle, which could arguably be used to require licensing, no U.S. court has upheld its application to an intellectual property right.[14]

In contrast, in a very few cases, EU antitrust authorities have declared such a refusal to be a violation of antitrust law. The EU Commission suggests a standard that includes requirements that the refusing undertaking is dominant, that the refusal is likely to have a negative effect on competition, that the refusal is not objectively justified, and that it "prevents the development of the market for which the license is an indispensable input, to the detriment of consumers."[15] Among the leading EU examples are *McGill TV*,[16] in which IP rights were used to prevent publication of integrated TV schedules, and *IMS Health*,[17] which involved an effort to protect a map used for reporting sales in different areas. Thus, this is one of the points of difference between U.S. and EU law.

For the developing nation, there is a strong argument that failure to make technology available in *any* way, that is, neither through licensing nor through product sale, can reasonably be considered improper. Otherwise, the patent system is not really encouraging innovation. Indeed, in the international context, considering that the local market is the one affected by such action, it is hard to see how a patent holder should be viewed as harmed by treating such an action as anti-competitive. (The case in which the holder is protecting one product against competition from a separate product on which it holds the patent is not a sympathetic one.) Moreover, even within traditional doctrine, there is a reasonable argument that damages, rather than an injunction, may be the appropriate

---

13. See *Continental Paper Bag v. Eastern Paper Bag*, 210 US 405 (1908) (Justice Harlan dissenting); *Independent Serv Orgs Antitrust Litig*, 203 F 3d 1322 (Fed Cir 2000). 35 USC § 271(d)(4); Hovenkamp et al. (cited in note 5).

14. Robert Pitofsky, Donna Patterson, and Jonathan Hooks, "The Essential Facilities Doctrine Under U.S. Antitrust Law," 70 *Antitrust Law Journal* 443 (2002); Paul D. Marquardt, and Mark Leddy, "The Essential Facilities Doctrine and Intellectual Property Rights; A Response to Pitofsky, Patterson, & Hooks," 70 *Antitrust L J* 847 (2003). There is a U.S. case that rejected the IP rights on other principles, but it was one in which the IP argument was generally irrelevant to the refusal to license, and the case has been strongly criticized. *Image Technical Services v. Eastman Kodak Co* 125 F 3d 1195 (9th Cir 1997). The criticism is presented in U.S. Department of Justice and Federal Trade Commission (cited in note 1).

15. DG Competition discussion paper, at ¶ 239 (cited in note 11).

16. *Radio Telefis Eireann (RTE) v. E.C. Commission*, [1995] ECR I-743.

17. For example, *IMS Health Inc v. Commission*, [2001] ECR II-02193, and see generally, James S. Venit, Article 82 "EC: Exceptional Circumstances; The IP/Antitrust Interface After *IMS Health*," EUI-RSCAS/EU Competition 2005/Proceedings, to be published in Claus-Dieter Ehlermann & Isabela Atanasiu, eds., *European Competition Law Annual 2005: The Interaction between Competition Law and Intellectual Property Law* (Hart).

remedy when a technology is not being practiced. Granting damages alone amounts to a judicially created, reasonable-royalty license. This has been done in the United States in the public-interest context of a process being used by a local government for treatment of raw sewage.[18] It may also be the result appropriately implied from the U.S. Supreme Court's recent interpretation of the appropriate standards for injunctions in patent cases.[19] Moreover, it is consistent with the TRIPS provisions on compulsory licensing (Article 31).

It is essential, however, to be careful with any extension that would apply such a doctrine when the technology *is* offered, but only on terms that may appear unreasonable to the developing-nation's national authorities. That issue arose in international debate over the newly adopted Chinese Anti-Monopoly Law.[20] And it is also an issue posed by the Taiwanese *patent* (not *antitrust*) principle that permits a compulsory license when an applicant is unable to reach a licensing agreement "under reasonable commercial terms and conditions within a considerable time period."[21] In a recent case in which a compulsory license was initially granted, Taiwan backed down under the threat of a WTO response.[22] In general, the market should be allowed to determine the price of an offered technology—that price should have to appear *extremely* unreasonable before it becomes appropriate to treat the refusal to deal as an antitrust offense.

5. Territorial Division It is today controversial whether market division, that is, the licensing or sale of products exclusively to one region with efforts to prevent their export to other regions, is a violation of antitrust law. In essence, a product is sold for marketing in one nation, but its re-export is prevented because it infringes

---

18. *Milwaukee v. Activated Sludge*, 69 F 2d 577 (7th Cir 1934).

19. *eBay v. MercExchange*, 126 S Ct 1847 (2006).

20. The Anti-Monopoly Law of the People's Republic of China was adopted on August 30, 2007, and takes effect on August 1, 2008. An English translation is available at http://www.fdi.org.cn/pub/FDI_EN/Laws/GeneralLawsandRegulations/BasicLaws/P020071012533593599575.pdf. Article 55 of the new law provides, "This law does not govern the conduct of business operators to exercise their intellectual property rights . . . ; however, business operators' conduct to eliminate or restrict market competition by abusing their intellectual property rights shall be governed by the Law." Like earlier drafts, the law as adopted does not define "abuse." For discussion, *see* Bruce Owen, Su Sun, and Wentong Zheng, "China's Competition Policy Reforms: The Antimonopoly Law and Beyond" (John M. Olin Program in Law and Economics, Stanford Law School, Working Paper No 339, 2007), available online at http://papers.ssrn.com/sol3/papers.cfm?abstract_id=978810 (collected online August 2, 2007) and *Joint Submission of the American Bar Association's Sections of Antitrust Law, Intellectual Property Law and International Law on the Proposed Anti-Monopoly of the People's Republic of China* (2005), available at http://www.abanet.org/intlaw/committees/business_regulation/antitrust/chinacommentsantimonopoly.pdf.

21. *See* Lily Lim, "Trends in Compulsory Licenses in Greater China," *IP Law* 360 (August 16, 2006).

22. *See* Kathrin Hille, "Taiwan Acts to Avoid WTO Ruling," *Financial Times* (April 26, 2007), p. 6.

on patents in other nations. The assumption among many antitrust authorities is that such arrangements, as least if made through the working of intellectual property law alone, facilitate price discrimination among different markets and thus both increase the return to the innovator and make products available to some customers who would otherwise be unable to purchase them. (Territorial division among competitors, however, remains a commonly agreed violation of antitrust principles and will be discussed in the next session.) Yet, when the underlying intellectual property issue was negotiated for TRIPS, the Article 6 agreement to disagree on exhaustion—that is, the ability to use IP to separate markets—was all that was politically available.

It follows that it is certainly legitimate under TRIPS for a developing nation to permit parallel imports to give its consumers the benefit of a lower foreign price. The question is how often this will be useful. After all, the normal expectation for price discrimination is that prices in developing-nation markets will be lower than those in developed-nation markets. Hence, the developing nation will normally benefit from price discrimination. This pattern is reversed only in unusual cases, such as the effort by South Africa to facilitate import of lower-cost drugs from India.[23]

6. Other Licensing Practices Dominant firms often seek to protect their position by imposing various provisions in their license or marketing agreements to harm the growth of competitors. Thus, among thc practices of Microsoft that were condemned were arrangements that created an incentive for computer suppliers not to market computers with competing operating systems installed or not to include icons on the computer screen that might make it easier for users to use alternative browsers.[24] (Some of these arrangements may be dealt with as agreements in restraint of trade under Sherman § 1, rather than under § 2.) Such practices, although sometimes acceptable for a firm with a small market position, may violate antitrust law by making it more difficult for a competitor to enter the market.[25] Save in extreme cases, the appropriate antitrust remedy in this context is to require a termination of such practices rather than to override a patent.

C. Related IP Circumstances

Finally, there are reasonable exceptions to the use of any IP, depending on the particular form of IP. In the case of patents, for example, it is reasonable to allow experimental use of patented inventions (normally under a statutory provision). In the case of copyrighted material, there are various forms of fair use to allow

---

23. This act was the basis of a major trade dispute. See, for example, Kara M. Bombach, "Can South Africa Fight Aids? Reconciling the South African Medicines And Related Substances Act with the Trips Agreement," 19 *Boston University International Law Journal* 273 (Fall 2001).

24. *Microsoft*, 253 F 3d 34 (cited in note 8).

25. *See*, for example, the Remarks of Thomas McCoy (Advanced Micro Devices) before Federal Trade Commission and Department of Justice Hearings on Section 2 of the Sherman Act, Berkeley, California, January 30, 2007.

limited copying—this is particularly significant in the case of software, where it is reasonable to allow decompilation and reverse engineering under at least some circumstances.[26] And, of course, there is sometimes the possibility of a compulsory license under TRIPS Article 31.

D. Implications of BITs and TRIPS-plus Agreements

Although the antitrust principles just described are certainly consistent with TRIPS, they may pose questions under the terms of recent Bilateral Investment Treaties (BITs) or TRIPS-plus bilateral trade agreements.[27] TRIPS includes a section, Article 40, that specifically protects the right to apply competition-law standards against IP. This section includes details on the vertical restraints that will be discussed in section III but not on the restraints discussed in this section. Nevertheless, a reasonable interpretation of the Article would certainly permit antitrust restrictions of the type discussed here.

The BITs are oriented primarily toward protecting investors' expectations. Some BITs require protection of investments—which is sometimes expected to include intellectual property rights—to the "Highest International Standards" or on a basis of "Fair and Equitable Treatment." Although this would seem to require fair procedures—and antitrust procedures should certainly be fair—it is not clear how such principles might apply to restrict compulsory licensing on antitrust grounds. Nor is it clear that a suspension of an intellectual property right on antitrust grounds is the same as an expropriation. The same is true for requirements of "reasonable and entire compensation." Similarly, it is not clear whether a TRIPS-plus principle is meant to apply to antitrust policy as distinguished from IP policy. But there are a number of contexts in which there may be a stronger argument. For example, some treaties place limits on parallel imports, and some restrict the "revocation" of patents to grounds such as fraud and misrepresentation. These are among the classic bases of "patent misuse" in U.S. law; a treaty with such a provision might complicate restrictions on a patent based on tying or other antitrust violations.

Also, a trend to include explicit provisions on antitrust law in Free Trade Agreements (FTAs) has emerged. As exemplified by the U.S.-Singapore FTA, these provisions typically require a nation to have an antitrust law and require transparency in the policy; in addition, they may allow for certain monopoly

---

26. It must be recognized that the Digital Millennium Copyright Act, Pub L 105-304 (1998), and the European Software Directive, Council Directive of 14 May 1991 on the legal protection of computer programs (91/250/EEC), attempt to restrict the circumstances of such reverse engineering.

27. For discussion, and a source for the examples in the paragraph, *see* Rosa Castro Bernieri, "Intellectual Property Rights in Bilateral Investment Treaties and Access to Medicines: The Case of Latin America," 9 *Journal of World Intellectual Property* 548 (2006).

exceptions (presumably in government-owned or -regulated industries).[28] This appears to be a typical pattern.[29] Thus, it seems unlikely that these provisions will be barriers to effective antitrust law.

E. International Enforcement

In all these cases, a developing nation can readily apply a reasonable antitrust principle to its own market; this is adequate for an import-substitution situation. But for an export situation, a nation or firm runs into the problem of the territoriality of patents. Patents are a right conveyed by national law, and, as implied by recent decisions by the Supreme Court and by the Court of Appeals for the Federal Circuit, the courts of one nation generally have no right to interfere with a foreign nation's patents.[30] The only way to obtain freedom to export against a patent in such a context is, therefore, to litigate in that nation based on a similar antitrust principle in the importing nation's courts, if such a principle exists. If such a principle does not exist, there is no possibility of achieving the export.

The obvious response to this problem is to seek a global agreement under which nations would agree reciprocally to recognize the limitation, invalidation, or compulsory licensing of a patent that such restrictions have made in accordance with antitrust law. This would obviously be politically possible only if there were a reasonable understanding as to the antitrust principles to be applied, and perhaps some form of appeal procedure—this is clearly both a difficult and a sensible goal to seek in the global antitrust context.

II. OLIGOPOLIES

A. Background

In most cases outside the pharmaceutical and entertainment contexts in which there are monopolies on individual products, the leading firms do not have monopolies. Instead, there are usually several firms in an industry, creating a

---

28. United States–Singapore, Free Trade Agreement, Chapter 12 (May 6, 2003), available at http://www.ustr.gov/Trade_Agreements/Bilateral/Singapore_FTA/Final_Texts/Section_Index.html. (Collected online August 2, 2007.)

29. *See* Ruth Okediji, "Negotiating Competition in the EPA Context," *Project Management Unit* (October 2006); Alden Abbott (U.S. Federal Trade Commission), *Competition Policy in Bilateral Trade Arrangements in the Context of Developing Country Economic Reform* (June 15, 2006).

30. The Supreme Court case is *Microsoft Corp v. AT&T Corp*, No 05-1056 (April 30, 2007), in which it gave a narrow interpretation to a statute giving limited extraterritorial scope to the patent law. The CAFC case is *Voda v. Cordis Corp*, 05-1238 (CAFC, Feb 1, 2007), decided on a 2-1 basis, which cited an earlier decision, which stated that "[o]nly a British court, applying British law, can determine validity and infringement of British patents," *Stein Associates v. Heat & Control, Inc.* 748 F 2d 653, 659 (CAFC 1984).

global oligopoly. As a matter of economics, such an oligopoly pattern is normal for a technology-based industry.

Two types of issues are posed. One is that such an oligopoly may be able to charge a higher-than-competitive price, either through some form of collusion or through "conscious parallelism" (i.e., a tacit recognition by each firm that it may be in its interest not to undercut its competitor's prices). The second is that the firms may be able to use their intellectual property to exclude new entrants, while not seeking to exclude one another. For example, the firms may have competitive products based on separate patents, or they may cross-license some or all of the relevant patent rights. The extreme example of this latter pattern is the semiconductor industry, in which each firm regularly infringes many of the patents of its competitors. To the extent the relationship between any single pair of firms is symmetrical, they will cross-license each other on royalty-free terms, or simply refrain from suing because they know that any suit would simply bring a countersuit. This amounts to a tacit cross-license. If the relationship is less symmetrical, there may be a cross-license in which the technologically weaker party must make a payment to the technologically stronger partner.

Economics suggests that there may be an optimal size for such an oligopoly.[31] As the number of oligopolists increases, their ability to gain rents decreases—but their incentive to do research increases at the same time. Moreover, it is probably in the interest of the oligopolists to keep the group smaller than the optimal size. Hence, it is economically understandable that they would not be ready to license to all, but they would probably license to fewer than would be economically optimal. And, of course, it is economically reasonable that any new entrants would be technologically strong and would actually bring something to their partners in the oligopoly.

A new, developing-nation firm may face difficulty in breaking into such an industry. For example, the technologies that the incumbents readily license to one another may not be available to it. The incumbents may not wish to encourage the entry of a new firm. Moreover, the oligopoly may work to raise the costs of products or technology to developing nations. Obviously neither pattern is true for all industries; nevertheless, this is probably an extremely important issue for developing nations, which face oligopolies that are usually (albeit not always) controlled by developed-nation firms that wish to maintain their competitive position. This is probably the most serious of the antitrust issues for developing nations.

The various issues in this area are generally handled as horizontal restraints under Sherman § 1 and EU Article 81. Moreover, certain of the practices are discussed in the 1995 U.S. Antitrust Guidelines for the Licensing of Intellectual Property.[32]

---

31. John H. Barton, "Antitrust Treatment of Oligopolies with Mutually Blocking Patent Portfolios," 69 *Antitrust L J* 851 (2001).

32. U.S. Department of Justice & Federal Trade Commission, *Antitrust Guidelines for the Licensing of Intellectual Property* (April 6, 1995).

B. Explicit Agreements to Exclude or to Fix Prices

There is no question as to the applicability of antitrust law to certain practices by such an oligopoly. For example, an agreement that amounts to explicit price-fixing is clearly a violation.[33] An agreement among firms to share technologies with one another will properly be evaluated on the basis of its effect on the individual firms' incentives to innovate. A cross-license that explicitly excludes a specific competitor will generally be regarded as improper under the antitrust laws, at least if it includes a significant share of the industry.[34]

C. Pools and Cartel Behavior

A patent cross-license can be structured as a pool, in which a separate entity holds the patents and licenses back to the members the rights to use the technology. The pool was the classic pattern of international cartel of the interwar period.[35] Firms would cross-license their patents subject to territorial restrictions so that each firm would be allocated a territory in which it would have freedom to act like a monopolist. These arrangements are clear violations of antitrust law: They may restrain the entry of a developing-nation firm into a global industry; they may slow the development of technology; they may lead to price increases. In one case, the development of synthetic rubber, licensing of technology was specifically prohibited by Germany, presumably in preparation for its war effort.[36] This kind of cartel has probably disappeared, but prosecutions in the 1990s indicate that there are many contemporary cartels, mainly to manage price—but in at least two cases (laminated plastic tubes and graphite electrodes) also to control access to technology.[37] The graphite-electrode case was particularly significant, for developing nations were harmed, and the technology is extremely significant to the steel industry.[38]

Some cross-licenses have also been created under specific, statutory antitrust exemptions that may be internationally discriminatory. For example, the United States has a number of arrangements under which competitors can cooperate in

33. Consider, for example, the current U.S. Department of Justice prosecution of price-fixing in the international DRAM industry. *See* Department of Justice Press Release, Oct 18, 2006, "Three executives indicted for their roles in the FRA price-fixing and bid-rigging conspiracy," available at http://www.usdoj.gov/opa/pr/2006/October/06_at_710.html. (Collected online August 2, 2007.)

34. *United States v. Singer Manufacturing Co.*, 374 US 174 (1963).

35. Robert P. Terrill, "Cartels and the International Exchange of Technology," *American Economic Review* 36: 745–757 (May 1946); Thurman Arnold, "The Abuse of Patents," *The Atlantic* (July 1942), reprinted in 24 *Journal of the Patent and Traremark Office Society* 521 (1942). (Thurman Arnold was U.S. Assistant Attorney General for Antitrust at the time.)

36. Id.

37. Margaret Levenstein and Valerie Suslow, "Contemporary International Cartels and Developing Countries: Economic Effects and Implications for Competition Policy," 71 *Antitrust L J* 801 (2004).

38. Id.

research without antitrust risk—but the exemptions are typically limited to U.S. firms or to firms that will manufacture in the United States.[39] There is serious question whether such exemptions have any real economic effect—indeed, the economic value of one of the key cooperative research arrangements, a semiconductor arrangement, has been seriously questioned.[40] But, to the extent that such exemptions do have such an effect, they amount to a national cartel and are obviously inconsistent with any rational global antitrust policy.

D. Standards-Based Pools

Standards present a further situation, for a patented technology is often required to practice a standard. There are frequent debates over whether, in essence, a patent needed to practice a standard must be licensed on reasonable-royalty terms, or, at least, whether a holder of such a patent should be prepared to enter into good-faith negotiations for a license on reasonable and non-discriminatory terms.[41] And firms involved in the negotiation of a standard often are asked to disclose any patents that they hold that may affect practice of the standard. The precise scope of such obligations is sometimes unclear and depends, in part, on the rules of the standards organization.[42] But many nations feel that technologies needed for use in a standard should be made available on some terms, and even the United States is suspicious of the activities of firms shaping standards in ways that favor their patent interests. The issue for developing nations is that a standard may effectively compel use of particular patented technologies; if these are imposed in an unfair way, then there is no reason that the nation

---

39. For example, National Cooperative Research Act of 1984 as amended by the National Cooperative Production Act of 1993; 15 USC §§ 4301 ff. *See*, generally, Mark A.A. Warner and Alan M. Rugman, "Competitiveness: An Emerging Strategy of Discrimination in U.S. Antitrust and R&D Policy," 25 *Law and Policy in International Business* 945 (1994).

40. Douglas A. Irwin and Peter J. Klenow, "High Tech R&D Subsidies: Estimating the Effects of Sematech" (NBER Working Paper No 4974 1994). As a framework for cooperative research, Sematech faced staffing and intellectual property management difficulties arising from the unwillingness of the participants to share key technologies. As a mechanism for developing standards among the different tiers of the industry (e.g., manufacturing equipment, chips, and software for the chips), it was a major contribution.

41. The conflict with traditional IP principles is exemplified by the debate over the rules of the European Telecommunications Standards Institute (ETSI). *See*, for example, Mark Shurmer and Gary Lea, "Telecommunications Standardization and Intellectual Property Rights: A Fundamental Dilemma," *StandardView* 3: 50–59 (June 1995). And see Mark A. Lemley, "Ten Things to Do About Patent Holdup of Standards (and One Not To)," 48 *Boston College Law Revue* 149 (2007).

42. For the leading U.S. example of the various disputes, *see* U.S. Federal Trade Commission, *In the Matter of Rambus, Inc*, Docket No 9302 (Aug 2, 2006); for the international debate, *see* World Trade Organization, Communication from the People's Republic of China, *Intellectual Property Right (IPR) Issues in Standardization*, G/TBT/W/251 (25 May 2005).

cannot, at least for domestic use, resist use of the standard or of the components of the particular supplier whose patent was used improperly.

In this context, as in some others, it is possible for a cross-license to be competitive and beneficial, particularly if the members of the arrangement allow entry of new firms into the arrangement. Thus, the agreements used to create a group license of the patents needed for compliance with new standards are generally carefully defined so that a non-member firm believing it has a relevant patent can obtain impartial consideration of its claim and possible entry into the group.[43] At least in the United States, the antitrust reviews ensure that the standards are set fairly as regards entry to the list of patents that will be compensated. Such groups are, therefore, unlikely to bar entry of new developing-world members unfairly—and are often very valuable in making new technologies available.

There is a separate question, however, regarding whether such arrangements are fair in their licensing terms. In at least some cases, developing-world firms have complained that the standards agreements require unreasonably high licensing fees: such high fees can be a barrier to competitiveness for the developing world firm and have been a basis for protest.[44] Developed-world antitrust authorities have generally avoided reviewing the financial terms in these cases, on the theory that markets are generally better determinants of price than are regulators.[45] Considering the near-monopoly position that a group licensor may hold, this is not necessarily an accurate assumption, and a developing-nation regulator might reasonably agree that a price is too high. It would be hard to make such an approach effective for international sales, although it might be possible for domestic sales. In one recent case, the Taiwan Administrative High Court held that such an arrangement amounted to price fixing.[46]

E. Tacit Pools

As just noted, it is solid antitrust doctrine that a cartel that makes an agreement to restrain the entry of new firms is acting in violation of antitrust law principles. But what if the arrangement is tacit rather than explicit? Here, the reasonable

---

43. For examples, *see* Letter from Joel I. Klein to Carey P. Ramos, Esq. (June 10, 1999); Letter from Joel I. Klein to Garrard R. Beeney, Esq. (December 16, 1998) (DVD pool); Letter from Joel I. Klein to Garrard R. Beeney, Esq. (June 26, 1997) (MPEG pool).

44. *See*, G. Linden, *Optical Storage in China: A Study in Strategic Industrial Policy*, Center for Work, Technology and Society, University of California, Berkeley, Report 2003-01 (September 2003).

45. *See*, for example, U.S. Department of Justice and Federal Trade Commission (cited in note 1).

46. Taipei Administrative High Court Decision of August 11, 2005, as described in Lim (cited in note 21). An effort to attack the same licenses as an improper package succeeded at the U.S. International Trade Commission but was reversed by the Court of Appeals for the Federal Circuit, *U.S. Philips v. Int'l Trade Commission*, 424 F 3d 1179 (Fed Cir 2005).

law is much less clear. After all, in the parallel situation of pricing, an agreement among competitors to fix prices is per se an antitrust offense. In contrast, a tacit arrangement in which competitors, looking over each others' shoulders, manage to keep their prices above the competitive level is generally not regarded as an antitrust violation. This is perhaps because the price is lower than the monopoly price that might be fixed by full agreement; it is perhaps because there is no practical way to prevent such tacit collusion; it is perhaps because the price increase that is achieved this way is often the way research is financed. Should a similar distinction be applied in the patent context? The arguments against it are those made in connection with the basic oligopoly analysis above—even in the tacit arrangement, the good of the society may be harmed if the oligopoly is allowed to remain too small. A strong counterargument is that it is extremely difficult, if not impossible, to decide whether the oligopoly really is too small economically.

F. The International Aspects of This Situation

As the above analysis shows, there are some situations in which oligopolies or their members act to set prices or to refuse to license out patents that are nearly uniformly agreed to violate antitrust law. And there are some cross-licenses or refusals to license that are certainly innocent as an antitrust matter and some in which there is substantial doubt. Even in the clear cases, however, it is difficult for a market nation to respond with antitrust prosecution because the oligopoly is almost always international. The offense lies in the interaction of firms from different nations—and the affected markets may be in still further nations. This always creates an incentive problem: Even where there is a price-fixing cartel, and antitrust authorities in some nations obtain jurisdiction over many or all of the firms, those authorities will typically achieve damages based only on the impact of the cartel in their own markets.[47] This may not be enough to deter the cartels, which will seek to obtain supranormal profits in all markets—and it is probable that cartels are under-prosecuted.[48] In addition, it is likely to be very difficult to obtain information about cartel activity.

Moreover, the analysis of mergers and of technical cooperation agreements, which contribute to concentration and define the effective size of the oligopoly, is often limited by the same territorial concerns. Nor is it clear how often merger analysis will consider technological effects, as opposed to static market concentration.[49]

---

47. *F. Hoffman La-Roche Ltd v. Empagran S.A.*, 542 US 155 (2004).

48. *See* John M. Connor, "Global Antitrust Prosecutions of Modern International Cartels," 4 *Journal of Industry, Competition and Trade* 239 (2004); Julian L. Clarke and Simon J. Evenett, *A Multilateral Framework for Competition Policy?*, prepared for *The Singapore Issues and the World Trading System: The Road to Cancun and Beyond* (Simon J. Evenett and Swiss State Secretariat of Economic Affairs, eds.).

49. When they do so, they utilize a potential competition analysis, and have, in some cases, required divestment of specific research programs in order not to decrease the

There is also a risk that home nations with large markets will be able to review, and approve or disapprove, a merger that affects the size and, therefore, the effective power of an oligopoly. Other nations may have less power over the transaction. Consider, as an example, the debate between U.S. and EU officials over the McDonnell-Douglas merger with Boeing, which was approved by U.S. authorities.[50] E.U. authorities were able to negotiate some changes but were almost certainly under enormous practical pressure to accept the merger as approved by the United States.

There is also an incentive problem, in that each nation's antitrust authorities will be more concerned with protecting the nation's own firms than with protecting global competition and technological advance. (This dynamic may have been at play in the McDonnell-Douglas/Boeing interplay discussed.) This is in spite of the fact that global society benefits from technological advance, perhaps even more than it does from free trade.

And there is a special problem in the patent area. Nations can certainly affect the licensing of patents that affect their market, but they find it hard to affect the licensing of patents in other nations. Formally, the issue of the validity of a patent license under antitrust law is certainly different from that of the validity of a foreign patent or of the infringement of that patent, and it is only the latter issues that have been held not subject to decision by U.S. courts.[51] Nevertheless, it is very difficult for the courts of a single jurisdiction to respond to territorial restrictions based on exclusive licensing. In a celebrated case involving the old DuPont-ICI arrangements to divide markets for nylon, a U.S. court declared the market-division agreement illegal and, as part of its remedy, directed that both parties license their patents to each other to reestablish competition in each nation. In particular, the various U.K. patents were to be licensed on reasonable royalty terms, including to DuPont, thus reestablishing competition in the United Kingdom. This arrangement was attacked in the United Kingdom, where the Court of Appeals rejected enforcement of such a foreign decree affecting British patent rights.[52] In the face of this opposition, the U.S. court backed down on the reciprocal U.S. provisions and allowed DuPont to exclude ICI.[53] The result was to reestablish the territorial division. In a later case, the courts avoided the issue by saying that

---

amount of research. This is typical in the pharmaceutical sector when the merging firms each have research programs oriented toward the same market, as exemplified by the U.S. Federal Trade Commission's consent decree in the Hoechst merger with Rhone-Poulenc, Consent Order 3919 (Jan 18, 2000).

50. William E. Kovacic, "Transatlantic Turbulence: The Boeing-McDonnell Douglas Merger, and International Competition Policy," 68 *Antitrust L J* 805 (2001).

51. See discussion of *Voda v. Cordis Corp* (cited in note 30).

52. *British Nylon Spinners v. Imperial Chemical Industries, Ltd* [1952] 2 All ER 780 (Cof A). And *see* "Conflict of Laws," 66 *Harvard Law Revue* 924 (1953).

53. *United States v. Imperial Chemical Industries*, 1954 Trade Case ¶67,739 (SDNY 1954).

grants of territorial patent rights were acceptable under the antitrust laws, as long as the market division was implicit in the patent licenses rather than achieved through an explicit agreement.[54] And, in a more recent U.S. case involving an offense of the type to be considered in the next section, the consent decree didn't even try to affect the technology development outside the United States.[55]

Thus, as in the previous situation, a developing nation can give its own firms protection in its own local markets against technological restraints imposed by a global oligopoly. But it cannot generally reach the origin of the problem—and, in contrast to the situation of section I—there is no other antitrust authority that can, either. It is essential to globalize damages, yet patent-law and antitrust principles currently prevent that. This is one of the central needs for global antitrust law to address, and it is difficult to see how it can be resolved without either a global antitrust authority or a new set of rules covering extraterritorial enforcement of patent-related antitrust decrees. It is unlikely that such an arrangement could be negotiated without a set of agreed-upon standards on the relevant patent-antitrust and oligopoly issues—and, perhaps, without agreement on how to deal with more traditional global cartel issues. Yet the problem is very serious.

III. THE LOCAL FIRM

The final situation to consider is that of the relationship between a foreign firm and a local one that is seeking to gain technology. Here, in contrast to section I, which emphasized unilateral refusal to license, the focus will be on the details of the contractual relationship between an international licensor and a local technology-oriented firm. It is some of these provisions that were at the heart of the technology transfer debates of the 1970s and 1980s.[56] Today the issues are typically handled as vertical restraints under U.S. § 1 or EU Article 81. And there are much more detailed analyses of these issues reflected in the U.S. *Antitrust Guidelines for the Licensing of Intellectual Property* and in the U.K. Block Exemption for Technology Transfer.[57] In addition, this section considers the economic wisdom of mergers between a foreign firm and a local firm, an issue typically handled under merger law principles.

54. *United States v. Westinghouse Electric Corp*, 648 F 2d 642 (9th Cir 1980) (electrical products).

55. *United States v. Pilkington*, Consent Decree (DC Ariz 27 December 1994) (float-glass technology).

56. *See*, for example, Surendra J. Patel, Pedro Roffe, and Abdulqawi Yusuf, eds., *International Technology Transfer: The Origins and Aftermath of the United Nations Negotiations on a Draft Code of Conduct* (Kluwer, 2001).

57. Commission Regulation (EC) No 772/2004 of 27 April 2004 on the application of Article 81(3) of the Treaty to categories of technology-transfer agreements.

Before exploring the detailed law in this area, it must be recognized that the relationship between a foreign firm and a local firm varies depending on the circumstances. When the foreign firm is licensing the local firm to produce a product for export to the global market, the interests of the two firms are, in the short run, quite complementary and parallel. The foreign firm wants a globally competitive product and is therefore willing to share technology as necessary for this purpose. But, in the long run, the global firm may fear that the local firm may eventually become a competitor—and may therefore hesitate to share its most important technologies, which it will likely seek to retain at its home office. Thus, the foreign firm may be willing to license the production of only some part of the product. In the case of production for a local market, the relationship is more immediately antagonistic. Both firms will benefit from the production, but they may be in greater disagreement as to the sharing of the profits in terms of pricing, license fees, and the like. And there will always be a fear of losing key technologies to a possible new global competitor.

Host-nation antitrust policy must, therefore, recognize that the foreign supplier of technology has options other than licensing technology. The supplier can instead directly invest and, save for situations of expropriation or employee misconduct, maintain complete control of its technology. Or, unless compelled by a compulsory license, it can avoid participation in any production or research ventures within the nation. To the extent to which national antitrust authorities attempt to strengthen competitive pricing in the national market or access to technology for national firms, they may have to pay a price in terms of foreign reluctance to participate in the national economy. The trade-offs for a typical developing-nation antitrust entity are thus different from those faced by an antitrust entity in a nation in which significant technology is generated.

A. Licensing Rules

1. The General Trend Before about 1980, developed-world antitrust regulators were very suspicious of many patent-licensing practices, such as territorial restrictions and resale-pricing requirements. These suspicions were reflected in the international technology-transfer debates. But then a major change occurred as the intellectual balance in both the United States and Europe shifted toward increased support for intellectual property and decreased support for antitrust. As a result, many of the practices that had been prohibited were now accepted, both by U.S. regulatory authorities and in revised European block exemptions for specific categories of license agreements. And, in the same time period, developing-world ideology changed, and technology-transfer code negotiations were essentially abandoned.

2. Specific Practices In light of the new economic understanding of the balance between antitrust and intellectual property, it is useful to consider which licensing practices might be competitive and which might be anti-competitive in the developing-nation context. The balances might still be different for the developed and the developing nation. In this paper, it would be absurd to attempt to detail all the principles, which take many pages to discuss in the U.S. *Guidelines* and the European *Block Exemptions.* And there were the classic "nine no-nos" once, but no longer, regarded as antitrust violations.[58] (These are not the only important practices.) Those practices that generally contribute to the patent holder's return on innovation will be discussed in the next paragraph, and export limitations, grant-backs, and non-contest clauses will be discussed in subsequent paragraphs below. The use of tying clauses was discussed in section I.

Licensing practices that contribute to the return on innovation, as by restricting the resale price, are now generally viewed as positive because the increased return may contribute to the incentive to innovate. On a global basis, this argument is solid, and it would probably not be wise (or politically feasible) to negotiate an international agreement that restricted such clauses. The difficulty for the developing nation is that the innovation is typically encouraged in the developed world, whereas an increased price may occur in the developing world. At the same time, the developing nation ultimately benefits from the innovation. In the face of this balance, it is economically plausible, but not necessarily economically or politically wise, for a developing nation to prohibit such clauses. In particular, whether restrictions are wise depends on whether there is need for investment to develop or modify the technology for the developing-nation market.

It is reasonable for a developing nation to be concerned about clauses prohibiting the export of products, a restriction not in the nine no-nos, but certainly in the traditional list of developing-nation concerns and, in the analogous form of territorial resale restrictions, a developed-nation concern, as well. For the patent holder, such clauses permit explicit price discrimination among different markets and thus permit an increased economic return on the invention. (As noted in section II, this can sometimes be achieved without an explicit clause by simply granting the rights arising under some nations' patents while not granting the parallel rights under other nations' patents.) In the new world of globalized production, such clauses will be less common, but they will sometimes be used to serve large markets, such as China. Given that such clauses undercut the benefits of free trade and comparative advantage, there is no economic reason for a developing nation to accept them, unless the nation receives a price benefit.

58. They included (a) tying of patent rights to other rights, (b) mandatory grant-backs, (c) restrictions on resale of patented products, (d) covenants not to purchase a competitor's product, (e) giving the licensee a veto over the licensor's grant of further licenses, (f) mandatory package licensing, (g) compulsory payment of royalties not reasonably related to the sales of the patented product, (h) restrictions on sale of unpatented products made by a patented process, and (i) regulating the price at which licenses can resell products made with licensed technology. This list is drawn from that presented in R. D. Anderson, "The Interface between Competition Policy and Intellectual Property in the Context of the International Trading System," 1998 *Journal of International Economic Law* 655 (1998).

Indeed, the reciprocal situation, a nation's freedom to allow parallel imports, is implied by the "agreement to disagree" of TRIPS Article 6 on parallel trade. Even a nation that generally rejects such clauses may still, of course, choose to allow them in contexts in which a particular technology is needed for domestic markets and available only under restriction.

One category of clause should clearly be prohibited: the exclusive grant-back, that is, a requirement that any improvements the licensor makes to a licensed invention be granted back to the licensor on an exclusive basis. This is anti-competitive, as seen in the *Pilkington* litigation,[59] because it removes any incentive for the licensee to innovate. In the *Pilkington* example, the result was stagnation in float-glass technology for a generation. It is still reasonable to permit non-exclusive grant-backs, giving the licensor assurance that it will be able to compete with its licensee as the latter makes product improvement. And it is important for developing nations that they not inadvertently restrict the provisions of open-source technology agreements that are designed to ensure that follow-on innovations to open-source technology remain open source.[60]

Another category of clauses that should be prohibited are those that prevent the licensee from contesting the validity of the intellectual property involved. Such clauses contribute to reducing the number of parties who may have an incentive to determine whether the particular monopoly right really was correctly granted. Although there are a number of doctrines, such as "licensee estoppel" and restrictions on the right to bring declaratory judgment actions to determine whether a patent is valid, one version of such doctrines, the declaratory-judgment version, was recently struck down by the U.S. Supreme Court.[61]

3. Monopoly and Technology Incentive Finally, a wise national regime will *not* offer a monopoly as a basis to encourage a foreign investor to come into a nation. This was typical, for example, in the telecommunications context, in which a national telecommunications entity could be privatized on a more lucrative basis if sold with some monopoly rights. This is understandable, considering the extent to which privatization has often derived from budgetary demands, but it is effectively a hidden tax on both innovation and the economy. There is no good reason to create monopoly intentionally unless there is also very sophisticated regulation. (This is an example of the much broader issue of effective regulation of technology-based industries, such as telecommunications and energy; it is easy to regulate such industries unwisely.)

59. United States v. Pilkington, Civil Action 94-345-TUC-WDB (DC Arizona, Dec 22, 1994).

60. *See* Robin Cooper Feldman, "The Open-Source Biotechnology Movement: Is It Patent Misuse?" 6 *Minnesota Journal of Law, Science & Technology* 1 (2004).

61. *Medimmune, Inc. v. Genentech, Inc.*, 127 S Ct 764 (2007).

B. Acquisition

A recurring issue will be the possible integration of national firms with foreign ones. Under what circumstances should an international firm be allowed to purchase a domestic technology-based firm, or vice-versa? Unless the foreign and domestic firms are already in a close relationship, such a purchase will generally reduce domestic competition and may thus contribute to higher prices. At the same time, the foreign firm may bring advanced technology—and this has been a reason both to favor foreign purchase of national firms and national firm purchase of foreign ones. The last point is exemplified by the rise of such developing nation–based global firms as the Indian steel company ArcelorMittal. In some cases, the integration of the two entities may enable the local firm to become a more effective player and contribute to competition on the local level, or contribute to exports and competition on the global level. Moreover, it is not always bad for a global industry to consolidate: sometimes the result of *some* global consolidation will be to facilitate greater innovation.

Ideally, such an issue would be evaluated on the basis of the impact on the global economy and the global incentive to innovate. But, in the absence of a solid, global antitrust authority, no nation is currently able to evaluate impartially the impact of global consolidation in an industry. Rather, it can evaluate only the impact in its own national market, and it is likely to favor its own firms in the process. Hence, as globalization proceeds, this is an issue that will have to be internationalized.

In this situation, a developing nation can certainly analyze such a merger from its own perspective. Is the benefit of the technological relationship brought by the global actor valuable enough to outweigh the loss in local competition? This is a manageable question. But it must be recognized that answering it requires serious economic expertise. The question cannot be resolved by legal principles alone; rather, it requires a balancing of two economic unknowns: the impact of the merger on product competition and the impact of the merger on technology development and access.

C. TRIPS

The antitrust-based restrictions described above in this section are certainly consistent with existing international regulation. Thus, Article 40 of TRIPS allows nations to control certain restrictive practices in licenses and specifies, in particular, exclusive grant-backs, restrictions on challenges to validity, and coercive package licensing. This is where TRIPS mentions and implicitly approves certain restrictions. Not only are restrictions on such behavior clearly acceptable, but the article requires the licensor's nation's authorities to enter into consultations with the licensee's nation under some circumstances and to assist in antitrust prosecution.

IV. IMPLEMENTATION AND REMEDIES

The analysis above describes a number of principles for international antitrust in areas that affect the availability of technology to developing nations. In each area, there is room for further judgment and detailing of the principles. Making the principles meaningful, in whatever form they might finally take, requires domestic action and, ideally, international action.

A. Legislative Texts and Principles

At the domestic level, antitrust requires a law. Presumably, this law will cover much more than just those principles related to intellectual property. Many nations are now adopting competition laws—the number of nations with such laws nearly doubled in the 1990s.[62] The difficulty (and it is true for both U.S. and EU laws), is that competition legislation rarely includes very specific principles governing IP questions. Thus, the new Indian Act prohibits anti-competitive agreements but includes a proviso affirming "the right of any person to restrain any infringement of, or to impose reasonable conditions, as may be necessary for protecting" specified intellectual property rights.[63] Even in the Chinese competition law, the issues are buried in the question of what constitutes an "abuse" of intellectual property rights.[64] There are already several model competition laws proposed by the World Bank and OECD together, by UNCTAD, and by the Commonwealth.[65] These are not, however, at all specific regarding intellectual property-related practices, although they do consider refusals to deal and abuses of a dominant position. The UNCTAD document, for example, mentions certain technology issues in passing but does not face the difficult problems involved in patent/antitrust balances.

The United States and the European Union have developed more specific principles, exemplified by the U.S. *Guidelines* and the EU *Block Exemption*. Almost certainly, most nations' laws could be interpreted with parallel, more detailed principles, and an ideal first step would be the creation of an analogous—and economically defensible—set of guidelines for developing nations to use in enforcing their existing antitrust laws. It is important to deal with at least

a) principles for the misuse of intellectual property, as discussed in section I above, including whatever principles are chosen for compulsory licenses on an antitrust basis;

---

62. Clarke and Evenett (cited in note 48).

63. "The Competition Act 2002," *The Gazette of India* § 3(5)(i) (January 14, 2003).

64. *See* note 20 supra.

65. *See* United Nations Conference on Trade and Development, *Model Law on Competition*, TD/RBP/CONF.5/7 (2002); Cassey Lee, *Model Competition Laws: The World Bank-OECD and UNCTAD Approaches Compared*, Working Paper No. 96 (Centre on Regulation and Competition, University of Manchester, January 2005).

b) principles for the acceptability of pooling arrangements and any principles to reject global pools, as discussed in section II above;
c) principles governing license agreements, as discussed in section III above; and
d) principles governing mergers in the high-technology area, again as discussed in section III above.

This is a task that could be undertaken in any of a number of international or expert fora. It is probably better that it be initially done by experts than by diplomats, for any early effort at diplomatic negotiation would face great tensions over the proper scope of intellectual property and the choice of antitrust principles. Moreover, the guidelines could generally be applied domestically without the need for international agreement.

B. TRIPS Requirements

These responses are consistent with TRIPS, because of the limitations contained in TRIPS Articles 8.2 and 40. Article 8.2 states that "Appropriate measures, provided that they are consistent with the provisions of this Agreement, may be needed to prevent the abuse of intellectual property rights by rights holders or the resort to practices which unreasonably restrain trade or adversely affect the international transfer of technology." Article 40 goes on to detail the rights of members to impose specific limitations on licensing practices and includes a list of practices that may be treated as abuses.

C. National (or Regional) Institutions

It is also essential to build the necessary enforcement institutions. This certainly includes a national public-enforcement entity that has the rights, under the legal procedures of the nation, to ensure compliance with the law. It is essential that there be an appeal procedure and that the institutions be as impartial as possible in order to ensure confidence for investors. It is also essential that there be solid economic expertise as well as legal expertise. Otherwise, antitrust law can be more harmful than helpful. This is not simply a matter of building regulatory institutions: it is also a matter of ensuring that the judiciary does not become a mechanism for delay during appeals from regulatory decisions.[66] And, because expertise in these areas is so difficult to develop, it may sometimes be wise to establish the key, new institutions at a regional level.

D. International Principles and Institutions

As noted in the analysis of the principles, a nation can achieve some competition and protection from misuse of intellectual property in its home market without

66. For an example of the problem, *see* Germano Mendes De Paula, "Competition Policy and the Legal System in Brazil: The Experience of the Steel Industry, Centre on Regulation and Competition," Working Paper No. 87 (University of Manchester, October 2004).

any new international arrangements. (It may face serious criticism and, perhaps, the potential of TRIPS sanctions, if its principles are out of step with those of solid economics.) But it cannot achieve protection of its balance of antitrust and intellectual property with respect to its exports in a globalized world without new international arrangements.

1. **History and Relevant Provisions** There have been two types of international antitrust discussions. One involves cooperation agreements among national antitrust authorities, looking particularly to the exchange of information to facilitate the prosecution of international antitrust defendants. This has gone quite far, leading, for example, to a concept of "positive comity," in which a nation can ask another to prosecute an alleged antitrust offender that it believes is hurting its economy. (Under "negative comity," a nation merely gives others an opportunity to comment before undertaking enforcement action that may affect the other nations.)[67] These discussions have now been formalized in a new International Competition Network (ICN). The ICN was founded in 2001 and concentrates on discussions among enforcement agencies, training for new agencies, and some committee-based studies of new issues.[68]

The other is negotiation toward an international antitrust treaty. There have been serious unofficial proposals.[69] And there have been two international fora (since the restrictive business practice discussions of several decades ago):[70] the Organisation for Economic Cooperation and Development (OECD) and the WTO.

The OECD has a Competition Committee, which was created in 1961 and includes senior representatives from OECD member nations. It often includes representatives of other nations and non-governmental organizations. It provides a forum within which competition issues can be studied and publishes a variety of reports. It does develop recommendations and best practices but does not appear to be oriented toward negotiating large-scale new agreements. It is,

---

67. OECD, Working Party No. 3 on International Cooperation, *CLP Report on Positive Comity: Note by the Secretariat* (June 14, 1999). *See* Sheridan Scott (Canadian Commissioner of Competition), *Canadian Perspectives on the Role of Comity in Competition Law Enforcement in a Globalized World; To Defer or Not To Defer? Is that the question?* Speech at American Bar Association's Section of Antitrust Law 2006 Spring Meeting (March 29, 2006).

68. *See* Maria C. Tineo (U.S. Federal Trade Commission), International Competition Network update, available at http://www.ftc.gov/bc/international/docs/03Intro-ftc.pdf. (Collected online August 2, 2007.)

69. *See*, for example, the *Draft International Antitrust Code* (July 10, 1993), reproduced at 65 *Antitrust & Trade Regulation. Reporter* (BNA) No 1628 (Aug 19, 1993). For a sample of academic proposals, *see* Eleanor M. Fox, "Antitrust and Regulatory Federalism: Races Up, Down, and Sideways," 75 *NYU Law Rev* 1781 (2000); Andrew T. Guzman, "Antitrust and International Regulatory Federalism," 76 *NYU Law Rev* 1141 (2001).

70. *See*, for example, *Set of Multilaterally Agreed Equitable Principles and Rules for the Control of Restrictive Business Practices*, TD/RBP/CONF/10/Rev. 2), 19 *ILM* 813 (1980).

rather, a place in which expertise can be developed and shared among member nations.[71]

The WTO discussion took place in the Working Group on Trade and Competition Policy. This group considered intellectual property/antitrust issues in one of its 1998 meetings.[72] It moved by 2003, however, toward a more minimal agreement that would require nations to enact an anti-cartel law, to apply core fairness principles (for example, transparency and non-discrimination) in enforcing antitrust law, and to encourage voluntary cooperation among, and strengthening of, competition agencies. There was, apparently, no intention to create a mandatory standard law: in this domain, one size would *not* fit all. And the focus was specifically on hard-core cartels, rather than on the vertical restraints that are often relevant to patent issues.[73] This forum, however, is now inactive, as a result of a 2004 decision by the General Council of the WTO.

So far, then, efforts toward a treaty have failed. There are probably several underlying reasons. One is fear on the part of the U.S. Department of Justice that a global treaty will not reflect the principles that it believes are appropriate for antitrust law. Although the differences are probably not as great as they once were, the U.S. antitrust authorities fear that antitrust principles will protect small competitors against large ones, rather than simply protecting competition. This statement oversimplifies the issues, but the difference and fear are real.[74] And, as is clear from the discussion above and from the *Microsoft* litigation, the United States and the European Union differ further on IP aspects of antitrust. Another issue is that the developing world has resisted including antitrust in the WTO negotiations. The reasons are not entirely clear. Probably, they primarily fear that this is one more context in which global negotiations might hurt the developing world. There are almost certainly doubts about how to handle state-owned enterprises—this was apparently an obstacle to China's adoption of an antitrust law.[75] And there must be concerns about protecting existing cartels—the United States, for example, has a legal provision permitting export cartels,[76] and there

---

71. *See Resolution of the Council* [C(87)138(Final)].

72. Report (1998) of the Working Group on the Interaction between Trade and Competition Policy to the General Council, WTO WT/WGTCP/2 (8 December 1998).

73. For an excellent review of the WTO situation as of 2003, *see* Clarke & Evenett (cited in note 48).

74. The differences are carefully reviewed in Spencer Waller, "An International Common Law of Antitrust," 34 *New England Law Revue* 163 (1999). For an example of the contemporary conservative U.S. concern about international antitrust, *see* John McGinnis, "The Political Economy of International Antitrust Harmonization," 45 William and Mary Law Revue 549 (2003–2004).

75. *See* Owen et al. (cited in note 20), and Maarten Roos, "Developing China's Antimonopoly Law," *AsiaLaw* (May 2007).

76. This is the Webb-Pomerene Act, 15 USC §§ 61–65.

are, of course, supporters of governmental cartels, such as the Organization of Petroleum Exporting Countries (OPEC).

2. **Possible New Rules** One thing that international rules could do is to bring confidence to developing nations with respect to their own choice of rules. Certainly, international rules can confirm the reasonableness of applying antitrust law against tying and other broadly agreed offenses. They can describe what cartel behavior is and is not reasonable with respect to antitrust offenses. They would rationally ensure that any research-oriented antitrust exemptions are open on a non-discriminatory basis to firms from all nations. And they can provide cover with respect to licensing principles on which there may be disagreement. Presumably any treaty in this area would include lists of licensing clauses that are clearly permitted, of clauses that are clearly prohibited, and of those on which nations may take diverging positions or which circumstances may determine whether the clause is a competition offense.

3. **Enforcement Questions** An international system can also provide new enforcement mechanisms. There are two obvious needs. One is the management of mergers and oligopolistic integration at the global level. This is obviously a serious issue that transcends the intellectual property area. And it will be difficult to manage internationally, because of problems of enforcement, of national favorites, of the link with government-encouraged cartels, and of the political power of the companies themselves. Yet it must be faced—and the political pressure to face it will come from consumers and antitrust authorities in developed as well as developing nations. It may require an international antitrust authority; it may be solvable instead through negotiation of a standard for such mergers, coupled with much deeper agreements to share information among antitrust authorities.

The other enforcement context is that of intellectual property. As noted above, intellectual property rights are still national, and it is difficult, even in a negotiated antitrust decree, to obtain extraterritorial effect for a restriction on the use of intellectual property. This point bedeviled the enforcement of both the *BNS* and the *Pilkington* decrees. The obvious goal here is an international agreement that gives transnational recognition to a nation's properly issued decree restricting a particular use of intellectual property. Considering that there are great differences around the world on which restrictions are properly placed on the use of intellectual property rights, it is hard to imagine that such an agreement can be achieved without first coming to agreement on standards to be used in the intellectual property/antitrust area, and perhaps, as well, a review process (which could be international or based in the nation in which the decree is being applied extraterritorially).

E. Recommendations

All developing nations should consider interpretations of their antitrust laws along the lines suggested in sections I and II. And those developing nations that have significant indigenous or foreign-owned technological capability should also consider laws along the lines suggested in section III. All should also ensure that they gain (perhaps through regional cooperation) the economic expertise needed to enforce the legislation wisely. This can be done without diplomatic conflict.

At least in my judgment, although the point is controversial, the developing nations should also encourage negotiation of an international agreement, either in the form of a WTO antitrust agreement or of a WIPO intellectual property/ antitrust agreement. The analysis above makes it clear that the current process of national enforcement of antitrust law is sub-optimal from a traditional competition-law perspective. Although there needs to be much more data and analysis before one can make a solid judgment, the failure of the international process *may* be particularly bad in the patent-antitrust context because it is important for the world to be able to benefit from the cross-fertilization of different economic streams. There is an obvious question of whether developing-nation power will be adequate to bring new negotiations to a favorable result rather than one dominated by an overly pro–intellectual property and overly anti-antitrust perspective. But the opportunity deserves exploration.

18. INNOVATION, COMPETITION POLICIES, AND INTELLECTUAL PROPERTY
An Evolutionary Perspective and Its Policy Implications

LEONARDO BURLAMAQUI*

Intellectual property laws are the legal sinews of the information age: They affect everything from the availability and price of AIDS drugs, to patterns of international development, to the communications structure of the Internet.
—James Boyle, 2004

I. INTRODUCTION

In our 21st-century globalized economy, innovation, competition policies, and intellectual property issues are at the forefront of every government, firm, and policymaking debate, North or South (Wells 2002, Landes and Posner 2003, Wu 2004). From the perspective of crafting development strategies, there is no way to circumvent those matters.

Largely because of the work of Richard Nelson and his collaborators, a "National System of Innovation" approach to policymaking was developed and is revealing itself to be extremely useful in evaluating innovation policies (Nelson 1993 and 2005; Kim and Nelson 2000). However, when it comes to competition policies and to the subtleties of the interaction among technology, law, and economics, the available perspectives at hand still hail from the so-called "Harvard School" or "Prophets of Regulation School" (McCraw 1984) and the now-hegemonic "Chicago School" (Posner 1976 and 2002, Bork 1993, Hovenkamp 1999). The Harvard School tracks the imperfect-competition models of neoclassical economics. It highlights the imperfections and failures of the market, thus carrying

* I would like to thank both Neil Netanel and an anonymous reviewer for the excellent suggestions concerning both form and content for this chapter. The usual caveat regarding responsibilities applies. This chapter represents my own personal views, and does not reflect those of the Ford Foundation.

a deep suspicion of industry concentration, firm consolidation, and business cooperation in general.

The Chicago School focuses on consumer welfare and holds efficiency as its core concept. The Chicago School of Law and Economics underscores the inevitable public-policy failures of government[1] and is aligned with the public-choice understanding of government as captive of private interests. Consequently, the Chicago School is much more libertarian and less hostile toward industry concentration and mergers than is the Harvard School. Additionally, the Chicago School is grounded in neoclassical economic theory: It relies on the perfect-competition model as its basic blueprint, with some inputs from contestable-markets theory. Accordingly, Chicago School theorists do not take market power very seriously (Bork 1993; Hovenkamp 1999, chapter 2). As mentioned, consumer welfare and efficiency are its main concerns, but they are (tentatively) measured by comparing two different points in time, with no attention to the evolution from one to the other (Langlois 2001).

Whatever the Harvard and Chicago Schools' differences may be regarding competition policy, it is on the intellectual property front that the most important issues and developments are taking shape (Benkler 2006, Boyle 2006, Landes and Posner 2003, Wu 2004, Jaffe and Lerner 2004). Interestingly from a neoclassical perspective, the whole new wave of intellectual property claims is about extending monopoly positions and market power (the right to patent generic knowledge, business models, etc.—cf. Merger 2003; Coriat, Cimoli, and Primi 2005) to leading firms, thereby protecting them from competition—or, to put it in mainstream language, these claims are designed to create or reinforce market failures in the sense of shielding firms from competition instead of exposing them to it.[2]

How do competition and intellectual property interact in the new economy? It appears there is no coherent analytical framework to address that interaction[3] and certainly no Schumpeterian perspective on these issues, either.[4] But that

1. One of most important influences in the foundation of that approach was George Stigler, whose "capture theory" and influence on what under James Buchanan and Gordon Tullock would become the "rational-choice approach" is well known.

2. *See* Arnold Plant's point below on that matter.

3. This does not imply a shortage of work discussing specific issues in what is called "the economics of intellectual property rights." *See* Menell 1999 for an excellent survey on general theories of IP. A very interesting review acknowledging the under-researched nature of the theme can be found in Dixon and Greenlalgh 2002. The shortcomings of most of that work are, from my perspective, the result of its concentration on "data," "measures," and "testing," with little attention paid to the theoretical framework within which they are conducted.

4. This was emphasized by David Teece in 1992 and restated in 2001. There have been some attempts to deal with this issue from business and legal scholars, and from policymakers, but one cannot say that they have achieved a great deal of success.

interaction is central to any meaningful discussion of both dynamic competition and development strategies in a global context today.

This chapter aims to be a very preliminary effort to contribute to a better understanding of the interaction between competition (construed more broadly than the Anglo-American emphasis on antitrust) and intellectual property policies from a Schumpeterian perspective. As such, it seeks to build a more coherent framework within which the discussions of both institution building and policy design for development can proceed.[5,6]

The chapter is structured as follows: after this brief introduction, section II attempts to link dynamic competition with intellectual property issues from the perspective of the dynamic efficiencies and inefficiencies that are bound to appear. Section III introduces the concept of a "market-features approach" conceived as a more suitable one than the market-failures approach for structuring competition policies from a Schumpeterian perspective. Section IV further develops the previous ones by linking market features, competition policies, and intellectual property rights. Special attention is given to how competition policies should address intellectual property issues under a market-features approach, as well as to the institutional design of public agencies dealing with intellectual property issues. Section V concludes the paper by suggesting some policy implications of that Schumpeterian approach.

II. INTELLECTUAL PROPERTY AND DYNAMIC EFFICIENCIES AND INEFFICIENCIES

From a Schumpeterian perspective, or in the context of Schumpeterian competition, intellectual property rights (IPRs)—patents, trade secrets, confidentiality contracts, copyrights, trademarks, and registered brand names—are powerful,

---

(*See*, e.g., Carlton and Gertner 2002 and Anthony 2003.) That includes the otherwise extremely knowledgeable treatise from Landes and Posner 2003 (on the relationship between antitrust and IP; *see* their chapter 14). The leading Schumpeterian-oriented author in that field is certainly Richard Nelson. (*See*, e.g., Mazzoleni and Nelson 1998 and Nelson et al. 2004.)

5. Incidentally, it should contribute, as well, to broadening the Schumpeterian research agenda by directing it into a scarcely explored (in the Schumpeterian domain) territory: that of "law and economics." But *see* Langlois 2001 for an interesting starting point in that direction.

6. F. Scherer (1994 and 1996) has dealt consistently with these issues but, I argue, in a much more structure–conduct–performance approach than in a genuinely Schumpeterian one. The neo-Schumpeterian legacy has dealt heavily on competition policies (or how to enforce competition) but has said very little on the relationship among innovation, intellectual property regimes, business cooperation, and abuses of economic power.

strategic weapons for generating sustained competitive advantages and Schumpeterian and Ricardian rents (cf. Teece 2001, Jolly and Philpott 2004).[7] In the evolutionary economics framework (see Box 18.1), it is quite clear that in the absence of legal protection for an invention, the inventor either will have less incentive to innovate or will try to keep his invention secret, thus reducing, in both cases, the stock of knowledge to society as a whole (Landes and Posner 2003, p. 294).

From an entrepreneurial perspective as well, patents and other IPRs are extremely effective means to reduce uncertainties—and, therefore, to ignite the animal spirits and long-term expectations—through building temporary monopolies around products, processes, market niches, and, eventually, whole markets (Burlamaqui and Proença 2003, Nelson 1996). However, the word *temporary* is crucial here because of creative destruction: as Schumpeter stated long ago, "a monopoly position is in general no cushion to sleep on" (1942, p. 102).

From an intellectual property perspective, patent law[8] itself internalizes the goal of promoting the diffusion of innovation. It requires, as a condition to granting a patent, that the patent application disclose the steps constituting the invention in sufficient detail to enable readers of the application, if knowledgeable about the relevant technology, to manufacture the patented product themselves. Of course, anyone who wishes to replicate a patented product or process legally will have to negotiate a license with the patentee (Jolly and Philpott 2004, part 1; Landes and Posner 2003, p. 294–295).

Significantly, moreover, any reader of the patent application will be free to "invent around" it: to achieve the technological benefits of the patent by other means without infringing on the patent. Translated to evolutionary-economics jargon, the requirement of public disclosure creates a situation of "incomplete appropriability" for the patent holder, and, therefore, it reinforces Schumpeter's insight on the temporary nature of monopolies: Incomplete appropriability allows for the possibility of technological inventiveness and borrowing from publicized information, both of which foster creative destruction processes which are the main challengers of established monopolistic positions.

In sum, intellectual property rights are sources of dynamic efficiencies that can help deliver the Schumpeterian positive-sum game represented by falling costs, falling prices, positive margins (market power), and increased consumer welfare.

7. Having said that, it is striking how little has been written about the crucial connection between Schumpeterian competition and IPR. And, of course, I include myself in that loophole. In that regard, legal theorists such as Landes and Posner are clearly ahead, in the sense that they are already doing the reverse track—using Schumpeterian concepts and insights to deal with IPR (cf. Landes and Posner 2003).

8. Reference here is to American Patent Law.

BOX 18.1 The Evolutionary Perspective on Economics

Capitalism is a historical process in which *change* (and not equilibrium) is the most relevant feature. "Economic change," therefore, should be *the* object of investigation in an evolutionary research program.[9]

Economic agents are *creative*, and firms—the main agents—are *agents of transformation.*

Competition, understood as *rivalry* among firms and as a *selection mechanism*,[10] is the *engine* that propels economic change.

Innovations, understood as applications of new ideas and/or methods to the economic sphere, are the main *fuel* of that engine.

Money is an *asset*,[11] and *markets* are sets of financial interrelations and cash flows in which production and distribution are *embedded.*[12]

The *main causal chain* in the operation of the economic system runs from the entrepreneurial decisions—expenditure decisions bound to financial commitments and directed to an unknown future—to the determination of the aggregate levels of investment, production, demand, and employment.

Finance and *innovations* function both as *"levers of riches"* and as *uncertainty creators.* Their interplay is at the root of the system's twin operating features: *progress* and *conflict.*[13]

Profit rates tend to *differentiate* (not to equalize[14]), and no "proportionality law between investments and profits" applies.

So much for the basics, but the picture can get much more complicated as we examine the details. Consider the following five observations.

First, as Arnold Plant, an almost forgotten analyst in the field, observed in the early 1930s, "In the case of physical property, the institution of private property

9. This roughly corresponds to Winter's methodological imperative: "dynamics first" (cf. Winter 1986).

10. Although, as Paul David and Brian Arthur have taught us, not necessarily of "best practices."

11. A "liquidity time-machine," as Davidson uses to call it.

12. This roughly corresponds to Minsky's "Wall Street" paradigm (cf. Minsky 1982, chapter 3).

13. A process wonderfully synthesized in Schumpeter's phrase "creative destruction."

14. Note that the equalization tendency of the rate of profit is an almost "holy" assumption shared by classical, Marxian, neoclassical, and neo-Ricardian economics. In evolutionary economics, there is neither theoretical basis nor empirical support for holding such an "heroic" assumption. In evolutionary theory, differentiation, not equalization, is the key theoretical outcome.

makes for the *preservation of scarce goods*. . . . In contrast, property rights in patents and copyrights make possible *the creation of scarcity* of the products appropriated. . . . *The beneficiary is made the owner of the entire supply of a product for which there may be no easily obtainable substitute*" (Plant 1974 [1934], pp. 65–67, emphasis added). In sum, intellectual property can easily give rise to dynamic inefficiencies,[15] and that alone leaves ground for competition policies[16] to enter the scene, as we will see shortly.

Second, the broader the patent protection (and IPRs, generally), the less the patentee's competitors will be able to benefit from the patent by "inventing around," or innovating on the shoulders of, the patent- (or copyright-) holder. Broad IPRs are thus bound to exacerbate the dynamic efficiencies that Plant and others have observed. Accordingly, especially given the complexity and diversity of patents and other IPRs, a one-size-fits-all prescription seems ill-advised. Competition policies surely have a place in limiting IPR scope, as well.

Third, intellectual property and competition policy must address the practice of *strategic patenting*, that is, the proliferating business strategy of applying for patents that the company has no intention to use, or exploit, solely to prevent others from profiting from the innovation (cf. Varian, Farrel, and Shapiro 2004, part 2; and Landes and Posner 2003, chapter 11). Obviously this is a major source of dynamic inefficiency. It has the effect of draining resources from true innovative activity. It also drastically increases the costs of patent prosecution and litigation and, therefore, of innovation. Such strategic patenting constitutes a paradigmatic example of what Baumol has called "unproductive entrepreneurship." As Baumol notes:

> . . . [a] variety of roles among which the entrepreneur's efforts can be reallocated . . . and some of those roles do not follow the constructive and innovative script conventionally attributed to that person. Indeed, at times the entrepreneur may even lead a parasitical existence that is actually damaging to the economy (cf. Baumol 1993, chapter 2, p. 25; see also chapter 4).

Evidently, this task of "reallocation of entrepreneurship" (from unproductive roles to productive ones) is a public policy matter as well as an institutional-design task in the junction of competition policy and intellectual property management.

Fourth, IPRs have a central role in the "new economy" (or "digitally renewed" economy, as Paul David would more precisely label it).[17] In so-called "new-economy industries," intellectual property, rather than the products and processes in and of themselves, is a firm's primary output or asset. Overlapping innovations, rapidly

15. Meaning the expected (negative) impact on future incentives for competitors to compete (innovate) and future consumer welfare. (*See* Anthony: 2003, section IV.)

16. We will use the term "competition policies" rather than "antitrust" here because of the outdated connotation of the latter. We will not be discussing "trust-busting," but a much more subtle and complex set of behaviors, institutions, and policy tools.

17. cf. David in Brynjolfsson and Kahin 2002, p. 85.

falling average total costs, zero marginal costs, strong network externalities and, therefore, fierce "standards battles" and path dependence are the hallmarks of new-economy industries (Shapiro and Varian 1999, Best 2001, De Long 2000, Brynjolfsson and Kahin 2002). These market characteristics might be seen to generate speeding waves of creative destruction and, thus, potentially more (not less) fiercely competitive challenges to incumbents. Although there is an element of truth in that picture, creative destruction in a world of increasing returns of scale, learning, adoption, and "winner-take-all" markets does not mean anything close to some idealized form of "perfect competition" or perfectly contestable markets. Rather, it merely brings the replacement of one, or a few, dominant firms by others, such as the replacement of Fairchild by Intel, of Wang and Compaq by Dell and Toshiba, and of IBM by Microsoft.

In the new economy, in other words, firms' abilities to combine first-mover advantages with trade secrets, patents, copyrights, brand loyalties, and network externalities may afford them secure monopolistic positions despite their low rate of (radical) innovations and not because of it.[18] There is an obvious role for competition policies here. However, the normative framework within which they should take place is far from certain. We will revisit it in section IV.

Fifth, if we think of innovation as a cumulative process in which cutting-edge knowledge and know-how rest on previous innovations, and of patents and IPRs, in general, as fences erected to protect those previous innovations, it is not difficult to perceive, depending on the institutional design within which IPRs are handled, the tension and potential trade-off between private and public interests. This is the so-called argument of the "second enclosure movement" or "information feudalism" which is now the subject of intense debate (cf. Drahos and Braithwaite 2002, Boyle 2003, Evans 2005, Technology Review 2005). According to Evans (discussing Boyle's ideas),

> There are really two halves to the second-enclosure movement. The defensive side focuses on intensifying the enforcement of protected monopoly rights to exclude others from using information that has been defined as private property. The offensive side of the agenda involves taking information that has been considered part of "nature," or the common, cultural and informational heritage of humankind, and transforming it into "private property." If both halves are successful, the

18. *See* Landes and Posner's somehow reluctant recognition of that point (pp. 395–96). The case of Microsoft itself can be used to illustrate the point. The lack of breakthroughs—technological innovations, or radical quality-price improvements—is notoriously known in Microsoft. It is well known that the "Windows" model was copied from Apple's user interface—which itself was a second-hand theft from Xerox PARC—as well as the tremendous lack of perception, by the company, of the Internet potential until the success of Netscape became obvious. It is also known that the differences between the versions of Windows and Office that I'm using right now, although "new," display very pale improvements in relation to their 1998 predecessors.

"second enclosure movement" would constitute a *global re-distribution of property* comparable to the eradication of the commons that ushered in agrarian capitalism in Western Europe 300 years ago (2005, p. 2, emphasis added).

Once more, we encounter strong forces of *global* dynamic inefficiencies, presenting an opportunity for competition policies to step in.

Last, it is necessary to underline the crucial role of the institutional structure—or institutional design—within which IPRs are enforced. I refer here not the rules, as such, but to their legal enforcement apparatuses, the state structures by which they are supported, and the sort of public bureaucracy available to administer the IP system. It is well known in the literatures on institutions and economic sociology that these are crucial elements in determining the degree of success any regulatory system (such as IPRs) can achieve (Evans 1995, Dobbin 2004, Smelser and Swedberg 2005, and Nee and Swedberg 2005 offer excellent discussions on this theme). Jaffe and Lerner's thoughtful and provocative work on the recent changes in the U.S. patent system (Jaffe and Lerner 2004) provides background for our discussion of the relationship between the institutional design of the patent system and problems related to the promotion of innovation and "productive entrepreneurship" (Section IV below).

III. COMPETITION, MARKET FAILURES, AND THE MARKET FEATURES APPROACH

Competition from a Schumpeterian perspective means *rivalry*. But it also allows room for cooperation. Competition policies are the regulatory devices used to build a competition-enhancing environment and steer firms' behaviors toward pro-competitive strategies. Competition policies must be framed against some sort of theoretical background. The most commonly used is the "market-failure approach."[19] But that approach to public policy adds more confusion than clarity to the matter.[20] It takes the perfect-competition model as its point of departure, yet, if perfect competition is our metric, all markets are laden with market failures

19. For a clear exposition of that approach, as well as for a public-choice-oriented critique of it, *see* Mitchell and Simmons 1994, part 1. Both the Chicago School and its heir, the public-choice perspective, have pioneered the criticisms to that approach by trying to show that most of what was presented by market failures turned out to be children of government failures. But their root is neoliberal in the sense that they stick to the notion of a self-regulated market and with the perfect-competition model as its "proof." Ours will be, instead, an evolutionary-institutionalist-based rejection that will leave spacious room for the "role of the state" in forging competition policies. (*See* Burlamaqui 2000 for a more general discussion of that matter.)

20. The paper by Nelson, Dosi, Cimoli, and Stiglitz given at the IPD meeting in Rio (March 17–18) makes the same point but does not pursue, in that work, an alternative theory (Nelson et al. 2005, pp. 2–3).

requiring correction. And according to which blueprint are we to correct the inevitable failures? The perfect-competition model, again. But where can we find empirical evidence to support that model's relevance for public-policy usage (although there is plenty to reject it)? Or, how can we test this model in order to be assured of its efficiency. (Has anyone ever heard of an actual measurement of a Pareto optimum?) It does not get us very far.[21]

In place of the market-failure approach, I proffer a *market-features* approach. By market-features approach, I mean an analytical perspective that takes into account institutional diversity, sector specificities, distinctive dynamics—in both their technological and industrial dimensions—as well as the regulatory and legal aspects of differentiated degrees of market power. It is a conceptual framework whose main advantage is that it does not *fight* the empirical evidence but, rather, accommodates it. It does not utilize a one-size-fits-all approach but relies instead on analytical flexibility. And, for our specific subject, it opens space for both sector-specific competition policies and differentiated intellectual property rules.

The idea of a market features approach is not new. It comes from that undeservedly neglected tradition that unites scholars such as George Shackle and Ludwig Lachmann, a tradition that could very well be labeled "Austrian Keynesianism" (see Lachmann 1986 and Vaughn 1994 on that matter). The specific idea of a market's taxonomy comes from Lachmann's last book in his discussion of markets as economic processes embedded in institutions. As Vaughn explains it, Lachmann argues that:

> Instead of examining the world through the lens of the "market" we need to develop ideal types *of particular kinds of markets:* assets markets versus production markets, fix-price versus flex-price markets, markets dominated by merchants versus markets dominated by salesmen. Such distinctions will make a difference as to how markets adjust to change (Lachmann 1986, p. 128, in Vaughn 1994, p.159, emphasis added).

This was a brilliant insight, but it was left more or less as it was first submitted. For our concerns, it offers as a very promising alternative point of departure both for positive and normative purposes. Some further elements to be used in mapping market features appear in Box 18.2.

---

21. After all, the perfect-competition model should be an ideal in the Weberian sense of the concept: a construct that accentuates certain properties found in reality and exaggerates them for purposes of organizing and making sense of the empirical data. That means that the construct should be abstract but empirically relevant. The problem is that none of the core assumptions supporting the hypothesis of the model—perfect information, product homogeneity, free entry and exit (absence of sunk costs), price-taking behavior (absence of market power), absence of increasing returns, and tendency toward equilibrium—is found in reality, thus making the model useless either for positive or normative functions—something that Frank Hahn (1984), for instance, spelled out several times in his works.

BOX 18.2 Mapping Market Features' Tools

- Concentration measures and market leaderships
- Level of technological complexity (measured by the ratio of R&D to sales)
- Rate of innovation, as measured by the number of patents and copyrights granted versus new products actually being marketed
- Patenting strategies (patents earned versus patents actually used or effectively licensed, plus degree of litigation involving patent claims)
- Price behavior (price changes *over time*—decreasing, increasing, stable?)
- Profits made by leading firms and their evolution
- Regulatory apparatuses embedding the market or sector (standards, requirements, frequency of government intervention)
- Legal characteristics (enforcement mechanisms available, types of contracts)

These, of course, do not exhaust the possibilities of mapping, but they allow for a much more realistic, although possibly less elegant, assessment of differentiated market workings and how they are likely to adjust (or give rise) to change. That perspective still has to be properly developed, but it will enable economic theory to be relevant and useful from the point of view of empirical reality and policy. It is also in line, for instance, with the recent findings by Carlton and Gertner (2002) in their NBER working paper "Intellectual Property, Antitrust and Strategic Behaviour," in which they state that "Only detailed study of the industry of concern has the possibility of uncovering reliable relationships between innovation and industry behaviour" (p. 30). There is clearly a very promising theoretical road to be traveled here. From a Schumpeterian perspective, the market-features perspective should be the departing point for a discussion of competition policies.

IV. MARKET FEATURES, COMPETITION POLICIES, AND INTELLECTUAL PROPERTY RIGHTS: POLICY AND INSTITUTIONAL BUILDING IMPLICATIONS

The market-features approach has as its policy counterpart a market-shaping perspective. It is possible, and desirable—through institution building, legal change, and administrative guidance—to redesign market features as well as regulatory mechanisms and proceedings in order to pursue the major, Schumpeterian policy outline of promoting and regulating entrepreneurial success. Within that approach, the main proposition is that the theory of Schumpeterian competition is the best for the simultaneous treatment of competition policies and intellectual property issues. The general rule under which both should be articulated is the promotion of innovation plus the assurance of its diffusion, and this implies, again, simultaneously, promoting and regulating entrepreneurial success. Promoting *and* regulating is a crucial link. Together they address both the private (profit-seeking) and the public (innovation-diffusion and technological upgrading) sides of competition policies and their respective institutional designs.

Competition policies should take the market-features approach as their point of departure and should use, extensively, market-shaping devices in order to design policies to manage the creative-destruction process. These policies would seek to shape markets in order to reduce dynamic inefficiencies and increase dynamic efficiencies coming from Schumpeterian competition, a form of competition that uses intellectual property rights as one of its core weapons to instigate competitive conflicts. From the perspective of firms, competition policies should not be about interfering with consolidation or preventing "market power" but should be about preventing "too secure monopolies"—and especially those not based in, and thriving on, higher productivity and superior technological performance.

More concretely, competition policies should shape markets and drive firms toward establishing research coordination, pushing common standards, preserving multiple sources of experimentation, monitoring patent pools, establishing variable patent and copyrights terms, and severely punishing both "unproductive patenting" behavior and attempts by firms to close markets through creating their own proprietary, closed systems. (See Carlton and Gertner 2002 for a similar line of reasoning.)

Competition policies can be crafted to deal with dynamic market inefficiencies. Plant argued that patents can make the beneficiary "*the owner of the entire supply of a product for which there may be no easily obtainable substitute,*" a troubling claim. A clever, but not radical, innovation (for instance, Post It® notes from 3M) should not raise major concerns among policymakers dealing with competition issues. But what about a nascent general-purpose technology (for instance, the new genetic engineering research tools or a particular DNA sequence)? Then Plant's point would hold completely, and the granting of the patent would create substantial monopoly for the owner—and potentially prevent others from exploiting it—thus slowing the diffusion of a new innovation.

Those examples highlight the importance of the market-features approach, including its technological dimension. In cases like those involving general-purpose technologies, the IPR policy should be much more rigorously examined and carefully constructed. A possible "tool" for dealing with that would be for the government to claim a *golden share* in the IPR system (especially patents and copyrights), by which it would be able to convert a property right previously granted[22] into a

22. That is, a *legally enforced* temporary monopoly.

general public license should the owner refuse, after establishing his first-mover advantage,[23] to behave cooperatively and to license broadly and fairly.

In sum, radical innovations—and, especially, general-purpose technologies—should be subjected to a special IPR regime in which the government's administrative guidance should be able, if needed, to "shape" the market toward a more competitive institutional design (away from too secure—even if temporary—monopolies). A legitimate, and fair, reason to do so is that, according to some recent studies, the U.S. government played a decisive part in the development of virtually all general-purpose technology, from interchangeable parts and mass production to Darpa[24] and biotech (cf. Ruttan 2006, Weiss 2007, Block 2008). Having financed the bulk of the basic R&D that enabled the emergence of champions such as Colt, Boeing, General Electric, IBM, and a whole host of high-tech giants in hardware, software, and biotech, it would not be unreasonable for the U.S government to have a stronger role in granting that technological achievements don't remain overly protected and scarcely diffused (cf. Roland 2002, Fong 2000)[25]. Although in other countries the privatization of publicly generated knowledge is not as acute as in the contemporary United States, the U.S. PTO is certainly setting standards for everyone else. The way we have it now, its "public virtues, private vices," an inversion of Mandeville's dictum.

Given both the complexity and diversity of patents and IPRs, in general, a one-size-fits-all prescription is perhaps not the best way to handle the matter. The 20-year length of a patent (or the terms of copyrights and registrations) is certainly not a "scientifically established outcome" (Landes and Posner 2003). It is, rather, a convention—that is, an institutional-legal construct that, as such, can

---

23. Meaning being able to recover his costs, establish a robust competitive advantage, and enjoy a sizable profit stream, but not being able to exclude others from using and inventing around his innovation or protecting its diffusion. Taking as an example the Microsoft case, the battle shouldn't be about "breaking" the company. The golden share would allow the government to force Microsoft to publish its source code. An open code would quickly get cleaned up and improved, consumers would benefit, and new entrants would probably arise helping ignite the innovation race and dislodging Microsoft from its monopoly position while preserving the company's market power and ability to innovate.

24. DARPA is the Defense Advanced Research Projects Agency, the central research organization of the United States Department of Defense. Its most radical innovation was the Internet (known first as "DARPA-Net").

25. In fact, this is already in the EU Competition Commission's radar. Its chief, Neelie Kroes, has recently argued in a speech that " industry standards for technology could be based on either proprietary or non-proprietary technologies, but when a market developed so that a proprietary technology became a *de facto* standard and the owner of that technology exploited that market power, competition authorities might have to intervene. One remedy would be to require disclosure of information at "fair rates" so that other companies could design compatible products and systems" (cf. Financial Times: June, 11, 2008).

very well be questioned and changed[26]. Conversely, as Jaffe and Lerner adduce (very much in line with the market features approach), "In the world of theoretical patent analysis, it is easy to show that the attributes of patent protection should vary depending on the characteristics of the technology" (p. 203).

But Jaffe and Lerner then expose several reasons why this differential-treatment approach would not work in practical terms (pp. 203–205). The difficulties of dealing with technologies—classifying and quantifying their impact empirically—plus the political lobbying by firms to get special treatment are the main arguments submitted by the authors. I am in partial agreement with them as to having pure technological considerations serving as the basis for policy, as well as to the rent-seeking dangers surrounding any sort of differential treatment. But note that if we look to the development histories of Japan, South Korea, China, Ireland, or the United States, differential treatment lay at the core of both their technological and industrial policies. That is, it *can* work (cf. Chang 2002, Reinert 2007).

To be less abstract on the matter, let us propose this broad guideline for competition policies: the length and breadth of patent protection, as well as innovations protected by copyrights, such as software, should be linked to the expenditures in R&D, made or to be made,[27] by applicants. Thus, big research budgets (in terms relative to the firm's size) would, in principle, qualify better than "historical accidents" to earn legitimate protection. Instead of one size fitting all, we would have something like—paraphrasing Rodrik—"Many recipes under the same rule."[28]

The third source of dynamic inefficiencies referred to above, *strategic patenting*, should be dealt with in a somewhat Ricardian way[29]—earned but unused patents

---

26. As a matter of fact, a century ago, copyrights lasted for 14 years—and could be extended another 14 if the copyright holder petitioned for an extension. Today, corporate copyrights last for 95 years, and individuals retain copyrights for 70 years after their deaths. There was nothing "scientific" to back these changes but rather the powerful lobby of the entertainment industry. As for patents, mind the reader that both in Switzerland (between 1850 and 1907) and in the Netherlands (between 1868 and 1912), industrialization occurred without enforcement of patent laws (cf. Schiff 1971).

27. R&D expenses as a percentage of the applicant's sales or assets, assuming that those R&D-intensive industries are also the ones bearing more fixed and sunk costs, plus near-future planned expenses tied to the "birth" of an innovation or technology, should be in the contract granting the rights and their actual production of the enabling mechanism to conclude the exam. Otherwise, patent pending would be a sort of "reasonable doubt" proviso.

28. A very difficult, emerging theme here is the protection to be given to traditional knowledge: DOC (Denominacione de Origine Controllata certifications that grant monopolies based on regional know-how and capabilities, like champagne versus sparkling wines) issues and related others. I acknowledge its importance but do not deal with that in this paper.

29. The parallel here would be between the example given by David Ricardo of the unique fertility of a piece of privately owned land, which would generate increasing revenues to its owner, regardless of efforts to improve the land's productivity, and the stream of revenue generated from a patent regardless of whether its owner keeps innovating.

should be classified like fertile but uncultivated pieces of land in an environment structurally constrained by scarcity. They should be taxed, and progressively so. After an initial "launching period," each year of idleness in the commercialization of the patent should give rise to a severe fine, the exact amount of which should be figured out by specialists in the field but could very well be an increasing percentage of the patentee's sales or assets. Rigorous? Yes, but patents and IPRs, in general, are subjects of public interest. They are too important to be left to markets and lawyers to craft. Additionally, the competition policy we are pointing to should discourage the sort of unproductive entrepreneurship that Baumol has been talking about for more than a decade, a type of legal entrepreneurship that turns law firms into very big and profitable corporations but with zero impact on the economy's real productivity. It would, in sum, help to trigger the "relocation of entrepreneurship"—from courts back to labs—as claimed by Baumol.

The fourth point outlined (in section II above) relates to the relationship between the "digitally renewed economy" and intellectual property issues, and particularly to the risk of winner-take-all market outcomes or, from the point of view of firms, to locking out competitors via the combination of increasing returns, network externalities, path dependency, and stronger IPRs protection (cf. Varian, Farrel, and Shapiro 2004; Carlton and Gertner 2002). Competition policies here should pursue, very aggressively if needed, public subsidization of standards development, cooperative standards setting, stimulus of (instead of restriction on) joint-research ventures and other forms of research coordination (Carlton and Gertner 2002, pp. 3–7) and venture-capital financing to multiple sources of experimentation (Bartzokas and Mani 2004). Our aim should be a "less kind, less gentle patent system," as Jaffe and Lerner (2003) put it, in which patents are much harder to acquire and relatively easier to share.

Also of concern is the recent wave of IPR expansion and its connection to a potential "information feudalism" or "second enclosure movement." This movement is seen by the so-called "progressive IP lawyers," software programmers, and a sizable number of social and natural scientists of various extractions as a recipe for global monopoly, one that is likely to stifle innovation at the same time it concentrates wealth (see Moglen 2003, Benkler 2003, and Evans 2005). A number of commentators have called for an alternative to this second enclosure, an alternative they term "the new commons."[30] As Evans has aptly put it, this alternative is "attractive both because of its distributional implications and because of its potential for raising the rate of innovation and value creation" (2005, p. 3). The basis of

30. A "commons" is a piece of land over which people can exercise certain traditional rights in common, such as allowing their livestock to graze upon it. Older texts use the word "common" to denote any such right, but more modern usage is to refer to particular rights of common and to reserve the name "common" for the land over which the rights are exercised. By extension, the term "commons" has come to be applied to other resources that a community has rights or access to.

the new commons comes from a redefinition of "ownership": from the focus on the right to exclude to the focus on the right to distribute (disseminate).

The key idea here is that once property rights are redefined along the lines pioneered by the open-source software movement, a much more egalitarian redistribution of intangible assets and a more powerful rationale to foster innovations will be able to emerge. This rationale is one that unfolds from the characteristics of the networked information economy—an economy of information, knowledge, and culture that flows over a ubiquitous, decentralized network. In that environment, as Benkler remarks, productivity and growth can be sustained in a pattern that differs fundamentally from the industrial information economy of the 20th century in two crucial characteristics. First, non-market production can play a much more important role than it could in the physical economy. Individuals working alongside firms can make a real difference in the creation of innovative solutions and productivity gains (Benkler 2003, p. 1, and 2006).[31] Second, radically decentralized production and distribution, whether market-based or not, can similarly play a much more important role by increasing the diversity of ways of organizing production and consumption and, therefore, by increasing the sources and possibilities for multiple forms of experimentation.

This is clearly a global issue and—because of its global scope, and also because of the undertheorized relationship between competition policies and intellectual property rights—a very difficult one to handle. It will certainly require the active involvement of governments in encouraging and assisting the development of open-source systems to move society toward more general-public-licenses-oriented IPR regimes. It will also require international cooperation—both very turbulent matters from a power-politics perspective. Nevertheless, the recent decisions by IBM and Nokia, for example, to put part of their patents into the public domain suggests that there is perhaps more room to maneuver than the skeptical analyst might expect.

Finally, the crucial role of the institutional structure—or institutional design—within which the IPRs are enforced must be examined. This brings us to Jaffe and Lerner's (2004) discussion of the recent institutional-design changes in the U.S. patent system and its deleterious effects on innovation.[32] Their story unfolds around two fundamental changes in the legal-institutional foundations of the system. The first, in 1982, was a change in the process by which patent cases were handled. From then on, instead of the 12 regional courts of appeal, one

31. And, he adds, one can clearly observe this behavior by noticing that most of what we do on the Internet runs on software produced by tens of thousands of volunteers, working together in a way that is fundamentally more closely related to a community than to a hierarchical big corporation standing alone.

32. Why do I want to illustrate that point with the U.S. system? Because, simply, it is the most powerful patent system in the world and also the most likely to be mimicked by "emergent economies."

single, specialized appeals court began to process all appeals in patent cases: the Court of Appeals for the Federal Circuit (CAFC). Consolidating patent appeals in one court had the salutary effect of injecting homogeneity into a fragmented system. However, because the CAFC's formative years coincided with the "Japanese challenge," "America's lost competitiveness," and the Reagan administration's extreme pro-business policies, the new homogeneity took the form of interpreting patent law "to make it easier to get, easier to enforce patents against others, easier to get large financial awards from such enforcement, and harder for those accused of infringing patents to challenge the patents' validity" (Jaffe and Lerner 2004, pp. 2–11).

The second change dates from the early 1990s, when Congress modified the Patent and Trademark Office's (PTO) financial basis, turning it into a profit center, a service agency whose costs of operation should be covered by the fees paid by patent applicants—or by its clients (id.).

According to Jaffe and Lerner, these two changes transformed a regime that had been committed to fostering and protecting innovation into a lawyers' paradise. The patent system then became a very powerful generator of unproductive entrepreneurship and, hence, a severely dysfunctional institution. In order to be "efficient," the PTO started to examine—and grant—as many patents as it could, regardless of the quality and reliability of the examination process. Between 1983 and 2006, the patents granted increased from about 62,000 to 196,000 per year. The number of patent applications also ballooned to 452,633 in 2006 (from 112,040 in 1983).[33]

In analytical terms, what happened was the replacement of a qualified bureaucracy committed to public service by a business-oriented "new public management" (NPM) cadre that was given the task of regulating a crucially important part of the knowledge-creation system of the new economy.[34] The results were dismal in that they incentivized strategic patenting and patent litigation (which consumes literally billions of dollars) without any clear impact in terms of innovation inducement or on the rate of innovation (see Noll 2004 on this issue). In sum, the economic benefits of stronger patent protection and increased room for strategic patenting have failed to materialize—except in the big patent–portfolio holders' licensing revenues and on the dedicated law firm's balance sheets. On the sort of detailed institutional redesign which ought to be done in order to

33. cf. http://www.uspto.gov/go/taf/us_stat.htm.

34. As Drechsler aptly sums it, NPM is the transfer of business and market principles and management techniques from the private into the public sector, symbiotic with and based on a neoliberal understanding of state and economy. The goal, therefore, is a slim, reduced, minimal state in which any public activity is decreased and, if at all, exercised according to business principles of efficiency. NPM is based on the understanding that all human behavior is motivated by self-interest and, specifically, profit maximization (cf. 2005, p. 1).

improve patent quality in the United States, I direct the reader to the excellent discussion by Jaffe and Lerner (2004).

Patents and intellectual property in general are too important to be left to lawyers, juries, and a single PTO. They should be institutionally restructured, in the form of a cross-cutting regulatory agency working in coordination with the existing ones, where field experts from specific agencies would get training in IP issues in order to become examiners. Dedicated judges and courts (but not juries) should be the "last resort" in those matters, not the first.

Additionally, this agency should be structured along "Weberian lines"—a set of offices in which appointed civil servants operate under the principles of merit selection, expertise, hierarchy, the division of labor, exclusive employment, career advancement, and legality. This type of rationality—Weber's key term—would increase speed, scope, predictability, and cost-effectiveness (Weber 1922, pp. 124–130; Drechsler 2005).

V. CONCLUSION

The policy-institutions framework I have proposed should be flexible and pragmatic and should have creative-destruction management—or the promotion and regulation of entrepreneurial success—as its main goal. In its competition-policies dimension, it should *not* be anti-consolidation but anti–unproductive entrepreneurship (Baumol 1993 and 2002); pro-efficiency but not libertarian (in the "Chicago School" sense of letting the market, almost always, take care of its own problems); and, especially, pro-cooperation, leaving room for business networks to thrive and for state-sponsored administrative-guidance initiatives. It should also engineer policies toward the development of multiple sources of experimentation and allow room for industrial and technology policies without jeopardizing its own core theoretical foundations.

In its intellectual property dimension, it should *not* point to a one-size-fits-all institutional design[35] and should *not* pursue the maximum protection of monopolistic rents as both the U.S. PTO and the WTO seem to be doing. It should, rather, search for the minimal common denominator, allowing for institutional and

35. It should *not*, therefore, be framed as Coriat, Cimoli, and Primi indicate in a just-released paper, as an American "export": it is essential to note that recent (dramatic) changes in IP law have been strongly embedded in the specificities of an American patent law that is predicated on a common-law regime wherein the essential criterion for patentability is the "utility" the invention is deemed to have. Utility, a property that refers to products of "useful arts," basically involves industrial and commercial advances enabled by this invention. Under these conditions, in my opinion, the aforementioned change was in fact that suddenly it was enough to relax or change the meaning of the word "utility" for non-patentable areas to become patentable (Coriat, Cimoli, and Primi 2005, p. 4).

technological diversity and for distinctive developmental strategies (Boyle 2004). It should take into account the asymmetries in the distance to the "development frontier" among countries and regions, echoing Joseph Stiglitz's recent, and wise, remark that "Intellectual property is certainly important, but the appropriate IPR system for an emerging country is different than the IPR system best fitting already developed nations" (Stiglitz 2005, retranslated into English [LB]).[36]

From an evolutionary-policy perspective, the key issue to deal with is how to separate innovation-rooted profits, which should be rewarded but understood as windfalls (dependent on continuous innovation), from legal monopoly-granted rents, which should be eliminated or, at least, closely monitored and curtailed.

None of these policy prescriptions will be achieved without a huge dose of "strategic state action," and most of them will require a high degree of international cooperation. This is an uneasy task; nonetheless, the expected result, to which this paper intends to be a small contribution, will be a theory-policy framework linking market features to Schumpeterian competition, and competition policies to intellectual property rights' management, which will allow room for catching-up initiatives and for the (re)construction of development strategies in order to reverse the dismal picture shown in Coriat, Cimoli, and Primi (2005, p. 16):

> To sum up, weak institutional and personnel capabilities in intellectual property systems' management, reduced capacity of negotiating intellectual property rights and regime domain and the existence of monopolistic markets where regional enterprises and economic agents perform at the lowest levels of international hierarchies, depict a displeasing scenario where . . . [emerging] Countries have weak negotiation powers in terms of intellectual property, scantly use the windows of opportunities that current agreements offer and suffer of structural weakness in terms of capacities of proposing regionally-tailored changes in the rules' games in order to support domestic technological and innovation capabilities.

REFERENCES

Anthony, S. 2000. Antitrust and Intellectual Property Law: From Adversaries to Partners. *AIPLA Quarterly Review* Vol. 28, Number 1.

Bartokas, A., and S. Mani, eds. 2004. *Financial Systems, Corporate Investment in Innovation and Venture Capital.* E. Elgar.

Baumol, W. 1993. *Entrepreneurship, Management and the Nature of Payoffs.* MIT Press.

36. One of the main reasons for that, although certainly not the only one, is that the big pharmaceutical companies perform obscene price discrimination among nations (cf. Varian, Farrel, and Shapiro 2004, p. 52) and almost always refuse to engage in poor and emerging countries' public policies oriented toward health care.

Baumol, W. 2002. *The Free-Market Innovation Machine.* Princeton University Press.

Benkler, Y. 2003. Freedom in the Commons: Towards a Political Economy of Information. *Duke Law Journal.* No. 52.

Benkler, Y. 2006. *The Wealth of Networks.* Yale University Press.

Best, M. 2001. *The New Competitive Advantage.* Oxford University Press.

Block, F. 2008. Where do Innovations Come From? Transformations in the U.S National Innovation System—1970–2006. Research paper for The Ford Foundation, Grant # 1075-1307.

Bork, R. 1993. *The Antitrust Paradox.* Free Press.

Boyle, J. 2003. The Second Enclosure Movement and the Construction of the Public Domain. Available at http://www.law.duke.edu/boylesite/.

Boyle, J. 2004. Manifesto on the Future of WIPO. Available at http://www.law.duke.edu/boylesite/.

Boyle, J. 2006. Bipolar Economics. Available at http://www.law.duke.edu/boylesite/.

Brynjolfsson and Kahin, eds. 2002. *Understanding the Digital Economy.* MIT Press.

Burlamaqui, L. 2000. Evolutionary Economics and the Role of State. In Burlamaqui, Castro, Chang, eds. *Institutions and the Role of the State: New Horizons in Institutional and Evolutionary Economics.* E. Elgar.

Burlamaqui, L., and A. Proença. 2003. "Inovação, Recursos e Comprometimento: Em Direção a uma Teoria Estratégica da Firma." In Revista Brasileira de Inovação, Ano 1, Vol 3.

Carlton, D., and R. Gertner. 2002. Intellectual Property, Antitrust and Strategic Behavior. NBER Working Paper, No. 8976.

Chang, H. J. 2002. *Kicking Away the Ladder.* Anthem Press.

Cimoli, M., G. Dosi, R. Nelson, and J. Stiglitz. 2005. *A Note on the Institutions and Policies Shaping Industrial Development.* Paper presented at the IPD meeting, Rio, March 17–18.

Coriat, B., M. Cimoli, and A. Primi. 2005. *Intellectual Property Right Regimes: Incentives and Constraints for Technological and Industrial Development.* Paper presented at the IPD meeting, Rio, March 17–18.

De Long, B. 2000. *The Dilemma of Antitrust—A Short History.* Available at http://econ161.berkeley.edu/.

Dixon, P., and C. Greenlalgh. 2002: The Economics of Intellectual Property: A Review to Identify Themes for Future Research. CRIC, Manchester.

Dobbin, F., ed. *The Sociology of the Economy.* Russell Sage Foundation.

Drahos, P., and J. Braithwaite. 2002. *Information Feudalism.* The New Press.

Drechsler, W. 2005. The Rise and Demise of the New Public Management. *Post-autistic Economics Review,* Issue 33, September 14, pp. 17–28, http://www.paecon.net/PAEReview/issue33/Drechsler33.htm.

Ellig, J., ed. 2001. *Dynamic Competition and Public Policy: Technology, Innovation, and Antitrust Issues.* Cambridge University Press.

Evans, P. B. 1995. *Embedded Autonomy: States and Industrial Transformation.* Princeton University Press.

Evans, P. B. 2005. The New Commons vs. the Second Enclosure Movement: Comments on an Emerging Agenda for Development Research. Forthcoming in *Studies in Comparative International Development.*

Fong, G. 2001. Arpa Does Windows: The Defense Underpinning of the PC Revolution. *Business & Politics* Vol. 3, Number.3 (November).

Hahn, F. 1984. *Equilibrium and Macroeconomics.* MIT Press.

Hovenkamp, H. 1999. *Federal Antitrust Policy*. West.
Jaffe, A., and J. Lerner. 2002. *Innovation and Its Discontents: How Our Broken Patent System Is Endangering Innovation and Progress, and What to Do About It*. Princeton University Press.
Jolly, A., and J. Philpott, eds. 2004. *A Handbook of Intellectual Property Management*. Kogan Page.
Kwoka Jr., J., and L. White, eds. 1999. *The Antitrust Revolution*. Oxford University Press.
Lachmann, L. 1986. *The Market as an Economic Process*. Blackwell.
Landes, W., and R. Posner. 2003. *The Economic Structure of Intellectual Property Law*. Belknap Press.
Langlois, R. 2001. Technological Standards, Innovation and Essential Facilities: Towards a Schumpeterian Approach. In J. Ellig, ed. *Dynamic Competition and Public Policy: Technology, Innovation, and Antitrust Issues*. Cambridge University Press.
Mazzoleni, R., and R. Nelson. 1998: The Benefits and Costs of Strong Patent Protection: A Contribution to the Current Debate. *Research Policy* Vol. 27.
Menell, P. 1999. *Intellectual Property: General Theories*. Working Paper, Berkeley Center for Law and Technology.
McCraw, T. 1984. *Prophets of Regulation*. Harvard University Press.
Mitchell, W., and R. Simmons. 1994. Beyond Politics—Markets, *Welfare and the Failure of Bureaucracy*. Westview Press.
Moglen, E. 2003. *Freeing the Mind: Free Software and the Death of Proprietary Culture*, Fourth Annual Technology and Law Conference, University of Maine Law School, Portland, June 29.
Nee, V., and R. Swedberg, eds. 2005. *The Economic Sociology of Capitalism*. Princeton University Press.
Nelson, R. 1996. *The Sources of Economic Growth*. Harvard University Press.
Nelson, R., et al. 2004. *Ivory Tower and Industrial Innovation: University-Industry Technology Transfer Before and After the Bayh-Dole Act in the United States*. Stanford University Press.
Nelson, R., et al. 2005. *A Program of Study of the Processes Involved in Technological and Economic Catch Up*. The Earth Institute/Columbia University.
Noll, R. 2004. The Conflict over Vertical Foreclosure in Competition Policy and in Intellectual Property Law. Stanford Institute for Economic Policy Research, Working Paper No. 03-22.
Plant, A. 1934. *Selected Economic Essays and Addresses*.
Posner, R. 2002 [1976]. *The Economic Analysis of Law*. Aspen Publishers. .
Reinert, E. 2007. *How Countries Got Rich . . . and Why Poor Countries Stay Poor*. Constable Books.
Roland, A. 1983–1993. *Strategic Computing: DARPA and the quest for Machine Intelligence*. MIT Press.
Ruttan, V. 2006. *Is War Necessary for Economic Growth?* Oxford University Press.
Scherer, F. 1994. *Competition Policies for an Integrated World Economy*. The Brookings Institution.
Scherer, F. 1996. *Industry Structure, Strategy and Public Policy*. Harper Collins.
Schiff, E. 1971. *Industrialization without National Patents*. Princeton University Press.
Schumpeter, J. 1997 [1934]. *The Theory of Economic Development*. Transaction Publishers.
Schumpeter, J. 1994 [1942]. *Capitalism, Socialism and Democracy*. Routledge.
Shapiro, C., and H. Varian. 1999. *Information Rules*. HBS Press.
Shelby, H. 2000. *A General Theory of Competition*. Sage Books.

Smelster, N., and R. Swedberg, eds. 2005. *The Handbook of Economic Sociology*. Princeton University Press.

Stiglitz, J. 2005. *"Erros e acertos da propriedade intelectual."* In *O Globo*, August 29.

Technology Review. 2005 (June). *Intellectual Property Issue*. MIT Press.

Teece, D. 2000. *Managing Intellectual Capital*. Oxford University Press.

Teece, D., and T. Jorde, eds. 1992. *Antitrust, Innovation and Competitiveness*. Oxford University Press.

Varian, H., J. Farrel, and C. Shapiro. 2004. *The Economics of Information Technology*. Cambridge University Press.

Vaughn, K. 1994. *Austrian Economics in America—The Migration of a Tradition*. Cambridge University Press.

Weber, M. 1922 [1976]. *Economy and Society*. Berkeley University Press.

Weiss, L. 2007. *Governing the Market for America*. Research paper for The Ford Foundation, Grant # 1075-1307.

Wells, W. 2002. *Antitrust & the Formation of the Postwar World*. Columbia University Press.

Wu, L. ed. 2004. *Economics of Antitrust: New Issues, Questions, and Insights*. NERA Economic Consulting.

PART EIGHT

INTELLECTUAL PROPERTY AND DEVELOPING-COUNTRY CITIZENS' FREEDOM

19. INTELLECTUAL PROPERTY AND DEVELOPMENT AS FREEDOM

MADHAVI SUNDER

I. INTRODUCTION

In late December 2004, I traveled to India to witness the social ruptures that India's entry into the modern intellectual property world would likely trigger. The deadline for developing nations to be fully compliant with the Agreement on Trade-Related Aspects of Intellectual Property (TRIPS), the preeminent global intellectual property law of the Information Age, was January 1, 2005. From that date on, India would have Western-style intellectual property rights in everything from medicines to seeds. For more than a decade, the developing world had resisted this moment. Since they had been pressured into signing TRIPS during the Uruguay Round of WTO negotiations, countries such as Brazil and India had argued that strong intellectual property rights would help the West but would devastate the rest.

Sadly, my visit to India that December bore witness to an all-too-literal tsunami that shook the Subcontinent. The tsunami focused the world's attention on the rural poor in the countries at the perimeter of the Indian Ocean. I will seek to keep my focus on these people here.

Much to my surprise, India rang in the New Year without much ill note of TRIPS. In the intellectual property storm, the dust had settled—at least temporarily. TRIPS was finally in India, seemingly to stay, and the intellectual property scholars and practitioners there with whom I spoke had little interest in prolonging the battles of the last decade. "TRIPS has entered, and India took a U-turn because it felt it could not [continue fighting against TRIPS]," V. C. Vivekanandan, an intellectual property professor at NALSAR, a leading national law school in Hyderabad, told me. "It has been grudgingly accepted."

But in that characteristically Indian way of absorbing every contradiction and all the diversity of life, this was not simply an expression of passive acceptance of destiny. After a decade of resisting the Western imposition of intellectual property, now many in India—from the intellectual property professors and lawyers in the cities to the farmers and artisans in the villages—were beginning to ask,

How can intellectual property rights work for us? TRIPS protected the knowledge and economic interests of the developed world, the rich corporations of the West. Can intellectual property be a tool for protecting poor people's knowledge as well? Many seem to think so. Take the case of an award-winning farmer in Kerala who developed a high-yield method for planting rubber trees. An intellectual property professor from Kerala related the farmer's story: "Later when somebody tried to plant [rubber trees] in the same way, [the farmer] said, 'No, I will get a patent in this.'" The professor noted, "Five years back this concept [of patenting] was totally lacking. This farmer had only studied up to [the] sixth or seventh [grade]. But he has some idea about this particular law where you can stop somebody else from using the method."

Certainly, the shift to appropriating intellectual property in India is neither complete nor uncontested. When the Kerala farmer took his claims to the Rubber Board, there was fierce debate among the farmers. "One young farmer stood up and said, 'I [wouldn't] want any monetary benefit from this. I [would] just want this to be propagated freely. Uncle, I [wouldn't] want a patent. For me the honor of the award [would be] enough.'" But if the daily headlines are any indication, the country's approach is shifting from this traditional view. The front pages chronicle a rising tide of applications filed with a national registry established pursuant to the Geographical Indication of Goods (Registration and Protection) Act of 1999 (GI Act). Required by TRIPS originally as a means to protect French makers of wines and champagnes, the law gives trademark-like protection to distinctive goods or services whose quality and reputation derive from the geographical area in which they are produced. In a country such as India, which has a vast cultural heritage and a store of traditional knowledge dating back to the Vedas, the GI Act is seen as a potentially important source of recognition and income for India's rural poor—the very same poor who otherwise have been displaced and forced further into poverty by globalization. One hope is that Geographical Indication (GI) protection will allow local artisans to stay in their communities and fend for themselves, without having to renounce their traditional work for life in the overcrowded cities. When I visited India in 2005, farmers and artisans from across the country were getting in line to register their wares, from Darjeeling tea to Alfonso mangoes, Kolhapuri *cheppals*, Mysore silk and sandalwood, and the uniquely woven sarees from the village of Pochampally in the shadow of high-tech Hyderabad.

Turn the clock back 10 years. When intellectual property had found its way into the sanctions regime of the international trade order, there were no marchers in the streets to mark the occasion. The White House issued a white paper declaring the need to strengthen intellectual property law in the face of the digital revolution. Congress was just about to undertake enormous giveaways to intellectual property holders—granting famous brands rights even in the absence of consumer confusion, extending copyright terms by another two decades, and securing technological copyright-protection schemes against hacking.

Courts signaled their willingness to accept patents on business methods. In the new economy of the Information Age, patents, trademarks, copyrights, and even domain names were being distributed with abandon. Conventional wisdom was that the digital world to come would require bigger and stronger intellectual property rights.

Amid this euphoria, some intellectual property scholars recognized a dark side of intellectual property. In this narrative of progress, academics saw us sowing the seeds of our own destruction. Just as the first enclosure of the commons and industrialization had threatened our natural environment, this new "land grab" in cyberspace and on our cultural commons, James Boyle observed, threatened to ruin our cultural landscape and deplete our cultural heritage. Boyle's critical insight was that expanding intellectual property rights were fed by the conceit of Romantic authorship: the idea that individuals (and even corporations) create out of thin air rather than borrow from a rich public domain of freely circulating sources and inspirations. "The author vision blinds us to the importance of the commons—to the importance of the raw material from which information products are constructed," he wrote in his 1996 book, *Shamans, Software, and Spleens: Law and the Construction of the Information Society*.[1] The process of creation, Boyle noted, requires the conservation of cultural raw materials; if these are themselves owned, the process of creation may be stunted.

Boyle's vision of a political movement to protect and preserve the public domain, complete with private institutions dedicated to the project modeled after Greenpeace, spurred the establishment of the Creative Commons.

Less noted but equally profound, the metaphor Boyle offered, "cultural environmentalism," helped lay the foundation for the recognition and protection of traditional knowledge and natural resources found in the developing world. Taking a cue implicitly from the environmental justice movement, which demonstrated the disparate effects of environmental harms on disadvantaged minorities, the *cultural* environmental movement illustrated how third-world peoples are disproportionately disadvantaged by intellectual property law, which historically has not recognized their cultural contributions. Indigenous people and those in the third world benefited from the attention to our cultural commons. It provided a moral and economic basis to reward their cultivation of the world's biodiversity and ancient cultural knowledge about that biodiversity, both of which were required inputs for innovation. By "reifying the negative" and focusing needed attention on the "other side" of intellectual property, Boyle, along with contemporary intellectual property scholars, "invented" the current concept of the public domain.

---

1. James Boyle, Shamans, Software & Spleens: *Law and the Construction of the Information Society*, xiv. (Cambridge, MA: Harvard University Press, 1996).

But Boyle's depiction suggests there are only two sides to the story. In fact, there are many views of the cathedral. Now, in the developing world, scholars, lawyers, and activists are turning the light on "poor people's knowledge."[2] For them, *this* is "the other half of intellectual property"—the knowledge that is not protected by TRIPS but perhaps should be. In this chapter, I consider how "cultural environmentalism" both bolsters and obstructs the project of protecting poor people's knowledge and promoting development through intellectual property. I argue that although the metaphor spurred the invention of traditional knowledge as a political and legal category, the same metaphor may also obscure the *inventiveness* of traditional knowledge. Reifying the public domain may have the unintended effect of congealing traditional knowledge as "the opposite of property," presenting poor people's knowledge as the raw material of innovation—ancient, static, and *natural*—rather than as intellectual property—modern, dynamic, *scientific* and *cultural invention*. Under this view, traditional knowledge holders may receive remuneration for conserving biodiversity and contributing the raw materials of innovation, but they are not recognized as intellectual property holders in their own right. What's more, a binary view of "intellectual property versus the public domain" rejects new claims for intellectual property in traditional knowledge on the premise that these rights would shrink the public domain.

In truth, the line between what the law considers "raw material" versus "intellectual property" is less stable and more fraught with bias than the binary approach would acknowledge. Although politically effective, reifying the negative may have the perverse effect of reinventing these categories as real and stable, obscuring the degree to which they are constructed and insecure.

II. WARDENS OF KNOWLEDGE

The invention of the public domain helped lay a foundation for "the invention of traditional knowledge" as a political and legal category worthy of rights. Boyle's metaphor for a politics of the public domain, "cultural environmentalism," helped focus the world's attention on the value of ecological and cultural diversity for the process of scientific and cultural innovation, and of the need to preserve those resources. Although Boyle offered cultural environmentalism as a metaphor, at points cultural environmentalism coincides with environmentalism itself. Recall the shamans of Madagascar. In this poverty-stricken nation, medicine men had developed therapeutic uses for the indigenously grown rosy periwinkle. Enter Eli Lilly & Company, which transformed this plant and the shaman's lore into a drug to treat Hodgkin's disease. At the time, the drug was

2. See generally J. Michael Finger and Philip Schuler, eds., *Poor People's Knowledge: Promoting Intellectual Property in Developing Countries* (Washington, DC: The World Bank, 2004).

valued at some $100 million annually. As Boyle pointed out, even a fraction of the company's profits would have been a significant boost to the economy of this poor country. But through the vagaries of Western intellectual property law, the people of Madagascar received nothing of the profits derived from this new drug. Western intellectual property, as Boyle explained, was premised upon an authorial regime that "values the raw materials for the production of intellectual property at zero," yet judges Eli Lilly's contribution, refining the shaman's traditional knowledge, in the hundreds of millions.[3]

For Boyle, the rosy periwinkle symbolized more than just a moral problem or a problem of postmodern authorship. The rosy periwinkle, Boyle wrote, "exemplifies *the utilitarian failures* of the current regime."[4] Absent any reward for their preservation of biodiversity and traditional knowledge, the people of Madagascar had "chopped down most of their forests to feed [their] people"[5]—an irony Boyle decried. In this context, the cultural environment was not merely metaphor. Boyle was concerned about the literal environment, the earth's forests and all of its abundant biodiversity, from which medicinal and other cultural knowledge could be derived. *Cultural* environmentalism called our attention to the *traditional knowledge* of the shaman and other people, often poor, who cultivated disease-resistant wheat and rice and held the secrets of which plants could cure our ills. Going further, cultural environmentalism highlighted the need to preserve diverse cultures, the repositories of such knowledge. "Who knows what other unique and potentially valuable plants disappear with the forest, what generations of pharmacological experience disappear as the indigenous culture is destroyed?" Boyle pointedly asked.[6]

The trope of the Romantic author obscured the contributions of biodiversity and traditional knowledge to innovation. "Who needs a public domain if you can create out of nothing?" Boyle asked.[7] By exposing how companies such as Eli Lilly did not, in fact, create out of thin air but, rather, often benefited from the rich biodiversity and knowledge found in the global South, Boyle made the strongest case for preserving the public domain: *the public domain saves lives.*

This theory of the public domain provided intellectual grounding to arguments for recognizing the value of the cultural contributions of indigenous and third-world peoples to innovation. Both the Convention on Biological Diversity (CBD, adopted in 1992) and, more recently, the draft of a proposed Access to Knowledge Treaty promote an international legal regime that would reward indigenous peoples for supplying the raw materials of innovation and preserving

---

3. Boyle, *Shamans*, p. 126.

4. Boyle, *Shamans*, p. 142 (emphasis added).

5. Boyle, *Shamans*, p. 128.

6. Boyle, *Shamans*, p. 128–29.

7. James Boyle, "The Second Enclosure Movement and the Construction of the Public Domain," 66 *Law & Contemp. Probs.* 33, 52 (Winter/Spring 2003).

the public domain. The CBD grants countries sovereign rights of ownership over genetic resources found within their borders. These rights serve as both ex post reward for biodiversity conservation and ex ante incentive for continued conservation. The CBD would grant both sovereignty in biological resources and the right to share in the benefits of patented products that arise from the appropriation of a country's biodiversity or traditional knowledge. Similarly, a draft Treaty on Access to Knowledge seeks to "protect, preserve and enhance the public domain, which is essential for creativity and sustained innovation,"[8] by similarly requiring patent holders to seek prior, informed consent for use of biological materials from the country of origin and to "equitably share the benefits derived from use of that biological material."[9] The dual recommendation of both resource sovereignty and equitable benefit sharing seeks to recognize indigenous peoples as the wardens of the world's "raw materials" and to benefit them materially for their role in preserving the public domain.

But whereas this theory of the public domain has served to undergird claims for traditional knowledge protection, so, too, has it proved a stumbling block. In the last decade, we have seen indigenous peoples and the poor, not unlike the Kerala rubber-tree farmer, turning their attention to appropriating intellectual property to their own ends. Today, claims by indigenous people and the poor go beyond equitable benefit sharing; increasingly, the poor seek to own copyrights, trademarks, and patents in their own cultural and scientific innovations. Strikingly, the traditional advocates for preserving the public domain have flipped. "Native peoples once stood for the commons,"[10] but with the imbalance of TRIPS being more and more apparent, advocates of the poor are turning their attention to securing affirmative intellectual property rights for their own cultural and scientific innovations. Paradoxically, however, the concepts of "traditional knowledge," the "public domain," and "cultural environmentalism" are now proving to be obstacles to understanding poor people's knowledge *as intellectual property*. Claims by native peoples to hold intellectual property are resisted as threats to the public domain, as the false consciousness of neoliberalism, or as a radical assault on the Western intellectual property tradition, which encourages and promotes cultivation, not stewardship.

We should be wary of these declarations and "the romance of the public domain" itself.[11] Anupam Chander and I have argued that, although the banner of the public domain is taken up for all of humanity, a binary view of "intellectual property

8. *Treaty on Access to Knowledge*, pt. 1, Preamble (draft, May 9, 2005). Available online at http://www.cptech.org/a2k/a2k_treaty_may9.pdf.

9. Id., at art 4(1)(b)(iii).

10. Anupam Chander and Madhavi Sunder, "The Romance of the Public Domain," 92 *California Law Review* 1331, 1335 (2004).

11. Chander and Sunder, p. 1331.

versus the public domain" may not be to the benefit of the world's poor.[12] Often, we argued, the benefits of an open-access commons go to the richest and the strongest. Differences in wealth, gender, and class determine whether one will, in fact, be able to convert the riches of the commons into lucrative property. This is what we call the "*romance* of the commons: the belief that because a resource is open to all by force of law, it will indeed be equally exploited by all."[13] Concerns arising from efficiency alone obscure the disparate effects of the commons on the poor. Staying attuned to the distributional effects of the public domain, in contrast, may require thinking about poor people's knowledge in un–common property terms, facilitating their capability to exert greater control over their property and to extract compensation from their knowledge.

In this chapter, I focus on the effects on the poor of the "cultural environmentalism" metaphor through its reification of the division between "raw" and "cooked" knowledge, a conceptual separation long fundamental to intellectual property law. Poor people benefited from this approach to the extent their contributions toward preserving the cultural environment were unrecognized in the past. At the same time, reifying the negative has the perverse effect of congealing poor people's knowledge as the *object* of property, the raw material from which real intellectual property is derived, and obscures its status as the *subject* of property, deserving of the label "intellectual property" in its own right.

Today we must consider how the law's reification of the negative invents tradition rather than discovers it. The lines between the inputs and outputs of innovation are anything but static. At the end of the last century, we witnessed the migration of many forms of knowledge from the public domain to intellectual property: university research, business methods, and even life forms entered the realm of intellectual property. In truth, our intellectual property traditions are more complex than political campaigns for the public domain allow us to recognize. Viewed in this light, we may begin to see how the invention of traditional knowledge as perennially raw rather than cooked erects a false wall between modernity and tradition. Worse still, it deprives diverse peoples of the world of their humanity and cultural creativity. As the Indian eco-feminist and property theorist Vandana Shiva describes, biodiversity is not simply the bounty of nature, guided by nothing but Providence." Far from it, "commons are resources shaped, managed and utilized through community control."[14] When law defines the contributions of the poor as *nature* rather than *culture*, the "creativity of both nature and other cultures is negated."[15] Boyle underlined "law and the *construction* of the Information Society." Our understanding of information and knowledge is not

12. Chander and Sunder, p. 1335.

13. Chander and Sunder, p. 1332.

14. Vandana Shiva, *Protect or Plunder? Understanding Intellectual Property Rights* 47 (London: Zed, 2001).

15. Shiva, p. 50.

preordained but involves political choices. Indeed, this is the insight of Shiva's own political act of defining as "biopiracy" the "patent claims over biodiversity and indigenous knowledge that are based on the *innovations, creativity and genius of the people of the Third World.*" "Since a 'patent' is given for invention," she argues, "*a biopiracy patent denies the innovation embodied in indigenous knowledge.*" [16]

I do not claim that our ability to distinguish the inputs and outputs of innovation is entirely indeterminate. Nor do I advocate law shifting continuously according to the changing political strength of either the rich or the poor in these matters. But I do call for legal decision-makers to recognize contingency, bias, and unreasoned orthodoxy in the legal definitions that begin to appear—every decade or so—as "natural." Today, we can see how constructing poor people's knowledge as raw material supports a model of "benefit sharing," permitting local communities to perhaps receive some compensation from Western patents derived from those communities' resources. But this approach rewards the poor only as wardens, not also as cultivators.

III. CULTIVATORS OF KNOWLEDGE

Today the poor seek to learn how to use the tools of intellectual property to recognize their own cultural and scientific contributions, not just those of the West. Witness the inventiveness of traditional knowledge: In Mysore, India, the makers of internationally famous silk sarees begin offering *waterproof* sarees. Inlaid marble designers in Agra, home of the Taj Mahal, who for years peddled "hackneyed tourist designs" to visitors now apply their craft to create "stunning dinnerware" to be served in the finest Indian and Western homes. Traditional people move, intermarry, share ideas, and modify their skills and products to the shifting demands of the market and their culture. These activities are not merely strategic and pragmatic, but are evidence of a healthy and dynamic culture. In short, traditional knowledge is more vibrant and innovative than the "environmentalism" metaphor, with its emphasis on conservation of nature's raw materials, acknowledges.

Debates over the protection of traditional knowledge, however, often fail to recognize its dynamic character. "Traditional knowledge" typically refers to knowledge handed down from generation to generation. This knowledge includes such forms of cultural expression as songs, dance, stories, artworks, and crafts, as well as "symbols, marks, and other recurring expressions of traditional concepts." Agricultural, scientific, and medical knowledge is also covered. It is often believed that this knowledge has existed for millennia and, remarkably, that it has remained static over time. We are told that proper authorship cannot be determined because the knowledge has passed through oral tradition and was not written down. Even if inscribed,

16. Shiva, p. 49.

we may not locate a single author; traditional knowledge is often communally held. Now mix in the historic conception of indigenous and third-world peoples as the anti-West: anti-commodification, anti-property, and anti-markets. The result is that, partly because of the difficulties of fitting poor people's knowledge into Western frameworks and partly because this knowledge is valued *as the opposite of property*, the wealth of creative knowledge and capacity for knowledge-creation of the poor is often overlooked. Instead, poor people's concerns are addressed by stimulating technology transfer, foreign direct investment, access to Western knowledge, and, at best, equitable benefit-sharing. Much less attention is given to how law can tap the innovation and productive knowledge capacities of the poor.

This is beginning to change. A recent World Intellectual Property Organization (WIPO) report on traditional knowledge finds that, in fact, "much [traditional knowledge] is not ancient or inert, but is a vital, dynamic part of the contemporary lives of many communities today." This should not be surprising. Many of the most ancient monuments survived because they remained in use. Traditional knowledge techniques survive in this way, as well, not as static but as continuously evolving as humans innovate around them to meet current needs and solve contemporary problems. Nothing comes naturally. Knowledge requires constant human ingenuity to sustain it. Traditional knowledge, WIPO tells us, "is being created every day and evolves as individuals and communities respond to the challenges posed by their social environment. . . . *This contemporary aspect is further justification for legal protection.*" [17]

Return to the example of Mysore silk sarees. The "grand old queen" of Indian silk has had a makeover since obtaining a Geographical Indication, updating its look with trendy, new (but interestingly, *natural*) colors—"lilac, ecru, coffee-brown and elephant-grey"—and "contemporary" designs inspired by temple architecture and tribal jewelry. Make no mistake: tradition is hard work. As an executive producer of Mysore silk sarees explained, revamping the designs without losing the sheen of the silk took "months of painstaking research and trials."

Consider another example. A San Francisco–based artist trained in the modernist textile tradition of Ray Eames receives a felt rug from her Iranian-American husband, which he purchased in 1999 on his first trip back to Iran after the Revolution. The felt rug, the product of a 7,000-year-old tradition, inspired the designer to apply her contemporary paintings to the rugs themselves—a collaboration across cultures and generations. This was an idea that the Internet and the Creative Commons could not assist. Indeed, the couple embarked on a four-year journey across Iran to learn more about felt rug-making and found that only a few living felters remain, sprawled all over that country and unconnected to one another. The couple put the felters in touch and established an Iranian factory employing

17. World Intellectual Property Organization, *Intellectual Property and Traditional Knowledge* 6. Available online at http://www.wipo.org/freepublications/en/tk/920/wipo_pub_920.pdf. (Collected on Feb 24, 2006.)

the best of their techniques, literally reviving an art on the verge of extinction and creating a profitable market for the rugs, both within and beyond Iran.

Tradition is cultivated, not discovered. The concept of traditional knowledge, too, is a modern invention. Those studying poor people's knowledge warn of the dangers of "overdrawing the distinction between [traditional knowledge] and modern knowledge." In truth, "no one's life is entirely traditional, and no one's life is entirely modern."[18] Indeed, forcing ourselves to see the modern aspects of traditional knowledge also helps us to view more critically our own Romantic notions of Western intellectual property as "new." As Boyle demonstrated so well, the line separating the public domain and intellectual property does not often involve the eureka discovery that the trope of the Romantic author suggests.

Developing marketable uses for third-world cultural products is "ultimately perhaps the most effective way to protect their traditions."[19] Increasingly, third-world artisans recognize that "[e]xcept in a museum setting, no traditional craft skill can be sustained unless it has a viable market."[20] And recent activity suggests that many third-world craftspeople and artisans are more market-accepting than is generally acknowledged. We see again that commerce and culture are not necessarily at odds, as demonstrated by the revitalization of felt rug-making by the introduction of global markets: preservation through commercialization. And vehicles like geographical indications help preserve geographical diversity. Weavers, artisans, farmers, and the makers of handicrafts do not have to leave their skills or homes for city life. If properly tapped, trained, and protected, they can remain at home and participate in global industry simultaneously.

Intellectual property rights in poor people's knowledge are increasingly considered a key to third-world development—not just in the defensive sense of resisting TRIPS but also in the offensive approach of writing rights into TRIPS. Partly, the development interest here is economic, although how much monetary value lies here is uncertain. Handicrafts alone were estimated to hold close to $3 billion annually in 2000.[21] The UN estimates that developing countries lose about $5 billion in royalties annually from the unauthorized use of traditional knowledge.[22] Poor people's turn to property is surely about economics, but it is about social and cultural values, as well. These claims recognize that the

18. J. Michael Finger, "Introduction and Overview," in *Poor People's Knowledge: Promoting Intellectual Property in Developing Countries* 31 (Washington, DC: The World Bank, 2004).

19. Maureen Leibl and Tirthankar Roy, "Handmade in India: Traditional Craft Skills in a Changing World," in *Poor People's Knowledge: Promoting Intellectual Property in Developing Countries* 70 (World Bank 2004).

20. Leibl and Tirthankar, p. 67.

21. Leibl and Tirthankar, p. 54.

22. Coenraad J. Visser, "Making Intellectual Property Laws Work for Traditional Knowledge," in *Poor People's Knowledge: Promoting Intellectual Property in Developing Countries* 213 (Washington, DC: The World Bank, 2004).

relationship between intellectual property and development goes beyond GDP. People, rich and poor alike, want recognition of their creativity and their contributions to science and culture. This capacity for innovation, work, and cultural sharing is part of what makes us human; this is the freedom-enhancing aspect of intellectual property. At the same time, humans require some amount of stability to develop their cultures and communities; this is the security-enhancing aspect of intellectual property.

WIPO and TRIPS have focused on teaching the poor how to protect the intellectual property of the West. We need to turn our attention to helping the poor to use intellectual property to protect their own inventions, as well. Only some of the people who hold traditional knowledge oppose the commodification of their knowledge on religious or cultural grounds; but *most* are poor, lack infrastructure for production, and are ignorant of intellectual property laws and commercial knowledge of marketing and branding. Intellectual property ownership does not come naturally.

> In many cases . . . poor people's knowledge meets the standard of novelty that modern IP law demands. . . . The development dimension lies in helping poor people to master the commercial/legal tools needed to collect the value of their novelty. This is about entrepreneurship, about finding clever ways to repackage traditional knowledge into products useful for consumers in mass markets, and about developing the capacity to produce and deliver these products in sufficient quantity and quality as to satisfy such markets.[23]

Increasingly, indigenous people and those in the third world seek "training on IP tools and how to use them."[24] The new Indian Geographical Indication Act offers an example. When the Act became effective in 2003, few were aware of its implications. NGOs thus embarked on extensive campaigns to educate local farmers and artisans about GIs.

TRIPS offers a foundation for international recognition of GIs. It defines GIs as "indications which identify a good as originating in the territory of a Member. . . where a given quality, reputation, or other characteristic of the good is essentially attributable to its geographical origin."[25] "Champagne," "Tequila," and "Roquefort" present examples of the types of goods recognized as GIs. Under TRIPS, member states must provide legal means to prevent uses of a designated GI that either mislead the public as to the geographical origin of the good or constitute "unfair

23. Finger, "Introduction," p. 35 (emphasis added).

24. Finger, "Introduction," p. 19.

25. "Agreement on Trade-Related Aspects of Intellectual Property Rights," Apr. 15, 1994, Marrakesh Agreement Establishing the World Trade Organization, Annex 1C, Legal Instruments—Results of the Uruguay Round, Art. 22(1), 1869 U.N.T.S. 299, 33 I.L.M. 1197 (2004).

competition" under Article 10*bis* of the Paris Convention.[26] In addition, TRIPS Article 23 mandates that further protection be extended to GIs for "wines and spirits,"[27] which must be protected even in the absence of consumer confusion.[28]

Two-tiered protection—a higher level of protection for wines and spirits and a lower one for everything else—has been a source of continuing conflict between Europe and the developing world. Partly, this is because of a perceived inequity in the current TRIPS system, and partly it is because GIs are considered to be where much of the wealth of poor people lies: in local production methods and cultural goods, from Darjeeling tea to Mysore silk to basmati rice. The patent provisions of TRIPS have posed clear challenges for developing countries, which typically lack capital for R&D-intensive breakthroughs or manufacturing capacity. GIs, in contrast, are hailed as the poor people's intellectual property rights, recognizing the knowledge of weavers, farmers, and craftspeople rather than just the high-technology contributions of multinational corporations. The structure of GIs does make them particularly suited to poor people's knowledge. First, GIs recognize collective intellectual property rights; under the Indian GI Act, multiple associations of artisans may be recognized as the authorized producers or users of a GI.[29] GI applications are also relatively cheap, at least for a group of artisans working together. Under the GI Act, it costs a modest 5,000 rupees to apply (little more than $100).[30]

---

26. Id., at art 22(2).

27. Id., at art 23.

28. Id., at art 23(1) (prohibiting use of the GI when the product does not originate "in the place indicated by the geographical indication. . . even where the true origin of the goods is indicated or the geographical indication is used in translation or accompanied by expressions such as 'kind,' 'type,' 'style,' 'imitation' or the like"). The designation "Napa Valley Champagne," for example, even when truthful as to the indication of the product's origin, would be impermissible under the heightened level of protection mandated by TRIPS for wines and spirits.

29. The Indian GI Act defines "geographical indication" in relation to goods as an indication that identifies such goods as agricultural goods, natural goods, or manufactured goods as originating, or having been manufactured in the territory of a country, or a region or locality in that territory, where a given quality, reputation, or other characteristic of such goods is essentially attributable to its geographical origin, and in the case where such goods are manufactured goods one of the activities of either the production or of processing or preparation of the goods concerned takes place in such territory, region, or locality, as the case may be. Geographical Indication of Goods (Registration and Protection) Act of 1999, No. 48, Acts of Parliament, 1999 § I-1(3)(e).

30. The cost to renew a GI is 3,000 rupees. The Geographical Indication of Goods (Registration and Protection) Rules, 2002, The First Schedule, 4A. Once approved, GIs and all producers and authorized users of the GIs are listed in a national register. Geographical Indication of Goods Act §II-5–6. Registration lasts for 10 years and is renewable "from time to time" for periods of an additional 10 years. Id,. § III-18.

Although GIs certainly hold promise for the poor, they have limits. The Indian GI Act protects only those goods or processes whose quality or reputation are shown to be "due exclusively or essentially to the geographical environment, with its inherent natural and human factors."[31] GI applications require "proof of origin" and a "historical record"[32] of continuous use of the goods or process. Registrants obtain the exclusive right to use the GI,[33] and licensing of GIs is prohibited.[34]

Such requirements and restrictions take a narrow view of traditional knowledge, linking culture to land. The rule against alienability poses special concerns. Even if this approach may enable people to *remain* within their communities (and preserve the physical environment, as well), what if they move? What rights do traditional weavers from Mysore have if they move to North India—or the United Kingdom? Of course, there are good reasons to prevent the alienation of the GI from the particular geographical community. It prevents the scenario in which a large foreign corporation hires a member of that community away and then begins to produce "authentic" work elsewhere, using that GI—and decimating the livelihoods of the traditional community left behind. At the same time, such a restriction could stifle opportunities for some individuals, as they remain within a traditional community by economic necessity, not choice. People move, intermarry, and change jobs. Culture flows with them. The GI Act does not recognize this dynamic nature of culture, ossifying authentic production in *today's* localities.

Within a recognized "association, traditional leaders may impose their will on members, reifying traditional hierarchies. Scholars such as Elizabeth Povinelli note that cultural rights often lead to the ironic production of authenticity or indigeneity, which conforms to traditional structures from the past, rather than celebrating cultures as diachronic peoples who are dynamic and heterogeneous. GIs also pose economic concerns. GIs may protect Darjeeling tea, for example, but also prohibit the Indian manufacture of Scotch whiskey, driving up the cost of Scotch in India. It is possible that the poor may reap greater economic rewards in a system with fewer production constraints. Boyle's concern about the public domain also applies: at which point does too much intellectual property impede the very processes of cultural sharing and innovation that law ought to promote, especially to aid the little guy in cultural production? These economic concerns raise an important question of liberal strategy. As critical legal theorists have aptly warned, we must stand ready to openly question when and how "rights" might work to the disadvantage of the poor rather than to the poor's benefit.

These concerns notwithstanding, GIs do potentially offer a range of benefits, from recognizing the innovation of collectives, to preserving geographic diversity

---

31. Id., § III-11(2).

32. Geographical Indication of Goods Rules § Form GI-1.

33. Geographical Indication of Goods Act § IV-21(1-b).

34. Id., § IV-24.

and stimulating some redistribution of wealth. It may be more important to think of GIs as part of a larger framework in which the poor learn the secrets of Madison Avenue. If one simply produces goods, then any successful product will eventually draw stiff competition from global mass production. But creating a protected *brand* allows one to stave off complete usurpation by mass-produced substitutes. The GI Act works on this principle. It rewards the local community for having created a valued reputation and protects that reputation from the forces of global commerce. It recognizes that consumers everywhere seek authentic products and that they may care about *who* produces something, not just the ultimate product. Fair Trade coffee, Rugmark carpets, and dolphin-safe tuna, for example, appeal to people's desire to consume free from the worry about exploitation in the process of production. In response to the commercialization of ghetto style by white-owned fashion houses, one African American company declares to the consumer its ghetto roots by branding itself "FUBU"—For Us, By Us. Such authenticity marks translate into profits in the marketplace.

The goal is "to help poor people get along in the modern world—to use modern instruments for managing the ownership of knowledge either to collect on the commercial value of that knowledge or to prevent its use in a way that its owners consider inappropriate."[35] New organizations, such as Light Years IP are emerging to address this need, specializing in marketing and branding a developing country's intellectual property. Given the ease with which work can be copied by mass-production techniques, local artisans must assert their IP rights in their designs to maintain their ability to receive compensation for the knowledge-based portion of the products.

The Danish artists' collective Superflex has pioneered this strategy. The Superflex "Supercopy" art collaboration employs what it calls a "counter-economic strategy" to teach local farmers in the third world how to convert their biodiversity and traditional knowledge into branded end-products, which will eventually compete with the products of global multinationals. In one ongoing collaboration, Superflex works with a farmers' cooperative in Maues, Brazil. This region in the Amazon is famous for cultivating the guarana berry, prized by the local population for its perceived medicinal and energy-giving properties. The Dutch multinational Ambev and Pepsi Co. have successfully marketed global energy drinks derived from this plant, most notably Ambev's "Antarctica" drink. The local Maues farmers complained that the multinationals have formed a cartel, driving down the price of the guarana berries from $25/kilo to $4/kilo. So, the cooperative is fighting back. In collaboration with Superflex, farmers held brainstorming sessions to begin developing their own product and designing a label for it. One member, for example, suggested a coffee drink called Maues Café, evoking the internationally popular Nescafé drink, as depicted in Figure 19.1.

35. Finger, "Introduction," p. 3.

FIGURE 19.1 MAUES CAFÉ.

Eventually, though, the cooperative decided to manufacture and distribute a soft drink: Guarana Power. Members designed a label for the drink, which comprises a photograph of local farmers affixed atop the familiar Antarctica label. Guarana Power's marketing slogan? "[O]riginal Maues guarana for energy and empowerment." (See Figure 19.2.)

The Superflex collaboration turns on a simple idea: empowerment for the poor will entail the poor learning to control and market their own knowledge products. In the words of Superflex (appropriated from Ani DiFranco), "Every tool is a weapon if you hold it right." The Maues collective spoke with lawyers about intellectual property rights, raised capital, paired with a production company in Denmark, and searched for global distributors for Guarana Power. Superflex's Guarana Power gallery floor reproduces the shop floor, taking visitors on a journey from producing to bottling, labeling, refrigerating, and literally tasting Guarana Power.

IV. DEVELOPMENT AS FREEDOM

Without ignoring the importance of economic growth, we must look well beyond it.
Amartya Sen, Development as Freedom[36]

36. Amartya Sen, *Development as Freedom* 14 (New York: Anchor Books, 1999).

FIGURE 19.2 GUARANA POWER, WITH LOGO PASTED OVER MULTINATIONAL BRAND LABEL.

In September 2007 the WIPO General Assembly declared that intellectual property law needs to incorporate a "development agenda." WIPO responded in part to the Geneva Declaration, a call from hundreds of scientists, scholars, and activists to reorient intellectual property law in favor of the "[l]ong-neglected concerns of the poor, the sick, the visually impaired and others."[37] The Development

37. Geneva Declaration on the Future of the World Intellectual Property Organization, Oct. 2004. Available at http://www.cptech.org/ip/wipo/futureofwipodeclaration.pdf.

Agenda and Geneva Declaration sound a common theme: that intellectual property law must confront its vast social effects and serve a broader range of human values.

So we must now think beyond incentives, but to what? The preamble to TRIPS stipulates that intellectual property rights must promote "development," but it leaves that concept undefined. For the United States, establishing intellectual property law is itself development—such law will attract foreign direct investment and spur indigenous creation.

But many see this understanding of development as much too narrow. Demands to expand the ambit of values served by intellectual property abound. Artists and students around the world are joining in a "Free Culture" movement. Indigenous peoples complain of the ransacking of their cultural knowledge and environment. HIV/AIDS activists work to secure access to lifesaving medicines for the world's poor. Farmers demand the right to replant seeds. Cultural environmentalists seek to preserve biodiversity and cultural communities.

We have already been here: Recall the brilliant move made by Mahbub Ul Haq 15 years ago when he fashioned the *Human Development Report* for the United Nations. That report countered the earlier dominance of GDP-based evaluations of social welfare. It built a positive measure of development from a number of disgruntled constituencies. Amartya Sen describes Mahbub Ul Haq's strategy as shaping the negative energy of these multiple constituencies into a single, positive vision:

> Mahbub [Ul Haq] took on the leadership of large armies of discontent that were gunning, somewhat sporadically, at the single-minded concentration on the GNP. There were activists arguing for the recognition of "basic needs." There were international interventionists lamenting "the state of the world's children." There were relief organizations concerned with hunger and epidemics. There were writers focusing on "disparities" between the actual lives of the rich and the poor. There were humanists voicing the need for social justice in the quality of life. There were advocates of measures of physical quality of life. There were even some philosophically oriented critics wondering about the bigger insights into social ethics provided in the far-reaching works of Aristotle, Adam Smith, Karl Marx, and even of John Stuart Mill. It is to the credit of Mahbub's integrating vision that he saw the possibility of harnessing these different discontents into the development of a capacious alternative outlook which would be, at once, both practical and broad, and which could accommodate—however roughly—these different concerns.[38]

Since 1990, the United Nations has understood development in the broad terms of expanding human capabilities, thanks in no small part to Sen himself.

38. Amartya Sen, "A Decade of Human Development," 1 *Journal of Human Development* 17, 21 (2000).

Ul Haq's *Human Development Report* and Sen's vision of "development as freedom" are pluralist, measuring development based on the capacity for many freedoms, including, but not limited to, market-oriented freedoms. These freedoms range from basic needs, such as the right to life and health, to more expansive freedoms of movement, creative work, and participation in social, economic, and cultural institutions. Furthermore, Sen's theory recognizes the interrelatedness of rights: the right to labor and remuneration for one's creations, including intellectual creations, affects the right to health, and vice versa.

Intellectual property law is essential to development, not just in the narrow sense of efficiency but in this broader view of expanding capability for central freedoms. Surely, copyrights and patents determine our access to basic needs, from educational materials to lifesaving medicines. What is less obvious is that failure to be recognized as an author or inventor may impede one's access to these essential life goods by diminishing one's material wealth and the capability for living a full life. Stated differently, the implications in intellectual property rights go well beyond incentives for innovation: These rights are related to questions of cultural relations, social development, and GDP growth.

The time has come to supplement our traditional economic analysis of intellectual property with a cultural analysis that takes note of the social and cultural effects of intellectual property law, but not to replace the economic lens with a cultural lens. Rather, neither lens alone is adequate either to describe positive intellectual property law or to guide normative analysis.

The traditional utilitarian understanding of intellectual property focuses on incentivizing the creation of more knowledge goods. Public-domain advocates would preserve a rich public domain in order to promote this goal. But utilitarianism does not ask who makes the goods or whether the goods are fairly distributed to all who need them. A broader understanding of intellectual property recognizes the importance not just of producing more knowledge goods but also of participating in the process of knowledge creation. Recognizing people's humanity requires acknowledging their production of knowledge of the world. The United Nations' conception of a "Knowledge Society" articulates this in terms of the *products* and *processes* of knowledge creation. In the Knowledge Age, social, cultural, and economic freedom will require not only access to knowledge *products*, but also access to the *processes* of creating knowledge. As a UN report puts it, "the Knowledge Society is not only about technological innovations, but also about human beings, their personal growth and their individual creativity, experience and participation . . . at its best, the Knowledge Society involves all members of a community in knowledge creation and utilization."[39] The principal

39. UN Division for Public Administration and Development Management, Department of Economic and Social Affairs, *Report: Understanding Knowledge Societies*, p. xi, UN Doc ST/ESA/PAD/SER E/66 (2005).

assets of a Knowledge Society are "information . . . that triggers people's creative reflection" and "people . . . as creative beings and carriers of tacit knowledge."[40]

Recognizing access to knowledge as consisting of both products and processes is essential as we integrate development into our international intellectual property law and policy. We may ask first, how might intellectual property law enhance access to knowledge *products*—such as, for example, by not making textbooks and pharmaceuticals cost prohibitive to people who live on two dollars a day? At the same time, we must consider how intellectual property law and policy may enhance the *capacity* for participating in the *processes* of knowledge creation. The Indian GI Act, for example, *recognizes the poor as producers of knowledge and promotes their participation in global markets.* Rather than focus just on the reception of knowledge goods, the GI Act—and a vast campaign by NGOs to teach poor people about it—focuses on teaching people how to recognize and market their own knowledge production. The GI Act takes an "agent-oriented" view of development, recognizing that "[w]ith adequate social opportunities, individuals can effectively shape their own destiny and help each other." These individuals, in Sen's words, "need not be seen primarily as passive recipients of the benefits of cunning development programs."[41]

Focusing on development as freedom and agency also gives us a metric by which to assess the Indian GI Act. For one thing, a geographical indication works by denying many the ability to identify a good by a particular name. But in so doing, it recognizes the quality and reputation cultivated by particular communities, and, like traditional trademarks, prohibits others from free-riding off that reputation. It thereby empowers local communities, which can continue to commercialize their products without fearing displacement by global mass production. Of course, GIs might circumscribe freedom if those within the community are forced to play defined roles in the production process or are prevented from leaving. As Sen writes, an economy premised upon agency and freedom will value "free labor contract and unrestrained physical movement" in contrast to the "bonded labor and forced work" characteristic of traditional economies. A core value in Sen's development-as-freedom approach is that "the people must be allowed to decide freely what traditions they wish or not wish to follow."[42]

V. CONCLUSION

The poor must be recognized as both receivers and producers of knowledge. Failing to promote poor people's capacity for creative work and their participation

40. UN Div. for Pub. Admin. and Dev. Mgmt., Dep't. of Econ. and Social Affairs, p. xi (cited in note 92).

41. Sen, *Development as Freedom*, p. 11.

42. Sen, *Development as Freedom*, p. 28.

in global culture and commercial markets hinders development as freedom. As Sen writes, "the rejection of the freedom to participate in the labor market is one of the ways of keeping people in bondage and captivity."[43] In the Knowledge Age, wealth lies not simply in access to other people's knowledge (although this is certainly important), but also in the ability to produce new knowledge and to benefit from this creation, culturally and economically.

43. Sen, *Development as Freedom*, p. 7.

20. CONTOURS OF AN INTERNATIONAL INSTRUMENT ON LIMITATIONS AND EXCEPTIONS*

P. BERNT HUGENHOLTZ AND RUTH L. OKEDIJI

* This chapter is an abridged version of a study sponsored by the Open Society Institute (OSI), available at http://www.ivir.nl/publicaties/hugenholtz/finalreport2008.pdf (last visited April 13, 2008). The study reflects contributions from leading copyright and IP experts who participated at a workshop sponsored by OSI and held at the Cardozo School of Law in New York on 16–18 December, 2007: Prof. Graeme B. Dinwoodie, Chicago-Kent College of Law; Prof. Rochelle C. Dreyfuss, New York University School of Law; Vera Franz, Open Society Institute; Prof. Daniel J. Gervais, Faculty of Law, University of Ottawa; Prof. Laurence R. Helfer, Vanderbilt University Law School; Prof. Reto M. Hilty, Max Planck Institute for Intellectual Property; Prof. Justin Hughes, Benjamin Cardozo School of Law; Sisule F. Musungu, Research Fellow, Information Society Project, Yale Law School; Prof. Jerome H. Reichman, Duke University School of Law; Dr. Manon A. Ress, Knowledge Ecology International; Prof. Pamela Samuelson, UC Berkeley School of Law; and Louis Villaroel, Ministry of Education, Chile. The authors also thank Tomas Felcman for invaluable research assistance. P. Bernt Hugenholtz is Professor of Intellectual Property Law & Director of the Institute for Information Law (IViR), University of Amsterdam. Ruth L. Okediji is William L. Prosser Professor of Law & Solly Robins Distinguished Research Fellow, University of Minnesota Law School.

INTRODUCTION

The issue of limitations and exceptions (L&Es) to copyright figures prominently on the agenda of international lawmakers today. It is one of many items short-listed for action by the Committee on Development and Intellectual Property (CDIP) at the World Intellectual Property Organization (WIPO), which was established to implement the WIPO Development Agenda.[1] More recently, at a meeting of the WIPO Standing Committee on Copyright and Related Rights (SCCR),[2] a proposal by the Chilean government to initiate what might eventually become an international instrument on L&Es received broad support and will remain on the future agenda of the SCCR, despite reservations by some developed countries. Thus, the time is clearly ripe to consider the ways in which such an instrument might be legally and institutionally conceived. This chapter suggests various approaches and offers recommendations.

As mechanisms of access, L&Es contribute to the dissemination of knowledge, which in turn is essential for a variety of human activities and values, including liberty; the exercise of political power; and economic, social, and personal advancement. Appropriately designed L&Es may alleviate the needs of people around the world who still lack access to books and other educational materials and may also open up rapid advances in information and communication technologies that are fundamentally transforming the processes of production, dissemination, and storage of information. As new technologies challenge copyright's internal balance, and as the costs of globalization heighten the vital need for innovation and knowledge dissemination, a multilateral instrument that can effectively harness various national practices with regard to L&Es, and which can provide a framework for dynamic evaluation of how global copyright norms can be most effectively translated into a credible system that appropriately

1. *See* World Intellectual Property Organization (WIPO), Committee on Intellectual Property and Development (CDIP), First Session, Summary by the Chair, March 3–7, 2008, available at http://www.wipo.int/edocs/mdocs/mdocs/en/cdip_1/cdip_1_summary.doc (last visited April 13, 2008).

2. *See* WIPO, Standing Committee on Copyright and Related Rights (SCCR), Sixteenth Session, Conclusions of the Sixteenth Session of the SCCR, March 10–12, 2008, available at http://www.wipo.int/edocs/mdocs/sccr/en/sccr_16/sccr_16_conclusions.doc (last visited April 13, 2008).

values author and user rights, is a necessity. This chapter examines policy options and modalities for framing an international instrument on limitations and exceptions to copyright within the treaty obligations of the current international copyright system. We consider this international copyright *acquis* as our general starting point and evaluate options for the design of such an instrument, including questions of political sustainability and institutional home.

Section I sketches the rationales for a multilateral approach to the question of limitations and exceptions. In section II, we explore flexibilities inside the international copyright *acquis*, review the three-step test, and assess its import for the validity of a proposed international instrument on L&Es, particularly given the expansion of the test in the TRIPS Agreement and the interpretive jurisprudence of the WTO dispute panels. Finally, in section III we set out in preliminary fashion the basic contours of a multilateral instrument on L&Es. Considerations of feasibility, political sustainability, and normative priorities, among others, are briefly explored and then situated along a continuum of possible modalities for such an instrument. We then offer some preliminary recommendations on the way forward.

I. RATIONALES FOR AN INTERNATIONAL INSTRUMENT

The rights-access balance struck in the current international *acquis* is largely reflective of the conditions that affected the outcome of negotiations on the initial iteration of the Berne Convention in 1886. Prior to the conclusion of negotiations, the copyright laws of individual European nations each reflected a balance between the protection of authorial rights on the one hand and access to creative works on the other. To eliminate discriminatory practices commonly employed by national laws with respect to foreign works, the Berne Convention at its genesis sought to serve a coordinative function and correlate existing national norms into a set of minimum baseline principles acceptable to a broad multilateral membership.

There are good historical reasons for the imbalanced treatment of L&Es in the *acquis*. Because L&Es reflect specific domestic welfare interests ranging from freedom of expression to cultural development, global mandatory obligations in this regard would unduly impose uniformity in a sphere that, at the time of the Berne Convention's negotiation, was uniquely designed to accomplish wholly domestic goals. Further, as a strategic matter, it can be argued that the presumed self-interest of a state in promoting its domestic welfare obviated any need to require mandatory global L&Es. In addition, although a global approach to copyright protection ensured a mutually beneficial return for authors' rights, the same could not be said for L&Es that were directed to the public good. L&Es enacted in one country are intended to address interests, needs, and conditions uniquely beneficial to that country and reflective of that country's markets.

Unlike the benefits of reciprocal rights protection, the benefits of L&Es are thus perceived to be limited to the domestic market. This may explain why an international approach to L&Es has historically never been pursued by developed countries that championed multilateralism in copyright relations. State-focused L&Es are deemed sufficient and preferred to an international mandatory approach, since unilateral action in this regard can be successful domestically without any corresponding public loss.[3]

Today, the vintage preoccupation with competing common and civil law rationalizations of IP and the expected gains of strong protection have given way to much larger considerations of the global effects of unlimited exclusive rights in knowledge goods. From public health to consumer protection, the high social costs of ever-expanding IP protection have compelled a demand from scholars, policymakers, international agencies, and civil society groups for accountability in the IP system to the fundamental public purpose that private rewards for innovation and creative works are intended to advance. As is now widely recognized, the unlimited grant or exercise of exclusive rights by copyright holders without corresponding and appropriate L&Es has serious adverse long-term implications not only for development priorities, but indeed for the creation and innovation process itself. It is well established that most innovation occurs incrementally by building on preceding technologies or existing knowledge, which underscores the crucial role that access plays in the achievement of copyright's fundamental goals.

A new international instrument on L&Es would offer a unique opportunity to coordinate, harmonize, and balance the heightened (and new) standards of protection set forth in the successive Berne Convention Revisions, the TRIPS Agreement, and the WIPO Internet Treaties. International harmonization of L&Es present in national copyright laws would diminish reliance on national courts for the interpretation of multilateral accords, therefore augmenting the benefits of substantive rights harmonization. For example, a new international instrument on L&Es could help to eliminate diverging interpretations of the three-step test across national jurisdictions. A new international instrument would also offset the TRIPS constriction of the three-step test as well as the nascent jurisprudence of WTO dispute panels, which emphasizes economic benefits of control over economic benefits of diffusion. A global approach to L&Es would further help: to facilitate transborder trade, both online and in traditional media, by eliminating inconsistency and uncertainty and encouraging uniformity of standards of protection and transparency; to alleviate institutional weakness of states that need diffusion most (DCs and LDCs); to counteract the recent shift to bilateralism and regionalism in international copyright policymaking;

3. *See* Ronald B. Mitchell and Patricia M. Keilbach, *Situation Structure and Institutional Design: Reciprocity, Coercion and Exchange*, 55 INT'L ORG. 891 (2001), at 892.

and to constrain unilateral ratcheting up of global standards. Finally, a new international instrument with a broad membership offers an opportunity to consolidate recent gains in integrating public interest goals in the international copyright system, as seen notably in the Preamble to the TRIPS Agreement, the Preamble to the WIPO Copyright Treaty (WCT), and its Agreed Statements.

II. IN SEARCH OF "WIGGLE ROOM"

Ideally, a new international instrument on L&Es should be compatible with the standards set by the international copyright *acquis*, while optimally exploiting flexibilities that exist within the current multilateral framework. In search of these flexibilities, it is important to understand the mechanics of the copyright system. Statutory limitations and exceptions are but one, albeit important, way of creating balance inside copyright. The toolbox of copyright law consists of several other balancing instruments as well, including, for example, the concept of a "work of authorship," which features a requirement of "originality";[4] the idea/expression dichotomy, which delineates the border between protected subject matter and the public domain; the delineation of economic rights of the right holder, such as the right of reproduction and the right of communication to the public; general limits to copyright, such as the exhaustion rule (first-sale doctrine) and the term of protection; and, finally, limitations and exceptions proper. In addition, outside the copyright toolbox, certain limits to copyright can be directly sourced in fundamental rights and freedoms, such as freedom of expression and the right to privacy, and others in competition law, such as the use of compulsory licenses. This section explores the "wiggle room"[5] that the main multilateral Conventions (BC, TRIPS, and the WCT) leave to the contracting states to set limits to copyright and, by implication, to enter into special agreements codifying such limits, without undercutting the *acquis*.

A. Minimum Standards

Characteristic of the international copyright regime is a structure of minimum standards that qualified right holders may invoke before the national courts of the contracting states. But these minimum standards need not apply in purely national contexts (BC art. 5.1). States have remained fully autonomous as regards works in their country of origin (BC art. 5.3). At least theoretically, this has left

---

4. *See* P. B. Hugenholtz, *Fierce Creatures. Copyright Exemptions: Towards Extinction?*, keynote speech, IFLA/IMPRIMATUR Conference, *Rights, Limitations and Exceptions: Striking a Proper Balance*, Amsterdam, 30–31 October 1997, available at http://www.ivir.nl/publications/hugenholtz/PBH-FierceCreatures.doc (last visited March 3, 2008).

5. The term is taken from J. H. Reichman, *From Free Riders to Fair Followers: Global Competition Under the TRIPS Agreement*, 29 N.Y.U. J. INT'L L. & POL. 11, 29 (1997).

contracting states complete freedom to derogate from the conventional minimum rights as they see fit. The main minimum standards set by the Berne Convention and other international agreements concern (1) protected subject matter ("works of authorship"); (2) economic (patrimonial) rights; and (3) limitations and exceptions subject to the "three-step test."

1. Limits to Protected Subject Matter Inherent to the minimum rights prescribed by the Berne Convention, and incorporated by reference into TRIPS and the WCT, are certain general limits to copyright protection that could be exploited in an international instrument on L&Es, as regards both the subject matter of copyright and the economic rights defined and prescribed by the Conventions. The notion of a "work of authorship," codified in BC art. 2(1), includes an implicit requirement of "originality,"[6] which rules out, for instance, mere factual accounts. This ground rule is illustrated by BC art. 2(8), which excludes from copyright protection "news of the day or miscellaneous facts having the character of mere items of press information." Similarly, TRIPS art. 10(2) and WCT art. 5 state that copyright in compilations of data "shall not extend to the data or material itself." A related balancing tool is the idea/expression (content/form) dichotomy, codified not in the BC, but in TRIPS art. 9(2) and in WCT art. 2. Accordingly, copyright protection extends "to expressions and not to ideas, procedures, methods of operation or mathematical concepts as such."

Note that BC art. 2(8), TRIPS arts. 9(2) and 10(2), and WCT arts. 2 and 5 are phrased as *mandatory* exclusions from copyright protection. The reasons for these exclusions are, however, not clear from the historical record. Are these objects excluded from copyright protection as a matter of public policy, expressing principles of free speech or freedom of competition? Or are they simply reminders of the general rule that copyright protects original expression?[7] If the former interpretation is correct, one could read into these exclusions an actual obligation upon contracting states not to protect these objects. If the latter is correct, the net effect of these exclusions would be more limited; for example, a Union "author" of news items could not invoke minimum protection in another Union country.[8]

2. Limits to Economic Rights The definition of the economic rights in the three main Conventions in the field of copyright offers additional "wiggle room." The BC enumerates the minimum rights in a rather haphazard fashion, reflecting the history of the Convention; rights were added incrementally as new modes of exploitation became mainstream. But not all economic rights normally found in national laws have found their way into the international copyright *acquis*.

---

6. *See* Sam Ricketson and Jane Ginsburg, INTERNATIONAL COPYRIGHT AND NEIGHBORING RIGHTS: THE BERNE CONVENTION AND BEYOND (Oxford University Press, 2006) 405.

7. *See* id., at 498–501.

8. *See* id., at 499.

A display right, for instance, is not recognized in any of the three main Conventions, whereas a right of commercial rental of films and software may not be required depending on market conditions (TRIPS art. 11; WCT art. 7), and an artist's resale right has voluntary status only (BC art. 14*ter*). Such unregulated or optional rights may therefore be subjected to unlimited limitations and exceptions.

But even a minimum right seemingly carved in stone, such as the right of reproduction, may leave contracting states latitude for limitation. Whereas BC art. 9(1) prescribes the "exclusive right of authorizing the reproduction of . . . works, in any manner or form," and the Agreed Statements to the WCT confirm its application in the digital environment,[9] neither instrument defines the act of "reproduction" as such. Scholars have convincingly argued that reproduction is basically a normative, not a technical, notion and should therefore be interpreted in the light of its objective.[10] This line of reasoning leaves room, for instance, for a statutory carve-out permitting acts of economically insignificant temporary copying.[11] Arguably, such carve-outs need not be subjected to the three-step test.[12] Further flexibilities can be derived from the notion of "public," which determines the scope of several other economic rights codified in the Berne Convention, some of which were eventually absorbed by the general right of communication to the public that was introduced in WCT art. 8.[13] Indeed, many countries have

---

9. *See* World Intellectual Property Organization (WIPO) Copyright Treaty, Dec. 20, 1996, S. Treaty Doc. No. 105-17, 36 I.L.M. 65 [hereafter WCT], Agreed statement concerning Article 1(4):

> The reproduction right, as set out in Article 9 of the Berne Convention, and the exceptions permitted thereunder, fully apply in the digital environment, in particular to the use of works in digital form. It is understood that the storage of a protected work in digital form in an electronic medium constitutes a reproduction within the meaning of Article 9 of the Berne Convention.

10. *See* Legal Advisory Board, *Reply to the Green Paper on Copyright and Related Rights in the Information Society, Brussels,* September 1995 (copy on file with the authors); *see also* generally P. Bernt Hugenholtz, *Adapting Copyright to the Information Superhighway*, in P. Bernt Hugenholtz (ed.), The Future of Copyright in a Digital Environment (Kluwer Law International, 1996) 81–102.

11. *See*, e.g., Dutch Copyright Act (as amended), art. 13, available at http://www.ivir.nl/legislation/nl/copyrightact1912_unofficial.pdf (last visited March 5, 2008) (unofficial translation by Ministry of Justice of the Netherlands):

> The reproduction of a literary, scientific or artistic work will not include temporary reproduction of a passing or incidental nature and forming an essential part of a technical procedure whose sole purpose is to enable a) the passing on by an intermediary through a network between third parties, or b) a lawful use and if it contains no independent economic value.

12. Note, however, that insofar as such carve-outs from the economic rights would fall under the rubric of "minor reservations," they might still fall within the ambit of the three-step test. See discussion below.

13. These rights include the right of public performance "by any means or process" (BC art. 11); the public recitation including the public communication of thereof (BC art. 11*ter*);

taken advantage of such flexibilities by permitting certain de minimis acts of public performance or communication to the public by way of legally defining the contours of these acts around such minimal uses.

The Berne Convention also warrants an exclusive right to make transformative uses, in the form of translations (art. 8), adaptations, arrangements and other alterations (art. 12), and cinematographic adaptations (art. 14(1)). Again, in the absence of clear definitions, these provisions leave some room for *de facto* limitations, for instance by determining in national law the criteria for copyright infringement. The exhaustion rule (first-sale doctrine) found in most national laws, and permitted under TRIPS art. 6 and WCT art. 6.2, is another boundary of copyright.[14] The same can be said of the limited term (duration) of copyright (BC art. 7). And although the minimum Berne term of life of the author plus 50 years (BC art. 7) is increasingly overrun by countries providing "life plus 70," the Berne minimum is in itself subject to several exceptions.[15]

3. Specific Limitations and Exceptions in the BC The Berne Convention recognizes two types of limitations: compensated limitations and uncompensated limitations. The difference is important especially in relation to the three-step test discussed below. The existence of a statutory compensation scheme may avoid causing "unreasonable prejudice" to authors or right holders and thereby makes it easier for limitations of the latter category to satisfy the third step of the test. Uncompensated limitations in the Berne Convention include provisions permitting public speeches (art. 2*bis*(2)), quotations (art. 10(1)), uses for teaching purposes (art. 10(2)), press usage (art. 10*bis*(1)), reporting of current events (art. 10*bis*(2)), and ephemeral recordings by broadcasting organizations (art. 11*bis*(3)).[16] Many of these provisions simply state the purpose of the permitted use and leave a considerable measure of freedom to contracting states for implementation at

the public performance of cinematographic adaptations (BC art. 14(1)); the rights of broadcasting, rebroadcasting, cable distribution, and public communication by loudspeaker (BC art. 11*bis*).

14. Note that neither the BC nor TRIPS prescribes a general right of distribution.

15. The standard minimum term may be reduced to 50 years from first communication to the public or from creation for cinematographic works. Contracting states may also offer shorter terms of 25 years from creation for photographic works and works of applied art. However, art. 9 of the WCT reinstates the normal BC term for photographic works by ruling out the application of Berne art. 7(4). For works in which copyright is initially vested in a corporate entity, minimum terms expire 50 years from first publication or creation (TRIPS art. 12).

16. *See* WIPO Standing Committee on Copyright and Related Rights, *WIPO Study on Limitations and Exceptions of Copyright and Related Rights in the Digital Environment*, Ninth Session, June 23–27, 2003, WIPO Doc. SCCR/9/7 (April 5, 2003) [hereafter WIPO Study], at 11–20. In addition to the limitations and exceptions discussed above, the Berne Convention allows, in a few well circumscribed situations, for statutory (compulsory) licensing, as in the case of the recording of musical works (art. 13(1)) and broadcasting and cable retransmission (art. 11bis(2)). In such cases, right holders have a right to equitable remuneration.

the national level. In some cases (e.g., arts. 10(1) and 10(2)), the norms of the Berne Convention refer to "fair practice," a notion which arguably leaves room for an interpretation that takes account of local conditions,[17] thus creating additional flexibilities. It is important to stress that Berne Convention art. 10(1) is phrased as a *mandatory* user freedom. The reason for this special status, most likely, lies in the exception's rationale: freedom of expression. Moreover, a right to quote might be considered an essential prerogative for authors, who traditionally occupy centre stage in the Berne Convention.

In addition to the specific limitations enumerated in the Convention, Berne art. 9(2) allows unspecified limitations to the right of reproduction, subject to the three-step test, which is discussed below. The TRIPS Agreement and the WCT do not contain any additional specific limitations to the rights newly introduced by these Conventions; both extend the rule of the three-step test to all rights covered by the respective treaties. However, the contracting parties to the WCT did underscore the importance of retaining a balance in copyright, as is clear from its preamble,[18] which may serve as a guideline to interpretation of the norms of the WCT, and arguably the Berne Convention as well.

Moreover, as the record of the Stockholm Conference reveals, certain exceptions to particular rights, although not expressed in the international instruments, might be nevertheless implied.[19] As their name "minor reservations" indicates, these implied limitations usually concern de minimis uses, such as use of works during religious ceremonies, or use by military bands.[20] Such minor reservations might be codified in a future instrument on L&Es. Finally, for developing nations, there exist additional flexibilities in the Berne Appendix. However, because of the complexity of its provisions and the administrative burdens it imposes on its users, to date the Appendix has largely remained unused.[21]

B. Three-Step Test

1. Overview of the Three-Step Test At the 1967 Stockholm Conference, the so-called three-step test of BC art. 9(2) was introduced in international copyright

---

17. Id., at 13.

18. *See* WCT, *supra* n. 9, pmbl. ¶5 ("*Recognizing* the need to maintain a balance between the rights of authors and the larger public interest, particularly education, research and access to information, as reflected in the Berne Convention . . ." [emphasis in original].

19. WIPO Study, *supra* n. 16, at 33; *see also* Report of the Panel, US—Section 110(5) Copyright Act, 15 June 2000, WTO Doc. WT/DS/160/R, § 6.33 et seq. [hereafter US—Section 110(5) Report].

20. M. Senftleben, COPYRIGHT, LIMITATIONS AND THE THREE-STEP TEST (Kluwer Law International, 2004) 198–201.

21. *See* R. L. Okediji, *Welfare and Digital Copyright in International Perspective,* in J. H. Reichman and K. Maskus (eds.), INTERNATIONAL PUBLIC GOODS AND TRANSFER OF TECHNOLOGY UNDER A GLOBALIZED INTELLECTUAL PROPERTY REGIME (Cambridge University Press, 2005).

law as a companion to the formal recognition of the general right of reproduction in art. 9(1) of the Berne Convention. The three-step test reappeared in TRIPS art. 13 and WCT art. 10. The three-step test has subsequently found its way, via WCT art. 10, into art. 5(5) of the European Copyright (Information Society) Directive of 2001, and from there into the national laws of some EU States.[22] Under TRIPS art. 13, Member States shall confine limitations and exceptions (1) to "certain special cases," (2) "which do not conflict with a normal exploitation of the work," and (3) which "do not unreasonably prejudice the legitimate interests of the right holder." Increasingly, variants of the test also appear in various regional instruments, such as the European harmonization directives, or in bilateral treaties, such as the U.S.-Australia Free Trade Agreement (art. 17.4(10)).

The evolution of the three-step test into the overriding norm of international copyright law through its incorporation into the TRIPS Agreement has attracted criticism from scholars and stakeholders alike.[23] The three-step test apparently negates the balance between exclusivity and access that should be inherent in any mature copyright system. Its focus, as with the entire structure of minimum rights, is geared toward protecting rights of authors or, in the case of TRIPS, "right holders," not the interests of society or the general public. Cumulative application of the three steps, as its wording requires, heavily tilts the balance in favor of the right holders. Through its incorporation into the TRIPS Agreement, what was essentially a norm of international copyright has morphed into a norm of international trade law. Finally, the test fails to take into account the justified needs of developing nations. We share much of this criticism. However, as a political reality, the existing *acquis*, including the three-step test, can hardly be ignored. Fortunately, as the analysis that follows reveals, despite its firm wording, the three-step test does afford states significant flexibilities, and leaves them sufficient room to enter into an instrument on L&Es with meaningful substantive content.

The three-step test is often portrayed as imposing a "limit to limitations." This is indeed what the language suggests. In this vein, the WTO Panel in the

22. *See* Directive 2001/29/EC of the European Parliament and of the Council of 22 May 2001 on the harmonisation of certain aspects of copyright and related rights in the information society, OJ L 167, June 22, 2001, art. 5.5 [hereafter Directive 2001/29/EC] ("The exceptions and limitations provided for in paragraphs 1, 2, 3 and 4 shall only be applied in certain special cases which do not conflict with a normal exploitation of the work or other subject-matter and do not unreasonably prejudice the legitimate interests of the rightholder.").

23. *See, e.g.*, R. Cooper Dreyfuss, *TRIPS—Round II: Should Users Strike Back?*, 71 U. CHI. L. REV. 21 (2004); R. Cooper Dreyfuss and G. Dinwoodie, *TRIPS and the Dynamics of Intellectual Property Lawmaking*, 36 CASE W. RES. J. INT'L L. 95 (2004); Ruth Okediji, *TRIPS Dispute Settlement and the Sources of (International) Copyright Law*, 49 JCPS 585 (2001); South Centre, *The TRIPS Agreement: A Guide for the South* (Geneva, November 1997), available at http://www.southcentre.org/publications/trips/tripsagreement.pdf (last visited March 5, 2008).

IMRO case, which pitted the European Union against the United States in a conflict concerning the interpretation of the so-called "business exemption" (Section 110(5) of the US Copyright Act), noted at the outset of its opinion "that [TRIPS] Article 13 cannot have more than a narrow or limited operation. Its tenor consistent as it is with the provisions of Article 9(2) of the Berne Convention (1971), discloses that it was not intended to provide for exceptions or limitations except for those of a limited nature."[24] However, the history of the three-step test tells a somewhat different story. As the drafting history of the Stockholm Revision of the Berne Convention reveals, art. 9.2 is more akin to a "grandfathering" clause, a purposefully vague reflection of a compromise among states of different copyright traditions,[25] which confirms that the broad array of—frequently broadly worded—statutory limitations that existed at the national levels in 1967[26] is in conformity with BC minimum standards. The same might be said in respect of art. 13 of the TRIPS Agreement adopted in 1994.[27]

2. What Are "Limitations and Exceptions"? Although BC art. 9(2), TRIPS art. 13, and WCT art. 10 expressly refer to "limitations and exceptions" as the object of the three-step test, surprisingly little has been written, even in the *IMRO* WTO Panel Report, on what actually constitutes "limitations and exceptions." In all likelihood, the term applies first and foremost to statutory limitations that directly curtail the rights of copyright owners in specific circumstances in order to advance the interests of certain user groups or the public at large. Given the structure of the three Conventions, the three-step test need not be applied to domestic codifications of the subject matter of copyright (i.e., to the definition of a "work of authorship") or of the exclusive economic rights of copyright owners as such. According to some scholars, the term also does not encompass provisions that restrict the *exercise* of economic rights, such as provisions mandating the collective exercise of rights found in a variety of European directives and national laws.[28]

Whether the compensated limitations permitted under the Berne Convention qualify as "limitations and exceptions" subject to the three-step test under

24. *See* US—Section 110(5) Report, *supra* n. 19, §6.97.

25. Ch. Geiger, *The Role of the Three-step Test in the Adaptation of Copyright Law to the Information Society*, UNESCO e-Copyright Bulletin, January–March 2007, p. 3, available at http://unesdoc.unesco.org/images/0015/001578/157848e.pdf (last visited March 3, 2008).

26. For an exemplary inventory of limitations and exception existing in national law in a number of contracting States (e.g., Germany, Netherlands, France, United Kingdom and India) prior to the 1967 Stockholm Conference, see M. Senftleben, *supra* n. 20, at 52–81.

27. *See* id., at 87.

28. *See*, e.g., S. von Lewinski, *Mandatory Collective Administration of Exclusive Rights—A Case Study On Its Compatibility With International and EC Copyright Law*, UNESCO e-Copyright Bulletin, January–March 2004, p. 5, available at http://unesdoc.unesco.org/images/0013/001396/139656e.pdf (last visited March 3, 2008).

TRIPS art. 13 is an unsettled question.[29] But even if they are, such compensated limitations are generally more likely to pass the test given the fact that prescribing compensation to authors or right holders is generally recognized as a crucial factor in assessing "unreasonable prejudice" under the third step. Surely, the term "limitations and exceptions"—and by implication the three-step test—cannot apply to exercises of state discretion that are done pursuant to public policy external to copyright issues, such as freedom of expression and competition law, because this would imply a hierarchy of copyright over other domains of law, which would effectively render the copyright system immune against such external sources. However, as case law from the highest courts in Europe and elsewhere reveals, such a hierarchy does not exist.[30]

3. Scope of the Three-Step Test The mother of all three-step tests, BC art. 9(2), applies only to the right of reproduction guaranteed in Berne art. 9(1). Other economic rights guaranteed under the Convention come either with corresponding specific limitations (e.g., quotation), or none at all. In the latter case, the "minor reservations" doctrine may apply. Given the structure of the Berne Convention, the three-step test arguably does not extend to a state exercise of discretion pursuant to those articles where such discretion has explicitly been granted, such as articles 2*bis*, 10, and 10*bis*. Thus, states may freely enact legislation with respect to the subjects covered in these provisions without the restrictions of the three-step test.[31]

Article 13 of the TRIPS Agreement takes the three-step test an important step further. The test now applies to all economic rights guaranteed by TRIPS as minimum standards. These include not only the rights newly recognized in TRIPS, such as the right of rental (TRIPS art. 11), but also the panoply of rights of the Berne *acquis* as incorporated into TRIPS (TRIPS art. 9(1)).[32] Likewise, TRIPS art. 13 most likely applies not only to express limitations but also to the "minor reservations" implied in the Berne Convention.[33] WCT art. 10 appears to be stricter and has a more pronounced dual function than TRIPS art. 13. Whereas WCT art. 10(1) concerns the rights newly granted in arts. 6, 7, and 8 of the WCT, art. 10(2) applies to limitations and exceptions to all the economic rights already

29. D. Gervais, *Making Copyright Whole: A Principle Approach to Copyright Exceptions and Limitations* (unpublished manuscript on file with the authors).

30. *See*, e.g., P. Bernt Hugenholtz, *Copyright and Freedom of Expression in Europe*, in Rochelle C. Dreyfuss, Diane L. Zimmerman, and Harry First (eds.), EXPANDING THE BOUNDARIES OF INTELLECTUAL PROPERTY. INNOVATION POLICY FOR THE KNOWLEDGE SOCIETY (Oxford University Press, 2001) 343–363 (demonstrating that European courts regularly subject copyright claims to external freedom expression norms); L. Guibault, General Report (ALAI 1998), 46–48 (external limiting of copyright by competition law well established in various national and supranational courts).

31. WIPO Study, *supra* n. 16, at 21; Ricketson and Ginsburg, *supra* n. 6, at 763.

32. US—Section 110(5) Report, *supra* n. 19, §6.80.

33. Id., §6.81.

recognized by Berne. The potential impact of WCT art. 10(2) on Berne limitations, however, is neutralized by the Agreed Statements concerning art. 10:[34]

> It is understood that the provisions of Article 10 permit Contracting Parties to carry forward and appropriately extend into the digital environment limitations and exceptions in their national laws, which have been considered acceptable under the Berne Convention. Similarly, these provisions should be understood to permit Contracting Parties to devise new exceptions and limitations that are appropriate in the digital networked environment. It is also understood that Article 10(2) of the WCT neither reduces nor extends the scope of applicability of the limitations and exceptions permitted by the Berne Convention.[35]

Following a literal reading of the test, as enshrined in various international treaties, the three steps of the test must apply cumulatively.[36] By necessity, such cumulative application implies that at least the first and second steps be applied in a liberal manner, so as to leave some relevance to the third and final step.[37] A narrow construction of these initial steps would otherwise rob the test of much of its meaning. For this reason, Dr. Geiger has advocated reading the test in reverse, i.e. starting with the third test and working backwards. Such a reading is likely to accentuate the normative considerations built into the third (then first) step of the test. Indeed, nothing in the wording of the three-step test would prevent a legislator, international court, or a WTO panel from following this approach.[38]

Another approach, which admittedly takes more liberties with the wording of the provision, would be to perceive the norms reflected in the three steps as a trio of factors to be taken into account by legislators or courts—much like the four factors of fair use in section 107 of the U.S. Copyright Act.[39] This approach has the obvious advantage of offering greater flexibility. A limitation might score low on, for instance, the first or second step, but could still be admitted by scoring high on the third step. Indeed, such a "holistic" approach would do more justice to the proportionality principle that in essence underlies the three-step test.[40]

Scholars tend to read different meanings into the three-step test. Although classic doctrine underscores its function as imposing limits on the "erosion" of copyright by limitations and exceptions, more progressive scholars perceive the three-step test as no more than a proportionality test allowing national legislatures a relatively broad measure of discretion in codifying limitations and

---

34. Senftleben, in Dreier/Hugenholtz, *Concise Copyright*, WCT, art. 10, n. 6(b).
35. WCT, *supra* n. 9, Agreed statements concerning Article 10.
36. US—Section 110(5) Report, *supra* n. 19, §6.87.
37. *See*, e.g., Senftleben, *supra* n. 20, at 244.
38. Geiger, *supra* n. 25, at 18.
39. K. J. Koelman, *Fixing the Three-Step Test*, 2006 E.I.P.R. 407; Geiger, *supra* n. 25, at 19.
40. Senftleben, *supra* n. 20, at 243.

exceptions while balancing the interests of right holders against those of users and society at large.[41] Read in a constructive and dynamic fashion, the three-step test becomes a clause not merely limiting limitations, but empowering contracting states to enact them, subject to the proportionality considerations that form its core and that fully take into account, inter alia, fundamental rights and freedoms and the general public interest.[42]

4. The Three Steps in Some Detail The WTO Panel Report in the *IMRO* case has inspired a voluminous literature, including one highly detailed monograph,[43] on the meaning of the individual steps of the three-step test. This literature need not be repeated here; we shall limit ourselves to a few general observations.

No authoritative interpretation of the three-step test has ever been given under the Berne Convention.[44] However, national courts have applied, or at least referred to, the three-step test on many occasions, even before the incorporation of the test in European copyright legislation. The interpretation and application of the test by national courts varies considerably. For instance, whereas some European courts have judged statutory limitations that allow unauthorized digital "press clipping" to be compliant with the three-step test, others—in almost identical cases—have not.[45]

In 2000, TRIPS art. 13 was interpreted in considerable detail by a WTO dispute panel in the *IMRO* casc.[46] Another panel has interpreted the test's patent law corollary—TRIPS art. 30—in similar detail.[47] Although both panel reports contain valuable analyses of the three-step test and of its place and function in the international law of intellectual property, it should be borne in mind that WTO panels are not courts and the legal framework within which they operate is the law of international trade, not of copyright. Thus, WTO panels are likely to

---

41. At a workshop titled "Rethinking the Three-Step Test," jointly organized by the Max Planck Institute for Intellectual Property Law and Queen Mary University in London, Paris, ULIP, 16 February 2007, participants agreed to work on a declaration on the three-step test, expressing the consensus opinion that the test should be applied in a liberal, holistic, normative, and dynamic manner.

42. *See*, e.g., Senftleben, *supra* n. 34; Ch. Geiger, *From Berne to National Law, via the Copyright Directive: The Dangerous Mutations of the Three-step Test*, 2007 E.I.P.R. 486, at 490–491.

43. Senftleben, *supra* n. 20.

44. Such an interpretation could have been given only by the International Court of Justice. *See* Ricketson and Ginsburg, *supra* n. 6, at 1152.

45. *See* Geiger, *supra* n. 42, at 489 (discussing individual national cases).

46. *See* US—Section 110(5) Report, *supra* n. 19.

47. WTO Panel Report, WTO Panel Report, Canada-Patent Protection of Pharmaceutical Products, April 7, 2000, WTO Doc. WT/DS114/R. See also Panel Reports for the trademark-related cases WT/DS174/R and DS2890/R (US and Australia v. EU). For a comparison of all three panel decisions, see M. Senftleben, *Towards a Horizontal Standard for Limiting Intellectual Property Rights?—WTO Panel Reports Shed Light on the Three-Step Test in Copyright Law and Related Rights in Patent and Trademark Law*, IIC 2006/4, at 407.

be relatively insensitive to arguments based on fundamental rights and freedoms or (other) non-economic (e.g., cultural or educational) public interests, even if art. 7 of the TRIPS Agreement mandates that the protection of intellectual property rights be "conducive to social and economic welfare, and to a balance of rights and obligations."[48] Also, it is unlikely for a variety of reasons that decisions of WTO panels qualify as definitive interpretations of the relevant norms in question.[49] In sum, WTO panel decisions ought to have only limited precedent value for international courts, such as the International Court of Justice (ICJ), which is competent to interpret the BC and the WCT, or national courts interpreting national norms of copyright law.

Under the first prong of the three-step test, limitations and exceptions must be confined to "certain special cases." Although one might argue that any purpose-specific limitation complies with this requirement almost by definition, making the first step basically superfluous,[50] the *IMRO* Panel Report does contain exhaustive discussion of this threshold criterion. The word "certain" implies, according to the panel, that, as a matter of legal certainty, a limitation must be well defined. However, this does not rule out broadly phrased limitations, such as the fair use exemption in the United States, as a matter of principle:[51]

> . . . there is no need to identify explicitly each and every possible situation to which the exception could apply, provided that the scope of the exception is known and particularised. This guarantees a sufficient degree of legal certainty.[52]

The panel subsequently interpreted the term "special" as meaning something akin to exceptional. "In other words, an exception or limitation should be narrow in quantitative as well as a qualitative sense."[53] The panel thus rejected the interpretation advanced by several scholars that "special" has normative meaning (i.e., that the purpose of the exempted use be objectively justifiable).[54] According to the panel, the term "special" does not imply that policy objectives pursued by the limitation or exception at issue need to be objectively justified, as was argued by the EC in the case.[55] In other words, it is left to the discretion of WTO members to determine the need for, and the objectives of, exceptions and limitations as they see fit.

48. *See* Ruth L. Okediji, *Toward an International Fair Use Doctrine*, 39 COLUM. J. TRANSNAT'L L. 75 (2000). *See also* Dreyfuss, *supra* n. 23, at 22.

49. Senftleben, *supra* n. 20, at 107–08.

50. Daniel J. Gervais, *Towards a New Core International Copyright Norm: The Reverse Three-Step Test*, 9 MARQ. INTELL. PROP. L. REV. 1 (2005).

51. Several scholars have questioned whether the fair use doctrine complies with (the first part of) the three-step test. *See*, e.g., WIPO Study, *supra* n. 16, at 68-769; Okediji, *supra* n. 48, at 148; Senftleben, *supra* n. 20, at 162.

52. US—Section 110(5) Report, *supra* n. 19, §6.108.

53. Id., §6.109.

54. WIPO Study, *supra* n. 16; Senftleben, *supra* n. 20, at 137 et seq.

55. US—Section 110(5) Report, *supra* n. 19, §6.112.

The second step is arguably more critical, and the WTO panel's interpretation thereof certainly more controversial. The panel's reading of "normal exploitation" is essentially economical, and consequently restrictive:

> We believe that an exception or limitation to an exclusive right in domestic legislation rises to the level of a conflict with a normal exploitation of the work (i.e., the copyright or rather the whole bundle of exclusive rights conferred by the ownership of the copyright), if uses, that in principle are covered by that right but exempted under the exception or limitation, enter into economic competition with the ways that right holders normally extract economic value from that right to the work (i.e., the copyright) and thereby deprive them of significant or tangible commercial gains.[56]

To avoid a circularity of reasoning that would effectively eclipse exceptions and limitations, Dr. Senftleben has proposed to revisit the preparatory works of the Stockholm Conference. According to the Conference record, normal exploitation would encompass "all forms of exploiting a work, which have, or are likely to acquire, considerable economic or practical importance."[57] In other words, there is a conflict with the second step if the exempted use would rob the right holder of a real or potential source of income that is substantial. As evident from the *IMRO* Panel Report, the WTO appears to subscribe to this historical reading.[58]

The third step seems to leave legislatures considerable flexibility. The terms "legitimate" and "reasonable" at last inject a measure of normative meaning into the three-step test.[59] Both terms allow, in principle, an infinite variety of public interests to be factored into the three-step equation.[60] By the same token, these terms allow fundamental rights and freedoms, such as the right to privacy (which might, for example, justify a freedom to make private copies) or freedom of expression (which could justify an entire spectrum of excepted uses), to be factored into the three-step test. At the 1967 Stockholm Conference, a principle was established that the payment of equitable remuneration could be taken into account in the context of the third criterion.[61] In other words, the third step (further) restricts the availability of *uncompensated* exceptions.[62]

From the preceding analysis we can conclude that limitations and exceptions that (1) are not overly broad, (2) do not rob right holders of a real or potential

---

56. Id., §6.183.

57. Senftleben, *supra* n. 20, at 177 et seq.; S. Dusollier, *L'Encadrement des Exceptions au Droit d'Auteur par le Test des Trois Etapes*, 2005 IRDI 212, at 219.

58. US—Section 110(5) Report, *supra* n. 19, §6.180.

59. Gervais, *supra* n. 50, at 17.

60. Note that the WTO panels in the corresponding patent and trademark law cases expressly referred to the interests of "third parties," as a factor in determining legitimacy.

61. Senftleben, *supra* n. 20, at 237.

62. Gervais, *supra* n. 29.

source of income that is substantial, and (3) do not disproportionally harm the right holders will pass the three-step test. The test does not prescribe a template for any preferred system of national limitations and exceptions and most likely permits both discrete European-style limitations and broader fair-use-style exemptions, or possibly a combination of both.[63]

C. Assessment

In conclusion, despite an unmistakable "ratcheting up" of levels of copyright protection at the international, regional and bilateral levels, enough "wiggle room" appears to be left to the parties to the main copyright Conventions to make framing an international instrument on L&Es within the confines of the international *acquis* a worthwhile exercise. Despite over a century of international norm-setting in the field of copyright, limitations and exceptions have largely remained an "unregulated space."[64] This is not to say, of course, that the international *acquis* is inherently balanced. What it does mean, however, is that there is ample scope for rebalancing without having to deviate from the current *acquis*.

Indeed, nothing in the international *acquis* would prevent parties to the Berne Convention, the WCT, or TRIPS from entering into a special agreement listing in an exhaustive or enumerative manner those copyright limitations that are permitted within the confines of the three-step test. One could imagine such an instrument as containing a preamble and a number of provisions, divided into several chapters—for example, (1) *exclusions from protection* (excluding, for instance, facts, ideas, laws, and government works); (2) *limits to economic rights* (permitting, for instance, exhaustion and various non-public acts of communication); and (3) *limitations and exceptions proper*. As concluded earlier, only the norms listed in the last section would have to comply with the three-step test. As to that chapter, the EU Information Society Directive of 2001[65] inspires a pragmatic, albeit not very elegant solution. Like the Directive, the instrument on L&Es could provide a list of (mandatory and optional) limitations and conclude with a general obligation upon contracting states to subject any transpositions thereof to the three-step test.[66] A preamble might then offer guidance to the contracting states in interpreting the test.[67]

63. M. Senftleben, *Beperkingen à la Carte: Waarom de Auteursrechtrichtlijn Ruimte Laat voor Fair Use*, AMI 2003/1, at 10 (arguing that the EU Copyright Directive, despite its positivist provenance, permits a broadly worded, fair-use style limitation within the confines of the three-step test).

64. Gervais, *supra* n. 29.

65. Directive 2001/29/EC, *supra* n. 22, art. 5.

66. *See* id., art. 5.5 ("The exceptions and limitations provided for . . . shall only be applied in certain special cases which do not conflict with a normal exploitation of the work or other subject-matter and do not unreasonably prejudice the legitimate interests of the right-holder.").

67. In following this approach, however, care should be taken to avoid a proliferation of the test into the norms of national law. *See* Geiger, *supra* n. 42.

III. CONTOURS OF AN INTERNATIONAL INSTRUMENT ON L&Es

With respect to the possibility of an international agreement on L&Es, important questions point to design elements that affect the feasibility of such an endeavor. Despite gains made possible through a multilateral approach, particular design features may vary how appealing an international agreement is to individual states and how effectively the agreement will accomplish the stated goals. For example, the breadth of membership could be a significant factor in determining the extent of positive gains that could be realized; if only a few countries join, it could imperil the legitimacy and credibility of the international solution. Similarly, a treaty that reflects membership only of developing countries is less likely to sufficiently reduce the uncertainty faced, for example, by innovators of new technology who need legal stability on a global basis, and in particular in the developed countries. Some important questions include the following: Should an instrument on limitations and exceptions be linked with specific institutional mandates? What should be the modalities of such an instrument? Should articulated public interests be universally shared? In the following sections, we offer a preliminary approach to these important questions.

A. Institutional Considerations

The objectives and activities of WIPO and the WTO are central to cooperation and coordination in the realm of international intellectual property law. The WTO in particular occupies a distinct role in the oversight of IP harmonization through the activities of the TRIPS Council, which is chiefly responsible for facilitating compliance with the TRIPS Agreement and is therefore deeply involved in the normative design of the current and future multilateral copyright framework.[68] The activities of the TRIPS Council constitute an important medium for generating and spreading copyright norms among WTO Member States and for securing at least formal compliance with TRIPS obligations.[69] Between its general oversight and interpretive/

68. *See* Ruth L. Okediji, *WIPO-WTO Relations and the Future of Global IP Norms*, in The Netherlands Yearbook of International Law (forthcoming 2008).

69. The TRIPS Council has also taken important actions affecting the uneven costs of harmonization. For example, the WTO TRIPS Council agreed in 2005 to grant LDCs an extension of time—until July 1, 2013—to implement the entire TRIPS Agreement, with the possibility of further extension. This came after the 2001 Doha Declaration on TRIPS and Public Health that extended implementation of TRIPS provisions on granted on pharmaceuticals products and related provisions on exclusive marketing rights until 2016. *See* Doha WTO Ministerial 2001, Declaration on the TRIPS Agreement and Public Health, Nov. 14, 2001, WTO Doc. WT/MIN(01)/DEC/2, available at http://www.wto.org/English/thewto_e/minist_e/min01_e/mindecl_trips_e.htm (last visited Feb. 24, 2008). The WTO Secretariat in its Trade Policy Reviews (TPR) also plays an important role in communicating norms to Member States. For a review of TPRs reflecting somewhat the view of the WTO with respect to IP issues, see www.wto.org.

compliance functions, it is easy to see why the WTO might offer an appealing institutional home for an instrument intended to promote innovation by restoring balance to the normative fabric of the international copyright system. There are, however, offsetting considerations to be taken into account.

First of all, the WTO is principally a *trade* regime. It does not have the primary responsibility for the development of IP norms *qua* IP norms; instead, IP protection is viewed through its impact on free trade, which provides a distinct gloss on the interpretation of TRIPS obligations that often disregards cultural and other relevant criteria central to both national and international copyright systems.[70] Secondly, the WTO lacks the important historical context and technical considerations to evaluate the need for an international instrument on L&Es and to analyze the nature and scope of what might be contained in such an instrument. Indeed, the agreements that the WTO is charged to enforce originate from WIPO,[71] and are equally subject to WIPO's oversight.[72] Thus, the WIPO-WTO Agreement creates a partnership in which WIPO can support the efforts of the WTO in interpretation of the various WIPO Conventions.[73] WTO TRIPS dispute panels have sought information and advice from WIPO on matters arising from the interpretation of WIPO treaties, suggesting deference to WIPO's expertise, although the legal implications of WIPO's role in WTO matters, and vice versa, remain largely unexplored.[74] Finally, given its founding Agreement, it is unclear whether the WTO can initiate a new international instrument exclusively for IP, much less a stand-alone one for copyright.[75]

As the historical site for generating norms for international copyright harmonization, we believe that WIPO offers unique advantages as an agency with the necessary experience, expertise, and mandate suitable for the proposed multilateral exercise. Already, WIPO has commissioned three major studies on

70. *See* generally Neil Netanel, *The Next Round: The Impact of the WIPO Copyright Treaty on TRIPS Dispute Settlement*, 37 VA. J. INT'L L. 441 (1997).

71. *See* Agreement on Trade-Related Aspects of Intellectual Property Rights, April 15, 1994, Marrakesh Agreement Establishing the World Trade Organization, Annex 1C, 1869 U.N.T.S. 299, 33 I.L.M. 81, art 2.2 (1994) [hereafter TRIPS Agreement]. *See also* id., art. 5 (excluding "agreements concluded under the auspices of WIPO relating to the acquisition or maintenance of intellectual property rights").

72. Accordingly, the TRIPS Agreement calls for a "mutually supportive relationship between the WTO and the World Intellectual Property Organization." *See* id., pmbl.

73. *See* Agreement Between the World Intellectual Property Organization and the World Trade Organization, Dec. 22, 1995, 35 I.L.M. 754 (1996) [hereafter WIPO-WTO Agreement].

74. *Cf.* Okediji, *supra* n. 68.

75. For the objectives and functions of the WTO, see Marrakesh Agreement Establishing the World Trade Organization, Apr. 15, 1994, THE LEGAL TEXTS—THE RESULTS OF THE URUGUAY ROUND OF MULTILATERAL TRADE NEGOTIATIONS 4 (1999), 1867 U.N.T.S. 154, 33 I.L.M. 1144 (1994) [hereafter Marrakesh Agreement or WTO Agreement].

L&Es[76] that could serve as a first step in identifying the nature and scope of current concerns by Member States in this regard. Also relevant is the fact that WIPO, as a United Nations specialized body, is bound by the UN Charter, which obligates it to a larger set of norms reflected in an array of international agreements concluded under the auspices of the UN. As with the WTO, there are, however, factors presenting a potential challenge toward using WIPO as the exclusive institutional home of the new instrument on L&Es, most important of which is the absence of a suitable enforcement framework ensuring the successful implementation of the instrument as well as the fact that WIPO's efforts to produce a treaty in the field of copyright and related rights have failed twice in recent years.

B. Minimum Goals and Features

Among the principal motivations for an international instrument on L&Es is the need to recognize limitations to copyright as internal to the copyright system and core to its effective functioning. Further, such an instrument would provide states with a coherent framework within which the principle of maximum protection might otherwise constrain unilateral efforts that undermine copyright's foundational commitment to the public good. With these principles in mind, we identify the minimum goals of an international approach to L&Es to include (i) elimination of barriers to trade, particularly in regard to activities of information service providers; (ii) facilitation of access to tangible information products; (iii) promotion of innovation and competition; (iv) support of mechanisms to promote and reinforce fundamental freedoms; and (v) provision of consistency and stability in the international copyright framework by the explicit promotion of the normative balance necessary to support knowledge diffusion. Each of the five goals is specifically referenced in one or more multilateral intellectual property agreements.[77] They also collectively reflect the important role of public goods in enhancing human welfare. As such, these goals should be explicitly reflected in the preambular provision of the new international instrument on L&Es. Most importantly, the preamble should also include a well-articulated statement of the purposes of copyright protection that should be reflective of the dynamic nature of the creative enterprise.

We further identify three vital attributes that should be reflected in an international instrument on L&Es—the instrument must (i) be flexible; (ii) be judicially manageable; and (iii) leave ample space for national cultural autonomy.

---

76. *See* WIPO Study, *supra* note 16; Judith Sullivan, *Study on Copyright Limitations and Exceptions for the Visually Impaired*, WIPO Doc. SCCR/15/7, Feb. 20, 2007. Both Reports are available on the website of WIPO (www.wipo.org). A third report focusing on L&Es for libraries written by Professor Ken Crews is expected this year.

77. *See*, e.g., TRIPS Agreement, *supra* n. 71, pmbl.; WCT, *supra* n. 9, pmbl.; World Intellectual Property Organization Performances and Phonograms Treaty, Dec. 20, 1996, 36 I.L.M. 76, pmbl. [hereafter WPPT].

1. **Flexibility** An international instrument on L&Es must retain flexibility on several levels. First, it must contain principles that are sufficiently flexible to accommodate technological change that invariably requires a recalibration of the copyright balance. This flexibility must also facilitate new dimensions/definitions of the "public interest" to reflect changes and gains in technology. In other words, it must be clear that not all surplus from technological developments automatically accrues to rights owners. Second, the instrument must be designed to accommodate exceptional circumstances that warrant adaptation or modification of the rules. Escape clauses in trade agreements are key examples of such "adaptive" flexibility,[78] as perhaps are so-called "safeguard" clauses in the GATT. Third, the instrument must accommodate differentiated market structures between rich and poor nations, thus allowing for specific provisions to address unique but persistent problems of concentrated market power and other forms of market failure in the global economy. Finally, the instrument must include a mechanism enabling periodic review and possible revision.

2. **Judicial manageability** The clarity of copyright doctrine has always been hostage to the vagaries of technological change and unwieldy compromises produced by competing industry interests.[79] In both the United States and the European Union, the increasing density and complexity of copyright law has been a source of significant concern to scholars, policymakers, and judges, as courts have grappled with practical application of the law simultaneously to new uses, new users, and new technologies. Because national courts will remain important actors in enforcing national and international copyright law, an instrument on L&Es must be written in a way that provides clear guidance with respect to how best competing interests might be resolved to reflect copyright's commitment to the protection of and access to creative goods.

3. **Space for national cultural autonomy** We recognize that there is inherent tension between the call for international harmonization of L&Es and the preservation of cultural autonomy of individual Member States. We therefore recommend explicit recognition, in the new instrument, of a principle of state autonomy over discrete areas and events necessary to address unique national conditions and culture-specific needs. An example would be regulations promulgated by a state addressing use of copyrighted materials in conjunction with national cultural/religious ceremonies and other episodic national events, or allowing translation of works into (official) minority languages.

C. Possible Modalities of an International Instrument on L&Es

As observed earlier, the range and complexity of international relations has greatly expanded over the years, producing a dense and intricate network of

78. Barbara Koremenos, Charles Lipson, and Duncan Snidal, *The Rational Design of International Institutions*, 55 Int'l Org. 761, 773 (2001).

79. *See* Jessica Litman, *Copyright, Compromise, and Legislative History*, 72 Cornell L. Rev. 857, 879 (1987).

obligations between and among states of different political, cultural, economic, and technological strengths. At one end of the spectrum are "hard law" options represented most usually by treaties that have entered into force. These are termed "hard law" because they are always binding. If an international agreement reflects the parties' intent to be bound, then in principle such an agreement could also constitute hard law even if technically it is not labeled as a treaty.[80] Soft law, on the other hand, is usually viewed as comprising non-binding international obligations which nevertheless have significant normative influence and may in some cases reflect existing law based on state practice or constitute early attempts to create new customary law.[81] Different forms and legal effects exist for soft law, and it is possible for hard law instruments to share certain features of soft law and vice versa.[82] For example, treaties cast in open-ended standards are functionally "soft" in effect,[83] whereas declarations or understandings may reflect norms that are firmly entrenched in state practices.[84]

An international instrument on L&Es cast in soft law has much merit. First, soft law instruments have been quite influential in international economic law and, given the TRIPS Agreement, this option would fit well within the current institutional cooperation between WIPO and the WTO.[85] Second, a soft instrument would have the same force of law for purposes of TRIPS interpretation pursuant to extant rules of international law[86] and it might even gradually evolve into a formal hard law international instrument.[87] A soft law instrument could have a great political calming effect on international copyright relations, much like

---

80. UN Security Council Resolutions adopted pursuant to Article 25 of the Charter are a prime example. *See* Alan Boyle, *Soft Law in International Law-Making*, in INTERNATIONAL LAW (Malcolm D. Evans, 2nd ed.) 141, 142 (2006).

81. Id.

82. Janet Koven Levit, *Bottom-Up International Lawmaking: Reflections on the New Haven School of International Law*, 32 YALE J. INT'L L. 393, 413–14 (2007) ("While instruments such as the Global Compact, the Voluntary Principles, and the General Understanding are admittedly 'soft,' the norms embedded in such instruments often become 'hard.'").

83. *See* Christine Chinkin, *Normative Development in the International Legal System*, in Dinah Shelton (ed.), COMMITMENT AND COMPLIANCE: THE ROLE OF NON-BINDING NORMS IN THE INTERNATIONAL LEGAL SYSTEM (2000) 21, 30 (providing six definitions of soft law, including vague or imprecise terms).

84. Levit, *supra* n. 82.

85. *See* Christine Chinkin, *The Challenge of Soft Law: Development and Change in International Law* (1989) 38 I.C.L.Q. 850; *see also supra* text accompanying notes 71–74.

86. *See* Vienna Convention on the Law of Treaties, May 23, 1969, 1155 U.N.T.S. 331, art. 31(3) [hereafter Vienna Convention].

87. *See* id. *See also* generally Susy Frankel, *WTO Application of "the Customary Rules of Interpretation of Public International Law" to Intellectual Property*, 46 VA. J. INT'L L. 365 (2006); JOOST PAUWELYN, CONFLICT OF NORMS IN PUBLIC INTERNATIONAL LAW, 25–29 (2003). *See* generally Boyle, *supra* n. 80.

the Doha Declaration had on the international patent framework.[88] Third, it is often easier to conclude agreements using soft law because although such instruments are carefully crafted, the limited consequences of non-compliance often encourage states to be more willing to negotiate in detail and precision.[89] Fourth, soft law agreements avoid the national ratification processes that in any event may weaken robust commitments made during treaty negotiations. The political costs of treaty ratification often make states less willing to engage in the treaty process or to agree to meaningful terms.[90] Fifth, soft law instruments have a higher degree of flexibility in that they are easier to upgrade, amend, or replace.[91] In an area where technological changes will require substantive flexibility, flexibility of institutional form is an important added value. Finally, soft law instruments can reflect agreements between state and non-state actors. Given the strong role of industry actors in international copyright law, this particular feature of soft law options is an important consideration in thinking about the various actors that need to be engaged in the process of developing an international instrument for L&Es.

An example of an instrument cast in soft law would be a declaration by WIPO Member States identifying a list of L&Es that are already reflected in national laws and thus presumptively valid under the TRIPS Agreement. Such a declaration would reflect existing law but could also establish guidelines or recommendations that affect member obligations as interpreted by the WTO. Whatever the form of soft law, what is important is that it can afford states a credible defense against threats in response to any challenges to behavior consistent with the codified norms. State practice would also strengthen the normative force and appeal of the instrument through its relationship to Berne Convention provisions.

D. Recommendations

In conclusion, we summarize our main recommendations:

1. **Multilateral Solution** We believe that to restore balance to the international copyright regime a multilateral solution is called for.[92] Although, for example, the strategic utility and relative simplicity of alternative options such as a moratorium on the further expansion of IP rights,[93] or an agreement by developed

---

88. *See* Frederick M. Abbott and Jerome H. Reichman, *The Doha Round's Public Health Legacy: Strategies for the Production and Diffusion of Patented Medicines Under the Amended TRIPS Provisions,* 10 JIEL 921 (2007).

89. Boyle, *supra* n. 80, at 143–44.

90. Id.

91. Id.

92. *See* generally Inge Kaul et al., *Why Do Global Public Goods Matter Today,* in Inge Kaul, Pedro Conceicao, Katell Le Goulven, and Ronald U. Mendoza (eds.), PROVIDING GLOBAL PUBLIC GOODS: MANAGING GLOBALIZATION (2002).

93. *See* Keith E. Maskus and Jerome H. Reichman, *The Globalization of Private Knowledge Goods and the Privatization of Global Public Goods,* in Keith Maskus and Jerome

countries not to sanction (or threaten to sanction) developing countries that employ existing access mechanisms, are useful, we feel strongly that in the digital age, welfare gains from dynamic competition and diffusion of information goods require positive access norms as integral features of an effective international copyright system. Multilateralism in the area of L&Es has important functional, facilitative, and normative advantages. As a functional matter, multilateralism invariably fosters centralization, which is a key factor in promoting international cooperation, particularly when there is a desire for broad-based membership in the regime.[94] A multilateral accord also offers protection against "forum-shopping" by owners of proprietary rights who may be willing to sacrifice long-term dynamic gains of access for short-term monopoly gains from rent payments.

2. Regional Experimentation While we underscore the value of multilateralism, regional experimentation during the early stages of the multilateral exercise[95] may be an important step in beginning the work toward a coherent global framework for L&Es. Regional incubators for harmonized minimum L&Es offer the advantage of incremental development of L&Es among like-minded countries. A string of regional successes with such experimentation over time will undoubtedly pave the way for a more general multilateral instrument.

3. Joint WIPO and WTO Initiative We believe that a joint initiative between WIPO and the WTO could be an ideal and appropriate expression of a soft law modality with real impact for collective action on an international instrument on L&Es. Notable examples of soft law initiatives within WIPO include the Joint Recommendation on Internet Use, developed by the WIPO Standing Committee on Trademarks (SCT) and adopted by the WIPO General Assemblies and the Paris Union in 2001,[96] and the WIPO Joint Recommendation Concerning Provisions on the Protection of Well-Known Marks.[97] Neither is a binding instrument,

---

Reichman (eds.), INTERNATIONAL PUBLIC GOODS & TRANSFER OF TECHNOLOGY UNDER A GLOBALIZED INTELLECTUAL PROPERTY REGIME (2005).

94. Barbara Koremenos, Charles Lipson, and Duncan Snidal, *Rational Design: Looking Back to Move Forward*, 55 INT'L ORG., 1051, 1054 (2001).

95. As noted by copyright experts, at present, the primary candidates for experimentation at the regional level appear to be the Southern Common Market (MERCOSUR) and the Association of Southeast Asian Nations (ASEAN).

96. WIPO, Joint Recommendation Concerning Provisions on the Protection of Marks, and Other Industrial Property Rights in Signs, on the Internet, adopted by Assembly of the Paris Union for the Protection of Industrial Property and General Assembly of the World Intellectual Property Organization, WIPO Doc. 845(E), pmbl. (Oct. 2001) (setting forth provisions intended to apply when determining whether "use of a sign on the Internet has contributed to the acquisition, maintenance or infringement of a mark or other industrial property right in the sign, or whether such use constitutes an act of unfair competition").

97. WIPO, Joint Recommendation Concerning Provisions on the Protection of Well-Known Marks adopted by Assembly of the Paris Union for the Protection of Industrial

but the latter clearly is evolving into an international legal standard through its incorporation by the United States into several bilateral agreements. It was also recently cited by a U.S. federal court as a potential source of guiding principles for the famous marks doctrine.[98]

A recommendation by the SCCR could similarly be an important contribution to developing coherence in the international law of L&Es. It might involve coordination between the SCCR and the TRIPS Council, particularly through the latter's activities in the implementation of the TRIPS Agreement. Even a recommendation solely authored by the SCCR could be used by the TRIPS Council to evaluate both rights implementation and user freedoms when assessing national copyright laws for compliance with the international copyright framework.

CONCLUSION

The task of developing a global approach to limitations and exceptions is one of the major challenges facing the international copyright system today. At risk are fundamental elements of the copyright system which were historically designed to require accountability to goals and purposes far beyond individual economic gain. This chapter has not answered all the questions, but we hope it has provided some direction on possible ways forward.

Property and General Assembly of the World Intellectual Property Organization, WIPO Doc. 833(E) (Sept. 1999), available at http://www.wipo.int/about-ip/en/development_iplaw/pub833.htm (last visited March 5, 2008).

98. *See ITC Limited v. Punchgini, Inc.*, 482 F.3d 135 (2d Cir. 2007).

INDEX